SECOND EDITION

Managerial Economics

Eugene F. Brigham
University of Florida

James L. Pappas
University of Wisconsin

The Dryden Press
Hinsdale, Illinois

Editorial - Production Services provided
by COBB/DUNLOP, Inc.

CONTENTS

PREFACE

The economic environment has undergone many significant changes in recent years. Strong inflationary pressures are having dramatic effects on both individuals and business firms. Energy shortages and rising energy costs are forcing drastic changes in production processes and techniques. The recession of 1975 has shown all too clearly that our economy is still subject to business cycles, and that neither individuals nor business firms can neglect this factor when planning for the future. In such a setting, economic analysis is assuming a growing importance in business decision making—firms are hiring professional economists, setting up economics departments, and using economic data and methods of analysis in all phases of their operations.

   With this background in mind, we designed this second edition of *Managerial Economics* to present those aspects of economic theory and analysis that are most relevant for students of business administration. The book provides a rigorous development of the elements of microeconomics that are most useful for managerial decisions, then illustrates with problems and cases the usefulness of the theory. Throughout, emphasis is placed on the actual decision process and on the role that economic analysis plays in this process.

Although virtually every aspect of both micro- and macroeconomic theory has important implications for managerial decisions, a number of microeconomic topics are of paramount importance. These include demand theory and estimation, production theory and cost estimation, analysis of market structures and their effects on pricing practices, antitrust policy, and capital expenditure decisions. *Managerial Economics* examines each of these topics.

Managers attempt to optimize under conditions of uncertainty. Accordingly, optimization techniques and methods of risk analysis are taken up early in the text, then used throughout the book. Although many students will have been introduced to these subjects in other courses, we have found that most either do not recall them or else never really had a grasp of how the techniques are applied in practice. Thus, in *Managerial Economics*, we presuppose no prior exposure to these basic tools and techniques.

An important feature of *Managerial Economics* is its attempt to show the firm as a cohesive, unified organization. Students of business administration take courses in marketing, finance, production, and so on, but they often fail to see the integration of these subjects. In *Managerial Economics*, we use a basic valuation model, show that value is determined as the present value of expected future profits, and then relate each topic in the text to an element of the valuation model. In the process, management is seen to involve an integration of the marketing, production, and finance functions. This integrating process is reinforced in the final chapter, which examines a long, integrated case that is particularly valuable, both for consolidating the materials and for demonstrating that important business decisions are interdisciplinary in the truest sense of the word. According to our students, setting forth the interrelationships within a business firm—or a business administration curriculum—as a unified whole rather than as a series of discrete, unrelated topics is one of the most valuable aspects of managerial economics.

The revisions made in this second edition include updating the descriptive materials, expanding the number and types of illustrations employed, smoothing out some of the more difficult presentations, and both modifications and additions to the end-of-chapter questions and problems. A *Study Guide* has also been developed, which outlines the major points in the text and provides a comprehensive set of solved problems. The basic framework for *Managerial Economics*, however, remains unchanged.

ACKNOWLEDGMENTS

We are grateful to the many individuals who aided in the preparations of both editions of *Managerial Economics*. Many helpful suggestions and valuable comments have been received from instructors (and students) using the first edition of the book, and numerous reviewers provided insightful assistance in clarifying difficult presentations. Among those who were especially helpful are B. Allen, R. Auerbach, C. Chittle, J. Elterich, R. Haas, E. Hale, T. Hogarty, R. Knapp, B. Mabry, G. Mellish, P. Nelson, T. Shin, K. Smith, J. Song, R. Thornton, D. Vrooman and D. Weigel. The Universities of California, Wisconsin, and Florida, and our students and colleagues on these campuses, also provided us with a stimulating environment and general intellectual support. Finally, we are indebted to the Dryden Press staff, particularly Jere Calmes and Sandy Nykerk, for their special efforts in helping us convert a manuscript into a bound book.

The field of managerial economics continues to undergo significant changes, and it is stimulating to participate in these exciting developments. We sincerely hope that *Managerial Economics* will contribute to a better understanding of the application of economic theory and methodology to managerial practices, and thus help lead to a more efficient economic system.

Eugene F. Brigham
James L. Pappas

Gainsville, Florida
Madison, Wisconsin
September, 1975

CHAPTER 1

Uses and Applications of Managerial Economics

WHAT IS MANAGERIAL ECONOMICS?

Although one finds the term *managerial economics* defined in a variety of ways, the differences are typically more semantic than real. To some, managerial economics is applied microeconomics. Others define the field in terms of management science and operations research concepts. There are also those who see managerial economics as primarily providing an integrative framework for analyzing business decision problems. In actuality, all of those views are correct, for each tells a part of the truth.

Managerial economics is the application of economic theory and methodology to business administration practice. More specifically, managerial economics uses the tools and techniques of economic analysis to analyze and solve business problems. In a sense, managerial economics provides the link between traditional economics and the decision sciences in managerial decision making, as is illustrated in Figure 1-1.

While we relate managerial economics to business administration decision problems in Figure 1-1, and while our focus is primarily on business applications throughout the text, it is important to recognize that the concepts of managerial economics are equally applicable to other types of or-

Figure 1-1 The Role of Managerial Economics in Business Decision Making

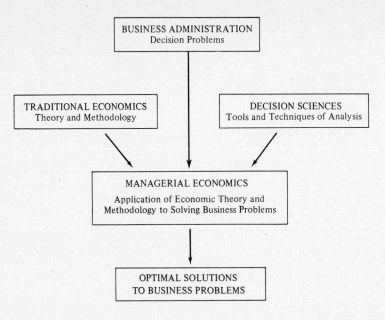

ganizations. That is, the principles of managerial economics are also relevant to the management of nonbusiness, nonprofit organizations—such as government agencies, schools, hospitals, museums, and similar institutions. We shall emphasize this point repeatedly through the use of examples from the not-for-profit sector at appropriate points in the chapters that follow.

Relationship of Managerial Economics to Traditional Economics

A clearer understanding of the generality of the concepts of managerial economics, as well as the complexities involved, can be gained by examining the relationship of managerial economics to traditional economics and the decision sciences. Understanding the relationship between managerial economics and traditional economics is facilitated by a consideration of the structure of traditional economics. Although this structure may be presented in several different ways, one common breakdown is given in Table 1-1.

The various aspects of traditional economics presented in Table 1-1 overlap to some extent. Not only are micro and macro theory interrelated but there are also micro and macro aspects to each area listed. Moreover, the areas themselves overlap to some extent; for example, econometric techniques provide a common set of tools of analysis applicable to each other area. Similarly, economic systems as studied in positive, or descriptive, economics must be understood before meaningful normative rules can be formulated. Never-

Table 1-1 Classifications of Traditional Economic Studies

Theory:	*Microeconomics* focuses on individual consumers and firms.
	Macroeconomics focuses on aggregations of economic units, especially national economies.
Specific Areas:	Agricultural Economics
	Comparative Economics
	Econometrics
	Economic Development
	Foreign Trade
	Industrial Organization
	Labor Economics
	Money and Banking
	Public Finance
	Stabilization Policy
	Urban and Regional Economics
	Welfare Economics
Emphasis:	*Normative* focuses on prescriptive statements; that is, establishes rules to help attain specified goals.
	Positive focuses on description; that is, describes the manner in which economic systems operate without attempting to state how they should operate.

theless, the focus of each item in the table is sufficiently well defined to warrant the breakdown.

Since each area of traditional economics has some bearing on business firms, managerial economics draws from all the areas. In practice some are more relevant to the business firm than others, and hence to managerial economics. To illustrate, although both microeconomics and macroeconomics are important in managerial economics, the micro theory of the firm is especially significant. It may be said that the theory of the firm is the single most important element in managerial economics. However, because the individual firm is very much influenced by the general economy, which is the domain of macroeconomics, managerial economics does involve macro theory.

The emphasis of managerial economics is certainly on normative theory. We want to establish decision rules that will help business firms attain their goals; this is the essence of the word "normative." If firms are to establish valid decision rules, however, they must thoroughly understand their environment; for this reason descriptive economics cannot be ignored.

Relationship of Managerial Economics to the Decision Sciences

Just as economics provides the theoretical framework for analyzing business decision problems, the tools and techniques of analysis derived from the decision sciences provide the means for actually constructing decision models, analyzing the impact of alternative courses of action, and evaluating the results obtained from the model. Managerial economics draws heavily from the area of *optimization techniques,* including differential calculus and mathematical programming, for developing decision rules aimed at assisting management in achieving the firm's established goals. *Statistical tools* are used to estimate relationships between important variables in decision problems. Because most business decision problems involve activities and events which will occur in the future, *forecasting techniques* also play an important role in managerial decision making and, therefore, in the study of managerial economics.

As in the economics area, the dichotomy used here to classify the decision sciences is not absolute. Optimization procedures are inherent in statistical relationships, and both optimization techniques and statistical relationships play important parts in developing forecasting methodologies.

In addition to the overlaps within the economics and decision science classifications, there is substantial overlap between them. For example, many of the basic corollaries of economics—including the well-known microeconomic axiom that profit maximization requires that marginal revenue equal marginal cost—are derived from the optimization procedures of differential calculus. It is because of these substantial interrelationships that we stated earlier that the definitional differences for managerial economics are largely semantic in nature.

Relationship of Managerial Economics to Business Administration

Now that we have established the role of economics and the decision sciences in managerial economics, it should prove useful to attempt to place managerial economics in perspective as a part of the study of business administration. In general, business administration is organized into four major categories, as is illustrated in Table 1-2. The functional areas are reasonably well situated because both businesses and business schools are generally structured to include these departments. The "special" areas are also fairly well defined, and their place in the business administration curriculum is relatively clearcut; the "tool" areas and integrating courses are not so easily categorized. Principles of management, for example, could be included as a tool or as an integrating course. It is not in the list of functional areas because no business firm has a management department. Yet management, in the sense of coordinating various aspects of the firm, is certainly a function, so there would be some justification for listing management within the functional areas. Accounting presents a similar problem—it is a function within the firm, but it is also a tool used throughout the firm. Accordingly, accounting is listed both as a functional area and as a tool.

The real question is this: Where does managerial economics fit into the picture? Again, the answer is not clearcut. Although many firms have economics departments, these departments are usually small, and "economics"

Table 1-2   Classifications of Business Administration Studies

Functional Areas:	Accounting
	Finance
	Marketing
	Personnel
	Production
"Tool" Areas:	Accounting
	Behavioral Science
	Computer Science
	Management
	Managerial Economics
	Quantitative Analysis, Including Operations Research
"Special" Areas:	Banking
	Insurance
	International Business
	Real Estate
	Transportation
Integrating Courses:	Management
	Managerial Economics

per se is not an important function within the firm. One possibility is to include managerial economics as a special area, but in our judgment it would be somewhat out of character there.

As we see it, managerial economics fits into the classification of business administration studies in two places. First, it serves as a tool course, wherein certain economic theories, methods, and techniques of analysis are covered in preparation for their later use in the functional areas. Second, it serves as an integrating course, combining the various functional areas and showing not only how they interact with one another as the firm attempts to achieve its goals, but also how the firm interacts with the environment in which it operates.

Role of Business in Society

One very important inquiry in managerial economics concerns the interrelationship between the firm and society. Managerial economics can help to clarify the vital role business firms play in our society and to point out ways of improving their operations for society's benefit. A business enterprise is a combination of people, physical assets, and information (technical, sales, coordinative, and so on). The people directly involved include stockholders, management, labor, suppliers, and customers. In addition to these direct participants, all society is indirectly involved in the firm's operations, because businesses use resources otherwise available for other purposes (including air and water), pay taxes if operations are profitable, provide employment, and generally produce most of the material output of our society.

Firms exist because they are useful in the process of allocating resources —producing and distributing goods and services. If social welfare could somehow be measured, business firms might be expected to operate in a manner that would lead toward maximizing some index of social well-being. Just which bundle of goods and services (including negative by-products such as pollution), as well as which distribution pattern for the bundle, would maximize social welfare is a complex, actually unanswerable, question. It is, however, one of the most vital questions facing us today, and as such is an important issue in managerial economics.

The traditional way of handling this matter in the United States has been through the economic and political systems. The economic system produces and allocates goods and services through the market mechanism. Firms determine what consumers desire, bid for the resources necessary to produce these products, and then make and distribute them. The participants—suppliers of capital, labor, and raw materials—must all be compensated out of the proceeds from the sale of the output, and competition (bargaining) takes place among these groups. Further, the firm competes for the consumer's dollar with other firms in the same and other industries. This process is "natural" in the sense that it occurs in all human societies as they develop.

A difficulty arises in the course of this development. Certain groups are likely to gain excessive economic power, permitting them to obtain too large a share of the value created by firms. To illustrate, the economics of producing and distributing electric power are such that only one firm can efficiently serve a given community. Further, there are no good substitutes for electricity for lighting purposes—and lighting is "essential." As a result, the electric companies are in a position to exploit consumers; they could charge high prices and earn excessive profits. Society's solution to this potential exploitation is rate regulation. Prices charged by electric companies and certain other monopolistic enterprises are controlled and held down to a level just sufficient to provide stockholders with a "fair" rate of return on their investment. The regulatory process is simple in concept; in practice, it is costly, difficult to operate, and in many ways arbitrary. It is a poor substitute for competition, but a substitute that is sometimes necessary.

A second problem in the economic development of society occurs when, because of economies of scale or other conditions, a limited number of firms serve a given market. If the firms compete with one another, no exploitation occurs; however, if they conspire with one another in setting prices, they may be able to obtain excessive profits. The antitrust laws are designed to prevent such collusion, as well as to prevent the merging of competing firms whenever the effect of the merger would be to lessen competition substantially. Like direct regulation, the antitrust laws contain arbitrary elements and are costly to administer, but they, too, are necessary if economic justice, as defined by the body politic, is to be served.

A third problem is that, under certain conditions, firms can exploit workers, so laws designed to equalize the bargaining power of firms and workers have been developed. These labor laws require firms to submit to collective bargaining and to refrain from certain "unfair" practices.[1]

A fourth problem faced by the economic system is that in their production processes, firms may impose costs on society; for example, by dumping wastes into the air or the water or by defacing the earth, as in strip mining. If a steel mill creates polluted air, which requires people to paint their houses in three years instead of in five years or to have their clothes dry cleaned more frequently or to suffer lung ailments, the mill is creating a cost to society in general, or a social cost. The steel company should be required to install pollution-control equipment or to pay fines equal to the social cost of the pollution; otherwise, either the steel company or its customers are gaining at the expense of society, because the company is not paying its full social costs.[2] Additionally, failure to shift social costs back onto the firm—and, ultimately, to the consumers of its output—results in an economically inefficient allocation of resources between industries and firms. Currently, much attention is being paid to this problem of internalizing social costs. Some of the practices being applied to achieve this end include the establishment of emissions limits both for manufacturing processes and for products that pollute (for example, autos), as well as the imposition of fines or outright closures of operations that do not meet these standards.

All the measures discussed above—utility regulation, antitrust laws, labor laws, and pollution control restrictions—are examples of actions taken by society to modify the behavior of business firms and to make this behavior more consistent with broad social goals. Since these social measures all constrain firms, the economy of the United States could be called a constrained-enterprise system as opposed to a free-enterprise system. As we shall see, these constraints have a most important bearing on the operations of a business firm.

THE BASIC VALUATION MODEL

In the preceding section we noted that firms are basically economic entities. As such, their activities can best be analyzed in the context of an economic

---

[1] In recent years the question of whether labor is too strong has been raised. For example, can powerful national unions such as the Teamsters use the threat of a strike to obtain "excessive" increases in wages, which may in turn be passed on to consumers in the form of higher prices and, thus, cause inflation? Those who believe this is the case have suggested that the antitrust laws should be applied to labor unions, especially to those bargaining with numerous small employers.

[2] Given the difficulty of estimating social costs, including the long-run effects on life itself, it is easy to see why political discussions of the subject run more toward prevention than toward compensation fines.

model of the firm. We now develop such a model and examine how it will aid in our study of managerial decision making.

The basic model of the business enterprise is what economists call the *theory of the firm*. In its earliest version, the goal of the firm was assumed to be profit maximization—the owner-manager of the firm was assumed to strive single-mindedly to maximize his firm's short-run profits. Later, when the emphasis on profits was shifted, or broadened, to encompass the time dimension, the primary goal became wealth maximization, rather than short-run profit maximization.

Simultaneously, the profit/wealth maximization criterion was questioned: Are not the owner-managers of firms interested, at least to some extent, in power, prestige, leisure, community well-being, and society in general? Further, do firms really try to *maximize*, or do they *satisfice;* that is, seek satisfactory results rather than *optimal* (that is, wealth-maximizing) results, as the economic theory asserts? Would the manager of a firm really seek the *sharpest* needle in a haystack (maximize); or would he stop when he found one sharp enough for sewing (satisfice)?

The economic theory of the firm, as it has evolved to date, states that a manager seeks to maximize the value of his firm, subject to constraints imposed by society. The theory does not explicitly recognize other goals, including the possibility that managers might take actions that not only would benefit someone other than stockholders—perhaps the managers themselves or society in general—but also might even *reduce* stockholder wealth. Thus, the model abstracts from the possibilities of satisficing, managerial self-dealing, and any voluntary social responsibility on the part of business.

Given these restrictions, is the economic model of the firm even worthy of consideration? We think it is. First, we believe that the very substantial competition both in the product market, where firms sell their output, and in the capital market, where they acquire the funds necessary to engage in productive enterprise, forces managements to pay close attention to valuation maximization in their decisions. Second, even if valuation maximization is an oversimplification of some multigoal objective of firms, it is realistic enough to provide decision rules that can increase the efficiency of firms; this will become clear as the theory is developed throughout this text. Third, the costs as well as the benefits of any action must be considered before a decision to take that action is made, including any decision to satisfice rather than to maximize. In other words, before a "satisfactory" level of activity can be decided upon, the managers of a firm must examine the "costs" of such an action. The analysis involved in the maximizing model provides information on such costs. Fourth, though at first glance the model seems to preclude the possibility of voluntary "social responsibility" activities on the part of the firm, it actually provides a great deal of insight into this area. Suppose the managers of a firm contemplate some action that may reduce short-run profits, yet may, at the same time, be socially beneficial. Such an action will probably be expected to have a favorable long-run impact on profits because of the good will it can create, and the valuation model is a useful device for considering such long-run effects.

Recognizing that business firms can be expected to analyze either voluntary or involuntary social responsibility in the context of the economic model of the firm is an important consideration in examining the set of inducements that can be used to channel the efforts of business in new directions as such changes are deemed desirable by society. Similar considerations should also be taken into account before political pressures or regulations are imposed on firms to constrain their operations. For example, from the consumer's standpoint it is preferable to pay lower rates for gas, electric, and telephone services, as well as lower fares for airline and train travel; but if public pressures on these regulated firms drive rates down too low, then profits will fall below the level necessary to provide an adequate return to investors, capital will not flow into the industries, and service will deteriorate. When such issues are considered, the economic model of the firm provides useful insights.

Definition of Value

Since the basis of the economic model is maximization of the value of the firm, it is appropriate to clarify the meaning of "value." Actually, a number of definitions of the term may be found in economic and business literature —book value, market value, liquidating value, going-concern value, and so on. *For our purposes, however, value may be defined as the present value of the firm's expected future cash flows.* Cash flows may, for now, be equated to profits; therefore the value of the firm today, its *present value*, is the value of its expected future profits, discounted back to the present at an appropriate interest rate.[3]

The essence of the model with which we are concerned throughout the book may be expressed as follows:

Value of the firm $= PV$ of expected future profits

$$= \frac{\pi_1}{(1+i)^1} + \frac{\pi_2}{(1+i)^2} + \cdots + \frac{\pi_n}{(1+i)^n}$$

$$= \sum_{t=1}^{n} \frac{\pi_t}{(1+i)^t}. \tag{1-1}$$

---

[3] We assume that the reader is familiar with the concepts of present value and compound interest. For those who are not, we have included a detailed treatment of the subject in Appendix A. This material is useful for a complete understanding of Chapter 3, "Risk Analysis"; it is essential to an understanding of Chapter 13, "Capital Budgeting."

To understand Chapter 1, however, one merely needs to recognize that $1 in hand today is worth more than $1 to be received a year from now, because the $1 today can be invested and, with interest, can grow to an amount larger than $1 by the end of the year. If we had 95 cents and invested it at 5 percent interest, it would grow to $1 in one year. Thus, 95 cents is defined as the present value of $1 due in one year when the appropriate interest rate is 5 percent.

PV is the abbreviation for present value; π_1, π_2, and so forth represent the expected profits in each year, t; i is the appropriate interest rate.[4]

Since profits are equal to sales revenues (S) minus costs (C), Equation 1-1 may be rewritten as follows:

$$\text{Value} = \sum_{t=1}^{n} \frac{S_t - C_t}{(1+i)^t}. \tag{1-2}$$

The marketing department of a firm has a major responsibility for sales; the production department a major responsibility for costs; and the finance department a major responsibility for the discount factor in the denominator. There are many important overlaps among these functional areas—the marketing department, for example, can help to reduce the costs associated with a given level of output, and the production department can stimulate sales by improving quality and making new products available to salesmen. Further, other departments within the firm—for example, accounting, personnel, transportation, and engineering—provide information or services vital to both sales expansion and cost control. We see, therefore, that various decisions in different departments of the firm can be appraised in terms of their effects on the value of the firm as expressed in Equations 1-1 and 1-2.

Some Fundamental Questions

A fundamental assumption in managerial economics is that, subject to constraints imposed by governments (antitrust laws, pollution control regulations, and so forth), the firm seeks to maximize its value as expressed in Equations 1-1 and 1-2. This statement is highly simplified; the remainder of this book is devoted to amplifying and qualifying it, and to showing how economic theory can be used to help management achieve the maximization goal. Some examples of the questions that we will attempt to answer include the following: Would the owner-manager of a business truly be interested in maximizing the value of the business; or would he not also be concerned with his own leisure time, his status with his employees and his community, and other matters, and might not these factors conflict with value maximization? What determines the profit stream, π_t, and how can this stream be increased? What determines the interest or discount rate, i, and how can this rate be decreased? These are the kinds of questions we will attempt to answer, or at least provide a basis for answering, throughout the book.

---

[4] The second form given for Equation 1-1 is simply a shorthand expression in which sigma (Σ) signifies "sum up" or add the present values of n profit terms. If $t = 1$, then $\pi_t = \pi_1$, and $(1+i)^t = (1+i)^1$; if $t = 2$, then $\pi_t = \pi_2$, and $(1+i)^t = (1+i)^2$; and so on, until $t = n$, the last year the project provides any profits. The term $\sum_{t=1}^{n}$ simply says "go through the following process; let $t = 1$ and find the PV of P_1; then let $t = 2$ and find the PV of π_2; continue until the PV of each individual profit has been found; then add the PVs of these individual profits to find the PV of the firm.

NATURE OF PROFITS

Although the central theme of this text focuses on the use of economic theory to increase the efficiency of the firm and thereby to maximize its value, an important secondary goal is to increase the reader's understanding of the firm and its place in the economy. The enterprise system, based as it is on the profit motive, has come under severe attack. While few would argue that the system cannot be improved (we certainly would not present such an argument), it does have tremendous advantages over the available alternatives. The attacks on the economic system have been made largely by people who do not thoroughly understand it, and it must be defended by people who do, including businessmen and students of business. Further, if the system is to be improved, changes must be formulated in large part by these groups. Because profit is a key element in the system, it is appropriate to analyze it in some depth.

Frictional Theory of Profit

A number of theories have been advanced to explain the existence of profit. One theory, the friction theory of profit, may be stated as follows: First, there exists a "normal rate of profit," which is simply the return on capital necessary to induce savers to invest some of their funds rather than to consume their entire income or "to put their savings in a mattress." In a static economy all businesses would be earning this normal rate of return, and the desired level of savings would be equal to the desired level of business investment. In other words, the normal rate of return is a market-clearing price for credit.[5]

Secondly, shocks occasionally occur in the economy, producing disequilibrium conditions that give rise to nonnormal profits for some firms. For example, the emergence of a new product such as the automobile might lead to a marked increase in the demand for steel, and this might cause profits of steel firms to rise above the normal level for a time. Alternatively, a rise in the use of plastics might drive the steel firms' profits down. In the long run, barring impassable barriers to entry and exit, resources would flow into or out of the steel industry, driving rates of return back to normal levels, but during interim periods profits might be above or below normal because of these frictional factors.

Monopoly Theory of Profit

A second rationale, the monopoly theory, is an extension of the frictional theory. It asserts that some firms—because of such factors as economies of scale, possession of unique natural resources, patent protection, or the like— are able to build up monopoly positions and to keep their profits above normal for indefinitely long periods. Monopoly, a most interesting topic, is dis-

---

[5] In Chapter 3 it is shown that if one business is inherently riskier than another, its normal profit rate should exceed that of the low-risk firm.

cussed at length in Chapters 10 and 12 of this book, where we consider in detail why it exists, its effects, and how it may be controlled.

Innovation Theory of Profit

The third theory of profit, the innovation theory, is also related to frictions. Under the innovation theory, above-normal profits arise as compensation for successful innovation. For example, the theory suggests that Xerox Corporation, which earns a high rate of return because it successfully developed and marketed a superior copying device, will continue to receive these super-normal returns until other firms enter the field to compete with Xerox and drive its high profits down to a normal level.

Compensatory Theory of Profit

The compensatory, or functional, theory holds that profits arise as payment for entrepreneurial services; that is, profits are the compensation for promoting, managing, and assuming the risks of a business enterprise.

Interaction of the Various Theories

It should be obvious that each theory has elements of truth—one theory applies in one instance, another in another instance, and perhaps all are applicable in some cases. To illustrate, a very efficient farmer may earn an above-normal rate of return in accordance with the compensatory theory, but during a wartime farming boom his already above-average profits may be supplemented by abnormal or frictional profits. Similarly, Xerox's profit position might be explained in part by all four theories: The company is exceptionally well managed and is earning "compensatory" profits; it is earning high "frictional" profits while 3M, IBM, and other firms are tooling up to enter the office copier field; it is earning "monopoly profits," because it is protected to some extent by its patents; and it is certainly benefiting from successful innovation.

Should Above-Normal Profits Exist?

If a firm is earning above-normal profits, should this condition be permitted to continue? Or should the successful farmer be taxed until his after-tax profits are down to the level of his less successful neighbor? Should Xerox be forced to give up its patents to competitors, enabling strong competition to come into the copying field sooner than it otherwise would? Should General Motors, which has a cost advantage in the automobile field because of economies of scale in both the production and the distribution of autos and, accordingly, a monopoly (or strong oligopoly) position, be "broken up"?

Difficulties would be encountered in any of these actions. Efficient farmers would have little incentive to be as productive as they could be; Xerox and other firms would have less motivation to innovate; and economies of mass production and distribution would be lost if GM and other large firms were broken up. Actions short of these extremes are practiced in the economy, however, to help alleviate "excessive" profits: Wealthy farmers as well as doctors, lawyers, and others who have "above-normal returns on personal services" are taxed at progressive rates. Patents expire after a time, and licensing agreements are used to reduce the monopoly power of holders of key patents. Antitrust laws are applied to prevent collusion and price fixing by large, oligopolistic firms.

Some monopoly firms, such as the utilities, are regulated to prevent them from charging exorbitant prices and from earning excessive rates of return. These and similar procedures have been evolved over the years to help reduce inequities while still retaining the profit system which provides an incentive for innovation and productive efficiency and serves as an allocator of scarce resources.

STRUCTURE OF THIS TEXT

Objectives

Reflecting the concept of managerial economics developed above, this text is designed to accomplish the following objectives:

1. To present those aspects of economics and the decision sciences which are most important and relevant in business decision making.
2. To provide a rationale, or framework, to help the student understand the nature of the firm as an integrated whole, as opposed to a loosely connected set of functional departments.
3. To demonstrate the interrelation between the firm and society, and illustrate the key role of business as an agent in social and economic change.

Outline of Topics

In this chapter the basic economic model of the firm has been presented, and value maximization, the central focus of the firm, introduced. Chapter 2 deals with optimization—the process of seeking the best way of accomplishing a stated objective. In Chapter 3 the basic model is expanded to include risk, and methods of measuring risk and incorporating it into the model are examined.

Demand theory, as well as application of the economic theory of demand to business decisions, is explored in Chapters 4 and 5. Production theory is discussed in Chapter 6; linear programming, a key element in production planning, is the subject of Chapter 7. Theoretical aspects of cost analysis are developed in Chapter 8; practical methods of estimating cost functions, as well as some difficulties in the estimation process, are explored in Chapter 9. Chapter 10—where the roles of demand, production, and costs are synthesized—explains the manner in which this synthesis affects the industry structure.

Chapter 11 sets forth the pricing policies called for under different market structures, then proceeds to show the limitations of economic theory in a world of uncertainty and how firms actually establish price policies. Since price/output decisions taken by firms operating in a completely unconstrained manner are not always in the public interest, certain rules and regulations, including antitrust laws and public utility regulations, have been developed to help make business decisions more consistent with the public interest; these topics are discussed in Chapter 12.

Chapter 13 explores long-run investment decisions, or capital budgeting, showing how firms combine demand analysis, production and cost theory, and risk analysis—all under constraints imposed by society—to make the strategic long-run investment decisions that shape the future of individual firms and of society itself.

SUMMARY

In the first section of this chapter we defined managerial economics as the application of economic theory and methodology to the practice of business administration. The traditional areas of study in both economics and business administration were delineated, and the place of managerial economics in this framework was discussed. As we see it, managerial economics fits into the business administration curriculum in two places: (1) as a tool course, wherein certain theories, methods, and techniques are covered in preparation for their later use in functional areas such as marketing, accounting, finance, and production; and (2) as an integrating course, which combines the various functional areas and shows how they interact with one another to help the firm achieve its goals.

The role of business in society was considered, and, on the basis of this discussion, the basic model of how a firm operates, or the *economic theory of the firm,* was developed. This model is based on the premise that managers seek to maximize the value of their firms, subject to constraints imposed by society. Although alternative models, including satisficing and multiple-goal models, were discussed briefly, the constrained economic model, which has proved to be most useful in solving actual business problems, was stressed.

A key element in the model is the firm's profit stream—the value of the firm is the present value of expected future profits. Because profits are so critical, the nature of profits, including both the theories used to justify their existence and the problems encountered in measuring them, received attention.

The reader should always have in mind the overall nature of managerial economics; only in this way can one see how each individual topic fits into the general scheme of things and understand how each section builds toward providing a general model of business behavior. To help provide a "road map" for managerial economics, a topical outline was set forth in the final section of the chapter.

QUESTIONS

1-1 In what sense could managerial economics be called an integrating course in a business-school curriculum?

1-2 What does the term "social responsibility of business" mean? What is the social responsibility of business?

1-3 Do you feel that it is reasonable to expect firms to take actions that are in the public interest, but detrimental to stockholders, on a voluntary basis, or must such actions be regulated or otherwise enforced?

1-4 Should the profit motive be retained as a major component of our economic system? What feasible alternative to profits can you suggest?

1-5 In terms of the valuation model discussed in this chapter, explain the effects of each of the following:

a) The firm is required to install new equipment to reduce air pollution.

b) The firm's marketing department, through heavy expenditures on advertising, increases sales substantially.

c) The production department purchases new equipment which lowers manufacturing costs.

d) The Federal Reserve System takes actions that lower interest rates dramatically.

e) The firm raises prices. Demand in the short run is unaffected, but in the longer run unit sales can be expected to decline.

SELECTED REFERENCES

Anthony, Robert N. "The Trouble with Profit Maximization," *Harvard Business Review*, November-December 1960, pp. 126-134.

Baumol, William J. "What Can Economic Theory Contribute to Managerial Economics?," *American Economic Review, Papers and Proceedings,* May 1961, pp. 142-146.

Friedman, Milton. "The Methodology of Positive Economics," *Essays in Positive Economics.* Chicago: The University of Chicago Press, 1953, pp. 3-43.

Machlup, Fritz. "Theories of the Firm: Marginalist, Behavioral, Managerial," *American Economic Review,* March 1967, pp. 1-33.

Shubik, Martin. "Approaches to the Study of Decision Making Relevant to the Firm," *Journal of Business,* April 1961, pp. 101-118.

―――. "A Curmudgeon's Guide to Microeconomics," *Journal of Economic Literature,* June 1970, pp. 405-429.

Solomons, David. "Economic and Accounting Concepts of Incomes," *The Accounting Review,* July 1961, pp. 374-383.

Whitin, Thomson. "Managerial Economics and the Firm," *American Economic Review,* May 1960, pp. 549-555.

CHAPTER 2

Optimizing Techniques

Optimization is the process of determining the best possible solution to a given problem. If only one solution, or action, is possible, no decision problem exists, and optimization is not involved. If a number of alternative courses of action are available, however, the course that produces a result most consistent with the decision-maker's goal is the optimal action. The process of finding this best action, or decision, is called optimization.

OPTIMIZATION: MAXIMIZING THE VALUE OF THE FIRM

In managerial economics the primary objective of management is assumed to be maximization of the firm's value. This objective is expressed in Equation 2-1:

$$\text{Value} = \sum_{t=1}^{n} \frac{\text{Profit}_t}{(1+i)^t} = \sum_{t=1}^{n} \frac{\text{Total Revenue}_t - \text{Total Cost}_t}{(1+i)^t}, \qquad (2\text{-}1)$$

which was introduced in Chapter 1.[1] Maximizing Equation 2-1 is a complex task, involving the determinants of revenues, costs, and the discount rate in each future year of some unspecified time horizon. Further, revenues, costs, and the discount rate are all interrelated, and this complicates the problem even more.

An example of the interrelationships involved in Equation 2-1 should help clarify both the concept and the difficulties. A firm's total revenues are determined in large part by the products it designs, manufactures, and sells; by the advertising strategies it employs; by the pricing policy it establishes; and by the general state of the economy. The firm's marketing department typically prepares a sales forecast on the basis of a set of assumptions about such variables as price charged, advertising expenditures, product quality, the general level of economic activity, and so on.

Simultaneously, the production department examines the cost relationships involved in producing the firm's products. This examination includes an analysis of the cost of alternative production systems. For example, on the one hand the firm could use a small plant and employ overtime; on the other hand it could build a larger plant, incur higher fixed costs, but avoid overtime. Using this and similar information, the production manager determines the least-cost method of producing each alternative combination of products.

Finally, the financial manager must analyze the relationship between the discount rate and the company's product mix, physical assets, and financial structure. These factors combine to determine the discount rate used by investors (in Equation 2-1) to establish a value for the firm.

The marketing, production, and financial decisions—as well as decisions related to personnel, transportation, and so on—must be combined into a single integrated system—one which shows how any action affects all parts of the firm—to truly determine the optimal course of action.

The complexity involved in this integrated, total optimization process typically limits the use of the procedure to major planning decisions. For many day-to-day operating decisions, much less complicated partial, or sub-optimizing, techniques are employed. Partial optimization abstracts somewhat from the complexity of the total optimization process by concentrating on more limited objectives within the firm's various operating departments. For example, the marketing department is usually required to determine the price and advertising policy that will maximize sales, given the firm's product line; the production department is expected to minimize the cost of producing a specified quantity of output of a stated quality level.

---

[1] In Chapter 1 it was pointed out that the firm operates subject to such constraints as antitrust laws, labor contracts, pollution-control requirements, and so on. We might also note that the firm seeks to maximize the wealth of its *existing owners*, so an action that raises the value of the entire firm but reduces the wealth of present owners would not be optimal. In subsequent chapters these and other qualifications are made more explicit, and the matter of wealth versus utility or happiness is considered.

The optimization process, regardless of whether it is partial or total, takes place in two steps. First, the economic relationships must be expressed in a form suitable for analysis—generally, this means expressing the problem in analytical terms. Second, various techniques are applied to determine the optimal solution to the problem at hand. In this chapter we first introduce a number of methods widely used for expressing economic relationships, and then examine several related analytical tools frequently used in the second part of the optimizing process.[2]

METHODS OF EXPRESSING ECONOMIC RELATIONSHIPS

Equations, tables in which relationships are enumerated, and graphs in which these relations are plotted are all frequently used to express economic relations. A table or a graph may be sufficient for the purpose at hand. When the problem is really complex, however, equations are necessary so that the powerful analytical tools of algebra and calculus may be used.

Functional Relationships: Equations

Perhaps the easiest way to examine the various means of expressing the economic relationships just mentioned and, at the same time, to gain an insight into the techniques of optimization is to consider several functional relationships which play key roles in the basic valuation model. Consider first a hypothetical relationship between output, Q, and total revenue, TR. Using functional notation, we can express the relationship in general terms as:

$$TR = f(Q). \qquad (2\text{-}2)$$

Equation 2-2 is read "Total revenue is a function of output." The value of the dependent variable, total revenue, is determined by the independent variable, output.[3]

Equation 2-2 does not indicate the specific relationship between output and total revenue; it merely states that some relationship exists. A more specific expression of the functional relationship is provided by the equation:

$$TR = \$1.50Q. \qquad (2\text{-}3)$$

Here the precise manner in which the value of the dependent variable is related to the independent variable is specified: Total revenue is always equal to $1.5 times the quantity of output sold.

---

[2] One important optimizing technique, linear programming, is deferred until Chapter 7, where it is analyzed in conjunction with production decisions.

[3] In an equation such as this one, the variable to the left of the equals sign is called the *dependent variable,* as its value *depends* on the size of the variable or variables to the right of the equals sign. The variables on the right-hand side of the equals sign are called *independent variables,* because their values are determined outside, or *independently,* of the model expressed in the equation.

Functional Relationships: Tables and Graphs

In addition to equations, tables and graphs are often used to express economic relationships. The data in Table 2-1, for example, express exactly the

Table 2-1 Relationship between Total Revenue and Output: Total Revenue = $1.50 · Output

Total Revenue	Output
$1.5	1
3.0	2
4.5	3
6.0	4
7.5	5
9.0	6

same functional relationship specified by Equation 2-3, and this same function is graphically illustrated in Figure 2-1. All three methods of expressing relationships play an important role in presenting and analyzing data for managerial decision making.

Figure 2-1 Graph of the Relationship between Total Revenue and Output

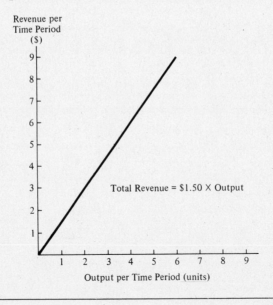

TOTAL, AVERAGE, AND MARGINAL RELATIONSHIPS

Total, average, and marginal relationships are very useful in optimization analysis. The definitions of totals and averages are too well known to warrant restating, but it is perhaps appropriate to define the term "marginal." *A marginal relationship is defined as the change in the dependent variable of a function associated with a unitary change in one of the independent variables.* In the total revenue function, marginal revenue is the change in total revenue associated with a one-unit change in output.

Because the very essence of the optimizing process involves analysis of changes, the marginal concept is of critical importance. Typically, we analyze a fully specified objective function by changing the various independent variables to see what effect these changes have on the dependent variable. In other words, we are examining the *marginal* effect of changes in the independent variables on the dependent variable. Obviously, the purpose of this analysis is to locate that set of values for the independent variables which optimizes the objective function.[4]

Relationship between Totals and Marginals

Table 2-2 shows the relationship between totals, marginals, and averages for a hypothetical profit function. Columns 1 and 2 show the assumed output/profit relationship; column 3 shows marginal profits for one-unit changes in output; and column 4 gives the average profit per unit of output.

Marginal profit refers to the change in profit associated with each one-unit change in output. The marginal profit of the first unit of output, for example, is $19. This is the change from the $0 profits related to an output of 0 units to the $19 profit earned when 1 unit is produced. Likewise, the $33 marginal profit associated with the second unit of output is the increase in total profits ($52 − $19) that results when output is increased from 1 to 2 units.

Notice that total profits for any level of output are always equal to the sum of all the marginal profits up to that output level. The $136 profit associated with 4 units of output, for example, is equal to the sum of the marginal profit of the first, second, third, and fourth units of output; that is, $136 = $19 + $33 + $41 + $43. *For any economic relationship, the total function will always be equal to the sum of all preceding marginal values.*

The importance of the total/marginal relationship in optimality analysis lies in the fact that when the marginal is positive, the total is increasing;

---

[4] In managerial economics we are frequently not interested in one-unit changes but, rather, in the effects of changes over wider ranges. An analysis of these wider changes, defined as *incremental analysis*, can be understood most easily after one understands the nature of the basic relationships as they are developed in *marginal analysis*. Accordingly, in this chapter, and throughout the text, we generally present the basic elements of economic theory in terms of marginal analysis, and then go on to show how the marginal concepts are modified and used in incremental analysis.

Table 2-2 Total, Marginal, and Average Relationships for a Hypothetical Profit Function

Units of Output (1)	Total Profits (2)	Marginal Profits = Change in Total Profits* (3)	Average Profits = (2) ÷ (1) (4)
0	$ 0	$ 0	—
1	19	19	$19
2	52	33	26
3	93	41	31
4	136	43	34
5	175	39	35
6	210	35	35
7	217	7	31
8	208	−9	26

* Marginal profits = Δ profits = Total profits$_q$ − Total profits$_{q-1}$. The symbol Δ, read "delta," denotes difference, or change.

and when the marginal is negative, the total is decreasing. The data in Table 2-2 can also be used to illustrate this point. The marginal profit associated with each of the first seven units of output is positive, and the total profits increase with output over this range. Since the marginal profit of the eighth unit is negative, however, profits are reduced if output is raised to that level. Thus, maximization of the profit function—or any function for that matter— occurs at the point where the marginal relationship shifts from positive to negative. This relationship is discussed in greater detail later in this chapter.

Relationship between Averages and Marginals

The relationship between average and marginal values is also important in optimization analysis. Since the marginal represents the change in the total, it follows that when the marginal is greater than the average, the average must be increasing. For example, if ten football players average 200 pounds, and an eleventh player (the marginal player), weighing 250 pounds, is added to the team, the average weight of the team increases. Likewise, if the marginal player weighs less than 200 pounds, the average will decrease.

Once again the data in Table 2-2 can be used to illustrate the marginal/ average relationship. In going from 4 units of output to 5, marginal profit, $39, is greater than the $34 average at 4 units; hence, average profit increases to $35. The marginal profit associated with the sixth unit, however, is $35, the same as the average, so average profit remains unchanged between 5 and 6 units. Finally, the marginal profit of the seventh unit is below the average, and this causes the average profit to fall.

Graphing the Total, Marginal, and Average Relationships

The relationships between totals, marginals, and averages can be demonstrated geometrically. Figure 2-2(a) presents a graph of the hypothetical profit output relationship given in Table 2-2. Each point on the curve represents a total profit/output combination, as do columns 1 and 2 of the table. Just as there is an arithmetic relationship between the totals, marginals, and

Figure 2-2 Geometrical Representation of Total; Marginal, and Average Relationships: (a) Total Profit; (b) Marginal and Average Profits

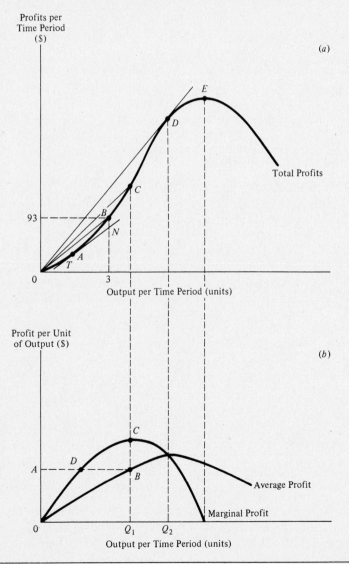

averages in the table, so, too, is there a corresponding geometrical relation-ship in the figure. The curves for the three quantities bear an exact mathe-matical relationship to one another; with any one curve given, the other two can be derived.

To see this relationship, consider first the average profit per unit of output at any point along the total profits curve. The average figure is equal to total profits divided by the corresponding number of units of output. Geometrically, this relationship is represented by the slope of a line from the origin to the point of interest on the total profits curve. For example, con-sider the slope of the line from the origin to point B in Figure 2-2 (a). Slope is a measure of the steepness of a line, and it is defined as the increase (or decrease) in height per unit of movement out along the horizontal axis. The slope of a straight line passing through the origin is determined by dividing the Y coordinate at any point on the line by the corresponding X coordinate.[5] Thus, the slope of the line $0B$ can be calculated by dividing \$93 (the Y coordinate at point B) by 3 (the X coordinate at point B). Notice, however, that in this process we are dividing total profits by the corresponding units of output. This is the definition of average profit at that point. *Thus, at any point along a total curve, the corresponding average figure is given by the slope of a straight line from the origin to that point.*

The marginal relationship has a similar geometrical association with the total curve. In Table 2-2 each marginal figure was shown to be the change in total profit associated with the last unit increase in output. This rise (or fall) in the total profit associated with a one-unit increase in output is the *slope* of the total profit curve at that point.

Slopes of nonlinear curves are typically found geometrically by draw-ing a line tangent to the curve at the point of interest and determining the slope of the tangent. (A tangent is a line which touches the curve at only one point.) In Figure 2-2(a), for example, the marginal profit at point A is equal to the slope of the total profit curve at that point, which is equal to the slope of the tangent labeled *TAN. Therefore, at any point along a total curve, the corresponding marginal figure is given by the slope of a line drawn tangent to the total curve at that point.*

Several important relationships between the total, marginal, and aver-age figures may now be examined. First, note that the slope of the total profit curve is increasing from the origin to point C. That is, lines drawn tangent to the total profit curve become steeper as the point of tangency approaches point C, so marginal profit is increasing up to this point. At point C, called an *inflection point,* the slope of the total profit curve is maximized; hence, marginal (but not average or total) profits are maximized at that point. Between points C and E, because marginal profit is still positive even though

---

[5] In general, slope $= \Delta Y/\Delta X = (Y_2 - Y_1)/(X_2 - X_1)$. Since X_1 and Y_1 are zero for any line going through the origin, slope $= Y_2/X_2$ or, more generally, slope $= Y/X$.

it is declining, total profit continues to increase. At point E a tangent to the total profit curve has a slope of zero and, thus, it is neither rising nor falling. Marginal profit at this point is therefore zero, and total profit is maximized. Beyond E the total profit curve has a negative slope, and marginal profit is negative.

In addition to the total/average and total/marginal relationships, the relation between marginals and averages is also demonstrated in Figure 2-2(a). Notice that the slopes of lines drawn from the origin to points on the total profit curve are increasing as one moves out along the curve to point D. Line $0C$, for example, is steeper than $0B$, and $0D$ in turn is steeper than $0C$. Over this range of total profits, the average is continuously increasing. Using the average marginal relationship discussed earlier, we know that if the average is rising, the corresponding marginal figure must be larger than the average. Geometrically, this means that the slope of the total profit curve at any point up to D is greater than the slope of a line drawn from the origin to that point on the curve.

At point D a line from the origin is tangent to the total profit curve. Its slope is exactly equal to the slope of the total curve, and at this point average profit equals marginal profit. Beyond D the slope of the total profit curve is smaller than that of a line drawn from the origin, so the marginal is less than the average, and average profit will decline if output is expanded beyond point D.

Marginal and Average Curves: An Alternative Graph
In Figure 2-2(a), marginal and average profits are graphed in terms of the slopes of the total profit curve and lines drawn from the origin to that curve. The average and marginal figures can also be plotted directly against output; such a graph is shown in Figure 2-2(b).

The relationships between marginals and averages discussed in the previous section are also apparent in Figure 2-2(b). At low output levels, where the marginal profit curve lies above the average, the average is rising. Although marginal profit reaches a maximum at output Q_1 and declines thereafter, the average curve continues to rise as long as the marginal lies above it. At output Q_2, marginal and average profits are equal, and here the average profit curve reaches its maximum value. Beyond Q_2, the marginal curve lies below the average, and the average is falling.

Deriving Totals from the Marginal or Average Curve
Just as it is possible to derive marginal and average profit figures from the total profit curve in Figure 2-2(a), we can also determine total profits from the marginal or average profit curves of Figure 2-2(b). Consider first the derivation of total profits from the average curve. Total profit is simply average profit times the corresponding number of units of output. The total profit associated with Q_1 units of output, for example, is average profit, A,

times output, Q_1, or, equivalently, total profit is equal to the area of the rectangle $0ABQ_1$. This relationship holds for all points along the average profit curve.

A similar relationship exists between marginal and total profits. Recall that the total is equal to the sum of all the marginals up to the specified output level. Thus, the total profit at any output is equal to the sum of the marginal profits up to that output quantity. Geometrically, this is the area under the marginal curve from the Y axis to the output quantity under consideration. At output Q_1 the total profit is equal to the area under the marginal profit curve, or the area $0DCBQ_1$.

Deriving a Marginal Curve from an Average Curve[6]
The fact that the area contained under both marginal and average curves represents the corresponding total figure enables us to construct marginal values when only average data are available. To see this, consider once more the total profit at output Q_1, in Figure 2-2(b). Using the average profit curve, total profit is equal to the area of the rectangle $0ABQ_1$; using the marginal curve it is the area $0DCBQ_1$. Since total profit at Q_1 must be the same regardless of which curve is used to derive it, these two areas must be equal. Further, the area $0DBQ_1$ is contained within both measures of total profit at Q_1. It follows therefore that area CDB, contained in the area under the marginal curve but not in the rectangle determined by the average profit figure, must be equal to the area $0AD$, which is in the rectangle $0ABQ_1$ but not under the marginal profits curve.

Linear Curves Since the two areas must be equal, there is a simple geometric relationship that allows the marginal curve to be constructed from the average. This relationship is somewhat easier to illustrate using linear curves, so consider first the average revenue curve shown in Figure 2-3. At output Q, total revenue as determined from the average revenue curve is equal to the area of the rectangle $0ABQ$. Proper construction of the marginal revenue curve requires that it begin at the point where the average curve cuts the Y axis,[7] because at the first unit of output, average and marginal revenues are equal. Further, the curve must be drawn so that triangles ACD and DBE have identical areas; otherwise the area $0ABQ$ will not equal $0CDEQ$, the area under the marginal curve.

Note that irrespective of the angle at which the marginal curve cuts the line AB, the triangles will have two identical angles; that is, they each have a right angle, and their respective angles at D are also equal. They must therefore be "similar" triangles. Now, reaching back for a little high-school geometry, recall that similar triangles of equal area are identical in

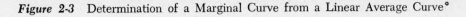

Figure 2-3   Determination of a Marginal Curve from a Linear Average Curve*

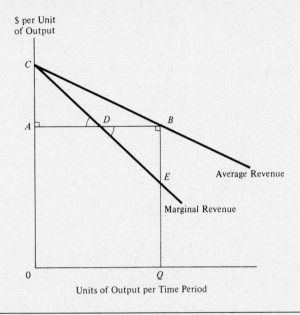

---

* For any linear average curve, the related marginal curve begins at the average curve's Y intercept and bisects any horizontal line from the Y axis to the average curve; that is, the marginal curve lies halfway between the average curve and the Y axis.

---

both size and shape. Thus, side AD in triangle ACD must be equal in length to side DB in triangle DBE. For this to occur, the marginal curve must bisect the horizontal line AB. This relationship is completely general: *For any linear average curve, the related marginal curve begins at the average curve's Y intercept and bisects any horizontal line from the Y axis to the average curve; that is, the marginal curve lies halfway between the average curve and the Y axis.*

Nonlinear Curves   Having demonstrated the geometrical determination of a marginal curve from a linear average curve, we now illustrate the procedure for nonlinear average curves. Although somewhat more difficult, it is similar to that illustrated above, consisting of the construction of linear tangencies for each point along the average curve and the use of these linear curves to determine *individual points* on the related marginal curve.

The technique is illustrated in Figure 2-4 with a standard U-shaped average cost curve. Here the point on the marginal cost curve associated with point A on the average curve, or, alternatively, the marginal cost for output Q_1, is determined: (1) By drawing the line tangent to that point; that is, line BAC. (2) By using the technique described above to find the

Figure 2-4 Construction of a Nonlinear Marginal Curve

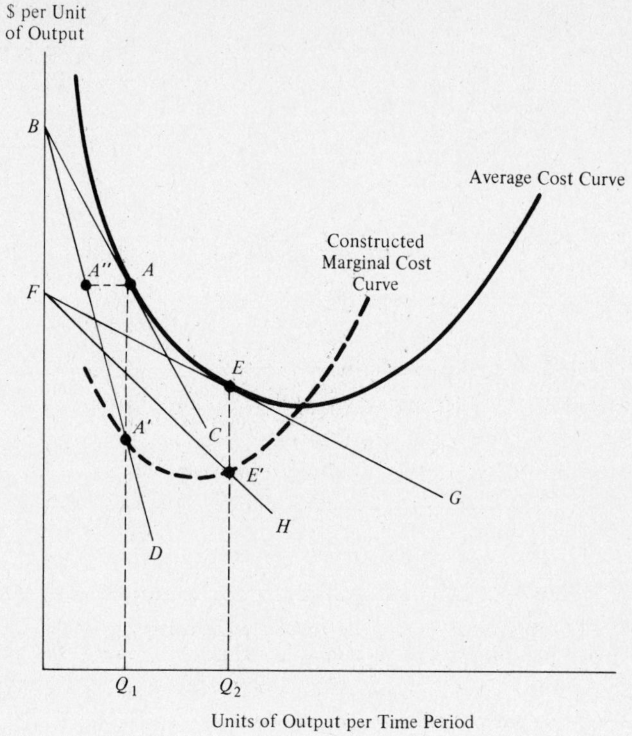

related linear marginal cost curve, $BA'D$. (3) By locating the related marginal cost figure at the intersection of a perpendicular line from A to the linear marginal cost curve, point A' in Figure 2-4.[8]

The process is repeated to locate a second point on the marginal curve, point E', the marginal cost associated with point E on the average curve. Line FEG is tangent to point E, and $FE'H$ is the associated linear marginal curve. Point E', which lies on that marginal curve directly below E, represents the marginal cost at Q_2 units of output. This procedure must be repeated for each point on the average cost curve, or at least for enough points to sketch out the marginal curve.

Because these average/marginal/total relationships are used repeatedly throughout the book, they should be thoroughly understood. The most common example of their use is in short-run profit maximization: Marginal cost and revenue curves are derived from average or total figures, and profits

---

[8] It should be emphasized that point A'' in Figure 2-4 is *not* on the marginal cost curve. The only point on line BD that is relevant for marginal cost determination is point A' which lies directly below the tangency at point A.

are maximized where marginal profit, equal to marginal revenue minus marginal cost, is zero. Thus, profit is maximized where marginal revenue is equal to marginal cost. This is only one illustration of the use of these concepts; many others will be encountered.

First, however, it is useful to consider some elementary calculus, which is exceptionally useful for finding optimal solutions to economic problems.

DIFFERENTIAL CALCULUS[9]

Although tables and graphs are useful for explaining concepts, equations are generally better suited for problem solving. One reason is that the powerful analytical technique of differential calculus can frequently be employed to locate maximum and minimum values.

Concept of a Derivative

Earlier, we defined a marginal value as *the change in the value of the dependent variable associated with a one-unit change in an independent variable.* Consider the unspecified function $Y = f(X)$. Using Δ (read delta) to denote change, we can express the change in the value of the independent variable, X, by the notation ΔX and the change in the dependent variable, Y, as ΔY.

The ratio $\Delta Y/\Delta X$ provides a very general specification of the marginal concept:

$$\text{Marginal } Y = \frac{\Delta Y}{\Delta X}. \qquad (2\text{-}4)$$

The change in Y, ΔY, divided by the change in X, ΔX, indicates the change in the dependent variable associated with a one-unit change in the value of X.

Figure 2-5, which is a graph of a function relating Y to X, illustrates this relationship. For values of X close to the origin, a relatively small change in X produces a large change in Y. Thus, the absolute value of $\Delta Y/\Delta X = (Y_2 - Y_1)/(X_2 - X_1)$ is relatively large, showing that a small increase in X induces a large decrease in Y. The situation is reversed further out the X axis. A large increase in X, say from X_3 to X_4, produces only a small decrease in Y, from Y_3 to Y_4, so $\Delta Y/\Delta X$ is small.

It is clear that the marginal relationship between X and Y, as shown in Figure 2-5, changes at different points on the curve. When the curve is rela-

[9] This section may be omitted by readers who are well grounded in calculus. While a knowledge of calculus is not necessary to follow the main ideas presented in the text, because we give both verbal and geometric interpretations to calculus formulations, we encourage all readers who do not have a good grasp of calculus to go through this section. Calculus was developed specifically for handling problems such as those found in managerial economics, so some concepts can be understood much more easily when expressed in these terms. Furthermore, the level of calculus we use is quite elementary and, therefore, not difficult to learn.

Figure 2-5   Illustration of Changing $\Delta Y/\Delta X$ over the Range of a Curve

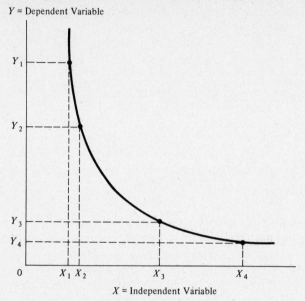

tively steep, the dependent variable Y is highly responsive to changes in the independent variable; but when the curve is relatively flat, Y is not influenced significantly by changes in X.

In concept, a *derivative* is a precise specification of the general marginal relationship, $\Delta Y/\Delta X$. Finding a derivative involves finding the value of the ratio $\Delta Y/\Delta X$ for extremely small changes in the independent variable. The mathematical notation for a derivative is:

$$\frac{dY}{dX} = \lim_{\Delta X \to 0} \frac{\Delta Y}{\Delta X}, \tag{2-5}$$

which is read: "The derivative of Y with respect to X equals the limit of the ratio $\Delta Y/\Delta X$, as ΔX approaches zero." [10]

---

[10] A limit can be explained briefly in the following manner: If the value of a function $Y = f(X)$ approaches a constant Y^* as the value of the independent variable X approaches X^*, then Y^* is called the limit of the function as X approaches X^*. This would be written as:

$$\lim_{X \to X^*} f(X) = Y^*.$$

For example, if $Y = X - 4$, then the limit of this function as X approaches 5 is 1; that is:

$$\lim_{X \to 5} (X - 4) = 1.$$

This says that as the value of X approaches, but does not quite reach, 5, the value of the function $Y = X - 4$ comes closer and closer to 1. This concept of a limit is examined in detail in any introductory calculus textbook.

This concept of the derivative as the limit of a ratio is precisely equivalent to the slope of a curve at a point. Figure 2-6 presents this idea, using the same curve relating Y to X shown in Figure 2-5. Notice that in Figure 2-6 the *average* slope of the curve between points A and D is measured as:

$$\frac{\Delta Y}{\Delta X} = \frac{Y_4 - Y_1}{X_4 - X_1},$$

and is shown as the slope of the chord connecting the two points. Similarly, the average slope of the curve can be measured over smaller and smaller intervals of X and shown by other chords, such as those connecting points B and C with D. At the limit, as ΔX approaches zero, the ratio $\Delta Y/\Delta X$ is equal to the slope of a line drawn tangent to the curve at point D. *The slope of this tangent is defined as the derivative, $\mathrm{d}Y/\mathrm{d}X$, of the function at point D, and it measures the marginal change in Y associated with a very small change in X.*

For example, the dependent variable Y might be total costs, and the independent variable might be output. The derivative dY/dX then shows precisely how costs and output are related at a specific output level. Since the change in cost associated with a change in output is defined as the marginal cost, the derivative of the total cost function provides a precise measure of marginal costs at any specific output level. A similar situation exists

Figure 2-6 Illustration of a Derivative as the Slope of a Curve

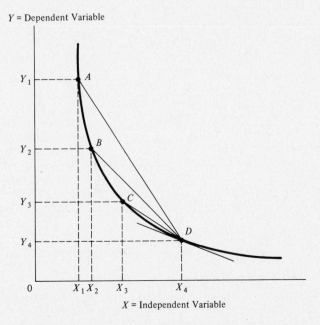

for total revenues: The derivative of the total revenue function at any output level indicates the marginal revenue at that output.

It is apparent that derivatives provide useful information in managerial economics. Other illustrations of their usefulness will be considered later, but first the rules for finding the derivatives of certain frequently encountered functions are provided.

RULES FOR DIFFERENTIATING A FUNCTION

Determining the derivative of a function is not a particularly difficult task; it simply involves applying a basic formula to the function. The basic formulas, or rules for differentiation, are presented below. Proofs are omitted here, but they can be found in any introductory calculus textbook.

Constants

The derivative of a constant is always zero; that is, if $Y =$ a constant, then:

$$\frac{dY}{dX} = 0.$$

This situation is graphed in Figure 2-7. Since Y is defined to be a constant, it does not vary as X changes, and hence dY/dX must be zero.

Powers

The derivative of a power function such as $Y = aX^b$, where a and b are constants, is equal to the exponent b multiplied by the coefficient a times the variable X raised to the $b - 1$ power:

$$Y = aX^b$$

$$\frac{dY}{dX} = b \cdot a \cdot X^{(b-1)}.$$

Figure 2-7 Graph of a Constant Function—$Y =$ Constant; $dY/dX = 0$

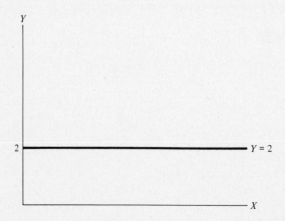

For example, given the function:

$$Y = 2X^3,$$

then:

$$\frac{dY}{dX} = 3 \cdot 2 \cdot X^{(3-1)}$$

$$= 6X^2.$$

Two further examples of power functions should clarify this rule. The derivative of the function $Y = X^3$ is given as:

$$\frac{dY}{dX} = 3 \cdot X^2.$$

The exponent, 3, is multiplied by the implicit coefficient, 1, and in turn by the variable, X, raised to the second power.

Finally, the derivative of the function $Y = 0.5X$ is 0.5:

$$\frac{dY}{dX} = 1 \cdot 0.5 \cdot X^{1-1} = 1 \cdot 0.5 \cdot X^0 = 0.5.$$

The implicit exponent, 1, is multiplied by the coefficient, .5, times the variable, X, raised to the zero power. Since any number raised to the zero power equals 1, the result is 0.5.

Again, a graph may help to make the power function concept clear. In Figure 2-8, the last two power functions given above, $Y = X^3$ and $Y = .5X$, are graphed. Consider first $Y = .5X$. The derivative of this function, $dY/dX = .5$, is a constant, indicating that the slope of the function is a constant. This can be seen readily from the graph. The derivative measures the *rate of*

Figure 2-8 Graphs of Power Functions

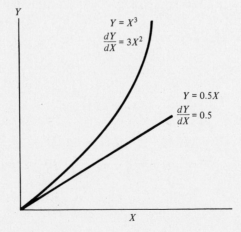

change. If the rate of change is constant, as it must be if the basic function is linear, then the derivative of the function must be a constant. The second function, $Y = X^3$, rises at an increasing rate as X increases. The derivative of the function, $dY/dX = 3X^2$, also increases as X becomes larger, indicating that the slope of the function is increasing, or that the rate of change is increasing.

Sums and Differences

The following notation is used throughout the remainder of this section to express a number of other important rules of differentiation:

$$U = g(X): U \text{ is an unspecified function, } g, \text{ of } X.$$
$$V = h(X): V \text{ is an unspecified function, } h, \text{ of } X.$$

The derivative of a sum (difference) is equal to the sum (difference) of the derivatives of the individual terms. Thus, if $Y = U + V$, then:

$$\frac{dY}{dX} = \frac{dU}{dX} + \frac{dV}{dX}.$$

For example, if $U = g(X) = 2X^2$, $V = h(X) = -X^3$, and $Y = U + V = 2X^2 - X^3$, then:

$$\frac{dY}{dX} = 4X - 3X^2.$$

Here the derivative of $2X^2$ is found to be $4X$ by the power rule; the derivative of $-X^3$ is found to be $-3X^2$ by that same rule; and the derivative of the function is the sum of the derivatives of the parts.

Consider a second example of this rule. If $Y = 300 + 5X + 2X^2$, then:

$$\frac{dY}{dX} = 0 + 5 + 4X.$$

The derivative of 300 is 0 by the constant rule; the derivative of $5X$ is 5 by the power rule; and the derivative of $2X^2$ is $4X$ also by the power rule.

Products

The derivative of the product of two expressions is equal to the sum of the first term multiplied by the derivative of the second, *plus* the second term times the derivative of the first. Thus, if $Y = U \cdot V$, then:

$$\frac{dY}{dX} = U \cdot \frac{dV}{dX} + V \cdot \frac{dU}{dX}.$$

For example, if $Y = 3X^2(3 - X)$, then letting $U = 3X^2$ and $V = (3 - X)$:

$$\frac{dY}{dX} = 3X^2 \left(\frac{dV}{dX}\right) + (3 - X)\left(\frac{dU}{dX}\right)$$
$$= 3X^2(-1) + (3 - X)(6X)$$
$$= -3X^2 + 18X - 6X^2$$
$$= 18X - 9X^2.$$

The first factor, $3X^2$, is multiplied by the derivative of the second, -1, and added to the second factor, $3-X$, times the derivative of the first, $6X$. Simplifying the expression results in the final expression shown.

Quotients

The derivative of the quotient of two expressions is equal to the denominator multiplied by the derivative of the numerator *minus* the numerator times the derivative of the denominator—all divided by the square of the denominator. Thus, if $Y = U/V$, then:

$$\frac{dY}{dX} = \frac{V \cdot \dfrac{dU}{dX} - U \cdot \dfrac{dV}{dX}}{V^2}.$$

For example, if $U = 2X - 3$ and $V = 6X^2$, then:

$$Y = \frac{2X - 3}{6X^2}$$

and

$$\begin{aligned}
\frac{dY}{dX} &= \frac{6X^2 \cdot 2 - (2X - 3)12X}{36X^4} \\
&= \frac{12X^2 - 24X^2 + 36X}{36X^4} \\
&= \frac{36X - 12X^2}{36X^4} \\
&= \frac{3 - X}{3X^3}.
\end{aligned}$$

The denominator, $6X^2$, is multiplied by the derivative of the numerator, 2. Subtracted from this is the numerator, $2X - 3$, times the derivative of the denominator, $12X$. The result is then divided by the square of the denominator, $36X^4$. Algebraic reduction results in the final expression of the derivative.

Function of a Function (Chain Rule)

The derivative of a function of a function is found as follows. If $Y = f(U)$, where $U = g(X)$, then:

$$\frac{dY}{dX} = \frac{dY}{dU} \cdot \frac{dU}{dX}.$$

For example, if $Y = 2U - U^2$, and $U = 2X^3$, then we find dY/dX as follows:

Step 1

$$\frac{dY}{dU} = 2 - 2U.$$

Substituting for U, we have:

$$\frac{dY}{dU} = 2 - 2(2X^3)$$

$$= 2 - 4X^3.$$

Step 2

$$\frac{dU}{dX} = 6X^2.$$

Step 3

$$\frac{dY}{dX} = \frac{dY}{dU} \cdot \frac{dU}{dX}$$

$$= (2 - 4X^3) \cdot 6X^2$$

$$= 12X^2 - 24X^5.$$

Further examples of this rule should indicate its usefulness in obtaining derivatives of many functions.

Example 1

$$Y = \sqrt{X^2 - 1}.$$

Let $U = X^2 - 1$. Then, $Y = \sqrt{U} = U^{1/2}$.

$$\frac{dY}{dU} = \frac{1}{2}U^{-1/2}$$

$$= \frac{1}{2U^{1/2}}.$$

Substituting $X^2 - 1$ for U in the derivative results in:

$$\frac{dY}{dU} = \frac{1}{2(X^2 - 1)^{1/2}}.$$

Since $U = X^2 - 1$:

$$\frac{dU}{dX} = 2X.$$

Using the function of a function rule, $dY/dX = dY/dU \cdot dU/dX$, so:

$$\frac{dY}{dX} = \frac{1}{2(X^2 - 1)^{1/2}} \cdot 2X$$

$$= \frac{X}{\sqrt{X^2 - 1}}.$$

Example 2

$$Y = \frac{1}{X^2 - 2}.$$

Let $U = X^2 - 2$. Then $Y = 1/U$, and, using the quotient rule, we find:

$$\frac{dY}{dU} = \frac{U \cdot 0 - 1 \cdot 1}{U^2}$$

$$= -\frac{1}{U^2}.$$

Substituting $(X^2 - 2)$ for U we obtain:

$$\frac{dY}{dU} = -\frac{1}{(X^2 - 2)^2}.$$

Since $U = X^2 - 2$:

$$\frac{dU}{dX} = 2X.$$

Therefore:

$$\frac{dY}{dX} = \frac{dY}{dU} \cdot \frac{dU}{dX} = -\frac{1}{(X^2 - 2)^2} \cdot 2X$$

$$= -\frac{2X}{(X^2 - 2)^2}.$$

Example 3

$$Y = (2X + 3)^2.$$

Let $U = 2X + 3$. Then $Y = U^2$, and:

$$\frac{dY}{dU} = 2U.$$

Since $U = 2X + 3$:

$$\frac{dY}{dU} = 2(2X + 3)$$

$$= 4X + 6,$$

and

$$\frac{dU}{dX} = 2.$$

Thus:

$$\frac{dY}{dX} = \frac{dY}{dU} \cdot \frac{dU}{dX} = (4X + 6)2$$

$$= 8X + 12.$$

Miscellaneous Rules for Differentiation

Although the preceding rules are those most commonly needed for differentiating economic expressions, other rules are used for special kinds of functions. A number of these are listed below for reference purposes only; they are not encountered in the functions discussed in this text.[11]

1. If $Y = ae^{bX}$, then $\dfrac{dY}{dX} = bae^{bX}$.

2. If $Y = a \log_e bX$, then $\dfrac{dY}{dX} = \dfrac{a}{X}$.

3. If $Y = a^X$, then $\dfrac{dY}{dX} = a^X \log_e a$.

4. If $Y = a \sin bX$, then $\dfrac{dY}{dX} = ab \cos bX$.

5. If $Y = a \cos bX$, then $\dfrac{dY}{dX} = -ab \sin bX$.

USE OF DERIVATIVES TO MAXIMIZE OR MINIMIZE FUNCTIONS

The process of optimization frequently requires us to find the maximum value for a function. For a function to be at a maximum (or a minimum), its slope must be zero, and since the derivative measures a function's slope, maximization occurs where the derivative is equal to zero. To illustrate, consider the following profit function:

$$\pi = -\$10{,}000 + \$400Q - \$2Q^2.$$

Here $\pi =$ total profit, and Q is output in units. As shown in Figure 2-9, if output is zero, the firm incurs a $10,000 loss (fixed costs are $10,000); but as output rises, profit also rises. A breakeven point is reached at 28 units of output; profit is maximized (at $10,000) at 100 units; and a second breakeven point is reached at 172 units.

The profit-maximizing output could be found by calculating the value of the function at a number of outputs, then plotting these as was done in Figure 2-9. The maximum can also be located by finding the derivative of the function, then determining the value of Q that makes the derivative equal to zero.

$$\frac{d\pi}{dQ} = 400 - 4Q,$$

[11] In these equations e is the Naperian constant, 2.718. It is used in growth models, continuous compounding, and as a base for natural logarithms.

Figure 2-9 Profit as a Function of Output

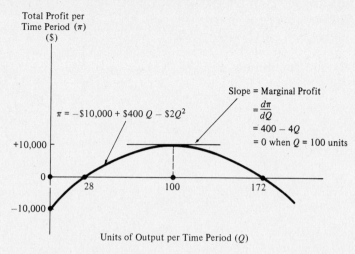

and setting the derivative equal to zero results in:

$$400 - 4Q = 0$$
$$4Q = 400$$
$$Q = 100.$$

Therefore, when $Q = 100$, profit is at a maximum. Even in this simple illustration it is easier to locate the profit-maximizing value by calculus than by graphic analysis; had the function been more complex, only the calculus solution would have been feasible.

Second-order Derivatives

A problem can arise when derivatives are being used to locate maximums or minimums. The first derivative of the total function provides a measure of whether the function is rising or falling at any point. To be maximized or minimized, the function must be neither rising nor falling; that is, the slope as measured by the first derivative must be zero. However, the condition $dY/dX = 0$ exists for both maximum and minimum values of a function, and further analysis is necessary to determine whether a maximum or a minimum has been located.

This point is illustrated in Figure 2-10, where we see that the slope of the total profit curve is zero at both points A and B. Point A, however, locates the output that minimizes profits, while B locates the profit-maximizing output.

The concept of a second-order derivative is used to distinguish between maximums and minimums along a function. The second-order derivative is simply the derivative of the original derivative; it is determined in

Figure 2-10 Locating Maximum and Minimum Values of a Function

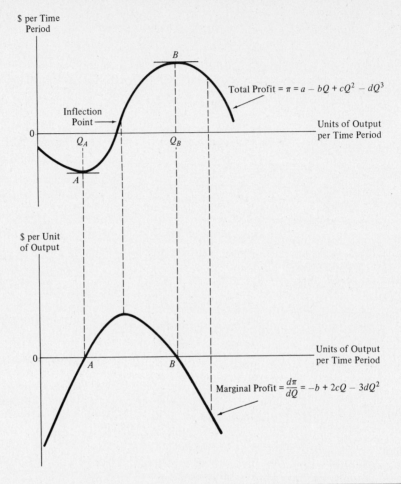

precisely the same manner as a first derivative. Thus, if $\pi = a - bQ + cQ^2 - dQ^3$, as in Figure 2-10, then the first-order derivative is:

$$\frac{d\pi}{dQ} = -b + 2cQ - 3dQ^2, \qquad (2\text{-}6)$$

and the second-order derivative is the derivative of Equation 2-6, or:

$$\frac{d^2\pi}{dQ^2} = 2c - 6dQ.$$

Just as the first derivative measures the slope of the total profit function, the second derivative represents the slope of the first derivative or, in this case, the slope of the marginal profit curve. We can use the second-derivative concept to distinguish between points of maximization and minimization due to the fact that the second derivative is always *negative* when evaluated at a point of *maximization* and *positive* at a point of *minimization*.

The reason for this inverse relationship can be seen by referring to Figure 2-10. Note that profits reach a local minimum at point A because marginal profits, which have been negative and therefore causing total profits to fall, suddenly become positive. Alternatively stated, marginal profits pass through the zero level from below at point A and, hence, are increasing or positively sloped. The reverse situation holds at a point of local maximization; the marginal value is declining and, hence, is negatively sloped.

A numerical example should help clarify this concept. Assume that the total profit function illustrated in Figure 2-10 is given by the following equation:

$$\text{Total Profit} = \pi = -\$3,000 - \$2,400Q + \$350Q^2 - \$8.333Q^3. \quad (2\text{-}7)$$

Marginal profit is given by the first derivative of the total profit function:

$$\text{Marginal Profit} = \frac{d\pi}{dQ} = -\$2,400 + \$700Q - \$25Q^2. \quad (2\text{-}8)$$

Total profit is either maximized or minimized at the points where the first derivative, marginal profits, is zero; that is, where:

$$\frac{d\pi}{dQ} = -\$2,400 + \$700Q - \$25Q^2 = 0. \quad (2\text{-}9)$$

Output quantities of 4 and 24 units satisfy Equation 2-9 and are therefore points of either maximum or minimum profits.[12]

---

[12] Any equation of the form $Y = a + bX + cX^2$ is a quadratic, and its two roots can be found by the general quadratic equation:

$$X = \frac{-b \pm \sqrt{b^2 - 4ac}}{2c}.$$

Substituting the values from Equation 2-9 into the quadratic equation, we obtain:

$$X = \frac{-700 \pm \sqrt{700^2 - 4(-2,400)(-25)}}{2(-25)} = \frac{-700 \pm \sqrt{490,000 - 240,000}}{-50}$$

$$X = \frac{-700 \pm \sqrt{250,000}}{-50} = \frac{-700 \pm 500}{-50}.$$

The minus root is:

$$X_1 = \frac{-700 - 500}{-50} = \frac{-1,200}{-50} = 24 \text{ units,}$$

and the plus root is:

$$X_2 = \frac{-700 + 500}{-50} = \frac{-200}{-50} = 4 \text{ units.}$$

One word of caution. Students may remember the quadratic equation as having 2a in the denominator rather than 2c. The reason is that in many mathematics books the functional relationship is written as $Y = aX^2 + bX + c$. We choose not to write the equation in this form because in *economic* expressions the constant term, which we call *a*, is generally placed first.

Evaluation of the second derivative of the total profit function at each of these points will indicate whether they are minimums or maximums. The second derivative of the total profit function is found by taking the derivative of the marginal profit function, Equation 2-8:

$$\frac{d^2\pi}{dQ^2} = +\$700 - \$50Q.$$

At output quantity $Q = 4$:

$$\frac{d^2\pi}{dQ^2} = \$700 - \$50 \cdot 4 = \$700 - \$200 = \$500.$$

Since the second derivative is positive, indicating that marginal profits are increasing, total profit is *minimized* at 4 units of output. In other words, total profit at 4 units of output corresponds to point A in Figure 2-10.

Evaluating the second derivative at 24 units of output, we obtain:

$$\frac{d^2\pi}{dQ^2} = \$700 - \$50 \cdot 24 = \$700 - \$1,200 = -\$500.$$

Since the second derivative is negative at 24 units, indicating that marginal profit is decreasing, the total profit function has reached a *maximum* at that point. This output level corresponds to point B in Figure 2-10.

Use of Derivatives to Maximize the Difference between Two Functions

The very important and well-known microeconomic corollary that marginal revenue equals marginal cost when profits are maximized has its basis in the calculus of optimization. It stems from the fact that the distance between two functions is maximized at the point where their slopes are the same; Figure 2-11 illustrates the point. Here hypothetical revenue and cost functions are shown. Total profit is equal to total revenue minus total cost and is, therefore, equal to the vertical distance between the two curves. This distance is maximized at output Q_B, where the slopes of the revenue and cost curves are equal. Since the slopes of the total revenue and total cost curves measure marginal revenues and marginal costs, where these slopes are equal, $MR = MC$.

The reason that Q_B is the profit-maximizing output can be seen in another way by considering the shapes of the two curves to the right of point A. At A total revenue equals total cost, and we have a breakeven point; that is, an output quantity where profits are zero. At output quantities just beyond Q_A, total revenue is rising faster than total cost, so profits are increasing and the curves are spreading farther apart. This diverging of the curves continues as long as total revenue is rising faster than total cost; in other words, as long as $MR > MC$. Once the slope of the total revenue curve is exactly equal to the slope of the total cost curve—in other words, where marginal revenue equals marginal cost—they will be parallel and no longer diverging.

Figure 2-11 Total Revenue, Total Cost, and Profit Maximization

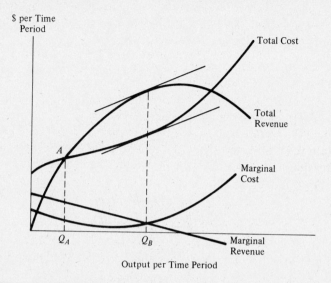

This occurs at output Q_B. Beyond Q_B the slope of the cost curve is greater than that of the revenue curve (marginal cost is greater than marginal revenue), so the distance between them is decreasing and total profits decline.

A numerical example will help to clarify this use of derivatives. Consider the following revenue, cost, and profit functions. Let:

$$\text{Total Revenue} = TR = 41.5Q - 1.1Q^2.$$
$$\text{Total Cost} \quad\; = TC = 150 + 10Q - 0.5Q^2 + 0.02Q^3.$$
$$\text{Total Profit} \quad = \pi = TR - TC.$$

The profit-maximizing output can be found by substituting the total revenue and total cost functions into the profit function, then analyzing the first and second derivatives of that equation:

$$
\begin{aligned}
\pi &= TR - TC \\
&= 41.5Q - 1.1Q^2 - (150 + 10Q - 0.5Q^2 + 0.02Q^3) \\
&= 41.5Q - 1.1Q^2 - 150 - 10Q + 0.5Q^2 - 0.02Q^3 \\
&= -150 + 31.5Q - 0.6Q^2 - 0.02Q^3.
\end{aligned}
$$

Marginal profit, the first derivative of the profit function is:

$$M\pi = \frac{d\pi}{dQ} = 31.5 - 1.2Q - 0.06Q^2.$$

Setting marginal profit equal to zero and using the quadratic equation to solve for the two roots, we obtain $Q_1 = -35$ and $Q_2 = +15$. Since negative output quantities are not possible, Q_1 is a nonfeasible root and can be discarded.

An evaluation of the second derivative of the profit function at $Q = 15$ will indicate whether this is a point of profit maximization or profit minimization. The second derivative is given by:

$$\frac{d^2\pi}{dQ^2} = -1.2 - 0.12Q.$$

Evaluating this derivative at $Q = 15$ indicates a value of -3.0; therefore, $Q = 15$ is a point of profit maximization.

To see the relationship of marginal revenue and marginal cost to profit maximization, consider once again the general profit expression $\pi = TR - TC$. Using the sums and differences rule of differentiation, note that a completely general expression for marginal profit is:

$$M\pi = \frac{d\pi}{dQ} = \frac{dTR}{dQ} - \frac{dTC}{dQ}.$$

Given that dTR/dQ is by definition the expression for marginal revenue, MR, and that dTC/dQ represents marginal cost, MC, we have:

$$M\pi = MR - MC.$$

Now, since maximization of any function requires that the first derivative be set equal to zero, profit maximization will occur where:

$$M\pi = MR - MC = 0,$$

or where:

$$MR = MC.$$

Continuing with our numerical example, marginal revenue and marginal cost are found by differentiating the total revenue and total cost functions:

$$MR = \frac{dTR}{dQ} = 41.5 - 2.2Q.$$

$$MC = \frac{dTC}{dQ} = 10 - Q + 0.06Q^2.$$

At the profit-maximizing output level, $MR = MC$; thus:

$$MR = 41.5 - 2.2Q = 10 - Q + 0.06Q^2 = MC.$$

Combining terms, we obtain:

$$-31.5 + 1.2Q + 0.06Q^2 = 0,$$

which is identical to the expression obtained when the first derivative of the profit function is set to zero. Solving for the roots of this equation (again using the quadratic equation) results in $Q_1 = -35$ and $Q_2 = 15$, the same values found above. This confirms the fact that marginal revenue does in fact equal marginal cost at the output where profit is maximized.

To conclude the example, Figure 2-12 presents graphs of the revenue, cost, and profit functions. The upper section of the graph shows the revenue and cost functions; at 15 units of output, the slopes of the two curves are equal, $MR = MC$. The lower section of the figure shows the profit function, and the profit-maximizing output is also 15 units, at which output $d\pi/dQ = 0$ and $d^2\pi/dQ^2 < 0$.

PARTIAL DERIVATIVES

Since most economic relationships involve more than two variables, it is necessary to extend the concept of differentiation to equations with three or more variables. Consider the demand function for a product where the quan-

Figure 2-12 Profit-maximizing Output Conditions

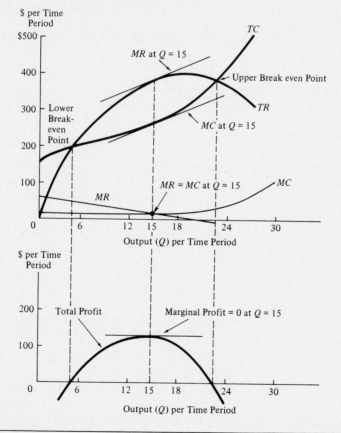

tity demanded, Q, is determined by the price charged, P, and the level of advertising expenditure, A. Such a function would be written as:

$$Q = f(P, A). \tag{2-10}$$

When analyzing multivariable relationships, such as the one in Equation 2-10, we need to know the marginal effect of each independent variable on the dependent variable. In other words, optimization in this case requires an analysis of how a change in each independent variable affects the dependent variable, *holding constant the effect of all other independent variables*. The partial derivative is the calculus concept used for this type of marginal analysis.

Using the demand function of Equation 2-10, we can examine two partial derivatives[13]:

1. The partial of Q with respect to price $= \partial Q / \partial P$.
2. The partial of Q with respect to advertising expenditure $= \partial Q / \partial A$.

The rules for determining partial derivatives are essentially the same as those discussed above. Since the concept of a partial derivative involves an assumption that all variables other than the one with respect to which the derivative is being taken remain unchanged, those variables are treated as constants in the differentiation process. Consider the equation $Y = 10 - 4X + 3XZ - Z^2$. In this function there are two independent variables, X and Z, so two partial derivatives can be evaluated. To determine the partial with respect to X, note that the function can be rewritten as $Y = 10 - 4X + (3Z)X - Z^2$. Since Z is being treated as a constant, the partial derivative of Y with respect to X is:

$$\frac{\partial Y}{\partial X} = 0 - 4 + 3Z - 0 = -4 + 3Z.$$

In determining the partial of Y with respect to Z, X is treated as a constant, so we can write:

$$Y = 10 - 4X + (3X)Z - Z^2,$$

and the partial with respect to Z is:

$$\frac{\partial Y}{\partial Z} = 0 - 0 + 3X - 2Z = 3X - 2Z.$$

Another example should help clarify the technique of partial differentiation. Let $Y = 2X + 4X^2Z - 3XZ^2 - 2Z^3$. Then, the partial with respect to X is:

$$\frac{\partial Y}{\partial X} = 2 + 8XZ - 3Z^2 - 0,$$

[13] The symbol ∂, called delta, is used to denote a partial derivative. In oral and written treatments of this concept, the word derivative is frequently omitted. That is, reference is typically made to the *partial* of Q rather than the *partial derivative* of Q.

and the partial with respect to Z is:

$$\frac{\partial Y}{\partial Z} = 0 + 4X^2 - 6XZ - 6Z^2.$$

MAXIMIZING MULTIVARIABLE FUNCTIONS

The requirement for maximization (or minimization) of a multivariate function is a straightforward extension of that for single variable functions. All first-order partial derivatives must equal zero. Thus, maximization of the function $Y = f(X, Z)$ requires:

$$\frac{\partial Y}{\partial X} = 0,$$

and

$$\frac{\partial Y}{\partial Z} = 0.$$

To illustrate this procedure, consider the function:

$$Y = 4X + Z - X^2 + XZ - Z^2, \tag{2-11}$$

whose partial derivatives are

$$\frac{\partial Y}{\partial X} = 4 - 2X + Z,$$

and

$$\frac{\partial Y}{\partial Z} = 1 + X - 2Z.$$

To maximize Equation 2-11, set the partials equal to zero:

$$\frac{\partial Y}{\partial X} = 4 - 2X + Z = 0,$$

and

$$\frac{\partial Y}{\partial Z} = 1 + X - 2Z = 0.$$

Here we have two equations in two unknowns. Solving them simultaneously, we find that the values $X = 3$ and $Z = 2$ maximize the function.[14] Inserting these values for X and Z into Equation 2-11, we find the value of Y to be 7; therefore, the maximum value of Y is 7.[15]

---

[14] Since $4 - 2X + Z = 0$, $Z = 2X - 4$. Substituting this value for Z into $1 + X - 2Z = 0$, we obtain $1 + X - 2(2X - 4) = 1 + X - 4X + 8 = -3X + 9 = 0$, or $X = 3$. Substituting this value of X into $Z = 2X - 4$, we obtain $Z = 2(3) - 4 = 2$.

[15] Actually, in order to prove that $Y = 7$ at $X = 3$ and $Z = 2$ is a point of maximization rather than minimization, we would have to examine the second-order conditions. Because the second-order requirements for determining maxima and minima are relatively complex and are not necessary for the materials that follow in this text, they are not developed here. A full discussion of these requirements can be found in any elementary calculus text.

With respect to our example, we can tell that $Y = 7$ is a maximum, not a minimum, by changing the values of X and Z slightly from 3 and 2 and noting that Y declines regardless of whether X and Z are increased or decreased.

The process involved here can perhaps be clarified by referring to Figure 2-13, a three-dimensional graph of Equation 2-11. Here we see that for positive values of X and Z, Equation 2-11 maps out a surface with a peak at point A. At the peak the surface of the figure is level. Alternatively stated, a plane that is tangent to the surface at point A will be parallel to the XZ plane, meaning that the slope of the figure with respect to either X or Z must be zero; this is the requirement for locating a maximum.

CONSTRAINED OPTIMIZATION

In a great many of the decision problems faced by business managers there are constraints imposed that limit the options available to the decision maker. For example, a production manager may be charged with minimizing total cost, subject to the requirement that specified quantities of each of the firm's products be produced. At other times the production manager may be concerned with maximizing output from a particular department, subject to limitations on the quantities of various materials and facilities available for use.

Figure 2-13 Finding the Maximum of a Function of Two Variables—$Y = 4X + Z - X^2 + XZ - Z^2$

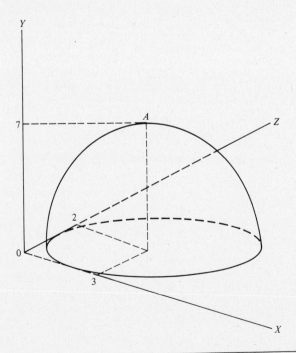

Other functional areas of the firm also face constrained optimization problems. Marketing managers are often charged with the task of maximizing sales, subject to the constraint that they not exceed a fixed advertising budget. Financial officers, in their efforts to minimize the cost of acquiring capital, must frequently work within constraints imposed by creditors.

Constrained optimization problems may be handled in several ways. In some cases, where the constraint equation is not too complex, we may solve for one of the decision variables, then substitute for that variable in the objective function—the function the firm wishes to maximize or minimize.[16] This procedure converts the problem to one of unconstrained maximization or minimization, which can be solved by the methods outlined above.

The procedure can be clarified by examining its use in a constrained minimization problem. Suppose a firm produces its product on two assembly lines and operates with the following total costs function:

$$TC = 3X^2 + 6Y^2 - XY,$$

where X represents the output produced on one assembly line and Y the production from the second. Management seeks to determine the least-cost combination of X and Y, subject to the constraint that total output of the product must be 20 units. The constrained optimization problem can be stated as follows:

Minimize

$$TC = 3X^2 + 6Y^2 - XY,$$

subject to

$$X + Y = 20.$$

Solving the constraint for X and substituting this value into the objective function results in:

$$X = 20 - Y,$$

and

$$
\begin{aligned}
TC &= 3(20 - Y)^2 + 6Y^2 - (20 - Y)Y \\
&= 3(400 - 40Y + Y^2) + 6Y^2 - (20Y - Y^2) \\
&= 1{,}200 - 120Y + 3Y^2 + 6Y^2 - 20Y + Y^2 \\
&= 1{,}200 - 140Y + 10Y^2.
\end{aligned}
\tag{2-12}
$$

---

[16] In this section we examine techniques for solving constrained optimization problems in those cases where the constraints can be expressed as equations. Frequently, constraints impose only upper or lower limits on the decision maker and, therefore, may not be "binding" or effective at the optimal solution. Constraints of this second, more general, type are properly expressed as inequality relationships, and in these cases another optimizing technique, mathematical programming, must be used to analyze the problem. Mathematical programming is discussed in Chapter 7.

Now we can treat Equation 2-12 as an unconstrained minimization problem. Solving it requires taking the derivative, setting that derivative equal to zero, and solving for the value of Y:

$$\frac{dTC}{dY} = -140 + 20Y = 0$$
$$20Y = 140$$
$$Y = 7.$$

A check of the sign of the second derivative evaluated at that point will insure that a minimum has been located:

$$\frac{dTC}{dY} = -140 + 20Y$$

$$\frac{d^2TC}{dY^2} = +20.$$

Since the second derivative is positive, $Y = 7$ must indeed be a minimum.

Substituting 7 for Y in the constraint equation allows us to determine the optimal quantity of X to be produced:

$$X + 7 = 20$$
$$X = 13.$$

Thus, production of 13 units of output on assembly line X and 7 units on line Y is the least-cost combination for manufacturing a total of 20 units of the firm's product. The total cost of producing that combination will be:

$$TC = 3(13)^2 + 6(7)^2 - (13 \cdot 7)$$
$$= 507 + 294 - 91$$
$$= \$710.$$

Lagrange Multipliers[17]

Unfortunately, the substitution technique used above is not always feasible; the constraint conditions are often too numerous or too complex for substitution to be employed. In these cases, the technique of *Lagrange multipliers* must be used.

The Lagrangian technique for solving constrained optimization problems is a procedure that calls for optimizing a function that combines the original objective function and the constraint conditions. This combined equation, called the Lagrangian function, is created in a way which insures (1) that when it has been maximized (or minimized) the original objective function will also be maximized (minimized), and (2) that all the constraint requirements will have been satisfied.

A re-examination of the constrained minimization problem illustrated above will clarify the use of this technique. Recall that the firm sought to minimize the function $TC = 3X^2 + 6Y^2 - XY$, subject to the constraint that

---

[17] This section may be omitted without loss of continuity.

$X + Y = 20$. Rearranging the constraint to bring all the terms to the left of the equals sign, we obtain:

$$X + Y - 20 = 0.$$

Multiplying this form of the constraint by the unknown factor λ[18] and subtracting the result from the original objective function results in:

$$L_{TC} = 3X^2 + 6Y^2 - XY - \lambda(X + Y - 20). \qquad \text{(2-13)}$$

L_{TC} is defined as the Lagrangian function for the constrained optimization problem under consideration.

Because it incorporates the constraint into the objective function, the Lagrangian function can be treated as an unconstrained optimization problem, and the solution to that problem will *always* be identical to the solution of the original constrained optimization problem. To illustrate this, consider the problem of minimizing the Lagrangian function constructed above in Equation 2-13. At a minimum point on a multivariable function, all the partial derivatives must be equal to zero. The partials of Equation 2-13 can be taken with respect to the three unknown variables, X, Y, and λ, as follows:

$$\frac{\partial L_{TC}}{\partial X} = 6X - Y - \lambda$$

$$\frac{\partial L_{TC}}{\partial Y} = 12Y - X - \lambda$$

$$\frac{\partial L_{TC}}{\partial \lambda} = -X - Y + 20.$$

Setting these three partials equal to zero results in a system of three equations and three unknowns:

$$6X - Y - \lambda = 0 \qquad \text{(2-14)}$$

$$-X + 12Y - \lambda = 0 \qquad \text{(2-15)}$$

$$-X - Y + 20 = 0. \qquad \text{(2-16)}$$

Notice that Equation 2-16, the partial of the Lagrangian function with respect to λ, is the constraint condition imposed on the original optimization problem. This result is not mere happenstance. The Lagrangian function is specifically constructed so that the derivative of the function taken with respect to the Lagrange multiplier, λ, will always give the original constraint. So long as this derivative is zero, as it must be at a local extreme (maximum or minimum), the constraint conditions imposed on the original problem will be met. Further, since under such conditions the last term in the Lagrangian expression must equal zero, that is, $(X + Y - 20 = 0)$, the Lagrangian function reduces to the original objective function and, thus,

---

[18] λ is the Greek letter lambda, which is typically used in formulating Lagrangian expressions.

the solution to the unconstrained Lagrangian problem will always be the solution to the original constrained optimization problem.

Completing the analysis for our example will clarify these relationships. We begin by solving the system of equations to obtain the optimal values of X and Y. Subtracting Equation 2-15 from Equation 2-14 gives:

$$7X - 13Y = 0. \tag{2-17}$$

Then, multiplying Equation 2-16 by 7 and subtracting Equation 2-17 from this product allows us to solve for Y:

$$
\begin{array}{ll}
7X + 7Y - 140 = 0 & 7 \cdot (2\text{-}16) \\
7X - 13Y \phantom{{}- 140} = 0 & (2\text{-}17) \\
\hline
\phantom{7X + {}} 20Y - 140 = 0 & \\
\phantom{7X + {}} 20Y = 140 & \\
\phantom{7X + {}} Y = 7. &
\end{array}
$$

Substituting 7 for Y in Equation 2-16 yields $X = 13$, the value of X at the point where the Lagrangian is minimized.

Since the solution of the Lagrangian is also the solution to the firm's constrained optimization problem, 13 units from assembly line X and 7 units from line Y will be the least-cost combination of output that can be produced subject to the restriction that total output must be 20 units. This is the same answer as was obtained previously by solving the constraint for one of the decision variables and substituting for it in the objective function.

In addition to being a more powerful technique for solving constrained optimization problems than is the substitution method—it is easier to apply the Lagrangian technique to a problem with multiple constraints—the Lagrangian method also provides the decision maker with some valuable supplementary information. This is due to the fact that the Lagrangian multiplier, λ, has an important economic interpretation. Substituting the values of X and Y into Equation 2-14 allows us to determine the value of λ in our example:

$$
\begin{array}{l}
6 \cdot 13 - 7 - \lambda = 0 \\
\lambda = +71.
\end{array}
$$

Here λ can be interpreted as the marginal cost of production at 20 units of output. It tells us that if the firm were required to produce only 19 instead of 20 units of output, total costs would fall by approximately \$71. Similarly, if the output requirement was 21 instead of 20 units, costs would increase by that amount.[19] More generally, any Lagrangian multiplier, λ, indicates

---

[19] Technically, λ indicates the marginal cost associated with an infinitesimally small change in the constraint requirement. Thus, it provides only a rough estimate of the change in total costs that would take place if 1 more (or less) unit of output were required. The interpretation of λ, the Lagrange multiplier, is examined more fully in Chapter 7, where linear programming techniques are introduced.

the marginal effect on the original objective function of incrementing the constraint requirement by 1 unit.

SUMMARY

Optimization is the process of determining the best possible solution to a given problem. In this chapter we first introduced a number of methods used to express economic relationships, then proceeded to examine several related tools of analysis used in the optimizing process.

Economic relationships may be expressed as tables, graphs, or equations. The key variables involve totals, averages, and marginals, and these values are themselves related in a unique manner. Given any one set of variables, the other two can be developed on the basis of the basic relationships that hold among the different variables.

Frequently, optimality analysis involves locating the maximum or the minimum value of a function. Values for the function could be calculated and entered in a table or plotted on a graph, and the point where the function is maximized (minimized) could be observed directly. It is frequently more convenient, however, to use calculus to locate the optimum point, simply calculating the derivative of the total function and setting it equal to zero; that is, $dY/dX = 0$. Accordingly, the process of taking derivatives was explained in some detail.

A function may have several values at which the derivative is zero, with some such points representing maximums and others minimums. To determine whether a maximum or a minimum has been found, the second derivative is calculated. If d^2Y/dX^2 is negative, a maximum has been found; if it is positive, a minimum has been located.

If a function contains more than two variables, partial differentiation comes into play; and so the process of finding partials, $\partial Y/\partial X$, was examined. To maximize a function of two or more variables, the partial with respect to each variable must be calculated, and these partials must simultaneously be set equal to zero.

The final topic covered was constrained optimization, the process of maximizing or minimizing a function subject to a set of constraints. Here we explained how the Lagrangian multiplier concept can be used to solve constrained optimization problems.

The tools developed in this chapter are used in all types of economic analysis, especially in managerial economics. Accordingly, they are employed throughout the remainder of the text.

QUESTIONS

2-1   What is the key relationship between totals and marginals that makes an understanding of the marginal concept so important in optimization analysis?

2-2   Why must a marginal curve always intersect the related average curve at either a maximum or a minimum point?

2-3   Considering the optimization procedures outlined in this chapter, what hazard is encountered in setting marginal revenue equal to marginal cost to solve for the profit-maximizing output level of a firm?

2-4   Economists have long argued that if you want to tax away excess profits from a firm without affecting the allocative efficiency of market-determined price/output relationships, you should use a lump-sum license tax instead of an excise or sales tax. Use the materials developed in this chapter to justify this statement.

PROBLEMS

2-1a) Given the total revenue (TR) and output (Q) data shown in the table below, calculate the related marginal revenue (MR) and average revenue (AR) figures needed to complete the table.

Q	TR	MR	AR
0	$ 0	—	$ 0
1	218	218	218
2	464	246	232
3	726		242
4	992	266	
5	1250	258	250
6	1488		248
7	1694	206	242
8	1856	162	232
9		106	
10	2000	38	200
11	1958		178
12	1824	(134)	

b) Using a two-part graph, like Figure 2-2, plot the total revenue, marginal revenue, and average revenue curves indicated by the data in the table constructed in Problem 2-1a. (*Note:* The relationships among totals, averages, and marginals are typically more accurately depicted by graphing the marginal values midway between the two output levels to which they relate. For example, the $218 marginal revenue associated with the first unit of output should be plotted at $Q = 0.5$.)

c) Locate on the total revenue curve graphed in Problem 2-1b the points at which marginal, average, and total revenues are maximized.

d) Locate the points of maximum total, average, and marginal revenues, using the average and marginal revenue curves constructed in Problem 2-1b.

e) Compare the relationships between the total, average, and marginal curves on your graph in Problem 2-1b and the table in Problem 2-1a with the relationships indicated in the chapter.

(*Note:* The total revenue function used to develop the data for this problem is shown in Problem 2-6. You may want to compare the solutions of this problem with those of Problem 2-6.)

2-2 A firm's total revenue (TR), total cost (TC), and output (Q) data are presented in the table below.

Q	TR	MR	TC	MC	π	$M\pi$
52	$3,848	—	$2,832	—	$1,016	—
53	3,896	$	2,875	$43		$ 5
54	3,942	46	2,918		1,024	
55	3,988	46	2,963	45	1,025	1
56	4,032	44	3,008	45	1,024	−1
57	4,076		3,055			
58	4,118	42	3,102	47	1,016	

a) Calculate the data necessary to complete the table.

b) Construct a two-part graph (like Figure 2-2) in which total profits are graphed in the upper part, and marginal revenue, marginal cost, and marginal profit are graphed in the lower. (*Note:* To enhance clarity, graph the marginal figures midway between the two output levels to which they relate.)

c) Examine the relationships between total profits, marginal profits, marginal revenue, and marginal cost at the point where total profits are maximized.

(*Note:* The total revenue and total cost functions used to generate the data in this problem are shown in Problem 2-7. It should prove instructive for you to compare the results of this problem with your solution to Problem 2-7.)

2-3 Data on a firm's cost/output function are supplied below. From that data, graph the firm's average cost curve and then use the average cost curve to construct geometrically the firm's marginal cost curve.

Quantity Produced	Average Cost
10	$65
20	50
30	40
40	35
50	30
60	30
70	35
80	45

2-4 Determine the first and second derivatives for the following:
a) $Y = 3 + 4X$
b) $Y = 50X - 0.3X^2$
c) $Y = 10 + 50X - 5X^2 + X^3$

    d) $Y = (2X + 2) \, (X - 3)$

    e) $Y = \dfrac{X^2 - 2}{X^3}$

    f) $Y = (3 + 2X)^3$

2-5a) Locate the maximum point on the function $Y = 100X - 0.25X^2$. Prove you have found a maximum rather than a minimum; that is, evaluate the second derivative at the point you locate.

    b) Locate all local maxima and minima points of the function $Y = 1{,}000 - 600X - 15X^2 + X^3$, and evaluate the second derivative to distinguish between them.

2-6 Given the total revenue function $TR = \$200Q + \$20Q^2 - \$2Q^3$, where Q represents the quantity of a particular product sold,

    a) Determine the output quantity that maximizes total revenue.

    b) Determine the output quantity at which marginal revenue is maximized.

    c) Determine the output quantity at which marginal and average revenue are equal.

    d) This total revenue function was used to construct the data for Problem 2-1. Check to see that your solutions to both problems are reconcilable.

2-7 Assume that a firm operates with the total revenue (TR) and total cost (TC) functions:

$$TR = \$100Q - \$0.5Q^2$$
$$TC = \$2{,}000 - \$10Q + \$0.5Q^2,$$

where Q represents the quantity of output produced and sold.

    a) Determine the profit-maximizing output level for this firm by maximizing its total profit function.

    b) Show that at the profit-maximizing output level determined in Problem 2-7a marginal revenue equals marginal cost.

    (*Note:* These are the revenue and cost functions used for generating the data in Problem 2-2. Your answers for the two problems should therefore be consistent.)

2-8 Determine the partial derivatives for the following functions:

    a) $Y = 20 - 2X - 3Z + XZ + Z^2$.

    b) $Y = 3X + Z + 2XZ - X^2 - Z^2$.

    c) $Y = 10 + X^2 + WXZ - 2WZ^2 + Z$.

    d) $Y = 8X^{0.4}Z^{0.6}$.

2-9 Inventory management is an area where the calculus tools of optimization provide a valuable technique for decision making. Assume that in a specific inventory problem usage of the item is evenly distributed over time, and delivery of additional units is instantaneous once an order has been placed. Under these conditions the costs associated with the purchase and inventory of the item are

    a) Purchase Costs $= P \cdot X$

    b) Order Costs $= \Theta \cdot \dfrac{X}{Q}$

    c) Carrying Costs $= C \cdot \dfrac{Q}{2}$

where P is the price per unit of the item, X is the total quantity of the item used annually, Θ is the cost of placing an order for the item, Q is the quantity," of the item ordered at any one point in time and C is the per-unit inventory carrying cost of the item. Thus, the total costs associated with this inventory item are given by the expression:

$$TC = P \cdot X + \Theta\frac{X}{Q} + C\frac{Q}{2}.$$

The cost of carrying this item in inventory can be minimized by selecting an optimal order quantity, Q, sometimes called the "economic order quantity," or EOQ. Develop an expression for determining the optimal EOQ by minimizing the above-cost function with respect to Q, the order quantity.

2-10 A firm produces its product using either of two production processes: A and B. The total cost function for the firm is:

$$TC = 50 - 10A + A^2 - AB - 4B + B^2,$$

where A and B represent the quantity of output produced by each process.
a)   Determine the least-cost combination of output for the firm.
b)   If the firm wishes to produce a total of 20 units of output, what would be the optimal quantities to be manufactured using each production process?
c)   What is the marginal cost of producing the twenty-first unit of output? (Assume that fractional units can be produced by each of the two processes.)

2-11 A firm has determined that the following relationship holds between its advertising expenditures in media A and media B and the total revenue generated by sales of its product:

$$TR = \$5A + \$5A^2 + \$5AB.$$

a)   If the price of A is \$5 a unit, the price of B is \$1 a unit, and the marketing manager faces a budget constraint of \$111, what is the optimal combination of advertising that he should engage in, assuming he desires to maximize total revenue?
b)   Interpret the Lagrangian Multiplier for this problem.

2-12 A field representative for a major pharmaceutical firm has just received the following information from a marketing research consultant who has been analyzing his recent sales performance. The consultant estimates that time spent in the two major metropolitan areas that comprise his sales territory will result in monthly sales as indicated by the equation

$$\text{Sales} = 500A - 20A^2 + 300B - 10B^2.$$

Here A and B represent the number of days spent in each metropolitan area respectively.
a)   Assuming that a working month is composed of twenty business days, what is the optimal number of days the salesperson should spend in each city? (Use the Lagrangian technique to solve this problem.)
b)   What is the value of λ, the Lagrangian multiplier in this problem, and how would you interpret it?

CASE—KANTELL ENGINEERING CORPORATION: OPTIMIZATION IN PRODUCT RELIABILITY DESIGN

Kantell Engineering Corporation is one of several manufacturers producing electrical switching equipment for use in chemical processing plants. Kantell's management is currently examining one standard switch, model SK4, with the objective of optimizing its market position and maximizing the profit from this product. It is management's firm belief that, given the nature of the market within which the SK4 is sold, price competition would be an ineffective way to enhance profits. The standard price of $200 is well established. Previous attempts to raise the price above $200 have resulted in substantial declines in market share, while attempts to increase market penetration by lowering the price have always led to retaliatory price reductions by competing firms.

On the basis of discussion with its sales representatives, Kantell's management believes that product reliability may hold the key to increasing profits on the SK4. Kantell's sales force has long claimed that there is an important relationship between product reliability and sales volume. While top management had considered this proposition indirectly in the past, no effort was made to determine the true parameters of this relationship. Now, Ed Major, president of Kantell, has requested such an analysis as part of the review of the SK4 profit position. Specifically, he has requested Jerry Scheilds, his administrative assistant, to prepare a report that will answer the following questions:

1. What relationship exists between sales volume and the reliability level of the product?
2. What is the relationship between product costs and reliability?
3. Assuming that the current $200 price is to be maintained, what reliability level results in maximum profits for the SK4?

Scheilds began his analysis by examining the relationship between demand and reliability. Reliability problems experienced with earlier design configurations for the SK4 provided data on reliability and sales for a number of years. Because of the stability of price and the lack of growth in the total market for the SK4 switch over the period covered by the data, Scheilds felt that these data accurately reflected the effect of variation in reliability on demand.

The data are shown in the following table. A graph of the data indicated a curvilinear relationship, and Scheilds fitted a quadratic equation to it, using the least squares regression technique (this statistical method is taken up in Chapter 5 of this book). The resulting equation was:

$$Q(000) = 92.7 - 6.15F - 0.154F^2.$$

Reliability Level (F = % failure per year)	Sales Volume, Q
1	83,000
2	80,000
3	77,000
5	60,000
10	15,000

Scheilds sought help from Kantell's engineering staff for determining the production costs/reliability relationship for the SK4 switch. The engineering personnel determined that total costs could best be separated into three relevant categories for purposes of the analysis:

1. *Per unit production costs* (C_p), which are defined as all costs that remain constant (per unit) regardless of the reliability level of the product. These production costs were estimated to be $90 a unit, and this cost figure is not expected to vary significantly with respect to the quantity produced over the output range that appears relevant to Kantell's decision problem—30,000 to 80,000 units.

2. *Per unit warranty costs* (C_w). The model SK4 switch is warranted for five years. On the basis of past service costs, it is estimated that warranty repair or replacement costs will average $100 for each failure. Thus, the warranty costs can be expressed as a function of the annual failure rate (F) by the following expression:

$$C_w = \text{cost per failure} \times \text{number of years warranted}$$
$$\times \text{failure rate per year}$$
$$= (\$100)\ (5)\ (F/100)$$
$$= 5F.$$

3. *Per unit reliability costs* (C_F). An extensive study by the engineering department of engineering alternatives which would provide different levels of product reliability as measured by the failure rate resulted in the following data:

Engineering Alternative	Reliability Level (F)	Reliability Costs per Unit (C_F)
1	1	$80
2	2	65
3	3	55
4	5	40
5	10	5

While a graphical plot of these data indicated that an exponential equation might best fit the data, the degree of curvature was not great; this fact, coupled with the complexities involved in utilizing an exponential equation, led Scheilds to conclude that a linear expression of the relationship between C_F and F would be acceptable. Calculations of the linear regression equation resulted in the following relationship:

$$C_F = 84.6 - 8.45F.$$

Scheilds received these cost equations from engineering and was preparing to calculate the optimal reliability level when Ed Major called to ask him to join Ed's Friday afternoon foursome. Jerry felt that he should accept the offer, but knowing that he would need the completed report for a Monday morning meeting of the executive committee, he has asked you, a new management trainee, to complete the analysis. He indicated that he wanted you to include the following points in your work:

1. The profit-maximizing reliability level.
2. The sales volume that will result from that reliability level.
3. The total profits from the SK4 switch, given that optimal reliability level.

SELECTED REFERENCES

Allen, R. G. D. *Mathematical Analysis for Economists*. London: Macmillan, 1956.
Draper, Jean E., and Jane S. Klingman. *Mathematical Analysis, Business and Economic Applications*. Second Edition. New York: Harper & Row, 1972.

CHAPTER 3

Risk
Analysis

To maximize the value of his firm, a manager seeks to increase the firm's stream of profits and at the same time to reduce the discount rate applied to its earnings. Since the discount (or "capitalization") rate depends on the riskiness of the firm, reducing the discount rate amounts to minimizing the risk level associated with any given profit level. If risk is to be minimized, it must be defined and measured. Accordingly, in this chapter we first provide a suitable definition of risk and a method for measuring it. Then we examine the effect of risk on the valuation model introduced in Chapter 1 and introduce several techniques designed to aid in decision making under conditions of risk.

RISK IN ECONOMIC ANALYSIS[1]

The riskiness of a decision alternative is typically defined in terms of the variability of possible future outcomes. For example, if one buys a $1 million

---

[1] Some writers distinguish between risk and uncertainty, but for our purposes this distinction is unnecessary. Accordingly, we define any decision whose outcome is uncertain as being risky, and we say that such decisions are subject to risk or uncertainty.

short-term government bond expected to yield 5 percent, then the return on the investment, 5 percent, can be estimated quite precisely, and the investment is defined to be relatively risk-free. If, however, the $1 million is invested in the stock of a company being organized to prospect for natural gas in Wisconsin, the probable return on the $1 million investment could range from minus 100 percent to some extremely large figure, and because of this high variability the project is defined to be relatively risky. Similarly, sales forecasts for different products of a single firm might exhibit differing degrees of riskiness. For example, The Dryden Press might be quite sure that sales of a certain fifth-edition introductory finance text will be in the range of sixty-five to seventy thousand copies for the first year, but be highly uncertain about the number of copies it will sell of a new first-edition statistics text.

Risk, then, is associated with variability—the more variable the expected outcome of a decision, the riskier the decision. It is useful, however, to define risk more precisely. This more precise definition requires a step-by-step development, which constitutes the remainder of this section.

Probability Distributions

Almost every business decision implies a forecast of future events, with the forecast being either explicit or implicit. Ordinarily, the forecast of outcomes is a single figure, or point estimate, frequently called the most likely or best estimate. For example, one might forecast that the returns from a particular activity will be $500 a year for three years.

How good is this point estimate; that is, how confident is the forecaster of his forecast? Is he certain, uncertain, or somewhere in between? This degree of uncertainty can be defined and measured in terms of the forecaster's probability distribution—the probability estimates associated with each possible outcome. In its simplest form a probability distribution could consist of just a few potential outcomes. For example, in forecasting profits we could make an optimistic estimate, a pessimistic estimate, and a most likely estimate; or, alternatively, we could make high, low, and best-guess estimates. We might expect our high, or optimistic, estimate to be realized if the national economy booms; our pessimistic estimate to hold if the economy is depressed; and our best guess to occur if the economy runs at a normal level. These ranges are illustrated in Table 3-1.

The figures in Table 3-1 represent some improvement over our earlier best-guess estimate of $500, because additional information has been provided. Some critical information is still missing, however: How likely is it that we will have a boom, a recession, or normal economic conditions? If we have estimates of the probabilities of these events, we can develop a weighted average profit estimate and a measure of our degree of confidence in this estimate.

Table 3-1   Expected Profits under Different Economic Conditions

State of the Economy	Profits
Recession	$400
"Normal"	500
Boom	600

Risk Comparisons

To illustrate how the probability distribution concept can be used to compare the riskiness of alternative decisions, suppose we are considering two investment alternatives, each calling for an outlay of $1,000 and each expected to produce a profit of $500 a year for three years. (The best-estimate profit is $500 a year for each project.) If the discount rate is 10 percent, we can use the methods developed in Chapter 1 and Appendix A to estimate each project's net present value:

$$NPV = \text{Present value of future profits} - \text{Initial investment}$$

$$= \sum_{t=1}^{3} \frac{\$500}{(1+0.10)^t} - \$1,000$$

$$= \$1,243.50 - \$1,000$$

$$= \$243.50 \text{ for each project.}$$

The projects have the same expected returns; does this mean that they are equally desirable? To answer this question, we need to know whether the projects are also equally risky, since desirability depends upon both returns and risk.

Assume that Project A calls for the replacement of an obsolete machine used in normal operations, and the benefits are savings in labor and raw materials if the old machine is replaced by a more efficient one. Project B, on the other hand, calls for the purchase of an entirely new machine to produce a new product, the demand for which is highly uncertain. The replacement machine (Project A) will be used more (hence savings will be greater) if demand for the firm's current product is high; product demand is high when the national economy is booming, and low when the national economy is in a recession. We can also expect demand for the new product (Project B) to be greatest when the economy is booming.

We stated above that the expected annual returns from each project are $500. Let us assume that these figures are developed in the following manner:

1. We begin by estimating project returns under different states of the economy as in Table 3-2. Tables of this kind are typically referred to as *payoff matrices*.

Table 3-2   Payoff Matrix for Projects A and B

State of the Economy	Annual Dollar Return	
	Project A	Project B
Recession	$400	$ 0
"Normal"	500	500
Boom	600	1,000

2. Next we estimate the likelihood of different states of the economy. Assume our economic forecasts indicate that, given current trends in economic indicators, the odds are 2 in 10 that a recession will occur, 6 in 10 that the economy will be normal, and 2 in 10 that there will be a boom.
3. Redefining "odds" as "probability," we find that the probability of a recession is 0.2, or 20 percent; the probability of normal times is 0.6, or 60 percent; and the probability of a boom is 0.2, or 20 percent. Notice that the probabilities add up to 1.0, or 100 percent: $0.2 + 0.6 + 0.2 = 1.0$, or 100 percent.
4. Finally, we calculate weighted values of the possible returns by multiplying each dollar return by its probability of occurrence, as in Table 3-3. When column 4 of the table is summed, we obtain a weighted average of the outcomes for each alternative under various states of the economy; this weighted average is defined as the *expected value* of cash flows from the project.[2]

We can graph the results shown in Table 3-3 to obtain a picture of the variability of actual outcomes; this is shown as a bar chart in Figure 3-1. The height of each bar signifies the probability that a given outcome will occur. The range of probable outcomes for Project A is from $400 to $600, with an average, or *expected value*, of $500. The expected value for Project B is also $500, but the range of possible outcomes is from $0 to $1,000.

Thus far we have assumed that only three states of the economy can exist: recession, "normal," and boom. Actually, the state of the economy could range from a deep depression, as in the early 1930s, to a tremendous boom, with an unlimited number of possibilities in between. Suppose we

---

[2] This weighted average or expected outcome need not be equal to the project's outcome for a normal state of the economy, although it is in this example.

Table 3-3   Calculation of Expected Values

State of the Economy (1)	Probability of this State Occurring (2)	Outcome if this State Occurs (3)	Expected Value (2) × (3) (4)
Project A			
Recession	0.2	$ 400	$ 80
"Normal"	0.6	500	300
Boom	0.2	600	120
	1.0		$500
Project B			
Recession	0.2	$ 0	$ 0
"Normal"	0.6	500	300
Boom	0.2	1,000	200
	1.0		$500

Figure 3-1   Relationship between State of the Economy and Project Returns

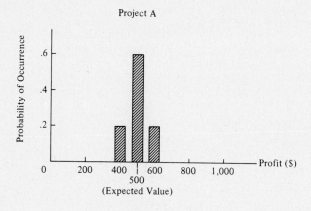

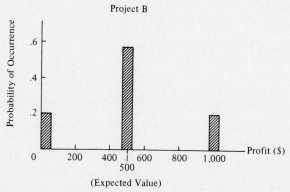

had the time and the patience to assign a probability to each possible state of the economy (with the sum of the probabilities still equaling 1.0) and to assign a monetary outcome to each project for each state of the economy. We would have a table similar to Table 3-3 except that it would have many more entries for "Probability" and "Outcome if this State Occurs." Both tables could be used to calculate expected values as shown above, and the probabilities and outcomes could be graphed as continuous curves, as they are in Figure 3-2. In this graph we have assigned a zero probability to the possibility that Project A will yield less than $400 or more than $600, and a zero probability that Project B will yield less than $0 or more than $1,000.

Figure 3-2 is a graph of the *probability distribution of returns* on Projects A and B. In general, the tighter the probability distribution—or, alternatively stated, the more peaked the distribution—the lower the risk on a project. The tighter the probability distribution, the more likely that the actual outcome will be close to the expected value, or, equivalently, the less likely it is that deviations of the actual outcome from the expected value will be large. Since Project A has a relatively tight probability distribution, its *actual* profit is likely to be closer to the *expected* $500 than is that of Project B.

Figure 3-2 Probability Distribution Showing Relationship between State of the Economy and Project Returns*

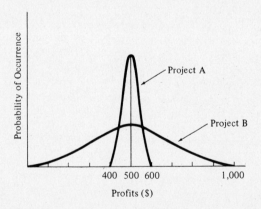

---

* The assumptions regarding the probabilities of various outcomes have been changed from those in Figure 3-1. The probability of obtaining *exactly* $500 was 60 percent in Figure 3-1; in Figure 3-2 it is *much smaller*, because here there are an infinite number of possible outcomes, instead of just three. With continuous distributions, as in Figure 3-2, it is generally more appropriate to ask "What is the cumulative probability of obtaining *at least* some specified value?" than to ask what the probability is of obtaining exactly that value. (Indeed, with a continuous distribution, the probability of occurrence for any single value is zero.) This cumulative probability is equal to 1 minus the area under the probability distribution curve up to the point of interest.

Measuring Risk

Risk is a difficult concept to grasp, and a great deal of controversy has surrounded attempts to define and measure it. The most common definition of risk, however, and one satisfactory for our purposes, is stated in terms of the probability distributions presented in Figure 3-2. This notion of risk is conveyed by the observation that the *tighter the probability distribution of possible outcomes, the smaller the risk of a given decision,* since the probability that the actual outcome will deviate greatly from the expected value is less. According to this definition, Project A is less risky than Project B in our example.

To be most useful, our measure of risk should have some definite value: we need a *measure* of the tightness of the probability distribution of project returns. One such measure, and the one we shall use, is the *standard deviation,* the symbol for which is σ, read "sigma." The smaller the standard deviation, the tighter the probability distribution and, accordingly, the lower the riskiness of the alternative.[3]

We should note that problems can arise when the standard deviation is used as the measure of risk. Specifically, in an investment problem, if one project is larger than another—that is, if it has a larger cost and larger expected cash flows—it will normally have a larger standard deviation without necessarily being more risky. For example, if a project has expected returns

---

[3] The standard deviation of a distribution is found as follows:

1. Calculate the expected value or mean of the distribution:

$$\text{Expected value} = \bar{R} = \sum_{i=1}^{n} (R_i P_i). \qquad (3\text{-}1)$$

   Here R_i is the return associated with the ith outcome; P_i is the probability of occurrence of that ith outcome; and $\bar{R}$, the expected value, is a weighted average of the various possible outcomes, each weighted by the probability of its occurrence.

2. Subtract the expected value from each possible outcome to obtain a set of deviations about the expected value:

$$\text{Deviation}_i = r_i = R_i - \bar{R}.$$

3. Square each deviation; multiply the squared deviation by the probability of occurrence for its related outcome; and sum these products. This arithmetic mean of the squared deviations is the variance of the probability distribution:

$$\text{Variance} = \sigma^2 = \sum_{i=1}^{n} r_i^2 P_i. \qquad (3\text{-}2)$$

4. The standard deviation is found by obtaining the square root of the variance:

$$\text{Standard deviation} = \sigma = \sqrt{\sum_{i=1}^{n} r_i^2 P_i} = \sqrt{\sum_{i=1}^{n} (R_i - \bar{R})^2 P_i}. \qquad (3\text{-}3)$$

   Using the equations, Project A's standard deviation is found to be $63.20, while that of Project B is $316.20. Since B's standard deviation is larger, B is the riskier project.

   Although some researchers have suggested that another dimension of the probability distribution, its skewness, may also affect risk, we shall not expand our treatment of risk analysis to encompass this factor.

of $1 million and a standard deviation of only $1,000, it is certainly less risky than a project with expected returns of $1,000 and a standard deviation of $500, the reason being that the *relative* variation for the larger project is much smaller.

One way of eliminating this problem is to calculate a measure of the relative risk involved by dividing the standard deviation by the mean expectation, or expected value, $\bar{R}$, to obtain the *coefficient of variation:*

$$\text{Coefficient of variation} = \nu = \frac{\sigma}{\bar{R}}. \qquad (3\text{-}4)$$

In general, when comparing decision alternatives whose costs and benefits are not of approximately equal size, the coefficient of variation should be used as a measure of relative risk.

UTILITY THEORY AND RISK AVERSION

The assumption of risk aversion is basic to many decision models used in managerial economics. Because this assumption is so crucial, it is appropriate to discuss why risk aversion holds in general.

In theory, we can identify three possible attitudes toward risk: a desire for risk, an aversion to risk, and an indifference to risk. A *risk seeker* is one who prefers risk; given a choice between more and less risky investments, with identical expected monetary returns, the *risk seeker* will select the riskier investment. Faced with the same choice, the *risk averter* will select the less risky investment. The person who is *indifferent to risk* is also indifferent to which investment he receives. *There undoubtedly are some who prefer risk and others who are indifferent to it, but both logic and observation suggest that business managers and stockholders are predominantly risk averters.*

Why would risk aversion generally hold? Given two alternatives, each with the same expected dollar returns, why do most decision makers prefer the less risky one? Several theories have been advanced in answer to this question, but perhaps the most logically satisfying one involves *utility theory.*

At the heart of utility theory is the notion of *diminishing marginal utility for money.* If a person with no money receives $100, he can satisfy his most immediate needs. If he then receives a second $100, he can use it, but the second $100 is not quite so necessary to him as the first $100. Thus, the "utility" of the second, or *marginal,* $100 is less than that of the first $100, and so on for additional increments of money. We therefore say that the marginal utility of money is diminishing.

Figure 3-3 graphs the relationship between income, or wealth and its utility, where utility is measured in units called "utils." Curve *A,* the one of primary interest, is for someone with a diminishing marginal utility for money. If this particular person has $2,500, he receives 6 utils of "happiness,"

Figure 3-3   Relationship between Money and Its Utility

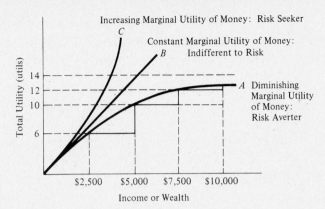

or satisfaction. If he receives an additional $2,500, his utility rises to 10 utils, *an increase of 4 units.* A second $2,500 increase in wealth (to $7,500) raises his utility to 12 utils, a *marginal gain of only 2 additional units of utility.* The marginal utility of each successive increment of income is lower than for the preceding ones and, thus, we state that the individual's marginal utility for income, or wealth, is diminishing.

Most business decision makers (as opposed to people who go to Las Vegas for the fun of it or because of psychological problems that make them gambling addicts) appear to have a declining marginal utility for money, and this directly affects their attitude toward risk. In essence, risk means the likelihood that a given outcome will turn out to be lower than was expected. Because an individual with a diminishing marginal utility for money will suffer more "pain" from a dollar lost than he will derive "pleasure" from a dollar gained, he will be very much opposed to risk. Thus, he will require a very high return on any investment that is subject to much risk. In Curve A of Figure 3-3, for example, a gain of $2,500 from a base of $5,000 brings 2 utils of additional satisfaction; but a $2,500 loss causes a 4-util satisfaction loss. A person with this utility function and $5,000 is therefore unwilling to make a bet with a 50-50 chance of winning or losing $2,500; the reason being that the 9 util expected utility of such a gamble [$E(u) = .5$ times the utility of $2,500 + .5$ times the utility of $7,500 = .5 \times 6 + .5 \times 12 = 9$] is less than the 10 units of utility obtained by foregoing the bet and keeping the $5,000 current wealth with certainty.[4]

---

[4] Since an individual with a constant marginal utility for money will value a dollar gained just as highly as a dollar lost, his expected utility from a fair gamble such as the one offered here will always be exactly equal to the utility of the expected outcome—10 utils in our example. Because of this, an individual indifferent to risk can make decisions on the basis of expected monetary outcomes and need not be concerned with possible variation in the distribution of outcomes.

A second example should help to clarify this relationship between utility and risk aversion. Let us assume that government bonds are riskless securities and that such bonds currently offer a 5 percent rate of return.[5] If an individual buys a $5,000 U.S. Treasury bond and holds it for one year, he will end up with $5,250, a profit of $250.

Suppose there is an alternative investment opportunity which calls for the $5,000 to be used to back a wildcat oil-drilling operation. If the drilling operation is successful, the investment will be worth $7,500 at the end of the year. If it is unsuccessful, the investor can liquidate his holdings and recover $2,500. There is a 60 percent chance that oil will be discovered, and a 40 percent chance of a dry hole, or no oil. If our investor has only $5,000 to invest, should he choose the riskless government bond or the risky drilling operation?

To analyze this question let us first calculate the expected monetary values of the two investments; this is done in Table 3-4. The calculation in the table is not really necessary for the government bond; the $5,250 outcome will occur regardless of what happens in the oil field. The oil venture calculation, however, shows that the expected value of this venture, $5,500, is higher than that of the bond. Does this mean that the investor should put his money in the wildcat well? Not necessarily—it depends on his utility function. If our investor's marginal utility for money is sharply diminishing, then the potential loss of utility that would result from a dry hole might not be compensated for by the potential gain in utility that would result from the development of a producing well. If the utility function shown in Curve A of Figure 3-3 is applicable, this is precisely the case. Four utils will be lost if no oil is found and only 2 will be gained if the well becomes a producer.

Let us modify the expected monetary value calculation to reflect utility considerations. Reading from Figure 3-3, Curve A, we see that this particular risk-averse investor will have 12 utils if he invests in the wildcat venture and

Table 3-4 Expected Returns from Two Projects

State of Nature	Drilling Operation			Government Bond		
	Probability (1)	Outcome (2)	(1) × (2) (3)	Probability (1)	Outcome (2)	(1) × (2) (3)
Oil	0.6	$7,500	$4,500	0.6	$5,250	$3,150
No oil	0.4	2,500	1,000	0.4	5,250	2,100
		Expected Value	$5,500		Expected Value	$5,250

[5] We shall abstract from any risk of price declines in bond prices caused by increases in the level of interest rates. Thus, the risk with which we are concerned at this point is *default risk,* the risk that principal and interest payments will not be made as scheduled.

Table 3-5 Expected Utility of the Oil-Drilling Project

State of Nature	Probability (1)	Monetary Outcome (2)	Associated Utility (3)	Expected Utility (utils) (1) × (3) (4)
Oil	0.6	$7,500	12.0	7.2
No oil	0.4	2,500	6.0	2.4
				9.6

oil is found, 6 utils if he makes this investment and no oil is found, and 10.5 utils with certainty if he chooses the government bond. This information is used in Table 3-5 to calculate the *expected utility* for the oil investment. No calculation is needed for the government bond; we know its utility is 10.5, irrespective of the outcome of the oil venture.

Since the *expected utility* from the wildcat venture is only 9.6 utils, versus 10.5 from the government bond, we see that the government bond is the preferred investment. Thus, even though the expected *monetary value* for the oil venture is higher, *expected utility* is greater for the bond; risk considerations therefore lead us to choose the safer government bond.[6]

ADJUSTING THE VALUATION MODEL FOR RISK

Diminishing marginal utility leads directly to risk aversion, and this risk aversion is reflected in the capitalization rate applied by investors in determining the value of a firm. Thus, if a firm takes an action that increases its risk level, this action affects its value. To illustrate, consider the basic valuation model developed in Chapter 1:

$$V = \sum_{t=1}^{n} \frac{\pi_t}{(1+i)^t}. \tag{3-5}$$

The stream of profits in the numerator, π_t, is really the *expected* value of the profits in each year. If the firm is choosing between two alternative methods of operation, one procedure may result in higher expected profits but also higher risk, while the other may have smaller expected profits but lower risk. Will the higher expected profits be sufficient to offset the higher risk? If so, the riskier alternative is the preferred one; if not, the low-risk procedure should be adopted.

[6] Although maximization of expected utility, a Bayesian decision criterion, is typically the soundest criterion for decision making under uncertainty, in some circumstances alternative decision rules may be appropriate. Several of these alternative criteria are examined in the appendix to this chapter.

Certainty Equivalent Adjustments

A number of procedures have been advanced for handling risk in the valuation context. One of these, the *certainty equivalent* approach, follows directly from the concept of utility theory as it is developed above.

Under the certainty equivalent approach, the decision maker must specify how much money he must be assured of receiving to make him indifferent between this certain sum and the expected value of a risky sum. To illustrate, suppose a rich eccentric offers you the following alternatives:

1. Flip a coin. If a head comes up, he gives you $1 million; if a tail comes up, you get nothing. The expected value of the gamble is $500,000 ($= 0.5 \times \$1,000,000 + 0.5 \times 0$).
2. $100,000 cash.

If you find yourself indifferent between the two alternatives, $100,000 is your certainty equivalent for the risky $500,000 expected return. In other words, the certain or riskless amount provides exactly the same utility as the risky alternative. Any certainty equivalent less than $500,000 indicates risk aversion.

The certainty equivalent concept is illustrated in Figures 3-4 and 3-5. The curve shows a series of risk-return combinations to which the decision maker is indifferent. For example, Point A represents an investment with a perceived degree of risk ν_A and an expected dollar return of $3,000. The person whose risk-return trade-off function, or indifference curve, is shown

---

Figure 3-4   Certainty Equivalent Returns

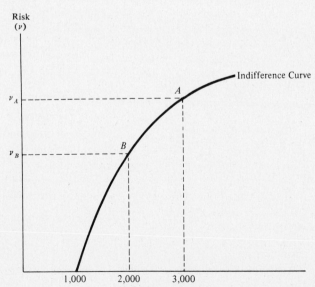

Figure 3-5   Hypothetical Market Risk Aversion Function[*]

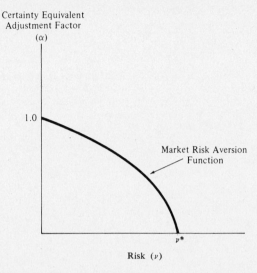

*As we have drawn it, the risk aversion function assumes that $\alpha = 0$ when $\nu \geqslant \nu^*$. Theoretically, α would never actually reach zero; rather, it would approach zero when risk becomes quite high.

here is indifferent among a sure $1,000, $2,000 expected with risk ν_B, and $3,000 expected with risk ν_A.

The indifference curve shown in Figure 3-4 can be used to construct a risk-aversion function such as the one illustrated in Figure 3-5. This conversion is gained by dividing each risky return into its certainty equivalent return to obtain a certainty equivalent adjustment factor, α, for each level of risk, ν. For example, the certainty equivalent adjustment factor for risk level ν_a is found as:

$$\alpha_A = \frac{\text{Certain return}}{\text{Risky return}} = \frac{\$1,000}{\$3,000} = 0.33 \text{ for } \nu_A,$$

and for ν_b we have:

$$\alpha_B = \frac{\$1,000}{\$2,000} = 0.50.$$

Conceptually, α values could be developed for all possible values of ν. The range of α would be from 1.0 for $\nu = 0$ to a value close to 0 for large values of ν, assuming risk aversion.

The risk-aversion functions of all individuals could conceptually be aggregated to form a market risk aversion function.[7] Given the market risk-

[7] Different investors have different α functions, depending on their degrees of risk aversion. Further, an individual's own α function shifts over time as his personal situation, including his wealth and his family status, changes. Nevertheless, we can conceive of a market risk-aversion function that exists at a given point in time.

aversion function and the degree of risk inherent in any risky return, the risky return could be replaced by its certainty equivalent:

$$\text{Certainty equivalent of } \pi_t = \alpha \pi_t,$$

and Equation 3-5 could then be converted to Equation 3-6, a valuation model that explicitly accounts for risk:

$$V = \sum_{t=1}^{n} \frac{\alpha \pi_t}{(1+i)^t}. \tag{3-6}$$

With the valuation model in this form, the effects of different courses of action with different risk (ν) and expected returns (π_t) can be appraised.

Risk-adjusted Discount Rates

An alternative procedure for taking risk into account calls for making adjustments to the discount rate, i. Like the certainty equivalent method, risk-adjusted discount rates are based on investors' trade-off functions between risk and return. For example, suppose a firm determines that its stockholders are willing to trade between risk and return, as is shown in Figure 3-6. The curve is defined as a *market indifference curve*, or a *risk/return trade-off function*. The average investor is indifferent to a riskless asset with a sure 5 percent rate of return, a moderately risky asset with a 7 percent expected return, and a very risky asset with a 15 percent expected return. As risk increases, higher and higher expected returns on investment are required to compensate investors for the additional risk.

The difference between the expected rate of return on a particular risky asset and the rate of return on a riskless asset is defined as the *risk premium* on the risky asset. In the hypothetical situation depicted in Figure 3-6 the riskless rate is assumed to be 5 percent; a 2 percent risk premium is required to compensate for a coefficient of variation of .5; and a 10 percent risk premium is attached to an investment with a coefficient of variation as high as 1.5. The average investor is indifferent between risky investments B, C, and D, and the riskless alternative A.

Since required returns are related to the level of risk perceived to be associated with a particular investment, we can modify the basic valuation model, Equation 3-5, to account for risk through an adjustment of the discount rate, i. Such a modification results in the valuation model:

$$V = \sum_{t=1}^{n} \frac{\pi_t}{(1+k)^t}, \tag{3-7}$$

where k, the risk-adjusted discount rate, is the sum of the riskless rate of return and the risk premium and, hence, a function of the variability of the firm's returns. Thus, for a firm whose coefficient of variation on profits was

Figure 3-6 Hypothetical Relationship between Risk and Rate of Return

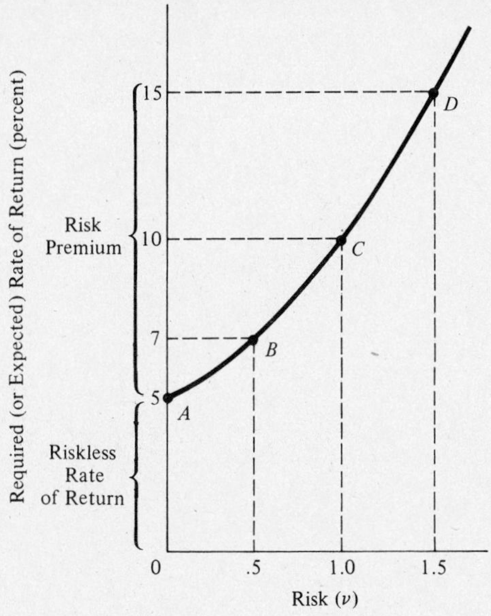

1.0, the appropriate discount rate would be 10 percent; a riskier firm with $v = 1.5$ would be evaluated with a 15 percent discount rate.

Use of Risk-adjusted Discount Rates: An Illustration

We can illustrate the use of risk-adjusted discount rates for managerial decision making with an example. The Walter Watch Company is considering the manufacture of two mutually exclusive types of watchbands. One band is specifically designed for Walter watches and cannot be used with those of other manufacturers; the other is adaptable to a wide variety of watches, both Walter's and those of competitive watch companies. The expected investment outlay for design, engineering, production setup, and so on is $100,000 for each alternative. Expected cash inflows are $20,000 a year for eight years if the bands are usable only with Walter watches (Project A), and $23,000 a year for eight years if the bands can be used with a wide variety of watches (Project B). Because of the captive market for Project A, however, the coefficient of variation of the expected annual returns from the project is only 1.0, while that of Project B is 1.5. In view of this risk differential, Walter Watch's management decides that Project A should be evaluated with a 10 percent cost of capital, while the appropriate cost of capital for Project B is 15 percent. Which project should be selected?

We can calculate the risk-adjusted value for each project as follows[8]:

$$\text{Value }_A = \sum_{t=1}^{8} \frac{\$20,000}{(1.10)^t} - \$100,000$$

$$= \$20,000 \left(\sum_{t=1}^{8} \frac{1}{(1.10)^t} \right) - \$100,000$$

$$= \$20,000 \times 5.335 - \$100,000$$

$$= \$6,700.$$

$$\text{Value }_B = \sum_{t=1}^{8} \frac{\$23,000}{(1.15)^t} - \$100,000$$

$$= \$23,000 \left(\sum_{t=1}^{8} \frac{1}{(1.15)^t} \right) - \$100,000$$

$$= \$23,000 \times 4.487 - \$100,000$$

$$= \$3,200.$$

Because the safer Project A will add more to the value of the firm than will risky Project B, the firm should choose Project A. This choice maximizes the value of the firm.

TECHNIQUES FOR DECISION MAKING UNDER UNCERTAINTY

Having considered the nature of risk, described a means of measuring it, and discussed the effect of risk on the value of the firm, we now examine two techniques used to help solve complex problems under conditions of uncertainty.

Decision Trees

Most important decisions are not made at one point in time but rather in stages. For example, a petroleum firm considering the possibility of expanding into agricultural chemicals might take the following steps:

1. Spend $100,000 for a survey of supply-demand conditions in the agricultural chemical industry.
2. If the survey results are favorable, spend $2 million on a pilot plant to investigate production methods.

[8] The terms in parentheses in the following equatons, $\left(\sum_{t=1}^{8} \frac{1}{(1.10)^t} \right) = 5.335$ and $\left(\sum_{t=1}^{8} \frac{1}{(1.15)^t} \right) = 4.487$, are defined as interest factors. Appendix A at the end of the text explains how the factors are calculated and presents tables of interest factors for various interest rates and years (t values).

3. Depending on the costs estimated from the pilot study and the demand potential from the market study, either abandon the project, build a large plant, or build a small one.

Thus, the final decision is actually made in stages, with subsequent decisions depending on the results of past decisions.

The sequence of events can be mapped out to resemble the branches of a tree; hence the term *decision tree*. As an example, consider Figure 3-7, in which it is assumed that the petroleum company has completed its industry supply/demand analysis and pilot plant study, and has determined that it should proceed to develop a full-scale production facility. The firm faces the alternative of building a large plant or building a small one. Demand expectations for the plant's products are 50 percent for high demand, 30 percent for medium demand, and 20 percent for low demand. Depending on demand, net cash flows (sales revenues minus operating costs), all discounted to the present, will range from $8.8 million to $1.4 million if a large plant is built, and from $2.6 million to $1.4 million if a small plant is built.

Since the demand probabilities are known, we can find the expected values of cash flows, which are given in Column 5 of Figure 3-7. Finally, we can deduct the investment outlays from the expected net revenues to obtain

Figure 3-7 Illustrative Decision Tree*

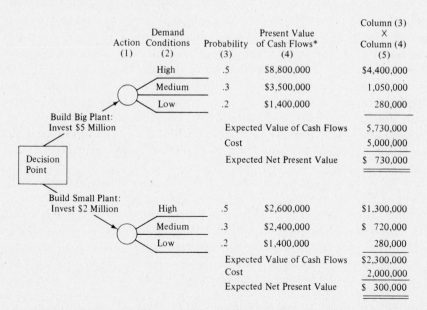

Action (1)	Demand Conditions (2)	Probability (3)	Present Value of Cash Flows* (4)	Column (3) X Column (4) (5)
	High	.5	$8,800,000	$4,400,000
	Medium	.3	$3,500,000	1,050,000
	Low	.2	$1,400,000	280,000
Build Big Plant: Invest $5 Million			Expected Value of Cash Flows	5,730,000
			Cost	5,000,000
			Expected Net Present Value	$ 730,000
Build Small Plant: Invest $2 Million	High	.5	$2,600,000	$1,300,000
	Medium	.3	$2,400,000	$ 720,000
	Low	.2	$1,400,000	280,000
			Expected Value of Cash Flows	$2,300,000
			Cost	2,000,000
			Expected Net Present Value	$ 300,000

Decision Point

* The figures in Column 4 are the annual cash flows from operation—revenues minus cash operating costs—discounted at the firm's cost of capital.

the expected net present value of each decision. In the example, the expected net present value is $730,000 for the large plant and $300,000 for the small one.

Since the net present value of the large plant is higher, should the decision be to construct it? Perhaps, but not necessarily. Notice that the range of outcomes is greater if the large plant is built, with the actual net present values (Column 4, present values, in Figure 3-7 minus the investment cost) varying from $3.8 million to *minus* $3.6 million. However, a range of only $600,000 to *minus* $600,000 exists for the small plant. Since the required investment for the two plants is not the same, we must examine the coefficients of variation of the net present value possibilities in order to determine which alternative actually entails the greater risk. The coefficient of variation for the large plant's present value is 4.3, while that for the small plant is only 1.5.[9] Risk is greater if the decision is to build the large plant.

The decision maker could take account of the risk differentials in a variety of ways. He could assign utility values to the cash flows given in Column 4 of Figure 3-7, thus stating Column 5 in terms of expected utility. He would then choose the plant size that provided the greatest expected utility. Alternatively, he could use the certainty equivalent or the risk-adjusted discount rate method in calculating the present values given in Column 4. The plant that offered the larger risk-adjusted net present value would then be the optimal choice.

The decision tree illustrated in Figure 3-7 is quite simple; in actual use, the trees are frequently far more complex and involve a number of sequential decision points. An example of a more complex tree is illustrated in Figure 3-8. The numbered boxes represent *decision points*, instances when the firm must choose between several alternatives; the circles represent the possible actual outcomes, one of which will follow the decisions. At Decision Point 1, the firm has three choices: to invest $3 million in a large plant; to invest $1.3 million in a small plant; or to spend $100,000 on market research. If the large plant is built, the firm follows the upper branch, and its position has been fixed—it can only hope that demand will be high. If it builds the small plant, it follows the lower branch. If demand is low, no further action is required; if demand is high, Decision Point 2 is reached, and the firm either must do nothing or must expand the plant at a cost of another $2.2 million. (Thus, if it obtains a large plant through expansion, the cost is $500,000 greater than if it had built the large plant in the first place.)

If the decision at Point 1 is to pay $100,000 for more information, the firm moves to the center branch. The research modifies the firm's information about potential demand. Initially, the probabilities were 70 percent for high demand and 30 percent for low demand. The research survey will show

[9] Using Equation 3-3 and the data on possible returns in Table 3-7, the standard deviation of return for the large plant is found to be $3.155 million, and that for the smaller to be $458,260. Dividing each of these standard deviations by the expected returns for their respective plant size, as in Equation 3-4, gives the coefficient of variation.

Figure 3-8 Decision Tree with Multiple Decision Points

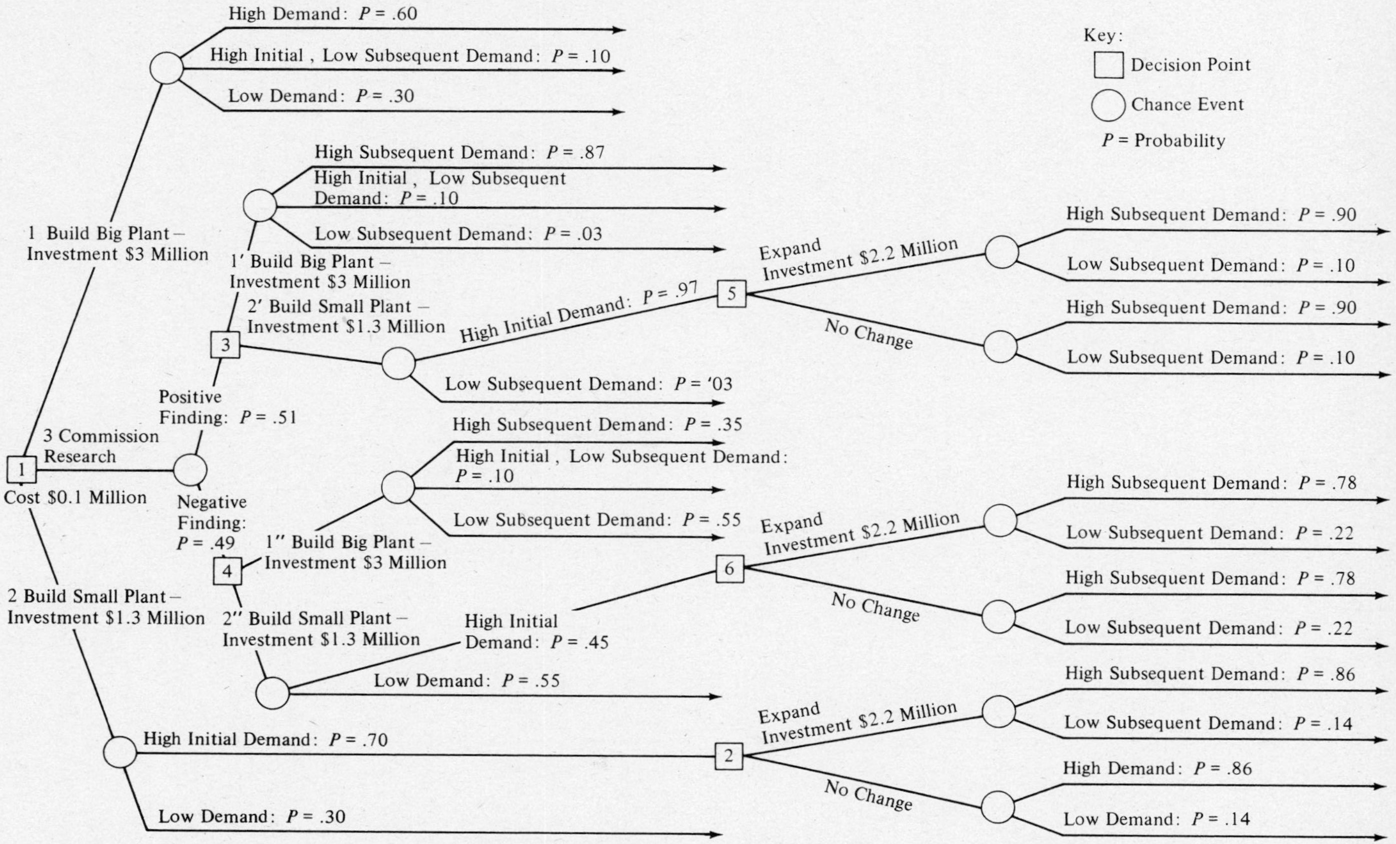

Key:

▢ Decision Point

◯ Chance Event

P = Probability

High Demand: P = .60

High Initial, Low Subsequent Demand: P = .10

Low Demand: P = .30

High Subsequent Demand: P = .87

High Initial, Low Subsequent Demand: P = .10

Low Subsequent Demand: P = .03

1′ Build Big Plant — Investment $3 Million

2′ Build Small Plant — Investment $1.3 Million

High Initial Demand: P = .97

Low Subsequent Demand: P = '03

High Subsequent Demand: P = .35

High Initial, Low Subsequent Demand: P = .10

Low Subsequent Demand: P = .55

1″ Build Big Plant — Investment $3 Million

2″ Build Small Plant — Investment $1.3 Million

High Initial Demand: P = .45

Low Demand: P = .55

1 Build Big Plant — Investment $3 Million

3 Commission Research Cost $0.1 Million

Positive Finding: P = .51

Negative Finding: P = .49

2 Build Small Plant — Investment $1.3 Million

High Initial Demand: P = .70

Low Demand: P = .30

Expand Investment $2.2 Million

No Change

High Subsequent Demand: P = .90

Low Subsequent Demand: P = .10

High Subsequent Demand: P = .90

Low Subsequent Demand: P = .10

Expand Investment $2.2 Million

No Change

High Subsequent Demand: P = .78

Low Subsequent Demand: P = .22

High Subsequent Demand: P = .78

Low Subsequent Demand: P = .22

Expand Investment $2.2 Million

No Change

High Subsequent Demand: P = .86

Low Subsequent Demand: P = .14

High Demand: P = .86

Low Demand: P = .14

5

6

2

3

4

1

79

either favorable (positive) or unfavorable (negative) demand prospects. If they are positive, we assume that the probability for high final demand will be 87 percent, and that for low demand will be 13 percent; if the research yields negative results, the odds on high final demand are only 35 percent, and those for low demand are 65 percent. These results will influence the firm's decision whether to build a large plant or a small plant.

If the firm builds a large plant and demand is high, sales and profits will be large. If, however, it builds a large plant and there is little demand, sales will be low and losses rather than profits will be incurred. On the other hand, if it builds a small plant and demand is high, sales and profits will be lower than they could have been had a large plant been built, but the chances of losses in the event of low demand will be eliminated. The decision to build the large plant is therefore riskier than the one to build the small plant. The cost of the research is, in effect, an expenditure serving to reduce the degree of uncertainty in the decision about which plant to build; the research provides additional information on the probability of high versus low demand, thus reducing the level of uncertainty.

The decision tree in Figure 3-8 is incomplete in that no dollar outcomes (or utility values) are assigned to the various situations. If such values are assigned, along the lines shown in the last two columns of Figure 3-7, expected values can be obtained for each of the alternative actions. These expected values can then be used to aid the decision maker in choosing among alternatives.

Simulation

Another technique designed to assist managers in making decisions under uncertainty is computer simulation. To illustrate the technique, let us consider a situation where a new textile plant is to be built. The exact cost of the plant is not known. It is expected to be about $150 million. If no difficulties arise in construction, the cost can be as low as $125 million; however, an unfortunate series of events—strikes, unprojected increases in material costs, technical problems, and the like—could result in an investment outlay as high as $225 million.

Revenues from the new facility, which will operate for many years, depend on population growth and income in the region, competition, developments in synthetic fabrics, research, and textile import quotas. Operating costs depend on production efficiency, materials and labor cost trends, and the like. Because both sales revenues and operating costs are uncertain, annual profits are also uncertain.

Assuming that probability distributions can be developed for each of the major cost and revenue determinants, a computer program can be constructed to simulate what is likely to occur. In effect, the computer selects one value at random from each of the relevant distributions, combines it with other values selected from the other distributions, and produces an estimated profit and net present value, or rate of return, on investment. This particular profit and rate of return occur only for the particular combination of values selected during the trial. The computer proceeds to select other sets of values and to compute other profits and rates of return for perhaps several hundred trials. A count is kept of the number of times each various rate of return is computed, and when the computer runs are completed, the frequency with which the various rates of return occurred can be plotted as a frequency distribution.

The procedure is illustrated in Figures 3-9 and 3-10.[10] Figure 3-9 is a flow chart outlining the simulation procedure described above; Figure 3-10 illustrates the frequency distribution of rates of return generated by such a simulation for two alternative projects, X and Y, each with an expected cost of $20 million. The expected rate of return on Investment X is 15 percent, and that of Investment Y is 20 percent. However, these are only the *average* rates of return generated by the computer; simulated rates ranged from −10 percent to +45 percent for Investment Y, and from 5 to 25 percent for Investment X. The standard deviation generated for X is only 4 percentage points; that for Y is 12 percentage points. From this we can calculate a coefficient of variation of .267 for Project X, and .60 for Project Y. Clearly, then, Investment Y is riskier than Investment X. The computer simulation has provided an estimate both of the expected returns on the two projects and of their relative risks. A decision about which alternative should be chosen can now be made on the basis of one of the techniques—certainty equivalents, risk-adjusted discount rates, or expected utility—discussed above.

One final point should be made about the use of computer simulation for risk analysis. The technique requires obtaining probability distributions about a number of variables—investment outlays, unit sales, product prices, input prices, asset lives, and others—and involves a fair amount of programming and machine-time costs. Full-scale simulation is therefore not generally feasible except for large and expensive projects such as major plant expansions or new product decisions. In these cases, however, when a firm is deciding whether or not to accept a major undertaking involving an outlay of millions of dollars, computer simulation can provide valuable insights into the relative merits of alternative strategies.

It should also be noted that a somewhat less expensive simulation technique is available as an alternative method of analyzing the outcomes of various projects or strategies. Instead of using probability distributions for each of the variables in the problem, we can simulate the results by starting with best-guess estimates for each variable, then change the values of the variables (within reasonable limits) to see the effects of such changes on the rate of return. Typically, the rate of return is highly sensitive to some variables, less so to others. Attention is then concentrated on the variables to which profitability is most sensitive. This technique, known as sensitivity

---

[10] Figure 3-9 is adapted from an article by David B. Hertz, "Risk Analysis in Capital Investment," *Harvard Business Review*, January-February 1964, pp. 95-106.

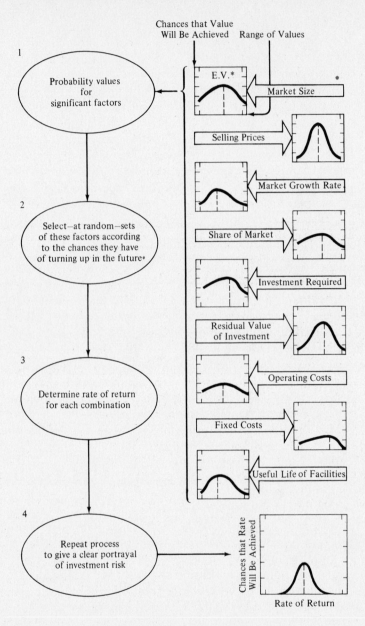

Figure 3-9 Simulation for Investment Planning*

* Expected value = highest point of curve.

Figure 3-10   Expected Rates of Return on Investments *X* and *Y*

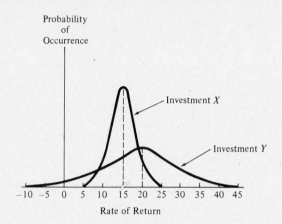

analysis, is considerably less expensive than the full-scale simulation and provides similar data for decision-making purposes.

SUMMARY

Risk analysis plays an integral role in the decision process for most business problems. In this chapter we defined the concept of risk, introduced it into the valuation model for the firm, and then examined several techniques for decision making under conditions of uncertainty.

Risk in economic analysis is characterized by variability of outcomes, and it is defined in terms of probability distributions of possible results. The tighter the distribution, the lower the variability, and hence the lower the risk. The standard deviation and coefficient of variation are two frequently used measures of risk in economic analysis.

The assumption of risk aversion by investors and managers is based on utility relationships. For most individuals, the marginal utility of money is sharply diminishing, and this leads directly to risk aversion. Investor risk aversion directly affects the valuation of the firm and must, therefore, be taken into account for managerial decision making. The basic valuation model can be adjusted to reflect this risk effect through the use of either certainty equivalent returns or risk-adjusted discount rates; when these two methods are properly applied, they are entirely consistent.

Decision making under conditions of uncertainty is greatly facilitated by two techniques used to structure the problems and to generate data necessary for optimization analysis: decision trees and simulation. Decision trees map out the sequence of events in a decision problem, providing a means for examining the branching that takes place at each decision point. Simulation techniques can be used to generate frequency distributions of possible outcomes for alternative decisions and to provide inputs for expected utility, certainty equivalent, or risk-adjusted discount rate analysis.

The concepts and techniques of analysis introduced in this chapter play major roles in the analyses used in subsequent chapters. We refer to them frequently in analyzing problems in the areas of demand, production, cost, pricing, and capital budgeting.

QUESTIONS

3-1 Define the following terms, using graphs to illustrate your answers where feasible:

a) Probability distribution
b) Expected value
c) Standard deviation
d) Coefficient of variation
e) Risk
f) Diminishing marginal utility for money
g) Certainty equivalent
h) Risk-adjusted discount rate
i) Decision tree
j) Simulation

3-2 The probability distribution of a less risky expected return is more peaked than that of a risky return. What shape would a graph of the probability distribution have for completely certain returns and for completely uncertain returns?

3-3 What is the main problem in making decisions based on strict comparisons between expected monetary values of alternative projects?

3-4 In this chapter we have defined risk in terms of the variability of expected future returns; that is, the standard deviation of these returns. In constructing this measure of risk, we have implicitly given equal weight to variations on both sides of the expected return—higher returns or lower returns. Can you see any problems resulting from this treatment?

3-5 "On reflection, the use of the market indifference curve concept illustrated in Figure 3-4 as a basis for determining certainty equivalents, or, alternatively, for determining risk-adjusted discount rates as in Figure 3-5 is all right in theory, but cannot be applied in practice. Market estimates of investors' reactions to risk cannot be measured precisely, so it is impossible to construct a set of certainty equivalents or risk-adjusted discount rates for the different classes of investment." Comment on this statement.

3-6 What is the value of decision trees in managerial decision making?

3-7 In computer simulation the computer makes a large number of "trials" to show what the various outcomes of a particular decision might be if the decision could be made many times under the same conditions. In practice, however, the decision will be made only once, so how can simulation results be useful to the decision maker?

PROBLEMS

3-1 The Maxfli Company's marketing department has been given an advertising budget of $100,000 for a new golf ball. Preliminary market research has indicated two feasible marketing strategies: (a) concentration on developing general consumer acceptance by advertising through newspapers, golf magazines, and other media; or (b) concentration on distributor acceptance of the ball by offering special retailer "deals" or "promotions," by personal sales calls by company representatives, and so forth. The marketing manager has developed estimates for sales under each alternative plan and has arranged rough "payoff" matrices according to his assessment of the "likelihood" of product acceptance under each plan. These matrices are illustrated below:

Strategy 1 (Advertising)		Strategy 2 (Promotions)	
Probability	Outcome (Sales)	Probability	Outcome (Sales)
0.2	$ 250,000	0.4	$ 500,000
0.3	750,000	0.4	750,000
0.3	1,250,000	0.2	1,000,000
0.2	1,750,000		

a) Assume that the company has a 50 percent profit margin on sales; that is, profits are equal to one-half of sales revenues. Calculate the expected profits for each plan.

b) Construct a simple bar graph of the possible profit outcomes for each plan. On the basis of the appearance of the two graphs, which plan appears to be the more risky?

c) Calculate the risk (coefficient of variation of the profit distribution) associated with each plan.

d) Assume that the company has a utility function like the one illustrated below. Which marketing strategy should the marketing manager recommend?

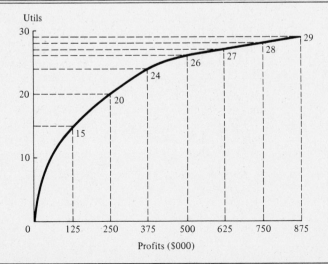

 e) Is such a decision process likely to be more valid, or easier to obtain agreement on, if Maxfli is owned by one stockholder or by a large number of stockholders? Why?

3-2 The Sport-time Equipment Company manufactures a line of tennis rackets. Part of its production facility is to be replaced by one of two innovative pieces of equipment. The benefits (net cash flows) will be generated over the four-year useful lives of the machines and have the following expectational characteristics:

	Probability	Annual Cash Flow
Alternative #1	.30	$2,900.
	.50	3,500.
	.20	4,100.
Alternative #2	.30	$ 0
	.50	4,000.
	.20	8,000.

Whichever piece of equipment is chosen, the total cost will be the same, $4,000.

 a) What are the expected annual net cash flows from each project?

 b) Given that the firm uses a discount rate of 12% for cash flows with a high degree of dispersion and a 10% rate for less risky cash flows, which machine has the highest expected net present value?

 c) Suppose we know that the firm is indifferent between a "certain" 4-year annuity of $3,292 per year and the payoff of alternative #1, and would also be indifferent between a "certain" 4-year annuity of $3,300 per year and the return from alternative #2. What certainty equivalent adjustment factors do these figures indicate for each project?

 d) Under these circumstances, which piece of equipment should be chosen if the firm uses an NPV certainty equivalent approach and an 8% riskless discount rate?

3-3 A manufacturer of novelty items has just designed a political button for a candidate in an upcoming election. It has contracted to sell the button to a campaign committee at five cents each, irrespective of the quantity purchased. The firm is trying to decide whether to use method A or method B for manufacturing the button. Under system A the costs of producing the button are three cents for each unit made plus a $2,000 setup cost. With method B the setup costs are $4,000 and unit costs are two cents each. The firm has approached you and requested information that will aid in their decision. You have examined the market for the button and estimate the probability distribution of sales volume for the primary election to be:

Sales Volume	Probability
10,000	.40
30,000	.60

Since the candidate is unopposed in the primary election, there is a virtual certainty that he will also campaign in the general election. You have estimated that sales of the campaign button in the general election are dependent upon whether or not the President actively campaigns for the candidate. If he campaigns, the distribution of sales is estimated to be:

Sales Volume	Probability
150,000	.70
300,000	.30

Without active Presidential support during the campaign, the sales distribution will probably be:

Sales Volume	Probability
100,000	.50
150,000	.50

There is a 50% chance that the President will actively campaign for this candidate.

a) Assuming the novelty company wants to choose between the two production systems on the basis of the profit distribution on the job, construct the decision tree that they might use to lay out the problem.

b) Calculate the potential profits associated with each possible route through the decision tree. (*Note:* The probability of each possible outcome is equal to the product of all the probabilities along each segment of that path through the tree.)

c) Which production system results in the largest expected profit?

d) Do the risks associated with each alternative appear to be similar, or is one production method more risky in terms of the potential profit variability?

e) Which production system should the company choose? Why?

3-4 The Fairfax Camera Company has been experiencing a leveling off in demand for its high-priced ($150) automatic camera. The variable cost of producing the camera is $100 a unit, irrespective of the quantity manufactured. Thus, Fairfax earns a $50 profit contribution (or profit margin, as it is frequently called) on each camera sold. Sales projections for the following two years show expected sales at a constant 25,000 units a year.

The firm's management has done research on three alternative programs for improving demand, and has come up with sales estimates and probability distributions for the following two years (the planning horizon):

Plan A calls for adding a built-in timer to the camera at a cost of $10,000 a year plus $2 for each unit sold; the $150 sales price would be continued.

Plan *B* calls for lowering the selling price from $150 to $146 a unit. Plan *C* requires increasing the advertising for the camera by $10,000 a year while retaining the $150 sales price.

For the first year, the following probabilities of success and failure, and corresponding expected sales changes, have been estimated:

Plan	Probability	Outcome in First Year
A	0.8 (success)	Increase 5,000 units
	0.2 (failure)	Increase 500 units
B	1.0 (success)	Increase 4,000 units
C	0.7 (success)	Increase 2,500 units
	0.3 (failure)	Increase 1,000 units

In the second year, the competition is likely to react (especially if the program is successful). The following probabilities of competitor retaliation and corresponding expected sales changes are given:

Plan	Probability	Competitor Reaction	Unit Sales Increase in Year 2 over Year 0
A	0.7 given 1st year success	Reaction	3,000
	0.3 given 1st year success	No reaction	4,500
	0.2 given 1st year failure	Reaction	0
	0.8 given 1st year failure	No reaction	400
B	0.6	Reaction	1,000
	0.4	No reaction	3,000
C	0.5 given 1st year success	Reaction	1,000
	0.5 given 1st year success	No reaction	2,000
	0.1 given 1st year failure	Reaction	0
	0.9 given 1st year failure	No reaction	500

a) Construct a decision tree for the firm to use in evaluating the three programs.
b) Assuming that all costs and revenues for a year are incurred at the end of the year for which they apply, compute the *NPV* of the incremental profit contribution at each branch terminal for each project using a discount rate of 10 percent. Next, find the expected *NPV* of each project as a weighted average of these terminal *NPVs*. (*Note:* The *NPVs* of the three projects could be computed in a simpler manner, but information needed for the risk analysis would not be generated.)

c) Which project is the most risky? The least risky? (Answer this question with the aid of graphs of the *NPV* distributions for all terminal branches. Do not calculate standard deviations.)

d) Which project should Fairfax select? Why?

SELECTED REFERENCES

Brown, Rex. "Do Managers Find Decision Theory Useful?" *Harvard Business Review,* May-June 1970, pp. 78-89.

Green, P. E. "Bayesian Decision Theory in Pricing Strategy," *Journal of Marketing,* January 1963, pp. 5-14.

Hertz, David B. "Risk Analysis in Capital Investment," *Harvard Business Review,* January-February 1964, pp. 95-106.

Hull, J., P. G. Moore, and H. Thomas. "Utility and Its Measurement," *Journal of the Royal Statistican Society,* 1973, 136, Part 2, pp. 226-247.

Magee, John F. "How to Use Decision Trees in Capital Budgeting," *Harvard Business Review,* September-October 1964, pp. 79-95.

Pratt, John, Howard Raiffa, and Robert Schlaifer. "Introduction to Statistical Decision Theory," in Edwin Mansfield, ed., *Managerial Economics and Operations Research,* New York: Norton, 1966, pp. 195-202.

Schlaifer, Robert. *Analysis of Decisions Under Uncertainty.* New York: McGraw-Hill Book Company, 1969.

Shubik, Martin. "A Note on Decision-making Under Uncertainty," in Edwin Mansfield, ed., *Managerial Economics and Operations Research,* New York: Norton, 1966, pp. 192-194.

APPENDIX: Alternative Decision Rules

The decision criterion stressed throughout this book is maximization of value. Ordinarily, the maximum value of a firm is obtained by maximizing expected utility as described in this chapter. Under certain circumstances, especially in situations where the environment is viewed as being malevolent rather than neutral and where probabilities of occurrence for states of nature are difficult to assign, other decision criteria may be appropriate. These rules are perhaps most relevant in oligopoly situations where firms can be expected to react to the actions taken by one of their competitors. A number of criteria for dealing with such cases have been advanced in the literature, and several are discussed in this appendix.

To simplify the analysis, the oil venture versus government bond example

Table 3A-1   Payoff Matrix

Alternatives	States of Nature	
	Oil	No Oil
Invest in Government Bonds	$5,250	$5,250
Invest in Oil Venture	$7,500	$2,500

developed in this chapter is re-examined. A slightly modified version of the payoff matrix for that example is reproduced in Table 3A-1.

MAXIMIN DECISION RULE

One decision criterion widely discussed in the literature on decision making under uncertainty is the extremely conservative *maximin* criterion. This criterion states that the decision maker should select that alternative which provides the best of the worst possible outcomes. This is done by finding the worst possible, or minimum, outcome for each alternative and then choosing that alternative whose worst outcome provides the highest, or maximum, payoff. Hence, this criterion instructs one to maximize the minimum possible outcome.

In our example the worst possible outcome from investing in the oil well venture is the $2,500 payoff that will result if the well turns out to be a dry hole. The government bond provides a payoff of $5,250 under either state of nature; therefore, $5,250 is the worst outcome possible with an investment in the bond. The maximin criterion would have us select the government bond, since its minimum possible outcome is greater than the $2,500 minimum payoff for the oil venture.

Although this decision criterion suffers from the obvious shortcoming of examining only the most pessimistic outcome for each alternative, we should not dismiss it immediately as being too naïve and unsophisticated for use in some decisions. The maximin criterion implicitly assumes a *very* strong aversion to risk, and we might therefore associate its use with decisions involving the possibility of a catastrophic outcome. In other words, at times when the alternative decisions available to the decision maker involve outcomes for various states of nature that endanger the survival of the organization, the maximin criterion may be an appropriate technique for decision making.

MINIMAX REGRET DECISION RULE

A second decision criterion that we might examine uses the relative "loss" of a decision rather than its absolute outcome for decision-making purposes. This decision rule, known as the *minimax regret* criterion, states that the decision maker should attempt to minimize the regret associated with the opportunity cost of a wrong decision *after the fact*. Alternatively stated, this criterion instructs one to minimize the difference between the possible outcomes of the chosen alternative and the best possible outcome for each state of nature.

Table 3A-2   Opportunity Loss or "Regret" Matrix

	States of Nature	
Alternatives	Oil	No Oil
Invest in Government Bonds	$2,250	0
Invest in Oil Venture	0	$2,750

In order to clarify this technique, we need to examine the concept of an opportunity loss or "regret" in greater detail. An *opportunity loss* can be defined as the difference between the payoff obtained from an alternative and the highest possible payoff for the resulting state of nature. It results from the fact that the return we actually receive using any decision criterion under conditions of uncertainty will frequently be lower than the maximum return obtainable if we had perfect knowledge of the outcomes beforehand.

Table 3A-2 is the opportunity loss, or regret matrix, associated with the investment problem we have been examining. It was constructed by finding the maximum payoff for each state of nature in Table 3A-1 and then subtracting the payoff associated with each alternative from that figure: The $2,250 in the upper left-hand box of Table 3A-2, for example, was obtained by subtracting the $5,250 outcome for an investment in the government bonds from the $7,500 payoff from the producing oil well. Notice that the opportunity loss is always a positive figure (or zero), since we are subtracting in each case from the largest payoff for each state of nature.

The minimax regret criterion would have the decision maker choose the investment in the government bonds, since this decision minimizes the maximum regret, or opportunity loss, that he can suffer. The maximum regret in this case is limited to the $2,250 that results if the oil venture is successful. Had our investor put his money in the oil venture and had it been unsuccessful, he would have suffered an opportunity loss of $2,750, or $500 more than the maximum regret associated with the investment in the bonds.[11]

AN ALTERNATIVE USE OF THE OPPORTUNITY-LOSS CONCEPT

This opportunity-loss concept can be used in yet another way in risk analysis. We have defined an opportunity loss as a cost associated with uncertainty. Therefore, the *expected opportunity loss* associated with a decision provides a measure of the expected monetary gain which would result from the removal of all uncer-

---

[11] Although the maximum and minimax regret criteria lead to the same decision in our example—that is, they both indicate that an investment in government bonds is optimal—such is not always the case. The two decision rules will frequently indicate different alternatives as being the best choice.

tainty about the occurrence of future events. It represents the difference between the highest expected payoff available from one of the decision alternatives and the expected payoff associated with choosing the correct alternative under each state of nature. Using the concept of an expected opportunity loss it is possible to determine in many cases whether additional information about the alternatives should be obtained before making a final decision.

Let us again examine our investment problem to illustrate this use of the opportunity loss. On the basis of the data in Table 3A-2 we can calculate the expected opportunity loss of each alternative as shown in Table 3A-3.

The minimum expected opportunity loss in this case is $1,100, an amount greater than 20 percent of the initial investment.[12] The decision maker might feel that with an expected opportunity loss of this magnitude, he would prefer to spend some more money in order to try to reduce the uncertainty in the original decision problem before making a final selection. In this example, our investor might hire a geologist to conduct additional tests of the rock formations or perhaps to make some seismic recordings in the area where the well is to be drilled.

We must emphasize that additional expenditures on information gathering will not guarantee that the costs associated with uncertainty will be reduced. (The geologist might make his examination of the area and be unable to change the predicted 60 percent odds that oil will be discovered.) The opportunity-loss concept merely informs the decision maker of the possible opportunity for reducing the cost of imperfect knowledge. We do, however, often see firms engaging in activities aimed at reducing the uncertainty of payoff for various alternatives before making an irrevocable decision. For example, a food-manufacturing company will employ extensive marketing tests in selected areas to gain better estimates of sales potential before going ahead with large-scale production of a new product, and an automobile manufacturer frequently installs new equipment in a limited number of models to ascertain reliability and customer reaction before including the equipment in all models.

PROBLEMS

3A-1   The Swift Bicycle Company has just designed a new, highly efficient reflector. It has priced the reflector to sell at 50¢ each to retail outlets. The firm is trying to decide whether to use Method *A* or Method *B* for producing the reflector. Under System *A*, the fixed costs of producing the reflector are $2,000 and variable costs are $.30 per unit. With Method *B* fixed costs are $3,000, and unit costs $.20. The firm has approached you and requested information that will aid in making the decision. You have

---

[12] Notice that this $1,100 is the *minimum* possible expected opportunity loss, and it results if the investor puts his money in the oil well. Use of the minimax regret criterion and investment in the bonds results in the larger expected opportunity loss of $1,350. Similarly, it is the difference between the expected return from a correct decision —irrespective of the state of nature—and the highest expected return from a single alternative—again the oil venture.

Table 3A-3 Calculation of Expected Opportunity Losses

From the Loss Matrix

	Oil Venture			Government Bonds		
State of Nature	Probability of this State of Nature (1)	Opportunity Loss of this State of Nature (2)	Expected Opportunity Loss (1) × (2) (3)	Probability of this State of Nature (1)	Opportunity Loss of this State of Nature (2)	Expected Opportunity Loss (1) × (2) (3)
Oil	0.6	0	0	0.6	$2,250	$1,350
No oil	0.4	$2,750	$1,100	0.4	0	0
			$1,100			$1,350

Minimum Expected Opportunity Loss = $1,100 = Cost of Uncertainty

From the Payoff Matrix

	Drilling Operation			Government Bond		
State of Nature	Probability (1)	Outcome (2)	(1) × (2) (3)	Probability (1)	Outcome (2)	(1) × (2) (3)
Oil	0.6	$7,500	$4,500	0.6	$5,250	$3,150
No oil	0.4	2,500	1,000	0.4	5,250	2,100
		Expected Value	$5,500		Expected Value	$5,250

Expected value of a "correct" decision after the fact = $7,500 × .6 + $5,250 × .4 = $6,600.
Cost of Uncertainty = Expected value of a "correct" decision − Expected value of the best alternative = $6,600 − $5,500 = $1,100.

examined the market for the reflector and estimate the probability distribution of sales volume to be:

Sales Volume	Probability
5,000	.25
30,000	.50
50,000	.25

- a) Construct a payoff matrix for this problem.
- b) Calculate the expected payoff for each alternative.
- c) Calculate the expected opportunity loss for each alternative.
- d) What is the cost of uncertainty in this problem?
- e) Should Swift be willing to spend an amount equal to the cost of uncertainty to remove all uncertainty in this case? Why? Or why not?

3A-2 Joe Albert, a young entrepreneur, is currently in the process of choosing between two facilities for the second location of a lawn and garden firm he owns and operates. One building is located in Central City, while the second is in Shelter Town, an adjacent suburb. Both buildings are located in middle-income areas where single-family housing predominates. Projected sales possibilities are nearly identical. Additionally, both facilities meet the requirements for space and layout equally well. Thus, Joe is going to make his choice between them solely on the basis of cost. The building in Central City can be purchased on terms that result in a $250 monthly payment. The Shelter Town location will cost somewhat more to purchase and with the same down payment, the monthly payment will be $300. The only other cost item which is relevant for the decision between the two buildings is the property tax. The facility in Central City has current property taxes of $150 per month while the Shelter Town building has a monthly property tax of $50. This wide discrepancy is due in part to the very high education and social welfare costs in Central City relative to Shelter Town. Currently, however, the U.S. Supreme Court is hearing a case concerning the constitutionality of using the property tax to finance those activities. Should the Court find in favor of the petitioners (those arguing against the use of the property tax) then taxes on the building in Central City will decline to $50 per month while those in Shelter Town will remain unchanged. (The costs of education and social welfare would be covered by an increase in income taxes and as such are invariant with respect to the decision facing Albert.)

- a) Assuming Joe Albert wants to choose between the two facilities on the basis of minimizing monthly costs, draw the decision tree that he would use to lay out the problem.
- b) Construct a payoff matrix for the problem.
- c) Assuming Joe is very risk adverse (so risk adverse in fact that he uses a maximin decision criterion) which facility will he purchase?
- d) What is the minimum probability of a positive finding by the Su-

preme Court (a decision in favor of the petitioners) that would cause Joe to prefer the Central City location?

e) Assume Joe has assessed the Supreme Court's probability of deciding in favor of the petitioners at .80. If he is making his decision strictly on the basis of minimizing the expected monthly cost, what is the maximum amount he would be willing to pay for an option allowing him to purchase either building *after* the Supreme Court's decision is rendered? That is, how much should he be willing to pay for the privilege of postponing the decision until after the tax issue has been settled?

CHAPTER 4

Demand
Theory

In many respects the most important determinant of a firm's profitability is the demand for its products. No matter how efficient its production processes and regardless of the astuteness of its financial manager, personnel director, or other officers, the firm cannot operate profitably unless a demand for its products exists or can be created, or unless it can find a new set of products for which a demand exists.

Because of the critical role of demand as a determinant of profitability, estimates of expected future demand constitute a key element in all planning activities. Production decisions are profoundly influenced by the firm's underlying demand function. For example, if demand is relatively stable, then long, continuous production runs may be scheduled; if demand fluctuates, either flexible production processes must be employed or sizable inventories must be carried. Financial decisions are also affected by demand conditions in the firm's product markets; if product demand is strong and growing, the financial manager must arrange to finance the firm's growing capital requirements. Similarly, the personnel director must set up recruitment and training programs to assure the availability of a sufficiently large work force to produce and sell the firm's products.

The demand function also interacts with the set of possible production technologies to determine the market structure of various industries and, hence, the level of competition in the economy. Where these demand and production factors would lead to monopoly or oligopoly, direct regulation or antitrust actions may be required to prevent exploitation. In Chapters 10, 11, and 12—where market structure, pricing, and antitrust policy are discussed —the importance of demand as a determinant of public policy will become quite apparent.

Demand is a complex subject, but its central importance requires that it be thoroughly understood. Accordingly, in this chapter we examine the theory of demand, emphasizing methods of analyzing the strength of demand for a product and the effect of changing conditions on this demand. Then, in the following chapter, we use the theoretical relationships developed here to formulate models that can be used to actually estimate demand functions.

THE DEMAND FUNCTION

The term "demand" is defined as the number of units of a particular good or service that customers are willing to purchase during a specified period and under a given set of conditions. The time period might, for example, be a year, and the conditions that must be specified would include the price of the good in question, prices and availability of competitive goods, expectations of price changes, consumer incomes, consumer tastes and preferences, advertising expenditures, and so on. The amount of the product that consumers wish to purchase—the *demand* for the product—is dependent on all these factors.

The *demand function* for a product is a statement of the relationship between the quantity demanded and the factors that affect this quantity. Written in general functional form, the demand function may be expressed as:

$$\begin{matrix} \text{Quantity of} \\ \text{Product } X \\ \text{Demanded} \end{matrix} = Q_X = f(\text{price of } X, \text{ prices of competitive goods,} \\ \text{expectations of price changes, consumer incomes, tastes and preferences, advertising expenditures,} \dots). \qquad (4\text{-}1)$$

The generalized demand function expressed in Equation 4-1 is really just a listing of the variables that influence demand; for use in managerial decision making, the demand function must be made explicit. That is, the precise relationship between quantity demanded and each of the independent variables must be specified. To illustrate what is involved, let us assume that we are analyzing the demand for automobiles, and the demand function has been specified as follows:

$$Q = a_1 P + a_2 Y + a_3 Pop + a_4 C + a_5 A. \qquad (4\text{-}2)$$

This equation states that the number of automobiles demanded during a given year, Q, is a linear function of the average price of cars, P; average per capita disposable income, Y; population, Pop; an index of credit availability, C; and advertising expenditures, A. The terms $a_1, a_2, \ldots, a_5$ are called the *parameters* of the demand function. We shall examine procedures for estimating their values, together with indicators of how confident we are in these estimates in the following chapter. For now, we shall simply assume that we know the parameters and that the demand function does accurately predict the quantity of the product demanded.[1]

Substituting a set of assumed parameter values into Equation 4-2, we obtain:

$$Q = -3,000P + 1,000Y + 0.05Pop + 1,500,000C + 0.05A. \qquad (4\text{-}3)$$

Equation 4-3 indicates that automobile demand falls by 3,000 units for each $1 increase in the average price charged; it increases by 1,000 units for each $1 increase in per capita disposable income; it increases by 0.05 units for each additional person in the population; it increases by 1.5 million units if the index of credit availability increases 1 unit; and it increases by 0.05 units for each $1 spent on advertising.

If we multiply each parameter in Equation 4-3 by the value of its respective variable, and then sum these products, we will have the estimated demand for automobiles during the coming year. Table 4-1 illustrates this

Table 4-1 Estimating the Demand for Automobiles Using a Hypothetical Demand Function

Independent Variable (1)	Estimated Value of the Independent Variable for Coming Year (2)	Parameter (3)	Estimated Total Demand (2) × (3) (4)
Average Price	$3,000	−3,000	−9,000,000
Disposable Income	$2,000	1,000	2,000,000
Population	200,000,000	0.05	10,000,000
Index of Credit Terms	1.00	1,500,000	1,500,000
Advertising Expenditures	$100,000,000	0.05	5,000,000
		Total Demand	9,500,000

[1] If all the variables that influence demand are not included in the demand function, or if the parameters are not correctly specified, the equation will not predict demand accurately, sales forecasts will be in error, and incorrect expansion and operating decisions will be made. Obviously, the more accurate the firm's demand estimates, the lower its risk. Thus, a close relationship exists between risk and the ability to estimate accurately the demand function. These points are elaborated on in Chapter 5, where techniques for estimating demand functions are developed.

process, showing that the estimated demand for autos, assuming the stated values of the independent variables, will be approximately 9.5 million units.

INDUSTRY DEMAND VERSUS FIRM DEMAND

Demand functions can be specified either for an entire industry or for an individual firm. Somewhat different independent variables would typically be used in industry, as compared to firm, demand equations, with perhaps the most important difference being the fact that variables representing competitors' actions would be stressed in firm demand functions. For example, in a firm's demand function the price charged by competing firms and a second advertising variable measuring competitors' advertising expenditures might be included. Demand for the firm's product would be negatively related to its own price, but positively related to the price charged by competing firms. Similarly, its demand would be positively related to its own advertising expenditures, but its demand would probably decrease with additional advertising by other firms.

Moreover, the parameters for specific variables would differ in the two functions. To illustrate, population would influence the demand for Ford's automobiles and for all producers' autos, but the parameter value in Ford's demand function would be smaller than that in the industry demand function. Only if Ford had 100 percent of the market—that is, if Ford *were* the industry—would the parameters for the firm and the industry be identical.

Since firm and industry demand functions differ, different models, or equations, must be specified for estimating the two kinds of demand. This matter need not concern us in the present chapter, however, because the theoretical demand relationships developed here are applicable to both firm and industry demand functions.

THE DEMAND CURVE

The *demand function* specifies the relationship between quantity demanded and *all* the variables that determine demand. The *demand curve* is that part of the demand function which expresses the relation between the price charged for a product and the quantity demanded, *holding constant the effects of all other independent variables*. Typically, a demand curve is shown in the form of a graph, and all independent variables in the demand function, except the price of the product, are assumed to be fixed. In the automobile demand function given in Equation 4-3 and Table 4-1, for example, we could hold constant income, population, credit restrictions, and advertising expenditures, then examine the relationship between price and quantity demanded.

To illustrate the process, consider the relationship depicted in Equation 4-3 and Table 4-1. Assuming that income, population, credit conditions, and advertising expenditures are all held constant at their Table 4-1 values, we can express the relationship between changes in price and changes in demand as:

$$Q = -3,000P + 2,000,000 + 10,000,000 + 1,500,000 + 5,000,000 \\ = 18,500,000 - 3,000P. \quad (4\text{-}4)$$

Equation 4-4, which represents the demand curve for automobiles, is presented graphically in Figure 4-1.[2] As is typical for most products, we see that a reduction in price causes an increase in demand and, conversely, an increase in price leads to a decrease in demand.

Figure 4-1   A Hypothetical Automobile Demand Curve

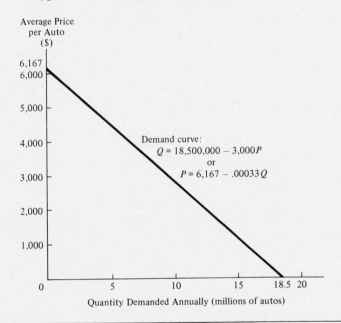

[2] Notice that the dependent variable (quantity demanded) is plotted on the horizontal axis and the independent variable (price) on the vertical axis. Ordinarily, we would expect to see the dependent variable on the vertical scale and the independent variable on the horizontal scale. This point can be confusing, because it is easy to write a demand equation as in Equation 4-4, then *incorrectly* graph it by treating the 18,500,000 as the Y-axis intercept instead of the X-axis intercept, and similarly misspecify the slope of the curve.
   The practice of plotting price on the vertical axis and quantity on the horizontal axis originated many years ago with the theory of competitive markets. Here firms have no control over price, but they can control output, and output in turn determines market price. Hence, in the original model, price was the dependent variable and quantity (supplied, not demanded) was the independent variable. For that reason, price/quantity graphs appear as they do.

RELATIONSHIP BETWEEN DEMAND
FUNCTION AND DEMAND CURVE

The interrelationship between the demand function and the demand curve can be demonstrated graphically. Figure 4-2 shows three demand curves for automobiles: D_1, D_2, and D_3. Each curve is constructed in a manner similar to Figure 4-1, and each represents the relationship between price and quantity, holding constant the values of all the other variables in the demand function. If D_1 is the appropriate curve, then 9.5 million units of a standard auto can be sold if the price is $3,000, while only 8 million autos will be demanded if the price is raised to $3,500. Changes such as these are defined as *movements along a demand curve.*

A *demand curve shift*—a shift from one demand curve to another—indicates a change in one or more of the nonprice variables in the product's

Figure 4-2   Hypothetical Automobile Demand Curves

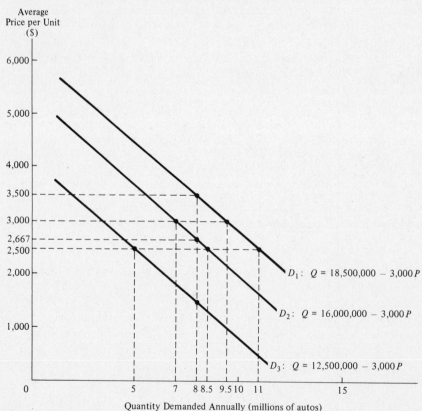

D_1: $Q = 18,500,000 - 3,000\,P$

D_2: $Q = 16,000,000 - 3,000\,P$

D_3: $Q = 12,500,000 - 3,000\,P$

Quantity Demanded Annually (millions of autos)

demand function. For example, a shift from D_1 to D_2 might be caused by a decrease in incomes or advertising expenditures, by more restrictive credit terms, or by a combination of these and other changes.

Consider the effect of shifts in the demand curve from D_1 to D_2 to D_3. At a price of $2,500 a car the number of autos that is demanded falls from 11 million to 8.5 million to 5 million. Alternatively, if the number of units is fixed at a constant amount, say 8 million, these cars could be sold only at successively lower prices, ranging from $3,500 to $1,500, as the demand curve shifts from D_1 to D_3. The *result* of the shift is a lower level of demand at each sales price; the *cause* of the shift could be lower disposable incomes, tighter credit, a less aggressive advertising campaign, or a combination of these and other factors. [3]

DEMAND RELATIONSHIPS AND MANAGERIAL DECISIONS

A firm must have reasonably good information about its demand function to make effective long-run planning decisions and short-run operating decisions. For example, a knowledge of the effect of changing prices on demand is essential in establishing or altering price policy, while knowledge of the effects of credit terms on demand is important in appraising the desirability of a new credit program or a credit card plan. In long-run planning good estimates of the sensitivity of demand to both population and income changes enhance a firm's ability to predict future growth potential and, thus, to establish effective long-range programs.

Measures of Responsiveness: Elasticity

For decision-making purposes, what the firm needs to know is: How sensitive is demand to changes in the independent variables in its demand function? Some variables can be controlled by the firm—prices and advertising, for example—and it is obviously essential to know the effects of altering them if good price and advertising decisions are to be made. Although other variables are outside the control of the firm—consumer incomes and competitors' prices, for example—the effect of changes in these variables must also be known if the firm is to respond effectively to changes in the economic environment within which it operates. Indeed, anticipating the values of variables outside the firm's control and estimating the response of demand to changes in these variables are major elements in the forecasting task.

The measure of responsiveness typically employed in demand analysis is *elasticity,* defined as *the percentage change in quantity demanded attrib-*

---

[3] If we were considering the demand curve for a *firm,* rather than for an *industry,* this shift might also occur because of competitors' price cuts, more aggressive promotional activities, and so on.

utable to a given percentage change in an independent variable. The equation for calculating any elasticity is:

$$\text{Elasticity} = \frac{\text{Percentage Change in } Q}{\text{Percentage Change in } X} = \frac{\Delta Q / Q}{\Delta X / X}$$

$$= \frac{\Delta Q}{\Delta X} \cdot \frac{X}{Q}. \tag{4-5}$$

Here Q is quantity demanded, X is any independent variable, and Δ designates the amount of change in the variable. There is, thus, an elasticity for each independent variable in a demand function. Frequently, price is the independent variable of concern, and the elasticity calculated is called "price elasticity"; but we are also concerned with other demand elasticities, as will be shown in later sections.

Point Elasticity and Arc Elasticity

Elasticity may be defined in two ways: point elasticity and arc elasticity. The elasticities of a demand function generally vary at different points on the function. *Point elasticity measures the elasticity at a given point; arc elasticity measures the average elasticity over some range of the function.*

Note that the first term in Equation 4-5, $\Delta Q / \Delta X$, is an approximate measure of the marginal relationship between X and Q. This term, when multiplied by the second term in the equation, X/Q, equals elasticity. At the limit, where ΔX is very small, $\Delta Q / \Delta X = \partial Q / \partial X$, the partial derivative of the function taken with respect to X. This precise marginal relationship at a specific point on the function is used in the equation for point elasticity.[4] Thus, using the Greek letter ϵ (epsilon) as the symbol for point elasticity, we have:

$$\text{Point Elasticity} = \epsilon = \frac{\partial Q}{\partial X} \cdot \frac{X}{Q}. \tag{4-6}$$

In other words, point elasticity is determined by multiplying the partial derivative of the demand function, at a given point, by the ratio X/Q at that point.

An example using the demand relationship described by Equation 4-3 and the variable values given in Table 4-1 will illustrate the construction of a point elasticity estimate. Assume that we are interested in analyzing the

---

[4] Since we are concerned with the response of quantity demanded to changes in X, *holding other variables constant*, we use the partial derivative $\partial Q / \partial X$ rather than dQ/dX. Note that the total change in Q in response to changes in the independent variables is given by the total differential:

$$dQ = \frac{\partial Q}{\partial P} \cdot dP + \frac{\partial Q}{\partial Y} \cdot dY + \frac{\partial Q}{\partial C} \cdot dC + \frac{\partial Q}{\partial A} \cdot dA + \cdots.$$

Here dP, dY, dC, and dA are the changes in the independent variables, and the partial derivatives are indicative of the responsiveness of Q to changes in the independent variables.

responsiveness of automobile demand to changes in advertising expenditures. The point advertising elasticity at the 9.5 million unit demand level shown in Table 4-1 is calculated as:

$$\text{Point Advertising Elasticity} = \epsilon_A = \frac{\partial Q}{\partial A} \cdot \frac{A}{Q}.$$

Since the partial derivative of the demand function, Equation 4-3, taken with respect to the advertising variable (that is, $\partial Q/\partial A$) is .05, and advertising expenditures at the 9.5 million unit demand are $100 million,

$$\epsilon_A = .05 \cdot \frac{100,000,000}{9,500,000}$$

$$\approx .53.$$

Thus, a 1 percent change in advertising expenditures results in approximately a ½ percent change in the number of automobiles demanded. The elasticity is positive, indicating a direct relationship between advertising outlays and automobile demand; that is, an increase in advertising expenditures leads to an increase in demand, and, conversely, a decrease in advertising expenditures leads to a decrease in demand.

For many business decisions managers do not have access to all of the data necessary to calculate point elasticities. They may, in fact, have only a single pair of data points from which to estimate a demand relationship. In these cases *arc elasticity* provides the relevant measure of responsiveness— *providing one can assume that all other demand-influencing variables have remained unchanged between the two data observations*. Arc elasticity is calculated as:

$$\text{Arc Elasticity} = E = \frac{\dfrac{\text{Change in } Q}{\text{Average } Q}}{\dfrac{\text{Change in } X}{\text{Average } X}} = \frac{\dfrac{Q_2 - Q_1}{(Q_2 + Q_1)/2}}{\dfrac{X_2 - X_1}{(X_2 + X_1)/2}} \tag{4-7}$$

$$= \frac{\dfrac{\Delta Q}{(Q_2 + Q_1)/2}}{\dfrac{\Delta X}{(X_2 + X_1)/2}} = \frac{\Delta Q}{\Delta X} \cdot \frac{X_2 + X_1}{Q_2 + Q_1}.$$

Again we divide the percentage change in quantity demanded by the percentage change in an independent variable, but here the bases used to calculate the percentage changes are averages of the two data points rather than the initially observed value. This use of an average results in a more accurate measure of the *average* relative relationship between the two variables over the range indicated by the data.

The demand relationship pictured in Figure 4-2 can be used to illustrate the calculation of an arc elasticity. Assume that rather than having all of the information provided by the demand curves in that figure, we only observed that with automobile prices held constant at \$3,000, the quantity of cars sold dropped from a level of 9.5 million units per year to 7 million when advertising expenditures in the industry were reduced from a \$100 million annual level to \$50 million. Assuming also that population, income, credit availability, and other factors that influence the level of automobile sales also remained unchanged, the arc advertising elasticity over this range can be calculated as:

Arc Advertising Elasticity

$$= \frac{\Delta Q}{\Delta A} \cdot \frac{A_2 + A_1}{Q_2 + Q_1} = \frac{-2,500,000}{-50,000,000} \cdot \frac{50,000,000 + 100,000,000}{7,000,000 + \quad 9,500,000}$$

$$= \frac{-2,500,000}{-50,000,000} \cdot \frac{150,000,000}{16,500,000} \approx .45.$$

Thus, on average a 1 percent change in the level of advertising expenditures in the range of \$50 million to \$100 million will result in a .45 percent change in the number of automobiles demanded.

The concept of elasticity is quite general—it involves simply the percentage change in one variable associated with a given percentage change in another variable. In addition to use in demand analysis, the concept is used in finance, where the impact of changes in sales on earnings under different production setups (operating leverage) and different financial structures (financial leverage) is measured by an elasticity factor. Elasticities are also used to compare the effects of output changes on costs. However, the concept is most frequently used in demand analysis, and several different types of demand elasticities are particularly useful in managerial economics.

PRICE ELASTICITY OF DEMAND

Probably the most widely used elasticity measure is the *price elasticity of demand*, which provides a measure of the responsiveness of the quantity demanded to changes in the price of the product, holding constant the values of all other variables in the demand function.

Using the formula for point elasticity, price elasticity of demand is found as:

$$\text{Point Price Elasticity} = \epsilon_p = \frac{\partial Q}{\partial P} \cdot \frac{P}{Q}, \qquad (4\text{-}8)$$

where $\partial Q/\partial P$ is the partial derivative of the demand function with respect to price, and P and Q are the price and quantity at a point on the demand curve.

The concept of point price elasticity can be illustrated by reference to Equation 4-3, which was used to construct demand curve D_1 in Figure 4-2.

$$Q = -3,000P + 1,000Y + 0.05Pop + 1,500,000C + 0.05A. \qquad (4\text{-}3)$$

The partial derivative with respect to price is:

$$\frac{\partial Q}{\partial P} = -3,000, \text{ a constant.}$$

Now let us calculate ϵ_p at two points on the demand curve: (1) where $P_1 = \$3,000$ and $Q_1 = 9,500,000$, and (2) where $P_2 = \$3,500$ and $Q_2 = 8,000,000$:

$$(1) \quad \epsilon_{p1} = (-3,000)\frac{3,000}{9,500,000} = -.95,$$

$$(2) \quad \epsilon_{p2} = (-3,000)\frac{3,500}{8,000,000} = -1.3.$$

Thus, on demand curve D_1 a 1 percent change in price from the $3,000 level results in a .95 percent change in the quantity demanded; but at a $3,500 price a 1 percent change results in a 1.3 percent change in demand. This example illustrates that price elasticity may vary along a demand curve, with ϵ_p increasing in absolute value at higher prices and lower quantities.[5]

Note also that the price elasticities are negative. This follows from the fact that the quantity demanded for most goods and services is inversely related to price. Thus, in the example, at a $3,000 price, a 1 percent *increase* (*decrease*) in price leads to a .95 percent *decrease* (*increase*) in the quantity demanded.

Using the arc elasticity concept, the equation for price elasticity is:

$$\text{Arc Price Elasticity} = E_p = \frac{(Q_2 - Q_1)/(Q_2 + Q_1)}{(P_2 - P_1)/(P_2 + P_1)}$$

$$= \frac{Q_2 - Q_1}{P_2 - P_1} \cdot \frac{P_2 + P_1}{Q_2 + Q_1}.$$

This form is especially useful for analyzing the average sensitivity of demand to price changes from one level to another. For example, the average price elasticity from $3,000 to $3,500 is:

$$E_p = \frac{8,000,000 - 9,500,000}{3,500 - 3,000} \cdot \frac{3,500 + 3,000}{8,000,000 + 9,500,000}$$

$$= \frac{-1,500,000}{500} \cdot \frac{6,500}{17,500,000} = -1.113.$$

Relationship between Price Elasticity and Revenue

The importance of the price elasticity concept lies in the fact that it provides a useful summary measure of the effect of a price change on revenues. Depending on the degree of price elasticity, a given change in price will result

[5] As we will show in a later section, price elasticity always varies along a linear demand curve. It can, however, under certain conditions, be constant along a curvilinear demand curve.

in an increase, decrease, or no change in total revenue. If we have a good estimate of price elasticity, we can estimate accurately the new total revenue that will follow a price change.

Elastic, Unitary, and Inelastic Demand The price elasticity for most goods lies in the range of 0 to about −10. However, for decision-making purposes, three specific ranges have been identified. Using $|\epsilon_p|$ to denote the absolute value of the price elasticity, the three ranges can be denoted as:

(1) $|\epsilon_p| > 1.0$, defined as "elastic demand."
   Example: $\epsilon_p = +3.0$.

(2) $|\epsilon_p| = 1.0$, defined as "unitary elasticity."
   Example: $\epsilon_p = +1.0$.

(3) $|\epsilon_p| < 1.0$, defined as "inelastic demand."
   Example: $\epsilon_p = +0.5$.

Consider first *unitary elasticity*, the situation where the percentage change in quantity divided by the percentage change in price equals 1. Since price and quantity are inversely related, this means that the effect on revenues of a price change is *exactly* offset by a change in quantity demanded, with the result that total revenue, the product of $P \cdot Q$, remains constant. If demand is *elastic* (that is, $|\epsilon_p| > 1$) the relative change in quantity is larger than that of price, so a given percentage increase in price causes demand to decrease by a larger percentage, resulting in a decrease in total revenue. Thus, if demand is elastic, a price increase will lower total revenue, and a decrease will raise total revenue. Finally, if demand is inelastic, a price increase will produce a less than proportionate decline in demand so total revenues will rise. These relationships are summarized below:

(1) Unitary Elasticity: $|\epsilon_p| = 1.0$. Total revenue
   is unaffected by changes in price.

(2) Elastic demand: $|\epsilon_p| > 1.0$. Total revenue
   declines with price increases; rises with price decreases.

(3) Inelastic demand: $|\epsilon_p| < 1.0$. Total revenue
   rises with price increases; declines with price decreases.

The Limiting Cases Price elasticity can range between 0 (completely inelastic) and $-\infty$ (perfectly elastic). To illustrate, consider first the case where the quantity demanded is independent of price, so that some fixed amount, Q^*, will be demanded irrespective of price. The demand curve of such a good is shown in Figure 4-3. Price elasticity is defined (using the point elasticity definition) as the partial derivative of the demand function taken with respect to price, $\partial Q / \partial P$, multiplied by the ratio P/Q. That is:

$$\epsilon_p = \frac{\partial Q}{\partial P} \cdot \frac{P}{Q}. \tag{4-8}$$

Figure 4-3 Completely Inelastic Demand Curve—$\epsilon_p = 0$

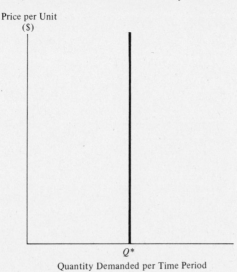

Price per Unit
($)

Q^*

Quantity Demanded per Time Period

Since demand in the case illustrated in Figure 4-3 remains constant regardless of price, the partial derivative $\partial Q/\partial P$ is equal to zero; hence, price elasticity for the product will be equal to zero.[6]

The other limiting case, that of infinite elasticity where $\epsilon_p = -\infty$, is shown in Figure 4-4. The slope of the properly oriented demand curve—that is, $\alpha Q/\alpha P$—is $-\infty$, so the value of ϵ_p in Equation 4-8 must be $-\infty$ irrespective of the P/Q ratio.

The economic as well as the mathematical properties of these limiting cases should be understood. A firm faced with the vertical, perfectly inelastic demand curve could charge any price and still sell Q^* units. Thus, it could exploit its market and, theoretically, appropriate all of its customers' incomes. Conversely, a firm facing a horizontal, perfectly elastic demand curve can sell an unlimited amount of output at the price P^*, but would lose all of its demand if it raised the price by even a small amount. Neither condition holds in the real world, but monopolistic firms selling necessities (for example, water companies) have relatively inelastic demand curves, while firms in highly competitive industries (for example, agriculture) face elastic curves.

---

[6] This can be confusing if one does not remember that the axes of Figure 4-3 are reversed in the sense that the dependent variable, Q, is plotted on the X axis. Now $Q = Q^* = $ a constant. In other words, $Q = Q^* + 0 \cdot P$, so $\partial Q/\partial P$ is zero or, alternatively, the slope of the demand curve properly oriented is zero. The reversal of the axis results in a demand curve whose slope is the inverse of the true marginal relationship between quantity and price. Thus, the slope in Figure 4-3 is $\partial P/\partial Q = \infty$, which is 1 divided by the true marginal relationship expressed by $\partial Q/\partial P = 0$; that is, the slope in Figure 4-3 equals $1/0 = \infty$.

Figure 4-4 Perfectly Elastic Demand Curve—$\epsilon_p = -\infty$

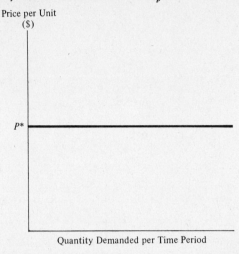

Quantity Demanded per Time Period

Varying Elasticity at Different Points on a Demand Curve

All linear demand curves, except perfectly elastic or perfectly inelastic ones, are subject to varying elasticities at different points on the curve. In other words, a particular demand curve may be elastic at one point but inelastic at another. To see this, recall again the definition of point price elasticity:

$$\epsilon_p = \frac{\partial Q}{\partial P} \cdot \frac{P}{Q}. \tag{4-8}$$

The slope of a linear demand curve, $1/(\partial Q/\partial P) = \partial P/\partial Q$, is constant. However, the ratio P/Q varies from 0 at a point on the horizontal axis to $+\infty$ at the Y-axis intercept. Since we are multiplying a negative constant by a ratio which varies between 0 and $+\infty$, the price elasticity of a linear curve must range from 0 to $-\infty$.

Figure 4-5 illustrates this relationship. As the demand curve approaches the vertical axis, the ratio P/Q approaches infinity, and so does ϵ_p. As the demand curve approaches the horizontal axis, the ratio P/Q approaches 0, causing ϵ_p also to approach 0. At some point along the demand curve $(\partial Q/\partial P)(P/Q) = 1.0$; this is the point of unitary elasticity.

Relationship between Price Elasticity,
Marginal Revenue, and Total Revenue

The relationship between price elasticity and revenue developed above can be illustrated graphically. Figure 4-6(a) reproduces the demand curve shown in Figure 4-5, but adds the associated marginal revenue curve. It can be seen that marginal revenue is positive in the elastic range, negative in the inelastic range, and zero where $\epsilon_p = -1$.

Figure 4-5   Elasticities along a Linear Demand Curve

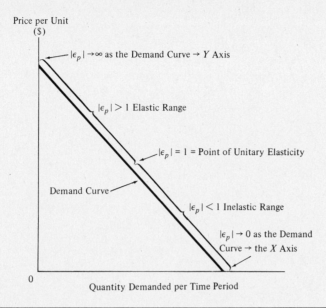

Price per Unit
($)

$|\epsilon_p| \to \infty$ as the Demand Curve $\to$ Y Axis

$|\epsilon_p| > 1$ Elastic Range

$|\epsilon_p| = 1$ = Point of Unitary Elasticity

Demand Curve

$|\epsilon_p| < 1$ Inelastic Range

$|\epsilon_p| \to 0$ as the Demand Curve $\to$ the X Axis

0

Quantity Demanded per Time Period

The associated total revenue curve is shown in Figure 4-6(b). Total revenue increases with price reductions in the elastic range, where $MR > 0$; peaks at the point of unitary elasticity, where $MR = 0$; and declines when price is reduced in the inelastic range, where $MR < 0$.

Determinants of Price Elasticity

Industry Demand   Why is the price elasticity of demand high for one product, low for another? In general, there are three major causes for differential price elasticities: (1) The extent to which a good is considered to be a necessity, (2) the availability of substitute goods which satisfy the need, and (3) the proportion of income spent on the product. A relatively constant quantity of such necessities as salt and electricity for residential lighting purposes will be purchased almost irrespective of price, at least within the price ranges customarily encountered. For these goods there are no close substitutes. Other goods—grapes, for example—while desirable, face considerably more competition, and their demand will be much more dependent on price.

Similarly, the demand for high-priced goods which account for a large portion of purchasers' incomes will be relatively sensitive to price. Demand for less-expensive products, on the other hand, will not be so sensitive to price—the small percentage of income spent on these goods means that it simply will not be worthwhile to waste time and energy worrying about

Figure 4-6 Relationship between Price Elasticity, Marginal Revenue, and Total Revenue: (a) Demand and Marginal Revenue Curves, (b) Total Revenue

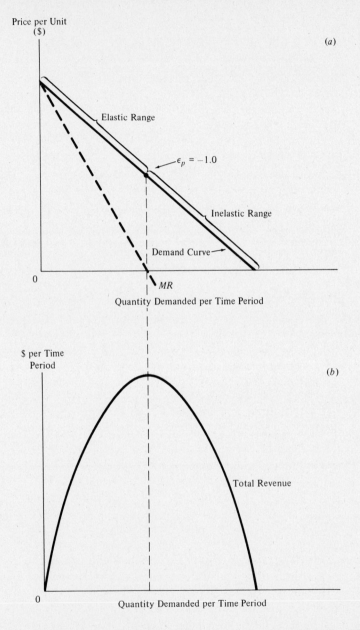

112

their prices. Accordingly, the elasticity of demand will typically be higher for major items than for minor ones. Thus, the price elasticity of demand for automobiles is higher than that for matches.

Firm Demand Are the price elasticities of an individual firm's demand curve the same as its respective industry demand curve? In general, the answer is an emphatic "No." The reason for this is discussed in detail in Chapter 10, which deals with market structure, but an intuitive explanation can be given here.

In pure monopoly the firm's demand curve is also the industry's demand curve, so obviously the firm's elasticity at any output is the same as that of the industry. Consider the other extreme—pure competition as exemplified by wheat farming. The industry demand curve for wheat is downward sloping: the lower its price, the greater the quantity of wheat that will be demanded. However, the demand curve facing any individual wheat farmer is horizontal: He can sell any amount of wheat at the going price, but if he raises his price by the smallest fraction of a cent he can sell nothing. The wheat farmer's demand curve—or that of any firm operating under pure competition—is therefore perfectly elastic. Figure 4-4 illustrated such a demand curve.

SOME USES OF PRICE ELASTICITY

Price elasticity is useful for a number of purposes. First, firms need to be aware of the elasticity of their own demand curves when they set product prices. For example, a profit-maximizing firm would never choose to lower its prices in the inelastic range of its demand curve—such a price decrease would decrease total revenue and at the same time increase costs, since output would be rising. The result would be a drastic decrease in profits. Even over the range where demand is elastic, a firm will not necessarily find it profitable to cut price; the profitability of such an action depends on whether the marginal revenues on new sales exceed the marginal cost of this added production. Price elasticities can be used to answer such questions as these:

1. What will be the impact on sales of a 5 percent price increase?
2. How great a price reduction is necessary to increase sales by 20 percent?

Two current illustrations of the importance of price elasticity developed during the 1973-1974 "energy crisis." First, electric utility companies were forced to raise prices dramatically because of rapid increases in fuel costs. The question immediately arose: How much of a cutback in demand and, hence, reduction in future capacity needs would these price increases entail; that is, what is the price elasticity of electricity? In view of the long lead times required to build electric generating capacity, and the major economic dislocations that arise from power outages, this was a most critical question, both for the companies and for the nation.

Similarly, price elasticity played a major role in the debate on a national petroleum policy during that same period. Some industry and government economists believed that the price elasticities for petroleum products were sufficiently large that the rather substantial price increases which occurred in late 1973 and early 1974 would reduce demand significantly and remove the imbalance between supply and demand. Others argued that the price elasticities were so low that only unconscionable price increases could reduce demand sufficiently to overcome the supply shortfall, and therefore a rationing system was needed as a replacement for market allocation of petroleum products.

Both of these issues continue unresolved; however, it is clear that price elasticity analysis is playing an increasingly important role in the debate.

These and other uses of price elasticity are examined in later chapters of this text. We now shift to an introduction of several other key demand relationships.

INCOME ELASTICITY OF DEMAND

For many goods, income is a major determinant of demand; it is frequently as important as price, advertising expenditures, credit terms, or any other variable in the demand function. This is particularly true of luxury items such as foreign sports cars, art treasures, and the like. On the other hand, the demand for such basic commodities as salt, bread, and matches is not very responsive to income changes. These goods are bought in fairly constant amounts regardless of changes in income.[7]

The income elasticity of demand provides a measure of the responsiveness of quantity demanded to changes in income, holding constant the impact of all other variables which influence demand. Using the calculus equation, and letting I represent income, point income elasticity is defined as:

$$\epsilon_I = \frac{\partial Q}{\partial I} \cdot \frac{I}{Q}. \tag{4-9}$$

Income and the quantity purchased typically move in the same direction. That is, income and sales are directly rather than inversely related, so $\partial Q/\partial I$ and hence ϵ_I are positive. For a limited number of products, termed *inferior goods*, this does not hold. For such products—beans and potatoes, for example—demand declines as income increases, because consumers replace them with more expensive products. More typical products, whose demand is positively related to income, are defined as *normal* or *superior goods*.

---

[7] "Income" can be measured in many ways. It might be on either a per capita or an aggregate basis. Gross national product, national income, personal income, and discretionary income have all been used in demand studies.

To examine income elasticity over a range of incomes rather than at a single point, we use the arc elasticity relationship:

$$E_I = \frac{(Q_2 - Q_1)/(Q_2 + Q_1)}{(I_2 - I_1)/(I_2 + I_1)}. \qquad (4\text{-}10)$$

Again, this provides a measure of the average responsiveness of demand for the product to a change in income from I_1 to I_2.

For most products income elasticity is positive, indicating that as the economy expands and national income increases, demand for the product will also rise. However, the actual size of the elasticity coefficient is also important. Suppose, for example, that ϵ_I for a particular product is 0.3. This means that a 1 percent increase in income will cause demand for this product to increase by only $\frac{3}{10}$ of 1 percent—the product would thus not be maintaining its relative importance in the economy. Another product might have an income elasticity of 2.5; for this product, demand will increase $2\frac{1}{2}$ times as fast as income. *We see, then, that if $\epsilon_I < 1.0$ for a particular good, producers of the good will not share proportionately in increases in national income. On the other hand, if $\epsilon_I > 1.0$, the industry will gain more than a proportionate share of increases in income.*

These relationships have important policy implications for both firms and governmental agencies. Firms whose demand functions have high-income elasticities will have good growth opportunities in an expanding economy, so forecasts of aggregate economic activity will figure importantly in their plans. Companies faced with low-income elasticities, on the other hand, are not so sensitive to the level of business activity. This may be good in that such a business is, to a large extent, "recession proof," but since the company cannot expect to share fully in a growing economy, it may seek entry into industries that provide better growth opportunities.

At the national level the question of income elasticity has figured importantly in several key areas. Agriculture, for example, has had problems for many years partly because the income elasticity of many food products is less than 1.0. This fact has made it difficult for farmers' incomes to keep up with those of urban workers, a problem that, in turn, has caused much consternation in Washington, D.C.

A somewhat similar problem arises in housing. Congress and all presidents since the end of World War II have stated that improving the United States' housing stock is one of our primary national goals. If, on the one hand, the income elasticity for housing is high, something in excess of 1.0, an improvement of the housing stock will be a natural by-product of a prosperous economy. On the other hand, if housing income elasticity is low, a relatively small percentage of additional income will be spent on houses; as a result, the housing stock will not improve much even if the economy is booming and incomes are increasing. In this case direct governmental actions such as public housing, rent and interest subsidies, and the like might be necessary to bring the housing stock up to the desired level. In any event not only has the income elasticity of housing been an important input in debates on national housing policy but these very debates have also stimulated a great deal of research into the theory and measurement of income elasticities.

CROSS-ELASTICITY OF DEMAND

The demand for many goods is influenced by the prices of other goods. For example, the quantity of beef demanded is related to the price of a close substitute, pork. As the price of pork increases, so does the demand for beef —consumers substitute beef for the now relatively expensive pork.

This direct relationship between the price of one good and the quantity of a second good purchased holds for all *substitute* products. Other goods —stereo record players and stereo records, as one example, or cameras and film—exhibit a completely different relationship. Here, price increases in one product typically lead to a reduction in demand for the other. Goods that are inversely related in this manner are known as *complements;* they are used together rather than in place of each other. If the two goods are always used together, as bottles and bottle caps, demand for such items is referred to as *joint demand.*

The concept of cross-elasticity is utilized to examine the responsiveness of demand for one product to changes in the price of another. Point cross-elasticity is given by the equation

$$\epsilon_{PX} = \frac{\partial Q_Y}{\partial P_X} \cdot \frac{P_X}{Q_Y}, \tag{4-11}$$

where Y and X are two different goods. The arc cross-elasticity relationship is constructed in the same manner as was previously described for price and income elasticity.

The cross-elasticity for substitutes is always positive—the price of one and the quantity demanded of the other always move in the same direction. Cross-elasticity is negative for complements—price and quantity move in opposite directions. Finally, cross-price-elasticity is zero, or nearly zero, for unrelated goods; variations in the price of one good have no effect on demand for the second.

We can illustrate the concept of cross-elasticity by considering the following unspecified demand function for Product Y:

$$Q_Y = f(P_W, P_X, P_Y, P_Z, I).$$

Here Q_Y is the quantity of Y demanded; P_W, P_X, P_Y, and P_Z are the prices of goods W, X, Y, and Z; and I is disposable income. For simplicity, assume that these are the only variables that affect Q_Y, and that the parameters of the demand equation have been estimated, using techniques developed in the next chapter, as follows:

$$Q_Y = 5,000 - 0.3P_W + 0.2P_X - 0.5P_Y + 0.000001P_Z + 0.0037I.$$

The partial derivatives of Q_Y with respect to the prices of the other goods are:

$$\frac{\partial Q_Y}{\partial P_W} = -0.3$$

$$\frac{\partial Q_Y}{\partial P_X} = 0.2$$

$$\frac{\partial Q_Y}{\partial P_Z} = 0.000001 \approx 0.$$

Since both P and Q are always positive, the ratios P_W/Q_Y, P_X/Q_Y, and P_Z/Q_Y are also positive. Therefore, the signs of the three cross-elasticities in the example are determined by their partial derivatives:

$\epsilon_{PW} = (-0.3)\left(\dfrac{P_W}{Q_Y}\right) < 0.$ Accordingly, W and Y are complements.

$\epsilon_{PX} = (0.2)\left(\dfrac{P_X}{Q_Y}\right) > 0.$ Accordingly, X and Y are substitutes.

$\epsilon_{PZ} = (0.000001)\left(\dfrac{P_Z}{Q_Y}\right) \approx 0.$ Accordingly, Z and Y are independent.

The concept of cross-elasticity is useful for two main purposes. First, it is obviously important for the firm to be aware of how the demand for its product is likely to respond to changes in the prices of other goods; this information is necessary for formulating the firm's own pricing strategy and for analyzing the risk associated with various products. Second, cross-elasticity is used in industrial organization to measure the interrelationships among industries. To illustrate, one firm may completely dominate a particular market—it is a monopolist in the market. If, however, the cross-elasticity between this firm's product and products in related industries is large and positive, the firm, even though it is a monopolist, will not be able to raise its prices without losing sales to other firms in related industries.[8]

OTHER KINDS OF ELASTICITIES

The elasticity concept is simply a way of measuring the effect of a change in an independent variable on the dependent variable in any functional relationship. The dependent variable in this chapter is the demand for a product, so the demand elasticity of any variable in the demand function may be calculated. We have emphasized the three most common demand elasticities—price elasticity, income elasticity, and cross-elasticity—but exam-

[8] This argument has been raised in connection with antitrust actions. In banking, for example, even though relatively few banks may exist in a given market, banks compete with savings and loan associations, credit unions, commerical finance companies, and the like. The extent of this competition has been gauged in terms of cross-elasticities of demand between various banking services and competing institutions.

ples of other demand elasticities will reinforce the generality of the concept.

In the housing market mortgage interest rates are an important determinant of demand; accordingly, the interest rate elasticity has been used in forecasting the demand for housing construction. Studies have indicated that the interest rate elasticity of residential housing demand is about −0.15. This indicates that a 10 percent rise in interest rates will result in a decrease of 1.5 percent in the quantity of housing demanded, provided all the other variables remain unchanged.[9] If Federal Reserve policy is expected to cause interest rates to rise from 8 to 8.8 percent, a 10 percent increase, we can project a 1.5 percent decrease $(-0.15 \times 10 = -1.5)$ in housing demand.

Public utilities calculate the "weather elasticity" of demand for their services, where "weather" is measured by "degree days," an indicator of average temperatures. This elasticity factor is used, in conjunction with long-range weather forecasts, to anticipate service demand and peak-load conditions.

We return to the topic of elastiscities in the following chapter, where we examine empirical techniques used in estimating demand. First, however, we must consider several other demand concepts useful for managerial decision making.

DIRECT VERSUS DERIVED DEMAND

The demand functions of some goods contain as one of the independent variables the aggregate demand for a second product. This relationship indicates that the quantity of the good purchased is derived from the demand for the other good, so we use the term "derived demand" to denote this kind of relationship. The demand for mortgage money is an example; the quantity of mortgage credit demanded is not determined autonomously or directly; rather, it is derived from the more fundamental demand for housing. Similarly, the demand for all producers' goods (those products used in the manufacture of goods for final consumption) is derived; the aggregate demand for consumption goods determines in large part the demand for the capital equipment used to manufacture them.

Acceleration Principle

This notion of derived demand for producers' goods leads to the economic concept known as the *acceleration principle*, which states that when the demand for a final good increases, the demand for the relevant producer's goods will increase at a faster rate. The reasoning behind the acceleration principle can be demonstrated by an example. Table 4-2 shows the situation

[9] Actually, this elasticity coefficent varies over time as other conditions in the economy change. "Other things" are held constant when measuring elasticity, but in the real world other things are *not* typically constant over time.

for a firm manufacturing automobile stereo tape decks. It produces and sells 1 million stereo units annually, using ten electronic welders in the production process. These welders must be replaced every ten years. The firm has been selling, roughly, the same number of units for several years and is now in an equilibrium situation where it replaces one welder a year. Purchases of the tape decks and the electronic welders under these conditions are shown for Years 1 and 2 in Table 4-2.

Now assume that demand for the tape players increases by 40 percent, to 1.4 million units, in Year 3. If the firm has been operating at capacity, it must add four electronic welders to produce the larger output. Therefore, in Year 3 demand for the welders rises to 5 units, 1 replacement unit and 4 expansion units, a 400 percent increase. Aggregate demand for the final product has increased 40 percent (Column 4), but demand for the capital good has increased 400 percent (Column 10).

Notice that once this process of accelerated demand for the producers' good has started, continued *increases* in sales of the final product are required to maintain the higher level of capital goods production. Thus, even though sales of tape decks increase by 11 percent in Year 5, expenditures on the welders decrease by 40 percent. The *rate* of increase in tape deck sales declined, so actual purchases of the electronic welders fell.

The data for Years 6 and 7 demonstrate that the acceleration principle works in reverse when the demand for the final product decreases. In Year 7 sales of the tape players decrease by 5 percent, and this decrease causes purchases of the welders to drop 100 percent. The firm will not even make replacement purchases—it uses the excess capacity caused by declining sales to replace the welder being retired. Aggregate demand for the producers' good in Years 9 and 10 is left for the reader to calculate.

The example explains one very important fact of economic life—that capital goods industries experience much greater cyclical fluctuations than consumer goods industries. This obviously has important implications for business firms and communities whose economic base is largely the manufacture of capital goods.

Limitation to the Acceleration Principle

The acceleration principle is an important tool for examining the derived demand for producers' goods. As with most theoretical concepts, however, it has empirical limitations. First, the accelerator effect will take place only if the original output of the final product made full use of the available capacity. If the added demand for the final product could be produced using the existing plant—either by making use of idle equipment or by running a second production shift—no additional spending on capital goods need take place. Second, the acceleration principle reflects only one kind of stimulus for demand of producers' goods, the stimulus of increased demand for the final product. It ignores technological change, which may render old equipment obsolete and lead to new investment in capital goods, as well as the

Table 4-2 The Acceleration Principle: The Relationship between Fluctuations in Demand for Final Consumption Goods and Related Producers' Goods

Year (1)	Unit Sales of the Tape Decks (millions) (2)	Absolute Δ in Unit Sales (thousands) (3)	Percent Δ in Sales of the Tape Players (4)	Number of Welders Necessary for Production (5)	Welder Replacement Purchases (units) (6)	Welder Expansion Purchases (units) (7)	Total Welder Purchases (8)	Absolute Δ in Total Welder Purchases (9)	Percent Δ in Welder Purchases (10)
1	1.0	0	0	10	1	0	1	0	0
2	1.0	0	0	10	1	0	1	0	0
3	1.4	400	40	14	1	4	5	+4	+400
4	1.8	400	29	18	1	4	5	0	0
5	2.0	200	11	20	1	2	3	−2	−40
6	2.0	0	0	20	1	0	1	−2	−67
7	1.9	−100	−5	19	0	0	0	−1	−100
8	2.0	100	5.5	20	1	1	2	+2	*
9	2.0	0	0	20					
10	2.2	200	10	22					

* The percentage increase in welder purchases in Period 8 is infinite, since no welders were purchased in Period 7.

cost and availability of funds required for long-term investments.[10] Finally, the increased demand for capital goods will occur only if the change in demand for the final product is viewed as more than just a temporary fluctuation.

TIME CHARACTERISTICS OF DEMAND

Time is another variable that enters the demand function of most goods. It may enter explicitly as a separate variable used to account for long-term trends in demand, such as might result from changing consumer tastes, or it may enter implicitly through lagged variables to account for frictions in the system—the absence of instantaneous reactions by consumers to changes in demand function variables. An example of this second phenomenon is the inclusion of *last year's* advertising expenditures in an equation used to determine this year's demand for a firm's product.

Short-run Effects

Time enters the demand function for goods in still other ways. In the short run, time affects demand through seasonal influences. Seasonal effects may be due to climatic variations between summer and winter. For example, we expect bathing suits to be in demand at a Lake Tahoe apparel store during the summer and ski parkas during the winter. Seasonality may also result from custom. Easter, Christmas, and St. Valentine's Day are holidays related to increased consumer spending on many goods. Some goods are more affected than others—Easter bonnet and Christmas tree sales are very closely related to these periods, as are sales of fireworks and flags to Independence Day.

Short-term influences on demand of such factors as temporary slowdowns in economic activity will typically vary, depending on the durability and income elasticity of the good. Demand for expensive durable products such as automobiles, homes, and appliances is more variable than that for nondurables, such as food and electricity. This is due to the fact that consumers can postpone the replacement of durable goods during temporary periods of low incomes, high prices, or high interest rates. Accordingly, purchases of durable goods tend to be "turned off and on," with the result that manufacturers and marketers of such products experience greater cyclical fluctuations than do nondurables producers.

The cyclic nature of durable goods industries is greater for manufacturers than for retailers. Retailers build up inventories as the economy expands, causing manufacturers' sales to grow faster than final demand. These inventories are then worked off in recessions, causing manufacturers' sales to decrease even faster than final sales to consumers.

---

[10] The cost of capital is considered in some detail in Chapter 13, which deals with capital budgeting.

Long-run Effects

Changes in population, income, consumer tastes, and technology take place slowly over extended periods, and people react slowly to changes in prices and other conditions. To illustrate this delayed, or lagged, effect, consider the demand for electric power. Suppose an electric utility raises its rates by 30 percent. What effect will this have on demand for electric power? In the very short ... the effect will be slight—customers may be more careful to turn off unneeded lights, but total demand would probably not be greatly affected. Prices would go up, demand would not fall very much, so total revenue would increase substantially. In other words, the short-run demand for electric power is *inelastic*.

Over the longer run, however, the increase in power rates has more substantial effects. Residential users would reduce their purchases of air-conditioners, electric heating units, and other appliances, and the use of outdoor lighting systems would be curtailed. These actions would reduce the demand for power. Similarly, industrial users would tend to switch to other energy sources or to relocate in areas where power costs are lower. Thus, the ultimate effect of the price increase on demand might be substantial, but it would take a number of years before the full impact was felt.[11]

This phenomenon of long-run elasticity exceeding short-run elasticity is discussed in more detail in the following chapter on demand estimation and in Chapter 11 on pricing practices.

Trend Factors in Demand Functions

Often, long-run effects of changes in tastes, the availability of substitutes and complements, and so on are lumped together in a *trend* term in a demand function. For example, the demand function for a product might be expressed as:

$$Q = a_0 + a_1X_1 + a_2X_2 + \cdots a_nT,$$

where the X_i's represent such factors as price, incomes, and so on; and T represents years. If the demand study covers the period 1921-1970, T would be set equal to 1 in 1921 and to 50 in 1970. Thus, demand would be $a_n \cdot 50$ units greater (or smaller if a_n is negative), other things being the same, in 1970 than in 1921, and demand would be changing by a_n units a year. Changing tastes, technology, and everything else not explicitly accounted for in the X variables would be embodied in the time variable.

The decline in the demand for central city transit systems in the United States during the second quarter of the twentieth century can be

---

[11] After the TVA project was completed, electric rates were much lower in that service district than the national average. These lower rates attracted large power-using industries such as aluminum producers, and appliance ownership rates became higher than the national average. However, these changes from the pre-TVA days occurred over a long period, variously estimated at between ten and twenty years.

traced in part to this phenomenon. Technological change resulted in the development of the automobile, a substitute product that provided transportation services in competition with streetcars, buses, and trains. Consumers' tastes also changed as they began moving from the city to the suburbs, reducing the value of fixed-route transit systems and further enhancing the desirability of the automobile. The combined effect helped lead to a secular decline in the demand for transit services, and the resulting decline in the services provided. Only recently have higher gasoline prices, congestion, and pollution in our major cities caused this trend to be slowed, if not reversed.

SUMMARY

The demand for a firm's products is a critical determinant of its profitability, and demand forecasts enter as key elements in virtually all long-run planning. To make a reliable demand forecast, one must have a thorough understanding of certain concepts and relationships. These concepts were discussed in general terms in this chapter; and they are used extensively in the following one, where we consider ways of actually estimating demand functions.

Several general points were noted. First, product demand is usually a function of several variables, including prices, incomes, advertising expenditures, and the like. The explicit statement of these relationships is the *demand function*. The partial relationship between demand and price is expressed by the *demand curve*. *Shifts in the demand curve* represent changes in variables other than price in the demand function; *movements along a demand curve* imply that factors other than price in the demand function are held constant.

A key concept introduced in the chapter is *elasticity,* the percentage change in demand associated with a percentage change in one of the determinants of demand. *Price* elasticity, ϵ_p and E_p, denoting *point* and *arc* elasticity respectively, relates changes in demand to changes in the product's own price. If $|\epsilon_p| > 1.0$, this is defined as *elastic* demand, and a price reduction leads to an increase in total revenue. If $|\epsilon_p| < 1.0$, we have *inelastic* demand, and a price reduction decreases total revenue.

Income elasticity, ϵ_I or E_I, relates demand to a measure of income. Ordinarily, ϵ_I is positive, signifying that higher incomes cause higher demand, but the size of the elasticity coefficient is also important. If $\epsilon_I > 1.0$, demand increases more than in proportion to income increases; if $\epsilon_I < 1.0$, the converse holds.

Cross-elasticity, ϵ_{pX} or E_{pX}, relates the demand for Product Y to the price of Product X. If $\epsilon_{PX} > 0$, an increase in P_X causes an increase in Q_Y, and the goods are *substitutes.* If $\epsilon_{PX} < 0$, the goods are *complements;* if $\epsilon_{PX} \approx 0$, the goods are *independent.*

Other kinds of elasticity may be calculated and used in demand analysis: Interest rate elasticity and advertising elasticity are two examples. We also employ the elasticity concept in connection with cost analysis in Chapters 8 and 9.

Another important point in demand analysis concerns the concept of *derived* demand, which refers to the fact that the demand for one product may be derived from a more fundamental demand for another. It was shown that the demand for capital goods is derived from the demand for consumer products. This discussion was extended to the *acceleration principle,* which was used to show why the demand for capital goods is more cyclical than that for consumer goods.

The last section indicated that, for many goods, certain factors in the demand function, especially tastes and preferences, may be changing slowly over time. In such cases a *trend factor* may be included in the demand function to take account of these changing variables. Time also enters the demand function for some goods and services through a seasonality factor.

All the concepts developed in this chapter are used in the following one, in which techniques for empirically measuring demand are discussed.

QUESTIONS

4-1 Explain the rationale for including each of the demand variables in Equation 4-1.

4-2 Distinguish between a demand function and a demand curve. What relationship is indicated by a shift in a demand curve?

4-3 Define each of the following terms, giving both a verbal explanation and the equation.
a) Point elasticity
b) Arc elasticity
c) Price elasticity
d) Cross-elasticity
e) Income elasticity

4-4 Arc price elasticity, as it is defined in this book, examines an average relationship over a given range of a demand curve:

$$\text{Arc Elasticity} = \frac{\Delta Q}{(Q_1 + Q_2)/2} \div \frac{\Delta P}{(P_1 + P_2)/2}.$$

An alternative definition is:

$$\text{Arc Elasticity} = \frac{\Delta Q}{Q_1} \div \frac{\Delta P}{P_1}.$$

Discuss the relationship between these two formulations, indicating by example when one might be more useful than the other.

4-5 What relationship do you think would exist between the shape of a firm's demand curve and the degree of competition existing in its industry (that is, is the industry highly competitive or is it monopolistic)?

4-6 How could the cross-elasticity concept be used in an analysis of the degree of competition in an industry?

4-7 Do you think that the point price elasticity of demand would be greater if computed for an industry or for one firm in the industry? Why?

4-8 Would elasticity be constant for the demand curve represented by the equation $Q = 5,000 - 0.5P$? Why?

4-9 Give some examples of industries where you think that price elasticity for individual firms would be (a) relatively elastic and (b) relatively inelastic. Explain your reasoning.

4-10 What is the acceleration principle? How is it related to each of the following: (a) derived demand, (b) capacity, (c) technological stability?

4-11 Assume that a time trend is thought to be operating in a demand function. How might this time trend be analyzed?

PROBLEMS

4-1 Before deciding on a proposed expansion in its production capacity, the Milton Company is analyzing the demand for its granulated sugar. Preliminary results indicate that the average daily demand in tons, Q, is a function of price, P, as given by the equation $Q = f(P) = 1,000 - 3P$.
a) Assume that the company plans to sell 400 tons a day. What price must it charge?
b) How many tons per day can the company sell at a price of $250 a ton?
c) At what price will sales be equal to 0?
d) What would be the demand for sugar if the company offers to give it away free?
e) Plot the demand, marginal revenue, and total revenue curves.
f) Determine the point price elasticity of demand at $P = \$200$ a ton.

4-2 The Golden Giant Company estimates that the demand/income relationship for its frozen corn is given by the function $Q = 100 + 0.2I$, where $I = $ consumer per capita income.
a) Determine the quantities demanded at each of the following income levels: $2,000, $3,000, $4,000, $5,000, $6,000.
b) Determine the point income elasticity of demand at income levels of $4,000 and $6,000.
c) Determine the arc income elasticity of demand for income ranges of $2,000 to $3,000 and $5,000 to $6,000.
d) The calculations in (b) and (c) should show $\epsilon_{I=6,000} > \epsilon_{I=4,000}$, $E_{I=5,000-6,000} > E_{I=2,000-3,000}$, and $\epsilon_{I=6,000} > E_{I=5,000-6,000}$. Explain why these relationships exist.
e) Would the relationships noted in (d) hold if the demand function was $Q = 0.2I$? Explain.
f) Assuming frozen corn is Golden Giant's only product, would you characterize the firm as highly sensitive to changes in the national economy or as relatively recession proof? Will it share proportionately in a growing economy? Explain.

4-3 You are given the following demand curve for Product X:

$$Q_X = a(P_X)^b(P_y)^c(A_X)^d(A_y)^e(I)^f.$$

Here $Q_X = $ quantity of X demanded in units, $P_X = $ price of X, $P_y = $ price of Y, $A_X = $ advertising expenditures on X, $A_y = $ advertising expenditures on Y, and $I = $ per capita income.
a) What is (1) the price elasticity of X, (2) the cross-elasticity between X and Y, (3) the income elasticity?
b) Suppose $f = -0.5$. What could you say about Product X?
c) Suppose $e = +0.8$. What could you say about the relationship between Products X and Y?

d) Suppose $c = -0.8$. Is this consistent with the condition stated in (c)? Explain.

e) Suppose $d = 5.0$. How many additional units of X will be demanded if A_X increases by \$1,000?

4-4 Northern Sports, Incorporated, is a large Midwestern manufacturer of recreational products. Northern's management is currently engaged in an analysis of the recreational vehicles division of the firm. As part of this analysis the future demand for the company's snowmobiles is being examined. Based on studies by the market research and economic analysis department, the firm believes that personal income and selling price are the two major economic variables affecting demand for the snowmobiles. The arc elasticity of income for the snowmobile has been estimated to be approximately 2.0 over the relevant income range, and arc price elasticity of demand has been estimated to be -3.0.

a) Using these elasticities and the data presented below, calculate the estimated sales for 1975 and 1976:

Year	Personal Income	Price	Quantity Sold
1974	1,100	800	1,000
1975	1,200	800	
1976	1,300	850	

b) Northern's management has information that a competitor plans to reduce the price of its snowmobile from \$1,000 to \$900 in 1975. The research department has estimated that the arc cross-price-elasticity between Northern's snowmobile and the competitor's is .5. What will be the impact of this price reduction on Northern's sales, assuming Northern maintains the \$800 price?

4-5 The Admiral Company conducted a research study to determine how the demand for its major product, Y, is affected by price changes of another product, X. The research staff estimated that the following function expressed the relationship between sales of Y and the price of X, holding other things constant: $Q_Y = 1,000 + 0.6P_X$.

a) How would you classify the relationship between Y and X: substitute, complement, or independent?

b) Determine the quantities demanded of Y for the following prices of X: $P_X = \$100, \$80, \$60, \$40$.

c) Determine the point cross-elasticity of demand at $P_X = \$80$ and at $P_X = \$40$.

d) Determine the arc cross-elasticity of demand for these price ranges: $P_X = \$100 - \$80$; $\$60 - \$40$.

e) Now reconsider your answer to (a). Can the word "close" be added to describe the relationship? Can you visualize the cross-elasticity concept being used in antitrust cases to help define markets?

4-6 The Belmount Company manufactures boots that currently sell for \$20 a pair. During 1971 its sales volume was about 10,000 pairs each month. In

January 1972 a competitor, the V. R. Nelson Company, cut the price of its boots from $25 to $18 a pair. The following month Belmount sold only 7,000 pairs of boots.

a) Determine the arc cross-elasticity of demand between Belmount's boots and Nelson's boots. (Assume that Belmount's price is held constant.)

b) Assume that the arc price elasticity for Belmount's boots is −2.0. Assume also that Nelson keeps the price of its boots at $18. What price cut must be made by Belmount to increase its sales volume back to 10,000 pairs a month?

c) Compare Belmount's total revenue under sales volumes of 7,000 and 10,000 after the Nelson Company price cut.

d) Does the analysis suggest that the two companies' boots are close or poor substitutes?

4-7 Airtight and Longlife are competitors in the commercial container industry. The demand curves for a major product of the two firms are:

Airtight $P_A = 1,000 - 5Q_A,$

Longlife $P_L = 1,600 - 4Q_L.$

The firms are currently selling 100 and 250 units of this product respectively.

a) What are the point price elasticities currently faced by the firms?

b) Assume that Longlife reduces its price and increases its sales to 300 units and that this action results in a reduction in Airtight's sales to 75 units. What is the indicated cross-price-elasticity between the Airtight and Longlife containers?

c) Does the hypothesized price reduction by Longlife make sense economically, assuming that Longlife's managers operate so as to maximize profits? Why?

d) Is the cross-elasticity calculated in Part b intuitively sound? Why?

SELECTED REFERENCES

Clarkson, Geoffrey P. *The Theory of Consumer Demand: A Critical Appraisal,* Englewood Cliffs, N.J.: Prentice-Hall, 1963.

Friedman, Milton. *A Theory of the Consumption Function,* Princeton: Princeton University Press, 1957.

Henderson, James M., and Richard E. Quandt. *Microeconomic Theory,* 2d ed., New York: McGraw-Hill, 1971, Chapter 2.

Hicks, J. R. *A Revision of Demand Theory,* London: Oxford University Press, 1959.

Knight, Frank H. "Realism and Relevance in the Theory of Demand," *Journal of Political Economy,* LII, 1944, pp. 289-318.

CHAPTER 5

Techniques
of Demand
Estimation

In Chapter 4 we introduced several concepts useful in demand analysis and indicated the key role that product demand plays in most business decisions. To use these important demand relationships in decision analysis, one must empirically estimate the structural form and parameters of the demand function, and in this chapter we consider procedures used in this estimation.

In some cases it is relatively easy to obtain accurate estimates of demand relationships, especially those necessary for short-run demand or sales forecasting. In other situations it is exceedingly difficult to obtain even the information needed to make short-run demand forecasts, and still more difficult to make long-run forecasts or to determine how changes in specific demand variables—price, advertising expenditures, credit terms, prices of competing products, and so on—will affect demand. These demand relationships are sufficiently important, however, to warrant devoting much time and effort in an attempt to estimate them, a task we will now examine.

We explore the three primary methods used to estimate the parameters (coefficients) of the demand function: the interview (or survey) method, market experimentation, and regression analysis. The first two techniques are covered extensively in marketing courses, so we will only introduce them and show how they are used to supplement regression analysis. Regression analysis, on the other hand, is examined in detail for two reasons. First, in many instances regression analysis is the best, or perhaps even the only, means of estimating the demand equation. Second, the technique of regression analysis is probably the single most important estimating technique used in managerial economics, and perhaps in all aspects of business administration. For example, in addition to its use in demand analysis, regression is used to study cost functions, cost of capital relationships, and the like. Accordingly, in this chapter we examine in some detail the technique of regression analysis in connection with demand, and in later chapters draw on this tool extensively.

THE IDENTIFICATION PROBLEM

One reason why it is difficult to obtain accurate estimates of demand relationships is the close interrelationships between most economic variables. To see why this poses a difficulty, consider the problem of estimating the demand curve for Product X. If we have data on the price charged and the quantity purchased at several points in time, a logical first step might be to plot this information as is shown in Figure 5-1. Can the line AB be interpreted as a demand curve and points 1, 2, and 3 as points on the demand curve? The curve connecting the points is negatively sloped, indicating the typical inverse relationship between the price charged for a product and the quantity demanded, and each data point does represent the quantity of

Figure 5-1   Price/Quantity Plot

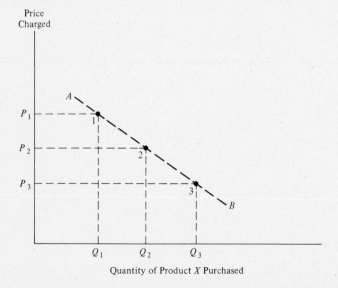

Quantity of Product X Purchased

X purchased at a particular price. Nevertheless, the available data is insufficient to allow us to conclude that AB is in fact the demand curve for X.

Let us see why this is so. For each of several points in time we have the price charged for X and the quantity purchased. But this will not necessarily trace out a demand curve. In the previous chapter we stated that the demand curve shows the relationship between the price charged for a good and the quantity demanded, *holding constant the effect of all other variables in the demand function.* Thus, in order to plot the demand curve, we must obtain data on the price/quantity relationship where the effects of all factors in the demand function other than price are constant.

The price/quantity data used to construct Figure 5-1 are insufficient to insure that the effects of all other demand-related variables have in fact been eliminated. The line AB might be the demand curve, but then again, it might not be. To see this, consider Figure 5-2, where the price/quantity data are again plotted, along with the hypothesized true supply and demand curves for Product X.[1] There we see that the data points indicate nothing more than the simultaneous solution of supply and demand relationships at three points in time. That is, the price/quantity data that we observe are the result of the interplay between the quantity of X supplied

---

Figure 5-2   Supply and Demand Curves

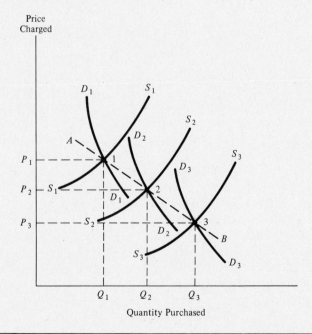

Quantity Purchased

---

[1] Supply curves indicate the relationship between the quantity of a product that producers will make available for purchase and the price they receive, holding constant the effect of all other factors in the firms' supply functions.

by producers and the quantity demanded by consumers. The intersection of the supply and demand curves at each point in time results in the observed price/quantity points, but the line AB is *not* the demand curve.

In Figure 5-2 we see that nonprice variables in both the supply and demand functions have changed between the data points. Suppose, for example, that new and more efficient facilities for producing X are completed between observation dates, and as a result the quantity supplied at any given price is larger. This causes a shift of the supply curve from S_1 to S_2 to S_3. Simultaneously, the price of a complementary product may have fallen or consumer incomes may have risen, so at any given price larger quantities of X are demanded in the later periods. This second phenomenon results in a shift of the demand curve from D_1 to D_2 to D_3.

Now observe what has occurred. Both the supply curve and the demand curve have shifted over time. This has resulted in a declining price and an increasing quantity purchased. The three intersection points of the supply and the demand curves in Figure 5-2—points 1, 2, and 3—are the same points plotted in Figure 5-1. But these *are not* three points on a single demand curve for Product X. Each point is on a *different* demand curve— one that is shifting over time—so connecting them does not trace out the product demand curve.

Observe the effect of erroneously interpreting the line AB (which connects the points 1, 2, and 3) as the demand curve. If a firm makes this mistake, it might assume that a reduction in price from P_1 to P_2 increases the quantity demanded from Q_1 to Q_2. An expansion of this magnitude may well justify the price reduction. In fact, however, such a price cut will result in a much smaller increase in demand—the true demand curve is much less elastic than is the line AB—so a price reduction is much less desirable than it first appeared.

Given the interrelationship between demand and supply curves, can data on prices and quantities purchased ever be used to estimate a demand curve? They can, but only under two sets of conditions: (1) the demand curve has *not* shifted, but the supply curve *has* shifted; or (2) we have enough information to determine just how each curve has shifted between data observations. For example, if a technological breakthrough occurs in the manufacture of Product Y, and if costs in the industry fall markedly within a short period during which demand conditions are stable, the situation depicted in Figure 5-3 may arise. The demand curve, which initially was unknown, is assumed to be stable. The supply curve shifts from S_1 to S_2 to S_3. Each price/quantity point represents the intersection of the supply and the demand curves. Since the demand curve is stable, points 1, 2, and 3 must all be on the demand curve, so the demand curve DD can be estimated by connecting the three points.

It is clear from this example that the problem of simultaneous relationships in demand analysis can be overcome only if one has enough information to *identify* the interrelated functions so that shifts in one curve

Figure 5-3   Shifting Supply Curve Tracing Out Stable Demand Curve

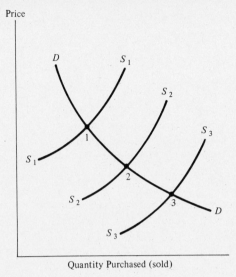

can be distinguished from shifts in the other. For this reason, the problem of estimating one function when simultaneous relationships exist is known as *the identification problem.* To separate shifts in demand from changes in supply we must have more information than just the price/quantity data; information about which curve is shifting and to what extent it is shifting is necessary to identify and estimate the demand relationship. Frequently this information is unavailable. In these cases, statistical techniques of demand estimation, such as regression analysis, are incapable of providing estimates of the demand function parameters. When the identification problem cannot be solved, such techniques as consumer interviews and market experiments must be used to obtain information about the important demand relationships.

CONSUMER INTERVIEWS

The consumer interview, or survey procedure, requires the questioning of a firm's customers or potential consumers in an attempt to estimate the relationship between the demand for its products and a variety of variables. The technique can be applied naïvely by simply stopping shoppers and asking questions about the quantity of the product they would purchase at different prices. At the other extreme, to elicit the desired information, trained interviewers may present sophisticated questions to a carefully selected population sample.

Theoretically, consumer surveys can provide excellent information on a number of important demand relationships. The firm might question each of its customers (or a statistical sample if the number of customers is large) about projected purchases under a variety of different conditions relating to price, advertising expenditures, prices of substitutes and complements, income, and any number of other variables in the demand function. Then, by aggregating the data, the firm can estimate its demand function.

Unfortunately, this procedure does not necessarily work smoothly in actual practice. The information obtainable by this technique, and its quality, is likely to be limited. Consumers are typically unable, and in many cases unwilling, to provide accurate answers to hypothetical questions about how they would react to changes in the key demand variables.

Consider the problem of attempting to determine the effect of just two variables, price and advertising expenditures, on the demand for automobiles. If an interviewer asks how you would react to a 1, 2, or 3 percent increase (or decrease) in the price of a specific model of car, could you respond accurately? What if the question relates to the effect of shifting the emphasis in the firm's advertising campaign from style to safety or to changing the advertising media—can you tell how this action will affect your demand for the car? Because most people are unable to answer such questions—even for major items such as automobiles, appliances, and houses—it is obviously difficult to use such a technique to estimate the demand relationships for most nondurable consumer goods.

We do not wish to imply that consumer survey techniques have no merit in demand analysis. Using subtle inquiries, a trained interviewer can extract a good deal of useful information from consumers. For example, an interviewer might ask questions about the relative prices of several competing goods and learn that most people are unaware of existing price differentials. This is a good indication that demand is not highly responsive to price changes, so a producer would not attempt to increase demand by reducing price—consumers would probably not even notice the reduction. Similar questions can be used to determine whether consumers are aware of advertising programs, how much exposure they receive, what their reaction is to the ads, and so on. Thus, some useful information is obtainable by surveys, and the quality of the results is adequate for some decision purposes.

Also, for certain kinds of demand information there is no substitute for the consumer interview. For example, in short-term demand or sales forecasting, consumer attitudes and expectations about future business conditions frequently make the difference between an accurate estimate and one that misses by a wide margin. Such subjective information can typically be obtained only through interview methods.[2]

---

[2] The use of interview or survey techniques for sales forecasting is covered more extensively in Appendix B on Forecasting.

MARKET STUDIES AND EXPERIMENTATION

An alternative technique for obtaining useful information about a product's demand function involves market experiments. One market experiment technique involves examining consumer behavior in actual markets. The firm locates one or more markets with specific characteristics, then varies prices, advertising, and other controllable variables in the demand function, with the variations occurring either over time or between markets. For example, Del Monte Corporation may have determined that uncontrollable consumer characteristics are quite similar in Denver and Salt Lake City. Del Monte could raise the price of sliced pineapple in Salt Lake City vis-à-vis that in Denver, then compare pineapple sales in the two markets. Alternatively, Del Monte could make a series of weekly or monthly price changes in one market, then determine how these changes affected demand. With several segregated markets, the firm may also be able to determine how such demographic characteristics as income, family size, educational level, and ethnic background affect demand.

As with consumer clinics, market experiments have several serious shortcomings. They are expensive and are therefore usually undertaken on a scale too small to allow high levels of confidence in the results. Related to this problem is the one of short-run versus long-run effects. Market experiments are seldom run for sufficiently long periods to indicate the long-run effects of various price, advertising, or packaging strategies. The experimenter is thus forced to examine short-run data and attempt to extend it to a longer period.

Difficulties associated with the uncontrolled parts of the experiment also reduce its value as an estimating tool. A change in economic conditions during the experiment is likely to invalidate the results, especially if the experiment includes the use of several separated markets; a local strike or layoffs by a major employer in one of the market areas, a severe snowstorm, or the like would probably ruin the experiment. Likewise, a change in a competing product's advertising expenditures, price, or packaging may distort the results. There is also the additional danger that customers lost during the experiment as a result of price manipulations cannot be regained when the experiment ends.

A second market experimentation procedure applies a controlled laboratory experiment wherein consumers are given funds with which to "shop" in a simulated store. By varying prices, product packaging, displays, and other factors, the experimenter can often learn a great deal about consumer behavior. The laboratory experiment, while providing similar information, has the advantage over field experiments because of its greater control of extraneous factors and its somewhat lower cost.

This "consumer clinic" or laboratory experiment technique is not without shortcomings, however. The primary difficulty is that the subjects invariably know that they are part of an experiment, and this knowledge may well distort their shopping habits. Moreover, the high cost of such experiments necessarily limits the sample size, which makes inference from the sample to the general population tenuous at best.

Demand for Oranges: An Illustrative Market Experiment[3]

During 1962 researchers from the University of Florida conducted a market experiment in Grand Rapids, Michigan, to examine the competition between California and Florida Valencia oranges. The experiment was designed to provide estimates of the price elasticities of demand for the various oranges included in the study, as well as measures of the cross-elasticities of demand between varieties of oranges.

The researchers chose Grand Rapids because its size, economic base, and demographic characteristics are representative of the Midwest market for oranges. Nine supermarkets located throughout the city cooperated in the experiment, which consisted of varying the prices charged for Florida and California Valencias daily for thirty-one days and recording the quantities of each variety sold. The price variations for each variety of orange covered a range of 32¢ a dozen (± 16¢ around the price per dozen that existed in the market at the time the study began. More than 9,250 dozen oranges were sold during the experiment.

The price and quantity data obtained in this study enabled the researchers to examine the relationship between sales of each variety of orange and its price, as well as the relationship between sales and the price charged for competing varieties. The results of the study are summarized in Table 5-1, in which the elasticities of these price variables are reported. The numbers along the diagonal represent the price elasticities of the three varieties of oranges, while the off-diagonal figures estimate the cross-price elasticities of demand.

The price elasticity for all three varieties was quite large. The −3.07 price elasticity for Florida Indian River oranges means that a 1 percent decrease in their price will result in a 3.07 percent increase in their sales. The other Florida orange had a very similar price elasticity, while the price elasticity of the California oranges was somewhat lower, indicating that demand for California oranges is less responsive to price changes than is demand for the Florida varieties.

The cross-elasticities of demand reveal some interesting demand relationships between these three varieties of oranges. First, note that cross-elasticities of demand between the two Florida varieties are positive and

[3] Adapted from Marshall B. Godwin, W. Fred Chapman, Jr., and William T. Hanley. *Competition between Florida and California Valencia Oranges in the Fruit Market*, Bulletin 704, December 1965, Agricultural Experiment Stations, Institute of Food and Agricultural Services, University of Florida, Gainesville, Florida, in cooperation with the U.S. Department of Agriculture, Florida Citrus Commission.

Table 5-1 Demand Relationships for California and Florida Valencia Oranges

A 1 Percent Change in the Price of	Percentage Change in the Sales of		
	Florida Indian River	Florida Interior	California
Florida Indian River	−3.07	+1.56	+0.01
Florida Interior	+1.16	−3.01	+0.14
California	+0.18	+0.09	−2.76

relatively large. This indicates that consumers view these two varieties as being close substitutes and therefore switch readily between them when price differentials exist. The cross-elasticities of demand between the Florida and California oranges, on the other hand, are all very small, indicating that consumers do not view them as close substitutes. That is, the market for California oranges in Grand Rapids is quite distinct from the market for Florida varieties.

This market study provided estimates of two important demand relationships, the price elasticity of demand for Florida and California oranges and their cross-elasticities of demand. The researchers were able to identify and measure these relationships because the thirty-one-day study period was brief enough to prevent changes in incomes, tastes, population, and other variables that would influence the demand for oranges; and they were able to insure that adequate supply quantities of the various Valencia oranges were available to consumers at each experimental price.

Summary on Market Experiments

The market experiment demand estimation technique can provide some valuable demand information, as was indicated by the example of Florida and California oranges. The rather sizable drawbacks associated with the cost and uncontrollable factors of such experiments, however, tend to limit their use to those situations where the information needed for statistical demand estimation cannot be obtained from historical records. Frequently a market experiment is used as a means of developing some of the data required for a statistical analysis of the demand relationships.

REGRESSION ANALYSIS

The statistical method most frequently employed in demand estimation is *regression analysis*. There are limitations to this technique, but regression analysis can frequently provide a good estimate of a demand function at a relatively small cost.

Specify the Variables

The first step in regression analysis is to specify the variables that are expected to influence demand. Product demand, measured either in units or in total dollar volume, is the dependent variable. The list of independent variables, or those which influence demand, always includes the price of the product and generally includes such factors as the prices of complementary and competitive products, advertising expenditures, consumer incomes, population of the consuming group, and other variables. The demand functions of expensive durable goods, such as automobiles and houses, include interest rates and other credit terms; those for ski equipment, beer, or air-conditioners include weather conditions. Demand determinants of capital goods, such as industrial machinery, include corporate profitability, output/capacity ratios, wage rate trends, and the like.

Obtain Data on the Variables

The second step in a regression analysis is to obtain accurate estimates of the variables: measures of price, credit terms, output/capacity ratios, advertising expenditures, incomes, and the like. Obtaining estimates of these variables is not always easy, especially if the study involves data for past years. Further, some key variables, such as consumer attitudes toward quality and their expectations about future business conditions—which are quite important in demand functions for many consumer goods—may have to be obtained by survey (questionnaire and interview) techniques, which introduces an element of subjectivity into the data, or by market or laboratory experiments, which may produce biased data.

Specifying the Form of the Equation

Linear Functions Once the variables have been specified and the data gathered, the next step is to specify the form of the equation or the manner in which the independent variables are assumed to interact to determine the level of demand. The most common specification is a linear relationship such as the following:

$$Q = a + bP + cA + dY. \tag{5-1}$$

Here Q represents the quantity of a particular product demanded, P is the price charged, A represents advertising expenditures, and Y is per capita disposable income. The quantity demanded is assumed to change linearly with changes in each of the independent variables. For example, if $b = -1.5$, demand will decline by $1\frac{1}{2}$ units for each $1 increase in the price of the product. The demand curve for a demand function such as that shown in Equation 5-1 is linear; that is, it is a straight line.

Linear demand functions have great appeal in empirical work for two reasons. First, experience has shown that many demand relationships are in fact approximately linear over the range for which data are typically encountered. Second, a convenient statistical technique, the method of least squares, can be used to estimate the parameters a, b, c, and d, the regression coefficients, for linear equations. More will be said about least squares below, but first it is useful to examine other forms of demand functions.

Power Functions The second most commonly specified demand relationship is the multiplicative form:

$$Q = aP^b A^c Y^d. \tag{5-2}$$

This equation is popular primarily because of two features. First, the multiplicative equation is frequently the most logical form of the demand function. It is the one with the most intuitive appeal, assuming as it does that the marginal effects of each independent variable on demand are not constant but, rather, depend on the value of the variable as well as on the value of all other variables in the demand function. This can be easily seen by considering the partial derivative of Equation 5-2 with respect to income, $\partial Q / \partial Y = adP^b A^c Y^{d-1}$, which includes all the variables in the original demand function. Thus, the marginal effect of a change in per capita disposable income on the product demand specified in Equation 5-2 depends on the level of income, as well as on advertising expenditures and the price charged for the product.

This changing marginal relationship is often far more realistic than the implicit assumption in a linear model; namely, that the marginal relation is constant. For example, as incomes increase from a low level to a higher level, the demand for sirloin steak might increase continuously. However, it is unlikely that the increase in demand will be linear. Instead, it will probably be more rapid at lower income levels, then gradually taper off at higher levels. A similar relationship probably holds for advertising expenditures. At low to moderate levels of spending the marginal impact on sales of an additional dollar of advertising is likely to be quite large. With very high spending levels, however, there may well be a saturation effect and a resultant decrease in the marginal effect on demand of each added advertising dollar. In such situations, use of a nonlinear demand function, such as a power function, is indicated.

The second reason for the popularity of the multiplicative demand function is that Equation 5-2 is an algebraic form which can be transformed into a linear relationship using logarithms, then estimated by the least squares regression technique. Thus, Equation 5-2 is equivalent to:

$$\log Q = \log a + b \cdot \log P + c \cdot \log A + d \cdot \log Y. \tag{5-3}$$

Equation 5-2 is "linear in logarithms," and when it is written in the form of Equation 5-3 the parameters of the equation ($\log a$, b, c, and d) can be estimated by least squares regression analysis.

An interesting and useful feature of a multiplicative relationship, such as the one specified in Equation 5-2, is that demand functions of this form have constant elasticities over the full range of data examined. Further, these elasticities are given by the coefficients estimated in the regression analysis. For example, consider the price elasticity of demand for the product whose demand function is represented by Equation 5-2. It was shown in Chapter 4 that point price elasticity is obtained by taking the partial derivative of the demand function with respect to price, then multiplying it by the ratio of price to quantity demanded:

$$\epsilon_p = \frac{\partial Q}{\partial P} \cdot \frac{P}{Q}. \tag{5-4}$$

Differentiating Equation 5-2 with respect to price, we obtain:

$$\frac{\partial Q}{\partial P} = abP^{b-1}A^cY^d. \tag{5-5}$$

Therefore,

$$\epsilon_p = abP^{b-1}A^cY^d \cdot \frac{P}{Q}. \tag{5-6}$$

Substituting Equation 5-2 for Q in Equation 5-6 gives:

$$\epsilon_p = abP^{b-1}A^cY^d \cdot \frac{P}{aP^bA^cY^d}. \tag{5-7}$$

Combining terms and canceling where possible in Equation 5-7, we obtain:

$$\epsilon_p = \frac{abP^{b-1}A^cY^d}{1} \cdot \frac{P}{aP^bA^cY^d}$$

$$= \frac{abP^bA^cY^d}{P} \cdot \frac{P}{aP^bA^cY^d}$$

$$= b.$$

Thus, the price elasticity of demand is equal to the exponent of price in the multiplicative demand function given as Equation 5-2. Since the elasticity is simply equal to b, it is not a function of the price/quantity ratio and hence is constant. This constant elasticity relationship holds for *all* the variables in any multiplicative demand relationship.

Constant elasticities, where they occur, are useful properties in demand equations. As an example, if the income elasticity of demand for housing is constant, then increases in income can be expected to produce proportionate changes in the demand for housing over wide ranges of income. If this feature does not hold—and recall from the discussion of Figure 4-5 that the elasticity of linear demand curves *always* changes over the range of the curve—decision makers concerned with housing demand have to worry about differing elasticities at different income levels. Thus, while we cannot force a demand curve into the multiplicative form of Equation 5-2, if it is in fact of this kind it will also have the useful property of constant elasticities.

Choosing the Form of the Equation The algebraic form of the demand function—linear, multiplicative, or other form—should always be chosen to reflect the true relationships between variables in the system being studied. In practice, however, there is often no a priori basis for choosing the form of the relationship. In such cases several different forms may be tested, and the one that best fits the data should be selected as being most likely to reflect the true relationship. Methods of fitting regression equations are described in the following section.

Estimating the Regression Parameters

Regression equations are typically fitted—that is, the parameters a, b, c, and d of Equation 5-1 or 5-2 are estimated—by the method of least squares. Using a very simple two-variable case, we can demonstrate the method as follows. Assume that data on XYZ Corporation's sales of Product Y and the advertising expenditures on this product have been collected over the past seven years. (The data are given in Table 5-2.) If a linear relationship between sales of Y and advertising expenditures, A, is hypothesized, the regression equation would take the following form:

$$\text{Sales } Y = a + bA. \tag{5-8}$$

Table 5-2 Sales and Advertising Data for XYZ Corporation

	1968	1969	1970	1971	1972	1973	1974	Mean
Sales (thousands of units)	37	48	45	36	25	55	63	$\bar{Y} = 44$
Advertising expenditures (millions of dollars)	$4.5	$6.5	$3.5	$3.0	$2.5	$8.5	$7.5	$\bar{A} = \$5.1$

The method of least squares is then applied to select the values of a and b which best fit the data in Table 5-2 to the regression equation. The procedure is presented graphically in Figure 5-4. Here each point represents the advertising expenditure and sales of Y in a given year. In terms of Equation 5-8, each point can be specified by the relationship:

$$\text{Sales}_t = Y_t = a + bA_t + u_t, \tag{5-9}$$

where u is a residual term that includes the effects of all determinants of sales that have been omitted from the regression equation, as well as a stochastic or random element, and t is used to denote the year of the obser-

Figure 5-4 Relationship between Sales and Advertising Expenditures for XYZ Corporation

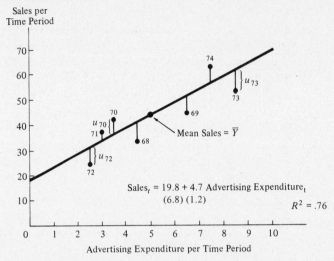

vation.[4] Notice that in this regression equation, a is the intercept of the regression line with the sales axis, b is the slope of the line, and u is the error term or residual which measures the vertical deviation of each tth data point from the fitted line. The sum of the squares of these error terms is minimized by the choice of a and b through the least squares technique.[5]

The least squares process for fitting a regression equation is nothing more than an application of the optimization procedure developed in Chapter 2 to the problem of minimizing the sum of the squared deviations from the fitted line. We can demonstrate this by continuing with the sales/advertising example for XYZ Corporation. Solving Equation 5-9 for the error term, u_t, results in:

$$u_t = Y_t - a - bA_t.$$

[4] One point that should be noted deals with the subscript t used to identify the year of each observation. When time series data are being examined, as they are in our example, the term t is used for the subscript. However, if cross-sectional data are being examined—for example, if we are examining the sales of Product Y during a given year in different markets where advertising expenditures had varied—we would designate the various markets with the subscript i. In other words, in time series work the subscript t is typically employed; while in cross-sectional work i is used.

[5] The error terms are squared because the deviations are both positive and negative and, hence, many different lines can be fitted that will result in the sum of the actual deviations being zero. That is, the *sum* of the deviations can be zero even though substantial positive and negative deviations exist. By squaring the deviations we are summing a set of positive numbers, and the line which minimizes this sum most accurately depicts the relationship between the dependent and the independent variables.

Thus the expression for the sum of the squared error terms is:

$$\sum_{t=1968}^{1974} u_t^2 = \sum_{t=1968}^{1974} (Y_t - a - bA_t)^2. \tag{5-10}$$

The least squares regression technique is a procedure for minimizing Equation 5-10 by choice of the two decision variables a and b, the parameters of the regression equation. Such minimization is accomplished by differentiating Equation 5-10 with respect to a and b, setting the partial derivatives equal to zero, and solving the resulting two-equation system for a and b:

$$\frac{\partial \sum_{t=1968}^{1974} u_t^2}{\partial a} = -2 \sum_{t=1968}^{1974} (Y_t - a - bA_t) = 0. \tag{5-11}$$

$$\frac{\partial \sum_{t=1968}^{1974} u_t^2}{\partial b} = -2 \sum_{t=1968}^{1974} A_t(Y_t - a - bA_t) = 0. \tag{5-12}$$

Equations 5-11 and 5-12 are called the *normal equations*, and when solved for a and b they result in:

$$b = \frac{\sum_{t=1968}^{1974} (A_t - \bar{A})(Y_t - \bar{Y})}{\sum_{t=1968}^{1974} (A_t - \bar{A})^2}. \tag{5-13}$$

Then,

$$a = \bar{Y} - b\bar{A}, \tag{5-14}$$

where $\bar{A}$ and $\bar{Y}$ are the mean values for the advertising and sales observations respectively. Inserting the data from Table 5-2 into Equations 5-13 and 5-14 results in estimates of 19.8 for a and 4.7 for b, so the sales/advertising regression for XYZ Corporation is estimated to be:

$$\text{Sales}_t = Y_t = 19.8 + 4.7A_t.$$

Notice that we have dropped the error term, u_t, at this point since its expected value is always zero.

While the relationships developed above are important for understanding regression analysis, it is seldom necessary to actually perform the calculations, since virtually all computers are equipped with "canned" regression programs, and all one need do is feed in data similar to those given in Table 5-2 to obtain the parameters of the equation. In fact, if the problem is small enough for the equation to be conveniently fitted by hand (or with a desk calculator), a freehand graphic fit is generally accurate enough, and the least squares estimating technique is unnecessary. However, if more than twenty or so data points are involved, or if two or more independent variables are included in the equation, then computer solutions are the only practical means of implementing the least squares technique. Accordingly, we shall concentrate on setting up regression problems for computer solution and interpreting the output, rather than dwelling on the mathematical process itself.

Interpreting the Regression Equation

Once we have estimates of the regression equation, how do we interpret the values of the coefficients? First, a, the intercept term, generally has no economic meaning. Caution must always be exercised when interpreting points outside the range of the observed data, and typically the intercept lies far outside this range. In our present example the intercept cannot be interpreted as the expected level of sales if advertising is completely eliminated. It *might* be true that the level of sales with zero advertising would equal the intercept term, a, but since we have no observations of sales at zero advertising expenditures, we cannot safely assume that 19,800 units can be sold with no advertising.[6]

The slope coefficient, b, gives us an estimate of the change in sales associated with a one-unit change in advertising expenditures. Since advertising expenditures were measured in millions of dollars for the regression estimation, while sales were in thousands of units, a one-million dollar increase in advertising will lead to a 4,700 unit expected increase in sales; a two-million dollar advertising increase to 9,400 additional units sold; and so on. Again, caution must be used when extending the analysis beyond the range of observed values in the data used to estimate the regression coefficients.

The results of this simple two-variable regression model can easily be extended to multiple variable models. To illustrate the extension, suppose that we also have information on the average price, P, charged for Product Y in each of the seven years. This new information can be added to the linear model given in Equation 5-9, resulting in the following regression equation:

$$\text{Sales } Y_t = a + bA_t + cP_t + u_t. \tag{5-15}$$

Again, computer programs using the method of least squares can be used to fit the data to the model and to determine the parameters a, b, and c. When this is done, we interpret the coefficients as follows: a is again an intercept term with little economic significance; b is the expected change in sales related to a one-unit change in advertising expenditure, *holding*

---

[6] Similarly, it would be hazardous to extend the sales/advertising curve very far upward from the range of observed values. For example, we could not extrapolate the sales curve out to advertising expenditures of $15 or $20 million and have much confidence in the predicted level of sales.

constant the price of X; and c is the expected change in sales related to a one-unit change in price, holding constant advertising expenditures.[7]

Graphic representations of multiple regression models are not generally feasible, but Figure 5-4 can be used to gain insights into the process. Note that actual sales in 1973 were well below the value predicted by the regression line, so u_{73} was large and negative. Similarly, note that actual sales exceeded the predicted level in 1970, so u_{70} was large and positive. Now suppose that our new information on prices reveals that the average price of X was relatively low in 1970 but high in 1973. Further, high prices prevailed in 1972, 1968, and 1969, while prices were low in 1971 and 1974 as well as in 1970. Thus, the price data seem to explain the deviations in the graph. Accordingly, we would expect that when the price data are added to the regression equation, the error terms, u_t, will be reduced; that is, the average absolute value of u in Equation 5-15 should be less than that of u in Equation 5-9 since more of the variation in sales can be explained by variables included in the model and, therefore, less need be absorbed by the error terms. Given that the sum of the squared error terms will be lower, Equation 5-15 is said to provide a better fit or explanation of the observed data.

REGRESSION STATISTICS[8]

When we use the least squares technique for estimating the parameters of a demand model, several available statistics greatly increase the value of the results for decision-making purposes. These statistics, which are included in the regular output of most computer regression routines, are described below.

Coefficient of Determination The coefficient of determination, typically indicated by the symbol R^2, is the statistic that indicates how well the regression model explains changes in the value of the dependent variable.[9] It is defined as *the proportion of the total variation in the dependent vari-*

---

[7] The parameters (coefficients) of a multiple regression model are, therefore, equivalent to the partial derivatives of the function:

$$\frac{\partial \text{ sales } Y}{\partial \text{ advertising}} = b, \text{ and } \frac{\partial \text{ sales } Y}{\partial \text{ price}} = c.$$

If the independent variables were related in some manner such that advertising *always* went up whenever the price was raised, then the least squares estimating equations break down because the assumption of "holding other things constant" is violated. This point, called "intercorrelation" or "multicollinearity," is discussed later in this chapter.

[8] This section may be omitted without loss of continuity. The statistics given here are developed more fully in statistics texts.

[9] In simple regression—that is, regression models with only one independent variable—the *correlation coefficient, r,* measures the goodness of fit. In multiple regression, R, the coefficient of multiple correlation, is used similarly. The square of the coefficient of multiple correlation R^2, is defined as the coefficient of determination.

able that is explained by the full set of independent variables included in the model. Accordingly, R^2 can take on values ranging from 0, indicating that the model is a bust and provides absolutely no explanation of variation in the dependent variable, to 1.0, indicating that all the variation has been explained by the independent variables. The coefficient of determination for the regression model illustrated in Figure 5-4 was .76, indicating that 76 percent of the total variation in XYZ Corporation's sales of Product Y are explained by variation in advertising expenditures. If the coefficient of determination is high, the deviations about a regression line, such as that shown in Figure 5-4 will be small—the actual observations will be close to the regression line and the values of u_t will be small.

This relationship can be clarified somewhat by examining the algebraic formulation of R^2. The total variation in Y, the dependent variable in a regression model, can be measured by summing the squares of the deviations about the mean of that variable:

$$\text{Total variation in } Y = \sum_{t=1}^{n} (Y_t - \overline{Y})^2. \tag{5-16}$$

The deviations of each observed value, Y_t, from the mean value, $\overline{Y}$, are squared; then these squares are summed to arrive at the total variation in Y. If Y were a constant, Y_t would equal $\overline{Y}$ for all observations, and there would be no variance in Y. In this case Equation 5-16 would equal 0. The greater the variability in Y, the larger the value of Equation 5-16.

Regression analysis breaks this total variation down into two parts: the variation explained by changes in the independent variables, and the variation that cannot be explained by the regression model. This breakdown is illustrated in Figure 5-5. The total variation at a given data observation is seen to be $Y_t - \overline{Y}$. The predicted value of Y at each data point, $\hat{Y}_t$, can be calculated as:

$$\hat{Y}_t = a + bX_t. \tag{5-17}$$

Using $\hat{Y}_t$ as derived in Equation 5-17, we define the value $\hat{Y}_t - \overline{Y}$ as the explained variation at point t, and the total variation explained by the regression equation is:

$$\text{Total explained variation} = \sum_{t=1}^{n} (\hat{Y}_t - \overline{Y})^2. \tag{5-18}$$

The unexplained variation is simply the sum of the squared deviations about the regression line:

$$\text{Unexplained variation} = \sum_{t=1}^{n} (Y_t - \hat{Y}_t)^2 = \sum_{t=1}^{n} u_t^2. \tag{5-19}$$

If all the data points in Figure 5-4 lay *exactly* on the regression line—that is, if $Y_t = \hat{Y}_t$ for all values of t—there would be no unexplained variation.

Figure 5-5   Explained and Unexplained Variation of the Dependent Variable in
a Regression Model

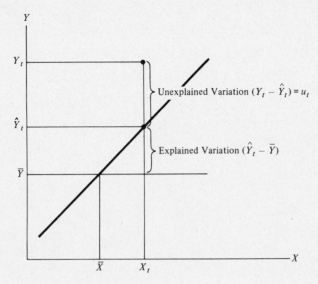

The total variation must equal the sum of the unexplained and explained variations, so we may write:

$$\text{Equation 5-16} = \text{Equation 5-18} + \text{Equation 5-19,}$$

or

$$\Sigma(Y_t - \overline{Y})^2 = \Sigma(\hat{Y}_t - \overline{Y})^2 + \Sigma u_t^2.$$

The coefficient of determination, R^2, is defined as the proportion of the total variation which is explained by the regression model. Thus:

$$R^2 = \frac{\Sigma(\hat{Y}_t - \overline{Y})^2}{\Sigma(Y_t - \overline{Y})^2}.$$

An R^2 of 1.0 indicates that all the variation has been explained. In this case, $\Sigma(\hat{Y}_t - \overline{Y})^2$ must exactly equal $\Sigma(Y_t - \overline{Y})^2$ or, alternatively, each predicted value for the dependent variable must exactly equal the corresponding observed value; that is, $\hat{Y}_t = Y_t$ for all t observations. Each data point will lie on the regression curve, and all residuals or error terms will be zero; that is, $u_t = 0$, for all t.

As the size of the deviations about the regression curve increases, the coefficient of determination will fall. At the extreme, the sum of the squared error terms will be equal to the total variation in the dependent variable, and R^2 will equal zero. In this case, the regression equation has been totally unable to explain variation in the dependent variable.

In an actual regression study the coefficient of determination will seldom be equal to either 0 or 1.0. For work in empirical demand estimation, values of R^2 of about 0.80, indicating that about 80 percent of the variation in demand has been explained, are quite acceptable. For some types of goods R^2's as high as 0.90 to 0.95 are obtainable; for others we must be satisfied with considerably less explanation of demand variation.

When the coefficient of determination is very low—say, in the range of 0.2 to 0.3—it is an indication that the model is inadequate for explaining the demand for the product. The most general cause for this problem is the omission of some important variable or variables from the model.

Standard Error of the Estimate Another statistic useful for examining the accuracy of the regression model as a whole is the standard error of the estimate. This statistic provides a means of estimating a confidence interval for predicting values of the dependent variable, *given* values for the independent variables. That is, the standard error of the estimate is used to determine a range within which we can predict the dependent variable with varying degrees of statistical confidence. Thus, although our best estimate of the tth value for the dependent variable is $\hat{Y}_t$, the value predicted by the regression equation, we must use the standard error of the estimate to determine just how accurate a prediction $\hat{Y}_t$ is likely to be.

Assuming the error terms are normally distributed about the regression equation, there is a 68 percent probability that future observations of the dependent variable will lie within the range $\hat{Y}_t \pm$ one standard error of the estimate. The probability that some future observation of Y_t will lie within two standard errors of its predicted value increases to 95 percent, and there is a 99 percent chance that an actual observed value for Y_t will lie in the range $\hat{Y}_t \pm$ three standard errors.[10] It is clear, then, that greater predictive accuracy is associated with smaller standard errors of the estimate.

This concept is illustrated graphically in Figure 5-6. Here we see the scatter of points between X and Y, the least squares regression line, and the upper and the lower 95 percent confidence limits. Ninety-five percent of all actual data observations will lie within two standard errors of the regression line. Thus, given the value of X, we can use the interval between the upper and the lower confidence bounds to predict the value of Y with a 95 percent probability that the actual outcome (Y value) will lie within that confidence interval. Notice that the confidence bounds are closest to the regression line in the vicinity of the mean values of X and Y—that is, at the center of the scatter diagram—then diverge from the regression line toward the extremes of the observed points. This underscores a point made earlier:

[10] The standard error is, in effect, equivalent to a standard deviation; it is the standard deviation of the dependent variable about the regression line. We should note that the standard error provides only an approximation to the true distribution of errors, and in actuality the confidence band widens as observations deviate from the mean values, as is shown in Figure 5-6.

Figure 5-6 Illustration of the Use of the Standard Error of the Estimate to Define Confidence Intervals

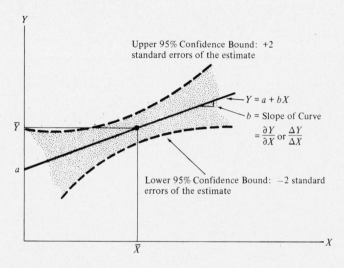

that not too much confidence can be put in the predictive value of a regression equation beyond the range of observed values.

Standard Error of the Coefficient Just as the standard error of the estimate indicates the precision with which the regression model can be expected to predict the dependent variable, the standard error of the coefficient provides a measure of the confidence we can place in the estimated regression parameter for each independent variable. We again use the properties of a normal distribution for determining the confidence to be placed in the estimated coefficient for each independent variable. There is a 68 percent probability that the true marginal relationship between X and Y, b^*, lies in the interval $\hat{b} \pm$ one standard error of the coefficient b, where $\hat{b}$ is the relationship between X and Y estimated by the regression technique. There is a 95 percent probability that b^* lies in the interval $\hat{b} \pm$ two standard errors of the coefficient; and a 99 percent probability that b^* is in the interval $\hat{b} \pm$ three standard errors of the coefficient. Thus, just as with the standard error of the estimate, the smaller the standard error of the coefficient, the greater the confidence we have that the regression equation has accurately estimated the marginal relationship between the independent and dependent variables.

A frequently encountered use of the standard error of the coefficient is to test whether the regression coefficient estimated for the independent variable, X, is greater in absolute value than twice its standard error.[11] If this is the case, one can reject at the 95 percent confidence level, the hypothesis that variation in the dependent variable, Y, is not significantly related to changes in X because a zero value for the parameter b^* does not lie within the range $\hat{b} \pm$ two standard errors of the coefficient.

A Problem in Regression Analysis: Multicollinearity

We have seen the usefulness of the coefficient of determination, R^2, and the standard errors of the slope coefficients, but additional information may be gained by comparing these statistics. Suppose that the coefficient of determination for a regression model is large, near 1.0, indicating that the model as a whole explains most of the variation in the dependent variable. However, assume also that the standard errors of the coefficients for the various independent variables are also quite large in relation to the size of the coefficients, so that little confidence can be placed in the estimated relationship between any single independent variable and the dependent variable. This condition indicates that, while the regression model demonstrates a significant relationship between the dependent variable and the independent variables as a group, the technique has been unable to separate the specific relationships between each independent variable and the dependent variable. This is the problem of simultaneous relationships, or multicollinearity, among the independent variables. It means simply that the "independent" variables are not really independent of one another, but rather have values that are jointly or simultaneously determined.

Home ownership and family income provide an example of this type of difficulty. A firm might believe that whether a given family will buy its product is dependent upon, among other things, the family's income and whether the family owns its home or rents. Because families who own their homes tend to have relatively high incomes, these two variables are highly correlated.

This problem can be troublesome in regression analysis, at the extreme resulting in arbitrary values being assigned for the coefficients of the mutually correlated variables. For example, if two "independent" variables move up and down together, the least squares regression technique *can* assign one variable an arbitrarily high coefficient and the other an arbitrarily low coefficient, with the two largely offsetting each other. In such a case neither coefficient would have any correspondence to the true relationships of the system being investigated. When this problem occurs, it is best to remove all but one of the correlated independent variables from the model before

---

[11] This is equivalent in most cases to observing a t value of approximately 2 for the regression coefficient, since the t statistic is merely the regression coefficient divided by its standard error, adjusted for the degrees of freedom.

the parameters are estimated using a single equation regression model.[12] Even then, the resulting regression coefficient assigned to the remaining variable can be used only for forecasting purposes rather than for "explaining" demand relationships. That is, the coefficient of the remaining variable indicates the joint effect on demand both, of it and of the removed correlated variable. Thus, the model is still unable to separate the effects of the two mutually correlated variables. The coefficient is not arbitrarily assigned in this case, however, and so long as the relationship between the correlated independent variables does not change, it can be used for predictive purposes.

Other Problems in Regression Analysis

In addition to the assumption of independence among the independent variables, or the problem of multicollinearity, least squares regression analysis requires four assumptions about the error terms, u_t, or the residuals, as they are commonly called:

1. Residuals are assumed to be randomly distributed.
2. Residuals are assumed to follow a normal distribution.
3. Residuals are assumed to have an expected value of zero.
4. Residuals are assumed to have a constant variance.

A violation of any one of these assumptions reduces the validity of the least squares technique for estimating demand relationships.

The residuals are typically calculated and printed as part of the output by most computer programs for regression analysis, and one can examine the residuals in a number of ways to determine if any of the assumptions have been violated. For most cases a graphic method is quite revealing and easy to use. Three basic graphs of the residuals will indicate most violations of the basic assumptions.

Frequency Distribution   Plotting the residuals on a linear scale, as in Figure 5-7, provides a frequency distribution of the residuals. This distribution can be examined to determine whether the residuals appear to be normally distributed and whether the mean of the residuals is approximately equal to zero. In most cases the frequency plots will not form a perfect bell-shaped (normal) curve, but any serious deviation from this shape will be readily indicated.

Sequence Plot   A plot of the residuals in order of occurrence provides another useful means of detecting violations of the regression assumptions.

---

[12] For a discussion of demand estimation using simultaneous equation models, see Chapter 12 of W. J. Baumol, *Economic Theory and Operations Analysis*, Third Edition, Prentice Hall, Englewood Cliffs, N.J.

Figure 5-7   A Frequency Distribution of the Residuals

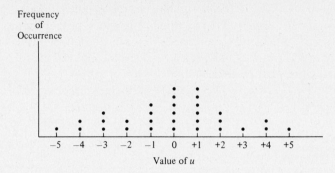

This plot is most beneficial for time series models, where the sequence of the data has an economic interpretation. In plotting the residuals over time (or, more generally, in their order of occurrence), we expect them to be randomly distributed about a mean of zero, as in Figure 5-8. Reviewing the

Figure 5-8   Sequence Plot of the Residuals

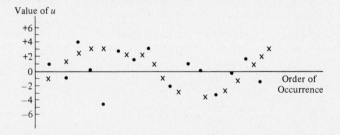

complete graph of the residuals plotted in sequence, we hope to see a horizontal band centered about the value zero, as is true of the dots in Figure 5-8. Within that band there should be no systematic patterns, indicating that the residuals are not occurring randomly, as is true of the "x"s in the figure; that is, any repetitive sequence in this plot, such as the "x"s, indicates that the residuals are not independent of one another but rather are serially correlated.

The problem of serial correlation (or autocorrelation, as it is called in time series regression) occurs frequently and is not always easily detected by the graphic technique discussed here. For this reason the Durbin-Watson statistic is often calculated and used to measure the extent of serial correlation in the residuals.[13] A value of approximately 2 for the Durbin-Watson statistic indicates the absence of serial correlation; deviations from this value indicate that the residuals are not randomly distributed.

When serial correlation exists, it may be removed by making a transformation of the data. Taking first differences is one such transformation. For example, in demand analysis, serial correlation of the residuals is often caused by slowly changing variables such as consumer tastes or the development of new competing or complementary products that are difficult if not impossible to measure and, hence, cannot be included in the statistical analysis. Specification of the demand model in terms of first differences—that is, in terms of the change in each variable from one period to the next—however, frequently overcomes this problem. Thus, in demand studies one often encounters regression models of the form[14]:

$$\Delta \text{ demand} = f(\Delta \text{ price}, \Delta \text{ income}, \Delta \text{ advertising, and so on}).$$

Returning to the sequence plot of the residuals, three general patterns indicate violation of one or more of the regression assumptions. These three patterns are illustrated in Figure 5-9(a), (b), and (c). The pattern shown in Figure 5-9(a) occurs frequently in time series regression where a trend variable has not been included in the model. In other words, the demand function is slowly changing over time (due perhaps to changing tastes, styles of living, and other factors); and the model can be improved by explicitly accounting for this trend by including time as one of the variables explaining demand for the product. Sometimes the trend effect is not constant over time but rather indicates an increasing or a decreasing rate of change. When this is the case, a sequence plot of the residuals might appear

[13] The Durbin-Watson statistic, d, is calculated by the equation:

$$d = \frac{\sum\limits_{i=1}^{N} (u_i - u_{i-1})^2}{\sum\limits_{i=1}^{N} u_i^2} \tag{5-20}$$

Essentially, the sum of the squared first differences of the residuals, $(u_i - u_{i-1})^2$, is divided by the sum of the squared residuals. Equation (5-20) can be rewritten as:

$$d = \frac{2 \sum\limits_{i=1}^{N} u_i^2 - 2 \sum\limits_{i=1}^{N} u_i u_{i-1}}{\sum\limits_{i=1}^{N} u_i^2} = 2(1 - \rho), \tag{5-21}$$

where ρ is the correlation coefficient between successive residuals. Thus, if $\rho = 0$, indicating that the residuals are serially independent, d will equal 2. As ρ approaches $+1$, indicating positive serial correlation, d will fall toward 0; and if ρ is negative, indicating negative serial correlation, d will increase, with an upper limit of $+4$ being associated with perfect negative serial correlation, $(\rho = -1)$.

[14] The use of first difference equations, while very popular, is not a panacea for serial correlation problems. *See* Chapter 7 in J. Johnston's *Econometric Methods*, McGraw-Hill, New York, 1960, for a more complete discussion of the problem.

Figure 5-9 Hypothetical Residual Patterns

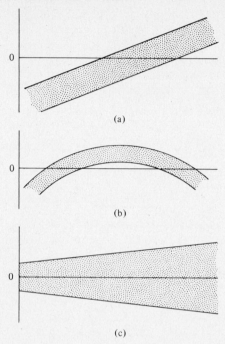

(a)

(b)

(c)

as in Figure 5-9(b). Inclusion of time variables in quadratic terms will correct this problem.

A sequence plot such as that illustrated in Figure 5-9(c) indicates a somewhat more serious problem. There, the plotted points indicate that the variance of the residuals about their expected value is not constant over the range of observation. This will invalidate many of the statistics used to determine the usefulness of the regression coefficients. A weighted least squares regression analysis can be used to correct for this difficulty.[15]

Plots against the Regression Variables   The third useful kind of plot of the residuals is against the variables of the regression model. In each case the desired pattern would appear as in Figure 5-8, a horizontal band centered on zero and with a constant dispersion, or variance.

Plots similar to those in Figure 5-9 all indicate difficulties of one form or another. A band that is positively (or negatively) sloped, as in Figure

[15] A discussion of the weighted least squares technique is outside the scope of materials that can be covered in a single course on managerial economics. The interested reader is referred to N. R. Draper and H. Smith, *Applied Regression Analysis,* John Wiley, New York, 1966, pp. 77-81.

5-9(a), indicates an error in the regression calculations when the residuals have been plotted against one of the independent variables in the model. Essentially, the linear effect of that variable has not been properly accounted for. If such a pattern appears in a plot of the residuals against the dependent variable, it indicates either an error in calculation as described above or else a misspecification of the regression model, such as omitting a key variable from the analysis or suppressing the intercept term in the regression model.

The curved band in Figure 5-9(b) again indicates the need for power terms in the equation. That pattern for residuals plotted against an independent variable indicates the need for a quadratic term in that same variable. If the plot is against the dependent variable, the indicated problem is probably the absence of a squared term; that is, $Y = a + bX - cX^2$, in the model.

A megaphone plot similar to Figure 5-9(c) in all cases indicates that the variance of the residuals is not constant. The corrective action in this case is either to use a weighted least squares regression technique or to make a transformation of the dependent variable (such as changing to the logarithm of the data or using a ratio) prior to estimating the regression parameters.

FROZEN FRUIT PIE DEMAND: AN ILLUSTRATIVE REGRESSION ANALYSIS PROBLEM

In late 1970 Wisco Foods, Incorporated, a regional food processor located in the upper Midwest, undertook an empirical estimation of the demand relationships for its frozen fruit pies. The firm was attempting to formulate its pricing and promotional plans for the following year, and management was interested in learning how certain decisions would affect sales of the frozen pies.

An analysis of earlier demand studies for its other prepared foods led Wisco to an hypothesis that demand for the fruit pies was a linear function of the price charged, advertising and promotional activities, the price of a competing brand of frozen pies, per capita income, and population in the market area. It was decided that a trend term should also be included in the hypothesized demand function to account both for the continuing shift to prepared foods and for the growth in sales resulting from increased consumer awareness of the product.

Wisco had been processing these frozen pies for about three years, and its market research department had two years of quarterly data for six regions on sales quantities, on the retail price charged for its pies, on local advertising and promotional expenditures, and on the price charged for the major competing brand of frozen pies. Statistical data published by *Sales Management* magazine on population and disposable incomes in each of the six locations was also available for the analysis; it was thus possible to include all the hypothesized demand determinants in the empirical estimation. The following regression equation was fitted to the data:

$$Q_{it} = a + bP_{it} + cA_{it} + dPX_{it} + eY_{it} + fPop_{it} + gT_t + u_{it}. \quad (5\text{-}22)$$

Here, Q is the quantity of pies sold during the tth quarter; P is the retail price in cents of Wisco's frozen pies; A represents the dollars spent for advertising and promotional activities; PX is the price, measured in cents, charged for competing pies; Y is dollars of per capita disposable income measured on an annual basis; Pop is the population of the market area; and T is the trend factor. The subscript i indicates the regional market from which the observation was taken, while the subscript t represents the quarter during which the observation occurred.

Least squares estimation of the regression equation on the basis of the forty-eight data observations (eight quarters of data for each of the six areas) resulted in the estimated regression parameters and statistics given in Table 5-3.

***Table* 5-3**   Estimated Demand Function for Frozen Pies

$$Q = -500 - 275P_{it} + 5A_{it} + 150PX_{it} + 7.25Y_{it} + 0.25Pop_{it} + 875T. \quad (5\text{-}23)$$
$$\quad\quad (52) \quad\quad (1.1) \quad\quad (66) \quad\quad (3.2) \quad\quad (0.09) \quad (230)$$

Coefficient of determination $= R^2 = 0.92$.
Standard error of the estimate $= 775$.

The terms in parentheses are the standard errors of the coefficients. An analysis of the error terms, or residuals, indicated that all the required assumptions regarding their distribution were met; hence the least squares regression procedure is a valid technique for estimating the parameters of this demand function.

The parameters of the regression equation can be interpreted as follows: The intercept term, -500, has no economic meaning—it lies far outside the range of observed data and obviously cannot be interpreted as the demand for Wisco's frozen fruit pies when all the independent variables take on zero values. The coefficient of each independent variable indicates the marginal relationship between that variable and sales of the pies, holding constant the effect of all the other variables in the demand function. For example, -275, the coefficient of P, the price charged for Wisco's pies, indicates that when we hold constant the effects of all other demand variables, each 1¢ increase in price will cause quarterly sales to decline by 275 pies. Similarly, the coefficient of A, the advertising and promotional variable, indicates that for each dollar spent on advertising during the quarter, 5 additional pies will be sold, and the coefficient of the disposable income variable, +7.25, indicates that an added dollar of disposable income leads on the average to an increase of 7.25 pies demanded quarterly.

The coefficient of determination ($R^2 = 0.92$) indicates that 92 percent of the total variation in pie sales has been explained by the regression model, a very satisfactory level of explanation for the model as a whole. Furthermore, each parameter estimate (the coefficients associated with each independent variable) is over twice as large as its standard error, which means that the estimates are all statistically significant. That is, we can reject at the 95 percent confidence level the hypothesis that any of the independent variables is unrelated to the demand for Wisco's frozen fruit pies. Further, the standard errors of the two key controllable decision variables, price and advertising, are very small in relation to their respective coefficients. This means that the regression coefficients for these two variables are probably very good estimates of the true relationship between them and the demand for Wisco's pies, so they can be used with a great deal of confidence for decision-making purposes.

The standard error of the estimate provides a measure of the confidence interval within which quarterly sales of Wisco's pies can be forecast. For example, assume that Wisco wishes to project next quarter's sales in Market Area B. It has set the price of its pies at $1.50 (or 150 cents) and promotional expenditures at $1,000. The prices of the competing pies are expected to remain at their current level of $1.40; population in the market area is 50,000; per capita disposable income is $5,000; and the quarter being forecast is the ninth quarter in the model. Inserting these values into the demand equation results in an estimated demand of 40,875 pies:

$$Q = -500 - 275(150) + 5(1,000) + 150(140) + 7.25(5,000)$$
$$+ 0.25(50,000) + 875(9) = 40,875.$$

While 40,875 is the best point estimate of demand, the standard error of the estimate allows us to construct a confidence interval for sales projection. For example, sales can be projected to fall within an interval of ±2 standard errors of the estimate about the expected sales level, with a confidence level of 95 percent. The standard error of the estimate for Wisco's pies is 775. Thus, an interval of ±1,550 pies about the expected sales of 40,875 pies represents the 95 percent confidence interval. This means that one can predict with a 95 percent probability of being correct that the sales of Wisco's pies during the next quarter in Market Area B will lie in the range of 39,325 to 42,425 pies. Wisco could use Equation 5-23 to forecast sales in each of the six areas, then sum these area forecasts to obtain the estimated demand for the firm as a whole.

SUMMARY

In this chapter we examined a variety of techniques for empirically analyzing demand relationships. At the outset we described the identification problem and demonstrated that it can be a serious obstruction to statistical demand estimation.

The identification problem results from the close interrelationships between many economic variables, and it can be overcome only if one has enough a priori information to identify and separate the individual relations so that shifts in a function can be distinguished from movements along the function.

Next, we considered the use of consumer interview and market experiment techniques for demand estimation in the situations where the data necessary for statistical analysis are not available. These techniques can provide valuable information about some important demand relationships. However, because of the high costs and severe limits on the information that can be obtained from them, statistical demand estimation is typically employed for empirical demand studies.

Because least squares regression analysis is by far the most widely used statistical estimating procedure in demand analysis, this technique was examined in some detail. The emphasis was on the specification of the regression model and the interpretation and use of the estimated parameters and associated regression statistics. Several problems that are frequently encountered in regression analysis were also examined. The chapter concluded with an example of the use of a regression model for empirically estimating a product's demand function.

The regression techniques introduced in this chapter are also widely used in empirical cost estimation. We shall therefore refer back to this material when cost studies are considered in Chapter 9.

QUESTIONS

5-1 What is the identification problem? Could it present a problem for statistical estimation of the demand/advertising relationship for a product? Would you expect this problem to be common for many products?

5-2 Why might a firm's customers be unwilling or unable to supply accurate information about their demand for its products?

5-3 What are some possible advantages that might cause a firm to give demand-related information to the suppliers of materials it uses?

5-4 The market research department of RAM Corporation recently completed a statistical study aimed at explaining the sales patterns of the firm's major product. The results are summarized in the following regression equation:

$$Q_t = 2.431 + 1.04A_{t-1} + 0.39Y_t - 49.8P_t$$
$$(0.41) \qquad (0.73) \quad (10.51),$$

$R^2 = 0.834$,

Standard error of the estimate $= 1,120$,

where Q_t = unit sales in Period t
A_{t-1} = advertising expenditures in the preceding period
P_t = price charged per unit of the product
Y_t = per capita disposable personal income in Period t.

a) Assume that the president of the firm, who is a nonquantitative person poorly trained in applied economics, has asked you to explain these results to him. Do so. (*Note*: The figures in parentheses are the standard errors of the coefficients.)

b) To what possible shortcomings or difficulties associated with such a study would you alert the president?

5-5 In the market study of the demand for oranges cited in the chapter, why do you suppose a lower cross-elasticity existed between California oranges and Florida oranges than between varieties of Florida oranges? Can these cross-elasticity relationships have anything to do with the lower price elasticity observed for California oranges?

PROBLEMS

5-1 You are given the following information:

	1969	1970	1971	1972	1973	1974	1975
Price	8.8	8.0	7.5	6.9	6.2	5.6	5.0
Quantity sold (000)	3.6	5.5	7.5	8.0	11.2	13.0	15.0

The quantity supplied is approximated by the following equation:

$$Q_S = -40,000 + 5,000P + 5,000T.$$

$T = 0.0$ in 1969 and increases by 1.0 each year.

a) Plot the supply curves. (*Hint:* You are to determine a *series* of curves, one for each year.) Determine the Y intercept first, letting $T = 0$ and $Q_S = 0$ for year 1969, and so on.
b) Now plot the price/quantity data given above. Use the same graph as in Part a.
c) Determine a linear approximation to the demand curve. What assumptions do you need in order to make this determination, other than the assumption of linearity?
d) What is the relationship of this problem to the "identification" problem?
5-2 The Winston Machine Tool Company has hired a management consulting firm to analyze the demand for one of its major products. A preliminary report from the consultant contained the following regression material:

$$Q = 50 - 5P + 2A + 1P_x - 2.5I$$
$$(0.2)\ (.6)\ (0.3)\ (1.5)$$

$$R^2 = .86$$
Standard Error of the Estimate $= 1$.

Here, Q is the annual demand for the machine tool in question; P is the price charged by Winston in hundreds of dollars; A is thousands of dollars of advertising expenditures; P_x is the average price of another product manufactured by Winston—also measured in hundreds of dollars—and I is the prime interest rate (measured in percents) charged by major New York banks. The terms in parentheses are standard errors of the coefficients.

a) Interpret this demand equation and explain the use of the regression statistics provided.
b) Assume that the consultant is not available and the management of Win-

ston is unsure whether the P_x variable in the equation is the price of a complementary or competing product. (Both were used in different regression runs and, due to a mixup in labeling, the P_x variable is unidentified.) Can you determine at the 99 percent confidence level whether x is a complement or a substitute? Why? Which is it?

c) Assuming that the current price is $1,100, advertising expenditures are $15,000, P_x is $1,000, and I is 8 percent—what is the point price elasticity of demand? Would a reduction in price result in an increase in total revenues? Why?

d) Given the data in Part c, what is the point cross-price-elasticity between the machine tool and Product x?

e) If Winston wished to use this equation for forecasting purposes what is the size of the 99 percent confidence interval for predicting Q?

5-3 Calculate the point price, advertising, income, and cross-price-elasticity for Wisco Foods' frozen fruit pies in the territory for which demand was forecast in the regression example in the chapter. Interpret each elasticity and comment on its use in Wisco's planning activities.

5-4 In 1962 the management of New York Equipment Company, a major distributor of office supplies and equipment in the New York City area, established a service plan for its most popular calculating machine. Any customer who purchased a machine could buy either a *one-year* or a *two-year* complete service contract, covering both labor and parts, to take effect at the end of the normal factory warranty period.

In early 1974 the marketing manager decided to evaluate sales of the contracts with respect to the sales volume during the preceding twelve years. The following data are available for analysis:

Year	Advertising Expenditures, A	Premium for 1-Year Contract, P_x	Premium for 2-Year Contract, P_Q	Number of 2-Year Contracts Purchased, Q
1962	$60,000	$25	$60	5,000
1963	60,000	25	65	4,900
1964	65,000	30	65	5,000
1965	65,000	35	65	5,100
1966	65,000	25	60	5,000
1967	65,000	30	60	5,100
1968	60,000	30	60	5,000
1969	65,000	30	70	5,100
1970	65,000	25	70	4,900
1971	65,000	25	75	4,800
1972	75,000	30	75	5,000
1973	80,000	30	75	5,100

You are to prepare data that will aid the sales manager in his analysis, then interpret the economic significance of the data. To determine the required elasticities, use years when all other factors are held constant. You are also to calculate averages of the elasticities for individual years.

a) What is the arc price elasticity of demand for the two-year contract?

b) What is the arc advertising elasticity of demand for the two-year contract?

c) What is the arc cross-elasticity of demand between the one-year contract and the two-year contract? Are the one-year and two-year contracts close substitutes?

d) On the basis of a linear regression model, the demand function for the two-year service contract is estimated to be:

$$Q = 4{,}589 + 0.010A + 16.403P_X - 10.829P_Q.$$
$$\quad\quad\quad (0.004) \quad\quad (5.357) \quad\quad (3.778)$$

(i) Calculate the *point* price, advertising, and cross-elasticities for 1970 and 1973, using the regression equation.

(ii) Compare the results in Part d-i to the results in Parts a, b, and c. Which elasticity figures do you feel provide better estimates of the true relationships? Why?

(iii) The following standard errors of the coefficients apply: (advertising) $= 0.004$, $(P_X) = 5.357$, and $(P_Q) = 3.778$. For each independent variable determine whether you can reject at 95 percent confidence level the hypothesis that no relationship exists between the independent variables and the dependent variable (Q).

(iv) The coefficient of determination, R^2, is 0.750. What proportion of the total variation in the dependent variable (Q) is explained by the full set of independent variables included in the model? What other independent variables might be added to the equation to obtain a better explanation of the variation in the dependent variable (Q)?

e) On the basis of a multiplicative demand relationship, the demand function for the two-year service contract is estimated as follows:

$$Q = 1500A^{0.134} \, P_X^{0.097} P_Q^{-0.144}.$$

(i) Calculate the point price, advertising, and cross-elasticities for the years 1970 and 1973. Compare the new elasticities with the results in Part d-i as well as with those found in Parts a, b, and c. What distinction can you make between these elasticities and those estimated in Part d-i?

(ii) The standard errors of the exponents[16] in the multiplicative demand function are as follows:

$$(b) = 0.047, \ (c) = 0.031, \text{ and } (d) = 0.041.$$

Can you reject at a 95 percent confidence level the hypothesis that no relationship exists between the independent variables and the dependent variable?

---

[16] The exponents are the coefficients in the linear equation $\log Q = \log a + b \log A + c \log P_x + d \log Pq$.

(iii) The coefficient of determination of the multiplicative demand equation, R^2, equals 0.761. Compare this R^2 with that for the linear model.

SELECTED REFERENCES

Adams, F. Gerard. "Consumer Attitudes, Buying Plans, and Purchases of Durable Goods: A Time Series Approach," *Review of Economics and Statistics*, November 1964, pp. 347-355.

Atkinson, L. Jay. "Factors Affecting the Purchase Value of New Houses," *Survey of Current Business*, August 1966, pp. 20-34.

Burstein, M. L. "The Demand for Household Refrigeration in the U.S.," in A. C. Harberger, ed., *The Demand for Durable Goods*. Chicago: University of Chicago Press, 1960, pp. 99-148.

Draper, N. R., and H. Smith. *Applied Regression Analysis*. New York: Wiley, 1966.

Dyckman, T. R. "An Aggregate-Demand Model for Automobiles," *Journal of Business*, July 1965, pp. 252-266.

Hammond, J. D., D. B. Houston, and E. R. Melander. "Determinants of Household Life Insurance Premium Expenditures," *The Journal of Risk and Insurance*, September 1967.

Houthaker, H. S., and L. D. Taylor. *Consumer Demand in the United States 1929-1970*. Cambridge, Mass.: Harvard University Press, 1966.

Katona, George. "On the Function of Behavioral Theory and Behavioral Research in Economics," *American Economic Review*, March 1968, pp. 146-149.

Lee, Tong Hun. "The Stock Demand Elasticities of Non-farm Housing," *The Review of Economics and Statistics*, February 1964, pp. 82-89.

Nevin, J. B. "Laboratory Experiments for Establishing Consumer Demand: A Validation Study," *Journal of Marketing Research*, August 1974, pp. 261-268.

Suits, Daniel B. "The Demand for New Automobiles in the United States 1929-1956," *Review of Economics and Statistics*, August 1958, pp. 273-288.

CHAPTER 6

Production
Theory

Given the demand for its product, how does a firm determine its optimal level of output? Given several alternative production methods, which one should the firm choose? If the firm undertakes an expansion program to increase productive capacity, will the cost per unit be higher or lower after the expansion? These questions are critically important to the firm, and answers, or at least insights useful in analyzing the questions, are provided by the study of production theory.

PRODUCTION FUNCTION

A production function relates inputs to outputs. It specifies the maximum possible output that can be produced for a given amount of inputs or, alternatively, the minimum quantity of inputs necessary to produce a given level of output. Inputs can be used inefficiently, but the production function concept assumes that firms operate efficiently and get the most from their inputs.

Production functions are determined by the technology and equipment available to the firm. That is, the input/output relationship for any production system is a function of the technological level of the plant, equipment, labor, materials, and so on employed by the firm. Any improvement in technology, such as the addition of a process control computer which permits steel companies to produce a given quantity of steel with fewer raw materials and labor, or a training program which increases the efficiency of labor, results in a new production function.

The basic properties of production functions can be illustrated by examining a simple two-input, one-output system. Consider a particular production process in which various quantities of two inputs, X and Y, can be used to produce the product, Q. The production function can then be written as the following unspecified relationship:

$$Q = f(X, Y). \tag{6-1}$$

Table 6-1 is a tabular representation of such a two-input, single-output production system. Each element in the table shows the maximum quantity of Q that can be produced with a specific combination of X and Y. The table shows, for example, that 2 units of X and 3 units of Y can be combined to produce 49 units of output; 5 units of X coupled with 5 units of Y results in 92 units of output; 4 units of X and 10 units of Y produce 103 units of Q; and so on.

The production relationships in Table 6-1 can also be displayed graphically as in Figure 6-1. There the height of the bars associated with each input combination indicates the output produced. The tops of the output bars map the production surface for the system.

Table 6-1   Representative Production Table

		Output Quantity								
10	70	82	92	103	113	122	127	129	130	131
9	71	82	91	102	111	120	125	127	128	129
8	69	80	90	99	108	117	122	124	125	126
7	67	77	87	96	104	112	118	120	121	123
6	62	72	82	91	99	107	113	114	115	117
Units of 5	55	66	75	84	92	99	104	107	109	110
Y Employed 4	47	58	68	77	85	91	96	100	102	103
3	35	49	59	69	76	82	88	91	93	93
2	22	38	51	59	66	73	79	82	83	82
1	10	24	37	48	56	63	68	71	72	70
	1	2	3	4	5	6	7	8	9	10

Units of X Employed

Figure 6-1 Representative Production Surface

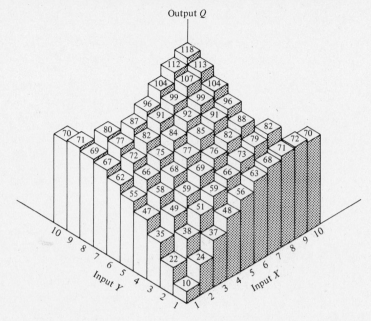

The discrete production data shown in Table 6-1 and Figure 6-1 can be generalized by assuming that the underlying production function is continuous in nature. This generalization will aid us in our examination of production concepts.

A continuous production function means the inputs can be varied in a continuous fashion rather than incrementally, as shown in the preceding example. For a continuous production function, all possible combinations of the inputs can be represented by the graph of the input surface, as shown in Figure 6-2. Each point in the XY plane represents a combination of inputs X and Y, which will result in some level of output, Q, determined by the relationship expressed in Equation 6-1.

The three-dimensional diagram in Figure 6-3 is a graphic illustration of a continuous production function for a two-input, single-output system. Following the X axis outward indicates that increasing amounts of input X are being used; going out the Y axis represents an increasing usage of Y; and moving up the Q axis means that larger amounts of output are being produced. The maximum amount of Q that can be produced with each combination of inputs X and Y is represented by the height of the production surface erected above the input plane. Q^*, for example, is the maximum amount of Q that can be produced using the combination X^*, Y^* of the inputs.

Figure 6-2 Input Surface for the Production Function—$Q = f(X, Y)$

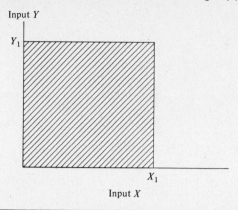

PRODUCTION ISOQUANTS

It is often simpler to examine the properties of production functions graphically by means of isoquants than by using three-dimensional production surfaces.[1] The term "isoquant"—derived from *iso*, meaning equal, and *quant*,

Figure 6-3 Production Surface

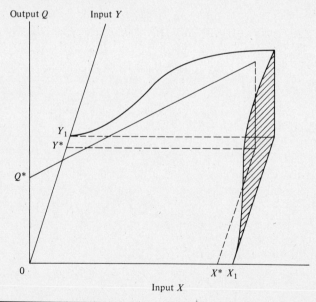

[1] Those familiar with topographic maps can see this relationship by visualizing the production surface as a mountain and the isoquant as a contour line, or isoelevation line, connecting all points of equal altitude.

meaning quantity—denotes a curve that represents all the different combinations of inputs which, when combined efficiently, produce a specified quantity of output. For example, we see in Table 6-1 and Figure 6-1 that 91 units of output can be produced by four input combinations: $X = 3$, $Y = 9$; $X = 4$, $Y = 6$; $X = 6$, $Y = 4$; and $X = 8$, $Y = 3$. Therefore, those four input combinations would all lie on the $Q = 91$ isoquant. Similarly, the combinations $X = 2$, $Y = 9$; $X = 2$, $Y = 10$; $X = 3$, $Y = 6$; $X = 6$, $Y = 3$; $X = 8$, $Y = 2$; and $X = 10$, $Y = 2$—all result in 82 units of production and, hence, lie on the $Q = 82$ isoquant.

The isoquants for the continuous production function displayed in Figure 6-3 can be located by passing a series of planes through the production surface, horizontal to the XY plane, at various heights. Each plane represents a different level of output. Two such planes have been passed through the production surface shown in Figure 6-4 at heights Q_1 and Q_2. Every point on the production surface with a height of Q_1 above the input plane—that is, all points along curve Q_1—represent an equal quantity, or isoquant, of Q_1 units of output. The curve Q_2 maps out the locus of all production possibilities that result in Q_2 units of production.

These isoquant curves can be transferred to the input surface, as indicated by the dashed curves Q'_1 and Q'_2 in Figure 6-4, then further transferred to the two-dimensional graph shown in Figure 6-5. These latter curves represent the standard form of an isoquant.

Suppose Q_1 represents 82 units of output. Each point on the Q_1 iso-

Figure 6-4   Isoquant Determination

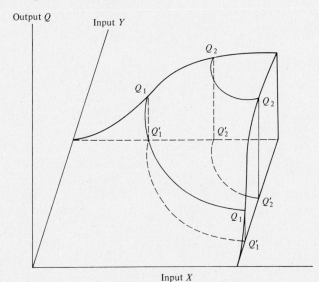

Figure 6-5 Production Isoquants

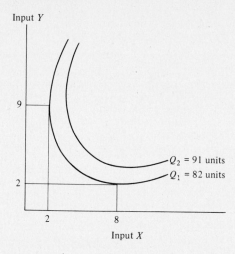

quant indicates a different combination of X and Y that can be used to produce 82 units of output. For example, 82 units can be produced with 2 units of X and 9 units of Y, with 8 units of X and 2 units of Y, or with any other combination of X and Y on the isoquant Q_1. A similar interpretation may be given Q_2, the isoquant for 91 units of output.

Substituting Input Factors

The shapes of the isoquants reveal a great deal about the substitutability of the input factors; that is, the ability to substitute one input for another in the production process. This point is illustrated in Figure 6-6(a), (b), and (c). Figure 6-6(a) shows isoquants for electric power generation. The technology, a power plant with a bank of boilers equipped to burn either oil or gas, is given; and various amounts of electric power can be produced by burning gas only, oil only, or varying amounts of each. Gas and oil are perfect substitutes here, and the isoquants are straight lines.

Figure 6-6(b), illustrating the isoquants for bicycles, represents the opposite case, complete nonsubstitutability. Exactly two wheels and one frame are required to produce a bicycle, and in no way can wheels be substituted for frames, or vice versa.

Figure 6-6(c) shows the more typical situation, that of a production process where inputs can be substituted for each other, but the substitutability is not perfect. A dress can be made with a relatively small amount of labor (L_1) and a large amount of cloth (C_1). The same dress can also be

Figure 6-6 Isoquants for Inputs with Varying Degrees of Substitutability: (a) Electric Power Generation; (b) Bicycle Production; (c) Dresses

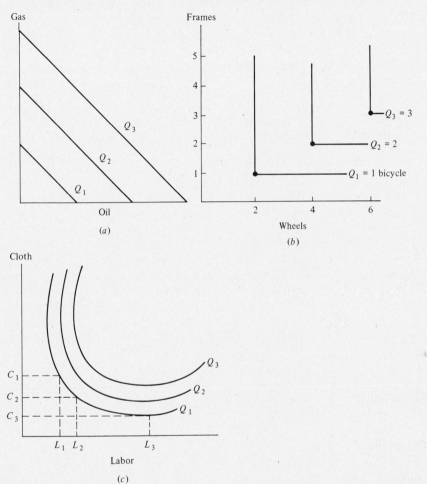

made with less cloth (C_2) if more labor (L_2) is used, because the worker can cut the material more carefully and reduce waste. Finally, the dress can be made with still less cloth (C_3), but the worker must be so extremely painstaking that the labor input requirement increases to L_3. Note that while a relatively small addition of labor, from L_1 to L_2, allows the input of cloth to be reduced from C_1 to C_2, a very large increase in labor, from L_2 to L_3, is required to obtain a similar reduction in cloth from C_2 to C_3. The substitutability of labor for cloth diminishes from L_1 to L_2 to L_3. The fact that the isoquant turns up beyond L_3 is discussed in the following section.

MARGINAL RATE OF SUBSTITUTION

The slope of the isoquant provides the key to the substitutability of input factors. In Figure 6-6(c), the slope of the isoquant is simply the change in Input Y (cloth) divided by the change in Input X (labor). This relationship, known as the *marginal rate of substitution (MRS) of factor inputs*, provides a measure of the amount of one input factor that must be substituted for one unit of the other factor if output is to remain unchanged. This can be stated algebraically:

$$MRS = \frac{\Delta Y}{\Delta X} = \frac{dY}{dX} = \text{Slope of the production isoquants.}$$

In the typical case the marginal rate of substitution is not constant but diminishes as the amount of substitution increases. In Figure 6-6(c), for example, as more and more labor is substituted for cloth, the increment of labor necessary to replace cloth is increasing. Finally, at the extremes, the isoquant may even become positively sloped, indicating that there is a limit to the range over which the input factors may be substituted for each other while the level of production is held constant.[2]

In Figure 6-7 the limits to the range of substitutability of X for Y are indicated by the tangencies between the isoquants and a set of lines drawn perpendicular to the Y axis. Similarly, the limits of substitutability of Y for X are shown by the tangencies of lines perpendicular to the X axis. The maximum and the minimum proportions of Y and X that can be combined to produce each level of output are determined by the tangencies of these lines with the production isoquants.

Note that it is irrational for a firm to use any input combination outside these tangencies, or *ridge lines*, as they are called. The reason such combinations are irrational lies in the fact that the marginal product (the change in output resulting from an incremental increase in an input factor) of the relatively more abundant input is negative outside the ridge lines. This means that addition of the last unit of the excessive input factor actually reduces the output of the production system. Obviously, if the input factor has a positive cost, it would be irrational for a firm to buy and employ additional units that caused production to decrease. To illustrate, suppose a firm is currently operating with a fixed quantity of Input Y equal to Y_1 units, as shown in Figure 6-7. In such a situation the firm would never employ more than X_3 units of Input X because employment of additional units of X results in successively lower output quantities being produced. For example, if the firm combines Y_1 and X_4, output is equal to Q_1 units.

---

[2] The classic example of this case is the use of land and labor to produce a given output of wheat. As labor is substituted for land, at some point the farmers trample the wheat. As more men are added, more land must also be added, if wheat output is to be maintained. The new men must have some place to stand.

Figure 6-7   Maximum Variable Proportions for Inputs X and Y

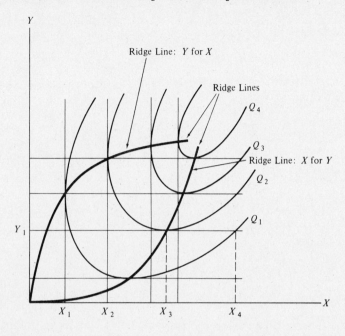

By reducing usage of X from X_4 to X_3, output can be increased from Q_1 to Q_2. Similar reasoning applies for all other input combinations lying outside the ridge lines, so we can henceforth eliminate all such combinations from serious consideration.

Diminishing Returns to Factor Inputs

The concept of diminishing returns to input factors can also be examined by means of *total product curves*. The total product for any Input X is defined as the schedule of output obtained as X increases, *holding constant the amounts of the other inputs employed*. This concept is illustrated in Figure 6-8, which shows output rising as Inputs X and Y are increased. Now suppose we fix, or hold constant, the amount of Input Y at the level Y_1. The total product curve of Input X, holding Input Y constant at Y_1, originates at Y_1 and rises along the production surface as the use of Input X is increased. Four other total product curves are shown in the figure: another for X, holding Y constant at Y_2, and three for Input Y, holding X fixed at X_1, X_2, and X_3, respectively.

Total product curves can also be drawn in two-dimensional space. A total product curve for Input X, holding Y constant at Y_1, is shown in Figure 6-9(a). This curve is developed directly from Figure 6-8, and a series of

Figure 6-8 Total Product Curves for X and Y

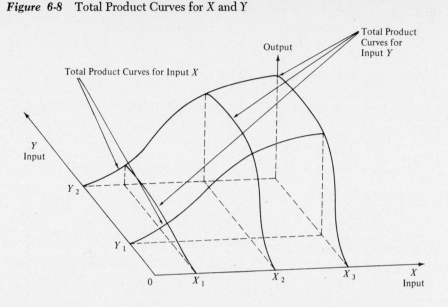

such curves can be drawn for various levels of Y. Similarly, total product curves can be drawn for Input Y, holding X constant at various levels.

Marginal and average product curves can be developed from the total product curve. First, recognize that *the marginal product of a factor,* MP_X, *is the change in output associated with a given change in the factor, holding other things constant, or:*

$$MP_X = \frac{\partial Q}{\partial X}.$$

The factor's average product, AP_X, *is the total output quantity divided by the units of the input employed, or:*

$$AP_X = \frac{Q}{X}.$$

The marginal product is equal to the slope of the total product curve, while the average product is equal to the slope of a line drawn from the origin of Figure 6-9(a) to a point on the total product curve. The average and marginal products for Input X can be determined in this manner, and these points are plotted to form the average and marginal product curves shown in Figure 6-9(b).

Three points of interest may be identified on the total product curve, A, B, and C, and each has a corresponding location on the average or marginal curves. Point A is the inflection point of the total product curve. The marginal product of X (the slope of the total product curve) increases until

Figure 6-9 Total, Marginal, and Average Product Curves: (a) Total Product Curve for X, Holding $Y = Y_1$; (b) Marginal Product Curve for X, Holding $Y = Y_1$

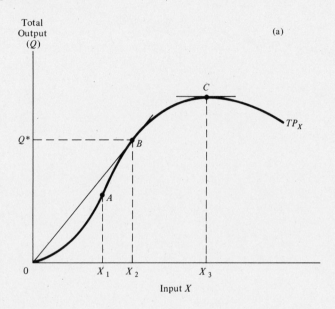

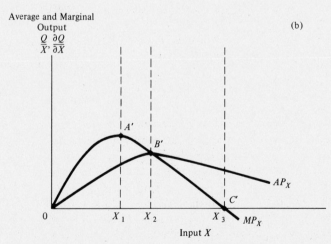

this point is reached, after which it begins to decrease. This phenomenon can be seen in Figure 6-9(b), as MP_X is at a maximum at A'.

The second point on the total product curve, B, indicates the output at which the average and the marginal products are equal. The slope of a line from the origin to any point on the total product curve measures the average product of X at that point, while the marginal product is equal to the slope of the total product curve. At Point B, where X_2 units of Input X are employed, such a line from the origin is tangent to the total product curve, so $MP_X = AP_X$. Note also that the slopes of successive lines drawn from the origin to the total product curve increase until Point B, after which their slopes decline. Thus, the average product curve rises until it reaches B, then declines; this feature is also shown in Figure 6-9(b) as point B'. Here we see again that $MP_X = AP_X$, and that AP_X is at a maximum.

The third point, C, indicates where the slope of the total product curve is zero and the curve is at a maximum. Beyond C the marginal product of X is negative, indicating that an increase in the usage of Input X results in a *reduction* of total product. The corresponding point in Figure 6-9(b) is C', the point where the marginal product curve cuts the X axis. Points C and C' occur at X_3 units of input, so X_3 is a point on the ridge line shown in Figure 6-7.

THE LAW OF DIMINISHING RETURNS TO A FACTOR

The total and the marginal product curves in Figure 6-9 demonstrate the well-known law of diminishing returns. This law states that as the quantity of a variable input is increased, with the quantities of all other factors being held constant, the *increases* in output eventually diminish. Alternatively stated, the law of diminishing returns holds that the marginal product of the variable factor must eventually decline. All this follows from the assumption of diminishing substitutability discussed above and illustrated in Figure 6-6(c).

THE THREE STAGES OF PRODUCTION[3]

Although not as general as isoquant analysis, the total product curve in Figure 6-9 can also be used to identify rational and irrational ranges of input combinations for a particular class of commonly encountered production functions. The curve can be divided into three segments, or stages. Stage I is the segment from the origin to point X_2.[4] In this stage the production function is characterized first by increasing returns to the variable factor, from the origin to Point X_1, and then by diminishing returns, from X_1 to X_2.

The second stage lies in the range from X_2 to X_3. In other words, Stage II begins in the range where the marginal product of the variable factor is decreasing, and it continues to the point at which total product is maximized and marginal product is zero. This stage of production is characterized by diminishing returns to the variable input over its entire range. That

---

[3] This section may be omitted without loss of continuity.

[4] X_2 is the point at which the average product is maximized, providing the production function exhibits constant returns to scale, a condition that is discussed later in this chapter.

is, although total product is increasing in this range of input proportions, it does so at a continuously decreasing rate.

Finally, we have Stage III, the area beyond X_3, where the total product curve is decreasing. In this range the marginal product of the variable factor is negative.

It is irrational for a firm to operate in either Stage I or Stage III. It is obvious that operation in Stage III is irrational because the marginal product of the variable factor, X, is negative in that range, and hence total product can be increased by using less of it. Therefore, even if Factor X were absolutely free, the firm would never use more than X_3 units of it in combination with Y_1 units of Input Y.

Stage I is also irrational. Here the fixed factor, Y, is so abundant in relation to the variable input that its marginal product is negative. This is illustrated in Figure 6-10, which reproduces the total product curve of Figure 6-9 and then shows two additional total product of X curves with Y held constant at Y_2 and Y_3. Here $Y_1 > Y_2 > Y_3$. Now consider the input combination X_1, Y_1, a Stage I combination with $Y = Y_1$, as in Figure 6-9. With X_1, Y_1 inputs used, Q_1 is the maximum attainable output. Note, however, that by reducing the usage of Y from Y_1 to Y_2, output is increased to Q_2 units. The reduction of the "fixed" factor has increased output. A further reduction from Y_2 to Y_3 also increases output associated with the usage of X_1 units of Input X.

This phenomenon of an output increase associated with *reduced usage*

Figure 6-10   Total Product Curves Illustrating the Negative Marginal Product of the Fixed Input Factor Y in Stage I

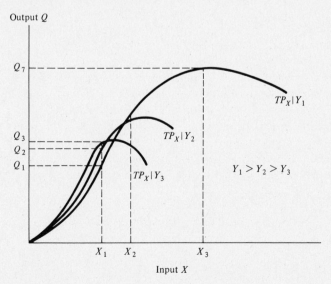

of the "fixed" factor, Y, implies that the marginal product of Y is negative. Since a firm producing in Stage I—that is, where the marginal product of the fixed factor is negative—can reduce the amount of the fixed factor employed and maintain or even increase output, it is irrational not to do so. So long as either factor has a positive cost, the input proportions found in Stage I cannot lead to cost minimization for any level of production.[5]

This concept of irrational stages of production can also be demonstrated by reference to the isoquant analysis discussed earlier. In Figure 6-11 the production isoquants for Product Q have been redrawn, and the ridge lines indicated. Holding the amount of Y fixed at Y_1, the output possibilities associated with varying quantities of X are shown at the points of intersection of the horizontal line $Y_1Y'_1$ with the production isoquants.

Moving out from the Y-axis, note that in the area above the upper ridge line the relative amount of Y is excessive. In this area it is possible to increase production (move to a higher isoquant) by reducing the amount of Y employed. For example, the input combination X_1Y_1 results in Q_1 units of output. However, by reducing to Y_2 the amount of Y employed while holding X constant at X_1, the firm produces a higher level of output, Q_2. A further reduction in Y again increases output to Q_3 units. This means that the marginal product of Y is negative, since reducing its usage increases production. Thus, the area above the upper ridge line in Figure 6-11 corresponds to the Stage I area of Figure 6-10. Note also that the input combination X_1Y_3 lies on the upper ridge line, which is the boundary between Stages I and II. The input combination X_2Y_1 also lies on the upper ridge in Figure 6-11 and is therefore a Stage I-Stage II boundary point, as described above.

The area between the ridge lines in Figure 6-11 corresponds to Stage II production combinations. All input proportions within this range are rational from the physical combination standpoint, and only by adding prices to the analysis—as we do in the following section—can the optimal combinations be determined.

The area below the lower ridge line corresponds to Stage III input combinations, assuming Input Y is the "fixed" factor. Here X is excessive in relation to Y, and its marginal product is negative. For example, the input combination X_3Y_1 in Figure 6-11 results in an output of Q_7 units. This corresponds to the point of maximum total product for Input X in Figure 6-9. That is, it is the input combination that maximizes the total product of X, holding Y fixed at Y_1 units. Increasing the amount of X utilized to X_4 units,

[5] One point should be made clear. The term "fixed factor" means that the factor is held constant in an analytical sense, as the other variables in a function are held constant when one is examining the partial derivative with respect to a particular variable. Thus, a fixed factor can actually be varied. However, once an operating plan has been determined and a plant constructed, the input combinations may be fixed in a very real sense, not in the analytic sense. This point is elaborated in the following chapter on linear programming.

Figure 6-11   Stages of Production: Isoquant Construction

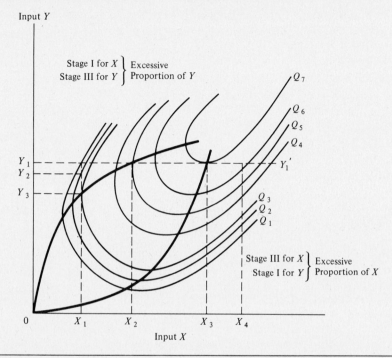

while maintaining Y at Y_1, reduces output to Q_6 units. No firm would operate by choice with input combinations in this range.

The isoquant analysis of Figure 6-11, while providing the same information as Figure 6-9, is somewhat more general. In Figure 6-11 we are able to specify the three stages of production for any combination of input factors, not just combinations in which one factor is held constant. Also, the symmetry of the stages of production is revealed. Stage I for variable Input X is identical with Stage III for variable Input Y, and both indicate an excessive usage of Input Y. Likewise, Stage III for X is the same as Stage I for Y, indicating that the relative proportion of X is larger than it should be. Stage II is identical for both, and it is within this stage that we must look for the optimal input combinations.

THE ROLE OF REVENUE AND COST IN PRODUCTION

To answer the question of what constitutes an optimal input combination in a productive process, we must move beyond technological relationships and introduce revenues and costs. In an advanced economy productive activity results in goods which are sold rather than *consumed* by the producer, so we must be concerned with returns to the owners of the various input factors—labor, materials, and capital—that result from those sales. Therefore, in order to gain an understanding of how the factors of production should be combined for maximum efficiency, it is necessary that we shift from an analysis of *physical* productivity of inputs to an examination of their *economic* productivity, or revenue-generating capability. The conversion from physical to economic relationships is accomplished by multiplying the marginal product of the input factors by the marginal revenue resulting from the sale of the goods or services produced, to obtain a quantity known as the *marginal revenue product* of the input:

Marginal Revenue Product of Input $X = MRP_X$
$$= (\text{Marginal Product}_X) \cdot (\text{Marginal Revenue Output})$$

The marginal revenue product is the value of a marginal unit of a particular input factor when used in the production of a specific product. For example, if the addition of one more laborer to a work force would result in the production of two incremental units of a product which can be sold for $5 per unit, the marginal product of labor is 2, and its marginal revenue product is $10 ($2 \times \$5$).

Optimal Use of a Single Product Factor

To see how the economic productivity of a factor, as defined by its marginal revenue product, is related to the use of the factor for productive purposes one need only consider the basic marginal principles of profit maximization developed in Chapter 2. Recall that so long as marginal revenue exceeds marginal cost, profits must increase. In the context of production decisions this means that if the marginal revenue product of an input—that is, the marginal revenue generated by its employment in a production system—exceeds its marginal cost, then profits are increased through such employment. Similarly, when the marginal revenue product is less than the cost of the factor, marginal profit is negative, so the firm would decline to employ additional units of that factor.

This concept of optimal resource use can be clarified by examining a very simple production system in which a single variable input, L, is used to produce a single product, Q. Profit maximization requires that production be at a level such that marginal revenue equals marginal cost. Since the only variable factor in the system is Input L, the marginal cost of production can be expressed as:

$$MC_Q = \frac{P_L}{MP_L}. \qquad (6\text{-}2)$$

That is, dividing the price of a marginal unit of L, P_L, by the number of units of output gained by the employment of an added unit of L, MP_L, provides a measure of the marginal cost of producing each additional unit of the product.

Since marginal revenue must equal marginal cost at the profit-maximizing output level, MR_Q can be substituted for MC_Q in Equation 6-2, resulting in the expression,

$$MR_Q = \frac{P_L}{MP_L} \qquad (6\text{-}3)$$

which must hold, since it was demonstrated immediately above that the right-hand side of Equation 6-3 is just another expression for marginal cost. Solving Equation 6-3 for P_L results in:

$$P_L = MR_Q \cdot MP_L,$$

or, since $MR_Q \cdot MP_L$ is defined as the marginal revenue product of L:

$$P_L = MRP_L. \qquad (6\text{-}4)$$

Equation 6-4 states the general result that a profit-maximizing firm will always employ an input up to the point where its marginal revenue product is equal to its cost. If the marginal revenue product exceeds the cost of the input, profits are increased by employing additional units of the factor. Similarly, when the resource's price is greater than its marginal revenue product, profit is increased by using less of the factor. Only at the level of usage where $MRP_{\text{INPUT}} = P_{\text{INPUT}}$ are profits maximized.

Optimal Combination of Multiple Inputs

The results of the preceding section can be extended to production systems employing several input factors. Although there are several possible approaches to this extension, one of the simplest involves combining technological and market relationships through the use of isoquant and isocost curves. That is, the optimal input proportions can be found graphically for a two-input, single-output system by adding an "isocost curve" (a line of constant costs) to the diagram of production isoquants. Each point on an isocost curve represents some combination of inputs, say X and Y, whose cost is equal to a constant expenditure. Isocost curves, which are illustrated in Figure 6-12, are constructed in the following manner: Let $P_X = \$500$ and $P_Y = \$250$; these are the prices of X and Y. For a given expenditure, say $E_1 = \$1,000$, the firm can purchase 4 units of Y ($\$1,000/\$250 = 4$ units) and no units of X, or 2 units of X ($\$1,000/\$500 = 2$ units) but none of Y. These two quantities represent the X and Y intercepts of an isocost curve, and a straight line connecting them provides the locus of all combinations of X and Y that can be purchased for $\$1,000$.

The equation for an isocost curve is merely a statement of the various combinations of the inputs that can be purchased for a given expenditure.

Figure 6-12 Isocost Curves

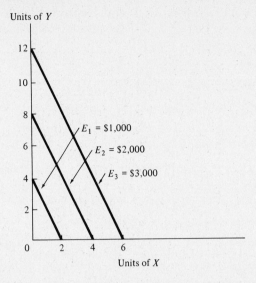

For example, the various combinations of X and Y that can be purchased for a fixed expenditure, E, are given by the expression:

$$E = P_X \cdot X + P_Y \cdot Y.$$

Solving this expression for Y so that it can be graphed, as in Figure 6-12, results in:

$$P_Y \cdot Y = E - P_X \cdot X,$$

and

$$Y = \frac{E}{P_Y} - \frac{P_X}{P_Y} X. \tag{6-5}$$

Note that the first term in Equation 6-5 is the Y-axis intercept of the isocost curve. It indicates the quantity of Input Y that can be purchased with a given budget or expenditure limit, *assuming zero units of Input* X *are bought*. The slope of an isocost curve dY/dX is equal to $-P_X/P_Y$ and, therefore, is a measure of the relative prices of the inputs. From this, it follows that a change in the expenditure level, E, leads to a parallel shift of an isocost curve, while changes in the prices of the inputs result in changes in the slope of the curve.

Extending the example introduced above and illustrated in Figure 6-12 will clarify these relationships. With a $1,000 expenditure level, the X-axis intercept of the isocost curve has already been shown to be 4 units.

The slope of the isocost curve is determined by the relative prices. Thus, in Figure 6-12 the slope of the isocost curves is given by the expression:

$$\text{Slope} = -\frac{P_X}{P_Y} = -\frac{\$500}{\$250} = -2.$$

Suppose a firm has only $1,000 to spend on inputs for the production of Q. Combining the production isoquants of Figure 6-11 with the isocost curve, E_1, of Figure 6-12 to form Figure 6-13, we find that the optimal input combination occurs at Point A, the point of tangency between the isocost curve and a production isoquant. At that point, X and Y are combined in proportions that maximize the output attainable for expenditure E_1. No other combination of X and Y that can be purchased for $1,000 will produce as much output. Alternatively stated, the combination X_1Y_1 is the least-cost combination of inputs that can be used to produce output Q_2. All other possible combinations for producing Q_2 are intersected by higher isocost curves.

The fact that optimal input combinations occur at a point of tangency between a production isoquant and an isocost curve leads to a very important economic principle. Recall that the slope of an isoquant curve is equal to the marginal rate of technical substitution of one input factor for the other when production is held constant at some level. The marginal rate of techni-

Figure 6-13 Optimal Input Combination

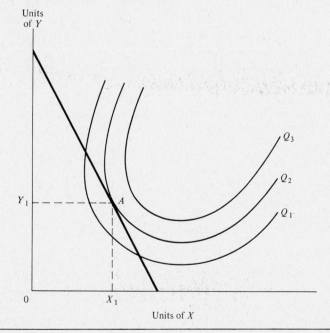

cal substitution can be shown to be equal to the ratio of the marginal products of the input factors as follows:

$$\text{Slope of an Isoquant} = MRTS = \frac{\Delta Y}{\Delta X} \text{ holding } Q \text{ constant.} \qquad (6\text{-}6)$$

Since output is held constant along an isoquant, if Input Y is reduced, causing output to decline, Input X must be increased sufficiently to return output to the original level. The loss in output resulting from a small reduction in Y is equal to the marginal product of Y, MP_Y, multiplied by the change in Y, ΔY. That is:

$$\Delta Q = MP_Y \cdot \Delta Y. \qquad (6\text{-}7)$$

Similarly, the change in Q associated with the increased use of Input X is given by the expression:

$$\Delta Q = MP_X \cdot \Delta X. \qquad (6\text{-}8)$$

For substitution of X for Y along an isoquant, ΔQ in Expressions 6-7 and 6-8 must be the same, and it follows that:

$$-MP_Y \cdot \Delta Y = MP_X \cdot \Delta X. \qquad (6\text{-}9)$$

Transposing the variables in Equation 6-9 produces the relationship:

$$\frac{\Delta Y}{\Delta X} = -\frac{MP_X}{MP_Y} = \text{Slope of an Isoquant.}$$

Thus, the slope of a production isoquant, shown in Equation 6-6 to be equal to $\Delta Y/\Delta X$, is seen to be determined by the ratio of the marginal products of the inputs.

At the point where inputs are combined optimally, there is a tangency between the isocost and the isoquant curves, and, hence, their slopes are equal. Therefore, for optimal input combinations the ratio of the prices of the inputs must be equal to the ratio of their marginal products, as is shown in Equation 6-10:

$$-\frac{P_X}{P_Y} = -\frac{MP_X}{MP_Y}. \qquad (6\text{-}10)$$

Or, alternatively, the ratios of marginal product to price must be equal for each input:

$$\frac{MP_X}{P_X} = \frac{MP_Y}{P_Y}. \qquad (6\text{-}11)$$

The economic principle for least-cost combinations of inputs, as given in Equation 6-11, states that the optimal proportions are such that an additional dollar's worth of each input adds as much to total output as would a dollar's worth of any other input. Any combination violating this rule is suboptimal in the sense that a change of inputs could result in the same quantity of output being produced for a lower cost.[6]

Consider the case of a firm combining X and Y in such a way that the marginal product of X equals 10, while that of Y equals 9. Assuming that X costs \$2 a unit and Y costs \$3, the marginal product per dollar spent is found to be:

$$\frac{MP_X}{P_X} = \frac{10}{2} = 5 \quad \text{and} \quad \frac{MP_Y}{P_Y} = \frac{9}{3} = 3.$$

This combination violates the optimal proportions rule: the ratios of the marginal products to prices are not equal. In this situation the firm can reduce its use of Y by 1 unit, reducing total output by 9 units and total costs by \$3. Then, by employing an additional nine-tenths of 1 unit of X at a cost of \$1.80, the 9 units of lost production may be regained. The result is production of the 9 units of output at a total cost which is less than in the original situation—the \$3 saved on Y is offset by only an additional \$1.80 spent on X.[7]

Combining a production system's input factors in proportions that meet the conditions of Equation 6-11 insures that *any* output quantity will be produced at minimum cost. At the optimal (profit maximizing) output level, meeting the conditions of Equation 6-11 is equivalent to employing each input up to the point where its marginal revenue product is equal to its price—the optimality condition developed in Equation 6-4. To see this, note that by the same reasoning that led to the development of Equation 6-2, the inverse of the ratios expressed in Equation 6-11 must necessarily measure the marginal cost of producing goods at any output level; that is:

$$\frac{P_X}{MP_X} = \frac{P_Y}{MP_Y} = MC_Q. \qquad (6\text{-}12)$$

Now since marginal cost will equal marginal revenue at the optimal output level, Equation 6-12 can be written as:

$$\frac{P_X}{MP_X} = MR_Q,$$

and

$$\frac{P_Y}{MP_Y} = MR_Q.$$

---

[6] The optimal input relationship shown in Equations 6-7 and 6-8 can also be derived using the Lagrangian technique to solve either a production maximization problem subject to a budget constraint or a cost minimization problem subject to an output requirement. Both approaches are developed in the Appendix to this chapter.

[7] This new input combination may still be suboptimal; that is, the example merely indicates that an alternative combination of inputs can lower production costs. It would be necessary to examine the new marginal product/price ratios for an input combination of 10.9 units of X and 8 units of Y to determine if further savings are possible.

Rearranging produces:

$$P_X = MP_X \cdot MR_Q = MRP_X,$$

and

$$P_Y = MP_Y \cdot MR_Q = MRP_Y,$$

the same condition stated in Equation 6-4 for the single factor production system.

RETURNS TO SCALE

Thus far the discussion of optimal input combinations has focused on the appropriate mix of the input factors. A closely related topic is the question of how a proportionate increase in *all* the input factors will affect total production. This is the question of *returns to scale*, and there are three possible situations. First, if the proportional increase in all inputs is equal to the proportional increase in output, *returns to scale are constant*. For example, if a simultaneous doubling of all inputs leads to a doubling of output, then returns to scale are constant. Second, the proportional increase in output may be larger than that of the inputs, which is termed *increasing returns to scale*. Third, if output increases less than proportionally with input increases, we have *decreasing returns to scale*.

Isoquant analysis can be used to examine returns to scale for a two-input, single-output production system. Consider in Figure 6-14 the production of Q_1 units of output using the input combination X_1Y_1. Doubling both inputs shifts production to Q_2. If Q_2 is precisely twice as large as Q_1, the system is said to exhibit constant returns to scale over the range X_1Y_1

Figure 6-14   Returns to Scale

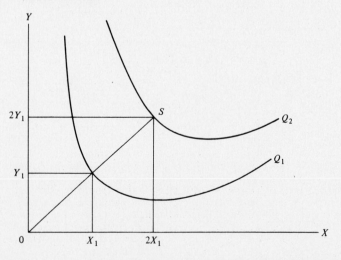

to X_2Y_2. If Q_2 is greater than twice Q_1, returns to scale are increasing, and if Q_2 is less than double Q_1, the system exhibits decreasing returns to scale.

The returns to scale implicit in a given production function can also be examined in terms of two- and three-dimensional graphs such as those drawn in Figures 6-15 through 6-18. In these graphs the slope of a curve drawn from the origin up the production surface indicates whether returns to scale are constant, increasing, or decreasing.[8] In the production system illustrated in Figure 6-15(a), for example, a curve drawn from the origin will have a constant slope, indicating that returns to scale are constant. Accordingly, the outputs for given (optimal) combinations of X and Y shown in Figure 6-15(b) are increasing exactly proportionally to increases in X and Y. In Figure 6-16, the "backbone" curve from the origin exhibits a constantly increasing slope, indicating increasing returns to scale. The situation is reversed in Figure 6-17, where the production surface is increasing at a decreasing rate, indicating that decreasing returns to scale are present.

The most typical situation is for a production function to have first increasing, then decreasing, returns to scale, as is shown in Figure 6-18. The region of increasing returns is attributable to specialization—as output increases, specialized labor can be used and efficient, large-scale machinery can be employed in the production process. Beyond some scale of opera-

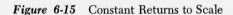

Figure 6-15   Constant Returns to Scale

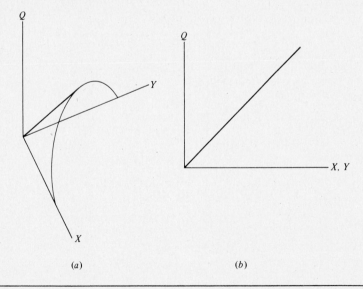

(a)   (b)

Figure 6-16 Increasing Returns to Scale

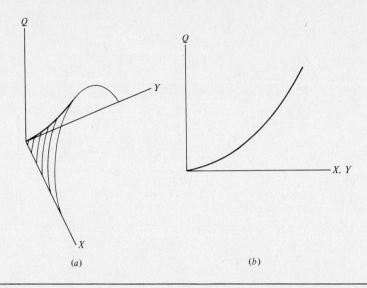

(a)   (b)

tions, however, not only are further gains from specialization limited but also problems of coordination may begin to increase costs substantially. When coordination expenses more than offset additional benefits of specialization, decreasing returns to scale set in.

Figure 6-17 Decreasing Returns to Scale

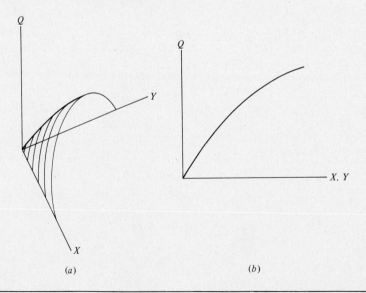

(a)   (b)

Figure 6-18 Variable Returns to Scale

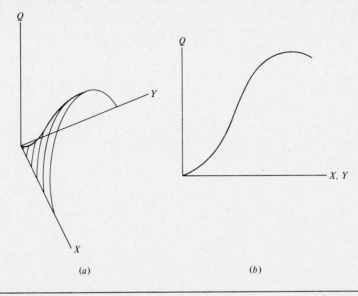

(a)   (b)

Algebraic Formulation of Returns to Scale

Returns to scale can be analyzed algebraically by examining the relationship between increases in the inputs and the quantity of output produced. Assume that all inputs in the unspecified production function $Q = f(X,Y,Z)$ are multiplied by the constant k. That is, all inputs are increased proportionally by the factor k. Then the production function can be rewritten as

$$hQ = f(kX, kY, kZ). \tag{6-13}$$

Here h is the proportional increase in Q resulting from a k-fold increase in each input factor. From Equation 6-13 it is evident that the following relationships hold:

If $h < k$, then the production function exhibits decreasing returns to scale.

If $h = k$, then the production function exhibits constant returns to scale.

If $h > k$, then the production function exhibits increasing returns to scale.

To illustrate, consider the production function $Q = 2X + 3Y + 1.5Z$. We can examine the returns to scale for this function by determining how a doubling of all inputs affects output. Initially, let $X = 1$, $Y = 2$, and $Z = 2$, so output is found to be:

$$Q_1 = 2(1) + 3(2) + 1.5(2)$$
$$= 2 + 6 + 3 = 11 \text{ units.}$$

Doubling all inputs (letting $k = 2$) leads to the input quantities $X = 2$, $Y = 4$, and $Z = 4$, and:

$$Q_2 = 2(2) + 3(4) + 1.5(4)$$
$$= 4 + 12 + 6 = 22 \text{ units.}$$

Since $k = 2$ and $h = Q_2/Q_1 = 22/11 = 2$, $k = h$, and the system exhibits constant returns to scale. A k-fold increase in all inputs leads to a k-fold increase in output.

Homogeneous Production Functions

Suppose a production function is such that, when each input factor is multiplied by a constant k, the constant can be *completely* factored out. Such a function is defined as *homogeneous*. To illustrate, if we have $Q = 2X + 3Y + 1.5Z$, and if we increase all inputs by some proportion k, then:

$$hQ = k(2X) + k(3Y) + k(1.5Z) = k(2X + 3Y + 1.5Z). \qquad \textbf{(6-14)}$$

Since k can be completely factored out, that is, each term contains the same power of the proportionality factor, this production function is homogeneous.

When k was factored in Equation 6-14, it had an exponent of 1.0, that is, $k = k^1$. This will not always be the case: Sometimes the factored k will have an exponent greater or less than unity. For example, consider Equation 6-15:

$$Q = X^{0.3}Y^{0.7}Z^{0.2}. \qquad \textbf{(6-15)}$$

Increasing each input proportionally results in:

$$hQ = (kX)^{0.3}(kY)^{0.7}(kZ)^{0.2},$$

and factoring out k gives[9]:

$$hQ = k^{(0.3+0.7+0.2)}[X^{0.3}Y^{0.7}Z^{0.2}]$$
$$= k^{1.2}[X^{0.3}Y^{0.7}Z^{0.2}].$$

In this case, $h = k^{1.2}$, so $h > k$, and increasing returns to scale are present.

These results may be generalized. First, when k is factored, we will obtain an expression of the form:

$$hQ = k^n f(X,Y,Z). \qquad \textbf{(6-16)}$$

From Equation 6-16 it can be seen that $h = k^n$, and n determines the *degree of homogeneity* of the production function. If $n = 1.0$, the function is homogeneous of degree 1. If $n < 1.0$, the equation is homogeneous of degree less than 1, for example, 0.95. If $n > 1.0$, the function is homogeneous of degree greater than 1, for example, 1.2, as in Equation 6-15.

The degree of homogeneity as indicated by the exponent n *provides*

[9] Recall from algebra that $(aX)^n = a^n X^n$. For example, $(2 \cdot 3)^2 = 2^2 \cdot 3^3 = 4 \cdot 9 = 36$. Alternatively, $(2 \cdot 3)^2 = 6^2 = 36$.

the key to the returns-to-scale question in this case. If n = 1, *then* h = k, *and the function has constant returns to scale. However, if* n > 1, *then* h > k, *and increasing returns to scale are present, while* n < 1 *indicates* h < k *and, hence, decreasing returns to scale.*

EMPIRICAL PRODUCTION FUNCTIONS

From a theoretical standpoint, the most appealing form of a production function is generally a cubic, such as the equation:

$$Q = a + bX + cX^2 - dX^3 + eY + fY^2 - gY^3. \qquad (6\text{-}17)$$

This form, graphed in Figure 6-18, is general in that it exhibits stages of first increasing and then decreasing returns to scale. Similarly, the marginal products of the input factors also exhibit this pattern of first increasing and then decreasing returns, as was illustrated in Figure 6-9.[10]

Given enough input/output observations, either over time for a single firm or at a point in time for a number of firms in an industry, regression techniques can be used to estimate the parameters (coefficients) of the production function. Frequently, however, the data observations do not exhibit enough dispersion to indicate the full range of increasing and then decreasing returns. In these cases simpler functional specifications can be used to estimate the production function within the range of data available. In other words, the generality of a cubic function may be unnecessary, and an alternative model specification, such as the power function described below, can be used for empirical estimation.

Power Functions
One function commonly employed in production studies is the power function, which indicates a multiplicative relationship between the various inputs, and takes the form:

$$Q = aX^bY^c. \qquad (6\text{-}18)$$

Power functions have several properties useful in empirical research. First, they are linear in logarithms and thus can be empirically estimated using linear regression analysis. That is, Equation 6-18 is equivalent to:

$$\log Q = \log a + b \log X + c \log Y. \qquad (6\text{-}19)$$

The least squares technique can be used to estimate the coefficients of Equation 6-19 and thereby the parameters of Equation 6-18.

Second, power functions are also homogeneous functions, and the degree of homogeneity is given by the sum of the exponents. Equation 6-18 is homogeneous of degree n, where n is the sum of the exponents b and c

---

[10] This can be seen by noting the partial derivatives, for example, $\partial Q / \partial X = b + 2cX - 3dX^2$, which first increases and then decreases as X increases, assuming $c > d$.

(or alternatively the sum of the regression coefficients b and c in Equation 6-19). Thus, whether returns to scale are increasing, are decreasing, or are constant can be easily determined.

Finally, if the sum of the exponents is exactly 1.0, the production function is homogeneous of degree 1, or linear and homogeneous. Returns to scale are constant, and in such cases the powerful analytical tool of linear programming, described in the following chapter, can be used to determine the optimal input/output relationships for the firm.

Power functions have been employed in a large number of empirical production studies, particularly since Charles W. Cobb and Paul H. Douglas' pioneering work in the late 1920s. The impact of this work was so great that power production functions are now commonly referred to as "Cobb-Douglas production functions."

Selection of a Functional Form for Empirical Studies

Many other alternative functional forms are available for empirical production study. As with empirical demand estimation, the primary determinant of the form of function to use in the empirical model should depend on the relationship hypothesized by the researcher. Selection of the functional form on this basis is difficult, however, and in many instances several alternative model specifications must be fitted to the data to determine which form seems most representative of actual conditions.

SUMMARY

In this chapter we learned that a firm's production function is determined by the technological level of the plant and equipment it employs. It relates inputs to outputs, showing the maximum product obtainable from a given set of inputs.

Several important properties of production systems were examined, including the substitutability of inputs—a characteristic expressed by the marginal rate of substitution—and diminishing returns to factor inputs. It was demonstrated that the properties combine to delimit three stages of production. Input combinations located in Stages I and III are irrational in that they involve excessive proportions of one input factor and thereby reduce output below a level obtainable with lower input requirements. Therefore, only those input combinations found in Stage II, where the marginal products of all input factors are positive, need be analyzed to determine the optimal input proportions.

Adding prices to the analysis enabled us to specify the necessary conditions for optimality in input combination. The least-cost combination of inputs requires input proportions such that an additional dollar's worth of each input adds as much to total output as does a dollar's worth of any other input. Algebraically, this relationship is given by the expression:

$$\frac{MP_X}{P_X} = \frac{MP_Y}{P_Y}.$$

The question of returns to scale was also examined, and several methods of measuring this property were illustrated. Returns to scale in production plays a major role in determining industrial organization and market structures, topics examined in Chapters 10 and 12.

Empirical estimation of production functions frequently makes use of the statistical methods of regression analysis. While theoretical considerations indicate that cubic equations, with their greater generality, might be preferred for estimation purposes, it was shown that simpler functional forms are often quite adequate for estimation of demand relationships over the range of data available. In fact, the power function, or the Cobb-Douglas production function, is by far the most frequently encountered form in empirical work.

QUESTIONS

6-1 Using the total product curve illustrated below:
   a) Describe both geometrically and verbally the marginal product and the average product associated with Output Q_1.
   b) At what points along the curve will the marginal and the average products be maximized?
   c) How could you use the related marginal product curve to delineate the maximum quantity of input for Factor X that is not irrational, holding constant the amounts of all other inputs? Illustrate graphically.

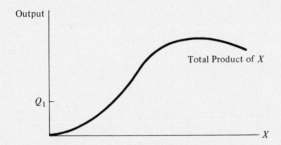

6-2 Given the isoquant diagram illustrated at the top of page 192, in which C^* and L^* indicate the optimal combination for producing Output Q^* as determined by a tangency between an isocost curve and an isoquant curve:
   a) What would be the effect of an increase in the relative productivity of labor in this production system on the isocost and the isoquant curves and on the optimal input combination?
   b) What would be the effect of a technological change which increased the productivity of capital on the curves and on the combination referred to in Part a?
   c) What would be the effect of a change that proportionally increases the effectiveness of both capital and labor simultaneously?

6-3 Using a diagram of isoquant and isocost curves, like those shown in Question 6-2, demonstrate that *both* relative input prices and factor productivity play roles in determining optimal input combinations.

6-4 Is the use of least cost input combinations a necessary condition for profit maximization? Is it a sufficient condition? Explain.

6-5 A labor economist discussing productivity once argued: "If you worked 2,000 hours last year at a $3.50 per hour wage rate and produced 10,000 widgets,

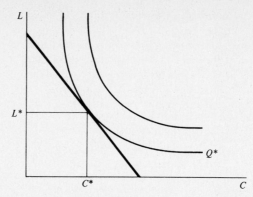

your output per hour was five widgets—total output divided by total hours worked. If you are averaging six widgets an hour this year, your productivity (output per hour) has gone up 20 percent. Assuming a widget sells for $2, the same as last year, and you still get paid $3.50 per hour, your employer's labor cost per widget has gone down from 70¢ to 58¢. He gets added profits on each widget, so he can afford to share his extra profits with his workers."

a)   Under what circumstances would this reasoning be correct?

b)   Is it possible to develop a case where such a productivity increase might *not* provide added profits to be shared with the labor factors? Explain.

PROBLEMS

6-1   You are given the cubic production function:

$$Q = bx + cx^2 - dx^3,$$

where $b = 0.2$, $c = 0.9$, $d = 0.005$, $Q =$ total product, and $x =$ input factor.

a)   Construct a table showing (1) total product (Q); (2) average product; and (3) marginal product for x values of 10, 20, 30, 40, 50, 60, 70, 80, 90, 100, 110, 120, 130, and 140 units of input. In order to compute the marginal product for each value of x, use the derivative of the production function as follows:

$$\text{Marginal Product} = \frac{dQ}{dx} = b + 2cx - 3dx^2.$$

In order to compute the average product for each value of x, use either the left or the right side of the average product formula:

$$\text{Average Product} = \frac{Q}{x} = b + cx - dx^2.$$

b)   Plot the curves of (1) total product, (2) average product, and (3) marginal product, using the vertical axis for output values and the horizontal axis for input values.

6-2   The following production table provides estimates of the maximum amounts of output possible with different combinations of two input factors, X and Y. (Assume that these are just illustrative points on a spectrum of continuous input combinations.)

Estimated Output per Day

5	66	95	116	134	150
Units 4	60	85	104	120	134
of X 3	52	73	90	104	116
Used 2	42	60	73	85	95
1	30	42	52	60	66
	1	2	3	4	5

Units of Y Used

a) Do the two inputs exhibit the characteristic of constant, increasing, or decreasing marginal rates of technical substitution? How do you know?

b) Assuming output sells for $2 per unit, complete the following tables:

X Fixed at 2 Units

Units of Y Used	Total Product of Y	Marginal Product of Y	Average Product of Y	Marginal Revenue Product of Y
1				
2				
3				
4				
5				

Y Fixed at 3 Units

Units of X Used	Total Product of X	Marginal Product of X	Average Product of X	Marginal Revenue Product of X
1				
2				
3				
4				
5				

c) Assume that the quantity of X is fixed at 2 units. If the output of this production system sells for \$2 and the cost of Y is \$25 a day, how many units of Y will be employed?

d) Assume that the company is currently producing 85 units of output per day, using 4 units of X and 2 units of Y. The daily cost per unit of X is \$1.50 and that of Y is also \$1.50. Would you recommend a change in the present input combination? Why or why not?

e) What is the nature of the returns to scale for this production system if the optimal input combination requires that $X = Y$?

6-3 Assume the case of a firm combining X and Y in such a way that the marginal product of X equals 10 while that of Y equals 8. Assume also that X costs \$2 a unit and Y costs \$2. Determine a better (why not necessarily the best?) combination of X and Y, maintaining the same level of output.

6-4 Determine whether the following production functions exhibit constant, increasing, or decreasing returns to scale:

a) $Q = aX^{1/6} Y^{1/8} L^{1/12} C^{15/24}$.
b) $Q = \frac{1}{2}x + 600y + 700z$.
c) $Q = \frac{1}{5}M + 600$.
d) $Q = bM_1 M_2 M_3 M_4$.
e) $Q = 4M_1 + 5M_2 + 3M_3 + 6M_4$.
f) $Q = bA_1{}^{1/4} A_2{}^{1/5} A_3{}^{1/6} A_4{}^{1/8}$.
g) $Q = \sqrt{aM_1{}^2 + bM_2{}^2 - cM_3{}^2 + dM_2 M_3}$.

6-5 Determine the degree of homogeneity and the returns to scale for the following homogeneous production functions:

a) $Q = 6M^{0.4} L^{0.2} Z^{0.3}$.
b) $Q = bX^p Y^q$.
c) $Q = 18X^{0.4} Y^{0.6} Z^{0.5} M^{0.3}$.
d) $Q = bM^2 + 3cMN + dL^2$.
e) $Q = \sqrt{2aM^2 + bM^2 - cM^2}$.

6-6 You are presented with the following production function:

$$Q = L^{3/4} \cdot C^{1/4}.$$

The function demonstrates constant returns to scale, since the sum of the exponents is equal to 1.

a) What is the optimal combination of L and C, given $P_c = \$10$, $P_L = \$20$.

b) Answer Part a for the production function $Q = L^{1/2} \cdot C^{1/2}$ given $P_c = \$10$, $P_L = \$5$.

c) Are the ratios you calculated in Parts a and b constant for all levels of output?

6-7 The Marpor Manufacturing Company's production function for its production scheduling department was found to be:

$$Q = f(x, y) = 4x^2 + 2xy + 3y^2,$$

where $Q =$ total output in terms of inventory orders, $x =$ number of computer-hours used, and $y =$ man-hours employed.

a) Determine the degree of homogeneity and the returns to scale in the above function.

b) Assume a weekly rate of use where $x = 40$ computer-hours and $y = 150$ man-hours. What will be the total product per week?

c) What will be the marginal product for computer-hours? For man-hours?

6-8 During legislative hearings on the energy crisis a spokesman for the paper and pulp industry in a northern Midwestern state has argued that a proposed reduction in energy inputs to the industry would result in approximately 9,000 workers losing their jobs. The short-run partial production function relating energy and labor to output in the industry is $Q = 2L^{.5}E^{.5}$ where L equals the units of labor employed (measured in thousands of employees) and E is the amount of energy used. Currently the industry, which receives 100 units of energy per production period, is employing 25,000 workers (measured as 25 units in the above production function). An average unit of output sells for $400, while employees receive a wage of $800 per period. The energy allocation scheme being considered would reduce the energy supplied to the paper and pulp industry to 64 units per production period.

The industry spokesman has just been asked by a legislator to show how he arrived at the employment reduction figure. Assume you are that spokesman and use your knowledge of production theory to develop an economically sound response.

6-9 *Productivity in Education: Issues in Defining and Measuring Output**

"I can't think of any other industry where the more experienced are less productive for more money," says Rexford Moon, vice-president of the Academy for Educational Development, Inc. Behind his statement lies the academic tradition that apportions the least teaching to the most prestigious professors.

The average class load has been decreasing over the past 15 years, making teaching "not a bad calling," says one professor. Joseph Garbarino, a Berkeley professor, says: "The way to get somebody you really want when you can't match salaries elsewhere is to offer him a reduced teaching load." The American Assn. of University Professors recommends six hours per week for professors in universities, nine hours in colleges, and 12 in community colleges. But some teachers may carry as little as four hours.

Educators, however, are quick to explain that class load and work load are not synonymous. Columbia Professor Walter Metzger says that a Nobel laureate earning $30,000, who works full-time with eight graduate students who pay a total of only $24,000 in tuition, "may not do much for the finances of the university, but does an immeasurable service for the nation." And, of course, he brings research and consulting contracts to the university. Princeton's Provost William Bowen maintains that "those that do get paid the most work the hardest—nights and weekends, too, like young pediatricians."

In a typical day recently, an associate professor of economics at Princeton reviewed a book, composed two PhD examinations, worked with students on a computer game, participated in examinations for masters' candidates, attended three committee meetings, and counseled a student who was failing. Along the way, he missed his lunch, and after dinner returned to the campus to work out a new program for the computer game. His class load: six hours a week. The emphasis on faculty-guided, independent student work also obscures the amount of time teachers really spend with students, and the American Council for Education's Logan Wilson says that "most aspects

* This material on productivity in education constitutes a small part of a *Business Week* article on the unionization of college faculties. The reader is referred to the original article for a fuller statement of the relationship between productivity and unionization. *See* "Unions Woo the College Faculties," *Business Week*, May 1, 1971, pp. 69-74. Reprinted from the May 1, 1971 issue of *Business Week* by special permission. © 1971 by McGraw-Hill, Inc.

of professorial work don't lend themselves to a quantitative evaluation—there is no per unit cost like an industrial model."

Nevertheless, Michigan and New York have set a regulated number of "student contact hours"—time spent in classroom and counseling. California has done the same thing by simply adding more students, but not more faculty. Kerry Smith, chief executive officer of the American Assn. for Higher Education, predicts this is doomed to fail because it is "artificial and arbitrary."

Allan Ostar, executive director of the American Assn. of State Colleges & Universities, feels that collective bargaining may promote "productivity clauses" like those in industrial unions. Bargainers would obtain a trade-off: higher salaries for more work by professors.

a) How would you define productivity for university faculty members?
b) Do you agree with Wilson's statement that "most aspects of professorial work don't lend themselves to a quantitative evaluation"? How might you go about measuring such productivity?
c) Do you agree with Moon's opening statement in the article? Think of this question in terms of your answers to Parts a and b; are they consistent with your answer to this question?
d) Would "productivity clauses" for professors as described in the article make sense economically? What problems do you see in implementing such clauses in actual practice?

SELECTED REFERENCES

Comitini, Salvatore, and David S. Huang. "A Study of Production and Factor Shares in the Halibut Fishing Industry," *Journal of Political Economy,* 1967, pp. 366-372.

Cookenboo, Leslie, Jr. *Crude Oil Pipe Lines and Competition in the Oil Industry.* Cambridge, Mass.: Harvard University Press, 1955.

Douglas, Paul H. "Are There Laws of Production?" *American Economic Review,* March 1948, pp. 1-41.

Heady, Earl O., and John L. Dillon. *Agricultural Production Functions.* Ames, Iowa: Iowa State University Press, 1961.

Johnston, J. "An Economic Study of the Production Decision," *Quarterly Journal of Economics,* 1961, pp. 234-261.

Stigler, George J. *The Theory of Price,* 3d ed. New York: Macmillan, 1966, Chapters 6 and 7.

Walters, A. A. "Production and Cost Functions: An Econometric Survey," *Econometrica,* January-April 1963, pp. 1-66.

APPENDIX: A Constrained Optimization Approach to Developing the Optimal Input Combination Relationships

It was noted in Chapter 6 that the determination of optimal input proportions could be viewed either as a problem of maximizing output for a given expenditure level or, alternatively, as a problem of minimizing the cost of producing a specified level of output. In this appendix we show how the Lagrangian technique for constrained optimization can be used to develop the optimal input proportion rule.

CONSTRAINED PRODUCTION MAXIMIZATION

Consider the problem of maximizing output from a production system described by the general equation:

$$Q = f(XY) \tag{6A-1}$$

subject to a budget constraint. The expenditure limitation can be expressed as:

$$E^* = P_X \cdot Y + P_Y \cdot Y, \tag{6A-2}$$

which states that the total expenditure on inputs, E^*, is equal to the price of input X, P_X, times the quantity of X employed, plus the price of Y, P_Y, times the quantity of that resource used in the production system. Equation 6A-2 can be rewritten in the form of a Lagrangian constraint, as developed in Chapter 2, as:

$$P_X \cdot X + P_Y \cdot Y - E^* = 0. \tag{6A-3}$$

The Lagrangian function for the maximization of the production function, Equation 6A-1, subject to the budget constraint expressed by Equation 6A-3 can then be written as:

$$\text{Max } L_Q = f(X, Y) - \lambda(P_X \cdot X + P_Y \cdot Y - E^*). \tag{6A-4}$$

Maximization of the constrained production function is accomplished by setting the partial derivatives of the Lagrangian expression taken with respect to X, Y, and λ equal to zero, and then solving the resultant system of equations. The partials of Equation 6A-4 are:

$$\frac{\partial L_Q}{\partial X} = \frac{\partial f(X, Y)}{\partial X} - \lambda P_X = 0 \tag{6A-5}$$

$$\frac{\partial L_Q}{\partial Y} = \frac{\partial f(X, Y)}{\partial Y} - \lambda P_Y = 0 \tag{6A-6}$$

$$\frac{\partial L_Q}{\partial \lambda} = -(P_X \cdot X + P_Y \cdot Y - E^*) = 0. \tag{6A-7}$$

Equating these three partial derivatives to zero results in a set of conditions that must be met for output maximization subject to the budget limit.

Note that the first terms in Equations 6A-5 and 6A-6 are the marginal products of X and Y respectively. That is, $\partial f(X, Y)/\partial X$ is $\partial Q/\partial X$, which by definition is the marginal product of X; and the same is true for $\partial f(X, Y)/\partial Y$. Thus, those two expressions can be rewritten as:

$$MP_X - \lambda P_X = 0$$

$$MP_Y - \gamma P_Y = 0,$$

or, alternatively, as:

$$MP_X = \lambda P_X \qquad (6A\text{-}8)$$

$$MP_Y = \lambda P_Y. \qquad (6A\text{-}9)$$

Now, the conditions required for constrained output maximization, expressed by Equations 6A-8 and 6A-9, are also expressed by the ratio of equations. Thus:

$$\frac{MP_X}{MP_Y} = \frac{\lambda P_X}{\lambda P_Y}. \qquad (6A\text{-}10)$$

Cancelling the lambdas in Equation 6A-10 results in the optimality conditions developed in the chapter:

$$\frac{MP_X}{MP_Y} = \frac{P_X}{P_Y}. \qquad (6A\text{-}11)$$

For maximum production, given a fixed expenditure level, the input factors must be combined in such a way that the ratio of their marginal products is equal to the ratio of their prices. Alternatively, transposing in Equation 6A-11 to derive the expression:

$$\frac{MP_X}{P_X} = \frac{MP_Y}{P_Y},$$

we see that optimal input proportions require that the ratio of marginal product to price for all input factors must be equal.

CONSTRAINED COST MINIMIZATION

The relationship developed above is also derivable from the problem of minimizing the cost of producing a given quantity of output. In this case the constrained-optimization problem is developed as follows. The constraint states that some level of output, Q^*, must be produced from the production system described by the function $Q = f(XY)$. Written in the standard Lagrangian format the constraint is $f(XY) - Q^* = 0$. The cost, or expenditure, function is given as $E = P_X \cdot X + P_Y \cdot Y$. The Lagrangian function for the constrained cost minimization problem, then, is:

$$L_E = P_X \cdot X + P_Y \cdot Y - \lambda(f(XY) - Q^*). \qquad (6A\text{-}12)$$

Again, as shown above, the conditions for constrained cost minimization are provided by the partial derivatives of Equation 6A-12.

$$\frac{\partial L_E}{\partial X} = P_X - \lambda \frac{\partial (fX, Y)}{\partial X} = 0 \qquad (6A-13)$$

$$\frac{\partial L_E}{\partial Y} = P_Y - \lambda \frac{\partial (fX, Y)}{\partial Y} = 0 \qquad (6A-14)$$

$$\frac{\partial L_E}{\partial \lambda} = - (f(X, Y) - Q^*) = 0. \qquad (6A-15)$$

Notice that the last terms on the left-hand side in Equations 6A-13 and 6A-14 are the marginal products of X and Y respectively, so those expressions can be rewritten as:

$$P_X - \lambda MP_X = 0$$
$$P_Y - \lambda MP_Y = 0,$$

or, alternatively, as:

$$P_X = \lambda MP_X \qquad (6A-16)$$
$$P_Y = \lambda MP_Y. \qquad (6A-17)$$

Taking the ratio of Equation 6A-16 to Equation 6A-17 and cancelling the lambdas again produces the basic input optimality relationship:

$$\frac{P_X}{P_Y} = \frac{MP_X}{MP_Y}.$$

PROBLEM

6A-1 Assume a firm produces its product in a system described in the following production function and price data:

$$Q = 2X + 3Y + 6XY$$
$$P_X = \$4$$
$$P_Y = \$6.$$

Here, X and Y are two variable input factors employed in the production of Q.
a) What are the optimal input proportions for X and Y in this production system? Is this combination constant irrespective of the output level?
b) It is possible to express the cost function associated with the use of X and Y in the production of Q as: Cost $= P_X \cdot X + P_Y \cdot Y$, or Cost $= \$4X + \$6Y$. Use the Lagrangian technique to determine the maximum output the firm can produce operating under a \$1,000 budget constraint for X and Y. Show that the inputs used to produce that output meet the optimality conditions derived in Part a.
c) What is the incremental output that could be obtained from an additional expenditure of \$1?

d) Assume that the firm is interested in minimizing the cost of producing 50,000 units of output. Use the Lagrangian method to determine what optimal quantities of X and Y to employ. What will the cost of producing that output be? How would you interpret λ, the Lagrangian multiplier, in this problem?

CHAPTER 7

Linear
Programming

In the preceding chapter we developed the basic elements of production theory, first showing the optimal conditions for combining inputs, then analyzing the conditions under which returns to scale are increasing, are decreasing, or are constant. In this chapter we will discuss linear programming, a most important analytical technique, and show how it can be used to reach optimal production decisions, as well as how it is applied to other aspects of managerial economics.[1]

APPLICATIONS OF LINEAR PROGRAMMING

Linear programming is used to solve maximization and minimization problems in which constraints are imposed on the decision maker. Many prob-

[1] Linear programming is only one of a series of analytical techniques, known collectively as *mathematical programming,* which are used to solve constrained optimization problems. Partly because linear programming has been developed much more highly, and has been used much more frequently, than nonlinear and other programming techniques, and partly because the nonlinear techniques are too complex to warrant including them in an introductory textbook, we restrict our discussion to linear programming.

lems of constrained optimization arise in business and economics. For example, an oil company has a specified quantity of crude oil and a fixed refinery capacity. It can produce gasoline of different octane ratings, diesel fuel, heating oil, kerosene, or lubricants. Given its crude oil supplies and refinery capacity, what mix of outputs should it produce? Integrated forest products companies face a similar problem. Because they have a limited supply of logs and limited mill capacity, their problem is to determine the optimum output mix of lumber, plywood, paper, and other wood products.

A somewhat different problem faced by many firms and government agencies relates to scheduling of deliveries. Goods must be delivered to customers. What is the least-cost method of routing delivery trucks?

Still another case involves determining the best way of producing a given output. A firm owns two plants that can be used to produce its products. The plants employ somewhat different technologies, so their cost functions are different. How should production be allocated between the two plants to minimize the total cost of production, subject to these constraints: (1) both plants must, because of a union contract, operate at least thirty hours a week and (2) at least 100,000 units of output must be produced each week to satisfy the firm's supply contracts.

In marketing, a frequently encountered issue is: What is the optimal advertising mix among various media, where optimal is defined as that mix which minimizes the cost of reaching a specified number of potential customers with certain characteristics of age, income, education, and other factors?

In finance, firms may have a large number of investment opportunities but be limited in the funds available for investment. What set of projects will maximize the value of new long-term investments, subject to the constraint that the total capital budget does not exceed the specified maximum? Moreover, firms must hold balances of cash, a nonearning asset. What is the minimum amount of cash that can be held, subject to the constraint that the probability of running short of cash must be kept below some minimum value?

From these examples it should be clear that linear programming is useful in a broad range of constrained maximization and minimization problems. It is indeed a powerful technique, one which promises to be applied to business problems with ever greater frequency in future years.

RELATIONSHIP OF LINEAR PROGRAMMING TO THE LAGRANGIAN TECHNIQUE

In Chapter 2 we described the Lagrangian-multiplier technique for solving constrained optimization problems. Linear programming is somewhat more complex and more difficult to apply than the Lagrangian method. Accordingly, one might question the reason for developing linear programming.

Why not just use the Lagrangian technique for solving constrained optimization problems?

The answer is that linear programming can handle a class of problems that cannot be solved by the Lagrangian technique. Specifically, with the Lagrangian method, the constraints must be stated in the form of equalities and must be met *exactly*. For example, a Lagrangian problem might be to minimize cost in a production system subject to the constraint that *exactly* 40 hours of machine time be used. The corresponding linear programming problem would be to minimize costs subject to the constraint that *no more than* 40 hours of time be used. In other words, in the Lagrangian system the constraints must be *equalities* (machine-time use = 40 hours); in linear programming the constraints may be *inequalities* (machine-time ≤ 40 hours).

Since most constraints in business problems are in fact inequalities rather than equalities, it is readily apparent why linear programming, not Lagrangian calculus, is more useful for practical applications in business.

ASSUMPTION OF LINEARITY

Linear programming is more general than the Lagrangian technique in that it permits inequalities in the constraints, but it is also more restrictive in that all relationships are assumed to be linear. What relationships are involved, and how important is the assumption of linearity likely to be?

The basic relationship involved in linear programming problems typically encountered in business and economics revolve around revenue functions, cost functions, and their composite, the profit function. Each of these must be linear; that is, as output increases, revenues, costs, and profits must increase linearly. For revenues to increase linearly with output, product prices must be constant. For costs to rise linearly with output, two conditions are required: (1) the firm's production function must be linear (that is, it must be homogeneous of degree 1), meaning that returns to scale are constant; and (2) input prices must be constant. Constant input prices, when coupled with a linear production function, result in a linear total cost function.[2]

Under what conditions are product and factor prices likely to be constant? In other words, when can a firm buy unlimited quantities of its inputs, and sell unlimited amounts of its products, without having to change prices? The answer is under conditions of pure competition. Does this mean that linear programming is applicable only for purely competitive industries and, further, only for competitive industries where returns to scale are constant? The answer is "No," because linear programming is used for decision making over limited output ranges. Because input and product prices are approxi-

[2] The relationship between production and cost functions when input prices are constant is developed more fully in Chapter 8.

mately constant over these ranges, the profit function can be approximated by a linear relationship.

To illustrate, if an oil company is deciding the optimal output mix for a refinery with a capacity of 50,000 barrels a day, it may be perfectly valid to assume that crude oil costs $10 a barrel, regardless of how much is purchased, and that products can be sold at constant prices, regardless of the quantities offered. The firm may have to pay more for crude oil and may have to sell its output at lower prices if it tries to expand the refinery by a factor of 10, but within the range of feasible outputs (up to 50,000 barrels a day) prices are approximately constant. Further, up to its capacity limits, it is reasonable to expect that a doubling of crude oil inputs leads to a doubling of output; therefore, returns to scale are constant. Roughly the same conditions hold for forest-product companies, office-equipment manufacturers, and automobile producers.

We see, then, that in many instances the linearity assumptions are valid. Further, in many more cases, when the assumption is not completely valid, linear approximations will not seriously distort the analysis.

LINEAR PROGRAMMING AND PRODUCTION PLANNING: ONE PRODUCT

Although linear programming has been applied in almost all aspects of business management, it has been developed most fully and is used most frequently in production decisions. Often the decision problem is to determine the least-cost combination of inputs needed to produce a particular product. In other cases, the problem may be concerned with obtaining the maximum level of output from a fixed quantity of resources. Both problems can be readily solved by linear programming. To see this more clearly, we start with a simple case and examine the problem faced by a firm that can use two inputs in various combinations to produce a single product. Then, in later sections, we examine more realistic but necessarily more complex cases.

Production Processes

Assume that a firm produces a single product, Q, using two inputs, L and K, which might stand for labor and capital. Further, instead of the possibility of continuous substitution between L and K, as was hypothesized in the preceding chapter, assume that there are only four possible input combinations with which the firm can produce Q. In other words, four different production processes are available to the firm for making Q, each of which uses a different but fixed combination of the two inputs, L and K.[3]

---

[3] In modern industry, this is an entirely reasonable assumption, much more reasonable than continuous substitution. The four "production processes" discussed here, for example, might be thought of as being four different plants, each with its own fixed asset configuration and each requiring a specific amount of labor to operate the equipment.

The four production processes are illustrated in Figure 7-1. Process A requires the combination of 15 units of L and 1 unit of K for each unit of Q produced. Process B uses 10 units of L and 2 units of K for each unit of output; while processes C and D use 7.5 units of L with 3 units of K, and 5 units of L with 5 units of K, respectively, for each unit of Q produced. The four production processes are illustrated as rays in the figure. Each point along the production ray for Process A combines L and K in the ratio 15 L to 1 K; and Process Rays B, C, and D are developed in the same way. Each point along a single production ray combines the two inputs in a fixed ratio, with the ratios differing from one production process to another.[4]

Figure 7-1 Production Process Rays in Linear Programming

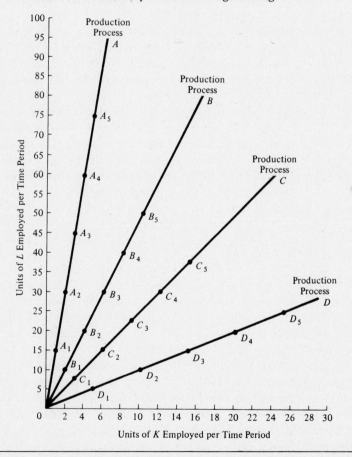

---

[4] If we assume that L and K represent labor and capital inputs, we can view the four production processes as being different plants employing different production techniques. Process A, for example, is very labor intensive in relation to the other production systems; while B, C, and D are based on increasingly capital-intensive technologies.

Examining Process A, we see that Point A_1 indicates the combination of L and K required to produce 1 unit of output using that production system. Doubling the quantities of both L and K doubles the quantity of Q produced; this is indicated by the distance moved along Ray A from A_1 to A_2. In other words, the line segment $0A_2$ is exactly twice the length of line segment $0A_1$, and thus represents twice as much output. Further, along Production Process Ray A, the distance $0A_1 = A_1A_2 = A_2A_3 = A_3A_4 = A_4A_5$. Each of these line segments indicates the addition of 1 unit of output, using increased quantities of L and K in the fixed ratio of 15 to 1.

Output along the ray increases proportionately with increases in the input factors. Thus, if each input is doubled, output is doubled; or if inputs are increased by a factor of 10, output increases in the same proportion. This follows from the linearity assumption noted above: Each production process must exhibit constant returns to scale.

Output is measured in the same way along the other three production process rays in Figure 7-1. For example, the point labeled C_1 indicates the combination of L and K required to produce 1 unit of Q using Process C. The production of 2 units of Q by that process requires the combination of L and K indicated at Point C_2, and the same is true for Points C_3, C_4, and C_5. Note that while the production of additional units by Process C is indicated by line segments of equal length, just as for Process A, the line segments are of different lengths between the various production systems. That is, although each production process exhibits constant returns to scale, allowing us to determine output quantities by measuring the length of the process ray in question, equal distances along *different* process rays do *not* ordinarily indicate equal output quantities.

Production Isoquants

Joining points of equal output on the four production process rays provides us with a set of isoquant curves, as illustrated in Figure 7-2, where isoquants for $Q = 1, 2, 3, 4$, and 5 are shown. These curves have precisely the same interpretation as the isoquants developed in the preceding chapter. They represent all possible combinations of input factors L and K that can be used to produce a given quantity of output.

The production isoquants in linear programming are composed of linear segments connecting the various production processes, and the segments of the various isoquants are always parallel to one another. For example, line segment A_1B_1 is parallel to segment A_2B_2; similarly, the isoquant segment B_3C_3 is parallel to B_2C_2.

The points along each segment of an isoquant between two process rays represent a combination of output from each of the two adjoining production processes. Consider Point X in Figure 7-2, which represents production of a total of 4 units of Q using 25 units of L and 16 units of K. None

***Figure* 7-2**   Production Isoquants in Linear Programming

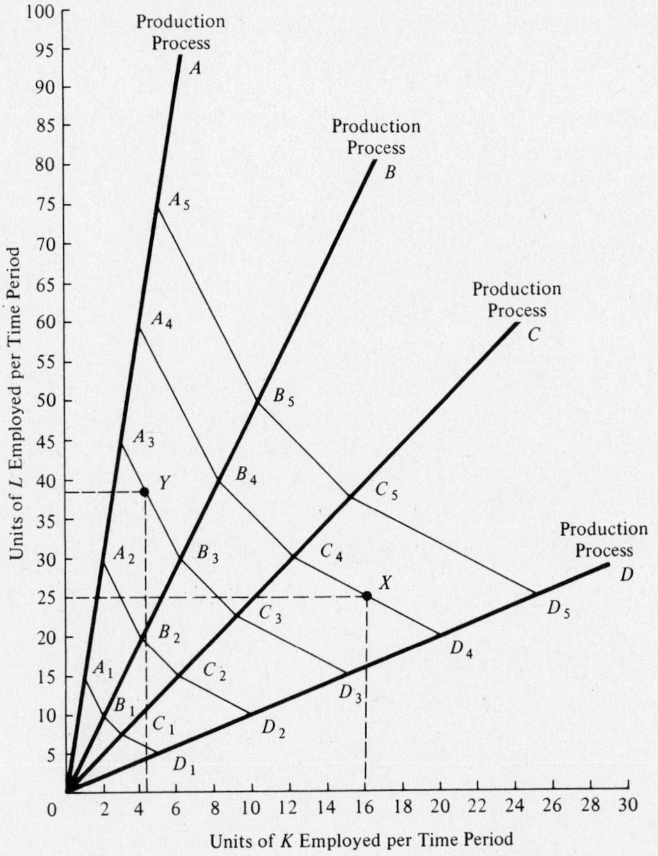

of the available production processes can be used to manufacture Q using L and K in the ratio 25 to 16, but that combination is possible by producing part of the output with Process C and part with Process D. In this case, 2 units of Q can be produced using Process C and 2 units using Process D. Production of 2 units of Q with Process C utilizes 15 units of L and 6 units of K. For the production of 2 units of Q with Process D, 10 units each of L and K are necessary. Thus, although no single production system is available with which the firm can produce 4 units of Q using 25 units of L and 16 units of K, Processes C and D together can produce in that combination.

All points lying on the production isoquant segments can be interpreted in a similar manner. Each point represents a linear combination of output using the production process systems which bound the particular segment. Point Y in Figure 7-2 provides another illustration of this. At Y,

3 units of Q are being produced, using a total of 38.5 units of L and 4.3 units of K.[5] That input/output combination is possible through a linear combination of Processes A and B. The reader can verify from Figure 7-2 that producing 1.7 units of Q using Process A and 1.3 units with Process B requires 38.5 units of L and 4.3 units of K.[6]

One method of determining the quantity to be produced by each production process at varying points along an isoquant is through the construction of parallelograms. This is shown in Figure 7-3, where the process combinations required to produce at Points X and Y are illustrated. Consider, first, production at Point X. A line through Point X parallel to Production Process Ray C intersects Process Ray D at Point D_2. This intersection indicates that the quantity of Q to be produced using Process D is 2 units. Notice also that this line completes the parallelogram $C_4XD_2C_2$. Therefore, segment C_2C_4 is equal in length to segment XD_2, which indicates that 2 units of Q will also be produced using Process C. In other words, the line segment $0D_2$ indicates how much of Q should be produced by Process D, while the line D_2X indicates the amount that should be produced by Process C.

The appropriate process combination for operating at Point Y can be determined in the same way. A line through Point Y parallel to Process Ray B intersects Process Ray A at the point A', indicating that 1.7 units of output are produced using Process A and 1.3 units with Process B. These combined three units of output require 38.5 units of L and 4.3 units of K.[7]

Least-cost Input Combinations

Adding isocost curves to the set of isoquants permits one to determine least-cost input combinations for the production of Product Q. This is shown in

---

[5] Another assumption of linear programming is that fractional variables are permissible. In most applications this assumption is not important. For example, in the present illustration we would probably be talking about thousands of man- and machine-hours and thousands of units of output. The solution value might call for $L = 39,640.5$. Rounding to 39,640 would not materially alter the final outcome.

In some cases, however, where inputs are large—whole plants, for example—the fact that linear programming assumes divisible variables is important. In such cases linear programming as described herein may be inappropriate, and a more complex technique, integer programming, may be required.

[6] This point can also be seen algebraically. To produce 1 unit of Q by Process A requires 15 units of L and 1 unit of K. Therefore, to produce 1.7 units of Q requires 25.5 (1.7×15) units of L and 1.7 (1.7×1) units of K. To produce a single unit of Q by Process B requires 10 units of L and 2 units of K, so 1.3 units of Q requires 13 (10×1.3) units of L and 2.6 (2×1.3) units of K. Thus, Point Y calls for the production of 3 units of Q in total, 1.7 units by Process A and 1.3 units by Process B, using a total of 38.5 units of L and 4.3 units of K.

[7] The reader can quickly verify from Figure 7-3 that it does not matter to which production process the line we construct is parallel—the resulting output quantities from each process are the same. For example, if we had constructed a line through Point Y parallel to Process A, it would have intersected Process B at Point B', indicating that 1.3 units of Q must be produced using Process B and that the remaining 1.7 units of Q would be produced using Process A.

Figure 7-3   Process Combinations along Production Isoquants

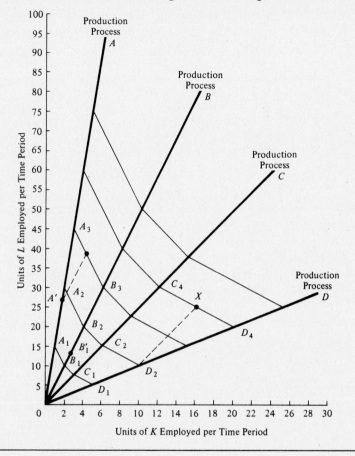

Figure 7-4, under the assumption that each unit of L costs $3 and each unit of K costs $10. The isocost curve illustrated indicates a total expenditure of $150.

The tangency between the isocost curve and the isoquant curve for $Q = 3$, at Point B_3, indicates that Production Process B, which combines the inputs L and K in the ratio 5 to 1, is the least-cost method of producing Q. For any expenditure level, production is maximized by using Process B, or, alternatively, Production Process B is the least-cost method for producing any quantity of Q, given the assumed prices for L and K.

Optimal Input Combinations with Limited Resources
Frequently, firms are faced with limited inputs during a production period and because of this may find it optimal to use inputs in proportions other than the least-cost combination. Examples of such constraints on resources

***Figure* 7-4**   Determination of Least-cost Production Process

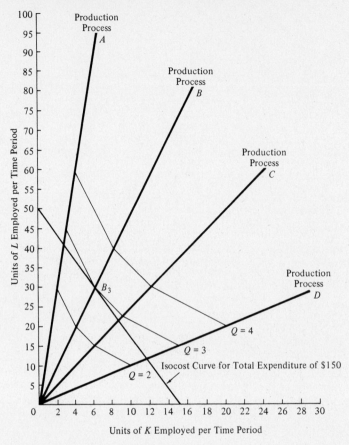

include limitations on the man-hours of skilled labor available, shortages of pieces of a particular type of equipment, insufficient raw materials, limited warehouse space, and other factors. In these cases the linear programming problem must be stated in terms of the physical constraints on inputs rather than in terms of the constraints on total expenditures.

To illustrate, consider the effect of limits on the quantities of L and K available in our illustrative case. Specifically, assume (1) that only 20 units of L and 11 units of K are available during each production period, and (2) that the firm seeks to maximize the output of Q. These constraints are shown in Figure 7-5. The horizontal line drawn at $L = 20$ indicates the upper limit on the quantity of L that can be employed during any production period; the vertical line at $K = 11$ indicates a similar limit on the quantity of K.

We can determine the production possibilities for this problem by

Figure 7-5   Optimal Input Combination with Limited Resources

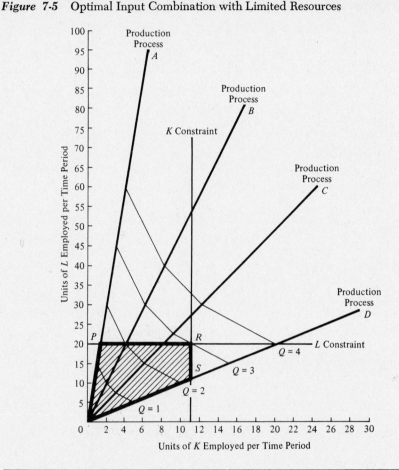

noting that, in addition to the limitations on the inputs L and K, the firm must operate within the area bounded by the Production Process Rays A and D. In other words, the firm is unable to combine L and K in ratios that lie either above Production Process Ray A or below Process Ray D. There are no combinations of production systems which result in those input ratios. Thus, we see that combining the production possibilities with the input constraints restricts the firm to operations within the shaded area $0PRS$ in Figure 7-5. This area is known as the *feasible space* in the programming problem. Any point within the space combines L and K in a technically feasible ratio, and availability limits on L and K are not exceeded.

Since the firm is trying to maximize the production of Q, subject to constraints on the use of L and K, it should operate at that point in the feasible space which touches the highest possible isoquant. This is Point R

in Figure 7-5, where $Q = 3$. The reader should be able to verify through the parallelogram method that at Point R the firm produces 1 unit of Q with Process D and 2 units with Process C.

LINEAR PROGRAMMING AND PRODUCTION PLANNING: MULTIPLE PRODUCTS

Most production decisions, as well as decisions in other areas, are considerably more complex than the preceding example. Accordingly, we must expand our discussion, moving first into the problem of the optimal output mix for a multiproduct firm facing restrictions on productive facilities and on other inputs. This problem, which is precisely the one faced by oil refineries, cereal-processing firms, and forest-products companies, among others, is readily solved by linear programming, as the following example reveals.

Consider a firm that produces two products, X and Y, and uses three inputs, A, B, and C. To maximize its total profits, the firm must determine the optimal quantities of each product to produce, subject to the constraints imposed by limitations on input availability.[8]

Specification of the Objective Function
We assume that the firm wishes to maximize total profits from the two products, X and Y, during each time period. If per-unit profit contribution, the excess of price over average variable cost, is \$12 for Product X and \$9 for Product Y, we can write the objective function as:

Maximize

$$\pi = 12Q_X + 9Q_Y. \tag{7-1}$$

Here Q_X and Q_Y represent the quantities of each product produced. The per-unit profit contribution of X times the units of X produced and sold, plus the unit contribution of Y times Q_Y, is the total profit contribution, π, earned by the firm. It is this total profit contribution that the firm wishes to maximize, for by maximizing profit contribution the firm also maximizes its net profit.

Specification of the Constraint Equations
Table 7-1, which specifies the available quantities of each input, as well as their usage in the production of X and Y, provides all the information necessary to construct the constraint relationships for this problem.

---

[8] In the typical linear programming problem we seek to maximize "profit contribution," defined as total revenue minus the *variable cost* of production. Fixed costs must be subtracted from the profit contribution to determine net profits. However, since fixed costs are constant, regardless of how much or how little output is produced, maximizing profit contribution is tantamount to maximizing profit, and the output mix that maximizes profit contribution also maximizes net profit. This concept of profit contribution is developed more fully in Chapter 9.

Table 7-1   Inputs Available for Production of X and Y

Input	Quantity Available per Time Period	Quantity Required per Unit of Output	
		X	Y
A	32	4	2
B	10	1	1
C	21	0	3

From the table we see that 32 units of Input A are available in each period, and that 4 units of A are required in the production of each unit of X, while 2 units of A are necessary to produce 1 unit of Y.

Since 4 units of A are required for the production of a single unit of X, the total amount of A used to manufacture X can be written as $4Q_X$. Similarly, 2 units of A are required to produce each unit of Y, so $2Q_Y$ represents the total quantity of A used in the production of Product Y. Summing the quantities of A used in the production of X and Y provides an expression for the total usage of A, and since this total cannot exceed the 32 units available, we can write the constraint condition for Input A as:

$$4Q_X + 2Q_Y \le 32. \tag{7-2}$$

The constraint for Input B can be determined in a like manner. One unit of Input B is necessary for the production of each unit of either X or Y, so the total amount of B that will be expended is $1Q_X + 1Q_Y$. The maximum quantity of B available for production in each time period is 10 units; thus, the constraint requirement associated with Input B is:

$$1Q_X + 1Q_Y \le 10. \tag{7-3}$$

Finally, there is the constraint relationship for Input C, which is used only in the production of Y. Each unit of Y requires an input of 3 units of C, and 21 units of Input C are available. Total usage of C, then, is given by the expression $3Q_Y$, and the constraint can be written as:

$$3Q_Y \le 21. \tag{7-4}$$

Constraint equations play major roles in linear programming. One further concept must be introduced, however, before we can completely specify the linear programming problem.

Nonnegativity Requirement

Because linear programming is nothing more than a mathematical tool for solving constrained optimization problems, nothing in the technique itself insures that an answer will "make sense." For example, in a production problem, for some very unprofitable product the optimal output level may be a *negative* quantity, clearly an impossible solution. Likewise, in a distribution problem, an "optimal" solution might include negative shipments from one point to another, again an impossible act.

To prevent such nonsense results, we must include a nonnegativity requirement. This is merely a statement that all variables in the problem must be equal to, or greater than, zero. Thus, for the production problem we are examining, we must add the expressions:

$$Q_X \geq 0$$

and

$$Q_Y \geq 0.$$

GRAPHIC SPECIFICATION AND SOLUTION OF THE LINEAR PROGRAMMING PROBLEM

Having specified all the component parts of the firm's linear programming problem, we first examine this problem graphically, then analyze it algebraically. Let us begin by restating the decision problem in terms of the system of expressions for the objective function and input constraints. The firm wishes to maximize its total profit contribution, π, subject to constraints imposed by limitations on its resources. This can be expressed as:

Maximize

$$\pi = 12Q_X + 9Q_Y, \tag{7-1}$$

subject to the following constraints:

$$\text{Input } A: \quad 4Q_X + 2Q_Y \leq 32, \tag{7-2}$$

$$\text{Input } B: \quad 1Q_X + 1Q_Y \leq 10, \tag{7-3}$$

$$\text{Input } C: \qquad\;\; 3Q_Y \leq 21, \tag{7-4}$$

where

$$Q_X \geq 0 \text{ and } Q_Y \geq 0.$$

Determining the Feasible Space

Figure 7-6 is a graph of the constraint equation for Input A, $4Q_X + 2Q_Y = 32$, which indicates the maximum quantities of X and Y that can be produced, given the limitation on the availability of Input A. A maximum of 16 units of Y can be produced if no X is manufactured; 8 units of X can be produced if the output of Y is zero. Any point along the line connecting these two outputs represents the maximum combination of X and Y that can be produced with no more than 32 units of A.

This constraint equation divides the XY plane into two half-spaces. Every point lying on the line or to the left of it satisfies the constraint ex-

Figure 7-6 Constraint Imposed by Limitations in Input *A*

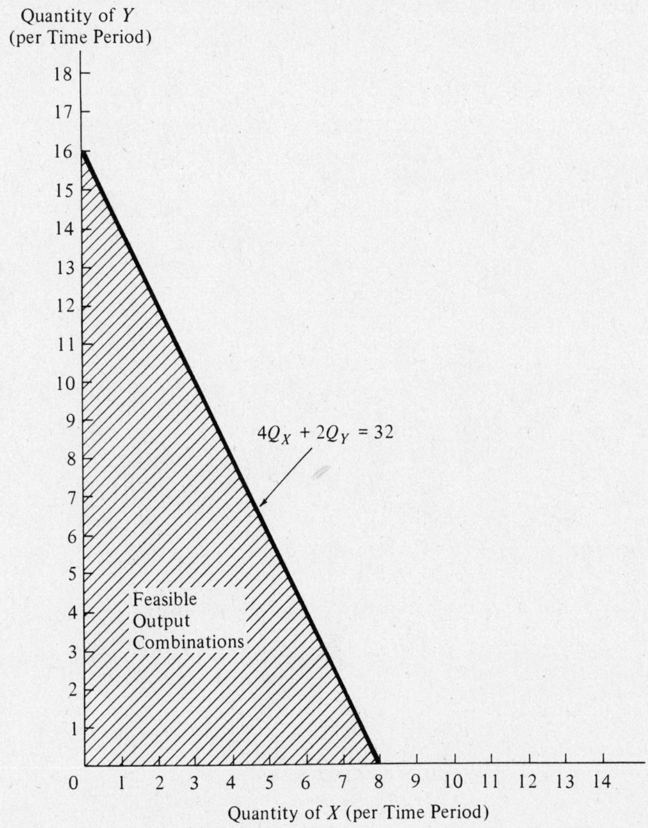

pressed by the equation $4Q_X + 2Q_Y \leq 32$; every point to the right of the line violates that expression. Thus, only points on the constraint line or to the left of it can be in the feasible space. The shaded area of Figure 7-6 represents the feasible area as delimited by the constraint on Input *A*.[9]

In Figure 7-7 we have further limited the feasible space by adding the constraints for Inputs *B* and *C*. The constraint on Input *B* can be expressed as $Q_X + Q_Y = 10$. Thus, if no *Y* is produced, a maximum of 10 units of *X* can be produced; if output of *X* is zero, 10 units of *Y* can be manufactured. All combinations of *X* and *Y* lying on, or to the left of, the line connecting these two points are feasible with respect to utilization of Input *B*.

[9] Although the half-space in the *XY* plane which satisfies the constraint conditions on Input *A* extends into the second, third, and fourth quadrants, only in the first are the nonnegativity requirements on the variables Q_X and Q_Y satisfied. Therefore, we can restrict the feasible space to those points in the first quadrant which satisfy the constraint conditions imposed by input restrictions.

Figure 7-7 Feasible Space

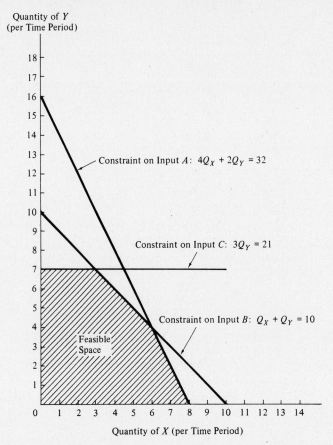

Quantity of Y
(per Time Period)

Constraint on Input A: $4Q_X + 2Q_Y = 32$

Constraint on Input C: $3Q_Y = 21$

Constraint on Input B: $Q_X + Q_Y = 10$

Feasible
Space

Quantity of X (per Time Period)

The horizontal line at $Q_Y = 7$ in Figure 7-7 represents the constraint imposed by Input C. Since C is used only in the production of Y, it does not constrain the production of X at all. Seven units of Y, however, are the maximum quantity that can be produced with the 21 units of C available.

The three input constraints, together with the nonnegativity requirement, completely delimit the feasible space of our linear programming problem, which is the shaded area of Figure 7-7. Only those points within this area meet all the constraints.

Graphing the Objective Function

The objective function in our example, $\pi = 12Q_X + 9Q_Y$, can be graphed in the $Q_X Q_Y$ space as a series of isoprofit curves. This is illustrated in Figure 7-8, where isoprofit curves for $36, $72, $108, and $144 are shown. Each isoprofit curve illustrates all possible combinations of X and Y that result in

Figure 7-8   Isoprofit Contribution Curves

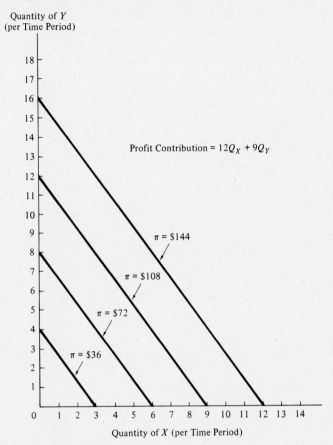

a constant total profit. For example, the isoprofit curve labeled $\pi = \$36$ is the locus of all points that satisfy the equation $\pi = 36 = 12Q_x + 9Q_Y$. Alternatively stated, each *combination* of X and Y lying along that curve results in a total profit of $36. Similarly, all output combinations along the $\pi = \$72$ curve satisfy the equation $72 = 12Q_x + 9Q_Y$ and thus provide a total profit contribution of $72. It is clear from Figure 7-8 that the isoprofit curves are a series of parallel lines which take on higher values as we move upward and to the right.

Isoprofit curves are identical in form to the isocost curves developed in Chapter 6. Here, the profit function $\pi = aQ_x + bQ_Y$, where a and b are the profit contributions of products X and Y respectively, is solved for Q_Y, resulting in an equation of the form:

$$Q_Y = \frac{\pi}{b} - \frac{a}{b} Q_x.$$

Given the individual profit contributions, a and b, the Q_Y intercept is determined by the profit level of the isoprofit curve, while the slope is given by the relative profitabilities of the products. Since the relative profitability of the products is unaffected by the output level, isoprofit curves in a linear-programming problem will always be a series of parallel lines. In the example, all the isoprofit curves have a slope of $-12/9$, or -1.33.

Graphic Solution of the Linear-programming Problem

Since the firm's objective is to maximize total profit, it should operate on the highest isoprofit curve obtainable. Combining the feasible space limitations shown in Figure 7-7 with the family of isoprofit curves from Figure 7-8 allows us to obtain the graphic solution to our linear-programming problem. The combined graph is illustrated in Figure 7-9.

Point Z in the figure indicates the solution to the problem. Here, the

Figure 7-9 Graphic Solution to the Linear-programming Problem

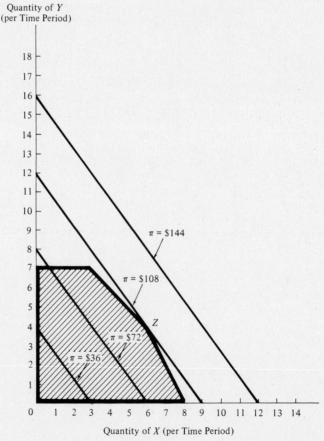

firm produces 6 units of X and 4 units of Y, and the total profit is \$108 [$(12 \times 6) + (9 \times 4)$], which is the maximum available under the conditions stated in the problem. No other point within the feasible space touches as high an isoprofit curve.

Notice that the optimal solution to the linear-programming problem occurs at a corner of the feasible space. This is not a chance result; rather it is a feature of the linearity assumptions underlying the linear-programming technique. When the objective function and all constraint relations are specified in linear form, there must be constant returns to scale. Because input and output prices do not change as production expands, it will always prove optimal to move as far as possible in the direction of higher outputs, provided that sales prices exceed variable costs per unit. This means that the firm will always move to a point where some capacity limit is reached; that is, to a boundary of the feasible space.

A final step is necessary to show that an optimal solution to any linear-programming problem always lies at a corner of the feasible space. Since all the relationships in a linear-programming problem must be linear by definition, every boundary of the feasible space is linear. Furthermore, the objective function is linear. Thus, the constrained optimization of the objective function takes place either at a corner of the feasible space, as in Figure 7-9, or at one boundary face, as is illustrated by Figure 7-10.

Figure 7-10 Graphic Solution of a Linear-programming Problem where the Objective Function Coincides with a Boundary of the Feasible Space

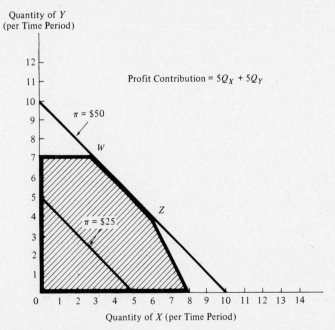

In Figure 7-10 we have modified the linear-programming example by assuming that each unit of either X or Y produced yields a profit of $5. In this case, the optimal solution to the problem includes any of the combinations of X and Y found along the line segment WZ, since all these combinations are feasible and all result in a total profit of $50. If all points along the line WZ provide optimal combinations of output, the combinations found at corners W and Z are also optimal. That is, since the firm is indifferent whether it produces the combination of X and Y indicated at Point W or at Point Z, or at any point between them, either corner location provides an optimal solution to the production problem. Thus, even when the highest obtainable isoprofit curve lies along a bounding face of the feasible space, it is possible to achieve an optimal solution to the problem at a corner of the feasible space.

From this result it follows that in linear-programming problems we can limit our analysis to just the corners of the feasible space. In other words, we can ignore the infinite number of points lying within the feasible space and concentrate our efforts solely on the corner solutions. This greatly reduces the computations necessary to solve linear-programming problems that are too large to solve by graphic methods.

ALGEBRAIC SPECIFICATION AND SOLUTION OF A LINEAR-PROGRAMMING PROBLEM

The graphic technique described above is useful to illustrate the nature of linear programming, but it can be applied only in the two-output case. Since most linear-programming problems contain far too many variables and constraints to allow solution by graphic analysis, we must use algebraic methods. These algebraic techniques are especially valuable in that they permit us to solve large, complex linear-programming problems on computers, and this greatly extends the usefulness of linear programming.

Slack Variables

In order to specify a linear-programming problem algebraically we must introduce one additional concept, that of *slack variables*. These variables are added to a linear-programming problem to account for the amount of any input that is *unused* at a solution point. One slack variable is introduced for each constraint in the problem. In our illustrative problem, the firm is faced with capacity constraints on Input Factors A, B, and C, so the algebraic specification of the problem contains three slack variables: S_A, indicating the units of Input A that are not used in any given solution; S_B, representing unused units of B; and S_C, which measures the unused units of C.

The introduction of these slack variables allows us to write each constraint relationship as an equation rather than as an inequality. Thus, the constraint on Input A, $4Q_X + 2Q_Y \leq 32$, can be written as:

$$4Q_X + 2Q_Y + S_A = 32. \tag{7-5}$$

Here $S_A = 32 - 4Q_X - 2Q_Y$, which is the amount of Input A not used in the production of X or Y. Similar equality constraints can be specified for Inputs B and C. Specifically, the equality form of the constraint on Input B is:

$$1Q_X + 1Q_Y + S_B = 10, \tag{7-6}$$

while for C the constraint equation is:

$$3Q_Y + S_C = 21. \tag{7-7}$$

Note that the slack variables not only allow us to state the constraint conditions in equality form, thus simplifying algebraic analysis, but also provide us with valuable information. In the production problem, for example, the slack variables whose value is *zero* at the optimal solution indicate the inputs that cause bottlenecks or are the limiting factors. Slack variables with *positive* values, on the other hand, provide measures of excess capacity in the related factor.[10] In either case, the information provided by slack variables is important, and we return to this subject when we examine the "dual linear-programming problem" later in this chapter.

Algebraic Solution

The complete specification of our illustrative programming problem can now be stated as follows:

Maximize

$$\pi = 12Q_X + 9Q_Y, \tag{7-1}$$

subject to these constraints:

$$4Q_X + 2Q_Y + S_A = 32, \tag{7-5}$$

$$1Q_X + 1Q_Y + S_B = 10, \tag{7-6}$$

$$3Q_Y + S_C = 21, \tag{7-7}$$

where

$$Q_X \geq 0, \, Q_Y \geq 0, \, S_A \geq 0, \, S_B \geq 0, \, S_C \geq 0.$$

In words, the problem is to find the set of values for variables Q_X, Q_Y, S_A, S_B, and S_C that maximizes Equation 7-1 and at the same time satisfies the constraints imposed by Equations 7-5, 7-6, and 7-7.

The problem stated in this form is underdetermined: We must obtain a simultaneous solution to the constraint equations, but there are more unknowns (five) than constraint equations (three), so we cannot "solve" the system for unique values of the variables. However, the requirement that the solution to any linear-programming problem must occur at a corner of

---

[10] Slack variables obviously can never take on negative values, since this would imply that the amount of the resource used exceeds the amount available. Thus, slack variables are included in the general nonnegativity requirements for all variables.

the feasible space provides enough information to allow one to obtain the final solution. To see how, let us first state the following facts:

1. The optimal output occurs at a corner point. Accordingly, we need examine only the corner locations of the feasible space.
2. There are a total of $M + N$ variables in the system, where M equals the number of products and N equals the number of constraints. Thus, in our example, $M = X + Y = 2$, and $N = A + B + C = 3$, so we have a total of five variables.
3. Each variable must be equal to or greater than zero.
4. At each corner point the number of nonzero-valued variables is equal to the number of constraint equations.[11] Consider Figure 7-11, where the feasible space for our illustrative problem has been re-graphed. At the origin, where neither X nor Y is produced, Q_X and Q_Y both equal zero. Slack exists in all inputs, however, so S_A, S_B, and S_C are all greater than zero. Now move up the vertical axis to point K. Here Q_X and S_C both equal zero, because no X is being produced and Input C is being used to the fullest possible extent. However, Q_Y, S_A, and S_B all exceed zero. At Point L, Q_X, Q_Y, and S_A are all positive; but S_B and S_C are equal to zero. The remaining corners, M and N, can be examined similarly, and at each of them the number of nonzero-valued variables is exactly equal to the number of constraints.

We see then that the optimal solution to a linear-programming problem occurs at a corner of the feasible space, and that at each corner the number of nonzero variables is exactly equal to the number of constraints. These properties enable us to rewrite the constraints as a system with three equations and three unknowns for each corner point; such a system can be solved.

Solving the constraint equations at each corner point provides values for Q_X and Q_Y as well as for S_A, S_B, and S_C. The profit contribution at each corner can be determined by inserting the values for Q_X and Q_Y into the objective function (Equation 7-1). The corner solution that produces the maximum profit is the constrained profit-maximizing output, the solution to the linear-programming problem.

The procedure described above is followed in actual applications of linear programming. Computer programs are available which find solution values of the variables at a corner point, evaluate profits at that point, and

---

[11] In almost all linear-programming problems, the number of nonzero-valued variables in all corner solutions is *exactly* equal to the number of constraints in the problem. Only under a particular condition known as "degeneracy," when more than two constraints coincide at a single corner of the feasible space, are there less nonzero-valued variables. This condition does not hinder the technique of solution considered in Chapter 7.

Figure 7-11   Determination of Zero-valued Variables at Corners of the Feasible
Space

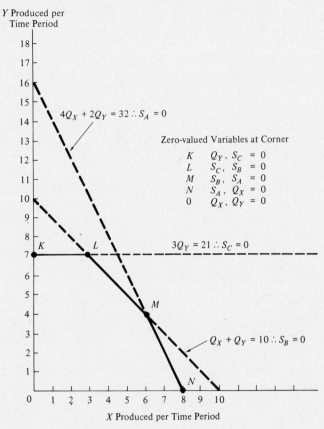

then iterate to an adjacent corner point with a higher profit, continuing until
the optimal corner point is located.

We can illustrate the technique somewhat more fully by examining the
algebraic determination of the corner solutions in our present example.
Although we could set any two of the variables equal to zero, it is convenient to begin by setting Q_X and Q_Y equal to zero and examining the
solution to the programming problem at the origin. Substituting those values
into the three constraint equations—7-5, 7-6, and 7-7—indicates that the
three slack variables are equal to the total units of their respective inputs
available to the firm; that is, $S_A = 32$, $S_B = 10$, and $S_C = 21$. This result is not
unexpected, because at the origin neither X nor Y is produced, and, therefore, none of the inputs is expended for production. The total profit contribution at the origin corner of the feasible space is zero.

Now let us examine the solution at a second corner, N in Figure 7-11, where Q_Y and S_A equal zero. Substituting into Constraint Equation 7-5 permits us to solve for Q_X:

$$4Q_X + 2Q_Y + S_A = 32$$
$$4 \cdot Q_X + 2 \cdot 0 + 0 = 32$$
$$4Q_X = 32$$
$$Q_X = 8.$$

With the value of Q_X determined, we can substitute into Equations 7-6 and 7-7 to determine values S_B and S_C:

$$Q_X + Q_Y + S_B = 10$$
$$0 + 8 + S_B = 10$$
$$S_B = 2,$$

and

$$3Q_Y + S_C = 21$$
$$3 \cdot 0 + S_C = 21$$
$$S_C = 21.$$

The total profit contribution is:

$$\begin{align} \pi &= 12Q_X + 9Q_Y \\ &= 12 \cdot 8 + 9 \cdot 0 \\ &= \$96. \end{align} \tag{7-1}$$

Next, we assign zero values to S_B and S_A, which permits us to reach solution values for Point M. Substituting zero values for S_A and S_B in Equations 7-5 and 7-6 gives us two equations in two unknowns:

$$4Q_X + 2Q_Y + 0 = 32. \tag{7-5}$$

$$Q_X + Q_Y + 0 = 10. \tag{7-6}$$

Multiplying Equation 7-6 by two and subtracting the result from Equation 7-5 provides the value for Q:

$$4Q_X + 2Q_Y = 32 \tag{7-5}$$
$$\underline{-2Q_X - 2Q_Y = -20} \qquad -2 \times (7\text{-}6)$$
$$2Q_X = 12$$
$$Q_X = 6.$$

Then, substituting 6 for Q_X in Equation 7-6, we find that $Q_Y = 4$. Total profit contribution in this case is $108 [(\$12 \cdot 6) + (\$9 \cdot 4)]$.

Similar algebraic analysis would provide the solution for the remaining two corners of the feasible space. However, rather than work through those corner solutions, we present the results in Table 7-2. Here it is apparent, just as we illustrated in the earlier graphic analysis, that the optimal solution occurs at Point M, where 6 units of X and 4 units of Y are produced. Total profit is $108, which exceeds the profit at any other corner of the feasible space.

***Table* 7-2**   Algebraic Solution to a Linear-programming Problem

Solution at Corner	Value of Variable					Total Profit Contribution
	Q_X	Q_Y	S_A	S_B	S_C	
O	0	0	32	10	21	$ 0
N	8	0	0	2	21	96
M	6	4	0	0	9	108
L	3	7	6	0	0	99
K	0	7	18	3	0	63

Slack Variables at the Solution Point

At each corner solution the values of the slack variables are determined by the linear-programming process. For example, at the optimal solution (Corner *M*) reached in the preceding section, S_A and S_B are both equal to zero, meaning that Inputs *A* and *B* are used to the fullest extent possible, but the value of S_C is determined as follows: First, note that $Q_Y = 4$ at the optimal corner. Next, substitute this value into Constraint Equation 7-7 to find the solution value of S_C:

$$3 \cdot Q_Y + S_C = 21$$
$$3 \cdot 4 \quad + S_C = 21$$
$$S_C = 9.$$

Production of the optimal combination of *X* and *Y* completely exhausts the available quantities of Inputs *A* and *B*, but 9 units of Input *C* remain unused. Thus, because Inputs *A* and *B* impose effective constraints on the firm's profit level, it may wish to acquire more of one or both of them in order to expand output. Input *C*, on the other hand, is in excess supply, so the firm would certainly not want more capacity of *C*; it might even attempt to reduce its purchases of *C* during future production periods. Alternatively, if *C* is a fixed facility, such as a computer, the firm might attempt to sell some of that excess capacity to other computer users.

Complex Linear-programming Problems

Our illustrative linear-programming problem is a simple one by design—we chose a problem that can be solved both graphically and algebraically so that we could first explain the theory of linear programming through the use of graphs, then rework the problem algebraically to show the symmetry between the two methods. The kinds of linear-programming problems encountered in the real world, however, are quite complex, frequently involving as many as 50 or 100 constraints and output variables. Such problems are obviously too complex to solve geometrically—the geometry is messy if we have three outputs, impossible for four or more. However, computer programs, which use the algebraic techniques, can handle very large numbers of variables and constraints.

THE DUAL IN LINEAR PROGRAMMING

For every maximization problem in linear programming there exists a symmetrical minimization problem; for every minimization problem there exists a symmetrical maximization problem. These pairs of related maximization and minimization problems are known as *dual linear-programming problems.* Convention specifies that for clarity we call one the "primal" problem and the other the "dual" problem.

The concept of duality in linear programming is significant for two reasons:

1. It is frequently easier to solve the dual programming problem than the original, or primal, problem. Because of the symmetry between the primal and the dual problems, either one can be used to determine the optimal values of the controllable variables. This feature is particularly beneficial for solving certain types of minimization problems, as the dual maximization problem is often much easier to solve.
2. Once the dual solution has been obtained, it can be used to determine the value to the firm of relaxing the various constraints. In the preceding example, we were trying to maximize profits subject to constraints on Inputs A, B, and C. The solution to the dual of this maximization problem gives us an indication of the value to the firm of increasing the availability of resources A, B, and C.

Imputed Values, or "Shadow Prices"

In the primal programming problem discussed above, we sought the values of Q_X and Q_Y that would maximize the firm's profit, subject to constraints on production imposed by limitations of Input Factors A, B, and C. In the dual problem we attempt to determine minimum values, or "shadow prices," for each of the inputs, such that these shadow prices will be just sufficient to absorb the firm's total profit. In other words, we seek to assign, or impute, "values" to each input (these "values" are called shadow prices) so as to minimize the total imputed value of the firm's resources. As we shall demonstrate, the output combination of X and Y indicated by this minimization of imputed values is identical to that combination of Q_X and Q_Y which maximizes profit. Also, the maximum profit figure determined in the primal solution is exactly equal to the minimum imputed value of inputs in the dual.

The concept of duality is a mathematical abstraction, not a straightforward intuitively obvious procedure such as the statement of the primal problem. Accordingly, it is hard to provide an intuitive explanation of the shadow price, or imputed value, concept. Why, logically, would we wish to *minimize* the "value" of the firm's resources? Why not maximize this value? The answer lies in the fact that by minimizing these artificial *imputed* values, subject to the constraints specified in the dual problem, we obtain an estimate of the marginal value of an additional unit of each of the firm's resources. That is, the shadow prices are equivalent to the partial derivatives of the primal objective function taken with respect to the various constraints and, hence, indicate the change in that function which results when one of the constraints is relaxed. This concept should become clear as we examine the dual to the linear-programming problem discussed above.

Dual Objective Function

In the primal problem, where the goal was to maximize profits, the objective function was stated in this way:

Primal Objective Function   Maximize

$$\pi = 12Q_X + 9Q_Y. \tag{7-1}$$

In the dual problem we seek to minimize the imputed values, or the shadow prices, of the firm's resources. Defining V_A, V_B, and V_C as the shadow prices for Inputs A, B, and C, respectively, and Z as the total imputed value of the firm's fixed resources, we may write the dual objective function as:

Dual Objective Function   Minimize

$$Z = 32V_A + 10V_B + 21V_C. \tag{7-8}$$

Since the firm has 32 units of A, the total imputed value of Input A is 32 times A's shadow price, or $32V_A$. If V_A, or Input A's shadow price, is found to be \$1.50 when the dual equations are solved, then the imputed value of A is \$48 ($= 32 \times \$1.50$). Inputs B and C are handled in the same way.

The Dual Constraints

In the primal problem the constraints stated that the total units of each input used in the production of X and Y must be equal to or less than the available quantity of the input. In the dual, the constraints state that the value assigned the inputs used in the production of 1 unit of X or 1 unit of Y must not be less than the profit contribution provided by a unit of these products. In other words, the shadow prices of A, B, and C times the amount of each of the inputs needed to produce a unit of X or Y must be equal to or greater than the unit profit of X or of Y. Recall that unit profit is defined as the excess of price over variable cost, that price and variable cost are both assumed to be constant, and that in our example the profit per unit of X is \$12 while that of Y is \$9.

As was shown in Table 7-1, each unit of X requires 4 units of A, 1 unit of B, and 0 units of C. Therefore, the total imputed value of the resources used to produce X is $4V_A + 1V_B$. The constraint requiring that this imputed cost of producing X be equal to or greater than the profit contribution of X may be written as:

$$4V_A + 1V_B \geq 12, \tag{7-9}$$

where $12 is the profit per unit of Product X. Moreover, since 2 units of A, 1 unit of B, and 3 units of C are required to produce each unit of Y, and the profit per unit of Y is $9, the second dual constraint is written as:

$$2V_A + 1V_B + 3V_C \geq \$9. \tag{7-10}$$

Because the firm produces only two products, the dual problem has but two constraint equations.

The Dual Slack Variables

Dual slack variables can be added to the problem, enabling us to express the constraint requirements as equalities. Letting L_X and L_Y represent the two slacks, the Constraint Equations 7-9 and 7-10 can be rewritten as:

$$4V_A + 1V_B - L_X = 12 \tag{7-11}$$

$$2V_A + 1V_B + 3V_C - L_Y = 9. \tag{7-12}$$

The dual slack variables measure the "opportunity cost" associated with production of the two products X and Y. This can be seen by examining the two constraint equations. Solving Constraint Equation 7-11 for L_X, for example, provides:

$$L_X = (4V_A + 1V_B) - 12.$$

This expression states that L_X is equal to the imputed cost of producing 1 unit of X minus the profit contribution provided by that product. Thus, L_X, the dual slack variable associated with Product X, is a measure of the opportunity cost of producing Product X. It compares the profit contribution, $12 of Product X with the value to the firm of the resources necessary to produce it.

A zero value for L_X indicates that the imputed value of the resources going into each unit of X is exactly equal to the profit contribution received from it; a positive value indicates that the resources expended in the production of X are more valuable in terms of the profit contribution they can generate by producing the other product. A nonzero value of L_X, then, measures the firm's opportunity cost associated with production of Product X.

The slack variable for the second dual constraint has a similar interpretation. That is, L_Y is the opportunity cost of producing Product Y. It will take on a value of zero if the imputed value of the resources used to produce 1 unit of Y exactly equals the $9 profit contribution provided by that product. A positive value for L_Y measures the opportunity loss in terms of the foregone profit contribution associated with the production of Y.

Since a firm would not choose to produce a product if the value of the resources needed to produce it were greater than the value of the product, it follows that a product with a positive opportunity cost will not be included in the optimal production combination in a linear-programming problem. The importance of this relationship is shown below when we interpret the dual solution to our own linear-programming example.

Solving the Dual Problem

The dual programming problem can be solved with the same algebraic technique that was employed to obtain the solution of the primal problem. Let us restate the equality form of the dual programming problem and examine the corner solutions to that problem. The dual problem is expressed by the following system:

Minimize

$$Z = 32V_A + 10V_B + 21V_C, \tag{7-8}$$

subject to

$$4V_A + 1V_B - L_X = 12, \tag{7-11}$$

and

$$2V_A + 1V_B + 3V_C - L_Y = 9, \tag{7-12}$$

where

$$V_A, V_B, V_C, L_X, L_Y \text{ all} \geq 0.$$

Since there are only two constraints in this programming problem, the maximum number of nonzero-valued variables at any corner solution will be two. Therefore, we can proceed by setting three of the variables equal to zero and solving the constraint equations for the values of the remaining two. By comparing the value of the objective function at each feasible solution, we can determine the point at which the function is minimized.

To illustrate the process, let us first set $V_A = V_B = V_C = 0$, and solve for L_X and L_Y:

$$\begin{aligned} 4 \cdot 0 + 1 \cdot 0 - L_X &= 12 \\ L_X &= -12 \end{aligned} \tag{7-11}$$

$$\begin{aligned} 2 \cdot 0 + 1 \cdot 0 + 0 + 3 \cdot 0 - L_Y &= 9 \\ L_Y &= -9 \end{aligned} \tag{7-12}$$

Since L_X and L_Y cannot be negative, this solution is outside the feasible set.

The values obtained above are inserted into Table 7-3 as Solution 1. All other solution values were calculated in a similar manner and used to complete Table 7-3. It is apparent from the table that not all the solutions lie within the feasible space of our linear-programming problem. Specifically, only solutions 5, 7, 9, and 10 meet the nonnegativity requirement of the pro-

***Table* 7-3**   Solutions for the Dual-programming Problem

Solution Number	Value of the Variable					Total Value Imputed to the Firm's Resources
	V_A	V_B	V_C	L_X	L_Y	
1	0	0	0	−12	−9	*
2	0	0	3	−12	0	*
3	0	0	**	0	**	*
4	0	9	0	− 3	0	*
5	0	12	0	0	3	$120
6	0	12	−1	0	0	*
7	4.5	0	0	6	0	$144
8	3	0	0	0	−3	*
9	3	0	1	0	0	$117
10	1.5	6	0	0	0	$108

* Outside the feasible space.
** No real solution.

gramming specification while simultaneously providing solutions in which the number of nonzero-valued variables is exactly equal to the number of constraints in the problem. Thus, these four solutions coincide with the corners of the dual problem's feasible space.[12]

At Corner Point 10 the total value imputed to the Inputs A, B, and C is minimized. Accordingly, Solution 10 is the optimum solution, about which we can make the following observations:

1. The total value of the firm's resources is exactly equal to the $108 maximum profit contribution which we found by solving the primal problem. Thus, the solutions to the primal and the dual programming problems are identical.

2. The shadow price for Input C, V_C, is zero. What does it mean to have a zero shadow price for an input? The shadow price measures the *marginal* value of the input to the firm. Hence, a zero shadow price implies that the resource in question has a zero marginal value to the firm; adding another unit of this input would add nothing to the firm's maximum obtainable profits. Thus, a zero shadow price for Input C is entirely consistent with our findings in the primal

[12] Note that while the number of nonzero-valued variables at a corner of the feasible space in a linear-programming problem is equal to the number of constraints, this does not mean that all solutions to the constraint set where the number of nonzero-valued variables is equal to the number of constraints will necessarily be corner points of the feasible space. This is because there exists the possibility of solutions involving negative values for the variables, and these solutions must obviously lie outside the feasible space since they violate the nonnegative restrictions on the variables.

problem: Input C is not a binding constraint. Excess capacity exists in C, so additional units of C will not result in increased production of either X or Y.

3. The shadow price of Input A is $1.50. A positive shadow price implies that this fixed resource imposes a binding constraint on the firm, and that, if an additional unit of A is added, the firm can increase its total profit by $1.50. The firm can afford to pay up to $1.50 for a marginal unit of Input A.[13]

4. The interpretation of Input B's shadow price is similar to that for A. Since B imposes an effective constraint on the firm's production, an additional unit of B would allow increased production of X and Y, with total profit increasing by $6. Thus, the firm can afford to pay up to $6 for a marginal unit of B.

5. Both of the dual slack variables are zero. This means that the imputed value of the resources required to produce a single unit of X or Y is exactly equal to the profit contribution provided by each of them. Thus, the opportunity cost of both X and Y is zero, indicating that the resources required for their production are *not* more valuable to the firm in some alternative use. Again, this is entirely consistent with the solution of the primal programming problem, as both X and Y were produced at the optimal solution. Any product with a positive opportunity cost would be nonoptimal and would not be produced in the profit-maximizing primal solution.

Use of the Dual Solution to Solve the Primal Problem

The dual solution, as we have developed it thus far, does not give us the optimal amounts of X and Y; it does, however, provide all the information necessary to determine the optimum output mix. First, note that the dual solution informs us that Input C does not impose a binding constraint on output of X and Y. Further, it tells us that at the optimum output of X and Y, $\pi = Z = \$108$. Now consider again the three constraints in the primal problem:

Constraint on A

$$4Q_X + 2Q_Y + S_A = 32,$$

Constraint on B

$$1Q_X + 1Q_Y + S_B = 10,$$

[13] It would pay the firm to buy additional units of Input A at any price less than $1.50 per unit until A is no longer a binding constraint. This statement concerning the interpretation of a shadow price assumes that the cost of the quantity of Input A used in the production of each unit of Products X and Y *was not* deducted from their selling prices to obtain the profit contribution figures used in the primal programming problem. If, in fact, those costs were included in the calculation of the profit contributions, then the shadow price must be intepreted as the amount *above* the current price of Input A that the firm could afford to pay for additional units.

Constraint on C

$$3Q_Y + S_C = 21.$$

We know that the constraints on A and B are binding, *because the dual solution found both of these inputs to have positive shadow prices.* Accordingly, the slack variables S_A and S_B are equal to zero, and the binding constraints may be rewritten as follows:

$$4Q_X + 2Q_Y = 32,$$

and

$$1Q_X + 1Q_Y = 10.$$

We have two equations in two unknowns, so the system can be solved for values of Q_X and Q_Y:

$$
\begin{aligned}
4Q_X + 2Q_Y &= 32 \\
-2Q_X - 2Q_Y &= -20 \\
\hline
2Q_X &= 12 \\
Q_X &= 6,
\end{aligned}
$$

and

$$6 + Q_Y = 10,$$
$$Q_Y = 4.$$

These values of Q_X and Q_Y, which were found after learning from the dual which constraints were binding, are identical to the values found by solving the primal problem. Further, having obtained the value for Q_Y, it is possible to substitute into the equation for Constraint C and solve for the amount of slack in that resource:

$$3Q_Y + S_C = 21$$
$$S_C = 21 - 3(4) = 9.$$

These relationships, which allow one to solve either the primal or dual specification of a linear-programming problem and then quickly obtain the solution to the other, can be generalized by the following two expressions:

$$Q_i \cdot L_i = 0. \tag{7-13}$$

$$S_j \cdot V_j = 0. \tag{7-14}$$

Equation 7-13 states that if an ordinary variable in the primal problem takes on a nonzero value in the optimal solution to that problem, its related dual slack variable must be zero. Only if a particular Q_i is zero-valued in the solution to the primal can its related dual slack, L_i, take on a nonzero value.

A similar relationship holds between the slack variables in the primal problem and their related ordinary variables in the dual. If the primal slack is nonzero-valued, then the related dual variable will be zero-valued and vice versa.

CONSTRAINED COST MINIMIZATION: AN ADDITIONAL LINEAR-PROGRAMMING PROBLEM EXAMPLE

The use of linear programming to solve constrained optimization problems is relatively complex, as is developing an understanding of the economic significance of the results. Gaining facility with the use of the technique requires substantial exposure and practice. Accordingly, in this section we provide an additional example of a typical managerial problem which can be solved with linear programming.

Constrained cost-minimization problems are frequently encountered in managerial decision making. One interesting example associated with a firm's marketing activities is the problem of minimizing advertising expenditures subject to meeting certain audience-exposure requirements. Consider, for example, a firm that is planning an advertising campaign for a new product. The goals that have been set for the campaign include exposure to at least 100,000 individuals, with no less than 80,000 of those individuals having incomes of at least $15,000 annually and no less than 40,000 of them being unmarried. For pedagogical reasons we will assume that the firm has only two media, radio and television, available for this campaign. One television ad costs $10,000 and is estimated to reach an audience numbering, on the average, 20,000 persons. Ten thousand of these individuals will have incomes of $15,000 or more, while 4,000 of them will be single. A radio ad, on the other hand, costs $6,000 and reaches a total audience of 10,000 individuals, all of whom have at least $15,000 in income. Eight thousand of the persons exposed to a radio ad will be unmarried. Table 7-4 summarizes these data.

Table 7-4 Advertising Media Relationships

	Radio	Television
Cost per ad	$ 6,000	$10,000
Total audience per ad	10,000	20,000
Audience per ad with income $\geq$ $15,000	10,000	10,000
Audience per ad single	8,000	4,000

The Primal Problem

The linear-programming problem the firm would use to solve this constrained-optimization problem is developed as follows. The objective is to minimize the cost of the advertising campaign. Since total cost is merely the sum of the amounts spent on radio and television ads, the objective function is given by the expression:

Minimize

$$\text{Cost} = \$6,000R + \$10,000TV,$$

where R and TV represent the number of radio and television ads, respectively, that are to be employed in the advertising campaign.

The linear-programming problem will have a total of three constraint equations: (1) the requirement for total audience exposure, (2) the income-related exposure requirement, and (3) the requirement that at least 40,000 single persons are among those exposed to the advertising campaign.

The restriction on the minimum number of individuals that must be reached by the ad campaign can be expressed as[14]:

$$10,000R + 20,000TV \geq 100,000.$$

This equation states that the number of persons exposed to radio ads (10,000 times the number of radio ads) plus the number exposed to television ads (20,000 times the number of television ads) must be equal to or greater than 100,000.

The remaining two constraints can be constructed similarly from the data in Table 7-4. The constraint on exposures to individuals with incomes of at least \$15,000 is written:

$$10,000R + 10,000TV \geq 80,000,$$

while the marital status-related constraint is given by:

$$8,000R + 4,000TV \geq 40,000.$$

Combining the cost-minimization objective function with the three constraints—written in their equality form through the introduction of slack variables—allows us to write the programming problem as:

Minimize

$$\text{Cost} = \$6,000R + \$10,000TV,$$

subject to

$$10,000R + 20,000TV - S_A = 100,000,$$
$$10,000R + 10,000TV - S_I = 80,000,$$

and

$$8,000R + 4,000TV - S_S = 40,000.$$
$$R, TV, S_A, S_I, S_S \geq 0.$$

[14] There is an implicit assumption in this formulation of the constraint that individuals are exposed *only once* to *either* a radio or a television ad. This could be accomplished by coordinating the times at which the ads were to run.

Here S_A, S_I, and S_S are the slack variables indicating the extent to which the minimums on total audience exposure, on exposure to individuals with incomes of at least $15,000, and on exposure to single individuals, respectively, have been exceeded. Note that the slack variables are *subtracted* from the constraint equations in this situation since we are dealing with equal-to or greater-than inequalities. That is, excess capacity or slack in any of the constraints implies that the audience exposure is greater than required. Thus, in order to make the exposures exactly equal to the required quantity, one must subtract the slack from the total.

The solution to this linear-programming problem is easily obtained graphically. Figure 7-12 illustrates that solution. There the feasible space for the programming problem is delimited by the three constraint equations and the nonnegativity requirements. Addition of an isocost curve allows one to determine that costs are minimized at Point *M*, where the constraints on total audience exposure and exposures to individuals meeting the income requirement are binding. The solution to the problem indicates that the firm should employ 6 radio and 2 television ads in its campaign in order to mini-

Figure 7-12   Advertising Cost-minimization Linear-programming Problem

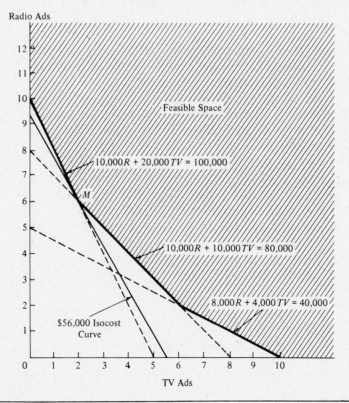

mize its expenditure while meeting the audience goals set for the program. The total cost for such a campaign would be $56,000.

The Dual Problem

The dual linear-programming problem for the advertising mix decision provides some very interesting and valuable information to the firm's management. It will prove instructive to formulate, solve, and interpret that form of the problem.

The dual programming problem in this situation will be a constrained-maximization problem, since the primal problem was a minimization problem. Also, we know that the objective function of the dual problem will be expressed in terms of shadow prices or imputed values for the constraints or restrictions in the primal problem. Thus, the dual objective function will contain three variables: (1) the imputed value, or shadow price, for the total audience exposure requirement, (2) the shadow price of the high income audience requirement, and (3) the shadow price associated with the marital status constraint. Since the constraint limits in the primal problem become the objective function parameters in the dual, the dual objective function can be written as:

Maximize

$$Z = 100{,}000V_A + 80{,}000V_I + 40{,}000V_S,$$

where V_A, V_I, and V_S are the three shadow prices described above.

The constraints in the dual problem are developed in terms of the objective function variables from the primal. Thus, there will be only two constraint conditions in the problem; one associated with radio ads, the other with television ads. Both of these constraints will be of an equal-to or *less-than* nature since the constraints in the primal were of an equal-to or *greater-than* form.

The limit on the constraint associated with radio advertising is the $6,000 coefficient of radio ads found in the objective function of the primal problem. The coefficients for the three shadow prices in the constraint equation are the numbers of exposures within each category provided by a single radio ad. The coefficient for the total audience exposure shadow price, V_A, therefore, will be 10,000, the number of individuals exposed to a radio ad. Similarly, the coefficient for V_I is 10,000, and that for V_S is 8,000. The constraint for radio ads, then, is given by:

$$10{,}000V_A + 10{,}000V_I + 8{,}000V_S \leq 6{,}000.$$

The constraint associated with television advertising is constructed in the same fashion. Since each TV ad reaches a total audience of 20,000, this is the parameter for the V_A variable in the second constraint equation. The parameters for V_I and V_S are 10,000 and 4,000, respectively, because these are the numbers of individuals in the income and marital categories exposed to one TV ad. With the \$10,000 cost of a television ad providing a limit to the constraint, the second constraint equation for the dual problem is:

$$20{,}000V_A + 10{,}000V_I + 4{,}000V_S \leq 10{,}000.$$

With the introduction of slack variables in the constraints, the dual programming problem may be stated:

Maximize

$$Z = 100{,}000V_A + 80{,}000V_I + 40{,}000V_S,$$

subject to

$$10{,}000V_A + 10{,}000V_I + 8{,}000V_S + L_R = 6{,}000,$$

and

$$20{,}000V_A + 10{,}000V_I + 4{,}000V_S + L_{TV} = 10{,}000.$$

$$V_A, V_I, V_S, L_R, L_{TV} \geq 0.$$

Solving the Dual   While it would be possible, although difficult, to solve the dual programming problem using either a three-dimension graph or the complete enumeration technique developed earlier in this chapter, there is a much easier way to obtain the solution, since we have already solved the primal problem. Recall that the solution to both the primal and dual statements of a single linear-programming problem will always be identical, and that the following relationships must always hold:

$$\text{Primal Objective Variable}_i \times \text{Dual Slack Variable}_i \equiv 0.$$

$$\text{Primal Slack Variable}_j \times \text{Dual Objective Variable}_j \equiv 0.$$

Thus, in this programming problem:

$$R \times L_R = 0 \ \& \ TV \times L_{TV} = 0,$$

and

$$S_A \times V_A = 0, S_I \times V_I = 0, \ \& \ S_S \times V_S = 0.$$

Since we know from the primal problem that both R and TV are non-zero-valued variables, L_R and L_{TV} in the dual problem must both be zero at the optimal solution. Further, since there was excess audience exposure in the unmarried category in the solution to the primal; that is, $S_S \neq 0$, we know that V_S in the dual must take on a value of zero in the optimal solution. This leaves only V_A and V_I as unknowns in the dual programming problem, and their values can be easily obtained by solving the two-equation constraint system for the two unknowns:

$$10{,}000V_A + 10{,}000V_I = 6{,}000,$$

$$20{,}000V_A + 10{,}000V_I = 10{,}000.$$

Subtracting the second constraint equation from the first results in:

$$-10,000V_A = -4,000$$

$$V_A = .4$$

Substituting the value .4 for V_A in either constraint equation produces a value of .2 for V_I. Finally, substituting the values for V_A, V_I, and V_S into the objective function of the dual problem results in a value for Z of $56,000 ($.4 \times 100,000 + .2 \times 80,000 + 0 \times 40,000$), exactly the same as the minimum cost figure obtained in the solution of the primal problem.

Interpreting the Dual Problem Results   The solution to the primal of our linear-programming problem tells management which advertising mix meets the various goals of its marketing program at the least cost, and, thereby, allows the firm to move ahead with the promotional campaign. However, the results of the dual problem are equally valuable for effective management. This is due to the fact that the dual program solution allows management to evaluate the goals that are being used to determine how best to advertise the new product.

Recall that the dual problem objective function variables, the various shadow prices, provide a measure of how the constraints affect the primal problem's objective function *at the margin.* That is, each shadow price indicates the change in the optimal solution value of the primal (and also dual) problem objective function that would accompany a very small (marginal) change in the limit of the related constraint.

Thus, in the problem we are examining, each dual problem shadow price indicates the change in total cost that would accompany a unitary change in the various audience-exposure requirements. They are, therefore, the marginal costs of the last audience exposure gained in each of the three categories; total, with incomes $\geq \$15,000$, and single. For example, the value of V_A is the marginal cost of reaching the last individual in the total audience that is exposed to the firm's ads. In this case V_A is .4, indicating that if the firm were to reduce by one the number of total individuals that must come in contact with an ad, there would be a $0.40 reduction in the $56,000 total cost of the advertising program. Similarly, the marginal cost of increasing total audience exposure from 100,000 to 100,001 individuals is 40¢.

V_I, the shadow price of reaching individuals with incomes of at least $15,000 is .2 or 20¢. This means that it would cost the firm an extra 20¢ per individual to reach more persons in the high-income category.

The zero value found for V_S, the shadow price for the restriction on exposures to unmarried individuals, indicates that the proposed advertising campaign already reaches more than the 40,000 required individuals in this category. Thus, a small change in that constraint will have no effect on the total cost of the promotion.

By comparing these marginal costs with the benefits it expects to derive from additional audience exposures in the various classes, the firm's management will be able to determine whether the goals on audience exposures are appropriate. If the expected return (profit) from one additional individual seeing an ad exceeds 40¢, it would prove profitable to design an advertising campaign for a larger audience. Likewise, if the expected return from an additional exposure to an individual in the $15,000 and above income class was greater than the 20¢ marginal cost of reaching one more person in that class, then again, the lower limit on exposures to that group should be raised. In both cases a determination that the marginal profitability of the last audience exposure was less than its marginal cost (shadow price) would indicate that the firm should reduce the size of the audience requirement for that particular category. Such a reduction would increase profits, since the costs of the advertising campaign would fall faster than the profits on lost sales.

The two slack variables in the dual problem also have an interesting interpretation. They represent the opportunity costs of using a specific advertising medium. L_R is thus a measure of the inefficiency associated with using radio in the promotion, while the value of L_{TV} indicates the added cost of including television in the media mix employed. Both L_R and L_{TV} were zero in the solution to the dual program, which indicates that neither medium is cost inefficient and that, in fact, both should be included in the promotional mix. This was also what we found in the solution to the primal problem.

This example has again demonstrated the oneness of the primal and dual specifications of a linear-programming problem. Either can be used to solve the basic problem, and the interpretations of both provide much valuable information for decision-making purposes.

Postscript on the Relation of Linear Programming to the Lagrangian Technique

In an earlier section we pointed out that linear programming is used to solve maximization and minimization problems, subject to inequality constraints, just as the Lagrangian technique was used to solve optimization problems, subject to constraints which can be stated as equalities. Recall from Chapter 2 that the Lagrangian multiplier, λ, is the marginal gain in the objective function obtained by relaxing the constraint by 1 unit. In the preceding section we learned that the values of the dual variables, the shadow prices, measure the value of relaxing input constraints by 1 unit. Thus, the shadow prices are the linear-programming equivalents to Lagrangian multipliers.

SUMMARY

Linear programming is a technique for solving maximization or minimization problems in which inequality constraints are imposed on the decision maker. This kind of problem occurs frequently in both business and government, so linear programming is rapidly becoming one of the most widely used tools in the sophisticated decision maker's kit.

Although linear programming has been applied to a wide variety of business problems, it has been developed most fully, and is used most frequently, in production problems. Accordingly, we used two production problems to explain the basic elements of the theory of linear programming. First, we presented the theory in graphic form, and then we showed that the same solution can be reached by an algebraic technique. The graphic method is useful to explain the theory; but the algebraic method is the one used in actual practice, because it can be adapted for solution by computers.

After discussing the *primal* linear-programming problem, we showed that for every primal problem there exists a *dual* problem. The primal is of interest because it provides us with values for the controllable variables—the output mix in our first illustrative problem. The dual is useful because the shadow prices which it generates for each input are an indication of the marginal value of adding additional capacity for each fixed input.

In the following chapter we assume that the firm has already determined its optimal production processes and output mix, either through linear programming or with some other technique, and go on to examine the relationship between cost and output.

QUESTIONS

7-1 What managerial problems can be solved by linear programming? Give some illustrations of situations where you think the technique is useful.

7-2 Why can linear programming *not* be used in each of the following situations?
   a) Strong economies of scale exist.
   b) As the firm expands output, the prices of variable factors of production increase.
   c) As output increases, product prices decline.
   d) The firm's resources must, by contract, be fully utilized at all times.

7-3 What is the major similarity between linear programming and the Lagrangian multiplier technique? The major difference?

7-4 Why is the fact that, at corners of the feasible space, the number of nonzero-valued variables exactly equals the number of constraints so critical in linear programming?

7-5 If the primal problem calls for determining the set of outputs that will maximize profits, subject to constraints on inputs:
   a) What is the dual objective function?
   b) What interpretation can be given to the dual variables, defined as the "shadow prices" or "imputed values"?
   c) What does it mean if a dual variable, or shadow price, is zero?

PROBLEMS

7-1 Assume that production of a particular product, X, makes use of two input factors, L and K, and that the production function can be expressed as $Q_X = 1/6L^{.5}K^{.5}$.
   a) Assuming that each unit of L costs $20 and each unit of K costs $10,

what is the optimal ratio in which to combine L and K in this production system?

b) Explain the difference between "returns to factors of input" and "returns to scale." What is the nature of each in the production system described in this problem?

c) Assume now and throughout the remainder of the problem that while the production function given above indicates the output produced from this system, it is valid only for input combinations in the ratio of $9L$ to $4K$. (Note that this means that 1 unit of Q could be produced with 9 units of L and 4 units of K, 2 units of Q would require 18 units of L and 8 units of K, and so forth.) What are the "returns to factors of input" and "returns to scale" under these conditions?

d) Assuming each unit of L costs $20 and each unit of K costs $10, what combination of L and K would be used to produce 4 units of X? Can you determine the quantity of L and K that would be used to produce 16 units of Q? If so, what is it? If not, why not?

e) Assume that the firm producing this product has 49 units of L and 16 units of K available during each production period. What is the maximum quantity of output the firm can produce in each period with these limits on input availability?

f) Given the assumptions in Part e, what are the marginal products of additional units of L and K?

7-2 Itex Electronics has just received an order for a large quantity of pressure switches (an electronic switch triggered by pressure changes). The company has been offered a substantial premium on the contract for rush delivery, but it must supply the switches at a rate of no fewer than 20 units a day to receive the premium. Because the production manager knows that the only production bottleneck will come in the final assembly department, he is concentrating on maximizing output from that department.

Final assembly of the switches requires two input factors, labor and a curing oven. Since it is impossible either to hire more labor with the proper skills or to purchase an additional curing facility in time to meet this contract, the quantities of these two inputs available for use are limited to the amounts on hand: a total of 70 labor-hours and of 20 curing-hours available each day.

The company is able to combine these two input factors in four different ratios, using different production techniques. These input ratios are fixed for each production method irrespective of the output level, and each method exhibits constant returns to scale. The input requirements for each method are provided in the table below:

Resource	Input Requirement per Unit of Output Using Process			
	A	B	C	D
Labor (hours)	9	5	4	3
Curing Facility (hours)	0.3	0.5	0.6	1.2

a) The optimal usage of inputs in the final assembly department for this problem can be determined by using linear-programming methods. Set up the appropriate linear-programming problem. (Define Q_A, Q_B, Q_C, and Q_D as the quantity of X produced by Processes A, B, C, and D, respectively. Use the equality form for expressing the constraint conditions.)

b) Solve the primal problem using graphic techniques. (*Hint:* Draw an isoquant for $X = 20$, then use the fact that all isoquants are parallel to determine the corner solution.)

c) Formulate the related dual linear-programming problem, again using the equality form for stating constraint requirements.

d) Use your solution of the primal (that is, your knowledge from the primal of which variables are zero) to obtain the solution to the dual.

e) Interpret all variables *and* equations in both the primal and the dual linear-programming problems.

f) Carefully examine the graph you constructed for Part b, then answer the following questions: (i) Will Process C or D be used more intensively if more labor is made available? (ii) How many additional units of labor will be required to make Itex cease to use Process D?

7-3 The Stephens Boat Company manufactures two models of boats—a 25-foot power cruiser and a 32-foot family sailboat. The market for both models is competitive, so Stephens can sell all the boats it can produce at the going prices—$6,000 for the power cruiser and $8,000 for the sailboat. Since variable costs are approximately $3,300 a unit for the power cruiser and $4,400 for the sailboat, the profit contributions are $2,700 for the power boat and $3,600 for the sailboat.

All inputs included as variable costs are available in unlimited quantities at constant prices, and the firm's production process provides constant returns to scale. However, three resources—the power engine assembly shop, the dry dock, and the boat assembly shop—are limited. The number of boat-unit-hours of each of these resources, together with the requirements for each model, is given in the table below. (Designate X = power boat, Y = sailboat. Assume that fractional inputs and outputs are permissible and are carried over to the next monthly production period.)

Available Inputs and Requirements

	Boat-unit-hours Available per Month	Hours Required per Boat	
		Power (X)	Sail (Y)
Boat Assembly (A)	9,600	600	1,200
Dry Dock (B)	3,000	300	300
Engine Shop (C)	6,300	900	0

a) Use an algebraic linear-programming model to determine the company's optimal output mix. You can use a graph to help set up the model, but solve it algebraically (for the values at the optimal corner as determined by the graph).

b) Assuming Stephens can purchase additional fixed inputs, what is the maximum it will pay for an additional unit of each input?

c) If dry-dock capacity is increased by 20 percent, would the output of sailboats increase or decrease? (This can be seen easily from a graph.)

7-4 Specialty Metal Products, Incorporated, finds itself facing a new production difficulty. Because of the nationwide energy shortage, the firms which supply Specialty with both natural gas and fuel oil have been forced to limit the quantities of these fuels that they can provide to the amount which Specialty purchased last year. This means that only 100 units of natural gas and 150 units of fuel oil will be provided this month.

Specialty Metal Products produces two basic items which are sold to heavy equipment manufacturers. One of the items is an extruded aluminum fixture that sells for $120 and has variable production costs of $60. This fixture is manufactured by a process in which the energy requirement must be supplied by the use of 3 units of natural gas and 6 units of fuel oil for each fixture produced.

The second product manufactured by Specialty is a copper clad steel plate used as a heat transfer mechanism in a complex machine tool. This plate sells for $140 and variable production costs are $50. Although the production costs are not affected, Specialty does have some flexibility in the production methods used to produce this plate. Specifically, there are two processes that can be used in its manufacture. Process 1 has energy requirements of 6 units each of natural gas and fuel oil, while Process 2 uses 7.5 units of gas and 4.5 units of oil. There are no other relevant differences in the production processes and the end product is indistinguishable.

a) Formulate both the primal and the dual linear-programming problems that Specialty might use to maximize short-run profit during the current period. (Use the equality form for the constraint equations.)

b) Solve the programming problem formulated in Part a. Be sure to solve it completely; that is, provide values for all the variables in both the primal and the dual.

c) Interpret the variables in the two problems you have set up in Part a. Be specific.

7-5 SoWis Beef, Incorporated, is engaged in a feedlot operation in a Midwestern state. The operating profits of SoWis have declined sharply over the past month due to substantial price increases for both corn and soybeans, the prime ingredients in the feed mixture used by SoWis, coupled with a weakening demand for beef.

Alex Swenson, the feedlot manager, believes that the firm's profits might be improved by cutting the costs of feeding the 1,000 head of beef that SoWis has on hand at any point in time. The daily feed mixture being used currently is composed of 3 tons of corn gluten feed and 2 tons of soybean meal. The corn has a cost of $80 per ton and the soybean meal costs $100 per ton. Swenson has obtained data from a State University Agriculture

Extentionist indicating that 1,000 head of beef cattle require at least 5 tons of feed per day and that the feed mixture should contain at least 3,000 units of protein, 3,200 units of carbohydrates, and 9,000 units of roughage.

a) Assuming that each ton of the corn mix contains 500 units of protein, 800 units of carbohydrates, and 3,000 units of roughage, and that a ton of soybean meal has 1,000 units of protein, 400 units of carbohydrates, and 1,000 units of roughage, set up the linear-programming problem Swenson would use to determine the best feed mixture for SoWis.

b) Solve the linear-programming problem you constructed in Part a.

c) Set up and solve the related dual programming problem.

d) Interpret your results in Parts b and c explicitly, explaining precisely what each variable in your linear-programming problem relates to and how you would make use of the information provided by your results.

SELECTED REFERENCES

Baumol, William J. *Economic Theory and Operations Analysis,* 3d ed. Englewood Cliffs, N.J.: Prentice-Hall, Inc., 1972, Chapters 5 and 6.

Dorfman, Robert. "Mathematical, or Linear, Programming: A Nonmathematical Approach," *American Economic Review,* December 1953, pp. 797-825.

————, Paul A. Samuelson, and Robert M. Solow. *Linear Programming and Economic Analysis.* New York: McGraw-Hill Book Co., 1958.

Wu, Yuan-Li, and Ching-Wen Kwang. "An Analytical Comparison of Marginal Analysis and Mathematical Programming in the Theory of the Firm," in Kenneth E. Boulding and W. Allen Spivey, eds., *Linear Programming and the Theory of the Firm.* New York: McGraw-Hill, 1960.

CHAPTER 8

Cost
Theory

Cost analysis plays a central role in managerial economics, because every managerial decision requires a comparison between the cost of an action and its benefits. For example, the expected benefits of an advertising program must be compared with the costs of the program. Likewise, a decision to expand capital assets requires a comparison between the revenues expected from the investment and the cost of funds used to acquire the new assets. Even a decision whether to pave an employees' parking lot requires a comparison between the cost of the project and the subjectively estimated benefits expected to result from improved employee morale. In each case, the marginal benefit resulting from the decision is compared to the marginal cost of the action.

In this chapter we examine a number of cost concepts, including alternative (or opportunity) costs, explicit versus implicit costs, marginal costs, and incremental costs. Further, we relate production costs to production functions, and develop long-run and short-run cost functions suitable for empirical measurement. The conclusions reached in this chapter are useful for managerial decisions; they also help one to understand how various industry structures develop and to see some of the implications of public policy designed to alter the structure of American industry.

RELEVANT COST CONCEPT

The term *cost* can be defined in a number of different ways, and the "correct" definition varies from situation to situation, depending upon how the cost figure is to be used. In general, cost refers to the price that must be paid for an item. If we buy a product for cash and use it immediately, no problems arise in defining and measuring its cost. However, if the item is purchased, stored for a time, and then used, complications can arise. The problem is even more acute if the item is a fixed asset that will be used at varying rates for some indeterminate period. What then is the cost of using the asset during any given period?

The cost figure that should be used in a specific application is defined as the *relevant cost*. When calculating costs for use in completing a firm's income tax returns, accountants are required by law to list the actual dollar amounts spent to purchase the labor, raw materials, and capital equipment used in production.[1] Thus, for tax purposes actual historical dollar outlays are the relevant costs. This is also true for Securities and Exchange Commission reports and for reports of profits to stockholders.

For managerial decisions, however, historical costs may not be appropriate; generally, current and projected future costs are more relevant than historical outlays. For example, consider a construction firm that has an inventory of 1,000 tons of steel purchased at a price of $250 a ton. Steel prices now double to $500 a ton. If the firm is asked to bid on a project, what cost should it assign to the steel used in the job—the $250 historical cost or the $500 current cost? The answer is the current cost. The firm must pay $500 to replace the steel it uses, and it can sell the steel for $500 if it elects not to use it on the proposed job. Therefore, $500 is the *relevant cost* of steel for purposes of bidding on the job. Note, however, that the cost of steel for tax purposes is still the $250 historical cost.

Similarly, if a firm owns a piece of equipment that has been fully depreciated—that is, its accounting book value is zero—it cannot assume that the cost of using the machine is zero. For example, if the machine could be sold for $1,000 now, but its market value is expected to be only $200 one year from now, the relevant cost of using the machine for one additional year is $800.[2] Again, there is little relationship between the $800 true cost

---

[1] The tax authorities also prescribe guidelines for estimating the depreciable life of capital equipment and methods for calculating depreciation.

[2] This statement contains a slight oversimplification. Actually, the cost of using the machine for one year is the current value minus the discounted present value of its value one year hence. This adjustment is necessary to account for the fact that dollars received in the future have a lower *present* worth than dollars received today.

of using the machine and the zero cost that would be reported on the firm's income statement.

Alternative Use Concept

Implicit in the preceding discussion of relevant costs is an alternative-use concept. Economic resources have value because they can be used to produce goods and services for consumption. When a firm purchases a resource for producing a particular product, it bids against alternative users. Thus, the firm must offer a price at least as great as the resource's value in an alternative use. This alternative value is often referred to as the *opportunity cost* of employing the resource. The cost of aluminum used in the manufacture of airplanes, for example, is determined by its value in alternative uses. An airplane manufacturer must pay a price equal to this value or else the aluminum will be used to produce alternative goods, such as cookware, automobiles, building materials, and so on.[3] Similarly, if a firm owns capital equipment that can be used to produce either Product A or Product B, the relevant cost of producing A for use in managerial decision making must include the profit of the alternative Product B that cannot be produced.

The alternative-cost concept, then, reflects the fact that all decisions are based on choices between alternative actions. The cost of a resource is determined by its value in its best alternative use.

Explicit and Implicit Costs

Closely related to the alternative-use concept is the distinction between explicit and implicit costs. Typically, the relevant cost of a resource is determined by the price paid for it; the cost of the resource is *explicitly* determined as the cash outlay required to obtain it. Wages paid, utility expenses, payment for raw materials, interest paid to the holders of the firm's bonds, and rent on a building are all examples of explicit expenses.

The implicit costs associated with any decision are much more difficult to compute. These costs do not involve cash expenditures and are therefore often overlooked in decision analysis. The rent a farmer could receive on his buildings and fields if he did not use them is an implicit cost of his own farming activities, as is the salary he can receive by working for someone else instead of operating his own farming enterprise.

Another example should clarify these cost distinctions. Consider the costs associated with the purchase and operation of a Mother Baker's Pie Shop. The franchise can be bought for $10,000; and an additional $5,000 working capital is needed for operating purposes. Jones has personal savings of $15,000 that he can invest in such an enterprise; Smith, another possible

---

[3] The value of aluminum must be sufficient to attract the labor and capital required to produce aluminum. In other words, the alternative-use concept also applies to determine the total amount of aluminum that will be produced.

franchisee, must borrow the entire $15,000 at a cost of 10 percent, or $1,500 a year. Assume that operating costs are the same irrespective of who owns the shop, and that Smith and Jones are equally competent to manage it. Does Smith's $1,500 annual interest expense mean that his costs of operating the shop are greater than those of Jones? For managerial decision purposes the answer is "no." Even though Smith has higher explicit expenses because of the interest on the loan, the true financing cost, implicit as well as explicit, might well be the same for both men. Jones has an implicit cost equal to the amount he can earn on his $15,000 in some alternative use. If he can obtain a 10 percent return by investing in other assets of equal risk, then Jones' opportunity cost of putting his own $15,000 in the pie shop is $1,500 a year. In this case, Smith and Jones each have a financing cost of $1,500 a year, with Smith's cost being explicit and Jones' implicit.

Can we then say that the total cost of operating the shop will be identical for both men? Not necessarily. Just as the implicit cost of Jones' capital must be included in the analysis, so, too, must be the implicit cost of management. If Jones is an assistant baker earning $10,000 a year and Smith is a master baker earning $17,000 annually, the implicit cost of management will not be equal for the two men. That is, the implicit management expense for Smith is equal to his value in his best alternative use, the $17,000 he would earn as a master baker. Jones, on the other hand, has an opportunity cost of only $10,000. Thus, Smith's relevant total costs of owning and operating the shop will be $7,000 greater than those of Jones.

Incremental Cost for Decision Analysis

The relevant-cost concept also entails the idea of incremental cost. This means that for any decision the relevant costs are limited to those which are affected by the decision. If a particular cost is unchanged by a given decision, the incremental cost for the action undertaken is zero. For example, if a firm has unused warehouse space that will otherwise stand idle, the cost of storing a new product in it will be zero, and zero is the incremental storage cost that should be considered in deciding whether to produce the new product.

The incremental-cost concept, although inherently simple, is often violated in practice. For example, a firm may refuse to sell excess computer time for $500 an hour because it figures its cost as $550 an hour, calculated by adding a standard overhead cost of $250 an hour to a marginal operating cost of $300 an hour. The relevant incremental cost of computer usage, however, is only $300, so the firm is foregoing a $200 per hour contribution to profit by not selling its excess time. Any firm that adds a standard allocated charge for fixed costs and overhead to the true incremental cost of production runs the risk of turning down profitable sales.

On the other hand, care must be exercised to insure against incorrectly assigning a low incremental cost to a given decision when a higher cost in fact exists. An example that came to the authors' attention involved a heat-treating plant where metal parts were hardened prior to final assembly in various products. At the time, the economy was depressed and the plant had unused capacity. A major steel company offered the firm in question a five-year contract to treat certain products, but at a price well below the normal charges. The price offered exceeded operating expenses, but was not sufficient to cover all overhead and provide a normal profit margin. That is, the offered price covered out-of-pocket costs but not full costs plus profits. The heat-treating company took the contract on the grounds that it would cover "incremental" costs and still have a little left over to contribute to total overhead expenses, which would not be affected by the decision.

A few months later the economy picked up and regular customers, who paid a higher price, began to bring in additional business. The plant was soon operating at full capacity, and the firm faced the prospect of being forced to turn away profitable business. At this point the plant manager realized his mistake—he had misjudged demand and had thereby miscalculated his costs. He had assumed that plant and equipment costs would be unaffected by the new contract, but in fact the contract forced him to expand at some considerable cost. If expansion had not been possible, then the *long-run* incremental costs of taking on the steel firm's business would have included the opportunity cost of the foregone regular business.

COST FUNCTIONS

Proper use of the relevant-cost concept for output and pricing decisions requires an understanding of the relationship between a firm's cost and output, or its *cost function*. Cost functions are dependent (1) on the firm's production function, and (2) on the market-supply function for its inputs. The production function specifies the technical relationship between combinations of inputs and the level of output, and this factor, combined with the prices of inputs, determines the cost function.

Assume that the prices of a firm's inputs are constant over the entire production range; in this case, a *direct* relationship exists between cost and production. Consider first a production function that exhibits constant returns to scale, such as was illustrated in Figure 6-15 on page 185. Such a production function is linear, and a doubling of inputs leads to a doubling of output. With constant input prices, a doubling of inputs doubles their total cost, producing a linear total cost function, as is illustrated in Figure 8-1.

If, however, a firm's production function is subject to decreasing returns to scale, as was illustrated in Figure 6-17, page 186 inputs must more than double in order to double output. Again, assuming constant input prices, the cost function associated with a production system of this kind will rise at an increasing rate, as is shown in Figure 8-2.

A production function exhibiting first increasing and then decreasing returns to scale was shown in Figure 6-18 on page 187. This production

Figure 8-1 Total Cost Function for a Production System Exhibiting *Constant* Returns to Scale

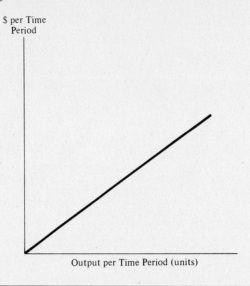

Figure 8-2 Total Cost Function for a Production System Exhibiting *Decreasing* Returns to Scale

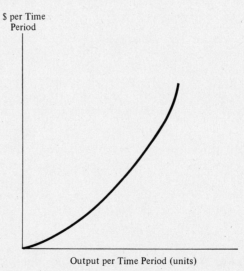

function implies the cubic cost function shown in Figure 8-3. Here costs increase less than proportionately with output over the range where returns to scale are increasing, but more than proportionately after decreasing returns set in.

All the direct relationships between production and cost functions described above are based on constant input prices. If input prices are a function of output, owing to such factors as discounts for volume purchases or, alternatively, to higher prices with greater usage because of a limited supply of inputs, the cost function will reflect this fact. For example, the cost function of a firm with constant returns to scale, but whose input prices increase with quantity purchased, will take the shape shown in Figure 8-2: Costs will rise more than proportionately as output increases. Quantity discounts, on the other hand, will produce a cost function that increases at a decreasing rate, as in the increasing returns section of Figure 8-3.

We see, then, that while cost and production are related, the nature of input prices must be examined before we attempt to estimate a cost function from the underlying production function. Input prices and productivity jointly determine the total cost function.

Before beginning a detailed examination of cost functions, it should prove useful to introduce several key cost relationships.

Figure 8-3   Total Cost Function for a Production System Exhibiting *Increasing* Then *Decreasing* Returns to Scale

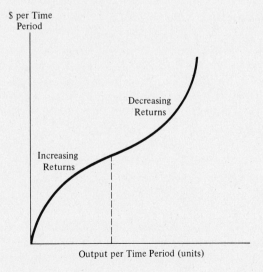

SHORT-RUN AND LONG-RUN COSTS

Two basic cost functions are used in managerial decision making: short-run cost functions, used in most day-to-day operating decisions, and long-run functions, typically used for long-range planning.

How does one distinguish the short run from the long run? The short run is defined as a period during which some inputs of a firm are fixed, while in the long run the firm can increase, decrease, or otherwise alter *all* factors of production without restriction. Thus, in the short-run period the firm's decisions are constrained by prior capital expenditures and other commitments; in the long run no such restrictions exist. For a public accounting firm operating out of a rented office, this period of constraint might be as short as several weeks, the time remaining on the office lease. A steel company, on the other hand, has a substantial investment in long-lived fixed assets, and until existing assets wear out and are replaced, its production and cost functions will be constrained.

In addition to the economic life of a firm's assets, their degree of specialization will also affect the period during which decisions are constrained. Consider, for example, a drugstore's purchase of an automobile for making deliveries. If the car is a standard model without modifications, it is essentially an unspecialized input factor; the car has a resale market consisting of the used-car market in general, and the pharmacy can sell it readily without an undue price reduction. If, however, the pharmacy has modified the car by adding refrigeration equipment for transporting perishable drugs, the car is a more specialized resource and its resale market is much more restricted, being limited to those individuals and firms who need a vehicle containing refrigeration equipment. In this case, the market price of the car might not equal its value in use to the pharmacy; hence, the short run is extended. We see, then, that at one extreme a firm operating with perfectly unspecialized factors has no short run; it can adjust to changes almost immediately by disposing of or purchasing assets in well-established markets. At the other extreme, when a firm employs highly specialized factors, no ready market exists, and the firm's short run extends for the entire economic life of the resources it currently owns.

The length of time required to order, receive, and install new assets also influences the duration of the short run. Electric utilities, for example, frequently must wait six to eight years to receive delivery of nuclear generating plants, and this obviously extends their short-run time horizon.

In summary, the long run is a period of sufficient length to permit a company to change its productive facilities completely by adding, subtracting, or modifying assets. The short run is the period during which at least some of the firm's productive equipment cannot be altered.[4] From this it is

[4] Within any firm, the long and short runs will vary for different decisions. If one division rents most of its equipment and deals with readily available and standardized

easy to see why long-run cost curves are often called *planning curves*, and short-run curves *operating curves*. In the long run, plant and equipment are variable, so management can plan the most efficient physical plant, given an estimate of the firm's demand function. Once the optimal plant has been determined and the resulting investment in equipment has been made, operating decisions will be constrained by this prior decision.

FIXED COSTS

Costs that are invariant with respect to output are defined as *fixed costs.* Included are interest on borrowed capital, rental expense on leased plant and equipment, depreciation charges associated with the passage of time, property taxes, and salaries of employees who cannot be laid off during periods of reduced output. No fixed costs exist in the long run.

VARIABLE COSTS

Variable costs, the opposite of fixed costs, vary with changes in output; they are a function of the output level. Included are such costs as raw materials expense, depreciation associated with the use of equipment, the variable portion of utility charges, some labor costs, sales commissions, and the costs of all other inputs that vary with output.[5] In the long run, all costs are variable.

SHORT-RUN COST CURVES

An illustrative short-run total cost curve is shown in Figure 8-4(*a*). As is apparent from the figure, total costs at each output level are the sum total of fixed costs (a constant) and total variable costs.

Since unit costs, either average or marginal, are used for most decision-making purposes, it is useful to examine these costs briefly. Defining *TC* as

---

inputs, its short run will be considerably shorter than that of another division that requires long-lived, nonstandardized facilities.

[5] Such a sharp distinction between fixed and variable costs is not always realistic. The president's salary may be fixed for most purposes, but if the firm went into a really severe depression, this "fixed" cost could certainly be reduced. Similarly, foremen's wages might be fixed within a certain range of outputs, but below a lower limit foremen might be laid off, while above the upper limit additional foremen would be hired. Also, the longer the duration of abnormal demand, the greater the likelihood that some fixed costs will actually be varied.

This recognition that certain costs are fixed only if output stays within prescribed limits, and that other costs can and will be varied if changed conditions are expected to persist, led to the development of the *semivariable* cost concept. In incremental cost analysis, it is essential that one consider the possibility of semivariable costs, which are fixed if incremental output does not exceed certain limits, but are variable outside these bounds.

Figure 8-4 Short-run Cost Curves: (*a*) Total Costs; (*b*) Unit Costs

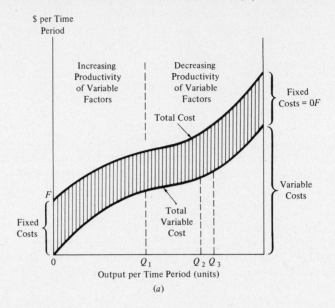

(*a*)

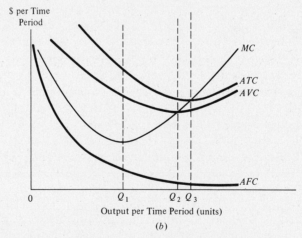

(*b*)

total cost, TFC as total fixed cost, TVC as total variable cost, and Q as the quantity of output produced during the relevant time span, the various unit costs are calculated as follows:

$$\text{Average Fixed Cost} = AFC = \frac{TFC}{Q}$$

$$\text{Average Variable Cost} = AVC = \frac{TVC}{Q}$$

$$\text{Average Total Cost} = ATC = \frac{TC}{Q} = AFC + AVC$$

$$\text{Marginal Cost}^6 = MC = \frac{\Delta TC}{\Delta Q} = \frac{dTC}{dQ}.$$

The unit cost curves corresponding to the total cost curve shown in Figure 8-4(a) are shown in Figure 8-4(b). Several important short-run cost relationships may be noted. First, the shape of the total cost curve is determined entirely by the total variable cost curve. That is, the slope of the total cost curve at each output level is identical to the slope of the total variable cost curve; fixed costs merely shift the total cost curve to a higher level. This means that marginal costs are totally independent of fixed cost. Marginal cost is the change in cost associated with a *change* in output, and because fixed costs are invariant with respect to output, fixed costs can in no way affect marginal cost.

Second, the shape of the total variable cost curve, and hence the total cost curve, is largely determined by the productivity of the variable input factors employed. Note that the variable cost curve in Figure 8-4 increases first at a decreasing rate, up to output level Q_1, and then at an increasing rate. Assuming constant input factor prices, this implies that the marginal productivity of the variable production inputs is first increasing, then decreasing. In other words, the variable input factors exhibit increasing returns in the range of 0 to Q_1 units and diminishing returns thereafter. This relationship is not unexpected. A firm's fixed factors, its plant and equipment, are designed to operate at some specific production level. Operating below that output level requires input combinations in which the variable factors are underutilized, so output can be increased more than proportionately to increases in variable inputs. At higher than planned output levels, however, the variable factors are being overutilized, the law of diminishing returns takes over, and a given percentage increase in the variable inputs will result in a smaller relative increase in output.

This relationship between short-run costs and the productivity of the variable input factors is also revealed by the unit cost curves. Marginal cost declines initially, over the range of increasing productivity, and rises thereafter. This imparts the familiar U shape to the average variable cost curve and the average total cost curve. Notice also that the marginal cost curve first declines rapidly in relation to the average variable cost curve and

---

[6] One frequently finds the term *incremental cost* used interchangeably with marginal cost when output changes are measured in descrete units; that is, when dealing with the relationship $\Delta TC/\Delta Q$. Actually, the term incremental cost is much broader than this. It refers to a change in total cost from any source—output related or not—and typically has no per-unit dimension. If the incremental cost is output related, then it refers to the total dollar cost difference associated with the change in output; that is, $\Delta TC =$ incremental cost. The incremental cost concept is examined in greater detail in Chapter 11.

the average total cost curve, then turns up and intersects each of these curves at its respective minimum point.[7]

LONG-RUN COST CURVES

In the long run the firm has no fixed commitments and, accordingly, no long-run fixed cost curve. Because all resources are variable, we need consider only long-run average total and long-run marginal cost curves.

Just as the short-run cost curves assumed optimal, or least-cost, input combinations for producing any level of output, *given the existing plant,* long-run cost curves are constructed on the assumption that an optimal plant, *given existing technology,* is used to produce any given output level.[8] Accordingly, long-run average cost curves can be thought of as an envelope of the short-run average cost curves for optimal plants of various scale.

This concept is illustrated in Figure 8-5, where four short-run average cost curves (*SAC*) representing four different scales of production are

Figure 8-5   Short-run Cost Curves for Four Scales of Plant

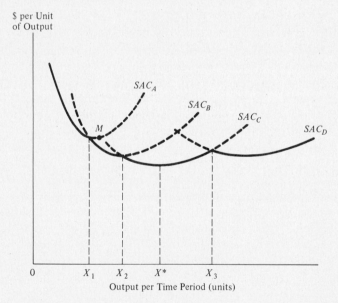

[7] The relationship between total, average, and marginal curves was discussed in Chapter 2, where we explained why the marginal cost curve intersects the average variable cost curve and the average total cost curve at their minimum points.
[8] "Existing technology" refers to the state of knowledge and abilities in the industry. If technological improvements occur, as in the development of more efficient electricity generation plants, the old production and cost functions no longer exist—they are replaced by new functions which can be quite different from the old ones.

shown. The four plants each have a range of output for which they are most efficient. Plant A, for example, provides the least-cost production system for output in the range 0 to X_1 units; Plant B provides the least-cost system for output in the range X_1 to X_2; Plant C is most efficient for output quantities X_2 to X_3; Plant D provides the least-cost production process for output above X_3.

The solid portion of each curve in Figure 8-5 indicates the minimum long-run average cost for producing each level of output, assuming only four possible scales of plant. We can generalize this by assuming that plants of many sizes, each one only slightly larger than the preceding one, are possible. As shown in Figure 8-6, the long-run average cost curve is then constructed so that it is tangent to each short-run average cost curve. At each tangency, the related scale of the plant is optimal; no other plant will produce that particular level of output at so low a total cost.

Notice that with a U-shaped long-run average cost curve, the most efficient plant for each output level will typically not be operating where its short-run average costs are minimized, as can be seen by referring to Figure 8-5. Plant A's short-run average cost curve is minimized at Point M, but at that output Plant B is more efficient; that is, B's short-run average costs are lower. In general, where increasing returns to scale exist, the least-cost plant

Figure 8-6 Long-run Cost Curve As the Envelope of All Short-run Curves

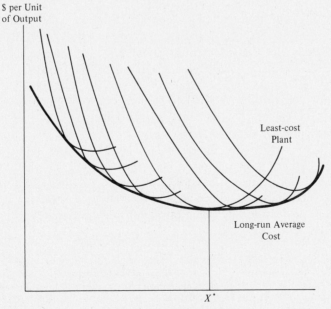

X^*

Output per Time Period (units)

will operate at less than capacity.[9] Only for that single output level at which long-run average cost is minimized—output X^* in Figures 8-5 and 8-6—will the optimal plant be operating at the minimum point on its short-run average cost curve. At all outputs in the range where decreasing returns to scale exist—that is, at any output greater than X^*—the most efficient plant will be operating at an output slightly greater than its capacity.

Economies of Scale

The cost systems illustrated in Figures 8-5 and 8-6 display first increasing, then decreasing returns to scale. Over the range of output produced by Plants A, B, and C in Figure 8-5, average costs are declining; these declining costs mean that total costs are increasing less than proportionately with output. Since Plant D's minimum cost is greater than that for Plant C, the system exhibits decreasing returns to scale at this higher output level.

Many factors combine to produce this pattern of first increasing, then decreasing returns to scale.[10] Economies of scale, which cause long-run average costs to decline, result from both production and market relationships. Specialization in the use of labor is one important factor that results in economies of scale. In the small firm a worker will probably have several jobs, and his proficiency at any of them is likely to be less than that of an employee who specializes in a single task. Thus, labor productivity is frequently greater in the large firm, where individuals can be hired to perform specialized tasks. This reduces the unit cost of production for larger scales of operation.

Technological factors also lead to economies of scale. As with labor, large-scale operations typically permit the use of highly specialized equipment, as opposed to the more versatile but less efficient machines used in smaller firms. Also, the productivity of equipment frequently increases with size much faster than does its cost. For example, a 500,000-kilowatt electricity generator costs considerably less than twice as much as a 250,000-kilowatt generator, and it also requires less than twice the fuel and labor inputs when operated at capacity.

The existence of quantity discounts also leads to economies through large-scale purchasing of raw materials, supplies, and other inputs. These economies extend to the cost of capital, as large firms typically have greater access to capital markets and can acquire funds at lower rates. These factors, and many more, lead to increasing returns to scale and hence to decreasing average costs.

---

[9] We define "capacity" not as a physical limitation on output but rather as the point where short-run average costs are minimized. We should note that businessmen and business writers use the term in many different ways, so its economic interpretation is not always obvious.

[10] The terms "economies of scale" and "increasing returns to scale" are used interchangeably.

Diseconomies of Scale

At some output level, however, the economies of scale may no longer hold, and average costs may begin to rise. Increasing average costs at high output levels are typically attributed to limitations in the ability of management to coordinate an organization after it reaches a very large size. This means (1) that staffs tend to grow more than proportionately with output, causing unit costs to rise, and (2) that managements become less and less efficient as size increases, again increasing the cost of producing a product. While the existence of such diseconomies of scale is disputed by some researchers, the evidence indicates that diseconomies may be significant in certain industries. Additional discussion of this point is included in the following chapter, where empirical cost relationships are analyzed.

FIRM SIZE AND PLANT SIZE

Production and cost functions exist both at the level of the individual plant and, for multiplant firms, at the level of the entire firm. The cost function of a multiplant (or multiproduct) firm can be simply the sum of the cost functions of the individual plants, or it can be greater or smaller than this figure. To illustrate, suppose that the situation as shown in Figure 8-6 holds; that is, there is a U-shaped long-run average cost curve at the plant level. If demand is sufficiently large, the firm will employ N plants, each of the optimal size and each producing Q^* units of output.

In this case, what would be the shape of the firm's long-run average cost curve? Figure 8-7 shows three possibilities. First, the long-run average cost would be constant, as in (a), if there are no economies or diseconomies of combining plants. Second, costs might decline throughout the entire range of output, as in (b), if multiplant firms are more efficient than single-

Figure 8-7   Three Possible Long-run Average Cost Curves for a Multiplant Firm: (a) Constant Costs; (b) Declining Costs; (c) U-shaped Cost Curve

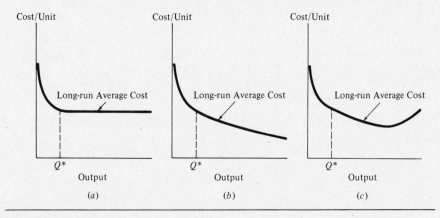

plant firms. Such cases, where they exist, are caused by economies of multi-plant operation. For example, all the plants may use a central billing service; purchasing economies may be obtained; centralized staffs of various types may serve all plants; and so on. The third possibility, shown in (c), is that costs may first decline (beyond Q^*, the output of the most efficient plant), and then rise. Here economies of scale for multiplant costs dominate initially, but later the cost of coordinating many operating units more than offsets these multiplant cost advantages.

All three kinds of long-run cost curves have been found in the United States economy, with different ones holding in different industries. Chapter 9 on empirical cost analysis includes additional discusson of this point, as do the chapters on market structure and market efficiency.

PLANT SIZE AND FLEXIBILITY

Is the plant that can produce a given output at the lowest possible cost necessarily the optimal plant for producing that expected level of output? The answer is an unequivocal "no." Consider the following situation. Although actual demand for a product is uncertain, it is expected to be 5,000 units a year. Two possible probability distributions for this demand are given in Figure 8-8. Distribution L exhibits a low degree of variability in demand; while Distribution H indicates substantially higher variation in possible demand levels.

Now suppose two plants can be employed to produce the required output. Plant A is quite specialized and is geared to produce a specified output

Figure 8-8 Probability Distributions of Demand

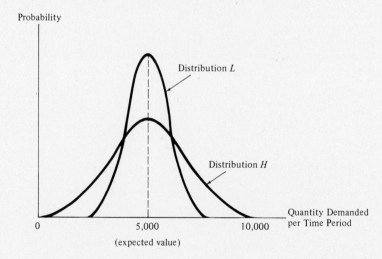

at a low cost per unit. If, however, more or less than the specified output is produced—in this case 5,000 units—unit production costs rise rapidly. Plant B, on the other hand, is more flexible. Output can be expanded or contracted without excessive cost penalties, but unit costs are not so low as those of Plant A at the optimal output level. These two cases are shown in Figure 8-9.

Plant A is more efficient than Plant B between 4,500 and 5,500 units of output, but outside this range B has lower costs. Which plant should be selected? The answer depends on the relative cost differentials at different output levels and the probability distribution for demand. The firm should select the plant with the lower expected average total cost.[11] In the example, if the demand probability distribution with the low variation—Distribution L—is correct, the more specialized facility will be optimal. If probability Distribution H more correctly describes the demand situation, however, the lower minimum cost of the more specialized facilities will be more than offset by the possibility of very high costs of producing outside the 4,500 to 5,500 unit range, and Plant B will have the lower expected costs.

Figure 8-9 Alternative Plants for Production of Expected 5,000 Units of Output

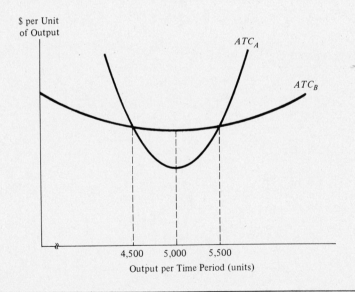

[11] The expected average total cost is defined as follows:

$$E(ATC) = \sum_{i=1}^{N} P_i ATC_i.$$

Here $E(ATC)$ is the expected ATC; P_i is the probability of the ith output; ATC_i is the ATC associated with the ith output level; and N is the number of possible output levels.

BREAKEVEN ANALYSIS

Breakeven analysis, or profit contribution analysis as it is often called, is an important analytical technique used to study the relationships between costs, revenues, and profits. The nature of breakeven analysis is depicted in Figure 8-10, a basic breakeven chart, composed of a firm's total cost and total revenue curves. The volume of output is measured on the horizontal axis, and revenue and cost are shown on the vertical axis. Since fixed costs are constant regardless of the output produced, they are indicated by a horizontal line. Variable costs at each output level are measured by the distance between the total cost curve and the constant fixed costs. The total revenue curve indicates the price/demand relationship for the firm's product, and profits (or losses) at each output are shown by the distance between the total revenue curve and the total cost curve.

Although Figure 8-10 is called a breakeven chart and can be used to

Figure 8-10   A Breakeven Chart

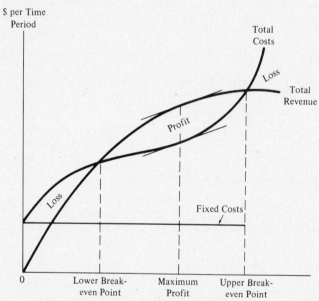

Units Produced and Sold per Time Period

Note: The slope of a line from the origin to a point on the total revenue line measures price—that is, total revenue/units sold = price—the slope of a line from the origin to the total cost curve measures average cost per unit. It can be seen that the angle of the line to the revenue curve declines as we move toward higher sales, which means the price is falling.

The slopes of the total cost and the total income lines measure marginal cost (*MC*) and marginal revenue (*MR*), respectively. At the point where the slopes of the two total curves are equal, *MR = MC*, and profits are at a maximum.

determine the output quantities at which the firm has zero profits, its analytical value goes well beyond indicating these breakeven output levels. The chart illustrates the relationship between revenues and costs at all levels of output and can therefore be used to analyze what happens to profits as volume varies.

Linear Breakeven Analysis

In practical applications of breakeven analysis, linear (straight-line) relationships are generally assumed in order to simplify the analysis. Nonlinear breakeven analysis is intellectually appealing for two reasons: (1) it seems reasonable to expect that in many cases increased sales can be achieved only if prices are reduced; and (2) our analysis of cost functions suggests that the average variable cost falls over some range of output and then begins to rise. Nevertheless, as our examples show, linear analysis is appropriate for certain uses.

Breakeven charts allow one to focus on key profit elements such as sales, fixed costs, and variable costs. In addition, even though linear breakeven charts are drawn extending from zero output to very high output quantities, no one who uses them would ordinarily be interested in, or even consider, the high and the low extremes. In other words, users of breakeven charts are really interested only in a "relevant range" of production, and within this range linear functions are probably reasonably accurate.

Figure 8-11 shows a typical linear breakeven chart. Fixed costs of $60,000 are represented by a horizontal line. Variable costs are assumed to be $1.80 a unit, so total costs rise by $1.80, the variable cost per unit, for each additional unit of output produced. The product is assumed to be sold for $3 a unit, so total revenue is a straight line through the origin. The slope of the total revenue line is steeper than that of the total cost line; this follows from the fact that the firm receives $3 in revenue for every $1.80 spent on labor, materials, and other variable input factors.

Up to the breakeven point, found at the intersection of the total revenue line and the total cost line, the firm suffers losses. After that point, it begins to make profits. Figure 8-11 indicates a breakeven point at a sales and cost level of $150,000, which occurs at a production level of 50,000 units.

Algebraic Breakeven Analysis

Although breakeven charts provide a useful means of illustrating profit/output relationships, algebraic techniques are typically a more efficient means for analyzing decision problems. The algebraic technique for solving a breakeven problem can be illustrated using the cost and revenue relationships shown in Figure 8-11. First, let:

$$P = \text{price per unit sold,}$$
$$Q = \text{quantity produced and sold,}$$
$$F = \text{total fixed costs, and}$$
$$V = \text{variable cost per unit.}$$

Figure 8-11 A Linear Breakeven Chart

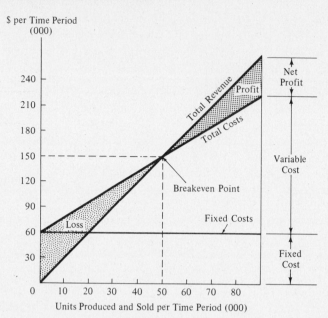

The breakeven quantity, defined as that volume of output at which total revenue ($P \cdot Q$) is exactly equal to total costs ($F + V \cdot Q$), is found as follows:

$$P \cdot Q = F + V \cdot Q$$
$$(P - V)Q = F \qquad \qquad (8\text{-}1)$$
$$Q = \frac{F}{P - V}.$$

In the example illustrated in Figure 8-11, $P = \$3$, $V = \$1.80$, and $F = \$60,000$, so the breakeven quantity is found as follows:

$$Q = \frac{\$60,000}{\$3 - \$1.80}$$
$$= 50{,}000 \text{ units.}$$

Example of Breakeven Analysis

The textbook publishing business provides a good example of the effective use of breakeven analysis for new product decisions. To illustrate, consider the following hypothetical example of the analysis for a college textbook:

Fixed Costs	
Copy Editing and Other Editorial Costs	$ 3,000
Illustrations	2,000
Typesetting	20,000
Total Fixed Costs	$25,000

Variable Costs per Copy	
Printing, Binding, and Paper	$ 1.60
Bookstore Discounts	2.40
Salesmen's Commissions	0.25
Author's Royalties	1.60
General and Administrative Costs	1.15
Total Variable Costs per Copy	$ 7.00

List Price per Copy	$12.00

The fixed costs can be estimated quite accurately; the variable costs, which are linear and which for the most part are set by contracts, can also be estimated with little error. The list price is variable, but competition keeps prices within a sufficiently narrow range to make a linear total revenue curve reasonable. Applying the formula of Equation 8-1, we find the breakeven sales volume to be 5,000 units:

$$Q = \frac{\$25,000}{\$12 - \$7}$$
$$= 5,000 \text{ units.}$$

Publishers can estimate the size of the total market for a given book, the competition, and other factors. With these data as a base, they can estimate the possibilities that a given book will reach or exceed the breakeven point. If the estimate is that it will do neither, the publisher may consider cutting production costs by reducing the number of illustrations, doing only light copy editing, using a lower grade of paper, negotiating with the author to reduce the royalty rate, and so on. In the publishing business—and also for new product decisions in many other industries—linear breakeven analysis has proved to be a useful tool.

Breakeven Analysis and Operating Leverage

Breakeven analysis is also a useful tool for analyzing the financial characteristics of alternative production systems. Here the analysis focuses on how total costs and profits vary with output as the firm operates in a more mechanized or automated manner and thus substitutes fixed costs for variable costs.

Operating leverage reflects the extent to which fixed production facilities, as opposed to variable production facilities, are used in operations. The relationship between operating leverage and profit variation is clearly indicated in Figure 8-12, in which three firms, A, B, and C, with differing degrees of leverage, are contrasted. The fixed costs of operations in Firm A are considered normal. It uses automated equipment, with which one operator can turn out a few or many units at the same labor cost, to about the same extent as the average firm in the industry. Firm B has lower fixed costs, but note the steeper rate of increase in variable costs of B over A. Firm B breaks even at a lower level of operations than does Firm A. For example, at a production level of 40,000 units, A is losing $8,000, but B breaks even.

Firm C has the highest fixed costs. It is highly automated, using expensive, high-speed machines that require very little labor per unit produced. With such an operation, its variable costs rise slowly. Because of the high overhead resulting from charges associated with the expensive machinery, C's breakeven point is higher than that of either A or B. Once Firm C reaches its breakeven point, however, its profits rise faster than do those of the other two firms.

Figure 8-12   Breakeven and Operating Leverage

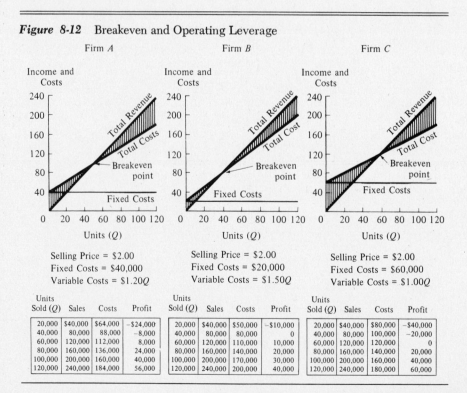

Selling Price = $2.00
Fixed Costs = $40,000
Variable Costs = $1.20Q

Selling Price = $2.00
Fixed Costs = $20,000
Variable Costs = $1.50Q

Selling Price = $2.00
Fixed Costs = $60,000
Variable Costs = $1.00Q

Units Sold (Q)	Sales	Costs	Profit
20,000	$40,000	$64,000	−$24,000
40,000	80,000	88,000	−8,000
60,000	120,000	112,000	8,000
80,000	160,000	136,000	24,000
100,000	200,000	160,000	40,000
120,000	240,000	184,000	56,000

Units Sold (Q)	Sales	Costs	Profit
20,000	$40,000	$50,000	−$10,000
40,000	80,000	80,000	0
60,000	120,000	110,000	10,000
80,000	160,000	140,000	20,000
100,000	200,000	170,000	30,000
120,000	240,000	200,000	40,000

Units Sold (Q)	Sales	Costs	Profit
20,000	$40,000	$80,000	−$40,000
40,000	80,000	100,000	−20,000
60,000	120,000	120,000	0
80,000	160,000	140,000	20,000
100,000	200,000	160,000	40,000
120,000	240,000	180,000	60,000

Degree of Operating Leverage

Operating leverage can be defined more precisely in terms of how a given change in volume affects profits. For this purpose we use the degree of operating leverage concept. *The degree of operating leverage is defined as the percentage change in profit that results from a percentage change in units sold.* Algebraically, this may be expressed as[12]:

$$\text{Degree of Operating Leverage} = \frac{\text{Percentage Change in Profit}}{\text{Percentage Change in Sales}}.$$

For Firm A in Figure 8-12, the degree of operating leverage at 100,000 units of output is 2.0, calculated as follows[13]:

$$DOL_A = \frac{\Delta\pi/\pi}{\Delta Q/Q} \tag{8-2}$$

$$= \frac{(\$56,000 - \$40,000)/\$40,000}{(120,000 - 100,000)/100,000} = \frac{16,000/40,000}{20,000/100,000}$$

$$= \frac{40\%}{20\%} = 2.0.$$

Here π is profit and Q is the quantity of output in units.

For linear relationships, a formula has been developed to aid in calculating the degree of operating leverage at any level of output Q[14]:

$$\text{Degree of Operating Leverage at Point } Q = \frac{Q(P-V)}{Q(P-V)-F}. \tag{8-3}$$

---

[12] Note that the degree of operating leverage is an elasticity concept, so we could call this measure "the operating leverage elasticity of profits." Since this elasticity measure is based on linear cost and revenue curves, it will vary depending on the particular part of the breakeven graph that is being considered. For example, the degree of operating leverage is always greatest close to the breakeven point, where a very small change in volume can produce a very large percentage increase in profits, simply because the base profits are close to zero near the breakeven point.

[13] To show the calculation, we arbitrarily assume that $\Delta Q = 20,000$. If we assume any other ΔQ—for example, $\Delta Q = 10,000$ or $\Delta Q = 40,000$—the degree of operating leverage will still turn out to be 2.0, because we are using linear cost and revenue curves. However, if we choose a base different from 100,000 units, we will find the degree of leverage different from 2.0.

[14] Equation 8-3 is developed as follows: The change in output is defined as ΔQ. Fixed costs are constant, so the change in profit is $\Delta Q(P-V)$, where $P =$ price per unit and $V =$ variable cost per unit.

The initial profit is $Q(P-V) - F$, so the percentage change in profit is:

$$\frac{\Delta Q(P-V)}{Q(P-V)-F}.$$

The percentage change in output is $\Delta Q/Q$, so the ratio of the change in profits to the change in output is:

$$\frac{\Delta Q(P-V)/[Q(P-V)-F]}{\Delta Q/Q} = \frac{\Delta Q(P-V)}{Q(P-V)-F} \cdot \frac{Q}{\Delta Q} = \frac{Q(P-V)}{Q(P-V)-F}.$$

Here P is the price per unit, V is the variable cost per unit, and F is fixed costs. Using Equation 8-3 we find Firm A's degree of operating leverage at 100,000 units of output to be:

$$DOL_A \text{ at } 100,000 \text{ units} = \frac{100,000(\$2.00 - \$1.20)}{100,000(\$2.00 - \$1.20) - \$40,000}$$
$$= \frac{\$80,000}{\$40,000} = 2.0.$$

The two methods must give consistent answers.

Equations 8-2 or 8-3 can also be applied to Firms B and C. When this is done, we find B's degree of operating leverage at 100,000 units to be 1.67 and that of C to be 2.5. Thus, for a 10 percent increase in volume C, the firm with the most operating leverage will experience a profit increase of 25 percent. For the same 10 percent volume gain B, the firm with the least leverage will have only a 16.7 percent profit gain.

In summary, the calculation of the degree of operating leverage shows algebraically the same pattern that Figure 8-12 shows graphically—that the profits of Firm C, the company with the most operating leverage, are most sensitive to changes in sales volume; while those of Firm B, which has only a small amount of operating leverage, are relatively insensitive to volume changes. Firm A, with an intermediate degree of leverage, lies between the two extremes.

PROFIT CONTRIBUTION ANALYSIS

In the short run, where many of a firm's costs are fixed and hence are invariant with respect to incremental sales and output decisions, management is often interested in determining the effects of a specific action on profits. Profit contribution analysis provides this information. Profit contribution is defined as the difference between revenues and variable costs and is therefore equal to price minus average variable cost on a per unit basis. For example, if a product sells for $10 and average variable costs are constant at $7, then $3 (= $10 − $7) is the per unit profit contribution of the product. The profit contribution can be applied to cover fixed costs or to increase reported profit.

Profit contribution analysis provides a convenient format for examining a variety of pricing and output decisions. To illustrate, consider again the textbook example discussed above. The variable costs of the proposed textbook are $7 a copy and the price is $12. This means that each copy sold provides $5 in profit contribution. Assume now that the publisher is interested in determining how many copies must be sold in order to earn a $10,000 profit on the text. Because profit contribution is the amount available to cover fixed costs and provide profit, the answer is found by adding the profit requirement to the book's fixed costs, then dividing by the per-unit profit contribution. The sales volume required in this case is 7,000 books, found as follows:

$$Q = \frac{\text{Fixed Costs} + \text{Profit Requirement}}{\text{Profit Contribution}}$$

$$= \frac{\$25,000 + \$10,000}{\$5}$$

$$= 7,000 \text{ units.}[15]$$

Consider a second decision problem that might confront the publisher. Assume that a book club has indicated an interest in purchasing the textbook for its members and has offered to buy 3,000 copies at $6 a copy. Profit contribution analysis can be used to determine the incremental effect of such a sale on the publisher's profits.

Since fixed costs are invariant with respect to changes in the number of textbooks sold, they can be ignored in the analysis. Variable costs per copy are $7, but note that $2.40 of this cost represents bookstore discounts. Since the 3,000 copies are being sold directly to the club, this cost will not be incurred, and hence the relevant variable cost is $4.60. Profit contribution per book sold to the book club then is $1.40 (= $6 − $4.60), and $1.40 times the 3,000 copies sold indicates that the order will result in a total profit contribution of $4,200. Assuming that these 3,000 copies would not have been sold through normal sales channels, the $4,200 profit contribution indicates the increase in profits to the publisher from accepting this order.

LIMITATIONS OF BREAKEVEN ANALYSIS

Breakeven analysis helps one understand the relations among volume, prices, and cost structure; and it is useful in pricing, cost control, and other financial decisions. However, breakeven analysis has limitations as a guide to managerial actions.

Linear breakeven analysis is especially weak in what it implies about the sales possibilities for the firm. Any given linear breakeven chart is based on a constant selling price. Therefore, in order to study profit possibilities under different prices, a whole series of charts is necessary, one chart for each price. Alternatively, nonlinear breakeven analysis can be used.

With regard to costs, breakeven analysis is also deficient—the linear relations indicated by the chart do not hold at all output levels. As sales increase, existing plant and equipment are worked beyond capacity, thus re-

---

[15] To see that 7,000 units will indeed produce a profit of $10,000, note the following calculations:

Sales Revenue $= \$12 \times 7,000 =$	$84,000
Total Cost $= FC + VC = \$25,000 + \$7(7,000) = \$25,000 + \$49,000 =$	74,000
Profit $=$ Sales Revenue $-$ Total Cost $=$	$10,000

ducing their productivity. This situation results in a need for additional workers and frequently longer work periods, which require the payment of overtime wage rates—all of which tend to cause variable costs to rise sharply. Additional equipment and plant may be required, thus increasing fixed costs. Finally, over a period the products sold by the firm change in quality and quantity. Such changes in product mix influence both the level and the slope of the cost function.

Although linear breakeven analysis has proved to be a useful tool for economic decision analysis, care must be taken to insure that it is not used in situations where its assumptions are violated so badly that the results of the analysis would be misleading. In other words, this decision tool, like all others, must be employed with a good deal of judgment.

SUMMARY

Cost relationships play a key role in most managerial decisions. In this chapter we introduced a number of cost concepts, showed the relationship between cost functions and production functions, and examined several short-run and long-run cost relationships.

Although the definition of relevant costs varies from one decision to another, several important relationships are common in all cost analyses. First, relevant costs are typically based on the alternative-use concept; the relevant cost of a resource is determined by its value in its best alternative use. Second, the relevant cost of a decision includes only those costs which are affected by the action being contemplated. This is the incremental cost concept. If a particular cost is unchanged by an action, the relevant incremental cost for decision purposes is zero. Finally, care must be taken to insure that all costs, both explicit and implicit, which are affected by a decision are included in the analysis.

Proper use of the relevant-cost concept requires an understanding of a firm's cost/output relationship, or its cost function. Cost functions are determined by the production function and the market-supply function for its inputs, with the production function specifying the technical relationship between inputs and output, and the prices of inputs converting this physical relationship to a cost/output function.

Two basic cost functions are used in managerial decision making—short-run cost functions, used in most day-to-day operating decisions; and long-run cost functions, used for planning purposes. The short run is the period during which some of the firm's productive facilities are unalterable; the long run is a period of sufficient length to permit the company to change its production system completely by adding, subtracting, or completely modifying its assets.

In the short run the shape of a firm's cost curves will be determined largely by the productivity of its variable input factors. Over that range of output where the marginal productivity of the variable inputs is increasing, costs will be increasing less than proportionately to output, so unit costs will be declining. Once diminishing returns to the variable factors set in, costs begin to increase faster than output, and unit costs will begin to rise.

A somewhat similar relationship holds for long-run cost curves. Here all inputs are variable, and the shape of the cost curve is determined by the presence of economies or diseconomies of scale. If economies of scale are present, unit costs will decline as output increases. Once diseconomies of scale begin to dominate, however, marginal and average cost curves will turn up.

Cost functions may be developed both at the level of the plant and, for multiplant firms, at the level of the firm. Frequently, because of economies of multiplant operation, the cost function of the multiplant firm is lower than the sum of the cost functions of the individual plants. These economies typically result from centralized computer facilities, financial activities, purchasing, marketing, and the like.

Although a firm desires to produce its output at the minimum possible cost, the existence of uncertainty often dictates a trade-off between lower costs and production flexibility. In these cases, the firm must examine the probability distribution of demand and the relative cost differentials of alternative production techniques, then select as the optimal system the one which maximizes the value of the firm.

Breakeven analysis was shown to be an important tool for analyzing the relations among fixed costs, variable costs, revenues, and profits. Its uses include analysis of the effects of varying the degree of operating leverage that a firm employs and incremental profit analysis using the profit-contribution concept.

QUESTIONS

8-1 The revelant cost for most managerial decision purposes is the *current* cost of an input. The relevant cost for computing income for taxes and stockholder reporting is the *historical* cost. Would it be preferable to use current costs for tax and stockholder reporting purposes?

8-2 What is the relationship among historical costs, current costs, and alternative or opportunity costs?

8-3 Are implicit costs reflected in income-tax calculations?

8-4 Explain in some detail the relationship between production functions and cost functions. Be sure to include in your discussion the impact of conditions in the input factor markets.

8-5 The president of a small firm has been complaining to his controller about rising labor and material costs. However, the controller notes that a just completed cost study indicates that average costs have not increased during the past year. Is this possible? What factors might you examine to analyze this phenomenon?

8-6 Given the short-run total cost curve in Figure 8-4, explain why (a) Q_1 is the minimum of the MC curve, (b) Q_2 is the minimum of the AVC curve, (c) Q_3 is the minimum of the ATC curve, and (d) the MC curve cuts the AVC and ATC curves at their minimum points.

8-7 Why is it possible for a multiplant firm to have either higher or lower unit costs than a single-plant firm?

8-8 How might the standard deviation of the probability distribution of sales influence plant design?

8-9 Of what use are cost curves to government officials?

PROBLEMS

8-1 Assume that output Q is a function of two inputs, or factors of production, X and Y. (In this problem, be *careful* with the geometry, as your graphs must reveal the required relationships.)

a) Construct a set of production isoquants that exhibit (i) diminishing marginal substitutability, and (ii) first increasing, then constant, and then decreasing returns to scale. Let the constant returns extend over a *range* of outputs. (Use a single two-dimensional graph.)

b) Assuming that factors X and Y are purchased in competitive markets, construct a *long-run total cost* curve that is consistent with the isoquant set constructed in Part a.

c) Construct average and marginal cost curves that are consistent with the total cost curve shown in Part b.

d) Explain what would happen to your graphs if the assumption of competitive factor markets in Part b is relaxed.

8-2 The Zipsaw Manufacturing Company markets a line of electric saws. The firm's current production capacity is 300,000 saws annually. Sales for next year have been forecast at 250,000 units, but Zipsaw has just received an offer to purchase 100,000 saws from a major tool distributor in a foreign market. The standard selling price for the saw is $50 in the domestic market, while the foreign offer calls for a price of $40. The costs associated with the manufacture of the saw are:

	Per Unit Cost
Raw Materials	$20.00
Direct Labor	10.00
Variable Overhead	3.00
Fixed Overhead (allocated on the basis of direct labor)	2.00
Total Cost	$35.00

a) Assuming that Zipsaw must either reject the offer or supply the entire 100,000 units, what are the relevant costs for the decision?

b) Using the profit contribution analysis concept, determine whether Zipsaw would increase or decrease its profits by accepting the offer.

8-3 The Edgewood Company manufactures a variety of electric appliances, several of which contain three units of a component known internally as Part B-0012, which is currently manufactured by the company in its own plant. The per-unit costs of B-0012 are:

Direct Material	$ 5.00
Direct Labor	3.00
Variable Overhead	2.00
Allocated Fixed Overhead	1.00
Total Cost per Unit	$11.00

Yearly usage of this item averages 2,000,000 units. The inventory manager wonders whether the company might save money by purchasing the component from an independent supplier at a price of $9 per unit. If the purchase program is instituted, storage costs would increase by $1,500,-000 a year, and an additional cost of $0.50 per unit would be incurred for ordering and receiving the part. No new investment would be needed, however, and there would be no impact on the plant's fixed overhead. Should the firm buy or make B-0012?

8-4 The Plentitude Products Company produces and markets three products: Long, Lang, and Ling. The company's current income statement is shown in the following table. The fixed production and selling costs are common to all three products and are allocated on the basis of sales revenue.

	Long	Lang	Ling	Total
Sales	$1,600,000	$1,200,000	$400,000	$3,200,000
Cost of Goods Sold:				
Variable	$ 800,000	$ 700,000	$300,000	$1,800,000
Fixed	$ 200,000	$ 150,000	$ 50,000	$ 400,000
Total Production Costs	$1,000,000	$ 850,000	$350,000	$2,200,000
Gross Margin	$ 600,000	$ 350,000	$ 50,000	$1,000,000
Selling Expenses:				
Variable	$ 80,000	$ 60,000	$ 20,000	$ 160,000
Fixed	$ 160,000	$ 120,000	$ 40,000	$ 320,000
Total Selling Expenses	$ 240,000	$ 180,000	$ 60,000	$ 480,000
Net Income (before tax)	$ 360,000	$ 170,000	$(10,000)	$ 520,000

The company management is considering dropping Ling from the line of products because it has consistently shown a loss. Would the removal of Ling improve the company's profit position?

8-5 Altec Corporation is engaged in the manufacture and sale of Product X. It has specialized facilities with a maximum annual capacity of 15,000 units. The marketing department has estimated that sales of 12,500 units can be realized if the price of X is reduced from the present $8 a unit to $5. The product is unprofitable at the current sales of 2,500 units, and the management, while in agreement with the sales estimate, is unsure that the greater output at the significantly lower revenue per unit will actually result in the product's becoming profitable. Current costs per unit of X can be summarized as follows:

Average Costs	
Labor	$2.50
Materials	1.90
Overhead (all fixed)	5.00
Total Average Cost	$9.40

The production function for X is such that labor productivity will increase by 50 percent if the higher output is produced. Additionally, a 10 percent quantity discount on material purchases will be available. The total overhead costs are not expected to change.

a) Assuming that the facilities for producing X are both expensive and new and that because of specialization they have a salvage value of $0, what short-run action would you recommend for Altec? Justify your recommendation.

b) Would your long-run recommendation for this decision problem be different? Why?

8-6 Bip Corporation manufactures and sells ballpoint pens. The current price received for the pens is $5.00 per gross, and the unit variable profit or profit contribution is $2.00 per gross. Sales of these pens—and profits—have been below expectations, and an attempt is being made to increase them. Bip is considering improving the quality of their pens at a cost of $0.25 per gross, and increasing advertising expenditure by $25,000 to promote the quality improvement. Current profits are $25,000 on sales of 200,000 gross of pens.

a) Determine the current total fixed costs for Bip.

b) What increase in sales must the quality improvement cause if Bip is to double its profits on this product? (Assume that Bip does not change the price of its product and that variable costs, other than the improvement cost, are constant.)

8-7 The Boxco Corporation produces and sells returnable containers to major food processors. The price received for the containers is $2 a unit. Of this amount $1.25 is profit contribution. Boxco is considering an attempt to differentiate its product through quality improvement at a cost of $0.05 a unit. Current profits are $40,000 on sales of 100,000 units.

a) Assuming that average variable costs are constant at all output levels, what is Boxco's total cost function before the proposed change?

b) What will the total cost function be if the quality improvement is implemented?

c) Assuming that the management does not feel it can raise the price of the containers above $2 and remain competitive, at least initially, what increase in sales would be necessary to increase profits to $45,000 with the quality improvement?

d) What would be the profit-maximizing price and output if Boxco is successful in differentiating its product so that it faces the demand curve $P = 3 - 0.000008Q$?

8-8 (Note: This problem should be assigned only if Problem 6-1 was also assigned.) Problem 6-1 presented a cubic production function, $Q = 0.2X + 0.9X^2 - 0.005X^3$, with $Q = $ output and $X = $ units of input. Now assume that the cost of the input factor is constant at $5 a unit, that total fixed costs are $20,000, and that the market price of a unit of output is $10.

a) Referring to Problem 6-1, use the already calculated total product (Q) for the units of input $X = 90, 100, 110, 120, 130,$ and 140 to compute (i) total variable costs (TVC), (ii) total fixed costs (TFC), (iii) total costs (TC), (iv) total revenue (TR), and (v) profit (π).

b) Determine the input and output levels where profit is maximized. What is the maximized profit? (Use *both* the table prepared in Part a and the calculus technique shown in Chapter 2.)

8-9   The Elek Company is a manufacturer of transitors for a variety of electronic applications. Elek's management is considering the possibility of producing a specialized transistor for one of its clients. Since only this client will be purchasing the new transistor, the managers of the firm have a very good estimate of the relationship between price and demand. Specifically, they have *estimated* that 30,000 units ($\pm3,000$) could be sold at a price of $3.00. The variable cost per unit for Elek would be $2.00, while fixed costs would increase by $25,000 if the new product was manufactured.
  a)   Graph the breakeven chart for the new product.
  b)   What is the breakeven point in units for the new transistor?
  c)   What would be the level of operating profits at the estimated demand level?
  d)   At the estimated demand level, what is the degree of operating leverage?
  e)   What would be the percentage change in profits if sales were to be at the lower end of the estimated range rather than at 30,000 units?
  f)   Given all the information from Parts a–e, do you think the managers should start production of the product?

8-10 Atlas Fasteners, Incorporated, is producing and selling 40,000 units of output. Because its plant capacity is 40,000 units, orders are being lost and the company is considering expanding capacity to 50,000 units. Its product sells for $6 a unit and management expects to maintain that price if capacity is expanded. Currently, output has a variable cost of $2 a unit and fixed costs are $80,000. Expansion of capacity to 50,000 units will increase fixed costs by 50 percent to $120,000, but variable costs per unit will decline by 40 percent to $1.20.
  a)   What is the firm's current breakeven output level?
  b)   What is the firm's current degree of operating leverage at 40,000 units?
  c)   What percentage increase in operating income (profit) would result from a 20 percent increase in output, assuming the firm continues operating with its current facilities?
  d)   Considered by itself (that is, assuming that variable cost per unit remains at $2), would the increase in fixed costs associated with expansion increase, decrease, or leave unchanged the degree of operating leverage at 40,000 units?
  e)   Considered by itself (that is, assuming that fixed costs remain at $80,000), would decrease in variable costs associated with expansion increase, or leave unchanged the degree of operating leverage at 40,000 units?
  f)   What is the combined effect in this case of the increase in fixed costs and the decrease in variable costs per unit on the degree of operating leverage at 40,000 units of output?
  g)   What is the importance of analyzing operating leverage in a decision problem such as this one?

SELECTED REFERENCES

Anthony, Robert N. "What Should 'Cost' Mean?" *Harvard Business Review*, May-June 1970, pp. 121-131.

Baumol, W. J., and C. Sevin. "Marketing Costs and Mathematical Programming," *Harvard Business Review,* September-October 1957, pp. 52-60.

Eiteman, W. J. "Factors Determining the Location of the Least Cost Point," *American Economic Review,* December 1947, pp. 910-918.

Henderson, James M., and Richard E. Quandt. *Microeconomic Theory,* 2d ed. New York: McGraw-Hill, 1971, Chapter 3.

Hirshleifer, J. "The Firm's Cost Function: A Successful Reconstruction," *Journal of Business,* July 1962, pp. 235-255.

Menger, K. "The Laws of Return," in O. Morgenstern, ed., *Economic Activity Analysis.* New York: Wiley, 1954, pp. 419-482.

Moroney, John R. "Cobb-Douglas Production Functions and Returns to Scale in U.S. Manufacturing Industry," *Western Economic Journal,* December 1967, pp. 39-51.

CHAPTER 9

Empirical Cost Analysis

The preceding chapter demonstrated the importance of a detailed knowledge of both long-run and short-run cost functions for many practical decision purposes. The short-run cost curve provides useful information for short-run pricing and output decisions; with the long-run curve, the firm can do a better job of planning its capacity requirements and future plant configurations.

Public officials are also interested in long-run and short-run cost functions. As will be shown in Chapters 10, 11, and 12, regulatory authorities (including the Antitrust Division of the Justice Department) can influence the size of business enterprises. If the size of a firm is held down below the least-cost level, economic efficiency suffers. On the other hand, if economies of scale are not important, regulators can perhaps justify a policy of limiting the size of a firm (by breaking up a large firm or by prohibiting mergers) in order to stimulate competition.

A number of analytical techniques have proved useful in the empirical estimation of cost functions. In this chapter we examine several of these techniques, illustrating their particular strengths and noting some of their weaknesses and limitations.

SHORT-RUN COST ESTIMATION

By assuming that the firm has been operating efficiently, or at least that inefficiencies can be isolated and accounted for, it is possible to estimate cost functions by statistical analysis. Time-series regression analysis is the most popular method used for estimating a firm's short-run variable cost function.[1] In such regression studies, total variable cost is regressed on output, typically in a model that includes a number of other variables whose effects on cost we wish to analyze or at least to account for. The total variable cost function rather than the total cost function is estimated in order to remove the very difficult problem of allocating fixed costs to a particular production quantity. Since these allocated costs are invariant with respect to output, they cannot affect the important average variable cost function and the marginal cost function that are used for short-run decision-making purposes; allocated costs can therefore be safely eliminated from the analysis.

Cost Specification and Data Preparation

Most difficulties encountered in statistical cost analysis arise from two causes: (1) errors in the specification of the cost characteristics that are relevant for decision-making purposes, and (2) problems in the collection and modification of the data to be analyzed. Thus, before examining the types of regression models actually used to estimate short-run cost functions, we should consider several caveats regarding specification, collection, and modification of cost data.

Conceptual Problems   Managerial decision making pertains to future activities and events, so the relevant costs for managerial decisions are future costs, as opposed to current or historical costs. Cost estimates based on accounting data—which record actual current or past costs and are thus historical—must therefore be considered as first approximations to the relevant costs in managerial economics. These accounting costs must be modified to account for likely changes before they are used for decision-making purposes.

A second conceptual problem, encountered when accounting data are used for cost analysis, stems from the failure of accounting systems to record opportunity costs. Since opportunity costs are frequently the largest and the most important costs in a short-run decision problem, cost functions derived from accounting data are often inappropriate. As Joel Dean, a pioneer in the development of managerial economics, has so aptly stated: "In business problems the message of opportunity costs is that it is dangerous to confine cost knowledge to what the firm is doing. What the firm is not doing but

---

[1] *See* Chapter 5 for a discussion of the least squares regression technique.

could do is frequently the critical cost consideration which it is perilous but easy to ignore." [2]

Cost/Output Matching   Another problem may arise in the attempt to relate certain costs to output. In short-run cost analysis, only the costs that vary with output should be included, but it is often difficult to distinguish between those costs which are and those which are not related to output. Economic depreciation of capital equipment is perhaps the best example of this difficulty. For most depreciable assets, both time and usage determine the rate of decline in value, but only the component related to usage should be included in the short-run cost estimation. Both components, however, are generally embodied in accounting data on depreciation costs, and it is often impossible to separate the use costs from the obsolescence or time-related costs.

Semivariable costs present a similar problem. Some costs may not vary with respect to output over certain ranges but may vary with output once a critical level has been exceeded for a long enough period. These cost/output relationships must be accounted for if accurate short-run cost functions are to be estimated.

Timing of Costs   An additional problem that arises from the use of accounting data is that of relating costs to the corresponding output. Care must be taken to adjust the data for leads and lags between cost reporting and output production. Maintenance expense provides a typical example of this problem: Production in one period causes additional maintenance expenses not in that period but, rather, in subsequent periods. During a period of high production, recorded maintenance expenses will be unusually low because the firm's equipment is being used at full capacity, so that maintenance must be postponed if possible. Repairs that are made will usually be temporary in nature, aimed at getting the equipment back into production rapidly until a period when some slack exists in the production system. Without careful adjustment, this problem can cause gross errors in statistically estimated cost functions.

Inflation   Price level changes present still another problem. In time-series analysis, recorded historical data are generally used for statistical cost analysis, and during most of the period for which data are available the costs of labor, raw materials, and other items have been rising. At the same time, an expanding population and greater affluence have caused the output of most firms to increase. The more recent output is therefore large and has a relatively high cost, and a naïve cost study might suggest that costs rise rapidly

[2] Joel Dean. *Managerial Economics.* Prentice-Hall, Englewood Cliffs, N.J., 1951, p. 260.

with increases in output when this is not the case. To remove this bias, cost data must be deflated for price level changes. The problem of adjusting for price variation is, however, compounded by the fact that price changes related to increases in demand for various inputs, when the firm's output rate increases (that is, when there are upward movements along an input supply curve) must not be removed. Only price changes that are independent of the production system under examination should be eliminated; otherwise, the statistically estimated cost function will understate the true cost of high-level production.[3]

Observation-period Problems Short-run cost curves are, by definition, cost/output relationships for a plant of specific scale and technology. If the short-run curve is to be accurately estimated, the period of examination must be one during which the product remains essentially unchanged and the plant facilities remain fixed. It should be noted that even though a firm's book value of assets remains relatively constant during the observation period, the plant may have actually changed significantly. Consider, for example, a firm that replaces a number of obsolete manual milling machines, which have been fully depreciated, with a single automated machine, which it leases. The firm's production function, and hence its total cost function, could have changed substantially even though the book value of assets remains constant. The problem of changing plant and product can be minimized by limiting the length of the period over which data are gathered. For satisfactory statistical estimation, however, the cost analyst needs an adequate sample size over a fairly broad range of outputs, and this requirement tends to lengthen the necessary period of data collection; this, in turn, necessitates a careful examination of a firm's total activities over the period of a cost study if accurate results are to be achieved.

Given the need for numerous data observations over a relatively short period, it is apparent that frequent data observations covering short production periods can improve the statistical results in empirical cost studies. Likewise, it is theoretically more satisfying to use frequent data observation points (for example, daily or weekly) so that output rates will be fairly constant *within* the observation period. At odds with this, however, is the fact that data collection and correction problems are magnified as the length of the observation period is shortened. Although the best length for the observation period will vary from situation to situation, one month is the period most frequently used. In other words, the various elements of vari-

---

[3] A further difficulty encountered in statistical cost studies when prices fluctuate during the period of examination results from the substitution among the various input factors that takes place when their relative prices change. That is, price level changes rarely result in proportional changes in the prices of all goods and services and, as was shown in Chapter 6, optimal input combinations depend in part on the relative prices of resources. Changes in optimal input combinations will affect the cost projections that are relevant for managerial decision analysis.

able costs incurred during each month are collected and compared with output produced during the month. A total period of perhaps three years (thirty-six months) can provide enough observations for statistical analysis, yet still be short enough that the plant and the product have remained relatively constant. It is not possible to generalize about the best period of study for all cases—the facts of the individual case must always be taken into account.

This brief examination of some of the major data problems encountered in short-run statistical cost analysis points up the importance of proper data collection within the firm. That is, the value of statistical cost analysis to a firm is in large part a function of its cost-accounting records. With this in mind, many firms are developing computerized management information systems in which cost and output data are recorded in sufficient detail to allow statistical analysis of their cost/output relations. It must be emphasized that, to be useful for managerial decision-making purposes, these management information systems must go well beyond the collecting and reporting of data found in standard accounting systems. Thus, careful planning and a clear understanding of the relevant cost concepts used for various business decisions are required for establishing an information system that will provide the necessary inputs for proper decision analysis.

Statistical Short-run Cost Functions

Once the data problems have been solved, cost analysts are faced with the problem of determining the proper functional form of the cost curve. A variety of linear and nonlinear models suitable for least squares regression analysis are available. If there are good theoretical or engineering reasons for using a particular model, that model will be selected. Often, however, there is no a priori reason for choosing one model over another, and in such cases the typical procedure is to fit several models to the cost/output data, then use the one that seems to fit best in terms of the statistical tests, especially R^2, the coefficient of determination. In other words, if one model has an R^2 of 0.80, indicating that the model explains 80 percent of the variation in total variable costs, and another model has an R^2 of 0.90, the second model will be relied upon for operating decisions.

Linear Short-run Cost Functions   For a great many production systems, a linear statistical cost curve of the form shown below provides an adequate fit of the cost/output data:

$$Y = a + bQ + \sum_{i=1}^{n} c_i X_i. \tag{9-1}$$

Here, Y refers to the total variable cost during an observation period; Q is the quantity of output produced during that period; X_i designates all other independent variables whose effects on cost the analyst wants to account for;

and a, b, and c_i are the parameters of the model as determined by the least squares regression technique. The "other" independent variables to be accounted for include such items as wage rates, fuel costs, weather, input quality, and so on. Including them in the model enables the analyst to obtain a better estimate of the relationship between cost and output.

The intercept parameter a in this model is typically irrelevant. It cannot be interpreted as the firm's fixed costs because such costs are not included in the data. Even if total costs, as opposed to total variable costs, are used as the dependent variable, the intercept parameter a still could not be interpreted as the firm's fixed costs. This parameter is nothing more than the intercept of the estimated cost curve with the vertical axis. This intersection occurs where output is zero and lies far outside the typical range of cost/output data observation points.

Although a linear form for the cost/output relationship may be very accurate for the range of available data, extrapolation far outside this range can lead to serious misstatements of the true relationship.[4] The problem of extrapolation outside the observation range is illustrated in Figure 9-1.

Figure 9-1 Linear Approximation of the Cost/Output Function

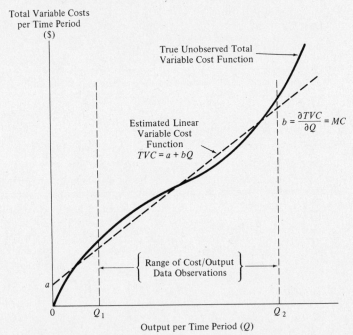

Within the observed output range, Q_1 to Q_2, a linear function closely approximates the true cost/output relationship. Extrapolation beyond these limits, however, leads to inaccurate estimates of the firm's variable costs.

The parameter b is the important one in a linear model of this type. As shown in both Figures 9-1 and 9-2, b provides an approximation to both marginal costs and average variable cost within the relevant output range.

Quadratic and Cubic Cost Functions Two other forms, the quadratic and the cubic, are also widely used in empirical cost studies. Figures 9-3 and 9-4 illustrate the average variable cost curve and the marginal cost curve associated with quadratic and cubic cost functions. Again, it should be emphasized that costs which are invariant with respect to output (fixed costs) are not typically included in the empirical estimates of short-run cost curves, so these curves are representative of variable costs only. An estimate of the fixed cost must be added to determine the firm's short-run total cost function.

Figure 9-2 Average Variable Cost and Marginal Cost for a Linear Estimated Cost Function—$TVC = a + bQ$

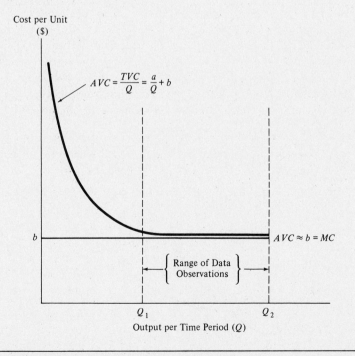

Note: If $a = 0$, $AVC = b = a$ constant. However, if $a > 0$, AVC declines continuously, but at a decreasing rate as output increases, because as Q becomes large, a/Q becomes smaller and smaller.

Figure 9-3 Average Variable Cost and Marginal Cost Curves for Quadratic Total Variable Cost Function—$TVC = a + bQ + cQ^2$

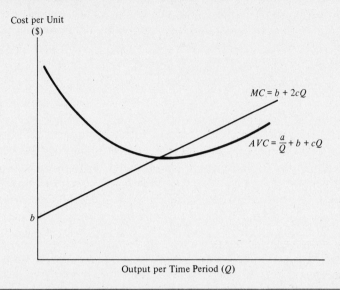

Empirically Estimated Short-run Cost Functions Many empirical studies have been undertaken in attempts to ascertain the nature of cost/output relationships in the short run. Joel Dean's pioneering studies of short-run costs in a furniture factory, a hosiery mill, and a leather belt shop in the late 1930s and early 1940s all indicated that costs and output were linearly related and, hence, that marginal costs were constant over the observed out-

Figure 9-4 Average Variable Cost and Marginal Cost Curves for a Cubic Variable Cost Function—$TVC = a + bQ - cQ^2 + dQ^3$

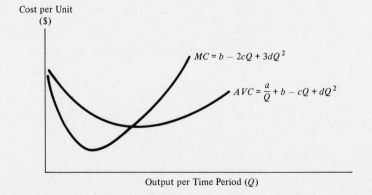

put ranges.[5] In another cost study[6] Dean estimated that marginal costs were constant in the hosiery and the shoe departments of a large department store, and slightly declining in the coat department. Dean concluded his report of the latter study by noting that while the regression results indicated a linear cost function for two of the three departments, "the unexplained scatter of observations is great enough to permit a cubic of the traditional form to be fitted in each case. However, the curvature would be so slight as to be insignificant from a managerial viewpoint, so that it could scarcely affect any economic conclusions which might be derived from the linear functions." [7]

Another early cost study was that conducted by T. O. Yntema on costs at United States Steel Corporation.[8] The statistical cost function he estimated was:

$$\text{Total Cost} = \$132{,}100{,}000 + \$55.73Q,$$

where Q was a measure of output in tons of steel. Thus, Yntema found that the company's cost function was linear and that the marginal cost of producing an additional ton of steel was \$55.73.

These early findings that short-run costs could be accurately estimated for many kinds of businesses by a linear function have been supported by more recent cost studies. By far the most complete statement of these empirical cost studies is found in J. Johnston's *Statistical Cost Analysis*,[9] in which Johnston summarizes a considerable number of cost studies performed by others and then examines both short-run and long-run cost functions for a variety of firms and industries. His short-run results tend to confirm the generality of the linear relationships reported earlier by Dean and by Yntema and they lend further support to the hypothesis that marginal costs for many firms remain fairly constant over a substantial output range.

LONG-RUN STATISTICAL COST ESTIMATION

Statistical estimation of long-run cost curves, although similar in many respects to short-run cost estimation, is typically somewhat more complex. In the long run, all costs are variable, and the problem is to determine the

[5] These studies were reported in the following: *Statistical Determination of Costs with Special Reference to Marginal Costs*, University of Chicago Press, Chicago, 1936; *Statistical Cost Functions of a Hosiery Mill*, University of Chicago Press, Chicago, 1941; "The Relation of Cost to Output for a Leather Belt Shop," National Bureau of Economic Research, New York, 1941.

[6] Joel Dean, "Department Store Cost Functions," in Oskar Lange, ed. *Studies in Mathematical Economics and Econometrics*. Cambridge Press, London, 1942.

[7] Dean, *op. cit.*, p. 254.

[8] T. O. Yntema. "Steel Prices, Volume and Costs," *United States Steel Corporation Temporary National Economic Committee Papers*, vol. 2, 1940.

[9] J. Johnston. *Statistical Cost Analysis*. McGraw-Hill, New York, 1960.

shape of the least-cost production curve for plants of different size. Total cost curves must be estimated, and this, in turn, introduces a number of additional difficulties.

As with short-run analysis, one can analyze the long-run cost/output relationship by examining a single firm over a long period. In this case the assumption that plant size is held constant during the examination period is removed, and total costs are regressed against output. The basic problem with this approach is that it is almost impossible to find a situation where the scale of a firm has been variable enough to allow statistical estimation of a long-run cost curve while, at the same time, technology and other extraneous conditions have remained constant. Without constant technology the function estimated in this manner will bear little resemblance to the relevant long-run cost function necessary for planning purposes.

Because of the difficulties encountered in using time-series data to estimate long-run cost functions, a different procedure, cross-sectional regression analysis, is frequently employed. This procedure involves a comparison of different size firms (or plants) at one point in time, regressing total costs against a set of independent variables. The key independent variable is again a measure of output, and other independent variables—such as regional wage rates, fuel costs, and the like—are included to account for the impact on cost of factors other than the level of output.

The use of cross-sectional analysis, as opposed to time-series analysis, for estimating long-run cost functions reduces some estimation problems and magnifies others. For example, since the data all represent factor prices at one point in time, the problem of price inflation (or deflation) is removed. A new problem arises, however, because factor input prices vary in different regions of the country; unless all the firms in the sample are located in the same region, interregional price variations may distort the analysis.

A second difficulty in cross-sectional studies can be traced to variations in accounting procedures. Differing depreciation policies among firms and varying techniques for amortizing major expenses such as research and development costs can substantially distort the true cost/output relationship.

A similar distortion in statistical cost analysis can arise if the firms examined use different means of factor payment. For example, one firm might pay relatively low wages to its employees but may have a substantial profit-sharing program. If this firm's costs are compared with those of a firm that pays higher wages but has no profit sharing, and if shared profits are not included in wage costs, it is clear that an adjustment must be made prior to estimating the cost function for the industry.

Finally, even if all these data problems are solved so that the effects on costs of all factors other than output are held constant, a last requirement must also be met if we are to estimate accurately the long-run cost function. A basic assumption in the use of cross-sectional data is that all firms are operating at the point along the long-run curve at which costs are minimized. That is, the cross-sectional technique assumes that all firms are operating in an efficient manner and are using the most efficient plant available for producing whatever level of output they are producing. If this assumption holds, the cost/output relationship found in the analysis does trace a long-run cost curve, such as that shown as *LRAC* in Figure 9-5. If this assumption is violated, however, the least squares regression line will lie above the true *LRAC* curve, and costs will be overstated.

Even more important than the uniform overstatement of average cost is the possibility that the true curvature in the long-run average cost curve may be accentuated and may thereby overstate any economies or diseconomies of scale available to firms in the industry being examined. For example, if the smaller firms in Figure 9-5 are operating well to the right of their optimal output, the estimated *LRAC* curve will have a downward slope much steeper than the true *LRAC* curve, and this bias will cause one to overestimate the extent of economies of scale in the industry.

Empirical Long-run Cost Functions

The great majority of empirically estimated long-run cost functions exhibit sharply increasing returns to scale at low output levels, but the extent of these scale economies declines as output increases and constant returns appear to hold at high output level. This means that the long-run average cost curve decreases at a decreasing rate as output increases, finally becoming horizontal. Very few studies have found evidence of decreasing returns to scale—an upturn in the average cost curve—at high output levels.

The results just discussed have caused researchers to hypothesize that typical long-run average cost curves are L-shaped as opposed to the U-shaped curves postulated in microeconomic theory. P. J. D. Wiles, for example, in discussing the results of his study of forty-four sets of data on long-run cost/output relations, states that "average costs descend like the

---

***Figure* 9-5**   Estimating Long-run Average Cost Curves with Cross-sectional Data

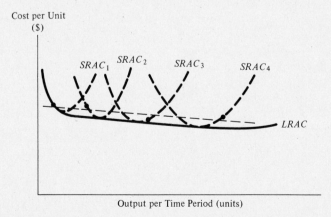

left-hand branch of a capital U, swiftly at first then more gently. Decreasing costs with size are almost universal. But the U seldom turns up. Sharply increasing costs with size are practically unknown and even slight increases are rare." [10] Wiles concludes that most of the cost functions "obey what we may call the law of L-shaped costs."

The study by Johnston led him to similar conclusions about the nature of long-run average costs. In examining the costs of electrical power generation in Great Britain, for example, Johnston found that average costs fell initially and then leveled off, indicating that "economies of scale in electricity generation can be fully exploited by firms of median size." [11]

Alternative Cost Estimation Techniques

Because of the difficulty of obtaining satisfactory statistical estimates of long-run cost/output relationships, several alternative means of empirically examining cost functions have been developed. Two of these, the survivor technique and the engineering technique, have proved to be very useful in certain situations where statistical cost estimation is tenuous, if not impossible, because of the absence of adequate data, or where checks on statistical cost estimates are sought. These techniques are discussed below.

Survivor Technique The survivor principle was developed by George Stigler.[12] The basic idea behind this technique is that more efficient firms—that is, those with lower average costs—will survive through time. Therefore, by examining the size makeup of an industry over time, one can determine the nature of its cost/output relations.

More specifically, Stigler proposes that one classify the firms in an industry by size and calculate the share of the industry output or capacity provided by each size class over time. If the share of one class declines over time, that size production facility is assumed to be relatively inefficient. If the relative share increases, however, firms of that size are presumed to be relatively efficient and hence to have lower average costs.

The survivor technique has been applied to several industries to examine the question of returns to scale. Stigler examined the distribution of steel production between firms of varying size in 1930, 1938, and 1951.[13] He found that over this period the percentage of industry output accounted for by the smallest and the largest size classes declined, while the output share of medium-sized firms increased. These findings indicate a long-run average cost curve such as that illustrated in Figure 9-6. Returns to scale are increasing at low output levels, are nearly constant over a wide range of intermediate output, and are decreasing at higher output levels.

[10] P. J. D. Wiles. *Prices, Cost, and Output*. Basil, Blackwell and Mott, Oxford, 1956.
[11] Johnston. *Op. cit.*, p. 73.
[12] George J. Stigler. "The Economics of Scale," *The Journal of Law and Economics*, vol. 1, no. 1, October 1958, pp. 54-71.
[13] Stigler. *Op. cit.*

Figure 9-6 Long-run Average Costs for Steel Production As Determined by the Survivor Technique

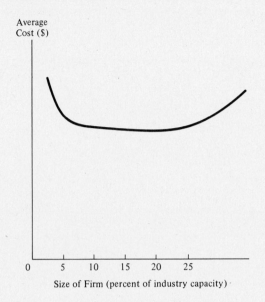

Average Cost ($)

0   5   10   15   20   25

Size of Firm (percent of industry capacity)

Stigler also applied the technique to the automobile industry. Again, he found that the smallest firms showed a continual decline in their share of total industry output; and he concluded from this that average costs decline with size. The small firms' losses were distributed equally among medium-sized and larger firms, indicating first increasing, then constant, returns to scale. Since there was no indication of diseconomies of scale at very high output levels, the conclusion was that the automobile industry's long-run average cost curve is L-shaped.

In a more recent study of economies of scale in the Portland cement industry Bruce T. Allen also found an L-shaped long-run average cost curve.[14] Table 9-1 provides data on the composition of cement production by plant size for the years 1965 and 1971. The data indicate that plant-size classes of less than 3.25 million barrels a year accounted for smaller shares of industry capacity in 1971 than in 1965, and that plant-size classes in excess of 3.25 million barrels accounted for larger shares of industry capacity in 1971 than in 1965.

[14] Bruce T. Allen. "Economies of Scale in the Portland Cement Industry, 1965-1971," working paper, Michigan State University, and "Vertical Integration and Market Foreclosure: The Case of Cement and Concrete," *The Journal of Law and Economics*, April 1971, pp. 251-274.

Table 9-1 Economies of Scale in the Portland Cement Industry, 1965 and 1971

Plant Capacity*	Percent of Industry Capacity	
	1965	1971
0- 0.79	0.86	0.00
0.8 - 1.24	4.45	3.63
1.25- 1.74	7.88	6.02
1.75- 2.24	12.87	11.00
2.25- 2.74	15.66	15.61
2.75- 3.24	14.90	9.97
. . .	. . .	. . .
3.25- 3.74	13.45	13.80
3.75- 4.24	7.56	8.71
4.25- 4.74	3.27	3.65
4.75- 5.24	1.05	8.03
. . .	. . .	. . .
5.25- 5.74	3.38	1.08
5.75- 6.24	2.51	3.61
6.25- 6.74	1.31	1.30
6.75- 7.24	1.46	2.81
8.25- 8.74†	3.51	3.05
9.75-10.24	2.09	5.12
10.75-11.24	0.00	0.00
13.00	0.00	2.61
16.00	3.34	0.00

* Millions of 376-pound barrels, annually.
† Size classes with no plants in either year are omitted.
SOURCE: Allen. *Op. cit.*

Allen's study does not reveal the conventional U-shaped long-run average cost curve; rather, it suggests that long-run average cost decreases as plant capacity increases to at least 3.25 million barrels, and that it does not rise beyond that point. Thus, although 3.25 million barrels does not represent a unique optimum size, it is at least a "minimum efficient" plant scale.

Beyond about 5 million barrels of annual capacity the picture is less clear. The changes in percentages of industry capacity do not appear to be related to plant scale; they are dominated by a single-plant construction and expansion. Returns to scale appear to be neither increasing nor decreasing beyond a plant scale of about 5 million barrels a year and are therefore best regarded as approximately constant.

Although the survivor technique is a valuable tool for examining cost/output relations, it does have some rather severe limitations. First, it is premised on the notion that survival is directly related to minimization of long-run average costs. As is demonstrated in more detail in Chapter 10, this premise implicitly assumes that the firms examined are operating in a very competitive market structure. Second, although the survivor technique may indicate the existence of increasing or decreasing returns to scale, it does not indicate the *relative* inefficiency of less than or greater than optimal-sized operations. Finally, because of the very long-run nature of the analysis, the survivor technique is particularly susceptible to the problem of changing technologies distorting the results.

Engineering Technique The engineering method of cost analysis is based directly on the physical relationship expressed in the production function for a particular product or firm. On the basis of a knowledge of the production technology involved, the optimal input combination for producing any given output quantity is determined. The cost curve is then formulated by multiplying each input in these least-cost combinations by its price and summing to develop the cost function.

The engineering technique probably comes the closest of any of the estimation procedures to reflecting the timeless nature of theoretical cost functions. It is based on the currently available technology, and it alleviates the possibility of confounding the results through improper data observations. That is, whereas the cost observations used for statistical cost estimation may be contaminated by any number of extraneous factors, engineering estimation abstracts from these complications by coupling current price quotations from suppliers with estimates of required quantities of various inputs.

The engineering method of cost estimation has proved to be useful for examining cost/output relationships in such areas as oil refining, chemical production, and nuclear power generation. Leslie Cookenboo, Jr., for example, used the technique to estimate cost functions for oil pipeline systems.[15] Cookenboo first analyzed the input/output relations for the three main factors in the system—pipe diameter, horsepower of pumps, and number of pumping stations—in order to determine the production function for the system. By adding input prices to the analysis, he was able to determine the least-cost combination of inputs for each production level and, hence, to develop the long-run cost curve for oil pipelines. His results showed that long-run costs decline continuously over the range of output levels examined.

The engineering method of cost estimation is not without pitfalls, and care must be exercised in using the method if accurate cost functions are to be developed. The difficulty often comes in trying to extend engineering production functions beyond the range of existing systems, or in going from pilot plant operations to full-scale production facilities. These problems are illustrated by the difficulties encountered by a major chemical company in

---

[15] Leslie Cookenboo, Jr. *Crude Oil Pipe Lines and Competition in the Oil Industry.* Harvard University Press, Cambridge, Mass., 1955.

developing a facility that made use of a new production technology. The firm completed an engineering cost study based on projected input/output relations developed from a small pilot facility. The estimated cost of constructing the new plant was $100 million; and it was projected that output would have a marginal cost of approximately $100 a ton, substantially below the costs in existing facilities. Once construction got underway, however, it became clear that the projection of production relations beyond the pilot plant's size were woefully inadequate. A planned two-year construction period dragged on for five years, and construction costs ballooned to $300 million. After completion of the plant, actual marginal costs of production were $150 a ton, a 50 percent increase over the estimated level. Although this is an extreme case, it does illustrate that while the engineering method can provide a useful alternative to statistical cost estimation, it, too, must be applied with care if accurate cost projection is to result.

SUMMARY

Empirical determination of a firm's cost function is a necessary requirement for optimal decision making. In this chapter a variety of techniques for analyzing both short-run and long-run cost/output relations were examined.

The primary statistical methodology used for cost estimation is least squares regression analysis. Properly conducted time-series analysis of a single firm's cost/output relations can provide an excellent estimate of the firm's short-run variable cost function. This function indicates the nature of marginal costs and average variable costs, the relevant cost concepts for short-run decision making.

Statistical estimation of long-run costs typically involves cross-sectional analysis as opposed to time-series regression analysis. Here the cost/output relationships for many firms of varying size are analyzed to determine the nature of the total cost function for firms of different scale.

Two major findings predominate the work of researchers in the area of cost analysis. First, in the short run the relationship between cost and output appears to be best approximated in most cases by a linear function. This means that marginal costs are constant over a significant range of output for most firms. Second, long-run estimation has typically indicated that sharply increasing returns to scale (decreasing average cost) are available over low output ranges in most industries, giving way to constant returns (constant average cost) at higher output levels. Decreasing returns to scale (increasing average costs), even at very high output quantities, appear to be the exception rather than the rule for most long-run cost functions.

Because of the difficulties encountered in statistical cost estimation, alternative techniques of empirical analysis are frequently employed. The survivor technique and the engineering technique are two methods commonly used for this purpose.

The survivor technique is premised on the assumption that more efficient firms—those with lower average costs—will have a greater probability of survival over time. Therefore, by examining the size makeup of an industry over time one can determine the nature of its cost/output relations.

The engineering technique is based on the physical relationships expressed in the production function for a firm. Using engineering estimates of input/output relationships, one determines the optimal production system and multiplies each required input by its cost to determine the cost function. This method is particularly useful for estimating cost relations for new products or plants involving new technologies where the historical data necessary for statistical cost analysis are unavailable.

QUESTIONS

9-1 The law of diminishing productivity in microeconomic theory leads one to expect that short-run marginal (and average variable) cost curves would be U-shaped. What factors do you suppose lead to the empirical finding of constant marginal costs for most firms?

9-2 For long-run statistical cost estimation, cross-sectional analysis, as opposed to time-series analysis, is typically used at least partly to overcome the problem of changing technology. Does the use of cross-sectional data necessarily eliminate this problem? Why or why not?

9-3 Does the survivor technique for estimating long-run cost/output relations overcome the problem of changing technology?

9-4 What is the significance for government antitrust activities of the finding that long-run average cost curves for many industries are L-shaped with constant average costs over substantial output ranges?

9-5 Short-run statistical cost studies have been reported for a wide variety of industries, ranging from autos to Xerox machines. Long-run cost studies, on the other hand, have been restricted to a few industries, such as steel manufacturing, banks, savings and loans, insurance, and utilities. Why do you suppose so many more short-run than long-run studies have been conducted?

HUNTER TEXTILES: A CASE ON COST ESTIMATION

Herbert A. Hunter IV, president and principal stockholder of Hunter Textiles, Incorporated, has for some time been viewing with alarm the rapidly shrinking profit margins in the clothing manufacturing operations of Hunter. Faced with rising labor and materials costs on the production side and with increased competition from imports and price declines on the sales front, the company has had declining profits annually over the past four years.

One afternoon Hunter came across the following article in *Business Week*:

A Laser to Cut the Garment Tangle
Hard-hit by imports and its failure to automate, the U.S. apparel industry this week could see, quite literally, a ray of light: It was a computer-driven laser that cuts out the 40 pieces of cloth that make up a man's suit at the rate of 25 suits an hour.

Genesco, Inc., industry giant and owner of the new machine, says the system will halve the time now needed to fill a retailer's order. And it will also slash inventory cost—now an estimated $3-billion annually for the industry.

The traditional practice in the cutting room is to stack up and machine-cut many plies of cloth—often several dozens—simultaneously, to minimize cost. Such cutting is not very accurate and it tends to result in either large inventories or long delivery times. The laser system handles one ply at a time, but eliminates 90% of the hand-cutting. Its speed is high enough to offset the advantage of cutting multiple plies in the standard way, Genesco says, and the resulting pieces are precise in size, with much cleaner edges.

But to Genesco the system's major selling point is that a garment maker can economically fill orders as they are received. "This enables us to get away from batch processing, the real foul-up in this business," says Franklin M. Jarman, Genesco's 39-year-old chairman. "Now, if we want to, we could have the laser cut out a man's sport jacket, a woman's skirt, and a child's pair of shorts, one right after the other."

"The real advantage is quick response," agrees Ross O. Runnels, vice-president of Kurt Salmon Associates, Inc., industry consultants. "You can deliver goods faster and meet changes in demand more quickly."

However, one industry consultant thinks that the real advantage of the one-at-a-time cutter is that it wastes 5% to 6% less fabric. "That alone could justify cost of the machine," he says.

The laser system was developed for Genesco by Hughes Aircraft Co. When a garment is to be cut, a computer selects the right pattern program from magnetic tape storage. This drives a positioning head—actually a fast-moving (70-in.-per-second) linear motor first developed by Xynetics Corp. for a numerically controlled drafting machine. An intricate array of mirrors transmits the beam of the stationary laser to the positioning head, which focuses the beam onto the cloth. The intense beam of coherent light vaporizes, or "burns," the cloth with high precision.

Genesco says it has no patents on the system, and Hughes plans to sell it to other garment makers. First, however, it will ship a second machine to Genesco late this year (the first is installed in Genesco's L. Greif & Bros. plant in Fredericksburg, Va.). It is committed to ship two dozen more after that, at two-month intervals, to Genesco plants across the country.

The laser cutter is expected to cost between $400,000 and $500,000. This will put the system out of reach of most apparel makers, and Hughes says it is looking at leasing arrangements.

One who does not share Jarman's enthusiasm for a laser cutter is H. Joseph Gerber, president of Gerber Scientific Instrument Co., which introduced a numerically controlled knife type of garment cutter two years ago. Gerber, who has not seen the Hughes machine, decided against a laser because it was restricted to a single ply—not practical for automotive fabrics —and because "we were concerned about fire and radiation."

Those who saw Gerber's machine in 1969 were enthusiastic, but because of the recession there have been few sales of it or of a competitive machine introduced by Cincinnati Milacron, Inc. On the other hand, if Genesco's machines do what the company expects them to, apparel makers who want to be equally responsive to the market may have little choice but to follow its lead.

Jarman thinks that is what will happen. The high cost of the development project—"several millions of dollars"—worried some in Genesco management, says Jarman. "But I was determined to see this through even if it meant a cut in dividends. This is the newest thing to the apparel industry since the introduction of the sewing machine." [16]

After reading the article Hunter gave it to L. R. Kent, one of the firm's management trainees who has shown an outstanding ability to formulate problems in a manner that facilitates thorough analysis, saying, "Here's an interesting article on a new application of laser technology to garment cutting. Take a look at it and see if you can structure a study that will suggest whether we should attempt to acquire such equipment."

Assuming you are Kent, prepare a report indicating (1) the factors that should be included in an analysis of the costs and benefits of acquiring a computer-driven laser cutter, (2) how you would obtain the inputs necessary for the analysis, and (3) the way in which you would analyze the data in order to reach a decision.

SELECTED REFERENCES

Allen, Bruce T. "Vertical Integration and Market Foreclosure: The Case of Cement and Concrete," *The Journal of Law and Economics*, April 1971, pp. 251-274.

Benston, George J. "Multiple Regression Analysis of Cost Behavior," *Accounting Review*, October 1966, pp. 657-672.

Cookenboo, Leslie, Jr. *Crude Oil Pipe Lines and Competition in the Oil Industry.* Cambridge, Mass.: Harvard University Press, 1955.

Dean, Joel. *Statistical Determination of Costs with Special Reference to Marginal Costs.* Chicago: University of Chicago Press, 1936.

———. *Statistical Cost Functions of a Hosiery Mill.* Chicago: University of Chicago Press, 1941.

———. "The Relation of Cost to Output for a Leather Belt Shop," New York: National Bureau of Economic Research, Technical Paper No. 2, December 1941.

———. "Department Store Cost Functions," in Oskar Lange, ed. *Studies in Mathematical Economics and Econometrics.* London: Cambridge Press, 1942.

Frech, H. E., and Paul B. Ginsberg. "Optimal Scale in Medical Practice: A Survivor Analysis," *Journal of Business*, January 1974, pp. 23-36.

Johnston, J. *Statistical Cost Analysis.* New York: McGraw-Hill, 1960.

Meyer, John R. "Some Methodological Aspects of Statistical Costing as Illustrated by the Determination of Rail Passenger Cars," *American Economic Reveiw*, May 1958, pp. 209-222.

Moore, Frederick T. "Economies of Scale: Some Statistical Evidence," *Quarterly Journal of Economics*, May 1959, pp. 232-245.

[16] Reprinted from the March 13, 1971 issue of *Business Week* by special permission. © 1971 by McGraw-Hill, Inc.

Stigler, George J. "The Economies of Scale," *The Journal of Law and Economics,* vol. 1, no. 1, October 1958, pp. 54-71.

Wiles, P. J. D. *Prices, Cost and Output.* Oxford: Basil, Blackwell and Mott, 1956.

Yntema, T. O. "Steel Prices, Volume and Costs," *Temporary National Economic Committee Papers,* vol. 2, United States Steel Corporation, New York, 1940.

CHAPTER 10

Market Structure
and the Theory
of Prices

The primary objective of management is to maximize the value of the firm subject to constraints imposed by society. This maximization process is exceedingly complex; it involves the full range of business functions, from decisions about producing totally new products or serving new markets to choices among public-relations programs designed to give the firm a favorable public image.

Thus far we have (1) considered the optimization process, (2) examined the nature of risk and its effects on the value of the firm, (3) studied the nature of the demand function and ways of estimating it, (4) analyzed the theory of production, (5) seen how linear programming can be used to reach optimal solutions, and (6) developed cost functions from information about the production function and input prices. We are now in a position to integrate these various topics and to show how demand, production, and cost interact to determine market structures.

CLASSIFICATION OF MARKET STRUCTURES

"Market structure" refers to the degree of competition in the market for a particular good or service. The most important characteristics of markets are the number and size distribution of sellers, and the extent of product differentiation. Markets are traditionally divided into four classifications; these four prototype structures are defined below and elaborated upon in the remainder of the chapter.

Pure competition is a market structure characterized by a large number of buyers and sellers, each of whose transactions are so small in relation to total industry output that they cannot affect the price of the product. No firm earns "above normal" profits in the long run.

Pure monopoly is a market structure characterized by the existence of a single producer. A monopolistic firm can earn above-normal profits, even in the long run.

Monopolistic competition is a market structure quite similar to pure competition, but distinguished from it by the fact that consumers perceive differences between the products of different firms. As in pure competition, above-normal profits are attainable only in the short-run.

Oligopoly is a market structure in which a small number of firms produce most of the industry's output. Oligopoly is subdivided into *differentiated oligopoly*, in which the product is not standardized (automobiles), and *undifferentiated oligopoly*, in which the product is standardized (steel). Under either class, the decisions of the firms are interdependent in the sense that if one firm changes its price, the other firms will react, and this knowledge is incorporated into the firm's price/output decision problem.

FACTORS DETERMINING MARKET STRUCTURE

Two key elements are involved in determining market structure: the number of buyers and sellers in the market and the extent to which the product is standardized. These factors, in turn, are influenced by the nature of the product, the form of the industry's production function, and the characteristics of consumers. These relationships are described in the following subsections.

Effect of Product Characteristics on Market Structures

A product's characteristics can affect the structure of the market in which it is sold. If other products are good substitutes for the one in question, this will increase the degree of competition in the market. To illustrate, rail service between two points is typically supplied by only one railroad. Transportation service is available from several sources, however, and railroads compete with bus lines, truck companies, airlines, and private autos. The substitutability of these other modes of transportation for rail service increases the degree of competition in the transportation service market.[1]

---

[1] In the 1800s and early 1900s—before the introduction of trucks, buses, autos, and airplanes—the railroads were subject to very little competition. Railroads could therefore charge excessive prices and earn monopoly profits. Because of this exploitation, laws were passed giving public authorities permission to regulate the prices railroads charge.

The physical characteristics of a product may also influence the competitive structure of its market. A low ratio of distribution cost to total cost, for example, tends to increase competition by widening the geographic range over which any particular producer can compete. Rapid perishability of a product produces the opposite effect.

Effect of Production Functions on Market Structure

The nature of the production function is perhaps the most fundamental determinant of market structure. Industries whose production functions exhibit increasing returns to scale out to a large output level in relation to total market demand are characterized by fewer producers and, hence, by less competition than are industries where constant or decreasing returns set in at an output that is small relative to total product demand.

Effect of Buyers on Market Structure

The degree of competition in a market is affected by buyers as well as sellers. If there are only a few buyers, there will be less competition than if there are many buyers. This situation, which is defined as *monopsony* (only one buyer) or *oligopsony* (a few large buyers), sometimes exists in local labor markets dominated by a single firm, in local agricultural markets dominated by a few large processors, in governmental purchases of complex systems, and in markets for certain components such as auto parts used by the major auto manufacturers.

Consumer education and mobility also affect the degree of competition in a market. Increasing consumer awareness of price and product differentials, coupled with the possibility of geographic mobility, increases competition by removing the constraints that allow isolated (and noncompetitive) submarkets to exist.

PURE COMPETITION

The market characteristics described in the preceding section, together with certain other factors, determine the degree of competition in the market for any good or service.[2] In this section we discuss pure competition in some detail; the other prototype market structures defined above are discussed in subsequent sections.

Pure competition exists when the individual producers in a market have no influence whatever on prices—they are "price takers" as opposed to

---

The concept of price regulation, which is discussed in detail in Chapter 12, was later extended to other forms of transportation and to telephone, gas, electric, and water utilities.

[2] The legal constraint on competition introduced by patents and copyrights is one obvious element that enters into this determination. The ability of certain groups—for example, physicians and certain labor unions—to limit entry into their professions by controlling licensing practices is another element that affects market structure.

"price makers." This total absence of influence on price requires the following conditions:

> *Large numbers of buyers and sellers.* Each firm in the industry produces a small portion of the industry output, and each customer buys only a small part of the total.
>
> *Product homogeneity.* The output of each firm is perceived by customers to be precisely equivalent to the output of any other firm in the industry.
>
> *Free entry and exit.* Firms are in no way restricted from entering or leaving the industry.
>
> *Perfect dissemination of information.* Cost, price, and quality information is known by all buyers and all sellers in the market.

These four basic conditions, which are necessary for the existence of a purely competitive market structure, are far too restrictive for pure competition to be commonplace in the real world. While security and commodity exchanges approach the requirements, imperfections occur even there.[3] Nonetheless, for certain individuals and firms, pricing decisions must be made under circumstances in which they have no control over price, and an examination of a purely competitive market structure provides insights into pricing decisions in these cases. More important, a clear understanding of pure competition provides a reference point from which to analyze the more typically encountered market structures—oligopoly and monopolistic competition.

Price/Output Decisions under Pure Competition

In a perfectly competitive market the firm takes price as a given: It can sell as much of its product as it desires at the going market price, but absolutely none at a higher price. The demand curve in this case is horizontal, as in Figure 10-1; at any price above P^*, the current market price, the firm can sell nothing; while at P^* it can sell whatever quantity it desires. Since it can sell all it wants at P^*, the firm will never cut its price below that level. *Management's decision problem, therefore, is to determine the output level that maximizes profit, given the going market price.*

Market Price Determination

Although the individual firms have no control over price, the market price for a competitive industry is still determined by supply and demand. There is a total industry demand curve for the product—an aggregation of the quantities that individual purchasers will buy at each price—and an industry supply curve—the summation of the quantities that individual firms are

---

[3] The sale by AT & T of $1.5 billion of new securities, for example, clearly affects the price of its stocks and bonds.

Figure 10-1   Demand Curve for a Firm in a Purely Competitive Market

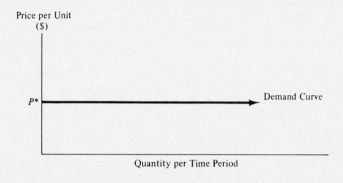

willing to supply at different prices. The intersection of the industry supply and demand curves determines the market price.

The data in Table 10-1 illustrate the process by which an industry supply curve is constructed. First, suppose there are five firms in an industry and that each firm is willing to supply varying quantities of the product at different prices. The summing of the individual supply quantities of these five firms for each price determines their combined supply schedule, shown in the column labeled "Partial Market Supply." For example, at a price of $2 the output quantities supplied by the five firms are 15, 0, 5, 25, and 45 units respectively, resulting in a combined supply of 90 units at that price. With a product price of $8, the supply quantities become 45, 115, 40, 55, and 75 for a total supply by the five firms of 330 units.

Table 10-1   Market Supply Schedule Determination

													Quantity Supplied by Firm					Partial Market Supply × 1,000 =	Total Market Supply
Price $	1	+ 2	+ 3	+ 4	+ 5	=		
1	5	0	5	10	30		50	50,000
2	15	0	5	25	45		90	90,000
3	20	20	10	30	50		130	130,000
4	25	35	20	35	55		170	170,000
5	30	55	25	40	60		210	210,000
6	35	75	30	45	65		250	250,000
7	40	95	35	50	70		290	290,000
8	45	115	40	55	75		330	330,000
9	50	130	45	65	80		370	370,000
10	55	145	50	75	85		410	410,000

Figure 10-2 Hypothetical Industry Supply Curve

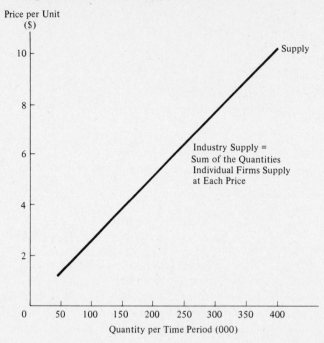

Now assume that the five firms, while representative of the firms in the industry, account for only a small portion of the industry's total output. Specifically, assume that there is actually a total of 5,000 firms in the industry, each with an individual supply schedule identical to one of the five firms illustrated in the table. Under this condition there are 1,000 firms just like each one illustrated in Table 10-1, so the total market supply—the total quantity supplied at each price—will be 1,000 times that shown under the partial market supply schedule. This supply schedule is illustrated in Figure 10-2, and adding the market demand curve to the industry supply curve, as in Figure 10-3, allows us to determine the equilibrium market price.

While it is apparent from Figure 10-3 that both total demand and total supply are dependent on price, a simple example should demonstrate the inability of an individual firm to affect price. Assume that the total demand function in Figure 10-3, which again represents the summation at each price of the quantities demanded by individual purchasers, can be described by the equation:

$$\text{Quantity Demanded} = Q = 400,000 - 10,000P, \qquad (10\text{-}1)$$

or, solving for price:

Figure 10-3 Market Price Determination in Perfect Competition

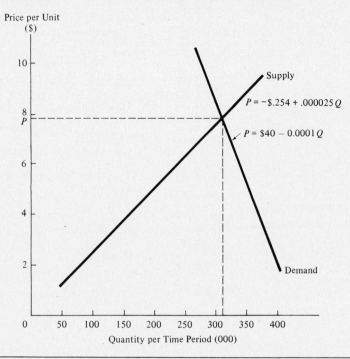

$$\$10,000P = \$400,000 - Q$$
$$P = \$40 - 0.0001Q. \qquad \textbf{(10-1a)}$$

According to Equation 10-1a, a 100-unit change in output would cause only a $0.01 change in price, or alternatively, a 1¢ price increase (reduction) would lead to a decrease (increase) in total market demand of 100 units.

The demand curve shown in Figure 10-3 is redrawn for an individual firm in Figure 10-4. The slope of the curve is −.0001, the same as in Figure 10-3; it is the derivative of Equation 10-1a in both cases.

The intercept $7.80 is the going market price as determined by the intersection of the market supply and demand curves in Figure 10-3.[4] At the scale shown in Figure 10-4, the firm's demand curve is seen to be a horizontal line, for all practical purposes. An output change of even 100 units by the individual firm results in only a 1¢ change in market price, and the data in Table 10-1 indicate that the typical firm would not vary output by this amount unless the market price changes by more than $10 a unit. Thus,

---

[4] The slopes of the demand curves in Figures 10-3 and 10-4 are identical; only the scales have been changed. Note also that at the equilibrium output shown in Figure 10-3, $P = \$40 - \$0.0001\,(322{,}000) = \$40 - \$32.20 = \$7.80.$

Figure 10-4 Demand Curve Faced by a Single Firm in Pure Competition

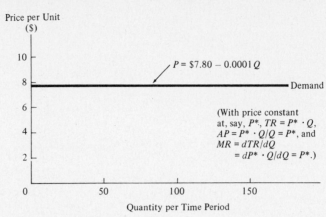

it is clear that under pure competition the individual firm's output decisions do not affect price in any meaningful way, and for pricing decisions the demand curve is taken to be perfectly horizontal. That is, price is assumed to be constant irrespective of the output level at which the firm chooses to operate.

THE FIRM'S PRICE/OUTPUT DECISION

Figure 10-5 illustrates the firm's price/output decision in a competitive market.[5] Profit maximization was shown in Chapter 2 to require that a firm operate at an output level where marginal revenue and marginal cost are equal to one another. With price a constant, average revenue, or price, and marginal revenue must always be equal (with price constant at, say, P^*, $TR = P^* \cdot Q$, $AR = P^* \cdot Q/Q = P^*$, and $MR = dTR/dQ = dP^* \cdot Q/dQ = P^*$), so the profit maximization requirement for a firm operating in a perfectly competitive market is that market price must be equal to marginal cost. In the example depicted in Figure 10-5, the firm chooses to operate at output level Q^*, where price (and, hence, marginal revenue) equals marginal cost and profits are maximized.

Notice that above-normal profits may exist in the short run even under conditions of pure competition.[6] For example, in Figure 10-5 the firm pro-

---

[5] For simplicity, in setting up graphic models in the sections on pure competition and monopolistic competition, we assume that the firm whose curves are graphed is a "representative" firm. Thus, the cost curves in Figure 10-5 are representative of an "average" firm in the industry.

[6] A "normal" profit, defined as a rate of return on capital just sufficient to provide the capital investment necessary to develop and operate a firm (See Chapter 1), is included as a part of economic costs. Therefore, any profit shown in a graph such as Fig-

Figure 10-5 Competitive Firm's Optimal Price/Output Combination

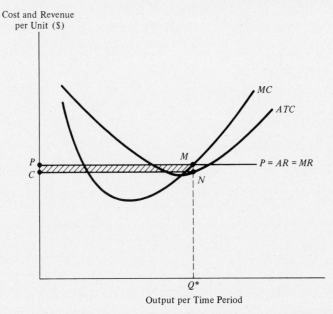

duces and sells Q^* units of output at an average cost of C dollars; and with a market price P, the firm earns economic profits of $P - C$ dollars per unit. Total economic profit, $(P - C)Q$, is shown by the shaded rectangle $PMNC$.

Over the longer run, however, positive economic profits will attract additional firms into the industry, will lead to increased output by existing firms, or will perhaps bring about both situations. As the industry supply is expanded, there will be a downward pressure on the market price for the industry as a whole—output can be expanded only by offering the product at a lower price—and simultaneously an upward pressure on cost, because of increased demand for factors of production. Long-run equilibrium will be reached when all economic profits and losses have been eliminated and each firm in the industry is operating at an output that minimizes average cost. The long-run equilibrium situation for a firm under pure competition is graphed in Figure 10-6. At the profit-maximizing output, price, or average revenue, equals average cost, so the firm neither earns economic profits nor incurs economic losses. When this condition exists for all firms in the industry, new firms are not encouraged to enter the industry nor are existing ones

---

ure 10-5 or 10-6 is defined as "economic profit," and it represents an "above-normal" profit. Notice also that economic losses are incurred whenever the firm fails to earn a normal profit. Thus, a firm might show a small accounting profit but be suffering economic losses because these profits are "below normal" and are thus insufficient to provide an adequate return to the firm's stockholders.

Figure 10-6 Long-run Equilibrium in a Competitive Market

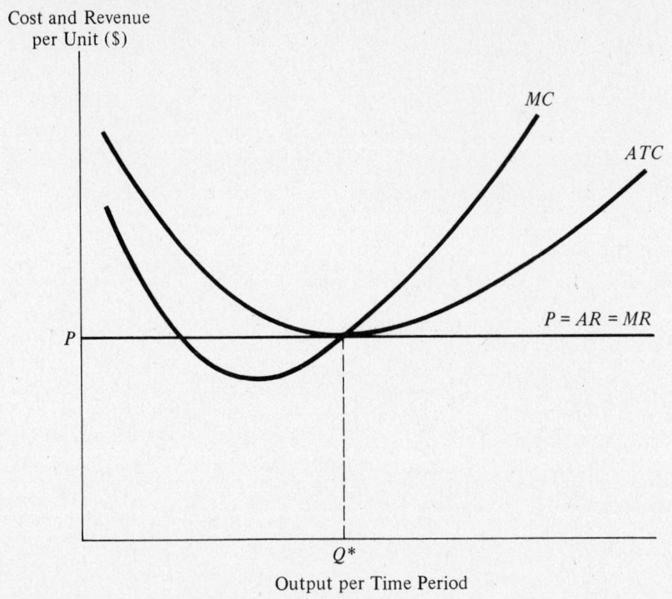

pressured into leaving it. Prices are stable, and each firm is operating at the minimum point on its short-run average cost curve.[7]

The Firm's Supply Curve

Market supply curves were seen above to be the summation of supply quantities of individual firms at various prices. We are now in a position to examine how the supply schedules for individual firms are determined.

In Figure 10-7 we add the firm's average variable cost curve to the average and marginal cost curves of Figure 10-5. *In the short run the competitive firm's supply schedule will correspond to that portion of the marginal cost curve which lies above the average variable cost curve; that is, the heavy portion of the marginal cost curve in Figure 10-7.*

To understand the reason for this, consider the options available to the firm. Profit maximization under pure competition requires that the firm operate at the output where marginal revenue equals marginal cost—if it produces any output at all. That is, the firm will either (1) produce nothing and incur a loss equal to its fixed costs, or (2) produce an output determined by the intersection of the horizontal demand curve and the marginal cost

---

[7] All firms must also be operating at the minimum cost point on the long-run average cost curve; otherwise firms would make production changes, decrease costs, and affect industry output and prices. Accordingly, a stable equilibrium requires that firms be operating with optimal-sized plants.

Figure 10-7 The Competitive Firm's Short-run Supply Curve

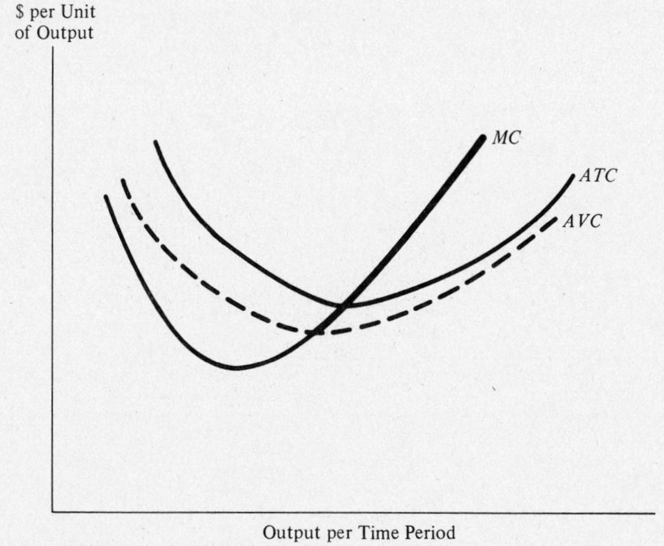

Output per Time Period

curve. It will choose the alternative that maximizes profits or, if losses must be incurred, minimizes losses. If the price is less than variable costs, the firm should produce nothing and incur a loss equal to its total fixed cost; if the firm produces any product under this condition, its losses will increase. But if price exceeds variable costs, then each unit of output provides some profit contribution which can be applied to cover fixed costs and provide profit; the firm should produce and sell its product because this production reduces losses or leads to profits. Accordingly, the minimum point on the firm's average variable cost curve determines the cutoff point, or the lower limit, of its supply schedule.

This conclusion is illustrated in Figure 10-8. At a very low price such as $1, $MR = MC$ at 100 units of output. But notice that at 100 units the firm has a total cost per unit of $2 and a price of only $1, so it is incurring a loss of $1 a unit. Notice also that the total loss consists of a fixed cost component, $2.00 - $1.40 = $0.60, and a variable cost component, $1.40 - $1.00 = $0.40.[8] Thus, the total loss is

$$\text{Total Loss} = (100 \text{ units}) \cdot (\$0.60 \text{ fixed cost loss} \\ + \$0.40 \text{ variable cost loss}) = \$100.$$

If the firm simply shuts down and terminates production, it would cease to

[8] The difference between the *ATC* and the *AVC* curves represents the fixed cost per unit of output.

Figure 10-8 Prices, Cost, and Optimal Supply Decisions for a Firm under Pure
Competition

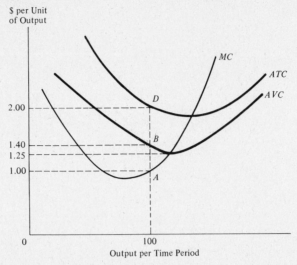

incur variable costs, and its loss would be reduced to the level of the fixed
cost loss; that is, to 100($0.60) = $60.

Variable cost losses will occur at any price less than $1.25, the mini-
mum point on the AVC curve, so this is the lowest price at which the firm
will operate. Above $1.25, the price more than covers variable costs, so,
even though total costs are not covered, it is preferable to operate and provide some contribution to cover a portion of fixed costs rather than to shut
down and incur losses equal to total fixed costs.

To recapitulate, *the short-run supply curve is that portion of the marginal cost curve which lies above the AVC curve.* Where marginal cost is
below average cost, but above average variable cost, the firm will incur
losses but will produce, nonetheless. Positive economic profits occur over
that part of the supply function where marginal cost (and price) is greater
than average total cost.

The firm's long-run supply function is similarly determined. Since all
costs are variable in the long run, a firm will choose to shut down unless
total costs are completely covered. Accordingly, that portion of the firm's
long-run marginal cost curve which lies above its long-run average total cost
curve represents its long-run supply schedule.

MONOPOLY

Pure monopoly lies at the opposite extreme from pure competition on the
market structure continuum. Monopoly exists when a single firm is the sole
producer of a good that has no close substitutes—in other words when the

industry consists of only one firm. Pure monopoly, like pure competition, exists primarily in economic theory—few goods are produced by a single producer and fewer still are free from competition of a close substitute. Even the public utilities are imperfect monopolists in most of their markets. Electric companies, for example, typically approach a pure monopoly in their residential lighting market, but they face strong competition from gas and oil suppliers in the heating market. Further, in all phases of the industrial and commercial power markets, electric utilities face competition from gas- and oil-powered private generators.[9]

Even though pure monopoly rarely exists, it is still worthy of careful examination. Many of the economic relationships found under monopoly can be used to estimate optimal firm behavior in the less precise, but more prevalent, partly competitive and partly monopolistic market structures that dominate the real world. In addition, an understanding of monopoly market relationships provides the background necessary to examine the economics of regulation, a topic of prime importance to business managers.

Price/Output Decision under Monopoly

Under monopoly, the industry demand curve is identical to the demand curve of the firm, and because industry demand curves typically are downward sloping, monopolists also face downward-sloping demand curves. In Figure 10-9, for example, 100 units can be sold at a price of $10 a unit. At an $8

Figure 10-9 The Firm's Demand Curve under Monopoly

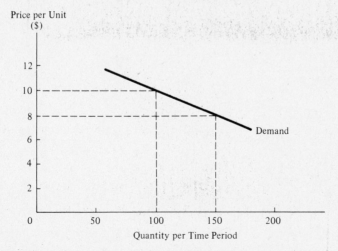

[9] During the late 1960s, as electric rates climbed rapidly and future supply capabilities became questionable, some of the larger apartment- and office-building complexes began installing their own power-generating facilities. This practice has long been followed by large industrial firms.

price, 150 units will be demanded. Alternatively, if the firm decides to sell 100 units, it will receive $10 a unit; if it wishes to sell 150 units, it must accept an $8 price. We see then that the monopolist can set either price or quantity, but not both. Given one, the value of the other is immediately determined by the relationship expressed in the demand function.

A monopolistic firm uses the same profit maximization rule as a firm in a competitive industry; it operates at the output where marginal revenue equals marginal cost. The demand curve facing the monopolistic firm, however, is not horizontal, or perfectly elastic, so marginal revenue will not coincide with price at any but the first unit of output. Marginal revenue is always less than price for output quantities greater than one.[10]

When the monopolistic firm equates marginal revenue and marginal cost, it simultaneously determines its output level and the market price for its product. This decision is illustrated in Figure 10-10. Here the firm produces Q units of output at a cost of C per unit, and it sells this output at price P. Profits, which are equal to $(P - C)$ times (Q), are represented by the area $PP'C'C$, and are at a maximum.

While Q is the optimal short-run output, the firm will engage in pro-

Figure 10-10   Price/Output Decision under Monopoly

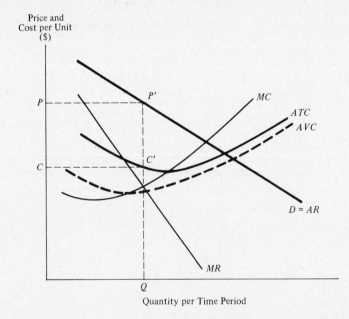

Price and
Cost per Unit
($)

Quantity per Time Period

duction only if average revenue, or price, is greater than average variable cost. This condition holds in Figure 10-10, but if the price had been below the average variable cost, losses would have been minimized by shutting down.

Long-run Equilibrium under Monopoly

In the long run a monopolistic firm will operate only if its price exceeds its long-run average cost. Because all costs are variable in the long run, the firm will not operate unless all costs are covered. No firm, monopolistic or competitive, will operate in the long run if it is suffering losses.

As was shown earlier, purely competitive firms must, in the long run, operate at the minimum point on the *LRAC* curve. This condition does not necessarily hold under monopoly. For example, consider again Figure 10-10 and assume that the *ATC* curve represents the long-run average total cost curve of the firm.[11] Here the firm will produce *Q* units of output at an average cost of *C* per unit, somewhat above the minimum point on the *ATC* curve. This firm is a *natural monopolist,* a condition that exists when the profit-maximizing output occurs at a point where *long-run* average costs are declining. A single firm can produce the total market supply at a lower total cost than could any number of smaller firms, hence the term "natural." Utility companies are the classic examples of natural monopoly, as the unnecessary duplication of production and distribution facilities would greatly increase costs if more than one firm served a given area.

Regulation of Monopoly

The existence of natural monopolies presents something of a dilemma. On the one hand, economic efficiency is enhanced by restricting the number of producing firms to one; on the other hand, where only one firm serves a market, the possibility of economic exploitation exists. Specifically, monopolistic firms tend to earn excessive profits and to underproduce. The term "excessive profits" is defined as profits so large that the firm earns a rate of return on invested capital that exceeds the risk-adjusted normal rate. Profits serve a useful function in providing incentive and in allocating resources, but it is difficult to justify above-normal profits that are the result of market and technological conditions, as opposed to exceptional performance. "Under production" is defined as a situation where the firm curtails production at a level where the value of the resources needed to produce an additional unit of output, as measured by the marginal cost of production, is less than the social benefit derived from the additional unit, which is measured by the price someone is willing to pay for the additional unit. Under monopoly, marginal cost is clearly less than price.

How can we escape from the dilemma posed by the twin facts (1) that

---

[11] All costs are variable in the long run and, therefore, average variable costs are equal to average total costs. Hence, the *AVC* curve should be disregarded.

monopoly may be efficient, but (2) that monopoly leads to excessive profits and underproduction? The answer lies in regulation, a topic discussed in Chapter 12.

MONOPOLISTIC COMPETITION

Pure competition and pure monopoly rarely exist in the real world; rather, most firms are subject to some competition, but not to the extent that would exist under pure competition. Even though most firms are faced with a large number of competitors producing highly substitutable products, firms still have some control over the price of their output—they cannot sell all they want at a fixed price, nor would they lose all their sales if they raised prices slightly. In other words, most firms do face downward-sloping demand curves, signifying less than perfect competition.

In 1933 Edward H. Chamberlain presented a theory of monopolistic competition that provided a more realistic explanation of the actual market structure faced by most firms. Chamberlain's theory retains two assumptions of a purely competitive market structure: (1) Each firm makes its decisions independently of all others; that is, each producer assumes that his competitor's prices, advertising, and so on are invariant with respect to his own actions. Thus, price changes by one firm are assumed not to cause other firms to react by changing their prices.[12] (2) There are a large number of firms in the industry all producing the same basic product. The assumption of completely homogeneous products is removed, however, so each firm is assumed to be able to differentiate its product to at least some degree from those of rival firms.

The assumption of no direct reactions by competitors should not be misconstrued as implying an independence between firms in a monopolistically competitive market. There is an assumed independence in decision making, just as in a perfectly competitive market. However, the demand function faced by each firm in such an industry is significantly impacted on by: (1) the existence of numerous firms all producing goods that consumers view as reasonably close substitutes; and (2) the fact that many demand and cost factors impact simultaneously on all firms, leading frequently to similar price movements by them. As Chamberlain pointed out, this latter phenomenon causes each firm's demand to be more price inelastic than would be the case if total interfirm independence prevailed.

Product differentiation takes many forms. A tube of Colgate toothpaste at a nearby drugstore is different from an identical tube available at a distant store. Quality differentials, packaging, credit terms, or maintenance service, such as IBM is reputed to supply, can lead to product differentiation, as can advertising and brand-name identification. The important factor

---

[12] If reactions occur, then the market structure is defined to be oligopolistic, a market structure examined later in this chapter.

in all these forms of product differentiation, however, is that some consumers prefer the product of one seller to that of others.

The effect of product differentiation is to remove the perfect elasticity of the firm's demand curve. Instead of being a price taker facing a horizontal demand curve, the firm determines its optimal price/output combination. The degree of price flexibility depends on the strength of a firm's product differentiation. Strong differentiation results in greater consumer "loyalty" and hence in more control over price. Alternatively stated, the more differentiated a firm's product, the lower the substitutability of other products for it. This is illustrated in Figure 10-11, which shows the demand curves of Firms A and B. Consumers view Firm A's product as being only slightly differentiated from the bulk of the industry's output, and since many other brands are suitable replacements for its own output, Firm A is close to being a price taker. Firm B, on the other hand, has successfully differentiated its product, and consumers are therefore less willing to substitute for B's output. Accordingly, B's demand is not so sensitive to changes in price.

Price/Output Decisions under Monopolistic Competition

The equilibrium situation for a "representative" firm producing in a monopolistically competitive market is shown in Figure 10-12. With the demand curve, D_1, and the related marginal revenue curve, MR_1, the optimum output, Q_1, is found at the point where $MR = MC$. But here, price, P_1, is just

Figure 10-11 Relationship between Product Differentiation and Elasticity of Demand

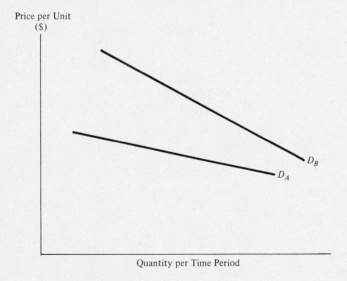

Price per Unit
($)

D_B

D_A

Quantity per Time Period

Figure 10-12 Long-run Equilibrium Price/Output Combination under Monopolistic Competition

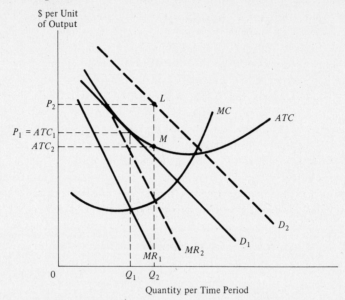

equal to the average cost per unit, ATC_1, so economic profits are zero.[13]

Now suppose that consumer incomes rise, causing the demand and the marginal revenue curves to shift to the right, say to D_2 and MR_2. The optimal output (the point where $MR = MC$) shifts out to Q_2; the price rises to P_2; the average cost declines to ATC_2; and profits, represented by the area P_2LMC_2, are earned. This is not a stable situation, however. The above-normal profits would attract new firms into the industry, and the output of these new competitors would cause the firm's demand curve to shift back to D_1. In other words, the entry of new firms would compete away the above-normal profits. Similarly, if an event occurred (such as a decline in consumer demand for the industry's product) that caused firms to incur losses, then in the long run firms would leave the industry, the demand curves of the remaining companies would shift to the right, and equilibrium would be re-established when the industry ceased to be in a loss position.

Notice that in equilibrium a monopolistically competitive firm will never be operating at the minimum point on its average cost curve—the demand curve is downward sloping, so it can be tangent to the ATC curve only at a point above the minimum of the ATC curve. Does this mean that a monopolistically competitive industry is inefficient? The answer is "no," ex-

---

[13] Recall that the term "cost" includes a normal profit sufficient to compensate the owners of the firm for their capital investment.

cept in a very superficial sense. The very existence of the downward-sloping demand curve implies that some consumers value the firm's products more highly than they do products of other producers. If the number of producers were reduced—perhaps by government edict—so that all the remaining firms could operate at their minimum cost point, some consumers would, by definition, suffer a loss in welfare, *because the products they desired would no longer be available*.

An example of this phenomenon is provided by the retail food industry. Grocery stores all sell similar goods, but the goods are differentiated in the eyes of consumers by factors such as location and hours—a closer store open twenty-four hours a day is preferable, other things being the same. A graph of the situation would be similar to Figure 10-12 in its equilibrium configuration, and firms *could* produce a larger output at a lower average cost. This could be accomplished, however, only if some stores closed and the remaining ones operated at higher output levels. Unfortunately, there would, in all likelihood, be a stronger economic incentive for the remaining firms to *reduce* rather than to increase their levels of operation in attempting to maximize profits, so that potential benefits from reduced firm costs are not likely to be achieved. Further, the total cost to society associated with the grocery industry operation might increase, because some customers would have to bear additional costs in terms of money, time, and effort to shop at greater distances. In other words, when all costs—implicit costs borne by consumers, as well as explicit costs borne by producers—have been considered, monopolistic competition does not appear to be an inherently inefficient market structure.

OLIGOPOLY

The theory of monopolistic competition borrows heavily from both pure competition and pure monopoly, but it provides a more accurate picture of the actual markets in which most businesses operate by recognizing that, while firms do have some control over price, their actions are limited by the large number of close substitutes for their products. The theory assumes, however, that firms make decisions without explicitly taking into account competitive reactions. Such a behavioral assumption is appropriate for some industries but inappropriate for others, and when an individual firm's actions will in fact produce reactions on the part of its competitors, *oligopoly* exists.

Examples of oligopolistic industries abound in the United States. Aluminum, automobiles, computers, electrical equipment, glass, steel, and petroleum products are all items produced and sold under conditions of oligopoly. Notice that in each of these industries a small number of firms produce all, or at least a very large percentage of, the total output. In the automobile industry, for example, General Motors, Ford, Chrysler, and American Motors—referred to as the Big Four—account for almost 100 percent of auto production in the United States. Aluminum production is also highly concentrated, with Alcoa, Reynolds, and Kaiser producing almost all the domestic output.

Oligopoly market structures also exist in a number of other industries where the market area for a single firm is quite small. Probably the best example of this type of oligopolistic structure is the market for gasoline. Here, a few sellers (service stations) compete within a small geographic area.

It is the fewness of sellers that introduces interactions into the price/output decision problem under oligopoly. Consider *duopoly,* a special form of oligopoly, under which only two firms produce a particular product. For simplicity, assume that the product is homogeneous and customers choose between the firms solely on the basis of price. Assume also that both firms charge the same price and that each has an equal share of the market. Now suppose Firm A attempts to increase its sales by lowering its price. All buyers will switch to Firm A, and Firm B will lose its entire market. To retain customers, B will react by lowering its price. Thus, neither firm is free to act independently—any action taken by one will lead to a reaction by the other.

Price/Output Decisions under Oligopoly

Demand curves relate the quantity of a product demanded to price, *holding constant the effect of all other variables.* One variable that is assumed to remain fixed is the price charged by competing firms. In an oligopolistic market structure, however, if one firm changes the price it charges, other firms will react by changing their prices. The "demand curve" for the initial firm shifts position, so that instead of moving along a single demand curve as it changes price, the firm moves to an entirely new demand curve.

This phenomenon of shifting demand curves is illustrated in Figure 10-13(a). Firm A is initially producing Q_1 units of output and selling them at a price, P_1. The demand curve, D_1, applies, *assuming* prices charged by other firms remain fixed. Under this assumption, a price cut from P_1 to P_2 would increase demand to Q_2. Assume, however, that only a few firms operate in the market and that each has a fairly large share of total sales. Therefore, if one firm cuts its price and obtains a substantial increase in volume, the other firms must lose a large part of their business. Further, they know exactly why their sales have fallen, and they react by cutting their own prices. This action shifts Firm A down to a new demand curve, D_2, which causes a reduction in Firm A's demand at P_2 from Q_2 to Q_3 units. The new curve is just as unstable as the old one, so a knowledge of its shape is useless to Firm A; if it tries to move along D_2, competitors will react, forcing the company to yet another curve.

Shifting demand curves would present no real difficulty in making price/output decisions *if Firm A knew for sure how its rivals would react to price changes.* The reactions would just be built into the price/demand relationship, and a new "demand curve," which includes interactions among

Figure 10-13 Shifting Demand under Oligopoly: (a) Demand Curves That Do Not Explicitly Recognize Reactions; (b) Demand Curve That Recognizes Reactions

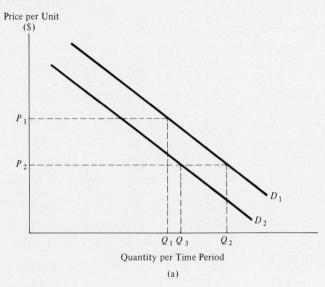

(a)

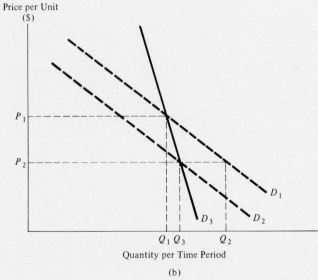

(b)

firms, could be constructed. Curve D_3 in Figure 10-13(b) represents such a reaction-based demand curve; it shows how quantity demanded will be affected by price reductions after competitive reactions have been taken into account. The problem with this approach, however, lies in the fact that there are many different theories about interfirm behavior, and each theory leads to a different pricing model and, hence, to different decision rules. Some of these theories are discussed in the following sections.

Reaction Not Recognized

The earliest model of oligopolistic pricing was developed in 1838 by Augustin Cournot, a French economist. Cournot's model was based on the assumption that each firm in an oligopolistic industry acts as though it can make price/output decisions independently; that is, that its demand curve is stable, because other producers will not react when the firm in question changes its price.

The oligopolistic price/output behavior that results from Cournot's model can best be examined by an example used in his original presentation. Two firms, A and B, each own a spring whose pure water is in great demand. For simplicity, assume that the cost of production is zero—consumers simply come to the spring, take water in their own containers, and pay a fee. Since marginal costs are zero, profits are maximized where $MR = MC = 0$; and since $MR = 0$ where total revenue is at a maximum, maximizing profits amounts to maximizing revenues. Finally, assume that the market demand curve for the water is given by the equation:

$$P = 500 - Q. \qquad (10\text{-}2)$$

The final Cournot solution does not depend on the initial output quantity of either firm, only on profit-maximizing behavior and assumed independence among decision units. To begin the analysis, however, assume that A was first to discover its spring. As a profit-maximizing company, A would begin selling 250 units of the water at a price of $250 a unit, determined as follows:

First, A's total revenue function is found by multiplying price, as given in Equation 10-2, by the quantity sold:

$$TR_A = P \cdot Q_A = (500 - Q_A) \cdot Q_A = 500Q_A - Q_A^2. \qquad (10\text{-}3)$$

Marginal revenue is the first derivative of the total revenue function:

$$MR_A = \frac{dTR_A}{dQ_A} = 500 - 2Q_A. \qquad (10\text{-}4)$$

Increasing output to the point where $MR_A = 0$ maximizes total revenue, and since $MC = 0$, this output also maximizes profits. The profit-maximizing output is found as follows:

$$MR = 500 - 2Q_A = 0 = MC$$
$$Q_A = 250.$$

Substituting this quantity into the demand equation, (10-2), we see that the optimal price is $250 a unit:

$$P = \$500 - Q = \$250.$$

Now Firm *B* locates a spring and decides to enter the market. In determining its profit-maximizing price/output combination, *B* assumes that its decision will not cause Firm *A* to change its output level. Given *A*'s production of 250 units, the demand curve facing *B* is determined as follows:

$$P_B = 500 - A\text{'s Output} - Q_B$$
$$= 500 - 250 - Q_B \qquad (10\text{-}5)$$
$$= 250 - Q_B.$$

The related total and marginal revenue functions are:

$$TR_B = 250Q_B - Q_B^2 \qquad (10\text{-}6)$$

and

$$MR_B = 250 - 2Q_B. \qquad (10\text{-}7)$$

Firm *B*'s total revenue and profit are maximized at an output level of 125 units. Notice, however, that if *B* sells 125 units and *A* sells 250, the market price must be at $125 a unit. This follows because the *industry* demand curve is $P = 500 - Q$, so:

$$P = 500 - (Q_A + Q_B)$$
$$= 500 - 375$$
$$= \$125.$$

Since Firm *A* is no longer able to sell 250 units at $250 a unit, it re-evaluates its price/output decision. Cournot's model assumes that reactions are not anticipated, so *A* assumes that *B* will continue to sell 125 units and that its own demand curve is:

$$P_A = 500 - B\text{'s Output} - Q_A$$
$$= 375 - Q_A. \qquad (10\text{-}8)$$

Firm *A* then attempts to maximize profit as above, producing an output of 187.5 units. The reduction in *A*'s output increases the market price to $187.50.

Now it is *B*'s turn to re-evaluate its position. *B* assumes that *A* will continue to produce 187.5 units and on this basis determines its profit-maximizing output to be 156.25 units. When *B* produces this output, the market price changes to $156.25.

Table 10-2, which shows these and successive price/output levels for the two firms, reveals several points of interest. First, note that the firms iterate toward equal market shares. (This holds true regardless of the original output levels and regardless of the number of firms in the market.) Further, the equilibrium output in the market is a function of the number of competing firms. Thus, when *A* was operating alone as a monopolist, the solution was 250 units at a price of $250 a unit. Once *B* entered, the equilibrium solution shifted to 333.33 units sold at a price of $166.67. With three firms, output would be 375 units, and the total output approaches the purely competitive level, 500 units, as the number of firms in the industry ap-

Table 10-2   Cournot's Pricing Model Assuming Two Identical Firms Each Operating Independently

| | Output | | | Market Price | Total Revenue (Profits) | | |
| | Firm A | Firm B | Total | | Firm A | Firm B | Combined |
	(1)	(2)	(3)	(4)	(1) × (4) (5)	(2) × (4) (6)	(3) × (4) (7)
(1)	250.00		250.00	$250.00	$62,500		$62,500
(2)	250.00	125.00	375.00	125.00	31,250	$15,625	46,875
(3)	187.50	125.00	312.50	187.50	35,156	23,438	58,594
(4)	187.50	156.25	343.75	156.25	29,297	24,414	53,711
(5)	171.88	156.25	328.13	171.88	29,543	26,856	56,399
(6)	171.88	164.06	335.94	164.06	28,198	26,915	55,113
(7)	167.97	164.06	332.03	167.97	28,213	27,557	55,770
(8)	167.97	166.02	333.99	166.02	27,886	27,563	55,449
.	.	.	.	.	.	.	.
.	.	.	.	.	.	.	.
Final solution*	166.67	166.67	333.33	166.67	27,775	27,775	55,550

* The final solution is found as follows:

(1) Notice that Firm A originally produced ½ the competitive output (500 units, where $P = MC - 0$).

(2) When B enters, A's output falls by 62.5 units, or ⅛ the competitive output.

(3) A's next reduction is 15.62 units, or 1/32 the competitive output.

(4) A's equilibrium output is thus:

$Q_A = $ (competitive output)$(1 - [1/2 + 1/8 + 1/32 + \ldots])$.

(5) The term in brackets is an infinite series whose sum is found as $a/(1 - r)$, where a is the initial proportion of the equilibrium output produced by A and r is the rate of decline in output between each iteration.

(6) Initially A is producing at one-half the competitive level, and at each iteration it reduces output by one-quarter, so:

$$\frac{a}{1 - r} = \frac{0.5}{1 - 0.25} = 0.67.$$

(7) Therefore, in equilibrium $Q_A = 500(1 - 0.67) = 500(0.33) = 166.67$.

(8) Since A and B will share the market equally in equilibrium, B's final output is also 166.67 units.

proaches infinity.[14] Thus, it is clear that Cournot's model of oligopolistic behavior is consistent with the pricing theory of both pure monopoly and pure competition.

[14] An equation for determining industry output is

$$Q = \frac{Na}{(N + 1)b},$$

where $Q = $ total industry output, $a = $ the intercept of the industry demand function, $N = $ the number of firms in the industry, and $b = $ the slope of the (linear) demand curve. Thus, for $N = 2$:

$$Q = \frac{2 \cdot 500}{3 \cdot 1} = \frac{1,000}{3} = 333.33 \ldots,$$

Numerous objections have, however, been raised to Cournot's theory of oligopolistic pricing. One relates to the assumption that firms fail to recognize the interdependent nature of the situation. Why assume that rival firms will maintain their current level of output? Would it not be just as logical to assume that they will react to actions of other firms by reducing their own prices? Further, Cournot's oligopolists seem incapable of learning. They doggedly hold to their belief that price/output decisions can be made with complete independence, even though past output changes have always caused a reaction by the rival firm. Introducing a learning capability into the model would result in higher equilibrium prices and lower output. This can be seen by examining columns 5, 6, and 7 in Table 10-2. If Firm A had recognized the true interdependence in decision analysis, it would have reacted to Firm B's initial price/output decision by maintaining output at 250 units. The $31,250 profit it is earning at that point is the best it can obtain. Even if it took A several successive iterations to learn the true interdependence pattern, it would always prove most profitable to react to B's latest price/output change by reverting to the 250-unit output level, provided B continues to operate in the established manner. A similar result would follow if B learned the nature of the reactions.

Once either firm discovers that the assumed independence in decision making is fallacious, it is faced with an added problem—has the rival also discovered the interrelationship? The answer to this question is critical for profit-maximizing price/output decisions. Again, reference to the two-firm example of Table 10-2 can be used to demonstrate this point. Assume that after A's second output change—and B's reaction to it—A realizes the true reaction pattern taking place. It can, as was shown above, shift back to 250 units of output and earn maximum profits of $31,250, assuming that B will react as before and reduce its output to 125 units. However, if B's management also recognizes what is happening, it will refuse to reduce output to 125 units, so A's profits will be considerably less than the expected $31,250.[15] Firm A, realizing this possibility, may well prefer to maintain output at 172 units and accept the accompanying profit level of $28,198.

This analysis shows that optimal price/output decisions under oligopoly ultimately depend on how rival firms react. If one firm knows that assumed independence will not lead to profit maximization, the other firms may

---

and for $N = 3$:

$$Q = \frac{3 \cdot 500}{4 \cdot 1} = \frac{1,500}{4} = 375.$$

The competitive output is determined by setting price (average revenue) equal to marginal cost (0 in this example); that is, $P = 500 - Q = 0$, so $Q = 500$.

[15] If Firm B maintains output at 164 units when A shifts to 250, A's profits will decline to $21,500, well below the $28,198 maximum profits it was earning. This will lead A to reverse its strategy and cut output back to 172 units. Firm B's profits of $26,915 at the 172-164 unit combination are considerably greater than the $15,625 profits it would earn by reducing output to 125 units in response to A's output increase.

well have discovered the same thing. The uncertainty about how a rival firm will react to price/output changes introduces a variety of complications into the theory of oligopolistic pricing.

Cartel Arrangements

At this point it should be obivous that it would benefit all the firms in an industry if they got together and set price so as to maximize total industry profits. In other words, the firms could reach an agreement whereby they set the same price as would a monopolist, and thereby extract the maximum amount of profits from consumers. In the preceding example Firms A and B could agree to charge a price of $250 and earn total profits of $62,500, which they would share equally, each earning $31,250. If such a formal, overt agreement were made, the group would be defined as a *cartel;* if a covert, informal agreement were reached, *collusion* would be taking place. Both practices are generally illegal in the United States.[16]

If a cartel has absolute control over all the firms in the industry, it can operate as a monopoly. To illustrate, consider the situation shown in Figure 10-14. The marginal cost curves of each firm are summed horizontally to arrive at an industry marginal cost curve. Equating the cartel's total marginal cost with the industry marginal revenue curve determines the profit-maximizing output and simultaneously the price, P^*, to be charged. Once this profit-maximizing price/output level has been determined, each individ-

Figure 10-14 Price/Output Determination for a Cartel

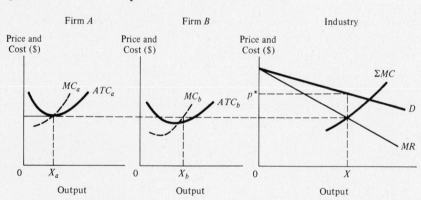

[16] Cartels are legal, however, in many parts of the world, and multinational United States corporations often become involved in them in foreign markets. Additionally, several important domestic markets are cartelized by producer associations and appear to operate without interference from the government. Certain farm products, including milk, are prime examples of products marketed under cartel-like arrangements.

ual firm's output is found by equating its own marginal cost to the previously determined industry profit-maximizing marginal cost level.

While profits are often divided between firms on the basis of their individual outputs, other allocating techniques can be used. Historical market shares, capacity as determined in a number of ways, and a bargained solution based on economic power have all been used in the past.

For numerous reasons cartels have typically been rather short lived. In addition to the long-run problems of changing products and of entry into the market by new producers, cartels are subject to much disagreement among the members. While firms usually agree that maximizing joint profits is mutually beneficial, they seldom agree on the equity of various profit allocation schemes, a problem leading to attempts to subvert the agreement.

Subversion of the cartel by an individual firm can be extremely profitable to that firm. With the industry operating at the monopoly price/output level, the demand curve facing an individual firm is highly elastic, provided it can lower its price without the cartel's learning of this action and retaliating. The availability of significant profits to a firm that cheats on the cartel, coupled with the ease with which secret price concessions can be made, makes policing a cartel agreement extremely difficult. This, in turn, makes it difficult for cartels to survive.

Price Leadership

A less formal but nonetheless effective means of reducing oligopolistic uncertainty is through price leadership. Price leadership results when one firm establishes itself as the industry leader and spokesman, and all other firms in the industry accept its pricing policy. This leadership may result from the size and strength of the leader firm, from cost efficiency, or as a result of the recognized ability of the leader to forecast market conditions accurately and to establish a price that produces satisfactory profits for all firms in the industry.

The most typical case is price leadership by a dominant firm, usually the largest firm in the industry. Here the leader faces a price/output problem similar to a monopolist, while the other firms face a competitive price/output problem.[17] This is illustrated in Figure 10-15, where the total market demand curve is D_T, the marginal cost curve of the leader is MC_L, and the horizontal summation of the marginal cost curves for all the price followers is labeled MC_f. Because the price followers take prices as given, they choose to operate at that output level at which their individual marginal costs equal price, just as they would in a purely competitive market structure. Accordingly, the MC_f curve represents the supply curve for the follower firms. This

---

[17] The leader allows the followers to sell as much as they please at the established price. This presents no problem for the price leader, since the followers' output is constrained by their marginal cost curves.

means that at price P_1, the followers would supply the entire market, leaving nothing for the dominant firm. At all prices below P_1, however, the horizontal distance between the summed MC_f curve and the market demand curve represents the demand faced by the price leader. At a price of P_2, for example, the price followers will provide Q_2 units of output, leaving a demand of $Q_4 - Q_2$ for the price leader.[18] Plotting of all the residual demand quantities for prices below P_1 results in the demand curve faced by the price leader, D_L in Figure 10-15, and the related marginal revenue curve MR_L.

Since the price leader faces the demand curve D_L as a monopolist, it maximizes profit by operating where marginal revenue equals marginal cost; that is, where $MR_L = MC_L$. At this output for the leader, Q_3, the market price is established to be P_3. The price followers will supply a combined output of $Q_5 - Q_3$ units. If no one challenges the price leader, a stable short-run equilibrium has been reached.

Kinked Demand Curve

An often-noted characteristic of oligopolistic markets is that once a general price level has been established, whether through a cartel or through some

---

Figure 10-15 Oligopoly Pricing with Dominant Firm Price Leadership

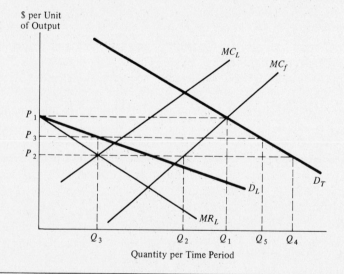

---

[18] More generally, the leader faces a demand curve of the form:

$$D_L = D_T - S_f,$$

where D_L is the leader's demand, D_T is total demand, and S_f is the followers' supply curve. Since D_T and S_f are both functions of price, D_L is likewise determined by price.

less formal arrangement, it tends to remain fixed for an extended period. This rigidity of prices is typically explained by yet another set of assumptions about firm behavior under conditions of price interdependence, which is known as the *kinked demand curve theory of oligopoly prices.*

The kinked demand curve theory describes a behavior pattern in which rival firms are assumed to follow any decrease in price in order to maintain their respective market shares but to refrain from following price increases, thereby allowing their market shares to increase at the expense of the price raiser. Thus, the demand curve facing an individual firm is kinked at the current price/output combination as illustrated in Figure 10-16. The firm is producing Q units of output and selling them at a price of P per unit; if it lowers its price, competing firms will retaliate by lowering their prices. The result of a price cut, therefore, is a relatively small increase in sales; that is, the demand curve associated with price reductions has very low elasticity.[19] Price increases, on the other hand, result in a significant reduction in the quantity demanded and in a related decrease in total revenue, because customers will shift to competing firms that do not follow the price increase.

Figure 10-16 Kinked Demand Curve

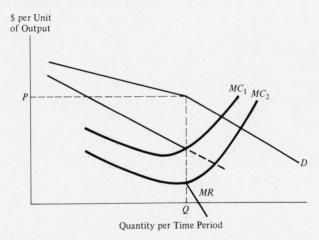

Associated with the kink in the demand curve is a point of discontinuity in the marginal revenue curve. That is, the firm's marginal revenue curve has a gap at the current price/output level, and it is this gap in the

[19] The reader is referred to Figure 10-13, where the shift in demand curves which results from a price cut was explained. The curve D_3 in Figure 10-13 is the counterpart of the steeper segment of D in Figure 10-16.

marginal revenue curve that explains the rigidity of price.[20] The profit-maximizing firm always chooses to operate at the point where marginal cost equals marginal revenue, and because of this gap in the marginal revenue curve, the price/output combination at the kink can remain optimal even though marginal cost fluctuates considerably. Thus, as illustrated in Figure 10-16, the firm's marginal cost curve can fluctuate between MC_1 and MC_2 without causing a change in the firm's optimal price/output combination.

NONPRICE COMPETITION

Because rival firms are likely to retaliate against price cuts, oligopolists tend to use nonprice competitive techniques to boost demand. What does nonprice competition mean? To explain the concept, let us first assume that a firm's demand function is given by Equation 10-9:

$$Q_A = f(P_A, P_X, Adv_A, SQ_A, SQ_X, I, Pop, \ldots)$$
$$= a - bP_A + cP_X + dA_A - eA_X + fSQ_A - gSQ_X + hI + iPop + \ldots, \quad \textbf{(10-9)}$$

where Q_A is the quantity of output demanded from Firm A, P_A is A's price, P_X is the average price charged by other firms in the industry, Adv_A is advertising expenditures, SQ denotes an index of styling and quality, I represents income, and Pop is population.[21] The firm can control three of the variables in Equation 10-9: P_A, Adv_A, and SQ_A. If it reduces P_A in an effort to stimulate demand, this will probably cause a reduction in P_X, offsetting the hoped-for effects of the initial price cut. Rather than get a substantial boost in sales, Firm A may have simply started a price war.

Now consider the effects of changing the other controllable variables in the demand function, Adv_A and SQ_A. Increased advertising could be expected to shift the demand curve to the right, thus enabling the firm to increase sales at a given price or to sell a constant quantity at a higher price. An improvement in styling or quality would have the same effect as a boost in the advertising budget, and similar results would follow from easing credit terms, training salespersons to be more courteous, providing more convenient retail locations, or any other improvement in the "product." Competitors can be expected to react to changes in nonprice variables, but the reaction rate is likely to be slower than for price changes. For one thing, these changes are generally less obvious, at least initially, to rival firms, so it will take them longer to recognize that a change has occurred. Then, too, advertising campaigns have to be designed, and media time and space must be purchased. Styling and quality changes frequently require long lead

---

[20] This gap occurs because MR_1 is the relevant marginal revenue curve for output to the left of the kink in the demand curve, while MR_2 depicts the appropriate marginal revenue for output to the right of the kink.

[21] There may be other variables such as credit terms, number of outlets (stores for a grocery chain or branches for a bank), and so on in the demand function.

times, as do training programs for salespeople, the opening of new facilities, and the like. Further, all these nonprice activities tend to differentiate the firm's products in the minds of consumers from those of other firms in the industry, and rivals may therefore find it difficult to regain lost customers even after they have reacted. So, while it may take longer to build up a "reputation" through the use of nonprice competition, once the demand curve has been shifted outward it will take rivals longer to counteract that shift. Thus, the advantageous effects of nonprice competition are likely to be more persistent than the fleeting benefits of a price cut.

How far should nonprice competition be carried? The answer is that such activities should be carried to the point where the marginal cost of the action is just equal to the marginal revenue produced by it. For example, suppose widgets sell for $10 a unit and the variable cost per unit is $8. If less than $2 of additional advertising expenditures will boost sales by 1 unit, the additional expenditure should be made.[22]

SUMMARY

Demand functions and cost functions interact to determine market structures, and the process by which this determination is made was explained in this chapter. If the average cost curve turns up at an output that is small in relation to total demand, then a large number of firms will operate, and a *competitive* market structure will emerge. However, if unit costs decline throughout the entire range of outputs, then in the absence of external controls (such as antitrust legislation) the industry is likely to consist of but one firm, a *monopolist*.

If a large number of firms exist in the industry and if a homogeneous product is produced, the result is likely to be *pure competition,* in which firms face horizontal demand curves. On the other hand, if the product is somewhat differenti-

---

[22] In theory, the firm should operate where the change in profit (π) associated with changing any variable (X_i) is zero: $\partial\pi/\partial X_i = 0$. To see this, consider the following:

(1) $\pi = TR - TC$.
(2) $TR = P \cdot Q$, where $Q = f_1(X_i)$. The X_i's include advertising expenditures, expenditures on quality improvements, and so on.
(3) $TC = f_2(X_i)$.
(4) Therefore, $\pi = P \cdot f_1(X_i) - f_2(X_i)$.
(5) To maximize profits, set $\partial\pi/\partial X_j = 0$ for all controllable variables X_j. This is equivalent to setting $\partial TR/\partial X_j - \partial TC/\partial X_j = 0$, or, alternatively, $MR_{X_j} - MC_{X_j} = 0$, which is the same as setting $MR_{X_j} = MC_{X_j}$.

This process requires that the cost and demand functions be specified and used to construct the profit function. The profit function is partially differentiated for every controllable variable X_j to obtain a set of j equations in j unknowns. The simultaneous solution of this system of equations provides the optimal value of all controllable variables: price, advertising expenditures, "quality," and so on.

It is much easier to say what to do than to do it. Nevertheless, a thorough understanding of the theoretical model provides us with insights about the probable direction if not magnitude of specific changes. Further, an understanding of the theory helps us to recognize what information would be most useful for decision purposes and, accordingly, what data we should attempt to collect.

ated, each firm will face a downward-sloping demand curve, and the market structure is defined as *monopolistic competition.*

Under competition, either pure or monpolistic, no individual firm is enough of a factor in the market so that its actions affect other firms seriously enough to cause them to react. Accordingly, competitive firms do not take into account reactions of other firms when making their price and output decisions. However, if only a few firms operate in the market, each of them will have a sizable share of the total market, and an action by one firm will have a noticeable effect on other firms.[23] Therefore, other firms will react to the actions of any individual firm, and all firms will recognize this fact and will take such reactions into consideration in their pricing decisions. This situation is defined as *oligopoly.*

The profit-maximizing decision rules are relatively simple and straightforward under monopoly, pure competition, and monopolistic competition. Under oligopoly, however, the rules become complex, almost to the point of being indeterminant. The firms all recognize that profits could be maximized by some form of cooperative behavior, so *cartels, price leadership arrangements,* and stable prices as explained by the *kinked demand curve* may develop. Also, because reactions may be delayed, oligopolistic firms are likely to engage in such forms of nonprice competition as advertising, styling and quality changes, and service improvements as much as or more than firms in direct price competition.

QUESTIONS

10-1 Explain the process through which above-normal profits are eliminated in a purely competitive industry and in a monopolistically competitive industry.

10-2 Would the demand curve for a firm in a monopolistically competitive industry be more or less elastic after any above-normal profits have been eliminated?

10-3 Assume that a Congressional committee is holding hearings on a proposed bill that would restrict the number of firms in monopolistically competitive industries, the idea being to help firms reach the minimum points on their *ATC* curves. (*See* Figure 10-12.) You have been retained as an economic consultant to analyze the proposal.

    a) What disadvantages can you see in the proposal?

    b) Consider how the trend from "mom and pop" grocery stores to supermarkets (with large parking lots) might be used as evidence in the hearing.

10-4 "One might expect firms in a competitive industry to experience greater swings in the price of their products over the business cycle than those in an oligopolistic industry. However, fluctuations in profits will not necessarily follow the same pattern." Do you agree with this statement? Why, or why not?

10-5 Explain how the following cost curve could be consistent with monopoly, oligopoly, or competition.

[23] The question of "how many" firms are required to produce a competitive outcome is deferred to Chapter 12.

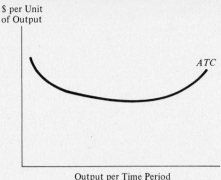

$ per Unit
of Output

ATC

Output per Time Period

10-6 Suppose strong economies of scale exist in the widget industry up to a large output. There are relatively few firms in the industry, so it is an oligopoly. Historically, Firm *A* has been the price leader in the industry. Explain the price action that each of the following conditions would cause *A* to take:

a) The industry demand curve shifts to the right.

b) *A*'s fixed costs and variable costs per unit rise.

c) A large conglomerate corporation announces that it might start a new division to produce widgets.

d) All governmental controls—on mergers, collusion in price setting, and cut-throat competition—are removed.

10-7 When a single buyer (or a few large buyers) faces many sellers, a condition known as *monopsony* exists. Describe the relationship between this form of market structure and the development of our labor laws.

10-8 When a single seller faces a large number of buyers, a condition known as *monopoly* exists.

a) Give an illustration of this form of market structure in United States labor markets.

b) Discuss the impact of such a structure on inflation.

c) Discuss the feasibility of modifying the antitrust laws to deal with such situations.

10-9 The following is taken from a talk given by a financial executive of a cement company to a trade association meeting:

> I presume that, in keeping with modern accounting concepts, many of you have an accounting system that breaks out your fixed and variable costs, and have financial people who tell you what they are per barrel. If you do, I suggest you use the system to control costs, which is what it was intended for in the first place. Extending its use as a tool for marketing decisions will result in some serious errors. *Every barrel of cement that is sold for less than fully-allocated costs plus an adequate return on investment represents giving money away rather than making it.*

Does the italicized statement make any sense for a competitive firm in the short run? Does this statement make any sense for a monopolist in the short run?

10-10 The automobile industry is marked by price leadership. Auto executives taking economics courses are always intrigued by the kinked demand curve and insist that this represents the situation they in fact face. Are price leadership and the kinked curve compatible?

PROBLEMS

10-1 Given the following market supply and demand equations for a certain Product X:

$$Q_S = 20,000P_X$$
$$Q_D = 60,000 - 12,000P_X,$$

a) Graph the demand and supply equations.
b) Determine both algebraically and graphically the equilibrium price for the industry; that is, at the point where quantity supplied equals quantity demanded.

10-2 The Coy Company is a small firm in the butternut-processing industry, which is purely competitive. The market price per unit of butternut is $640; the company's cost function is given by the equation $TC = \$240Q - \$20Q^2 + \$1Q^3$. A "normal" profit is included in the cost function.
a) Determine
   (i) the output at which profit is maximized,
   (ii) the average cost per unit at this output, and
   (iii) total profits.
b) If this firm is typical of all firms in the industry, is the industry in equilibrium? How do you know?
c) Assume that this firm's input factors are perfectly unspecialized such that there is no difference between the short-run and the long-run cost curves. If the firm and the industry are not now in equilibrium, when they do reach an equilibrium what will be:
   (i) the output per firm,
   (ii) the cost per unit of output, and
   (iii) the price per unit of output?
d) Describe the process that will drive the industry into equilibrium.

10-3 The Demming Corporation is a medium-sized electronics company specializing in alarm devices. Demming's demand schedule is estimated to be $Q = 4,500 - P$, and the company's accounting department, after consulting with the production and marketing managers, has reported the following total cost function for the near future: $TC = \$150,000 + \$400Q$. This total cost function includes a normal return of 10 percent on capital resources.
a) Determine the profit-maximizing output.
b) What is the profit at this output?
c) What price will be charged under profit maximization?

d) What price will be charged under the assumption that the company is no longer interested in profit maximization but seeks to maximize the dollar sales volume? Compute profits under this assumption.

e) Assume that Demming operates in a monopolistically competitive industry. If Demming is typical of other firms in the industry, and if "normal" profits are implicit in the cost function, is the industry in equilibrium? If not, what will output, price, and profits (as calculated above) be under equilibrium? Assume equilibrium occurs through a (parallel) shift in the demand curve. Use a graph to aid in your explanation.

10-4 Consider an industry with just two firms where the actions of each firm affect the profits of the other firm; that is, the profits of each firm are a function of the output decision of the other firm. The profit functions for the two firms are:

$$\pi_1 = 10Q_1 - 2Q_1{}^2 - Q_2{}^2 + 10$$
$$\pi_2 = 6Q_2 - 3Q_2{}^2 - 2Q_1{}^2 + 14.$$

a) Assuming the Cournot model—that is, the firms continuously assume that the other firm will not react to their output decisions—what will be the outputs and profits of each firm, and what will be the total industry output and profits?

b) Assuming the firms decide to maximize joint profits via collusion, what will be the output level and profits of each firm, and what will be the industry output level and profits?

10-5 The Henderson Company faces the following segmented demand curve:

$$P = 25 - 0.25Q \text{ over the range 0-20 units of output.}$$
$$P = 35 - 0.75Q \text{ when output exceeds 20 units.}$$

The company's total cost function is as follows:

$$TC_1 = 200 + 5Q + 0.125Q^2.$$

a) Graph the demand, marginal revenue, and marginal cost curves.

b) How would you describe the market structure of the Henderson Company's industry? Explain your answer in some detail, including an explanation of why the demand curve takes the shape given above.

c) What is the firm's optimal price and quantity, and what will its profits (or losses) be at this output?

d) What will be the optimal price and quantity, assuming the cost curve is:

$$TC_2 = 200 + 8Q + 0.125Q^2?$$

e) What will be the optimal price and quantity, assuming the cost curve is:

$$TC_3 = 200 + 8Q + 0.25Q^2?$$

f) Would a new kink be likely to develop at the price indicated in Part e? Assume that the same factors which caused Henderson's costs to rise affected all firms in the industry.

10-6   In the inland waterways shipping industry, bulk carriers (barges) are char-
tered on an annual basis to haul grain, oil, ore, and other bulk commodities.
As far as the shippers are concerned, the barges of any given class are
homogeneous products. The total industry demand for carriers varies over
time, depending on grain and oil movements; at present the industry demand curve is given by the following linear approximation:

$$Q = 40,000 - 0.2P.$$

The industry consists of one large firm, Mississippi Barge and Trans-
port Company (MBT), and ten smaller firms of about equal size. MBT is
the industry leader with regard to pricing decisions, and its marginal cost
curve is given by the following linear approximation:

$$MC_L = -20,000 + 6Q.$$

The follower firms' marginal cost curve, derived by summing the MC
curves of the ten follower firms, is given by the linear approximation:

$$MC_F = 44,000 + 4Q.$$

It must be stressed that these curves are *approximations*, empirically derived over a limited range of outputs. If observations were available over
the full range of outputs, the curves would not be linear, but these are good
approximations over the probable output ranges.

MBT has the following characteristics: It controls most port facilities.
Follower firms are permitted to use these facilities on a fee basis, but this
permission could be terminated. MBT has a reputation for "fairness" and
for having "good business judgment." MBT has great financial strength;
should the need arise, it could conduct an extended price war.

a)   Construct a graph showing
   (i)   the industry demand curve,
   (ii)   the leader's and the followers' cost curves,
   (iii)   the leader's demand and marginal revenue curves. To construct
this graph, make the following calculations and use them to
help draw the curves:

$$Q_F, \text{ when } P = \$114,000$$
$$Q_F, \text{ when } P = \$\ 60,000$$
$$Q_L, \text{ when } P = \$114,000$$
$$Q_L, \text{ when } P = \$\ 60,000$$

b)   What price will MBT establish, and what will its output be at this
price?
c)   How many units of output will the follower firms supply?
d)   Is price leadership as described here consistent with the kinked demand curve theory of oligopoly pricing?
e)   Reconsider your graph. Could a price leadership situation exist, given
the other facts of this problem, if MC_L lay above MC_F for all output
quantities where the MC_F curve is below the industry demand curve?

10-7   Computer Management Corporation specializes in the development of
management information and decision assistance computer programs which
it markets throughout the United States. CMC has just finished develop-

ment of a new program package that will permit small retail firms to computerize their inventory management at a cost lower than has previously been possible. The company is now confronted with the problem of setting a price for the product in the face of uncertain demand. On the basis of sales data for similar program packages CMC has marketed in the past, management believes that demand for the product will be greatly influenced by the reactions of other computer software companies to the introduction of CMC's new product. A minimal reaction will result in the demand function:

$$P = 150 - 0.1Q.$$

A major reaction will lead to the more elastic demand curve:

$$P = 130 - 0.4Q.$$

CMC's total cost for marketing this product is composed of $3,000 additional administrative expenses and $50 a unit for direct production and distribution costs. That is, the relevant cost function is given by the expression:

$$TC = \$3,000 + 50Q.$$

a) What is the profit-maximizing price for CMC's product, assuming
   (i) no reaction, and
   (ii) a reaction?
b) Develop the payoff matrix for this pricing problem under the assumption that CMC's management views its alternative courses of action as follows:
   (i) It can set price so as to maximize profits if competitors do not react, or
   (ii) it can set the price so as to maximize profits if competitors do react.
   (*Hint:* The prices you developed in Part a indicate the two alternative courses of action.)
c) If CMC's management is averse to risk—so risk-averse that it wishes to use a maximin decision criterion—what is the optimal price to set on this product?
d) Now assume that management is concerned with the relative performance of the firm as opposed to its absolute performance. Specifically, it makes decisions so as to minimize the difference between the actual outcome and the best possible outcome, given the resulting state of nature (this implies a regret decision criterion). Develop the relevant "payoff" matrix for the decision problem, given this decision criterion, and indicate the optimal price.
e) If CMC's management subjectively estimates the probabilities that competitors would react at 0.9 and that competitors would not react at 0.1, and makes decisions so as to minimize the *expected* regret, what price would it set?
f) What is the cost of uncertainty in this decision problem, and of what value is knowledge of that cost to CMC?
g) Do the probabilities assigned to a reaction versus no reaction by com-

petitors in Part e seem reasonable for this problem? Why? What factors do you think are important in determining the probability of a reaction?

h) How would you classify the industry structure within which CMC operates? Be as specific as you can.

SELECTED REFERENCES

Baumol, William J. *Economic Theory and Operations Analysis,* 3d ed. Englewood Cliffs, N.J.: Prentice-Hall, 1972, Chapter 14.

Chamberlin, Edward. *The Theory of Monopolistic Competition,* Cambridge, Mass.: Harvard University Press, 1933.

Friedman, Milton. "Monopoly and the Social Responsibility of Business and Labor," in *Capitalism and Freedom,* by Milton Friedman. Chicago: University of Chicago Press, 1962.

Harrod, Roy. "Doctrines of Imperfect Competition," *Quarterly Journal of Economics,* vol. 48, May 1934, pp. 442-470.

Modigliani, Franco. "New Developments on the Oligopoly Front," *Journal of Political Economy,* June 1959, pp. 215-232.

Murdock, Lawrence C., Jr. *The Price System,* Federal Reserve Bank of Philadelphia, reprinted in Heinz Kohler, ed., *Readings in Economics.* New York: Holt, Rinehart and Winston, 1969.

Schwartzman, David. "The Effect of Monopoly on Price," *Journal of Political Economy,* vol. LXVII, no. 4, August 1959, pp. 352-361.

———. "The Effect of Monopoly: A Correction," *Journal of Political Economy,* vol. LXIX, no. 5, October 1961.

CHAPTER 11

Pricing
Practices

Chapter 10 demonstrated that profit maximization is based on a careful analysis of the relationship between marginal cost and marginal revenue, regardless of the market structure within which the firm operates. Research into the question of actual pricing practices, however, indicates that most firms set prices without an explicit analysis of the marginal relationships. Hall and Hitch, for example, found that most firms use "cost-plus" pricing, setting prices to cover all direct costs plus a percentage markup for overhead and profit instead of determining the specific price at which $MR = MC$.[1] Similar findings were reported by Kaplan, Dirlam, and Lanzillotti in their study of pricing practices in big business,[2] and by Haynes in his analysis of small-business pricing decisions.[3]

[1] R. L. Hall and C. J. Hitch. "Price Theory and Business Behavior," *Oxford Economic Papers*, The Clarendon Press, Oxford, 1939, p. 19.

[2] A. D. H. Kaplan, Joel B. Dirlam, and Robert F. Lanzillotti. *Pricing in Big Business*. The Brookings Institution, Washington, D.C., 1958. *See also* Robert F. Lanzillotti, "Pricing Objectives in Large Companies," *The American Economic Review*, December 1958, pp. 921-940.

[3] W. W. Haynes, *Pricing Decisions in Small Business*. Lexington: University of Kentucky Press, 1962.

How can this conflict between economic theory and observed pricing practices be reconciled? If one thoroughly understands microeconomic theory, especially its weaknesses and limitations, and fully comprehends the procedures used in actual pricing decisions, one can see that the so-called conflict between theory and practice is more apparent than real. In this chapter we examine a variety of pricing practices, indicate their value in real-world situations, and demonstrate the economic rationale for their use.

COST-PLUS PRICING

Surveys of actual business pricing indicate that cost-plus pricing, or full-cost pricing as it is sometimes called, is by far the most prevalent pricing method employed by business firms. There are many varieties of cost-plus pricing, but a typical one involves estimating the average variable costs of producing and marketing a particular product, adding a charge for overhead, and then adding a percentage markup, or margin, for profits. The charge for indirect costs, or overhead, is usually determined by allocating these costs among the firm's products on the basis of their average variable costs. For example, if a firm's total overhead for the year was projected to be $1.3 million, and the estimated total variable costs of its planned production was $1.0 million, then overhead would be allocated to products at the rate of 130 percent of variable cost. Thus, if the average variable costs of a product are estimated to be $1, the firm would add a charge of 130 percent of that variable cost, or $1.30, for overhead, obtaining an estimated fully allocated average cost of $2.30. To this figure the firm might add a 30 percent markup for profits, or $0.69, to obtain a price of $2.99 a unit.[4]

Cost-plus pricing has long been criticized as a naïve pricing technique based solely on cost considerations—and the wrong costs at that. The failure of the technique to examine demand conditions, coupled with its emphasis on fully allocated accounting costs rather than marginal costs, is said to lead to suboptimal price decisions. While it is true that firms which use cost-plus pricing naïvely may fail to make optimal decisions, the widespread use of the technique by many successful firms should cause one to question the

---

[4] Profit margins, or markups, are often calculated as a percentage of price instead of cost. It is a simple matter to convert from one to the other by use of the following expressions:

$$\text{Markup on Price} = \frac{\text{Markup on Cost}}{1 + \text{Markup on Cost}} \qquad (11\text{-}1)$$

$$\text{Markup on Cost} = \frac{\text{Markup on Price}}{1 - \text{Markup on Price}}. \qquad (11\text{-}2)$$

Thus, a 30 percent profit margin on a cost basis is equivalent to a 23 percent margin on price:

$$\text{Markup on Price} = \frac{0.3}{1 + 0.3} = 0.23.$$

charge that it has no place in managerial decision making. In fact, a closer examination of the technique indicates both its value and its limitations in pricing analysis.

Role of Costs in Cost-plus Pricing

Although several different cost concepts are employed in cost-plus pricing, most firms use a "standard" or "normal" cost concept. These fully allocated costs are determined by first estimating the per-unit direct costs, then allocating the firm's expected indirect expenses, or overhead, assuming a "standard" or "normal" output level. The resulting standard cost per unit is then used for price determination, irrespective of short-term variations in actual unit costs.

The standard cost concept is typically based on historical accounting costs, with adjustments to account for wage and price changes that are expected to affect costs during the period for which prices are being established. The use of historical accounting costs as the basis for cost-plus pricing gives rise to several potential problems. First, firms often fail to properly adjust the historical cost data to reflect recent *or expected* price changes for key input factors. Unadjusted historical accounting costs have little relevance for decision making. The firm should use estimates of future costs; that is, costs that will be incurred during the period for which prices are being set. A further problem is that accounting costs seldom reflect true economic costs. The concept of opportunity, or alternative, costs must be employed for optimal decision making. Additionally, for many pricing decisions the use of fully allocated costs is erroneous, because incremental costs, rather than full costs, should typically be used for optimization in pricing decisions.

Role of Demand in Cost-plus Pricing

The structure of profit margins among different products for firms using cost-plus pricing provides clear evidence that demand analysis does, in fact, play an important role in price determination. James S. Earley, for example, reported that most of the firms he examined differentiated their markups for different product lines on the basis of competitive pressure and demand elasticities.[5] Kaplan, Dirlam, and Lanzillotti reported a similar finding in their study of pricing practices.[6] There is no evidence, however, that the markups used in cost-plus pricing result in optimal prices—that is, prices which would be established by setting $MR = MC$—so cost-plus pricing may not produce optimal results.

Explanation for the Existence of Cost-plus Pricing

Given the possibility that cost-plus pricing might result in a nonoptimal price/output decision, is there a rationale for its continued use by many

---

[5] James S. Earley. "Marginal Policies of Excellently Managed Companies," *The American Economic Review*, March 1956, pp. 44-70.

[6] A. D. H. Kaplan, Joel B. Dirlam, and Robert F. Lanzillotti. *Pricing in Big Business*. The Brookings Institute, Washington, D.C., 1958.

business firms? There are, indeed, reasons for this use, and an examination of the deviations between the basic microeconomic model of the firm and the actual environment faced by businesses explains why cost-plus pricing is so popular.

Although microeconomic theory is based on an assumption of profit maximization, it is a static concept in that the firm is assumed to operate so as to maximize *short-run* profits. Implicit in this prescribed behavior pattern is the assumption that continual maximization of short-run profits, coupled with proper adjustments to the physical plant as technology and demand change, will lead to long-run profit maximization.

The real world is more complicated than this model suggests. Actions taken in one period affect results in subsequent periods, and businessmen must and do recognize this fact. Accordingly, because short-run profit maximization seldom is consistent with long-run wealth maximization, firms do not typically attempt to maximize short-run profits.

An example will help to clarify the point. Consider the case of a firm that sets the current price of its product below the short-run profit-maximizing level in order to expand its market rapidly. Such a policy may lead to long-run profit maximization if the firm is able to secure a larger permanent market share by its action. A similar policy might be used to forestall competitive entry into the market or to prevent labor unions from using a recent high-profit record as a bargaining point in wage negotiations. From a legal standpoint, this policy of accepting less than maximum short-run profits might well reduce the threat of antitrust suits or government regulations, thereby again leading to long-run profit and wealth maximization.

The pricing practices of United States automobile manufacturers in the years just after World War II provide an example of this kind of behavior. Prices on most models were maintained well below the short-run profit-maximizing level. Automobile manufacturers felt that the rapid expansion of both automobile ownership and dealerships which would result from this policy would lead to higher long-run profits. Further, there was some fear of alienating consumers by charging high prices during this period of extremely heavy demand; moreover, the possibility of antitrust action also affected automobile-pricing decisions.

The existence of uncertainty in the real world is another complication that causes firms to depart from the theoretical microeconomic pricing solution. In pricing problems, microeconomic theory is based on the assumption that firms have precise knowledge of the marginal relationships in their demand and cost functions. Given this knowledge, it would be easy to operate so as to equate marginal revenue and marginal cost. However, firms know their cost and revenue functions only to an approximation. Consider first the demand function. In addition to the statistical problems described in Chapter 5, the element of interdependence discussed under the section on oligopoly in Chapter 10 is a most severe barrier to precise demand function estimation. The same statistical problems plague cost function estimation, and such considerations as joint costs, overhead costs, and the like present additional difficulties. This brief discussion makes clear the problems involved in empirically estimating historical demand and cost functions. When the uncertainties of the future—economic conditions, the weather, labor contract settlements, and so on—are added, it is abundantly clear why businessmen might be observed doing something other than equating marginal revenue and marginal cost when making price/output decisions.

Although the pricing corollaries of microeconomic theory are far too limited to be applied without modification in actual pricing problems, the theory does provide some useful tools for determining proper corporate action. For example, any attempt to reduce uncertainty and to estimate more precisely the marginal revenue and cost relations results in added costs. Marginal analysis indicates that the firm must weigh the added expense against the possible gain and act accordingly. That is, the firm must determine whether the added expense associated with obtaining better estimates of the marginal relationships is more than offset by the gain in profits expected to result. It follows from this that "short-cut" decision techniques may actually be resulting in maximum profits when full consideration is given to the added expense of obtaining the data necessary for complete marginal analysis.

INCREMENTAL ANALYSIS IN PRICING

The real world counterpart to marginal analysis is *incremental profit analysis,* which deals with the relationship between the *changes* in revenues and costs associated with managerial decisions. The emphasis on only the costs or revenues that are actually affected by the decision insures proper economic reasoning in decision analysis. That is, proper use of incremental profit analysis results in accepting any action that increases net profits and in rejecting any action that reduces profits.[7]

The statement that incremental analysis involves only those factors which are affected by a particular decision does not mean that the concept is easy to apply. Proper use of incremental analysis requires a wide-ranging examination of the *total* effect of the decision. Consider, for example, a firm's decision to introduce a new product. Incremental analysis requires that the decision be based on the net effect of changes in revenues and costs. An analysis of the effect on revenues involves an estimate of the net revenues to be received for the product and, additionally, a study of how sales of the new product will affect the firm's other products. It may well be that the

---

[7] In this section we are abstracting from changing the firm's risk posture. However, the true goal of the firm is constrained wealth maximization, and, as was pointed out in Chapter 1, an action might increase expected profits but be so risky that it would raise the firm's capitalization rate so much that the value of the firm might decline. The question of risk is considered more fully in Chapter 13.

new product will, in fact, compete with the firm's existing products; if so, even though the new product has a high individual revenue potential, the net effect on revenue might not justify the added expense. At the other extreme, although a new product may not be expected to produce much profit on its own, if it is complementary to the firm's other products, the expected gain in sales of these other products could result in a large incremental increase in total profit. Kodak's Instamatic camera series is an example of a product introduced, in part at least, because of the complementarity between it and a major component of the firm's existing product line, photographic film.

Incremental cost analysis is just as far reaching. In addition to the direct incremental costs associated with the new product, the firm must consider any impact on the costs of existing products. For example, introduction of a new product might cause production bottlenecks that would raise the cost of other products.

Incremental analysis involves long-run as well as short-run effects. A new product may appear to be profitable in an incremental sense in the short run because the firm has excess capacity in its existing plant and equipment. Over the longer run, however, this commitment to produce the new item may require a substantial investment when the necessary equipment wears out and must be replaced. There may also be high opportunity costs associated with future production if either expansion of other product lines or development of future alternative products is restricted by the decision to produce the new product.

It is important to stress once again that incremental analysis is based on the changes associated with the decision. For short-run analysis fixed cost (overhead) is irrelevant and must not be included in incremental analysis.

An Illustration of Incremental Analysis[8]

An example of how Continental Airlines has used incremental analysis in its flight service decisions demonstrates the usefulness of the technique. When considering adding a new flight (or dropping an existing one that appears to be doing poorly), Continental engages in a very thorough incremental analysis along the lines of Figure 11-1. The corporate philosophy is clear: "If revenues exceed out-of-pocket costs, put the flight on." In other words, Continental compares the "out-of-pocket," or incremental, costs associated with each proposed flight to the total revenues generated by that flight. An excess of revenues over incremental costs leads to a decision to add the flight to Continental's schedule.

The "out-of-pocket costs" figure that Continental uses is obtained by circulating a proposed schedule for the new flight to every operating department concerned and finding out what added expenses will be incurred by each of them. Here, an alternative cost concept is used. If a ground crew is

[8] Adapted from the April 20, 1963 issue of *Business Week* by special permission. © 1963 by McGraw-Hill, Inc.

Figure 11-1 Incremental Analysis as Employed by Continental Airlines

Problem:	Shall Continental run an extra daily flight from City X to City Y?	
The Facts:	Fully allocated costs of this flight	$4,500
	Out-of-pocket costs of this flight	$2,000
	Flight should gross	$3,100
Decision:	Run the flight. It will add $1,100 to net profit by adding $3,100 to revenues and only $2,000 to costs. Overhead and other costs totaling $2,500 [$4,500 minus $2,000] would be incurred whether the flight is run or not. Therefore, fully allocated or "average" costs of $4,500 are not relevant to this business decision. It is the out-of-pocket, or incremental, costs that count.	

on duty and between work on other flights, the proposed flight is not charged a penny of their salary. Some costs may even be reduced by the additional flight. For example, on a late-night round trip flight between Colorado Springs and Denver, Continental often flies without any passengers and with only a small amount of freight. Even without passenger revenues, these flights are profitable because their net costs are less than the rent for overnight hanger space at Colorado Springs.

On the revenue side, Continental considers not only the projected revenues for the flight but also the effect on revenues of competing and connecting flights on the Continental schedule. Several Continental flights which fail to cover even their out-of-pocket costs directly bring in passengers for connecting long-haul service. When the excess of additional revenue over cost on the long-haul flight is considered, Continental earns a positive net profit on the feeder service.

Continental's use of incremental analysis extends to its scheduling of airport arrival and departure times. A proposed schedule for the Kansas City Municipal Airport, for example, had two planes landing at the same time. This was expensive for Continental, because its facilities in Kansas City at that time were not sufficient to service two planes simultaneously. Continental would have been forced to lease an extra fuel truck and to hire three new employees at an additional monthly cost of $1,800. However, when Continental began shifting around proposed departure times in other cities to avoid the congestion at Kansas City, it appeared that the company might lose as much as $10,000 in monthly revenues if passengers switched to competing flights leaving at more convenient hours. Needless to say, the two flights were scheduled to be on the ground in Kansas City at the same time.

PRICE DISCRIMINATION

Additional complexities are involved in pricing when the firm sells its product in multiple markets. We now face this difficulty and examine price discrimination, or differential pricing.

In a general sense price discrimination can be said to exist whenever different classes of customers are charged different prices for the same product, or when a multiproduct firm prices closely related products in such a manner that the differences in their prices are not proportional to the differences in their costs of production. In other words, price discrimination occurs whenever a given firm's prices in different markets are not related to differentials in production and distribution costs. For example, a practice of nationwide uniform pricing for fountain pens by the Parker Pen Company of Janesville, Wisconsin, would be a form of price discrimination. The transportation cost of selling these pens in Chicago is lower than transportation cost to the Los Angeles market; thus a uniform price for the product reflects a lower markup in Los Angeles than in Chicago.

"Price discrimination" should not be given a bad connotation in a moral or ethical sense. It is merely a term used in economics to describe a particular condition that must be judged "good" or "bad" on other grounds. An opera company may charge lower prices for students than for nonstudents, and through this pricing practice it enables students who could not otherwise afford the price to attend performances. The company may still be losing money and may require a subsidy. Is such price discrimination bad? Of course, price discrimination can also be used by a predatory monopolist to increase already excessive profits, in which case most of us would agree with the antitrust laws designed to thwart such behavior.

Requirements for Profitable Price Discrimination

There are two necessary conditions for profitable price discrimination. First, the firm must be able to segment the market for a product; that is, to identify submarkets and to prevent transfers among customers in the different submarkets. When markets are segmented, the firm can isolate one group of buyers from another. If this is possible, the firm can sell at one price to some buyers and at a different price to others, without the possibility of intermarket leakages.

Second, different price elasticities of demand for the product must exist in the various submarkets. Unless price elasticities differ among the submarkets, there is no point in segmenting the market; with identical elasticities, the profit-maximizing price policy calls for charging the same price in all the segments. This point is elaborated in a later section.

Methods of Price Discrimination

Price discrimination can be based on a variety of factors. Geographical differentials may be used when a product's supplier feels that he can isolate regional markets through control of the product distribution system. For example, East Coast steel users may be charged a higher price than West Coast users because Japanese competition makes the West Coast market more price-elastic than the East Coast market. (Price differentials between geographically separated markets that are proportional to transportation costs are not classified as discriminatory.)

Product use provides another basis for price discrimination. Railroads, for example, typically charge different prices per ton-mile depending on the value of the product being hauled. Electric, gas, and water utilities' rate differentials between commercial and private consumers is another example of price discrimination based on product use. The utilities face very different demand elasticities in the residential and the industrial sectors of their markets.[9] The demand for electricity from residential users is inelastic, because these customers have no good substitutes for the electricity supplied by the power utility. Industrial buyers, on the other hand, have a much more elastic demand, because many of them could generate their own power if electricity prices should rise above the cost of operating in-plant generating equipment.

Time, either clock or calendar, provides another common basis for price discrimination. Segmenting the day for long-distance telephone rates is one example of such price discrimination; rates are higher during periods of the day when demand is greatest, as, for example, during business hours. Theater pricing provides another example of price discrimination based on clock time. The price differentials between matinee and evening performances are based on demand elasticity differentials rather than on any cost differentials. Also, calendar-time price discrimination is often reflected in "peak-season" and "off-season" pricing for resort facilities.

Age, sex, and income provide still other bases of discrimination, particularly for services as opposed to physical products. For example, lower prices for children's haircuts and movie tickets are discriminatory practices based on age; "ladies day" admission prices for sports events illustrates price discrimination based on sex. Doctors' fee schedules are often discriminatory between low-income and high-income patients.[10]

Profit Maximization under Price Discrimination

The firm that can segment its market will maximize profits by operating in such a way that marginal revenue equals marginal cost *in each market segment*. This can be demonstrated by an example. Suppose a firm is selling the same product in two separate markets, A and B. The demand curves for the two markets are given by Equations 11-3 and 11-4:

$$\text{Market } A: P_A = 60 - 0.5Q_A. \tag{11-3}$$
$$\text{Market } B: P_B = 110 - 3Q_B. \tag{11-4}$$

P_A and P_B are the prices charged in the two markets and Q_A and Q_B are the

---

[9] Utility users are prohibited from selling services to other users; otherwise, those paying low rates could make sales to those who are charged high rates by the utility.

[10] The AMA asserts that such discrimination is philanthropic; in many cases it no doubt is, but one can be just as sure that in other cases it represents profit-maximizing behavior.

quantities demanded. The firm's total cost function for its single homogeneous product is:

$$TC = 1,000 + 9Q + 0.1Q^2. \tag{11-5}$$

Here, Q equals the sum of the quantities sold in Markets A and B; that is, $Q = Q_A + Q_B$.

Figure 11-2 illustrates this pricing situation. The demand curve for Market A is shown in the first panel, that for Market B in the second. The aggregate demand curve shown in the third panel represents the horizontal sum of the quantities demanded at each price in Markets A and B. The associated marginal revenue curve, MR_{A+B}, has a similar interpretation. For example, marginal revenue equals $20 at 40 units of output in Market A and $20 at 15 units of output in Market B. Accordingly, one point on the firm's total marginal revenue curve will have output equal to 55 units and marginal revenue equal to $20. From a production standpoint it does not matter whether the product is being sold in Market A or Market B; therefore, the single marginal cost curve shown in panel three is applicable to both markets. If distribution costs had differed between the two markets, this fact would have had to be taken into account.

Obtaining the solution to this pricing problem can be thought of as a two-part process. First, the firm must determine the profit-maximizing total output level. Profit maximization occurs at that aggregate output level at which marginal cost and marginal revenue are equal. As shown in Figure

---

Figure 11-2 Price Discrimination for an Identical Product Sold in Two Markets

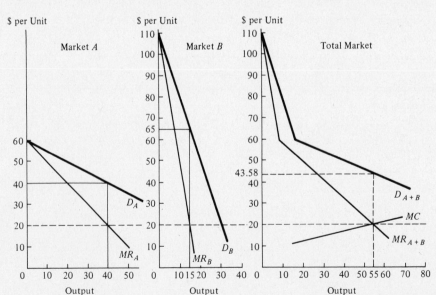

11-2, the profit-maximizing output is 55 units, where marginal cost and marginal revenue are both equal to $20. Second, the firm must allocate this output between the two submarkets. Proper allocation of the total output between the two submarkets can be determined graphically by drawing a horizontal line through the graphs in the first two panels at $20 to indicate that $20 is the marginal cost in *each* market at the indicated aggregate output. The intersection of this horizontal line with the marginal revenue curve in each submarket indicates the distribution of sales and the optimal pricing structure. According to the figures, our illustrative firm maximizes profits by producing a total of 55 units, then selling 40 units in Market A at a price of $40 and 15 units in Market B at a price of $65.

The price charged in the less elastic Market B is over 50 percent higher than the price charged in Market A, where demand is relatively elastic, and this differential adds significantly to the firm's profits. This can be seen by comparing profits earned with discrimination to profits if the firm was unable to segment the market. In the nondiscrimination case the firm acts as though it faced only the single total market demand curve shown in the third panel of Figure 11-2. Profit maximization requires that the firm operate at the output level where $MR = MC$; that is, at 55 units. Here, however, the single price that would prevail is $43.58, the price determined by the intersection of a vertical line at 55 units of output with the total market demand curve.

Because the optimal output level for the firm is 55 units irrespective of whether or not the firm can engage in price discrimination, total costs are the same in either case, and we need only consider the total revenues to determine the effect of price discrimination on the firm's profits. With price discrimination, the firm's total revenue is equal to $2,575, found as $40 × 40 units = $1,600 revenue in Market A plus $65 × 15 units = $975 revenue in Market B. Without price discrimination total revenue is $2,397 (= $43.58 × 55 units). The difference between these total revenue figures, $178, indicates the incremental profits the firm can obtain through differential pricing.

Calculus of Price Discrimination[11]

Since the effect of price discrimination on profits can be illustrated through the use of calculus as well as with graphs, this technique is employed below to re-examine the economics of differential pricing.

Step 1: Set Up the Total Revenue Function. The firm seeks to maximize the total profits from the sale of its product in Markets A and B. The total revenue function is given by Equation 11-6:

$$TR = P_A \cdot Q_A + P_B \cdot Q_B. \tag{11-6}$$

---

[11] This section re-examines the economics of price discrimination using the calculus tools developed in Chapter 2. It is useful as another illustration of the use of the Lagrangian technique, but is may be omitted without loss of continuity.

Substituting Equations 11-3 and 11-4 into Equation 11-6, we obtain:

$$TR = 60Q_A - 0.5Q_A{}^2 + 110Q_B - 3Q_B{}^2. \tag{11-7}$$

Step 2: Set Up the Total Cost Function. Total costs were previously given in Equation 11-5. Recognizing that Q in 11-5 equals the sum $Q_A + Q_B$, the total cost function can be rewritten as:

$$\begin{aligned}
TC &= 1{,}000 + 9(Q_A + Q_B) + 0.1(Q_A + Q_B)^2 \\
&= 1{,}000 + 9Q_A + 9Q_B + 0.1Q_A{}^2 + 0.2Q_AQ_B + 0.1Q_B{}^2.
\end{aligned} \tag{11-8}$$

Step 3: Set Up the Total Profit Function. Combining Equations 11-6 and 11-8, we can express the firm's total profit function as follows:

$$\begin{aligned}
\pi &= TR - TC \\
&= \text{Equation 11-7} - \text{Equation 11-8} \\
&= 60Q_A - 0.5Q_A{}^2 + 110Q_B - 3Q_B{}^2 - 1{,}000 - 9Q_A \\
&\quad - 9Q_B - 0.1Q_A{}^2 - 0.2Q_AQ_B - 0.1Q_B{}^2 \\
&= 51Q_A - 0.6Q_A{}^2 + 101Q_B - 3.1Q_B{}^2 - 0.2Q_AQ_B - 1{,}000.
\end{aligned} \tag{11-9}$$

Step 4: Determine the Marginal Profit Functions for Each Market. Taking the partial derivatives of this profit function with respect to Q_A and Q_B, we obtain the following expressions:

$$\frac{\partial \pi}{\partial Q_A} = 51 - 1.2Q_A - 0.2Q_B$$

$$\frac{\partial \pi}{\partial Q_B} = 101 - 6.2Q_B - 0.2Q_A.$$

Step 5: Determine Profit-maximizing Output Quantities. Setting these partial derivatives equal to zero and solving the two equations simultaneously, we can determine the profit-maximizing quantities to be sold in each market:

(a)
$$51 - 1.2Q_A - 0.2Q_B = 0 \tag{11-10}$$
$$101 - 0.2Q_A - 6.2Q_B = 0. \tag{11-11}$$

(b) Multiply Equation 11-11 by 6 and subtract the result from Equation 11-10 to eliminate Q_A, then solve for Q_B:

$$\begin{aligned}
51 - 1.2Q_A - 0.2Q_B &= 0 \\
-(606 - 1.2Q_A - 37.2Q_B &= 0) \\
\hline
-555 + 37Q_B &= 0 \\
37Q_B &= 555 \\
Q_B &= 15 \text{ units.}
\end{aligned}$$

(c) Substitute the 15 units of output for Market B into Equation 11-10, then solve for Q_A:

$$51 - 1.2Q_A - 0.2(15) = 0$$
$$51 - 1.2Q_A - 3 = 0$$
$$1.2Q_A = 48$$
$$Q_A = 40 \text{ units.}$$

Step 6: Determine the Optimal Prices in Each Market. As in the graphic analysis, we see that profits are maximized by selling 40 units of the product in Market A and 15 units in Market B. Substituting these values into the two demand equations, we calculate the price for each market:

$$P_A = 60 - 0.5(40)$$
$$= 60 - 20$$
$$= \$40,$$

and

$$P_B = 110 - 3(15)$$
$$= 110 - (45)$$
$$= \$65.$$

These prices correspond to those found graphically in Figure 11-2, as they must.

Step 7: Determine the Total Profits. The firm's total profits are found by substituting the optimal values of Q_A and Q_B into the profit function, Equation 11-9:

$$\pi = 51(40) - 0.6(40)^2 + 101(15) - 3.1(15)^2 - 0.2(40)(15) - 1,000$$
$$= \$777.50.$$

Step 8: Compare Total Profits with and without Price Discrimination. It is possible to illustrate the value of differential pricing by examining the maximum profits that could be achieved without price discrimination. Analytically, the problem is similar to the one just completed. The firm attempts to maximize its profit function as given by Equation 11-9, but here it must operate under the constraint that the price charged in Market A must be equal to the price charged in Market B; that is, $P_A = P_B$. Substituting Equations 11-3 and 11-4 for P_A and P_B, this constraint can be written as:

$$P_A = 60 - 0.5Q_A = 110 - 3Q_B = P_B,$$

or

$$50 + 0.5Q_A - 3Q_B = 0. \tag{11-12}$$

Writing the price constraint in this form allows us to use the Lagrangian multiplier technique for constrained optimization. Thus, we want to maximize the following Lagrangian function:

$$L\pi = 51Q_A - 0.6Q_A{}^2 + 101Q_B - 3.1Q_B{}^2 - 0.2Q_AQ_B \\ - 1{,}000 - \lambda(50 + 0.5Q_A - 3Q_B). \qquad (11\text{-}13)$$

Taking the partial derivatives of this expression with respect to Q_A, Q_B, and λ, and setting them equal to zero results in the following system of equations[12]:

$$\frac{\partial L\pi}{\partial Q_A} = 51 - 1.2Q_A - 0.2Q_B - 0.5\lambda = 0. \qquad (11\text{-}14)$$

$$\frac{\partial L\pi}{\partial Q_B} = 101 - 6.2Q_B - 0.2Q_A + 3\lambda = 0. \qquad (11\text{-}15)$$

$$\frac{\partial L\pi}{\partial \lambda} = -50 - 0.5Q_A + 3Q_B = 0. \qquad (11\text{-}16)$$

The system can be solved by first multiplying Equation 11-14 by 6 and adding the result to Equation 11-15, obtaining:

$$407 - 7.4Q_A - 7.4Q_B = 0. \qquad (11\text{-}17)$$

Solving Equation 11-16 for Q_A results in:

$$Q_A = 6Q_B - 100, \qquad (11\text{-}18)$$

and substituting this into Equation 11-17 allows us to determine Q_B:

$$407 - 7.4(6Q_B - 100) - 7.4Q_B = 0 \\ 407 - 44.4Q_B + 740 - 7.4Q_B = 0 \\ 51.8Q_B = 1{,}147 \\ Q_B = 22.14.$$

Substituting the 22.14 units of Q_B into Equation 11-18 provides the quantity that will be sold in Market A[13]:

$$Q_A = 6(22.14) - 100 \\ Q_A = 32.84.$$

Examination of the prices at which these quantities can be sold in each market reveals that a single price for the product, $43.58, does in fact exist:

$$P_A = 60 - 0.5(32.84) = \$43.58. \\ P_B = 110 - 3(22.14) = \$43.58.$$

Total profit for the nondiscrimination solution is found as follows:

---

[12] Notice that setting the partial derivative of $L\pi$ with respect to λ equal to zero insures that the constraint expressed in Equation 11-12 must be met at the optimum. That is, at the profit-maximizing solution, Equation 11-16 = Equation 11-12 = 0, so the prices are equal in the two markets.

[13] $Q_A + Q_B = 54.98$ rather than 55 units because of rounding.

$$\pi = 51(32.84) - 0.6(32.84)^2 + 101(22.14) - 3.1(22.14)^2$$
$$- 0.2(32.84)(22.14) - 1,000$$
$$= \$598,$$

or $178 less than the maximum profits obtained with differential pricing. Thus, we see that the firm gains an additional $178 profit by segmenting its markets and charging a higher price in that segment where demand is relatively inelastic.[14]

Optimal price discrimination in this case, where an identical product is being sold in two markets, requires that the firm operate so that the marginal revenues in both markets are equated not only to marginal costs but also to each other; that is, $MR_A = MR_B = MC$. This is the result of the products being indistinguishable in both markets from a production standpoint. If the marginal costs of production and distribution of the product in the two markets were different, profit maximization would have required the equation of marginal revenues to marginal costs in *each separate market*. The results obtained in this more general case of price discrimination with slightly differentiated products are similar to those shown here, so we shall not extend our analysis to the general case.

MULTIPLE-PRODUCT PRICING

The basic microeconomic model of the firm typically assumes that the firm produces a single homogeneous product. Yet we would be hard-pressed to name even one firm that does not produce a variety of products. Almost all firms produce at least multiple models, styles, or sizes of their output, and for pricing purposes each of these variations should be considered a separate product. Although multiple-product pricing requires the same analysis as that for a single product, the analysis is complicated by demand and production interrelationships.

Demand Interrelationships

Demand interrelations arise because of competition or complementarity between the firm's various products. Consider, for example, a firm which produces two products. If the products are interrelated, either as substitutes or as complements, a change in the price of one will affect the demand for the other. This means that in multiple-product pricing decisions these interrelationships—perhaps among dozens of products—must be taken into account.

Precise Specification of Demand Interrelationships   In the case of a two-product firm, the total revenue function can be specified as:

$$TR = f(P_1, Q_1, P_2, Q_2), \tag{11-19}$$

---

[14] The "extra" profit of $178 in this case is a single period short-run profit. The firm might well want to analyze the long-run effects of discriminatory pricing before embarking on such a strategy.

where P_1, P_2 and Q_1, Q_2 are the prices and quantities of the two products. The marginal revenues of the products can be obtained by partially differentiating Equation 11-19 with respect to Q_1 and Q_2:

$$MR_1 = \frac{\partial TR}{\partial Q_1} = P_1 + Q_1 \frac{\partial P_1}{\partial Q_1} + P_2 \frac{\partial Q_2}{\partial Q_1} + Q_2 \frac{\partial P_2}{\partial Q_1} \qquad (11\text{-}20)$$

$$MR_2 = \frac{\partial TR}{\partial Q_2} = P_2 + Q_2 \frac{\partial P_2}{\partial Q_2} + P_1 \frac{\partial Q_1}{\partial Q_2} + Q_1 \frac{\partial P_1}{\partial Q_2}. \qquad (11\text{-}21)$$

Equations 11-20 and 11-21 are completely general statements describing the revenue/output relationships for the two products. The first two terms on the right-hand side of each equation represent the marginal revenue directly associated with each product. The last two terms illustrate the problem of demand interrelationships. They indicate the change in total revenues associated with the second product that results from a change in the sales of the first. For example, the terms $P_2(\partial Q_2/\partial Q_1)$ and $Q_2(\partial P_2/\partial Q_1)$ in Equation 11-20 show the effect on the revenues generated by Product 2 when an additional unit of Product 1 is sold. Likewise, $P_1(\partial Q_1/\partial Q_2)$ and $Q_1(\partial P_1/\partial Q_2)$ in Equation 11-21 represent the change in revenues received from the sale of Product 1 when an additional unit of Product 2 is sold.

These "cross-marginal revenue" terms showing the demand interrelationships between products can be positive or negative, depending on the nature of the relationship. For complementary products the net impact will be positive, demonstrating that increased sales of one product will lead to increased revenues associated with the other. For competitive products the reverse is true: Increased sales of one product will reduce demand for the second, and hence the cross-marginal revenue term will be negative.

This brief examination of demand interrelations demonstrates that proper price determination in the multiple-product case requires a thorough analysis of the total effect of the decision on the firm's revenues. In practice this implies that optimal pricing must be based on a proper application of incremental reasoning so that the total impact of the decision is considered.

Production Interrelationships

Just as the multiple products of a firm can be related through their demand functions, so, too, they are often interrelated in production. Products may be jointly produced in a fixed ratio, as, for example, in the case of cattle, where hide and beef are obtained from each animal; or in variable proportions as in the refining of crude oil into gasoline and fuel oil. Products may compete with one another for the resources of the firm, as in the case of alternative products; or they may be complementary, as when one product uses wastes generated in the production of another or when increased production of one results in lower costs of another because of economies of scale at the firm level. In each case the production interrelationships must be considered if proper pricing decisions are to be made.

Joint Products Produced in Fixed Proportions The simplest case of joint production is that of joint products produced in fixed proportions. In this situation it makes no sense to attempt to separate the products from a production or cost standpoint. That is, if the products must be produced in fixed proportions with no possibility of adjusting the ratio of output, they are not really "multiple products" from a production standpoint but should, rather, be considered a package of output. The reason for this stems from the impossibility of determining the costs for the individual products in the package. Since the products are jointly produced, all costs are incurred in the production of the *package,* and there is no economically sound way of allocating them to the individual products.

Optimal price/output determination requires an analysis of the relationship between the marginal revenue of the output package and its marginal cost of production. So long as the total marginal revenue of the combination—the sum of the marginal revenues obtained from each product in the package—is greater than the marginal cost of producing it, the firm gains by expanding output.

Figure 11-3 illustrates the pricing problem for the case of two joint products produced in fixed proportions. The demand and the marginal revenue curves for the two products and the single marginal cost curve associated with the production of the combined output package are shown. A *vertical* summation of the two marginal revenue curves indicates the total marginal revenue generated by the package of products. Thus, it is the intersection of this total marginal revenue curve, MR_T in the figure, with the marginal cost curve that locates the profit-maximizing output level.

The optimal price for each product is determined by the intersection of a vertical line at the profit-maximizing output quantity with the demand curves for each separate product. Q_1 represents the optimal quantity of the output package to be produced, and P_1 and P_2 are the prices to be charged for the individual products.[15]

Note that the MR_T curve in Figure 11-3 coincides with the marginal revenue curve for Product 2 at all output quantities greater than Q_2. This is so because MR_1 becomes negative at that point, and hence the firm would never sell more than the quantity of Product 1 represented by the output package Q_2. That is, the total revenues generated by Product 1 are maximized at output Q_2, and, therefore, sales of any larger quantity must reduce revenues and profits.

If the marginal cost curve for producing the package of output intersects the total marginal revenue curve to the right of Q_2, profit maximization requires that the firm increase output up to this point of intersection—price Product 2 as indicated by its demand curve at that point, and price Product

[15] To illustrate, if we are dealing with cattle, the point package would consist of one hide and two sides of beef. Q_3 for the firm in question, a cattle feed lot, might be 3,000 steers, resulting in 6,000 sides of beef sold at a price of P_2 and 3,000 hides sold at P_1 per unit.

Figure 11-3 Optimal Pricing for Joint Products Produced in Fixed Proportions

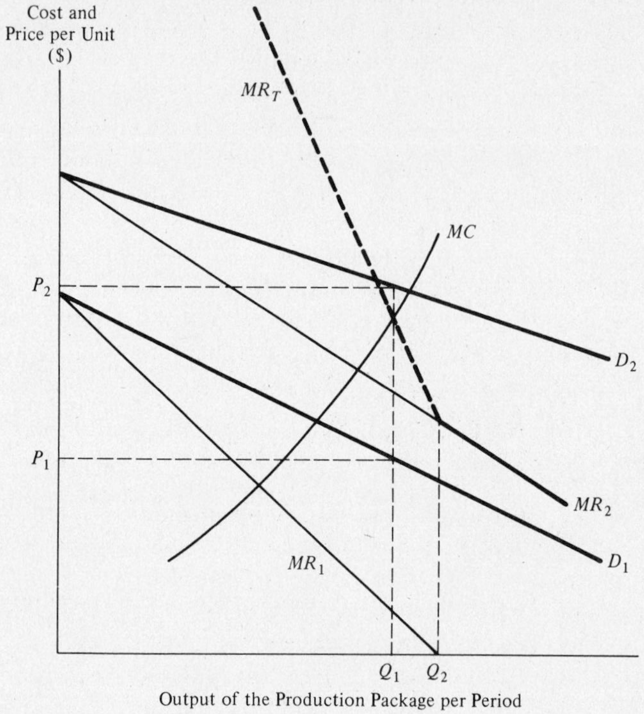

Output of the Production Package per Period

1 so as to maximize its total revenue. This pricing situation is illustrated in Figure 11-4, where the same demand and marginal revenue curves presented in Figure 11-3 are shown, along with a new marginal cost curve. The optimal output quantity is Q_3, determined by the intersection of the marginal cost curve and the total marginal revenue curve. Product 2 is sold in the amount indicated by output package Q_3 and is priced at P_2. The sales quantity of Product 1 is limited to the amount in output Q_2 and is priced at P_1. The excess quantity of Product 1 contained in the production, $Q_3 - Q_2$, must be destroyed or otherwise kept out of the market so that its price—and total revenue—is not lowered from that indicated at Q_2.[16]

[16] A case in point involves pineapple, where sliced pineapple and pineapple juice are joint products, the juice being produced as a by-product as pineapples are peeled and sliced. An excessive amount of juice was produced, and rather than put it on the market and depress prices, the excess was destroyed. This did not continue long, however; Dole, DelMonte, and other producers advertised heavily to shift the demand curve for juice, and created new products, such as pineapple-grapefruit juice, to bring about a demand for the "waste" product. Moreover, the canning machinery was improved to reduce the percentage of the product going into juice.

Figure 11-4 Optimal Pricing of Joint Products Produced in Fixed Proportions with Excess Production of One Product

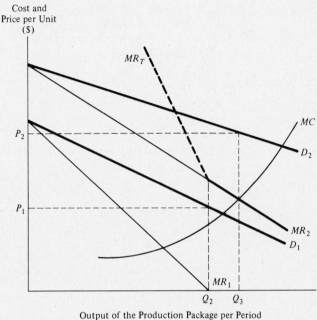

Output of the Production Package per Period

Pricing Example for Products Produced in Fixed Proportions An example of a price/output decision for two products produced in fixed proportions will clarify the relationships developed above. Assume that a firm produces two products in a joint production process where output must be in the ratio of 1:1. That is, the two products, say A and B, must always be produced in equal quantities due to the nature of the production process. The total cost function for this system is:

$$TC = 500 + 5Q + 2Q^2, \tag{11-22}$$

where Q is a unit of output consisting of one unit of Product A and one unit of Product B. Assume further that the price/demand relationship for the two products, given current market conditions, can be described by the demand curves:

$$P_A = \$395 - Q_A \tag{11-23}$$

and

$$P_B = \$100 - .5Q_B. \tag{11-24}$$

The profit-maximizing firm would view its price/output decision as being one of determining the optimal quantity of Q (the units of production composed of equal quantities of A and B) to produce, and of setting prices and sales quantities for the individual products, A and B. The problem is most conveniently analyzed by developing the proper profit function for the firm.

Although there are several ways in which one could express the profit function for this pricing problem, the most appropriate is an expression in terms of Q, the unit of production, since the individual products, A and B, must be produced in the one to one *fixed* proportions. Consider first the revenues associated with the firm's output. For each unit of Q produced, the firm obtains one unit of Product A and one unit of Product B for sale to its customers. Therefore, the revenue derived from the production and sale of a unit of Q (again the combined product package consisting of one unit each of A and B), is a simple summation of the revenues obtained from the sales of a unit of Product A and a unit of Product B. Similarly, the total revenue function for the firm expressed as a function of Q is merely the summation of the revenue functions for Products A and B. This relationship can be developed algebraically as:

$$TR_{FIRM} = TR_A + TR_B$$
$$= P_A \cdot Q_A + P_B \cdot Q_B$$

Substituting Equations 11-23 and 11-24 for P_A and P_B, respectively, results in the total revenue function:

$$TR_{FIRM} = (395 - Q_A)\, Q_A + (100 - .5Q_B)\, Q_B$$
$$= 395Q_A - Q_A{}^2 + 100Q_B - .5Q_B{}^2. \qquad \text{(11-25)}$$

Now, since one unit of Product A and one unit of Product B are contained in each unit of Q produced by the firm, Q_A, Q_B, and Q must all be equal. This means that we can substitute Q for Q_A and Q_B in Equation 11-25 to develop a total revenue function in terms of Q, the unit of production:

$$TR = 395Q - Q^2 + 100Q - .5Q^2$$
$$= 495Q - 1.5Q^2 \qquad \text{(11-26)}$$

Note that this revenue function is constructed under the assumption that equal quantities of Products A and B are *sold*. That is, it assumes no dumping or other withholding from the market of either product. Thus, it is the appropriate revenue function for use if the solution to the output determination problem is as shown in Figure 11-3; that is, with no excess production of one product. The only way to determine whether in fact this condition holds is to solve the problem and then check to ascertain that the marginal revenues of both products are in fact positive at the indicated profit-maximizing output level.

Because the firm's total cost function for the production of these joint products was expressed in terms of Q, the unit of production, in Equation

11-22, the profit function can be formed by combining that cost function with the total revenue function, Equation 11-26:

$$PROFIT = \pi = TR - TC$$
$$= 495Q - 1.5Q^2 - (500 + 5Q + 2Q^2)$$
$$= 490Q - 3.5Q^2 - 500.$$

Differentiating the profit function to solve for the profit-maximizing output level results in:

$$\frac{d\pi}{dQ} = 490 - 7Q = 0$$

$$7Q = 490$$
$$Q = 70 \text{ units.}$$

The optimal solution to the output quantity decision will be 70 units of production—70 units each of Products A and B—*provided that at a 70 unit output level the marginal revenues of both A and B are nonnegative.* This condition can be checked by evaluating the derivatives of the revenue functions for the two products at the 70 unit sales level:

$$TR_A = 395Q_A - Q_A{}^2$$

$$MR_A = \frac{dTR_A}{dQ_A} = 395 - 2Q_A$$

$$= 395 - 2(70) \quad \text{(at 70 units)}$$

$$= +225$$

$$TR_B = 100Q_B - .5Q_B$$

$$MR_B = \frac{dTR_B}{dQ_B} = 100 - Q_B$$

$$= 100 - 70 \quad \text{(at 70 units)}$$

$$= +30.$$

Since the marginal revenues are both positive, the solution to the problem is correct and one can then proceed with the determination of the proper prices for the two products.[17] The prices are obtained by substituting into the two demand curves, Equations 11-23 and 11-24:

[17] Had one product's marginal revenue been negative at 70 units of output, a problem solution with excess production of one product, as illustrated in Figure 11-4, would have been indicated. In such a situation the firm stops selling additional units of the product with a negative marginal revenue at the point where marginal revenue is zero. Hence, the relevant marginal revenue figure for use in determining the optimal output level is that associated with the other product. This would require use of the revenue function for only the one product being sold at the margin in the profit function used to determine the optimal output level. Equating the marginal revenue of

$$P_A = 395 - Q_A \qquad\qquad (11\text{-}23)$$
$$P_A = 395 - 70$$
$$= \$325$$

and

$$P_B = 100 - .5Q$$
$$= 100 - .5(70)$$
$$= \$65.$$

Thus, in this example, the firm should produce 70 units of output selling the resultant 70 units of Product A at \$325 per unit, and the 70 units of B at a price of \$65 per unit.

Joint Products Produced in Variable Proportions   Typically, the firm has the ability to vary the proportions in which joint products are produced. Even the classic example of fixed proportions in the joint production of beef and hides holds only over short periods, because cattle can be bred to provide an output package with differing proportions of these two products.

When the firm can vary the proportions in which the joint output is produced, it is possible to construct separate marginal cost relationships for each of the joint products. This is illustrated in Table 11-1, a matrix of the total cost/output relationships for two joint products, A and B. Since the marginal cost of either product is defined as the increase in total costs associated with a unit increase in that product, *holding constant the quantity of the other product produced*, the marginal costs of producing A can be determined by examining the data in the rows of the table, and the marginal costs of B are obtained from the columns. For example, the marginal cost of the 4th unit of A, holding the production of B at 2 units, is \$5($= \$23 - \$18$);

Table 11-1   Cost/Output Matrix for Two Joint Products

	Total Cost of Package				
	Output of *A*				
Output of *B*	1	2	3	4	5
1	\$5	\$ 7	\$10	\$15	\$ 22
2	10	13	18	23	31
3	20	25	33	40	50
4	35	43	53	63	75
5	55	67	78	90	105

that product to the marginal cost of producing a unit of output results in the optimal output determination, as is illustrated in Figure 11-4.

the marginal cost of the 5th unit of *B* when output of *A* is 3 units is $25(= $78 − $53).

Optimal price/output determination for joint products in this case requires a simultaneous solution of their cost and revenue relationships. The procedure can be illustrated graphically through the construction of isorevenue and isocost curves, as in Figure 11-5. The isocost curves map out the locus of all production combinations that can be produced for a given total cost; the isorevenue curves indicate all combinations of the products which, when sold, result in a given revenue.[18] At the points of tangency between the isocost and the isorevenue curves, the marginal costs of producing the products are proportionate to their marginal revenues. The tangencies therefore indicate the optimal proportions in which to produce the products. Since profits are equal to revenue minus cost, the firm maximizes profits by oper-

Figure 11-5 Optimal Price/Output Combinations for Joint Products Produced in Variable Proportions

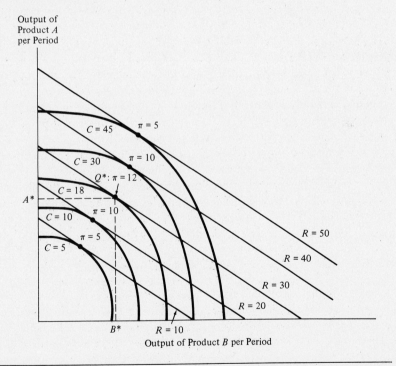

[18] The isorevenue relations in Figure 11-5 have been drawn as straight lines for simplicity. This implies that the products are sold in competitive markets; only if the demand curve is horizontal will prices be invariant with respect to changing quantities of the two products. If pure competition does not exist and prices change as output changes, the isorevenue curves will not be straight lines, but the optimum output combinations will still be indicated by tangencies between isocost and isorevenue curves.

ating at the tangency between the isorevenue and the isocost curves whose positive difference is greatest. At that tangency the marginal cost of producing each product is just equal to the marginal revenue it generates.

Point Q^* in Figure 11-5 indicates the profit-maximizing combination of Products A and B in the example illustrated in the figure. Production and sale of A^* units of A and B^* units of B result in a profit of 12, the maximum possible under the conditions shown here.

We should note that while the preceding discussion demonstrates the possibility of determining the separate marginal costs of production for goods produced jointly in variable proportions, it is impossible to determine the individual average costs. These individual costs cannot be determined because the common costs of production—costs associated with raw materials and equipment used for both products, management expenses, and other overhead—cannot be allocated to the individual products on any economically sound basis. Therefore, any allocation of common costs that affects the price/output decision is necessarily arbitrary and possibly irrational. This point is stressed because of the frequency with which businessmen and regulatory commissioners use fully allocated average costs in pricing problems of this kind.

Optimal multiple-product pricing requires a complete marginal (or incremental) analysis of the total effect of the decision on the firm's profitability. This analysis must include an examination of the demand interrelations of the products to be sure that a complete picture of the marginal revenue to be accrued from a decision is drawn. Likewise, complementarity and competition in production must be accounted for in the analysis of marginal costs. For alternative goods produced from a common production facility, this means that opportunity costs of foregone production must be considered in determining the relevant marginal costs of a decision. Linear programming has proved useful for cost/output analyses of this type when common facilities must be allocated among a variety of products.

SUMMARY

In this chapter a number of pricing topics were examined. *Cost-plus pricing*, the pricing technique most frequently used in practice, was shown to be closely related to marginal analysis. Proper use of cost-plus pricing requires that close attention be paid to both cost and demand relationships, but the wide variation in product margins, coupled with the empirical finding of an inverse relation between the size of a product's margin and the competitiveness of the market in which it is sold, indicates such analysis does, in fact, play a major role in cost-plus pricing as applied by successful businessmen.

Incremental profit analysis was also shown to be a powerful tool for optimal pricing decisions. Its emphasis on only the costs and revenues associated with the decision under consideration insures proper economic reasoning in decision analysis.

When a firm sells its product in multiple markets, it may be able to increase profits by charging different prices in the various markets, a practice known as *price discrimination*. In order to engage successfully in price discrimination, the firm (1) must be able to segment its market and isolate the various submarkets to prevent transfers, and (2) must face differing price elasticities of demand in the various market segments. Profit maximization under discrimination requires that the firm operate so as to equate marginal revenue and marginal cost in each separate submarket.

Multiple product pricing was shown to be based on the same economic concepts used for single-product pricing. The pricing analysis is complicated, however, by demand and production externalities, which arise because of competition or complementarity between the products on either the demand or the production side. Proper use of the incremental profit concept to insure that the total impact of a pricing decision on the firm is analyzed leads to optimal pricing in the multiple-product case, just as with a single product.

QUESTIONS

11-1 "Marginal cost pricing, as well as the use of incremental analysis illustrated by the example of Continental Airlines, is looked upon with favor by economists, especially those on the staffs of regulatory agencies. With this encouragement, regulated industries do indeed employ these 'rational' techniques quite frequently. Unregulated firms, on the other hand, use marginal or incremental cost pricing much less frequently, sticking to cost-plus, or full-cost, pricing except under exceptional circumstances. In my opinion, this goes a long way toward explaining the problems of the regulated firms, especially the airlines, vis-à-vis unregulated industry." Discuss this statement.

11-2 Why is it possible to determine the marginal costs associated with the production of joint products produced in variable proportions, but not joint products produced in fixed proportions?

PROBLEMS

11-1 Tucson Electronic Equipment Company produces a variety of precision measurement devices which it sells primarily to medical laboratories. The company's pricing policy currently consists of a cost-plus procedure. More specifically, prices are typically set at 200 percent of average variable cost; that is, the margin is 100 percent. The firm has just received an offer for the sale of 80 units of a slightly modified version of one of its products at a price of $7,000 a unit.

The production manager has estimated the cost of producing the instruments to be:

Raw materials	$120,000
Direct labor	80,000
Variable overhead	40,000
Fixed overhead allocation (80% of direct labor)	64,000
Production setup costs	20,000
Cost of special tools and dies	4,000
Total cost	$328,000

The offer specifies that delivery of the 80 units must be made within the next six months. To meet this schedule Tucson will have to forgo sales of its other products in the amount of $560,000, because of the limited excess capacity currently available at the firm. However, this inability to supply the standard products now will not affect future demand for them.

Using this information, determine whether Tucson Electronic should accept the order.

11-2 On November 1, 1974, Poulton Corporation received an invitation to submit a bid to Abext Company for the construction of an automated production line. As of January 1, 1975, Poulton had spent $200,000 in design and development costs and had submitted a bid of $2.673 million for the job. The bid was based on the following projected cost budget:

Costs:	
Design and development expenses	$ 200,000
Materials	1,110,000
Labor	700,000
Overhead (60% of direct labor)	420,000
Total costs	$2,430,000
Profit Requirement (10% of total costs)	243,000
Bid price	$2,673,000

Abext has just notified Poulton that it is enthusiastic about the Poulton design but that it is unwilling to pay more than $2 million for the job. Assuming that Poulton has excess capacity so that acceptance of the order will not require any increase in fixed expenses, should it accept this offer at the $2 million price? Why? Or why not?

11-3 Schoeps Beverage Company produces and sells a variety of soft drinks. Among the company's products is a drink called Lime Slush, which has been marketed for the previous five years. Sales of Lime Slush were strong during the first three years, but they have declined substantially during the last two. The introduction of competing flavors by other soft drink companies at a significantly lower price is believed to have been the major cause of this decline in sales. Lime Slush's retail price is $1.20 for an eight-bottle package, with the retailer paying 90¢ for the eight-pack. The principal competing brands of soft drink are retailed at 96¢ for an eight-pack, with retailers paying 75¢ a pack.

Schoeps' sales manager believes that sales of Lime Slush will continue to decline unless the rather large retail price difference between it and the competing brands is reduced. He has therefore undertaken an examination of the cost and revenue relationships of the product in order to formulate a new pricing policy. This examination has provided the following cost data. Variable production and distribution costs appear to be approximately constant at 40¢ a pack. The fixed production overhead is allocated among the firm's various soft drinks at a rate of 10¢ for each eight-pack produced, and fixed selling and administrative costs are allocated to all soft drink brands at a rate of 15 percent of total sales revenue. Schoeps' production facilities are common to all soft drinks. The only fixed distribution costs directly traceable to Lime Slush are annual promotional expenses of $300,000. These advertising expenses are believed to be necessary to generate any significant sales volume for Lime Slush.

a) What is the company's breakeven price to retailers for Lime Slush, assuming a 2.5 million eight-pack volume annually?

b) Assuming that 13¢ a bottle is the maximum price at which Lime Slush can effectively compete with other soft drinks and that retailers will not stock and push Lime Slush unless their percentage gross margin on it is as large as on competing brands, what price to retailers would Schoeps set on this product?

c) What factors should Schoeps' sales manager consider in his final price decision?

11-4 Centeck Appliance Company manufactures an electric mixer-juicer. Sales of the appliance have increased steadily during the previous five years and, because of its recently completed expansion program, annual capacity is now 500,000 units. Production and sales for next year are forecast at 400,-000 units, and projected standard production costs are estimated as:

Materials	3.00
Direct labor	2.00
Variable indirect labor	1.00
Overhead	1.50
Standard costs per unit	$7.50

In addition to production costs, Centeck projects fixed selling expenses and variable warranty repair expenses of 75¢ and 60¢ a unit respectively. Centeck is currently receiving $10 a unit from its customers (primarily retail appliance stores) and expects this price to hold during the coming year.

After making these projections, Centeck received an inquiry for the purchase of a large quantity of mixers from a discount department store chain. The discount chain's inquiry contained two purchase offers:

Offer 1. The chain would purchase 80,000 units at $7.30 a unit. These units would bear the Centeck label and the Centeck warranty would be provided.

Offer 2. The chain would purchase 120,000 units at $7 a unit. These units would be sold under the buyer's private label and Centeck would not provide warranty service.

a) Evaluate the effect of each offer on net income (pretax) for next year.

b) Should other factors be considered in deciding whether to accept one or the other of these offers?

c) Which offer (if either) should Centeck accept? Why?

11-5 Midcontinent Railroad Company runs a freight train daily between Indianapolis and Chicago. Its two major users of this service are Indiana Steel Corporation and Midwest Agriculture Company. The demand for freight cars by each firm is given by the equations:

$$P_1 = 500 - 8Q_1 \text{ for Indiana Steel}$$
$$P_2 = 400 - 5Q_2 \text{ for Midwest Agriculture}$$

P_i is the price charged by Midcontinent for hauling one freight car of materials between Indianapolis and Chicago and Q_i represents the number of cars demanded by each user. Midcontinent's total cost function for the daily train service is given by:

$$TC = \$10,000 + \$20Q,$$

where Q is the number of freight cars hauled on a particular trip. Midcontinent's pricing problem can be illustrated graphically as:

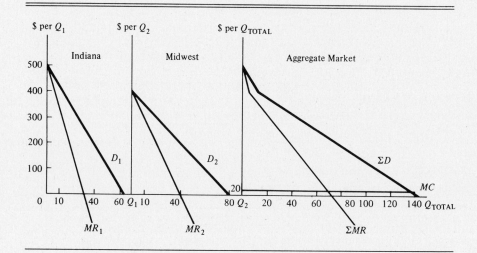

a) What conditions are necessary for profitable price discrimination by Midcontinent?

b) What profit-maximizing rule will Midcontinent Railroad Company employ to set prices as a discriminator? Determine the profit-maximizing quantity of freight service Midcontinent will supply, show how it will divide this quantity between Indiana Steel and Midwest Agriculture, and indicate the corresponding prices to be charged each company. Show that marginal revenue is equal in the two markets, and calculate Midcontinent's total profit.

c) Assume that Midcontinent is prevented by law from engaging in price discrimination. What is the profit-maximizing rule for determining profit and output under these conditions? Determine Midcontinent's profit-maximizing output and price under these conditions. Compare Midcontinent's profits in this case to those determined above under conditions of price discrimination.

11-6 The Dayton Company produces a line of expensive toys. One major item, a talking doll, has the following demand curves in the domestic (United States) and overseas markets:

Market A (maybe United States, maybe overseas) $P_A = 25 - Q_A$

Market B (maybe United States, maybe overseas) $P_B = 10 - 0.25Q_B$.

a) Dayton has patent protection and advertises heavily in the domestic market, but it faces severe competition overseas. Use this information to identify which market is the domestic one and which is the overseas market. Explain your answer.

b) Exactly the same doll is sold in both markets, and the cost function is as follows:

$$TC_1 = 40 + 5Q + 0.5Q^2.$$

Assume that Dayton can operate in Market A only, in Market B only, or in both markets. If it operates in both markets, it may or may not practice price discrimination.

(i) In which market or markets will Dayton operate? (*Note:* Check your answer by calculating the maximum profits when operating in Market A only, Market B only, and then in A and B together.)

(ii) What will be the total quantity produced and sold in each market served, and what will the prices be in each market?

(iii) What are Dayton's profits (or losses) from the doll operation? (*Hint:* Use a graph to help set up the problem.)

c) Now assume that Dayton shifts its production facilities overseas, and its total cost function changes to:

$$TC_2 = 100 + Q + 0.05Q^2.$$

It has the same sales possibilities as in Parts a and b.

(i) In which market or markets will Dayton now operate?

(ii) What will be the total quantity produced and sold in each market served, and what will the prices be in each market?

(iii) What are Dayton's profits (or losses) from the doll operation?

d) Now assume that price discrimination cannot be practiced; that is, the dolls can sell at only one price.

(i) Will Dayton choose to sell at a uniform price only in Market A, only in Market B, or in both markets?

(ii) What will total profits be under the best alternative?

e) The United States (and most other countries) has antidumping laws that prevent a foreign firm from selling in the United States at a price which is *both* lower than the price charged in the country in which the product is made *and* below the *average* cost of producing the product. In Part c of this problem, would Dayton be open to such a charge?

SELECTED REFERENCES

Baumol, William J., and Tibor Fabian. "Decomposition, Pricing for Decentralization and External Economies," *Management Science*, September 1964, pp. 1-32.

Earley, James S. "Marginal Policies of Excellently Managed Companies," *American Economic Review*, March 1956, pp. 44-70.

Eckstein, Otto, and Gary Fromm. "The Price Equation," *American Economic Review,* December 1968, pp. 1159-1183.

Hall, R. L., and C. J. Hitch. "Price Theory and Business Behavior," *Oxford Economic Papers,* Oxford: The Clarendon Press, 1939.

Haynes, W. Warren. *Pricing Decisions in Small Firms.* Lexington: University of Kentucky Press, 1962.

Hirshleifer, Jack. "On the Economics of Transfer Pricing," *Journal of Business,* July 1956, pp. 172-184.

————. "Economics of the Divisionalized Firm," *Journal of Business,* April 1957, pp. 96-108.

Kaplan, A. D. H., Joel B. Dirlam, and Robert F. Lanzillotti. *Pricing in Big Business.* Washington, D.C.: The Brookings Institution, 1958.

Lanzillotti, R. F. "Pricing Objectives in Large Companies," *The American Economic Review,* December 1958, pp. 921-940.

Oxenfeldt, Alfred R., and William T. Baxter. "Approaches to Pricing: Economist vs. Accountant," *Business Horizons,* Winter 1961, pp. 77-90.

Scherer, F. M. *Industrial Pricing.* Chicago: Rand-McNally, 1972.

Solomons, David. *Divisional Performance: Measurement and Control.* New York: Financial Executives Research Foundation, 1965.

Tarshis, Louie. *Modern Economics.* Boston: Houghton Mifflin Company, 1967, Chapter 7.

Udell, Jon G. "How Important Is Pricing in Competitive Strategy?" *Journal of Marketing,* January 1964, pp. 44-48.

APPENDIX: Transfer Pricing

Technological advances and expanding markets brought on by a continually larger and wealthier population have, over time, led to the development of large, multi-product firms. This trend has been accelerated by financial factors—large, diversified firms have greater access to capital markets and are frequently thought to be less risky than small, undiversified companies, and both these factors cause larger firms to have a lower cost of capital than smaller ones. Larger size results in increasing costs of internal communications and coordination, so if production, marketing, and financial economies of scale are to be realized, these coordination costs must be kept within reasonable bounds.

Perhaps the most significant management innovations in recent years—the establishment of divisional profit centers and decentralized operations—were designed to combat the problem of increasing costs of coordinating large-scale enterprises. Here separate profit centers are established for different products, and the individual profit centers are kept small enough so that their managers can control them without the need for excessive, expensive staffs to coordinate the various phases of the operation.

Decentralization into semiautonomous profit centers, while absolutely necessary for large-scale enterprises, creates problems of its own. Perhaps the most critical of them is that of *transfer pricing,* or the pricing of products transferred between divisions. United States Steel, for example, owns coal mines and iron mines as well as steel mills, and the coal and iron divisions sell to the steel division as well as to outsiders.[19] How much should the steel division pay for the coal and iron ore it obtains internally? Should it buy its entire requirements of these materials from the coal and iron divisions, or should it meet part of its needs from outside sources? Further, should the coal and iron divisions be required to produce whatever amounts of coal and iron the steel division requires? Suppose the steel division offers to pay $15 a ton for coal, but the coal division can sell to outsiders for $20; should the coal divisions be required to sell to the steel mills?

The answers to these questions are critically important for at least two reasons. First, the way they are answered will influence the output of each division, hence the output of the firm as a whole. If they are answered incorrectly, the firm will not produce at the optimal level. Second, transfer prices are an important determinant of divisional profits, and since promotions, bonuses, stock options, and so on are typically based on divisional performance, if a system of transfer prices is arbitrary and inequitable it can completely wreck morale and literally destroy the firm.

While the topic of transfer pricing is one of the more complex in managerial economics, and we cannot hope to more than scratch the surface in an introductory book of this kind, its importance dictates that we at least demonstrate the nature of the problem and point the direction toward optimal transfer rules. For the reader who wishes to pursue the topic further, the works of Jack Hirshleifer[20] and David Solomons[21] provide excellent expositions of both the theoretical and the practical problems in transfer pricing.

TRANSFER PRICING WITH NO EXTERNAL MARKET FOR THE INTERMEDIATE PRODUCT

The basic criterion by which to judge any internal transfer pricing scheme is the impact it will have on the operating efficiency of the firm. Optimally, a transfer pricing system will lead to activity levels in each division of the firm that are consistent with profit maximization for the entire enterprise. Alternatively stated, a well-designed transfer pricing scheme will lead to activity levels for the various decentralized divisions of a firm that are precisely identical to the activity levels

---

[19] United States Steel also owns steamship lines, cement mills, coking ovens, construction companies, and so on, and all these divisions buy and sell among one another.

[20] Jack Hirshleifer. "On the Economics of Transfer Pricing," *Journal of Business,* July 1956, pp. 172-184, and "Economics of the Divisionalized Firm," *Journal of Business,* April 1957, pp. 96-108.

[21] David Solomons. *Divisional Performance: Measurement and Control.* Finanical Executives Research Foundation, New York, 1965.

that would prevail with centralized decision making without provision for divisional profit centers.

This relationship can be examined in the context of a two-division firm producing a single product. Such a case is illustrated in Figure 11A-1 which shows the demand, marginal revenue, and marginal cost curves for the entire operation of the firm.

Profit maximization requires that the firm expand its output so long as the marginal revenue of additional units is greater than their marginal costs. In terms of Figure 11A-1, this means that the firm's profits are maximized at output Q^*, indicating a market price of P^* for the firm's product.

To clarify the relationship we are developing, it will prove useful to introduce a specific set of cost and demand functions. Assume that the demand curve illustrated in Figure 11A-1 is:

$$P = 100 - Q, \tag{11A-1}$$

and that the firm's total cost function is:

$$TC = 70 + 10Q + 1.5Q^2, \tag{11A-2}$$

so that the marginal revenue and marginal cost curves in Figure 11A-1 are[22]:

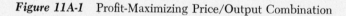

Figure 11A-1 Profit-Maximizing Price/Output Combination

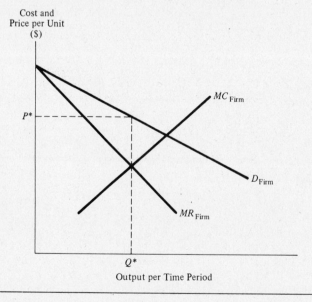

---

[22] The marginal revenue function is found as the derivative of the total revenue function; that is:

$$
\begin{aligned}
TR &= P \cdot Q \\
&= (100 - Q)Q \\
&= 100Q - Q^2
\end{aligned}
$$

(*continued*)

$$MR = 100 - 2Q \qquad \text{(11A-3)}$$
$$MC = 10 + 3Q. \qquad \text{(11A-4)}$$

Profit maximization occurs at the point where marginal revenue equals marginal cost, so the optimal output level is found as:

$$MR = MC$$
$$100 - 2Q = 10 + 3Q$$
$$90 = 5Q$$
$$Q = 18.$$

Thus, $Q°$ in Figure 11A-1 is 18 units and $P°$ is \$82 ($100 - 18$).

Consider now the situation if the firm we are examining is divisionalized into a manufacturing and a distribution division. The demand curve facing the distribution division is precisely the same demand curve the firm faced initially. The total cost function of the firm is unchanged, but can be broken down into the costs of manufacture and the costs of distribution. Assume that such a breakdown results in the divisional cost functions:

$$TC_{MFG.} = 50 + 7Q + .5Q^2$$

and

$$TC_{DISTR.} = 20 + 3Q + Q^2.$$

The total cost function for the firm would be:

$$TC_{FIRM} = TC_{MFG.} + TC_{DISTR.}$$
$$= 50 + 7Q + .5Q^2 + 20 + 3Q + Q^2$$
$$= 70 + 10Q + 1.5Q^2,$$

precisely the same as Equation 11A-2 above. Obviously in this situation no substantive changes have taken place and the firm should still operate at an 18-unit output level for profit maximization.

When no external market exists for the intermediate product (that is, if the manufacturing division is not able to sell its product externally), it can be shown that intrafirm transfers should take place based on prices that are set equal to the marginal costs of the transferring division—the manufacturing division in this case. This relationship is shown in Figure 11A-2, which adds the net marginal revenue ($MR_{FIRM} - MC_{DISTR.}$) curve for the distribution division and the marginal cost curve for the manufacturing division to the revenue and cost curves illustrated in Figure 11A-1. The *net marginal revenue curve* for the distribution division is found by subtracting the marginal costs of that division from the marginal revenues generated by its marketing activities. It is essentially nothing more than a net marginal profits curve for that division prior to taking account of the cost of the product that has been transferred to it from the manufacturing division.

$$MR = \frac{dTR}{dQ} = 100 - 2Q.$$

The marginal cost curve is given by the derivative of the total cost curve, so:

$$MC = \frac{dTC}{dQ} = 10 + 3Q.$$

Figure 11A-2 Transfer Pricing with No External Market for the Intermediate Product

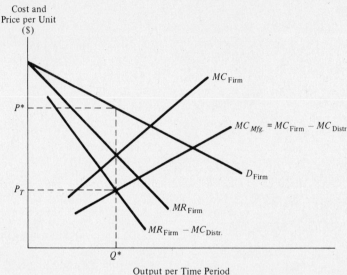

Note that in Figure 11A-2 the net marginal revenue curve for the distribution division intersects the marginal cost curve for the manufacturing division at Q^*, the firm's profit-maximizing activity level. This is not mere happenstance but must always occur. The reason is simple. Recall that the distribution division's net marginal revenue curve is nothing more than the firm's marginal revenue curve less the marginal cost of the distribution division. Similarly, the manufacturing division's marginal cost curve is nothing more than the firm's marginal cost curve less the marginal cost of the distribution division. If the firm's marginal revenue and marginal costs are equal at Q^* units of output, then obviously the distribution division's net marginal revenue must be equal to the manufacturing division's marginal cost at that same output level. Algebraically, if:

$$MR_{FIRM} = MC_{FIRM}$$

then:

$$MR_{FIRM} - MC_{DISTR.} = MC_{FIRM} - MC_{DISTR.} = MC_{MFG.}$$

This means that the correct transfer price for intermediate products for which there is no external market is the marginal cost of production. In Figure 11A-2 this transfer price is P_T.

Continuing with the numerical example, the net marginal revenue curve for the distribution division is given by the expression:

$$MR_{FIRM} - MC_{DISTR.} = 100 - 2Q - (3 + 2Q)$$
$$= 97 - 4Q.$$

Equating this to the marginal cost curve of the manufacturing division results in:

$$MR_{FIRM} - MC_{DISTR.} = MC_{MFG.}$$
$$97 - 4Q = 7 + Q$$
$$90 = 5Q$$
$$Q = 18.$$

This result indicates once again that at an optimal activity level the net marginal revenue of the distribution division will equal the marginal cost of the manufacturing division. This leads to the profit-maximizing condition that internal transfers of intermediate products for which no external market exists must take place at marginal production costs.

It still remains to demonstrate that by setting the transfer price equal to the marginal cost of production, the two decentralized divisions will choose to operate at the firm profit-maximizing activity level. Consider first the manufacturing division. If the firm's central management specifies that transfers are to take place at marginal manufacturing costs, then the marginal cost curve of the manufacturing division becomes its supply curve, just as the marginal cost curve is the supply curve for a firm operating in pure competition. Given a transfer price P_T, the manufacturing division *must* supply a quantity such that $MC_{MFG.} = P_T$.

Now consider the distribution division. The profit function for that division can be written as:

$$Profit = TR_{FIRM} - TC_{DISTR.}$$
$$= 100Q - Q^2 - (20 + 3Q + Q^2 + P_T \cdot Q) \qquad \text{(11A-5)}$$
$$= 97Q - 2Q^2 - 20 - P_T \cdot Q.$$

Notice that in this expression we have added the term $P_T \cdot Q$ to the total cost function for the distribution division to account for the fact that this division must now pay a price of P_T for each unit of product it receives from the manufacturing division.

Since profit maximization requires that marginal profit be zero, the profit maximization requirement for the distribution division is that the derivative of Equation 11A-5 be set equal to zero; that is:

$$M\pi = 97 - 4Q - P_T = 0,$$

or, solving for P_T, the transfer price:

$$P_T = 97 - 4Q. \qquad \text{(11A-6)}$$

Thus, profit maximization for the distribution division requires that the transfer price be equal to $97 - 4Q$. Therefore, $97 - 4Q$ can be considered a demand function indicating how the transfer price of the product is related to the quantity that the distribution division will seek to purchase. Note, however, that this demand function is identical to the net marginal revenue curve for the distribution division developed above.

Now if the distribution division determines the quantity it will purchase by movement along the net marginal revenue curve, and the manufacturing division is supplying output along its marginal cost curve, then the only "market" clearing transfer price is that price which occurs where $MR_{FIRM} - MC_{DISTR.} = MC_{MFG.}$. In the example, this is at 18 units of output with a transfer price, P_T, equal to \$25 ($MC_{MFG.} = 7 + Q = 25$ at $Q = 18$). At a transfer price above \$25 the distribution division will accept fewer units of output than the manufacturing division wants to supply, while if P_T is less than \$25, the distribution division will seek to purchase more units than the manufacturing division desires to produce. Only at a \$25 transfer price are the supply and demand forces in balance.

The marginal cost pricing rule can be implemented in actual practice in either of two ways: First, the distribution division could be given the manufacturing division's marginal cost curve and told that this is the supply function it must use in determining the quantity it desires to purchase internally. Alternatively, the manufacturing division could be supplied with data on the net marginal revenue curve for the distribution division and told to use this as its relevant marginal revenue curve in determining the quantity it should supply. In either case the divisions should choose to operate at output Q^* and a transfer price of $P_T = MC_T$ should prevail.[23]

TRANSFER PRICING OF A PRODUCT HAVING A COMPETITIVE MARKET

A second transfer pricing problem involves goods that can be sold externally in a competitive market. In this case, where the transferred good is sold in a competitive market, the market price of the good is also the appropriate transfer price; its use will lead to firm profit-maximizing levels of operation for all the divisions involved in the transfer.

Figure 11A-3 illustrates the economics of the competitive case. There, the demand, D_F, and the marginal revenue, MR_F, curves for the final product, F, are shown along with the demand, D_T, marginal revenue, MR_T, and marginal cost, MC_T, curves for T, the intermediate or transferred product. The line $MR_F - MC_F$ represents the net marginal contribution to overhead and profits of the final product *before the transfer price is deducted*.[24] That is, $MR_F - MC_F$ shows the excess of the marginal revenue of F over its marginal cost prior to a payment for the transferred good, T. At output Q_1, for example, Product F would sell at a price of \$100 and would have a marginal revenue equal to \$90. Since $MR_F - MC_F = \$70$, MC_F, *before any charge for the intermediate product*, is equal to \$20. The marginal cost of the transferred product at output Q_1 is \$30. Since the firm earns a contribution margin of \$70 on the final product at Q_1, and since the intermediate good costs only \$30, output should be expanded beyond Q_1.

Profit maximization requires that both the final product and the intermediate product divisions operate at the output levels at which their marginal costs equal marginal revenues. At any lower output level the marginal revenue obtained from sales of additional units is greater than the marginal costs of their production, and profits are increased by expanded production. At higher output levels the reverse

---

[23] Note, however, that the choice of rules *will* affect divisional profits, so divisional profits in such a case should *not* be used as the basis for rewarding personnel.

[24] The area under the curve $MR_F - MC_F$ represents the total contribution *before* paying for the transferred product.

is true; marginal costs exceed marginal revenues, and a reduction of output increases profits.

The optimal outputs for the two divisions are shown in Figure 11A-3. Division F should purchase Q_F units of the intermediate good, paying the market price P_T for it.[25] At that point the marginal cost of producing F is equal to its marginal revenue, and divisional profits—the area under the $MR_F - MC_F$ curve which lies above the horizontal line $P_T D_T$—are maximized. Division T should supply Q_T units of the product, the quantity at which its marginal cost equals its marginal revenue.[26] At Q_T units of output its divisional profits—the area under the curve D_T which lies above the curve MC_T—are maximized.

Note that this solution to the transfer pricing problem results in Division F's demanding more units of the intermediate product than Division T is willing to supply at price P_T. This situation presents no problem to the firm; it merely indicates that profit maximization requires Division F to purchase Q_T units of the intermediate product internally from Division T, and $Q_F - Q_T$ units in the marketplace. No other solution results in as great a total profit for the firm. For example,

---

Figure 11A-3　Transfer Price Determination with the Intermediate Product Sold Externally in a Competitive Market: Excess Internal Demand

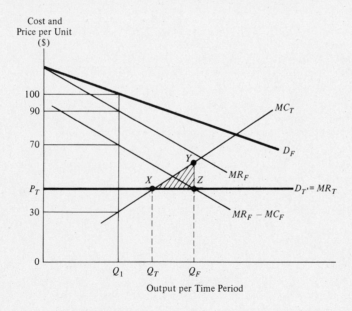

---

if Division T attempts to supply the entire quantity demanded by F, the cost to the firm would exceed the cost incurred by purchasing it in the market. The shaded triangle XYZ in Figure 11A-3 indicates the excess cost, and hence the reduction in profits, that would result from such a decision.

The use of the market price for transferring the intermediate product remains optimal even if the quantity of the intermediate product supplied by Division T is greater than the demand by Division F at the market price. Division T merely transfers the quantity demanded by F and sells the remainder in the market. This situation is depicted in Figure 11A-4.

Figure 11A-4   Transfer Price Determination with the Intermediate Product Sold Externally in a Competitive Market: Excess Internal Supply

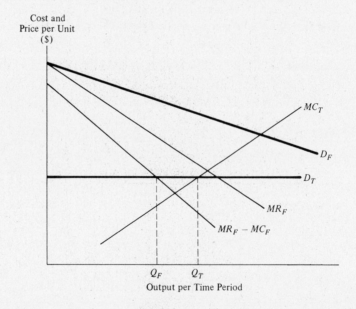

Here, although the marginal cost of producing the intermediate product, T, is below the net marginal revenue obtainable from an additional unit of F at the optimal quantity, Q_F, the marginal cost of producing T, *plus* the opportunity cost of not selling that additional unit in the competitive market, is greater than the net marginal revenue received from F. Therefore, the transfer of additional units to Division F would result in lower total firm profits.

So long as the intermediate product being transferred within the firm can be sold in a competitive market, the market price remains the proper transfer price. Only by transferring at that price can the firm's management insure that the level of activities in both the supplying and the using divisions will be optimal for firm, as opposed to divisional, profit maximization.

Transfer Pricing with an Imperfect External Market
for the Intermediate Product

Where an imperfect outside market exists for the intermediate product, transfer pricing is only slightly more complex than the case cited above. Again, transfer pricing at marginal costs results in optimal activity levels for both the supplying and the using divisions of the firm.

This case is illustrated in Figure 11A-5. Figure 11A-5(a) shows the demand and the net marginal revenue curves for the final product, F; (b) contains the external demand and the marginal revenue curves for the intermediate product, T. In (c) the net marginal revenue curve for Product F and the marginal revenue curve for T have been horizontally summed to arrive at an aggregate net marginal revenue curve, NMR_A, for product T. The marginal cost of producing T is also shown in (c).

Figure 11A-5 Transfer Pricing with an Imperfect Market for the Intermediate Product: (a) Market for Final Product; (b) Market for Intermediate Product; (c) "Aggregate" Market

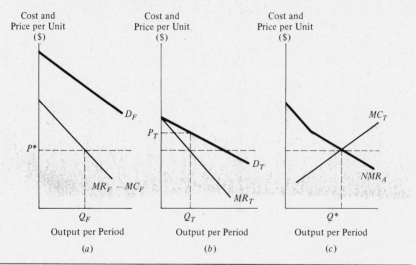

The profit-maximizing output of T occurs where the marginal cost of producing it and the aggregate net marginal revenue obtained from it are equal: output Q^* in Figure 11A-5(c). That output is divided between internal transfers and external sales by equating the net marginal revenue in part (a) of the figure and the marginal revenue in part (b) to the marginal cost of the optimal output as determined in part (c).[27] Setting an internal transfer price equal to that marginal

---

[27] Note that the distribution of the intermediate product follows the same pattern as a discriminating monopolist allocating output among his various segmented markets. In this case T acts as a "monopolist," selling part of its output in one internal market at the transfer price P^* and part in the external market at P_T.

cost, P^*, insures that Division F will demand the quantity of T that leads to profit maximization not only of that division but also of the firm as a whole. The price to be charged in the external market—P_T in Figure 11A-5(b)—is determined by the height of the demand curve for the product at a point directly above the intersection of the marginal revenue curve and the transfer price, or marginal cost of production.

SUMMARY STATEMENT ON TRANSFER PRICING

The material we have presented on transfer pricing barely scratches the surface of this important but complex subject. It by no means exhausts the possible cases for intrafirm transfers of goods and services. There are, for example, situations where several internal divisions are competing for the products of yet another division, or where two or more divisions supply intermediate products to a third. Still another whole set of transfer pricing problems arises when the demand and production externalities in multiple-product firms are considered.[28] Nonetheless, the material we have presented introduces the basic problem and demonstrates the kind of economic analysis necessary to obtain optimal solutions. To the extent that we can generalize, our analysis suggests that transfers should take place at the market price for inermediate products that are traded externally in a competitive market and at marginal cost in most other cases.

PROBLEMS

11A-1   The Bartlet Corporation manufactures and retails a single product. The monthly demand relationship for the product has been estimated to be:

$$P = 60 - 0.35Q.$$

The firm's cost analysts have estimated that the total manufacturing cost, TC_M, and the total distribution cost, TC_D, can be represented by the expressions:

$$TC_M = 1,000 + 8Q + 0.1Q^2$$
$$TC_D = 100 + 2Q + 0.05Q^2.$$

These cost functions pertain to monthly cost and output levels.
a)   On the basis of the above cost and demand estimates:
  (i)   What quantity of output should the corporate management of Bartlet schedule for production each month?
  (ii)   What price should be established?
  (iii)   What will be the firm's monthly profits at this output level?
b)   Suppose the management of Bartlet decides to decentralize the decision-making process by setting up a manufacturing division and a distribution division. Each division constitutes a profit center, and each division manager is to be rewarded on the basis of profit per-

[28] Mathematical programming has been shown to be a useful analytical tool for these more complex cases. *See,* for example, William J. Baumol and Tibor Fabian. "Decomposition, Pricing for Decentralization and External Economies," *Management Science,* September 1964, pp. 1-32.

formance. To handle the intrafirm transfer of the product between the manufacturing and the distribution divisions, the manufacturing division is to have the right to set a transfer price on the product it will "sell" to the distribution division. The distribution division will then have the right to "buy" any quantity of the product it desires at that price for resale to the outside market. Under this arrangement, the quantity of the product "demanded" by the division at each transfer price, P_T, is given by the expression:

$$P_T = 58 - 0.8Q.$$

(Consider this expression, which is the "demand curve" facing the manufacturing division, as "given" at this point; you will be asked to discuss it later.)

(i)   Assuming that the management of the manufacturing division has knowledge of the function given above, what transfer price would it set to maximize its own (the manufacturing division's) profits and how many units would be "sold" to the distribution division at this price?

(ii) What total monthly profit would each division report if the internal transfer price is established at this level?

(iii) How does this compare with the maximum profits determined Part a?

(iv) What modification to the manufacturing division's price determination will result in an optimal transfer price from a firm, as opposed to divisional, profit standpoint?

(v)   What is the optimal transfer price?

(vi) What profits or losses will each division have with the transfer price developed in (v)? What problems might this cause, and how might the problems be solved?

(vii) Explain why the distribution division would make purchases in accordance with the demand expression given above, $P_T = 58 - 0.8Q$.

11A-2   Among the products manufactured and sold by MFP Corporation is a child's clock radio. The demand curve facing the firm for this product is $P = 610 - 9Q$. Manufacture and sale of the radio is done by MFP's Home Products Division (HPD), with a major component part being supplied by a second division, the Electronics Specialty Division (ESD). The cost function for the radio and the electronic component are:

$$Total\ Cost_{HPD} = 3,000 + 10Q$$
$$Total\ Cost_{ESD} = 7,000 + 10Q + Q^2.$$

a)   The divisions are operated as separate profit centers. Internal transfers of goods and services are accomplished by allowing the using division to offer to purchase at a given price, and the supplying division to determine how much it will sell. Assuming that there is no outside market for the component supplied by the ESD, what is the optimal quantity (from the firm's standpoint) of product that should be transferred and what transfer price will lead to operation at this level?

b) Assume that the electronic component supplied by ESD could be sold to an outside firm for use in another product (one that doesn't compete with MFP's) for $190. This firm will purchase up to 100 units at this price. What is the optimal transfer price in this situation? How many units will ESD sell to HPD? How many will it sell to the outside firm?

c) Assume now that external demand for the component manufactured by ESD is described by the function $P = 410 - 9.1Q$. What is the optimal transfer price? The optimal price in the external market? How many units will ESD supply to each of these two markets?

d) Explain how an assumption that sales of the electronic component in the external market would affect sales of the radios, and that production of the component by ESD affected the cost of other products of that division, would impact on the analysis of this problem.

CHAPTER 12

Regulation and
Antitrust

Thus far we have assumed that firms seek to maximize their value, subject to two kinds of constraints. One set of constraints is unique for each firm: included are the personal characteristics of the owners and the managers, such as their desire for leisure or their awareness of social problems, which constrain them from the single-minded pursuit of wealth. Because this group of constraints is both subjective and unique for each firm, no useful purpose is served by attempting to generalize about it. However, because the other set of constraints—those imposed by governments—is well defined and is applied to all firms of a class, both the rationale for and the effects of this set are amenable to economic analysis. Accordingly, in this chapter we examine the three major kinds of governmental constraints: (1) operating controls, such as pollution abatement requirements, wage and price controls, and restrictions under the Pure Food and Drug Act; (2) constraints designed to reduce monopolistic profits; and (3) antitrust and related laws designed to maintain a "workable" level of competition in the economy.

OPERATING CONTROLS

What kinds of operating controls are imposed on business firms? Controls over environmental pollution immediately come to mind, but businesses are also subject to many other kinds of constraints. For example, federal legislation sets limits for automobile safety standards, and firms handling food products, drugs, and other substances that could harm consumers are constrained under the Pure Food and Drug Act. Industrial work conditions are governed under various labor laws and health regulations: included are provisions related to noise levels, noxious gases, and safety standards. Antidiscrimination laws designed to protect minority groups and women are also forcing firms to modify their hiring and promotional policies. Wage and price controls, used in an attempt to reduce high rates of inflation, restrict the freedom of firms in setting prices and affect the usage of resources throughout the economic system.

The Steam Boiler Industry[1]

Economic analysis can be used to analyze the effects of the above constraints and similar ones. As an illustration, consider the case of the steam boiler industry. Studies released in 1972 indicated that the noise level in steam boiler plants was having a serious impact on employees' hearing, causing permanent ear damage to many workers. The study also suggested that the noise level in boiler factories produced stresses which led to frequent mental breakdowns, as well as to such internal disorders as hypertension, high blood pressure, ulcers, and heart attacks.

On learning of the results of the study, the International Union of Steam Boilermakers immediately began discussions with the Boiler Manufacturers of America, the industry trade association. At the same time union officials contacted officials of the U.S. Department of Labor and the U.S. Department of Health, Education, and Welfare. The full-time staff economists of the manufacturers' association and the union immediately began examining the economic consequences of a major effort to control noise conditions.

In the negotiations between union leaders and the trade association, two facts became apparent: (1) the economic impact studies of the two groups differed significantly, and (2) both studies appeared to have major weaknesses. Accordingly, an outside consulting economist was requested to conduct a comprehensive study of the situation. Both the companies and the union promised the economist full cooperation, with the companies agreeing to make all necessary cost and revenue data available to him.

As a result of the economist's analysis, the following demand curve for the United States industry was estimated:

[1] The "steam boiler industry" is fictional; the example is actually a composite based on data from several industries that have faced similar problems.

$$P = \$25,000 - 0.1Q.$$

The industry's total and marginal cost functions were estimated as follows:

$$TC_1 = \$255,745,000 + \$5,000Q + \$0.25Q^2.$$
$$MC_1 = \$5,000 + \$0.5Q.$$

The marginal cost function, together with the revenue function, is shown in Figure 12-1. The profit-maximizing industry price/output position calls for the production of 28,571 boilers to be sold at a price of $22,143 a unit.

Total industry profits were approximately $30 million in 1973, representing a 5 percent return on invested capital of $600 million; this was one of the lowest rates of return on invested capital in United States industry. Naturally, some firms were more efficient than the industry average, and these firms earned relatively high returns; other firms suffered losses but still operated because revenues exceeded variable costs. Total factory employment, which approximated the union's membership, was 26,000 in 1973, and the average wage was $16,538, one of the highest among all blue-collar industries.

Several points should be noted. First, the industry produces many sizes and grades of boilers, but a "standard unit" is used in the trade to estimate production levels. Our example is stated in terms of this standard unit. Sec-

---

Figure 12-1 Cost and Demand Functions in the Steam Boiler Industry

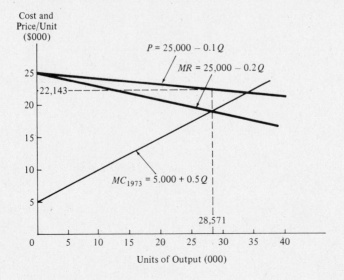

ond, the industry cost functions were developed from the cost data of the individual firms in the industry. Third, the industry's demand curve is relatively elastic because it faces severe competition from European and Japanese firms. This competition, which has intensified in recent years, has seriously eroded profits in the industry. Fourth, the price/output relationship called for in Figure 12-1 is a monopoly solution. The industry is not a monopoly; it is an oligopoly. Price leadership by the dominant firm, enforced by low profits and strong foreign competition, has caused the industry to reach approximately the monopoly position. Finally, although sales are somewhat cyclical, the figures shown in the graph were judged to be good approximations for a "normal" year in the foreseeable future.

Engineering studies indicated that reducing plant noise to the level recommended by the medical study would require the addition of approximately $250 million of new equipment. Assuming that all firms would continue in production, the fixed cost (depreciation and interest) of this noise control equipment would amount to $25 million annually, and variable costs would also increase. The resulting cost functions were estimated as follows:

$$TC_2 = \$280,745,000 + \$10,000Q + 0.35Q^2$$
$$MC_2 = \$10,000 + 0.7Q.$$

Under these conditions, *which assume that $250 million will be spent on new equipment,* output would decline to about 16,700 units and labor requirements would drop to about 15,000 men. However, this outcome was considered to be highly unrealistic because, under these conditions, the industry would be losing over $155 million a year as against the $30 million profits it had earned previously. In other words, *if* the industry installed the noise control equipment, *then* production would total 16,700 units and 15,000 men would be employed. However, the industry would be suffering huge losses, so it was not realistic to assume that all firms would install the new equipment. Rather, marginal, high-cost firms would simply close, and a completely new industry configuration would emerge.

The estimates for the new industry cost structure were admittedly subject to considerable uncertainty, but the economic consultant judged—and the trade association and union economists agreed—that only four of the present thirty-eight plants would remain open, so the industry cost functions would change to:

$$TC_3 = \$28,000,000 + \$15,000Q + 0.66Q^2$$
$$MC_3 = \$15,000 + \$1.32Q.$$

The four remaining plants, which were already quite modern and highly automated, would produce about 6,600 units, earn profits of about $5 million, and employ approximately 4,000 men.

The revised economic analysis, which is graphed in Figure 12-2, left the union, the federal government, and the industry in a quandary. On the

Figure 12-2 Cost and Demand Functions in the Steam Boiler Industry Before and After Noise Control

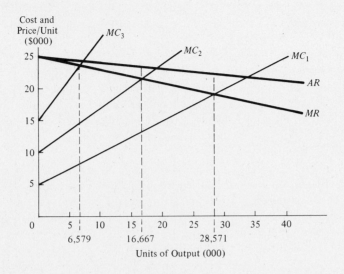

Units of Output (000)

one hand, all parties were convinced that some physical damage was being caused by the current plant noise levels, and because of this they all felt that noise levels should be reduced. They were not at all sure, however, that the problem was as serious as had been indicated by the medical report.

On the other hand, the economic implications were quite clear—if noise levels were to be reduced to the recommended levels, industry output would decline from a current level of 28,600 units to 6,600 units, and employment would fall from 26,000 to 4,000. Further, the employment losses would not be distributed uniformly, but would be concentrated in specific firms and regions. Moreover, because the men who would be laid off were highly skilled, well-paid craftsmen whose skills could not be transferred easily to other industries, they and their families would suffer severe hardships. This last point was compounded by two additional facts: (1) heavy industry as a whole was weak in 1974, and (2) many of the boilermakers were relatively older men (the average age of union members was 49 years), who would have difficulty relocating and breaking into new jobs.

Faced with these facts, the union leadership, after sounding out the feelings of its members, decided not to insist upon immediate noise level reductions. The federal officials were more inclined to press for changes, but faced with a reluctant union and with the fact that enforcement of new regulations would aggravate both the balance of payments problem and national unemployment in an election year, they agreed to abide by the union's wishes. The companies were willing to forego the changes. They did volunteer, however, to include noise abatement equipment as part of all expansion and modernization programs. All parties agreed to conduct a major educational program designed to encourage the men to use such existing safety equipment as ear plugs and sound-resistant helmets.

Generality of the Analysis

The analysis illustrated in the preceding example is quite general. It can be applied to all situations involving regulations and controls. Similar studies, for example, have been conducted to determine the economic impacts of other types of pollution controls, various kinds of taxes, increases in such factor costs as wages, and restrictions on prices charged, as in the case of regulated public utilities.

Although we shall discuss some of these types of analysis in the remainder of the chapter and illustrate them further in the end-of-chapter case and problems, two points should be made now. First, the outcomes of cases such as the one illustrated are critically dependent on the elasticity of demand for the product in question. In the steam boiler industry example, elasticity was found to be quite high, because foreign boilers are good substitutes for domestically produced ones. Thus, if prices were raised on United States boilers, demand for them would fall drastically. This meant, in effect, that the cost of noise control equipment could not be passed on to customers. Further, the poor profit position of the companies made it untenable to attempt to force them to absorb the added costs out of profits.

In other industries, where demand elasticity is low, costs can be raised without disrupting the industry. Thus, for example, electric utilities can afford to install pollution control equipment and to run new distribution lines underground much more easily than they could if they faced a highly elastic demand curve.

The second point we wish to make relates to the importance of analyzing the political as well as the economic feasibility of economic decisions. In the "steam boiler" example, action aimed at producing an immediate reduction in noise pollution was seen to be unacceptable because of the impact such action would have on the economic well-being of the individuals the noise abatement was aimed at benefiting. Thus, even though there were compelling health reasons to immediately establish noise abating standards in the industry, it was not politically feasible for the government to force such a change.

In a more typical situation the group that is likely to benefit most from a specific government control or regulation of business activity will not be the group upon whom the cost of the control activity falls. In such cases, an analysis of the political feasibility becomes considerably more complex because of the opposing forces at work. We shall return to this topic when considering antitrust activities later in this chapter.

MONOPOLY CONTROL: UTILITY REGULATION

In Chapter 10 we saw that, depending on the economics of the particular industry, monopoly or oligopoly may develop, possibly resulting in too little production and excess profits. Two methods are used to control monopolistic situations: (1) controls over industry structure, and (2) direct controls designed to prevent monopolistic industries from taking advantage of their customers. The antitrust laws, designed to decrease industrial concentration and to prevent collusion among oligopolistic firms, represent the primary example of the first kind of control. Public utility regulation, which fixes prices at a level designed to prevent firms from earning monopolistic profits, is the principal method of the second kind of control. In the remainder of this chapter we shall examine these contraints on managerial decisions, concentrating first on profit regulation, then turning to antitrust matters.

Natural Monopolies

Competitive firms must, in the long run, operate at the minimum point on the $LRAC$ curve. This condition does not necessarily hold under monopoly (or oligopoly). For example, consider Figure 12-3. Here the firm will produce Q units of output at an average cost of C per unit, somewhat above the minimum point on the $LRATC$ curve; and it will earn a profit equal to the rectangle $PP'C'C$, or $Q(P-C)$. This firm is a *natural monopolist*, a condition that exists when the profit-maximizing output occurs at a point where long-run average costs are declining. A single firm can produce the total market supply at a lower total cost than could any number of smaller firms, hence the term "natural." Electric and gas utility companies are the classic examples of natural monopolies, as the unnecessary duplication of production and distributing facilities would greatly increase costs if more than one firm served a given area. A similar situation exists for transportation companies, especially railroads, and for communications companies—for example, telephone companies.

This situation presents something of a dilemma—economic efficiency is enhanced by restricting the number of producing firms to one, but where only one firm serves a market, the possibility of economic exploitation exists. Specifically, monopolistic firms tend to earn excessive profits and to underproduce. "Excessive profits" is defined as profits so large that the firm earns a rate of return on invested capital that exceeds the risk-adjusted normal rate. That is, the profit rectangle $PP'C'C$, when divided by the asset base necessary to produce and distribute Q units of output, provides a greater than normal risk-adjusted rate of return to the firm's owners. Profits are useful both for allocating resources and as an incentive for efficiency, but it is difficult to justify above-normal profits caused by market structure instead of by exceptional performance.

"Underproduction" occurs when the firm curtails production at a level

Figure 12-3 Price/Output Decision under Monopoly

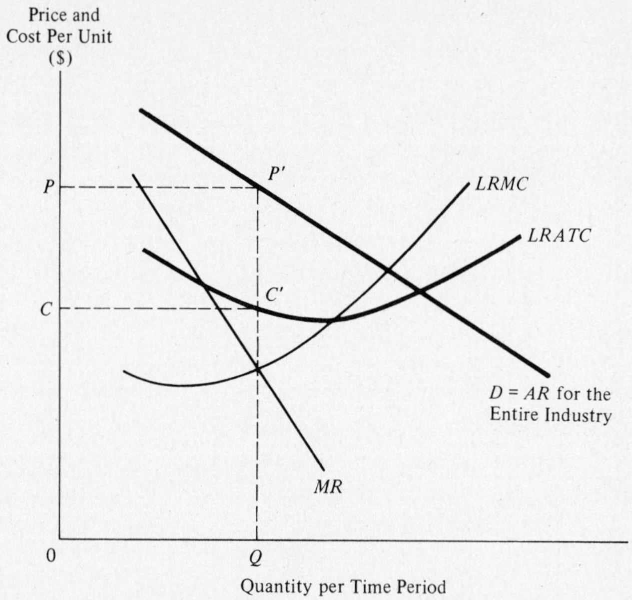

where the marginal resources needed to produce an additional unit of output (that is, the marginal cost) are less than the benefit derived from the additional unit, which is measured by the price consumers are willing to pay for it. In other words, at outputs just greater than Q in Figure 12-3, consumers are willing to pay approximately P dollars per unit, so the value of additional units must be P. However, the marginal cost of producing an additional unit is somewhat less than C dollars and well below P, so cost is not equal to gains. Accordingly, expansion of output is desirable.

How can we escape from the dilemma posed by the twin facts (1) that monopoly may be efficient, but (2) that monopoly may lead to excessive profits and underproduction? One answer is to permit certain monopolies to exist, then to regulate them by the government.

PRICE REGULATION

The most common method of monopoly regulation is through price controls. Price regulation typically results (1) in a larger quantity of the product being sold than would be the case with an unrestricted monopoly, (2) in a reduced dollar profit, and (3) in a lower rate of return on investment by the firm's owners. This situation is illustrated in Figure 12-4. The monopolist,

Figure 12-4 Price Regulation and Monopoly Optimal Price/Output Decision
Making

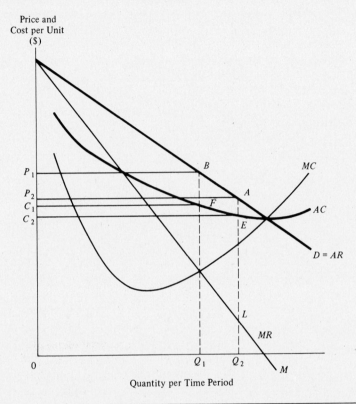

operating without regulation, would produce Q_1 units of output and charge
a price P_1. If regulators set a ceiling on prices at P_2, the firm's effective demand curve is the kinked curve P_2AD. Since price is a constant from 0 to
Q_2 units of output, marginal revenue equals price in this range; that is, P_2A
is the marginal revenue curve over the output range $0Q_2$. For output beyond Q_2, marginal revenue is given by the original marginal revenue function, the line LM. Thus, the marginal revenue curve is now discontinuous
at output Q_2, with a gap between Points A and L. This regulated firm will
maximize profits by operating at output Q_2 and by charging the ceiling price
P_2. Marginal revenue is greater than marginal cost up to that output, but
less than marginal cost beyond it.

Profits are also reduced by the regulatory action. Without price regulation, a price, P_1, would be charged; a cost of C_1 per unit would be incurred;
and an output, Q_1, would be produced. Profit would be $(P_1 - C_1)(Q_1)$,
which is equal to the area P_1BFC_1. With price regulation, the price is P_2,

the cost is C_2, Q_2 units are sold, and profits are represented by the smaller area P_2AEC_2.

How does the regulatory authority determine a "fair" price? This is a very complex question which has been the subject of many books. In essence, the theory is as follows. The regulatory commission has in mind a "fair" or "normal" rate of return, given the risk inherent in the enterprise. The regulators also know how much capital investment will be required to produce a given output. The commission then sets a price such that the profits earned, when divided by the required investment at the resultant output level, will produce the target rate of return. In the case illustrated in Figure 12-4, if the profit at price P_2, when divided by the investment required to produce Q_2, should produce a rate of return greater than the target, the price would be cut until the actual and the target rates of return are equalized.[2]

Problems of Direct Regulation

Uncertainty Although the concept of price regulation is simple, serious problems exist in practical regulation. First, it is impossible to determine exactly the cost and the demand schedules, as well as the asset base necessary to support a specified level of output. Utilities also serve several classes of customers, which means that a number of different demand schedules with varying price elasticities are involved; therefore, any number of different rate schedules can be used to produce the desired profit level. If telephone company profits are too low, should rates be raised for business subscribers or for residential customers; or should they be raised on local calls or on long-distance calls? If electric utilities need more profits, should business or residential users bear the burden? To produce higher airline profits, should fares be increased more on first class or coach seats? An appeal to cost considerations for a solution to this problem is of no avail, because all the services mentioned are joint products, a factor that makes it extremely difficult if not impossible to separate costs and allocate them to specific classes of customers.

Optimal Output Second, the regulators can make mistakes with regard to the optimal output, growth, and service levels. For example, if AT & T is permitted to charge excessively high rates, more funds will be allocated to the Bell Labs, and communication services will improve at a faster than optimal rate. Similarly, if prices allowed to natural gas producers, which are also regulated, are too low (1) consumers will be encouraged to use gas at a high rate, (2) producers will not seek new gas supplies, and (3) a shortage of gas will occur. Too low a price structure for electricity will,

[2] Determination of required rates of return on investment is examined more closely in Chapter 13.

similarly, encourage the use of power but discourage the addition of new generating equipment.

Inefficiency   Third, price regulations can lead to inefficiency. If the regulated companies are guaranteed a minimum return on their invested capital, then, provided demand conditions permit, operating inefficiencies can be offset by higher prices. To illustrate, consider the situation depicted in Figure 12-5. A regulated utility faces the demand curve AR and the marginal revenue curve MR. If the utility operates at peak efficiency, the average cost curve AC_1 would apply.[3] At a regulated price P_1, Q_1 units would be demanded, cost per unit would be C_1, and profits equal to the rectangle $P_1P_1'C_1'C_1$ would be earned. These profits are, let us assume, just sufficient to provide a "reasonable" return on invested capital.

Now assume that another company, but one with less capable managers, is operating under similar conditions. Because this management is less efficient than that of the first company, its cost curve is represented by AC_2. If its price is set at P_1, it, too, would sell Q_1 units, but its average cost would be C_2, its profits would be only $P_1P_1'C_2'C_2$, and the company would be earning less than a "reasonable" rate of return. In the absence of regulation,

Figure 12-5   Efficient and Inefficient Utility Companies

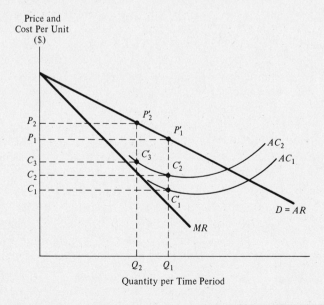

Price and
Cost Per Unit
($)

Quantity per Time Period

---

[3] The average costs illustrated in Figure 12-5 are exclusive of capital costs. That is, they *do not* include a normal return on capital investment.

inefficiency and low profits go together, but under regulation the inefficient company would request—and probably be granted—a rate increase to P_2. Here it would sell Q_2 units of output, incur an average cost of C_3 per unit, and earn profits of $P_2P_2'C_3'C_3$, resulting in a rate of return on investment approximately equal to that of the efficient company. We see, then, that regulation can reduce if not eliminate the profit incentive for efficiency.[4]

Investment Level A fourth problem with regulation is that it can lead to overinvestment or underinvestment in fixed assets. The allowed profits are calculated as a percentage of the rate base, which is approximately equal to fixed assets. If the allowed rate of return exceeds the cost of capital, it will benefit the firm to expand fixed assets and to shift to capital-intensive methods of production. Conversely, if the allowed rate of return is less than the cost of capital, the firm will not expand capacity rapidly enough and will produce by methods that require relatively little capital. This is related to the second point raised above in connection with optimal output, growth, and service levels.

Regulatory Lag and Political Problems Another related problem is that of regulatory lag, which is defined as the period between the time it is recognized that a price increase (or decrease) is appropriate and the effective date of the price change. Because of the often lengthy legal proceedings involved in these price change decisions, substantial periods can pass between the time at which the need for utility rate level adjustments is recognized and the time at which they are implemented.

The problem of regulatory lag is particularly acute during periods of rapidly rising prices. During the late 1960s and the 1970s, for example, inflationary pressures have exerted a constant upward thrust on costs, so if normal profits and a fair rate of return on capital are to be maintained, timely price increases must be implemented.

However, public utility commissioners are either political appointees or elected officials, and either those who appoint them or the commissioners themselves must periodically stand for election. Further, most voters are consumers of utility services, and, like all consumers, utility customers dislike price increases, whether these increases are justified or not. Unlike the

---

[4] Utility commissions attempt to consider efficiency when setting rates. For example, a particular commission might feel that 8 percent is a reasonable rate of return, but might allow efficient companies within its jurisdiction to earn up to 8.5 percent and penalize inefficient companies by holding them to a return of less than 8 percent. The difficulty with this approach is that each utility operates in a unique setting, so it is extremely difficult to make valid comparisons. One electric company might have a cost of 2 mils per kwh, while another in the same state might have a cost of 2.5 mils. Is the first company more efficient than the second, or is the cost difference due to fuel cost differences, different plant sizes, labor cost differentials, differing depreciation charges caused by construction during a more or less inflated period, and so on? Because of these difficulties, utility commissions do not frequently make explicit use of efficiency differentials in setting profit rates.

consumers of unregulated goods and services, however, utility customers can and do exert great pressure on public utility commissioners to deny or at least delay rate increases.

At least in part because of regulatory lag, a number of major utility companies experienced severe financial difficulties during 1974. The largest U.S. electric utility, Consolidated Edison (which serves New York City and the surrounding area), was almost forced into bankruptcy, and many other companies were forced to curtail construction programs because they were unable to obtain the funds necessary to purchase new plant and equipment. Profits were simply inadequate to induce investors to purchase the companies' stocks and bonds.

Cost of Regulation   By this time the sixth problem with price regulation should be obvious. A great deal of careful analysis, which is costly, must be conducted before regulatory decisions can be made. Maintaining public utility commission staffs is expensive, but an even more important cost element—maintaining required records and processing rate cases—is borne directly by the company. Ultimately the costs of both the commissions and the companies' regulation-related activities are borne by consumers.

It should be pointed out that we emphatically favor utility regulation. Indeed, we can see no other reasonable alternative to such regulation for electric, gas, telephone, and private water companies. It is evident, however, that serious problems arise from efforts to regulate industry through price determination. The market system, if competition is present, is a much more efficient allocator of goods and services, and it is for this reason that efforts are made to maintain a "workable" level of competition in the economy.

We turn next to the primary device used to stimulate competition, the antitrust laws.

ANTITRUST POLICY[5]

In the late nineteenth century a movement toward industrial consolidations developed in the United States. Industrial growth was rapid, and because of economies of scale, an oligopolistic structure emerged in certain industries. Reactions such as those discussed in Chapter 10 became apparent to the leaders of these industries, who concluded that higher profits could be attained through cooperation rather than through competition. As a result, voting trusts were formed, whereby the voting rights to the stocks of the various firms in an industry were turned over to a trust, which then managed the firms and sought to reach a monopoly price/output solution. The oil and the tobacco trusts of the 1880s are well-known examples.

---

[5] Antitrust is a complex subject, and many courses in law, economics, and marketing are devoted to it. A complete, comprehensive review of the subject is well beyond the scope of this text, but we do feel that the highlights of antitrust policy should be brought out here.

Although profitable to the firms, the trusts were socially undesirable, and public indignation resulted in the passage of the first significant antitrust measure in 1890, the Sherman Act. Other important legislation subsequently passed includes the Clayton Act (1914) and the Federal Trade Commission Act (1914), the Robinson-Patman Act (1936), and the Celler Anti-merger Act (1950). Each of these acts was designed to prevent anticompetitive actions, actions whose impact is more likely to reduce competition than it is to lower costs by increasing operating efficiency. In this section we present a brief chronology of major antitrust legislation.

Sherman Act

The Sherman Act of 1890 was the first federal antitrust legislation. In substance, it was brief and to the point. Section 1 forbade contracts, combinations, or conspiracies in restraint of trade (then an offense at common law), and Section 2 forbade monopolization. Both sections could be enforced by civil court decrees or by criminal proceedings, with the guilty liable to fines or jail sentences.

Despite some landmark decisions against the tobacco, powder, and Standard Oil trusts, enforcement proved to be sporadic. Moreover, the Sherman Act was alleged to be too vague. On the one hand, business people claimed not to know what was illegal; on the other, it was widely felt that the Justice Department was ignorant of monopoly-creating practices and did not bring suit against them until it was too late and monopoly was a fait accompli.

Clayton Act and Federal Trade Commission Act

Congress passed two additional measures in 1914 that were designed to overcome weaknesses in the Sherman Act—the Clayton Act and the Federal Trade Commission (FTC) Act. The principal features of these are summarized below.

Enforcement The Federal Trade Commission Act established and funded the FTC for the expressed purpose of initiating actions to prevent and punish antitrust violations.

Mergers Voting trusts that lessened competition were prohibited by the Sherman Act, but the act's interpretation did not always prevent one corporation from acquiring the stock of other, competing firms and then merging them into itself. Section 7 of the Clayton Act prohibited such mergers if they were found to reduce competition. Either the Antitrust Division of the Justice Department or the FTC can bring suit under Section 7, and mergers can be prevented or, if consummated prior to the suit, divestment can be ordered.

Interlocking Directorates   The Clayton Act also prevented individuals from serving on the boards of directors of two competing companies. Obviously, if two "competitors" had any common directors, they would probably not compete very hard.

Price Discrimination   The Clayton Act made it illegal for a seller to discriminate in prices between its customers (1) unless cost differentials in serving the various customers justified the price differentials, or (2) unless the lower prices charged in certain markets were offered to meet competition in the area. The primary concern was that a large, strong firm might employ selective price cuts in local markets to eliminate weak local firms. Once the competitors in one market were eliminated, monopoly prices would be charged in the area and the excessive profits could be used to subsidize cut-throat competition in other areas.

Tying Contracts and Related Arrangements   A firm, particularly one with the patent on a vital process or a monopoly on a natural resource, can use licensing or other arrangements to restrict competition. One such procedure is the *tying contract*, through which a firm ties the acquisition of one item to an agreement to purchase other items. For example, the International Business Machines Corporation for many years refused to sell its business machines. It rented these machines to customers, who were required to buy IBM punch cards and related materials, as well as machine maintenance. This clearly had the effect of reducing competition in the maintenance and service industry, as well as in the punch card and related products industry. After the IBM lease arrangement was declared illegal under the Clayton Act, the company was forced to offer its machines for sale and to cease tying leasing arrangements to agreements to purchase other IBM materials and services.

Robinson-Patman Act

The Robinson-Patman Act was passed in 1936 as an amendment to the section of the Clayton Act dealing with price discrimination. Specific forms of price discrimination, especially related to chain-store purchasing practices, were declared to be illegal.

Celler Anti-merger Act

Although the Clayton Act made it illegal for firms to merge through stock transactions when the effect would be to lessen competition, a loophole existed in the law. A firm could purchase the *assets* of a competing firm, integrate the operations into its own, and effectively reduce competition. The Celler Act closed this loophole, making asset acquisitions illegal when the effect of such purchases is to reduce competition. By a slight change in wording, it also made clear that the policy of Congress was to attack all mergers between a buyer and a seller (vertical), between potential competitors (product and market extension, or horizontal), and between entirely unrelated firms (pure conglomerate), whenever competition was threatened.

Economic Analyses in Antitrust Actions

In the main, the various antitrust provisions listed above apply *if a particular action would tend to lessen competition substantially.* Mergers are attacked if they would alter industry structure in a manner that reduces competition, but they are not illegal if competition is not reduced. When is competition reduced? If two firms, each with 1 percent of a market served by one hundred competitors, merge, few would argue that the merger reduces competition for ninety-nine firms would still remain after the merger. If, however, each of the firms had 5 percent of the market, and only nineteen firms would remain, the merger might affect competition. Surely competition would be affected if the merging firms each had 20 percent of a market served by only four or five firms. But where should the line be drawn?

Further, if it is judged that a *particular* merger would not, in and of itself, reduce competition but that a series of similar mergers would, should the merger in question be permitted? To illustrate, suppose twenty firms, each with a 5 percent share of the market, are in competition. A judgment is made, perhaps in a court of law after hearing much economic evidence, that a particular merger will not harm competition. If the merger is approved, however, other firms will also seek to merge, and the result will be a reduction in competition. When should the trend toward concentration be stopped? [6]

Market concentration is a key element in making judgments about the effect of a merger on the competitive posture of an industry, but how should an industry or a market be determined? To illustrate, suppose two banks in lower Manhattan seek to merge. There are about 14,000 banks in the United States, and the national banking concentration ratio is low. However, the entire United States is not a relevant market for most banking services—a local area is the relevant market. But what local area? Should metropolitan New York be deemed the market? The City of New York? The Borough of Manhattan? Or lower Manhattan only? The answer really depends on the nature of the banks. For certain classes of services, especially loans to major national corporations, the nation as a whole constitutes the market. But for small checking account and personal loan services, the local area is the relevant market.

[6] Industrial concentration is usually measured by the percentage share of a given market served by the four largest firms in an industry. The higher the concentration ratio, the less likely that workable competition will exist in an industry. The classic work in this area is by Joe S. Bain, *Industrial Organization*, Wiley, New York, 1959. Bain distinguishes between "highly concentrated oligopoly" (75 to 100 percent of sales by the top four firms in an industry), "moderately concentrated oligopoly" (50 to 75 percent concentration ratio), "slightly concentrated (or low-grade) oligopoly" (25 to 50 percent concentration ratio), and "atomistic oligopoly" for concentration ratios below 25 percent.

The problem is even more complex when competing products or industries are considered. A particular bank might, for example, be the only one serving a given neighborhood, but the bank might still face intense competition from savings and loan associations, credit unions, and distant banks that offer mail-deposit service.

Similar problems are found in other aspects of antitrust policy. Given the difficulties we have noted in determining costs, when is price discrimination based on quantity discounts legal because of low production costs on large orders? Here, just as in merger cases, the answer is not likely to be clearcut; a comprehensive economic cost analysis is required before a determination can be made—even then a large degree of arbitrariness is likely to be inherent in the decision.

Recently the question of whether bigness and concentration in business necessarily leads to reduced competition has once again become a centerstage issue in the debate on regulation and antitrust. On one side of the issue are those economists, social scientists, and politicians who believe that concentration and monopoly exploitation go hand in hand. They argue that government should move rapidly to break up the largest industrial concerns and prevent all activities that are likely to increase concentration in any single industry or to create larger conglomerate firms that control vast resources covering many different industries.

The opposing forces argue that antitrust activities must be oriented toward more specific anticompetitive behavior than mere growth. They cite the need for U.S. firms to expand in size in order to compete effectively against giant foreign competitors in both the U.S. and world markets. Those holding this position also rely on the evidence showing substantial economies of scale in most industries when developing their arguments that economic efficiency and bigness frequently are closely related.

There is no clearcut answer to this question of just what is the optimal antitrust policy the government should follow. Clearly, there are many instances of business practices that are anticompetitive in nature and, hence, socially undesirable. On the other hand, it is equally clear that economic efficiency and increased competition frequently result from mergers and combinations which create an additional firm of sufficient size to successfully challenge the dominating firm or firms in an industry. Additionally, as trade barriers continue to fall, it is increasingly important to analyze market structure and competition on an international basis so as not to hamstring domestic firms in their attempts to remain effective competitors.[7]

As we stated at the outset of this section on antitrust, the whole area is quite complex, with its complete coverage being well beyond the scope of this text. Further, generalizations are difficult in the antitrust arena—the

---

[7] For the reader who is interested in an expanded discussion of the current status of antitrust activity in the U.S., we recommend "Is John Sherman's Antitrust Obsolete?" *Business Week,* March 23, 1974, pp. 47-56.

fact that so many antitrust decisions are made in the courts is testimony to this point. Nevertheless, because antitrust policy does constitute a serious constraint to many business decisions, antitrust considerations are an important, if nebulous, aspect of managerial economics. Because of the importance of the role played by the court in determining antitrust activity, we have included an appendix to this chapter containing U.S. Supreme Court opinions of three of the most significant recent cases to show both the nature of the judicial process and the use the courts make of economic analysis in reaching their decisions.[8]

SUMMARY

Our primary purpose in this chapter has been to indicate the nature of the types of constraints society imposes on business operations. As we have seen, governments impose (1) direct operating controls, (2) controls over profits in the case of regulated utilities, and (3) antitrust controls designed to maintain competition.

Operating controls abound in the United States, and there seems to be a trend in the direction of more controls. Auto makers are being required to meet certain safety and pollution control standards (although these emission requirements may be modified in light of the emerging awareness of their compounding impact on energy shortages); the Pure Food and Drug Act constrains certain firms; companies that sell on credit or lend money to consumers are now required to make explicit statements of their interest charges; the validity of statements made in advertisements is being checked more carefully; increases in wages and prices are being controlled; and so on.

On balance, some of these controls are unquestionably good; for others the issues are less clearcut. In many cases the economic consequences of an action can be analyzed, and the results of this analysis, along with inputs from other disciplines, can be used to help reach "good" final decisions. Such an analysis for the steam boiler industry was presented as an illustration.

If an industry experiences such strong economies of scale that only a very few firms can exist and still be efficient, and if the product is a vital one with no good substitutes, monopolistic exploitation is likely unless some kind of regulation is imposed. Because this situation is common with public utilities, these companies are regulated. In essence, the regulator sets a price (lower than the profit-maximizing price) designed to give the company only a "normal" profit.

Because direct regulation, such as that imposed on public utilities, presents many problems, where it is possible to maintain "workable" competition this course of action is generally thought to be better than permitting monopolies to exist and then regulate them. Accordingly, a series of laws, known collectively as "antitrust laws," has been passed by Congress for the express purpose of maintaining competition. These laws deal with collusion, price discrimination, mergers, tying con-

---

[8] The interested reader may wish to consult one of the following books for a more thorough development of this interesting area.

R. Caves, *American Industry: Structure, Conduct, and Performance,* Prentice-Hall, Englewood Cliffs, N.J., 1967, Chapter 4; E. Mansfield, *Monopoly Power and Economic Performance,* Norton, New York, 1968, pp. 142-150; L. Stern and J. Grabner, *Competition in the Marketplace,* Scott, Foresman, Glenview, Illinois, 1970, Chapters 5-8.

tracts, and other practices designed to reduce competition and thus obtain monopoly profits.

QUESTIONS

12-1 What role does the price elasticity of demand play in determining the effect of operating controls on an industry when these controls lead to increased fixed costs and to increased variable costs?

12-2 It has been suggested that given the difficulties encountered in regulating the various utility industries in the United States, nationalization might lead to a more socially optimal allocation of resources. Do you agree? Why or why not?

12-3 The antitrust statutes in the United States have been used primarily to attack monopolization by big business. Should monopolization of labor supply by giant unions be as "vigorously" prosecuted?

12-4 Do "bigness" in business and absence of competition necessarily go hand in hand?

12-5 Do the United States antitrust statutes protect competition or competitors? What is the distinction between the two?

12-6 One of the major airlines recently proposed a "modified standby" fare scheme. A passenger would be able to buy a ticket without a reservation for half-fare but would have to wait until the last minute to board. If he were bumped (that is, if all seats were reserved and claimed), he would have a guaranteed seat on the next flight.

    a) What are the necessary preconditions for price discrimination?

    b) How are they met (or might they be met) in this case?

    c) In what sense is this scheme *not* price discrimination?

12-7 The Brown Shoe Company was a retailer of shoes, primarily in central-city areas. In 1955, it bought the Kinney Shoe Company, which sold shoes at roadside outlets and in suburban shopping centers. The Justice Department sued to prevent the merger, charging that it substantially lessened competition in violation of Section 7 of the Clayton Act. Brown lost in the District Court, which held, *inter alia*, that the Justice Department's depiction of the (horizontal) relevant market was correct. On appeal, the Supreme Court noted:

> The District Court found that the effects of this aspect of the merger must be analyzed in every city with a population exceeding 10,000 and its immediate contiguous surrounding territory in which both Brown and Kinney sold shoes at retail.... [Brown] claims that such areas should, in some cases, be defined so as to include only the central business districts of large cities, and, in others, so as to encompass the "standard metropolitan areas" within which smaller communities are found.... [370 U.S. 294, 338-39 (1962)]

    a) Why did the company try to define the relevant market in the ways it did?

    b) Why did the government try to define the relevant market the way it did?

    c) Using the economic data provided in the U.S. Supreme Court opinion (reprinted in the Appendix of this chapter), which market structure do you think is more appropriate?

PROBLEMS

12-1 In a recent hearing before the State Pollution Control Board, members of the Sierra Club clashed with representatives of the paper industry over the extent to which the companies should be permitted to discharge wastes into the Limpopo River. The Sierra Club, whose representatives were supported by the Resort Owners League, argued for quite stringent rules, whereas the paper companies sought less severe control regulation and more time in which to implement the rules. The companies were backed by representatives of Kaibab and Supai, the two largest towns on the river and both the sites of several large paper mills.

There was no argument about the need for *some* controls—everyone agreed that mercury emissions must cease and also that organic wastes should be reduced. The arguments were over the *degree* of controls, with the conservationists calling for a return of the river to its preindustrial state and the companies arguing that such tight controls would cause (1) a severe reduction in production, (2) industry to move to other states with less severe restrictions, and (3) large losses both to stockholders and to property owners in the mill towns. Besides, the companies argued, many other rivers in the state were still unspoiled, and it made good sense to industrialize some areas and keep others "pure."

As the hearings progressed, it became clear that insufficient facts were available. The companies suggested that the costs of tight pollution controls would be quite high and would drive industry out. The conservationists argued that the companies were overstating costs and understating the probability that other states would pass similarly tough control laws, thus making it impossible for paper mills to escape pollution control laws by relocating. The companies retorted that if all states passed legislation similar to that backed by the Sierra Club, the companies would not be able to pass their cost increases on to customers because of an elastic demand for paper products and because of foreign imports, especially from Canada.

After several days of emotion-packed debate the Pollution Control Board adjourned the hearings, commissioned a team of economists and engineers from State University to develop some facts on the case, and rescheduled the hearings for a later date when this information would be available. As a result of this analysis, the following data were developed:

1. Demand curve for raw paper facing all United States producers (Q in millions of tons):

$$P_A = \$650 - \$10Q. \tag{1}$$

2. Aggregate total cost curve (ignoring the required return on capital) facing all United States producers (dollars in millions, Q in million-unit increments):

$$TC_A = \$1,800 + \$200Q + \$5Q^2. \tag{2}$$

3. Total equity investment of all two hundred United States paper producers: $5 billion. A normal rate of return is 10 percent. The state in question has 8 percent of the United States paper industry. Assume all firms operate with similar cost functions.
4. Demand curve facing each individual producer:

$$P = \$425 - \$0.0Q. \tag{3}$$

5. Increased operating costs of $1 billion a year, excluding any return on the required new investment, would be required to bring the United States paper industry pollution standards up to the level recommended by the Sierra Club.

a) What price/output solution would be reached if the United States paper industry operated as a monopolist?
b) What profits would be earned?
c) Would above-normal or below-normal profits be earned if the industry operated as a monopolist? What would the profits amount to?
d) In fact, what price/output solutions would be reached? (Assume that monopoly outcome is *not* reached.) (*Note:* To find the realized output, equate MC_A to P_A, as determined in Equation 3.)
e) What is the industry profit? Is it above or below normal?
f) What would occur to the paper industry if the Sierra Club recommendation is adopted nationwide, assuming all data given thus far are valid and the firms all continue to operate?
g) In fact, what would be likely to occur? What assumptions in the data would likely be incorrect, causing the result in Part f *not* to occur?
h) What market structure would you judge the paper industry to have, assuming the facts given above?
i) What would become of the state paper industry if only this one state put in pollution control restrictions? What bearing has this on federal pollution control legislation?

12-2 Red River Chemical Corporation produces two products in a joint production process. The two chemicals (A and B) must be produced in the constant ratio of 1:1. Red River Chemical has long followed the practice of dumping its wastes (including excess production) into the Red River, and currently incurs no cost from this activity. The total cost function for Red River Chemical is:

$$TC = 100 + 10Q + 4Q^2,$$

where Q represents a unit of production consisting of 1 unit of A and 1 unit of B.

a) If the demand curves for the two products are $P_A = 600 - Q_A$ and $P_B = 100 - Q_B$ respectively, what would be the optimal price/output combination for the two products, assuming Red River Chemical operates as a profit-maximizing firm?
b) Assume now that the State Pollution Control Board imposed pollution abatement requirements, including a fine on waste disposal that resulted in Red River Chemical's cost function shifting to:

$$TC = 100 + 20Q + 4Q^2 + 10Q_A{}^* + 10Q_B{}^*,$$

where Q_A^* and Q_B^* are excess quantities of A and B that are dumped in the Red River. What are the optimal prices and sales levels for the firm's products now?

c) Determine the smallest fine per unit of B dumped that would cause Red River to stop dumping excess production altogether.

12-3 Aviation Electronics produces accelerometers and strain gauges for the Air Force. It has just received a rush order for 320 accelerometers and 150 strain gauges for replacement purposes. A one-week delivery is required. Aviation has two employees who can assemble these instruments. Employee A receives a wage of $5 an hour and can assemble a combination of 3 accelerometers and 2 strain gauges per hour. Employee B earns $4 an hour and can make 4 accelerometers and 1.5 strain gauges per hour. Because of the nature of the production system, these output ratios are fixed.

a) Assuming that Aviation Electronics' labor contract requires a minimum of 30 paid hours for each employee, what is the least-cost combination of hours that these employees should work to satisfy the delivery requirement specified by the Air Force? (*Hint:* Set up the problem algebraically and then use a graph to locate the optimal combination.)

b) Assuming
  (i) that Aviation is located in a state that prohibits females from working more than 40 hours a week, and
  (ii) that Employee B is in fact female, what would be the least-cost number of hours that A and B should each work?

c) What is the cost to Aviation on this particular job because of the state's employment restriction for women?

d) How could you develop an economic argument illustrating that the state's restriction on working hours of females might be a major determinant of the wage differential between Employee A and Employee B?

12-4 Forest Products Company is the major employer in Lakeland County, an economically depressed area in a northern Midwest state. Forest Products produces a single product the demand curve for which is given by $P = 1,000 - .02Q$, where Q is the quantity demanded per year. Production of each unit of output requires 100 man-hours of labor, .25 hours of capital equipment time, and $50 of raw materials. Forest Products has a total of 5,000 hours of capital equipment time available in its production facility each year and can purchase all the labor and materials it desires. The capital equipment investment by Forest Products is $50,000,000 and the firm requires a 12 percent return on capital. Assume for simplicity that these are the only costs incurred by the firm.

a) You have been employed by the State Unemployment Service to evaluate the impact on employment at Forest Products of a proposed minimum wage law. As a first step in this analysis, develop the short-run demand curve for labor by Forest Products.

b) Forest Products currently pays $2.00 per hour for labor. Calculate the short-run impact on employment of a $3.00 minimum wage law.

c) Would the long-run impact on employment be likely to differ significantly from the short-run impact in this case? Justify your answer.

12-5 The Eastern State Power Company is currently engaged in a rate case with the regulatory commission under whose jurisdiction it operates. The firm has assets of $30,000 and the utility commission desires that the firm earn an 8 percent return on investment. The demand curve faced by Eastern is given by:

$$P = \$107 - \$.5Q,$$

and its total cost (excluding capital costs) function is:

$$TC = \$1,000 + \$5Q.$$

a) Eastern has requested a price for its output of $50 per unit. What will Eastern's return on investment be if the commission allows that price?

b) What price should the commission set if it wishes to limit Eastern's return on investment to 8 percent?

STERLING DRUG COMPANY VERSUS FEDERAL TRADE COMMISSION: A NEW LOOK AT MARKET STRUCTURE FOR ANTITRUST ACTION*

In 1966 Sterling Drug Company purchased Lehn and Fink, makers of Lysol disinfectant, and Tussy and Dorothy Gray cosmetics. Sterling makes several nationally known proprietary drug items, including Bayer aspirin, Phillips milk of magnesia, Campho-Phenique external antiseptic, Cope and Vanquish pain relievers, Dr. Lyons tooth powder, Z-B-T baby powder, and pHisoHex skin cleanser. Lehn and Fink's consumer products included Lysol disinfectant—spray and liquid—Medi-Quik antiseptic, Stri-Dex medicated pads, Dorothy Gray and Tussy cosmetics, and Ogilvie and Noreen hair preparations.

The Federal Trade Commission attacked the merger between Sterling and Lehn and Fink, and in early 1971 a hearing on the matter was held.

The Commission had originally planned to challenge the merger solely on the basis of Lysol's dominant position in the aerosol deodorant market. This would have followed the precedent established by the Commission in setting aside the merger of Procter & Gamble Company and Clorox Company. That case, which was upheld by the United States Supreme Court, was built on the theory that large companies that hover just outside a market are part of the competitive picture and should not be allowed to buy leading producers.

However, after conversations with John C. Narver, a professor of economics at the University of Washington, who was serving as "visiting professor" at the Commission during 1968, the lawyers decided to broaden the case into a basic challenge to any tie-ups between producers of drug and toilet products. That meant that the Sterling case would establish a precedent that would be a clue to the legality of a host of other mergers involving cosemtic companies, including those between American Cyanamid and Shulton, Eli Lilly and Elizabeth Arden, and American Brands and Jurgens.

The FTC's case against the merger was based on an economic theory called the "supply space" concept, propounded by Narver. The concept is Narver's way of defining the "relevant market" for antitrust enforcement in the age of conglomerate mergers.

* Adapted from the May 22, 1971 issue of *Business Week* by special permission. © 1971 by McGraw-Hill, Inc.

The traditional way of looking at the market has been in terms of the products a company makes and the geographical areas in which it sells. This, Narver maintains, is a "preoccupation with the narrow" that has led to "much weaker and less rational" enforcement of the antimerger laws.

"The most realistic view of a firm is its capacity, its capabilities, for engaging in activities," Narver says. He sees a corporation as "a pool of resources"—managerial, financial, technological, marketing—that can be drawn on to fill any of a variety of demands, depending on where the front office thinks the biggest profits lie.

According to Narver's theory, the whole range of demands that a certain kind of company can easily satisfy constitutes a single "supply space," regardless of how different the industries in which it operates may look on the surface. For example, Narver says, the resources of tobacco companies can easily be applied to food production and distribution; the food and tobacco industries are therefore really contained in the same supply space. By the same reasoning, producers of cloth and producers of clothing can be lumped together, as can drug companies and cosmetic companies.

Narver does not contend that all mergers between companies within the same supply space should be barred. But, he says, if a relatively few firms control the bulk of the assets in that supply space, it should be illegal for any of them to buy other companies operating in that market. This, at any rate, is the contention of the FTC staff in its case against Sterling Drug's acquisition of Lehn and Fink, makers of Lysol disinfectant, and Tussy and Dorothy Gray cosmetics.

Narver's role in the case was more direct and more public than is usual for an economist. He was the Commission's chief witness, and spent a rancorous two and one-half days on the witness stand explaining his theory to the hearing examiner.

Narver's testimony was based on an application of his theory to the particular supply space involved in this merger.

First, he found that a significant and growing number of companies made products which the Census Bureau classifies as "pharmaceutical preparations" and also products which the Bureau calls "perfumes, cosmetics, and other toilet preparations." He reasoned that if the executives of these companies see a relationship between the two areas, they must be in the same supply space.

He then looked for the smallest company operating in the two areas, and found it was Lehn and Fink. If L and F could operate in both categories, so could any company bigger than L and F, he figured.

He found fifty-eight such big enough companies operating in one or the other of the census categories—Sterling ranked nineteenth—and branded them all competitors, since they were occupying the same supply space. If they are competitors, the FTC is on firm legal ground in opposing the merger of any two of them under the antitrust laws.

Narver also found empirical support for his theory in the research of some other young economists into corporate behavior. He cited a study of 111 large manufacturers by Michael Gort of the State University of New York, which he says shows that companies are quick to move resources into "economically related activities." He also referred to a study of 494 corporations by Princeton University's Charles Berry, which indicated that companies often shed product lines without getting rid of old plants and move into new areas without building new ones.

One problem with Narver's approach is that the standard industrial classifications used by the Census Bureau are less than perfect, and often do not conform to actual market usage. It was on this basis that Sterling's own expert witness, Almarin Phillips, head of the economics department at the University of Pennsylvania, lambasted Narver. He argued that the economic effects of a merger can be assessed only by reviewing the specifics of two companies, not the general categories.

It should be obvious that the approach of the Commission staff was very controversial. As reported in *Business Week* (June 12, 1971, p. 32), the FTC hearing examiner rejected the economic theory proposed by Narver and ruled the merger lawful. The decision was appealed to the full FTC Commission, which upheld the hearing examiner in dismissing the complaint.

1. Is Narver's economic concept of competitors sound? Why?
2. How would this concept affect the use of cross-elasticities of demand to distinguish competing products?
3. Do the facts of this case—particularly as regards Lehn and Fink's premier position in the household deodorant market with its Lysol disinfectant—appear similar to those of the Procter & Gamble-Clorox case; and if so, why do you think the FTC dismissed the complaint in this case in light of the U.S. Supreme Court decision in the Procter & Gamble case (the U.S. Supreme Court Opinion is given in the Appendix to this chapter)?

SELECTED REFERENCES

Ansoff, H. Igor, and J. Fred Weston. "Merger Objectives and Organization Structure," *Quarterly Review of Economics and Statistics,* vol. 2, August 1962, pp. 49-58.

Bain, J. S. "Economics of Scale, Concentration and the Condition of Entry in Twenty Manufacturing Industries," *American Economic Review,* vol. 44, March 1954, pp. 15-39.

————. *Industrial Organization.* New York: Wiley, 1959.

————. *International Differences in Industrial Structure.* New Haven: Yale University Press, 1966.

Bock, Betty. *Mergers and Markets: An Economic Analysis of Case Law.* New York: National Industrial Conference Board, 1960.

Caves, R. *American Industry: Structure, Conduct, and Performance.* Englewood Cliffs, N.J.: Prentice-Hall, 1967.

Kaysen, Carl, and Donald L. Turner. *Antitrust Policy: An Economic and Legal Analysis.* Cambridge, Mass.: Harvard University Press, 1959.

Kuhlman, John M. "The Procter and Gamble Decision," *Quarterly Review of Economics and Business,* Spring 1966, pp. 29-36.

Mansfield, E. *Monopoly Power and Economic Performance.* New York: Norton, 1968.

Markham, Jesse. "Antitrust Trends and New Constraints," *Harvard Business Review,* May-June 1963, pp. 84-92.

Shepherd, W. G. "Trends of Concentration in American Manufacturing Industries, 1947-1958," *Review of Economics and Statistics,* vol. 46, May 1964, pp. 200-212.

Stern, L., and J. Grabner. *Competition in the Marketplace*. Glenview, Ill.: Scott, Foresman, 1970.

Turner, Donald F. "Conglomerate Mergers and Section 7 of the Clayton Act," *Harvard Law Review*, May 1966, pp. 1313-1395.

APPENDIX: Selected Supreme Court Antitrust Cases

Since the legislation passed by Congress in the antitrust area is subject to various interpretations in its application, the courts must establish the parameters of antitrust regulation. Many important cases have been decided—far too many to be included here—but we present highlights, taken directly from the United States Supreme Court opinions, of three significant cases to show both the nature of the judicial process and the use the courts make of economic analysis. The opinions presented are in the cases of (1) the Brown Shoe Company, (2) Procter & Gamble, and (3) Anheuser-Busch.

BROWN SHOE COMPANY

This suit was initiated in November 1955 when the Government filed a civil action in the United States District Court for the Eastern District of Missouri alleging that a contemplated merger between the G. R. Kinney Company, Inc. (Kinney), and the Brown Shoe Company, Inc. (Brown), through an exchange of Kinney for Brown stock, would violate Section (§) 7 of the Clayton Act. The Act, as amended, provides in pertinent part:

> No corporation engaged in commerce shall acquire, directly or indirectly, the whole or any part of the stock or other share capital . . . of another corporation engaged also in commerce, where in any line of commerce in any section of the country, the effect of such acquisition may be substantially to lessen competition, or to tend to create a monopoly.

The complaint sought injunctive relief under § 15 of the Clayton Act, to restrain consummation of the merger.

A motion by the Government for a preliminary injunction *pendente lite* was denied, and the companies were permitted to merge provided, however, that their businesses be operated separately and that their assets be kept separately identifiable. The merger was then effected on May 1, 1956.

In the District Court, the Government contended that the effect of the merger of Brown—the third largest seller of shoes by dollar volume in the United States, a leading manufacturer of men's, women's, and children's shoes, and a retailer with over 1,230 owned, operated or controlled retail outlets[9]—and Kinney—the eighth largest company, by dollar volume, among those primarily engaged in selling shoes, itself a large manufacturer of shoes, and a retailer with over 350 retail outlets— "may be substantially to lessen competition or to tend to create a monopoly" by eliminating actual or potential competition in the production of shoes for the national wholesale shoe market and in the sale of shoes at retail in the Nation, by foreclosing competition from "a market represented by Kinney's retail outlets whose annual sales exceed $42,000,000," and by enhancing Brown's competitive advantage over other producers, distributors and sellers of shoes. The Government argued that the "line of commerce" affected by this merger is "footwear," or alternatively, that the "line[s]" are "men's," "women's," and "children's" shoes, separately considered, and that the "section of the country," within which the anticompetitive effect of the merger is to be judged, is the Nation as a whole, or alternatively, each separate city or city and its immediate surrounding area in which the parties sell shoes at retail.

In the District Court, Brown contended that the merger would be shown not to endanger competition if the "line[s] of commerce" and the "section[s] of the country" were properly determined. Brown urged that not only were the age and sex of the intended customers to be considered in determining the relevant line of commerce but that differences in grade of material, quality of workmanship, price, and customer use of shoes resulted in establishing different lines of commerce. While agreeing with the Government that, with regard to manufacturing, the relevant geographic market for assessing the effect of the merger upon competition is the country as a whole, Brown contended that with regard to retailing, the market must vary with economic reality from the central business district of a large city to a "standard metropolitan area" [10] for a smaller community. Brown further contended that, both at the manufacturing level and at the retail level, the shoe industry enjoyed healthy competition and that the vigor of this competition would not, in any event, be diminished by the proposed merger because Kinney manfactured less than 0.5% and retailed less than 2% of the Nation's shoes.

The District Court rejected the broadest contentions of both parties. The District Court found that "there is one group of classifications which is understood and recognized by the entire industry and the public—the classification into 'men's,' 'women's,' and 'children's' shoes separately and independently." On the other hand, "[t]o classify shoes as a whole could be unfair and unjust; to classify them further would be impractical, unwarranted and unrealistic."

[9] Of these over 1,230 outlets under Brown's control at the time of the filing of the complaint, Brown owned and operated over 470, while over 570 were independently owned stores operating under the Brown "Franchise Program" and over 190 were independently owned outlets operating under the "Wohl Plan." A store operating under the Franchise Program agrees not to carry competing lines of shoes of other manufacturers in return for certain aid from Brown; a store under the Wohl Plan similarly agrees to concentrate its purchases on lines which Brown sells through Wohl in return for credit and merchandising aid. In addition, Brown shoes were sold through numerous retailers operating entirely independently of Brown.

[10] "The general concept adopted in defining a standard metropolitan area [is] that of an integrated economic area with a large volume of daily travel and communication between a central city of 50,000 inhabitants or more and the outlying parts of the area. ... Each area (except in New England) consists of one or more entire counties. In New England, metropolitan areas have been defined on a town basis rather than a county basis." II U.S. Bureau of the Census, United States Census of Business: 1954, p. 3.

Realizing that "the areas of effective competition for retailing purposes cannot be fixed with mathematical precision," the District Court found that "when determined by economic reality, for retailing, a 'section of the country' is a city of 10,000 or more population and its immediate and contiguous surrounding area, regardless of name designation, and in which a Kinney store and a Brown (operated, franchise, or plan) store are located."

The District Court rejected the Government's contention that the combining of the manufacturing facilities of Brown and Kinney would substantially lessen competition in the production of men's, women's, or children's shoes for the national wholesale market. However, the District Court did find that the likely foreclosure of other manufacturers from the market represented by Kinney's retail outlets may substantially lessen competition in the manufacturers' distribution of "men's," "women's," and "children's" shoes, considered separately, throughout the Nation. The District Court also found that the merger may substantially lessen competition in retailing alone in "men's," "women's," and "children's," shoes, considered separately, in every city of 10,000 or more population and its immediate surrounding area in which both a Kinney and a Brown store are located.

Brown's contentions here differ only slightly from those made before the District Court. In order fully to understand and appraise these assertions, it is necessary to set out in some detail the District Court's findings concerning the nature of the shoe industry and the place of Brown and Kinney within that industry.

The District Court found that although domestic shoe production was scattered among a large number of manufacturers, a small number of large companies occupied a commanding position. Thus, while the 24 largest manufacturers produced about 35% of the Nation's shoes, the top 4—International, Endicott-Johnson, Brown (including Kinney) and General Shoe—alone produced approximately 23% of the Nation's shoes or 65% of the production of the top 24.

In 1955, domestic production of nonrubber shoes was 509.2 million pairs of which about 103.6 million pairs were men's shoes, about 271 million pairs were women's shoes, and about 134.6 million pairs were children's shoes. The District Court found that men's, women's, and children's shoes are normally produced in separate factories.

The public buys these shoes through about 70,000 retail outlets, only 22,000 of which, however, derive 50% or more of their gross receipts from the sale of shoes and are classified as "shoe stores" by the Census Bureau. These 22,000 shoe stores were found generally to sell (1) men's shoes only, (2) women's shoes only, (3) women's and children's shoes, or (4) men's, women's, and children's shoes.

The District Court found a "definite trend" among shoe manufacturers to acquire retail outlets. For example, International Shoe Company had no retail outlets in 1945, but by 1956 had acquired 130; General Shoe Company had only 80 retail outlets in 1945 but had 526 by 1956; Shoe Corporation of America, in the same period, increased its retail holdings from 301 to 842; Melville Shoe Company from 536 to 947; and Endicott-Johnson from 488 to 540. Brown, itself, with no retail outlets of its own prior to 1951, had acquired 845 such outlets by 1956. Moreover, between 1950 and 1956 nine independent shoe-store chains, operating 1,114 retail shoe stores, were found to have become subsidiaries of these large firms and to have ceased their independent operations.

And once the manufacturers acquired retail outlets, the District Court found there was a "definite trend" for the parent-manufacturers to supply an ever increasing percentage of the retail outlets' needs, thereby foreclosing other manufacturers from effectively competing for the retail accounts. Manufacturer-dominated stores were found to be "drying up" the available outlets for independent producers.

Another "definite trend" found to exist in the shoe industry was a decrease in the number of plants manufacturing shoes. And there appears to have been a concomitant decrease in the number of firms manufacturing shoes. In 1947, there were 1,077 independent manufacturers of shoes, but by 1954 their number had decreased about 10% to 970.

Brown Shoe was found not only to have been a participant, but also a moving factor, in these industry trends. Although Brown had experimented several times with operating its own retail outlets, by 1945 it had disposed of them all. However, in 1951, Brown again began to seek retail outlets by acquiring the Nation's largest operator of leased shoe departments, Wohl Shoe Company (Wohl), which operated 250 shoe departments in department stores throughout the United States. Between 1952 and 1955 Brown made a number of smaller acquisitions: Wetherby-Kayser Shoe Company (three retail stores), Barnes & Company (two stores), Reilly Shoe Company (two leased shoe departments), Richardson Shoe Store (one store), and Wohl Shoe Company of Dallas (not connected with Wohl) (leased shoe departments in Dallas). In 1954, Brown made another major acquisition: Regal Shoe Corporation which, at the time, operated one manufacturing plant producing men's shoes and 110 retail outlets.

The acquisition of these corporations was found to lead to increased sales by Brown to the acquired companies. Thus, although prior to Brown's acquisition of Wohl in 1951, Wohl bought from Brown only 12.8% of its total purchases of shoes, it subsequently increased its purchases to 21.4% in 1952 and to 32.6% in 1965. Wetherby-Kayser's purchases from Brown increased from 10.4% before acquisition to over 50% after. Regal, which had previously sold no shoes to Wohl and shoes worth only $89,000 to Brown, in 1956 sold shoes worth $265,000 to Wohl and $744,000 to Brown.

During the same period of time, Brown also acquired the stock or assets of seven companies engaged solely in shoe manufacturing. As a result, in 1955 Brown was the fourth largest shoe manufacturer in the country, producing about 25.6 million pairs of shoes or about 4% of the Nation's total footwear production.

Kinney is principally engaged in operating the largest family-style shoe-store chain in the United States. At the time of trial Kinney was found to be operating over 400 such stores in more than 270 cities. These stores were found to make about 1.2% of all national retail shoe sales by dollar volume. Moreover, in 1955 the Kinney stores sold approximately 8 million pairs of nonrubber shoes or about 1.6% of the national pairage sales of such shoes. Of these sales, approximately 1.1 million pairs were of men's shoes or about 1% of the national pairage sales of men's shoes; approximately 4.2 million pairs were of women's shoes, or about 1.5% of the national pairage sales of women's shoes; and approximately 2.7 million pairs were of children's shoes or about 2% of the national pairage sales of children's shoes.

In addition to this extensive retail activity, Kinney owned and operated four plants which manufactured men's, women's, and children's shoes and whose combined output was 0.5% of the national shoe production in 1955, making Kinney the twelfth largest shoe manufacturer in the United States.

Kinney stores were found to obtain about 20% of their shoes from Kinney's own manufacturing plants. At the time of the merger, Kinney bought no shoes from Brown; however, in line with Brown's conceded reasons for acquiring Kinney, Brown had, by 1957, become the largest outside supplier of Kinney's shoes, supplying 7.9% of all Kinney's needs.

It is in this setting that the merger was considered and held to violate Section 7 of the Clayton Act. The District Court ordered Brown to divest itself completely of all stock, share capital, assets or other interests it held in Kinney, to operate Kinney to the greatest degree possible as an independent concern pending complete divestiture, to refrain thereafter from acquiring or having any interest in Kinney's business or assets, and to file with the court within 90 days a plan for carrying into effect the divestiture decreed. The District Court also stated it would retain jurisdiction over the case to enable the parties to apply for such further relief as might be necessary to enforce and apply the judgment. Prior to its submission of a divestiture plan, Brown filed a notice of appeal in the District Court. It then filed a jurisdictional statement in this Court, seeking review of the judgment below as entered.

This case is one of the first to come before us in which the Government's complaint is based upon allegations that the appellant has violated § 7 of the Clayton Act, as that section was amended in 1950. The amendments adopted in 1950 culminated extensive efforts over a number of years, on the parts of both the Federal Trade Commission and some members of Congress, to secure revision of a section of the antitrust laws considered by many observers to be ineffective in its then existing form. Sixteen bills to amend § 7 during the period 1943 to 1949 alone were introduced for consideration by the Congress, and full public hearings on proposed amendments were held in three separate sessions. In the light of this extensive legislative attention to the measure, and the broad, general language finally selected by Congress for the expression of its will, we think it appropriate to review the history of the amended Act in determining whether the judgment of the court below was consistent with the intent of the legislature.

As enacted in 1914, § 7 of the original Clayton Act prohibited the acquisition by one corporation of the *stock* of another corporation when such acquisition would result in a substantial lessening of competition *between the acquiring and the acquired* companies, or tend to create a monopoly in any line of commerce. The Act did not, by its explicit terms, or as construed by this Court, bar the acquisition by one corporation of the *assets* of another. Nor did it appear to preclude the acquisition of stock in any corporation other than a direct competitor. Although proponents of the 1950 amendments to the Act suggested that the terminology employed in these provisions was the result of accident or an unawareness that the acquisition of assets could be as inimical to competition as stock acquisition, a review of the legislative history of the original Clayton Act fails to support such views. The possibility of asset acquisition was discussed, but was not considered important to an Act then conceived to be directed primarily at the development of holding companies and at the secret acquisition of competitors through the purchase of all or parts of such competitors' stock.

It was, however, not long before the Federal Trade Commission recognized deficiencies in the Act as first enacted. Its Annual Reports frequently suggested amendments, principally along two lines: first, to "plug the loophole" exempting asset acquisitions from coverage under the Act, and second, to require companies proposing a merger to give the Commission prior notification of their plans. The

Final Report of the Temporary National Economic Committee also recommended changes focusing on these two proposals. Hearings were held on some bills incorporating either or both of these changes but, prior to the amendments adopted in 1950, none reached the floor of Congress for plenary consideration. Although the bill that was eventually to become amended § 7 was confined to embracing within the Act's terms the acquisition of assets as well as stock, in the course of the hearings conducted in both the Eightieth and Eighty-first Congresses, a more far-reaching examination of the purposes and provisions of § 7 was undertaken. A review of the legislative history of these amendments provides no unmistakably clear indication of the precise standards the Congress wished the Federal Trade Commission and the courts to apply in judging the legality of particular mergers. However, sufficient expressions of a consistent point of view may be found in the hearings, committee reports of both the House and Senate, and in floor debate, to provide those charged with enforcing the Act with a usable frame of reference within which to evaluate any given merger.

The dominant theme pervading congressional consideration of the 1950 amendments was a fear of what was considered to be a rising tide of economic concentration in the American economy. Apprehension in this regard was bolstered by the publication in 1948 of the Federal Trade Commission's study on corporate mergers. Statistics from this and other current studies were cited as evidence of the danger to the American economy in unchecked corporate expansions through merger. Other considerations cited in support of the bill were the desirability of retaining "local control" over industry and the protection of small business. Throughout the recorded discussion may be found examples of Congress' fear not only of accelerated concentration of economic power on economic grounds, but also of the threat to other values a trend toward concentration was thought to pose.

What were some of the factors, relevant to a judgment as to the validity of a given merger, specifically discussed by Congress in redrafting § 7?

First, there is no doubt that Congress did wish to "plug the loophole" and to include within the coverage of the Act the acquisition of assets no less than the acquisition of stock.

Second, by the deletion of the "acquiring-acquired" language in the original text, it hoped to make plain that § 7 applied not only to mergers between actual competitors, but also to vertical and conglomerate mergers whose effect may tend to lessen competition in any line of commerce in any section of the country.

Third, it is apparent that a keystone in the erection of a barrier to what Congress saw was the rising tide of economic concentration, was its provision of authority for arresting mergers at a time when the trend to a lessening of competition in a line of commerce was still in its incipiency. Congress saw the process of concentration in American business as a dynamic force; it sought to assure the Federal Trade Commission and the courts the power to brake this force at its outset and before it gathered momentum.

Fourth, and closely related to the third, Congress rejected, as inappropriate to the problem it sought to remedy, the application to § 7 cases of the standards for judging the legality of business combinations adopted by the courts in dealing with cases arising under the Sherman Act, and which may have been applied to some early cases arising under original § 7.

Fifth, at the same time that it sought to create an effective tool for preventing all mergers having demonstrable anticompetitive effects, Congress recognized the stimulation to competition that might flow from particular mergers. When concern as to the Act's breadth was expressed, supporters of the amendments indicated that it would not impede, for example, a merger between two small companies to enable the combination to compete more effectively with larger corporations dominating the relevant market, nor a merger between a corporation which is financially healthy and a failing one which no longer can be a vital competitive factor in the market. The deletion of the word "community" in the original Act's description of the relevant geographic market is another illustration of Congress' desire to indicate that its concern was with the adverse effects of a given merger on competition only in an economically significant "section" of the country. Taken as a whole, the legislative history illuminates congressional concern with the protection of *competition,* not *competitors,* and its desire to restrain mergers only to the extent that such combinations may tend to lessen competition.

Sixth, Congress neither adopted nor rejected specifically any particular tests for measuring the relevant markets, either as defined in terms of product or in terms of geographic locus of competition, within which the anticompetitive effects of a merger were to be judged. Nor did it adopt a definition of the word "substantially," whether in quantitative terms of sales or assets or market shares or in designated qualitative terms, by which a merger's effects on competition were to be measured.

Seventh, while providing no definite quantitative or qualitative tests by which enforcement agencies could gauge the effects of a given merger to determine whether it may "substantially" lessen competition or tend toward monopoly, Congress indicated plainly that a merger had to be functionally viewed, in the context of its particular industry. That is, whether the consolidation was to take place in an industry that was fragmented rather than concentrated, that had seen a recent trend toward domination by a few leaders or had remained fairly consistent in its distribution of market shares among the participating companies, that had experienced easy access to markets by suppliers and easy access to suppliers by buyers or had witnessed foreclosure of business, that had witnessed the ready entry of new competition or the erection of barriers to prospective entrants, all were aspects, varying in importance with the merger under consideration, which would properly be taken into account.

Eighth, Congress used the words *"may* be substantially to lessen competition" (italics supplied), to indicate that its concern was with probabilities, not certainties. Statutes existed for dealing with clear-cut menaces to competition; no statute was sought for dealing with ephemeral possibilities. Mergers with a probable anticompetitive effect were to be proscribed by this Act.

It is against this background that we return to the case before us.

Economic arrangements between companies standing in a supplier-customer relationship are characterized as "vertical." The primary vice of a vertical merger or other arrangement tying a customer to a supplier is that, by foreclosing the competitors of either party from a segment of the market otherwise open to them, the arrangement may act as a "clog on competition," which "deprive[s] . . . rivals of a fair opportunity to compete." [11]

---

[11] In addition, a vertical merger may disrupt and injure competition when those independent customers of the supplier, who are in competition with the merging customer, are forced either to stop handling the supplier's lines, thereby jeopardizing the

Every extended vertical arrangement by its very nature, for at least a time, denies to competitors of the supplier the opportunity to compete for part or all of the trade of the customer-party to the vertical arrangement. However, the Clayton Act does not render unlawful all such vertical arrangements, but forbids only those whose effect "may be substantially to lessen competition, or to tend to create a monopoly" "in any line of commerce in any section of the country." Thus, as we have previously noted,

> [d]etermination of the relevant market is a necessary predicate to a finding of a violation of the Clayton Act because the threatened monopoly must be one which will substantially lessen competition "within the area of effective competition." Substantiality can be determined only in terms of the market affected.

The "area of effective competition" must be determined by reference to a product market (the "line of commerce") and a geographic market (the "section of the country").

The outer boundaries of a product market are determined by the reasonable interchangeability of use or the cross-elasticity of demand between the product itself and substitutes for it.[12] However, within this broad market, well-defined submarkets may exist, which, in themselves, constitute product markets for antitrust purposes.

The boundaries of such a submarket may be determined by examining such practical indicia as industry or public recognition of the submarket as a separate economic entity, the product's peculiar characteristics and uses, unique production facilities, distinct customers, distinct prices, sensitivity to price changes, and specialized vendors. Because § 7 of the Clayton Act prohibits any merger which may substantially lessen competition "in *any* line of commerce" (emphasis supplied), it is necessary to examine the effects of a merger in each such economically significant submarket to determine if there is a reasonable probability that the merger will substantially lessen competition. If such a probability is found to exist, the merger is proscribed.

Applying these considerations to the present case, we conclude that the record supports the District Court's finding that the relevant lines of commerce are men's, women's, and children's shoes. These product lines are recognized by the public; each line is manufactured in separate plants; each has characteristics peculiar to itself rendering it generally noncompetitive with the others; and each is directed toward a distinct class of customers.

Appellant, however, contends that the District Court's definitions fail to recognize sufficiently "price/quality" and "age/sex" distinctions in shoes. Brown argues that the predominantly medium-priced shoes which it manufactures occupy a product market different from the predominantly low-priced shoes which Kinney sells. But agreement with that argument would be equivalent to holding that me-

---

goodwill they have developed, or to retain the supplier's lines, thereby forcing them into competition with their own supplier.

[12] The cross-elasticity of production facilities may also be an important factor in defining a product market within which a vertical merger is to be viewed. However, the District Court made but limited findings concerning the feasibility of interchanging equipment in the manufacture of nonrubber footwear. At the same time, the record supports the court's conclusion that individual plants generally produced shoes in only one of the product lines the court found relevant.

dium-priced shoes do not compete with low-priced shoes. We think the District Court properly found the facts to be otherwise. It would be unrealistic to accept Brown's contention that, for example, men's shoes selling below $8.99 are in a different product market from those selling above $9.00.

This is not to say, however, that "price/quality" differences, where they exist, are unimportant in analyzing a merger; they may be of importance in determining the likely effect of a merger. But the boundaries of the relevant market must be drawn with sufficient breadth to include the competing products of each of the merging companies and to recognize competition where, in fact, competition exists. Thus we agree with the District Court that in this case a further division of product lines based on "price/quality" differences would be "unrealistic."

Brown's contention that the District Court's product market definitions should have recognized further "age/sex" distinctions raises a different problem. Brown's sharpest criticism is directed at the District Court's finding that children's shoes constituted a single line of commerce. Brown argues, for example, that "a little boy does not wear a little girl's black patent leather pump" and that [a] male baby cannot wear a growing boy's shoes." Thus Brown argues that "infants' and babies'" shoes, "misses' and children's" shoes and "youths' and boys'" shoes should each have been considered a separate line of commerce. Assuming *arguendo*, that little boys' shoes, for example, do have sufficient peculiar characteristics to constitute one of the markets to be used in analyzing the effects of this merger, we do not think that in this case the District Court was required to employ finer "age/sex" distinctions than those recognized by its classifications of "men's," "women's," and "children's" shoes. Further division does not aid us in analyzing the effects of this merger. Brown manufactures about the same percentage of the Nation's children's shoes (5.8%) as it does of the Nation's youths' and boys' shoes (6.5%), of the Nation's misses' and children's shoes (6.0%) and of the Nation's infants' and babies' shoes (4.9%). Similarly, Kinney sells about the same percentage of the Nation's children's shoes (2%) as it does of the Nation's youths' and boys' shoes (3.1%), of the Nations' misses' and children's shoes (1.9%), and of the Nation's infants' and babies' shoes (1.5%). Appellant can point to no advantage it would enjoy were finer divisions than those chosen by the District Court employed. Brown manufactures significant, comparable quantities of virtually every type of nonrubber men's, women's, and children's shoes, and Kinney sells quantities of virtually every type of men's, women's, and children's shoes. Thus, whether considered separately or together, the picture of this merger is the same. We, therefore, agree with the District Court's conclusion that in the setting of this case to subdivide the shoe market further on the basis of "age/sex" distinctions would be "impractical" and "unwarranted."

We agree with the parties and the District Court that insofar as the vertical aspect of this merger is concerned, the relevant geographic market is the entire Nation. The relationship of product value, bulk, weight, and consumer demand enable manufacturers to distribute their shoes on a nationwide basis, as Brown and Kinney, in fact, do. The anticompetitive effects of the merger are to be measured within this range of distribution.

Once the area of effective competition affected by a vertical arrangement has been defined, an analysis must be made to determine if the effect of the arrangement "may be substantially to lessen competition, or to tend to create a monopoly" in this market.

Since the diminution of the vigor of competition which may stem from a vertical arrangement results primarily from a foreclosure of a share of the market otherwise open to competitors, an important consideration in determining whether the effect of a vertical arrangement "may be substantially to lessen competition, or to tend to create a monopoly" is the size of the share of the market foreclosed. However, this factor will seldom be determinative. If the share of the market foreclosed is so large that it approaches monopoly proportions, the Clayton Act will, of course, have been violated; but the arrangement will also have run afoul of the Sherman Act. And the legislative history of § 7 indicates clearly that the tests for measuring the legality of any particular economic arrangement under the Clayton Act are to be less stringent than those used in applying the Sherman Act. On the other hand, foreclosure of a *de minimus* share of the market will not tend "substantially to lessen competition."

Between these extremes, in cases such as the one before us, in which the foreclosure is neither of monopoly nor *de minimus* proportions, the percentage of the market foreclosed by the vertical arrangement cannot itself be decisive. In such cases, it becomes necessary to undertake an examination of various economic and historical factors in order to determine whether the arrangement under review is of the type Congress sought to proscribe.

A most important such factor to examine is the very nature and purpose of the arrangement. Congress not only indicated that "the tests of illegality [under § 7] are intended to be similar to those which the courts have applied in interpreting the same language as used in other sections of the Clayton Act," but also chose for § 7 language virtually identical to that of § 3 of the Clayton Act, which had been interpreted by this Court to require an examination of the interdependence of the market share foreclosed by, and the economic purpose of, the vertical arrangement. Thus, for example, if a particular vertical arrangement, considered under § 3, appears to be a limited term exclusive-dealing contract, the market foreclosure must generally be significantly greater than if the arrangement is a tying contract before the arrangement will be held to have violated the Act. The reason for this is readily discernible. The usual tying contract forces the customer to take a product or brand he does not necessarily want in order to secure one which he does desire. Because such an arrangement is inherently anticompetitive, we have held that its use by an established company is likely "substantially to lessen competition" although only a relatively small amount of commerce is affected. Thus, unless the tying device is employed by a small company in an attempt to break into a market, the use of a tying device can rarely be harmonized with the strictures of the antitrust laws, which are intended primarily to preserve and stimulate competition. On the other hand, requirement contracts are frequently negotiated at the behest of the customer who has chosen the particular supplier and his product upon the basis of competitive merit. Of course, the fact that requirement contracts are not inherently anticompetitive will not save a particular agreement if, in fact, it is likely "substantially to lessen competition, or tend to create a monopoly." Yet a requirement contract may escape censure if only a small share of the market is involved, if the purpose of the agreement is to insure to the customer a sufficient supply of a commodity vital to the customer's trade or to insure to the supplier a market for his output and if there is no trend toward concentration in the industry.

Similar considerations are pertinent to a judgment under § 7 of the Act.

The importance which Congress attached to economic purpose is further demonstrated by the Senate and House Reports on H.R. 2734, which evince an intention to preserve the "failing company" doctrine of *International Shoe Co. v. Federal Trade Comm'n.* Similarly, Congress foresaw that the merger of two large companies or a large and a small company might violate the Clayton Act while the merger of two small companies might not, although the share of the market foreclosed be identical, if the purpose of the small companies is to enable them in combination to compete with larger corporations dominating the market.

The present merger involved neither small companies nor failing companies. In 1955, the date of this merger, Brown was the fourth largest manufacturer in the shoe industry with sales of approximately 25 million pairs of shoes and assets of over $72,000,000 while Kinney had sales of about 8 million pairs of shoes and assets of about $18,000,000. Not only was Brown one of the leading manufacturers of men's, women's, and children's shoes, but Kinney, with over 350 retail outlets, owned and operated the largest independent chain of family shoe stores in the Nation. Thus, in this industry, no merger between a manufacturer and an independent retailer could involve a larger potential market foreclosure. Moreover, it is apparent both from past behavior of Brown and from the testimony of Brown's President, that Brown would use its ownership of Kinney to force Brown shoes into Kinney stores. Thus, in operation this vertical arrangement would be quite analogous to one involving a tying clause.

Another important factor to consider is the trend toward concentration in the industry. It is true, of course, that the statute prohibits a given merger only if the effect of *that* merger may be substantially to lessen competition. But the very wording of § 7 requires a prognosis of the probable *future* effect of the merger.

The existence of a trend toward vertical integration, which the District Court found, is well substantiated by the record. Moreover, the court found a tendency of the acquiring manufacturers to become increasingly important sources of supply for their acquired outlets. The necessary corollary of these trends is the foreclosure of independent manufacturers from markets otherwise open to them. And because these trends are not the product of accident but are rather the result of deliberate policies of Brown and other leading shoe manufacturers, account must be taken of these facts in order to predict the probable future consequences of this merger. It is against this background of continuing concentration that the present merger must be viewed.

Brown argues, however, that the shoe industry is at present composed of a large number of manufacturers and retailers, and that the industry is dynamically competitive. But remaining vigor cannot immunize a merger if the trend in that industry is toward oligopoly. It is the probable effect of the merger upon the future as well as the present which the Clayton Act commands the courts and the Commission to examine.

Moreover, as we have remarked above, not only must we consider the probable effects of the merger upon the economics of the particular markets affected but also we must consider its probable effects upon the economic way of life sought to be preserved by Congress. Congress was desirous of preventing the formation of further oligopolies with their attendant adverse effects upon local control of industry and upon small business. Where an industry was composed of numerous independent units, Congress appeared anxious to preserve this structure. The Senate Report, quoting with approval from the Federal Trade Commission's 1948 report on the merger movement, states explicitly that amended § 7 is addressed, *inter alia,* to the following problem:

> Under the Sherman Act, an acquisition is unlawful if it creates a monopoly or constitutes an attempt to monopolize. Imminent monopoly may appear when one large concern acquires another, but it is unlikely to be perceived in a small acquisition by a large enterprise. As a large concern grows through a series of such small acquisitions, its accretions of power are individually so minute as to make it difficult to use the Sherman Act test against them. . . .
>
> Where several large enterprises are extending their power by successive small acquisitions, the cumulative effect of their purchases may be to convert an industry from one of intense competition among many enterprises to one in which three or four large concerns produce the entire supply.

The District Court's findings, and the record facts convince us that the shoe industry is being subjected to just such a cumulative series of vertical mergers which, if left unchecked, will be likely "substantially to lessen competition."

We reach this conclusion because the trend toward vertical integration in the shoe industry, when combined with Brown's avowed policy of forcing its own shoes upon its retail subsidiaries, may foreclose competition from a substantial share of the markets for men's, women's, and children's shoes, without producing any countervailing competitive, economic, or social advantages.

An economic arrangement between companies performing similar functions in the production or sale of comparable goods or services is characterized as "horizontal." The effect on competition of such an arrangement depends, of course, upon its character and scope. Thus, its validity in the face of the antitrust laws will depend upon such factors as: The relative size and number of the parties to the arrangement; whether it allocates shares of the market among the parties; whether it fixes prices at which the parties will sell their product; or whether it absorbs or insulates competitors. Where the arrangement effects a horizontal merger between companies occupying the same product and geographic market, whatever competition previously may have existed in that market between the parties to the merger is eliminated. Section 7 of the Clayton Act, prior to its amendment, focused upon this aspect of horizontal combinations by proscribing acquisitions which might result in a lessening of competition between the acquiring and the acquired companies. The 1950 amendments made plain Congress' intent that the validity of such combinations was to be gauged on a broader scale: their effect on competition generally in an economically significant market.

Thus again, the proper definition of the market is a "necessary predicate" to an examination of the competition that may be affected by the horizontal aspects of the merger. The acquisition of Kinney by Brown resulted in a horizontal combination at both the manufacturing and retailing levels of their businesses. Although the District Court found that the merger of Brown's and Kinney's *manufacturing* facilities was economically too insignificant to come within the prohibitions of the Clayton Act, the Government has not appealed from this portion of the lower court's decision. Therefore, we have no occasion to express our views with respect to that finding. On the other hand, appellant does contest the District Court's finding that the merger of the companies' *retail* outlets may tend substantially to lessen competition.

Shoes are sold in the United States in retail shoe stores and in shoe departments of general stores. These outlets sell: (1) men's shoes, (2) women's shoes, (3) women's or children's shoes, or (4) men's, women's or children's shoes. Prior to the merger, both Brown and Kinney sold their shoes in competition with one another through the enumerated kinds of outlets characteristic of the industry.

We hold that the District Court correctly defined men's, women's, and children's shoes as the relevant lines of commerce in which to analyze the vertical aspects of the merger. We also hold that the same lines of commerce are appropriate for considering the horizontal aspects of the merger.

The criteria to be used in determining the appropriate geographic market are essentially similar to those used to determine the relevant product market.

Moreover, just as a product submarket may have § 7 significance as the proper "line of commerce," so may a geographic submarket be considered the appropriate "section of the country." Congress prescribed a pragmatic, factual approach to the definition of the relevant market and not a formal, legalistic one. The geographic market selected must, therefore, both "correspond to the commercial realities" of the industry and be economically significant. Thus, although the geographic market in some instances may encompass the entire Nation, under other circumstances it may be as small as a single metropolitan area. The fact that two merging firms have competed directly on the horizontal level in but a fraction of the geographic markets in which either has operated, does not, in itself, place their merger outside the scope of § 7. That section speaks of "any . . . section of the country," and if anticompetitive effects of a merger are probable in "any" significant market, the merger—at least to that extent—is proscribed.[13]

The parties do not dispute the findings of the District Court that the Nation as a whole is the relevant geographic market for measuring the anticompetitive effects of the merger viewed vertically or of the horizontal merger of Brown's and Kinney's manufacturing facilities. As to the retail level, however, they disagree.

The District Court found that the effects of this aspect of the merger must be analyzed in every city with a population exceeding 10,000 and its immediate contiguous surrounding territory in which both Brown and Kinney sold shoes at retail through stores they either owned or controlled.[14] By this definition of the

---

[13] To illustrate: If two retailers, one operating primarily in the eastern half of the Nation, and the other operating largely in the West, competed in but two mid-Western cities, the fact that the latter outlets represented but a small share of each company's business would not immunize the merger in those markets in which competition might be adversely affected. On the other hand, that fact would, of course, be properly considered in determining the equitable relief to be decreed.

[14] In describing the geographic market in which Brown and Kinney competed, the District Court included cities in which Brown "Franchise Plan" and "Wohl Plan" stores were located. Although such stores were not owned or directly controlled by Brown, did not sell Brown products exclusively and did not finance inventory through Brown, we believe there was adequate evidence before the District Court to support its finding that such stores were "Brown stores." To such stores Brown provided substantial assistance in the form of merchandising and advertising aids, reports on market and management research, loans, group life and fire insurance and centralized purchase of rubber footwear from manufacturers on Brown's credit. For these services, Brown required the retailer to deal almost exclusively in Brown's products in the price scale at which Brown shoes sold. Further, Brown reserved the power to terminate such franchise agreements on 30 days' notice. Since the retailer was required, under this plan, to invest his own resources and develop his good will to a substantial extent in the sale of Brown products, the flow of which Brown could readily terminate, Brown was able to exercise sufficient control over

geographic market, less than one-half of all the cities in which either Brown or Kinney sold shoes through such outlets are represented. The appellant recognizes that if the District Court's characterization of the relevant market is proper, the number of markets in which both Brown and Kinney have outlets is sufficiently numerous so that the validity of the entire merger is properly judged by testing its effects in those markets. However, it is appellant's contention that the areas of effective competition in shoe retailing were improperly defined by the District Court. It claims that such areas should, in some cases, be defined so as to include only the central business districts of large cities, and in others, so as to encompass the "standard metropolitan areas" within which smaller communities are found. It argues that any test failing to distinguish between these competitive situations is improper.

We believe, however, that the record fully supports the District Court's findings that shoe stores in the outskirts of cities compete effectively with stores in central downtown areas, and that while there is undoubtedly some commercial intercourse between smaller communities within a single "standard metropolitan area," the most intense and important competition in retail sales will be confined to stores within the particular communities in such an area and their immediate environs.[15]

We therefore agree that the District Court properly defined the relevant geographic markets in which to analyze this merger as those cities with a population exceeding 10,000 and their environs in which both Brown and Kinney retailed shoes through their own outlets. Such markets are large enough to include the downtown shops and suburban shopping centers in areas contiguous to the city, which are the important competitive factors, and yet are small enough to exclude stores beyond the immediate environs of the city, which are of little competitive significance.

Having delineated the product and geographic markets within which the effects of this merger are to be measured, we turn to an examination of the District Court's finding that as a result of the merger competition in the retailing of men's, women's and children's shoes may be lessened substantially in those cities in which both Brown and Kinney stores are located. We note, initially, that appellant challenges this finding on a number of grounds other than those discussed above and on grounds independent of the critical question of whether competition may, in fact, be lessened. Thus, Brown objects that the District Court did not examine the competitive picture in each line of commerce and each section of the country it had defined as appropriate. It says the Court erred in failing to enter findings with respect to each relevant city assessing the anticompetitive effect of the merger on the retail sale of, for example, men's shoes in Council Bluffs, men's shoes in Texas City, women's shoes in Texas City and children's shoes in St. Paul. Even assuming a representative sample could properly be used, Brown also objects that the District Court's detailed analysis of competition in shoe retailing was limited to a single city—St. Louis—a city in which Kinney did not operate. The appellant says this analysis could not be sufficiently representative to establish a standard image of the shoe trade which could be applied to each of the more than 100 cities in

---

these stores and departments to warrant their characterization as "Brown" outlets for the purpose of measuring the share and effect of Brown's competition at the retail level.

[15] The District Court limited its findings to cities having a population of at least 10,000 persons, since Kinney operated only in such areas.

which Brown and Kinney sold shoes, particularly as some of those cities were much smaller than St. Louis, others were larger, some were in different climates and others were in areas having different median per capita incomes.

However, we believe the record is adequate to support the findings of the District Court. While it is true that the court concentrated its attention on the structure of competition in the city in which it sat and as to which detailed evidence was most readily available, it also heard witnesses from no less than 40 other cities in which the parties to the merger operated. The court was careful to point out that it was on the basis of all the evidence that it reached its conclusions concerning the boundaries of the relevant markets and the merger's effects on competition within them. We recognize that variations of size, climate and wealth as enumerated by Brown exist in the relevant markets. However, we agree with the court below that the markets with respect to which evidence was received, provide a fair sampling of all the areas in which the impact of this merger is to be measured. The appellant has not shown how the variables it has mentioned could affect the structure of competition within any particular market so as to require change in the conclusions drawn by the District Court. Each competitor within a given market is equally affected by these factors, even though the city in which he does business may differ from St. Louis in size, climate or wealth. Thus, we believe the District Court properly reached its conclusions on the basis of the evidence available to it. There is no reason to protract already complex antitrust litigation by detailed analyses of peripheral economic facts, if the basic issues of the case may be determined through study of a fair sample.

In the case before us, not only was a fair sample used to demonstrate the soundness of the District Court's conclusions, but evidence of record fully substantiates those findings as to each relevant market. An analysis of undisputed statistics of sales of shoes in the cities in which both Brown and Kinney sell shoes at retail, separated into the appropriate lines of commerce, provides a persuasive factual foundation upon which the required prognosis of the merger's effects may be built. Although Brown objects to some details in the Government's computations used in drafting these exhibits, appellant cannot deny the correctness of the more general picture they reveal.[16] We have appended the exhibits to this opinion. They show,

---

[16] Brown objects, for example, to the fact that these exhibits are drafted on the basis of the *cities* concerning which census information was available, rather than on the basis of the *cities and their environs*—as the relevant markets were defined by the District Court. However, the record shows that the statistics of shoe sales in cities by and large conform to statistics of shoe sales in counties in which those cities are the principal metropolitan area. Thus, we find no error in a conclusion drawn as to a slightly larger market from the available record of sales in cities alone. Brown also objects to the use of pairage sales, rather than dollar volume, as the basis for defining the size, and measuring Brown's shares, of the market. However, since Brown and Kinney sold shoes primarily in the low and medium price ranges, and in the light of the conceded spread in shoe prices, we agree that sales measured in pairage provide a more accurate picture of the Brown-Kinney shares of the market than do sales measured in dollars. Detailed statistics of shoe sales were available only in terms of dollar volume, however, and Brown objects to the method by which the Government has converted those figures into those reflecting sales in terms of pairage. The Government's conversion was, with some exceptions, based on national median income and national averages of shoe prices and the ratio of men, women and children in the population. The District Court accepted expert testimony offered by the Government to the effect that shoe price and population, age, sex, and income variations in the relevant cities produced, at most, a 6% error in the converted statistics, and

for example, that during 1955 in 32 separate cities, ranging in size and location from Topeka, Kansas, to Batavia, New York, and Hobbs, New Mexico, the combined share of Brown and Kinney sales of women's shoes (by unit volume) exceeded 20%.[17] In 31 cities—some the same as those used in measuring the effect of the merger in the women's line—the combined share of children's shoes sales exceeded 20%; in 6 cities their share exceeded 40%. In Dodge City, Kansas, their combined share of the market for women's shoes was over 57%; their share of the children's shoe market in that city was 49%. In the 7 cities in which Brown's and Kinney's combined shares of the market for women's shoes were greatest (ranging from 33% to 57%) each of the parties alone, prior to the merger, had captured substantial portions of those markets (ranging from 13% to 34%); the merger intensified this existing concentration. In 118 separate cities the combined shares of the market of Brown and Kinney in the sale of one of the relevant lines of commerce exceeded 5%. In 47 cities, their share exceeded 5% in all three lines.

The market share which companies may control by merging is one of the most important factors to be considered when determining the probable effects of the combination on effective competition in the relevant market. In an industry as fragmented as shoe retailing, the control of substantial shares of the trade in a city may have important effects on competition. If a merger achieving 5% control were now approved, we might be required to approve future merger efforts by Brown's competitors seeking similar market shares. The oligopoly Congress sought to avoid would then be furthered and it would be difficult to dissolve the combinations previously approved. Furthermore, in this fragmented industry, even if the combination controls but a small share of a particular market, the fact that this share is held by a large national chain can adversely affect competition. Testimony in the record from numerous independent retailers, based on their actual experience in the market, demonstrates that a strong, national chain of stores can insulate selected outlets from the vagaries of competition in particular locations and that the large chains can set and alter styles in footwear to an extent that renders the inde-

---

that this error was as likely to favor Brown (by increasing the universe of sales against which Brown's shares were to be measured) as it was to disfavor it. We find no error in the District Court's acceptance of the Government's evidence as to the propriety of the accounting methods its experts employed. Lastly, Brown objects that the statistics concerning its own pairage sales were improperly derived since they included sales by its wholesale distributors to the retail outlets on its franchise plans in the same category as sales to ultimate consumers by its owned retail stores. Again, while recognizing a possible margin of error in statistics combining sales at two levels of distribution, we believe they provide an adequate basis upon which to gauge Brown sales through outlets it controlled. Particularly as the franchise stores were required to finance their own inventory, does it seem reasonable to conclude that most of their purchases from Brown's distributors were eventually resold. In summary, although appellant may point to technical flaws in the compilation of these statistics, we recognize that in cases of this type precision in detail is less important than the accuracy of the broad picture presented. We believe the picture as presented by the Government in this case is adequate for making the determination required by § 7: whether this merger *may* tend to lessen competition substantially in the relevant markets.

[17] Although the sum of the parties' pre-existing shares of the market will normally equal their combined share of the immediate post-merger market, we recognize that this share need not remain stable in the future. Nevertheless, such statistics provide a graphic picture of the immediate impact of a merger, and, as such, also provide a meaningful base upon which to build conclusions of the probable future effects of the merger.

pendents unable to maintain competitive inventories. A third significant aspect of this merger is that it creates a large national chain which is integrated with a manufacturing operation. The retail outlets of integrated companies, by eliminating wholesalers and by increasing the volume of purchases from the manufacturing division of the enterprise, can market their own brands at prices below those of competing independent retailers. Of course, some of the results of large integrated or chain operations are beneficial to consumers. Their expansion is not rendered unlawful by the mere fact that small independent stores may be adversely affected. It is competition, not competitors, which the Act protects. But we cannot fail to recognize Congress' desire to promote competition through the protection of viable, small, locally owned businesses. Congress appreciated that occasional higher costs and prices might result from the maintenance of fragmented industries and markets. It resolved these competing considerations in favor of decentralization. We must give effect to that decision.

Other factors to be considered in evaluating the probable effects of a merger in the relevant market lend additional support to the District Court's conclusion that this merger may substantially lessen competition. One such factor is the history of tendency toward concentration in the industry.[18] As we have previously pointed out, the shoe industry has, in recent years, been a prime example of such a trend. Most combinations have been between manufacturers and retailers, as each of the larger producers has sought to capture an increasing number of assured outlets for its wares. Although these mergers have been primarily vertical in their aim and effect, to the extent that they have brought ever greater numbers of retail outlets within fewer and fewer hands, they have had an additional important impact on the horizontal plane. By the merger in this case, the largest single group of retail stores still independent of one of the large manufacturers was absorbed into an already substantial aggregation of more or less controlled retail outlets. As a result of this merger, Brown moved into second place nationally in terms of retail stores directly owned. Including the stores on its franchise plan, the merger placed under Brown's control almost 1,600 shoe outlets, or about 7.2% of the Nation's retail "shoe stores" as defined by the Census Bureau and 2.3% of the Nation's total retail shoe outlets.[19] We cannot avoid the mandate of Congress that tendencies toward concentration in industry are to be curbed in their incipiency, particularly when those tendencies are being accelerated through giant steps striding across a hundred cities at a time. In the light of the trends in this industry we agree with the Government and the court below that this is an appropriate place at which to call a halt.

[18] A company's history of expansion through mergers presents a different economic picture than a history of expansion through unilateral growth. Internal expansion is more likely to be the result of increased demand for the company's products and is more likely to provide increased investment in plants, more jobs and greater output. Conversely, expansion through merger is more likely to reduce available consumer choice while providing no increase in industry capacity, jobs or output. It was for these reasons, among others, Congress expressed its disapproval of successive acquisitions. Section 7 was enacted to prevent even small mergers that added to concentration in an industry.

[19] Although statistics concerning the degree of concentration and the rank of Brown-Kinney in terms of controlled retail stores in each of the relevant product and geographic markets would have been more helpful in analyzing the results of this merger, neither side has presented such statistics. The figures in the record, based on national rank, are, nevertheless, useful in depicting the trends in the industry.

At the same time appellant has presented no mitigating factors, such as the business failure or the inadequate resources of one of the parties that may have prevented it from maintaining its competitive position, nor a demonstrated need for combination to enable small companies to enter into a more meaningful competition with those dominating the relevant markets. On the basis of the record before us, we believe the Government sustained its burden of proof. We hold that the District Court was correct in concluding that this merger may tend to lessen competition substantially in the retail sale of men's, women's, and children's shoes in the overwhelming majority of those cities and their environs in which both Brown and Kinney sell through owned or controlled outlets.

The judgment is

Affirmed.

MR. JUSTICE FRANKFURTER took no part in the decision of this case.

MR. JUSTICE WHITE took no part in the consideration or decision of this case.

PROCTER & GAMBLE

This is a proceeding initiated by the Federal Trade Commission charging that respondent, Procter & Gamble Co., had acquired the assets of Clorox Chemical Co. in violation of Section 7 of the Clayton Act, 38 Stat. 731, as amended by the Celler-Kefauver Act.[20] The charge was that Procter's acquisition of Clorox may substantially lessen competition or tend to create a monopoly in the production and sale of household liquid bleaches.

Following evidentiary hearings, the hearing examiner rendered his decision in which he concluded that the acquisition was unlawful and ordered divestiture. On appeal, the Commission reversed, holding that the record as then constituted was inadequate. and remanded to the examiner for additional evidentiary hearings. After the additional hearings, the examiner again held the acquisition unlawful and ordered divestiture. The Commission affirmed the examiner and ordered divestiture. The Court of Appeals for the Sixth Circuit reversed and directed that the Commission's complaint be dismissed. We find that the Commission's findings were amply supported by the evidence, and that the Court of Appeals erred.

As indicated by the Commission in its painstaking and illuminating report, it does not particularly aid analysis to talk of this merger in conventional terms, namely, horizontal or vertical or conglomerate. This merger may most appropriately be described as a "product-extension merger," as the Commission stated. The facts are not disputed, and a summary will demonstrate the correctness of the Commission's decision.

At the time of the merger in 1957, Clorox was the leading manufacturer in the heavily concentrated household liquid bleach industry. It is agreed that household liquid bleach is the relevant line of commerce. The product is used in the home as a germicide and disinfectant, and, more importantly, as a whitening agent in washing clothes and fabrics. It is a distinctive product with no close sub-

---

[20] "No corporation engaged in commerce shall acquire, directly or indirectly, the whole or any part of the stock or other share capital and no corporation subject to the jurisdiction of the Federal Trade Commission shall acquire the whole or any part of the assets of another corporation engaged also in commerce, where in any line of commerce in any section of the country, the effect of such acquisition may be substantially to lessen competition, or to tend to create a monopoly."

stitutes. Liquid bleach is a low-price, high-turnover consumer product sold mainly through grocery stores and supermarkets. The relevant geographical market is the Nation and a series of regional markets. Because of high shipping costs and low sales price, it is not feasible to ship the product more than 300 miles from its point of manufacture. Most manufacturers are limited to competition within a single region since they have but one plant. Clorox is the only firm selling nationally; it has 13 plants distributed throughout the Nation. Purex, Clorox's closest competitor in size, does not distribute its bleach in the northeast or mid-Atlantic States; in 1957, Purex's bleach was available in less than 50% of the national market.

At the time of the acquisition, Clorox was the leading manufacturer of household liquid bleach, with 48.8% of the national sales—annual sales of slightly less than $40,000,000. Its market share had been steadily increasing for the five years prior to the merger. Its nearest rival was Purex, which manufactures a number of products other than household liquid bleaches, including abrasive cleaners, toilet soap, and detergents. Purex accounted for 15.7% of the household liquid bleach market. The industry is highly concentrated; in 1957, Clorox and Purex accounted for almost 65% of the Nation's household liquid bleach sales, and, together with four other firms, for almost 80%. The remaining 20% was divided among over 200 small producers. Clorox had total assets of $12,000,000; only eight producers had assets in excess of $1,000,000 and very few had assets of more than $75,000.

In light of the territorial limitations on distribution, national figures do not give an accurate picture of Clorox's dominance in the various regions. Thus, Clorox's seven principal competitors did no business in New England, the mid-Atlantic States, or metropolitan New York. Clorox's share of the sales in those areas was 56%, 72%, and 64% respectively. Even in regions where its principal competitors were active, Clorox maintained a dominant position. Except in metropolitan Chicago and the west-central States Clorox accounted for at least 39%, and often a much higher percentage, of liquid bleach sales.

Since all liquid bleach is chemically identical, advertising and sales promotion are vital. In 1957 Clorox spent almost $3,700,000 on advertising, imprinting the value of its bleach in the mind of the consumer. In addition, it spent $1,700,000 for other promotional activities. The Commission found that these heavy expenditures went far to explain why Clorox maintained so high a market share despite the fact that its brand, though chemically indistinguishable from rival brands, retailed for a price equal to or, in many instances, higher than its competitors.

Procter is a large, diversified manufacturer of low-price, high-turnover household products sold through grocery, drug, and department stores. Prior to its acquisition of Clorox, it did not produce household liquid bleach. Its 1957 sales were in excess of $1,100,000,000 from which it realized profits of more than $67,000,000; its assets were over $500,000,000. Procter has been marked by rapid growth and diversification. It has successfully developed and introduced a number of new products. Its primary activity is in the general area of soaps, detergents, and cleansers; in 1957, of total domestic sales, more than one-half (over $500,000,000) were in this field. Procter was the dominant factor in this area. It accounted for 54.4% of all packaged detergent sales. The industry is heavily concentrated—Procter and its nearest competitors, Colgate-Palmolive and Lever Brothers, account for 80% of the market.

In the marketing of soaps, detergents, and cleansers, as in the marketing of household liquid bleach, advertising and sales promotion are vital. In 1957, Procter was the Nation's largest advertiser, spending more than $80,000,000 on advertising and an additional $47,000,000 on sales promotion. Due to its tremendous volume, Procter receives substantial discounts from the media. As a multi-product producer Procter enjoys substantial advantages in advertising and sales promotion. Thus, it can and does feature several products in its promotions, reducing the printing, mailing, and other costs for each product. It also purchases network programs on behalf of several products, enabling it to give each product network exposure at a fraction of the cost per product that a firm with only one product to advertise would incur.

Prior to the acquisition, Procter was in the course of diversifying into product lines related to its basic detergent-soap-cleanser business. Liquid bleach was a distinct possibility since packaged detergents—Procter's primary product line—and liquid bleach are used complementarily in washing clothes and fabrics, and in general household cleaning. As noted by the Commission:

> Packaged detergents—Procter's most important product category—and household liquid bleach are used complementarily, not only in the washing of clothes and fabrics, but also in general household cleaning, since liquid bleach is a germicide and disinfectant as well as a whitener. From the consumer's viewpoint, then, packaged detergents and liquid bleach are closely related products. But the area of relatedness between products of Procter and of Clorox is wider. Household cleansing agents in general, like household liquid bleach, are low-cost, high-turnover household consumer goods marketed chiefly through grocery stores and presold to the consumer by the manufacturer through mass advertising and sales promotions. Since products of both parties to the merger are sold to the same customers, at the same stores, and by the same merchandising methods, the possibility arises of significant integration at both the marketing and distribution levels.

The decision to acquire Clorox was the result of a study conducted by Procter's promotion department designed to determine the advisability of entering the liquid bleach industry. The initial report noted the ascendancy of liquid bleach in the large and expanding household bleach market, and recommended that Procter purchase Clorox rather than enter independently. Since a large investment would be needed to obtain a satisfactory market share, acquisition of the industry's leading firm was attractive. "Taking over the Clorox business . . . could be a way of achieving a dominant position in the liquid bleach market quickly, which would pay out reasonably well." The initial report predicted that Procter's "sales, distribution and manufacturing setup" could increase Clorox's share of the markets in areas where it was low. The final report confirmed the conclusions of the initial report and emphasized that Procter could make more effective use of Clorox's advertising budget and that the merger would facilitate advertising economies. A few months later, Procter acquired the assets of Clorox in the name of a wholly owned subsidiary, the Clorox Company, in exchange for Procter stock.

The Commission found that the acquisition might substantially lessen competition. The findings and reasoning of the Commission need be only briefly summarized. The Commission found that the substitution of Procter with its huge assets and advertising advantages for the already dominant Clorox would dissuade new entrants and discourage active competition from the firms already in the industry due to fear of retaliation by Procter. The Commission thought it relevant that retailers might be induced to give Clorox preferred shelf space since it would be manufactured by Procter, which also produced a number of other products marketed by the retailers. There was also the danger that Procter might under-price Clorox in order to drive out competition, and subsidize the underpricing with revenue from other products. The Commission carefully reviewed the effect of the acquisition on the structure of the industry, noting that "[t]he practical tendency of the . . . merger . . . is to transform the liquid bleach industry into an arena of big business competition only, with the few small firms that have not dis-appeared through merger eventually falling by the wayside, unable to compete with their giant rivals." Further, the merger would seriously diminish potential competition by eliminating Procter as a potential entrant into the industry. Prior to the merger, the Commission found that Procter was the most likely prospective entrant, and absent the merger would have remained on the periphery, restraining Clorox from exercising its market power. If Procter had actually entered, Clorox's dominant position would have been eroded and the concentration of the industry reduced. The Commission stated that it had not placed reliance on post-acquisition evidence in holding the merger unlawful.

The Court of Appeals said that the Commission's finding of illegality had been based on "treacherous conjecture," mere possibility and suspicion. It dis-missed the fact that Clorox controlled almost 50% of the industry, that two firms controlled 65%, and that six firms controlled 80% with the observation that "the fact that in addition to the six . . . producers sharing eighty per cent of the market, there were two hundred smaller producers . . . would not seem to indicate any-thing unhealthy about the market conditions." It dismissed the finding that Proc-ter, with its huge resources and prowess, would have more leverage than Clorox with the statement that it was Clorox which had the "know-how" in the industry, and that Clorox's finances were adequate for its purposes. As for the possibility that Procter would use its tremendous advertising budget and volume discounts to push Clorox, the court found "it difficult to base a finding of illegality on dis-counts on advertising." It rejected the Commission's finding that the merger elimi-nated the potential competition of Procter because "there was no reasonable prob-ability that Procter would have entered the household liquid bleach market but for the merger." "There was no evidence tending to prove that Procter ever in-tended to enter this field on its own." Finally, "there was no evidence that Procter at any time in the past engaged in predatory practices, or that it intended to do so in the future."

The Court of Appeals also heavily relied on post-acquisition "evidence to the effect that the other producers subsequent to the merger were selling more bleach for more money than ever before," and "there [had] been no significant change in Clorox's market share in the four years subsequent to the merger," and concluded that "this evidence certainly does not prove anti-competitive effects of the merger." The Court of Appeals, in our view, misapprehended the standards for its review and the standards applicable in a § 7 proceeding.

Section 7 of the Clayton Act was intended to arrest the anticompetitive effects of market power in their incipiency. The core question is whether a merger may substantially lessen competition, and necessarily requires a prediction of the merger's impact on competition, present and future. The section can deal only with probabilities, not with certainties. And there is certainly no requirement that the anticompetitive power manifest itself in anticompetitive actions before § 7 can be called into play. If the enforcement of § 7 turned on the existence of actual anticompetitive practices, the congressional policy of thwarting such practices in their incipiency would be frustrated.

All mergers are within the reach of § 7, and all must be tested by the same standard, whether they are classified as horizontal, vertical, conglomerate[21] or other. As noted by the Commission, this merger is neither horizontal, vertical, nor conglomerate. Since the products of the acquired company are complementary to those of the acquiring company and may be produced with similar facilities, marketed through the same channels and in the same manner, and advertised by the same media, the Commission aptly called this acquisition a "product-extension merger":

> By this acquisition . . . Procter has not diversified its interests in the sense of expanding into a substantially different, unfamiliar market or industry. Rather, it has entered a market which adjoins, as it were, those markets in which it is already established, and which is virtually indistinguishable from them insofar as the problems and techniques of marketing the product to the ultimate consumer are concerned. As a high official of Procter put it, commenting on the acquisition of Clorox, "While this is a completely new business for us, taking us for the first time into the marketing of a household bleach and disinfectant, we are thoroughly at home in the field of manufacturing and marketing low priced rapid turn-over consumer products."

The anticompetitive effects with which this product-extension merger is fraught can easily be seen: (1) the substitution of the powerful acquiring firm for the smaller, but already dominant, firm may substantially reduce the competitive structure of the industry by raising entry barriers and by dissuading the smaller firms from aggressively competing; (2) the acquisition eliminates the potential competition of the acquiring firm.

The liquid bleach industry was already oligopolistic before the acquisition, and price competition was certainly not as vigorous as it would have been if the industry were competitive. Clorox enjoyed a dominant position nationally, and its position approached monopoly proportions in certain areas. The existence of some 200 fringe firms certainly does not belie that fact. Nor does the fact, relied upon by the court below, that after the merger, producers other than Clorox "were selling more bleach for more money than ever before." In the same period, Clorox increased its share from 48.8% to 52%. The interjection of Procter into the market considerably changed the situation. There is every reason to assume that the smaller firms would become more cautious in competing due to their fear of retaliation by Procter. It is probable that Procter would become the price leader and that oligopoly would become more rigid.

The acquisition may also have the tendency of raising the barriers to new entry. The major competitive weapon in the successful marketing of bleach is advertising. Clorox was limited in this area by its relatively small budget and its inability to obtain substantial discounts. By contrast, Procter's budget was much larger; and, although it would not devote its entire budget to advertising Clorox, it could divert a large portion to meet the short-term threat of a new entrant. Procter would be able to use its volume discounts to advantage in advertising

---

[21] A pure conglomerate merger is one in which there are no economic relationships between the acquiring and the acquired firm.

Clorox. Thus, a new entrant would be much more reluctant to face the giant Procter than it would have been to face the smaller Clorox.[22]

Possible economies cannot be used as a defense to illegality. Congress was aware that some mergers which lessen competition may also result in economies but it struck the balance in favor of protecting competition.

The Commission also found that the acquisition of Clorox by Procter eliminated Procter as a potential competitor. The Court of Appeals declared that this finding was not supported by evidence because there was no evidence that Procter's management had ever intended to enter the industry independently and that Procter had never attempted to enter. The evidence, however, clearly shows that Procter was the most likely entrant. Procter had recently launched a new abrasive cleaner in an industry similar to the liquid bleach industry, and had wrested leadership from a brand that had enjoyed even a larger market share than had Clorox. Procter was engaged in a vigorous program of diversifying into product lines closely related to its basic products. Liquid bleach was a natural avenue of diversification since it is complementary to Procter's products, is sold to the same customers through the same channels, and is advertised and merchandised in the same manner. Procter had substantial advantages in advertising and sales promotions, which, as we have seen, are vital to the success of liquid bleach. No manufacturer had a patent on the product or its manufacture, necessary information relating to manufacturing methods and processes was readily available, there was no shortage of raw material, and the machinery and equipment required for a plant of efficient capacity were available at reasonable cost. Procter's management was experienced in producing and marketing goods similar to liquid bleach. Procter had considered the possibility of independently entering but decided against it because the acquisition of Clorox would enable Procter to capture a more commanding share of the market.

It is clear that the existence of Procter at the edge of the industry exerted considerable influence on the market. First, the market behavior of the liquid bleach industry was influenced by each firm's predictions of the market behavior of its competitors, actual and potential. Second, the barriers to entry by a firm of

---

[22] The barriers to entry have been raised both for entry by new firms and for entry into new geographical markets by established firms. The latter aspect is demonstrated by Purex's lesson in Erie, Pennsylvania. In October 1957, Purex selected Erie, Pennsylvania —where it had not sold previously—as an area in which to test the salability, under competitive conditions, of a new bleach. The leading brands in Erie were Clorox, with 52%, and the "101" brand, sold by Gardner Manufacturing Company, with 29% of the market. Purex launched an advertising and promotional campaign to obtain a broad distribution in a short time, and, in five months captured 33% of the Erie market. Clorox's share dropped to 35% and 101's to 17%. Clorox responded by offering its bleach at reduced prices, and then added an offer of a $1-value ironing board cover for 50¢ with each purchase of Clorox at the reduced price. It also increased its advertising with television spots. The result was to restore Clorox's lost market share and, indeed, to increase it slightly. Purex's share fell to 7%.

Since the merger Purex has acquired the fourth largest producer of bleach, John Puhl Products Company, which owned and marketed "Fleecy White" brand in geographic markets which Purex was anxious to enter. One of the reasons for this acquisition, according to Purex's president, was that:

"Purex had been unsuccessful in expanding its market position geographically on Purex liquid bleach. The economics of the bleach business, and the strong competitive factors as illustrated by our experience in Erie, Pennsylvania, make it impossible, in our judgment, for us to expand our market on liquid bleach."

Procter's size and with its advantages were not significant. There is no indication that the barriers were so high that the price Procter would have to charge would be above the price that would maximize the profits of the existing firms. Third, the number of potential entrants was not so large that the elimination of one would be insignificant. Few firms would have the temerity to challenge a firm as solidly entrenched as Clorox. Fourth, Procter was found by the Commission to be the most likely entrant. These findings of the Commission were amply supported by the evidence.

The judgment of the Court of Appeals is reversed and remanded with instructions to affirm and enforce the Commission's order.

MR. JUSTICE HARLAN, concurring with the majority decision, stated:

> I agree that the Commission's order should be sustained, but I do not share the majority opinion's view that a mere "summary will demonstrate the correctness of the Commission's decision" or that "[t]he anticompetitive effects with which this product-extension merger is fraught can easily be seen." I consider the case difficult within its own four corners, and beyond that, its portents for future administrative and judicial application of § 7 of the Clayton Act to this kind of merger important and far-reaching. From both standpoints more refined analysis is required before putting the stamp of approval on what the Commission has done in this case. It is regrettable to see this Court as it enters this comparatively new field of economic adjudication starting off with what has almost become a kind of *res ipsa loquitur* approach to antitrust cases.

The type of merger represented by the transaction before us is becoming increasingly important as large corporations seek to diversify their operations, and "[c]ompanies looking for new lines of business tend to buy into those fields with which they had at least some degree of familiarity, and where economies and efficiencies from assimilation are at least possible." Application of § 7 to such mergers has been troubling to the Commission and the lower courts. The author of the Commission's exhaustive opinion in this case later explained that "the elaborateness of the opinion . . . reflected the Commission's awareness that it was entering relatively uncharted territory." The Sixth Circuit was equally troubled in this case by the lack of standards in the area and had difficulty in perceiving any effect on competition from the merger since "Procter merely stepped into the shoes of Clorox."

I thus believe that it is incumbent upon us to make a careful study of the facts and opinions below in this case, and at least to embark upon the formulation of standards for the application of § 7 to mergers which are neither horizontal nor vertical and which previously have not been considered in depth by this Court. I consider this especially important in light of the divisions which have arisen in the Commission itself in similar cases decided subsequent to this one. My prime difficulty with the Court's opinion is that it makes no effort in this direction at all, and leaves the Commission, lawyers, and businessmen at large as to what is to be expected of them in future cases of this kind.

The Court's opinion rests on three separate findings of anticompetitive effect. The Court first declares that the market here was "oligopolistic" and that interjection of Procter would make the oligopoly "more rigid" because "[t]here is every reason to assume that the smaller firms would become more cautious in competing due to their fear of retaliation by Procter." The Court, however, does not indicate exactly what reasons lie behind this assumption or by what standard such an effect is deemed "reasonably probable." It could equally be assumed that smaller firms would become more aggressive in competing due to their fear that otherwise Procter might ultimately absorb their markets and that Procter, as a new entrant in the bleach field, was vulnerable to attack.

But assumption is no substitute for reasonable probability as a measure of illegality under § 7, and Congress has not mandated the Commission or the courts "to campaign against 'superconcentration' in the absence of any evidence of harm to competition." Moreover, even if an effect of this kind were reasonably predictable, the Court does not explain why the effect on competition should be expected to be the substantial one that § 7 demands. The need for substantiality cannot be ignored, for as a leading economist has warned: "If society were to intervene in every activity which might possibly lead to a reduction of competition, regulation would be ubiquitous and the whole purpose of a public policy of competition would be frustrated."

The Court next stresses the increase in barriers to new entry into the liquid bleach field caused primarily, it is thought, by the substitution of the larger advertising capabilities of Procter for those of Clorox. Economic theory would certainly indicate that a heightening of such barriers has taken place. But the Court does not explain why it considers this change to have significance under § 7, nor does it indicate when or how entry barriers affect competition in a relevant market. In this case, for example, the difficulties of introducing a new nationally advertised bleach were already so great that even a great company like Procter, which the Court finds the most likely entrant, believed that entry would not "pay out." [23] Why then does the Court find that a further increase of incalculable proportions in such barriers substantially lessens competition? Such a conclusion at least needs the support of reasoned analysis.[24]

Finally, the Court places much emphasis on the loss to the market of the most likely potential entrant, Procter. Two entirely separate anticompetitive effects might be traced to this loss, and the Court fails to distinguish between them. The first is simply that loss of the most likely entrant increases the operative barriers to entry by decreasing the likelihood that any firm will attempt to surmount them.[25] But this effect merely reinforces the Court's previous entry-barrier argument, which

[23] Thus the Procter memorandum which considered the question of entry into the liquid bleach market stated: "We would not recommend that the Company consider trying to enter this market by introducing a new brand or by trying to expand a sectional brand. This is because we feel it would require a very heavy investment to achieve a major volume in the field, and with the low 'available' [a reference to profit margin] the payout period would be very unattractive."

[24] The need for analysis is even clearer in light of the fact that entry into the market by producers of nonadvertised, locally distributed bleaches was found to be easy. There were no technological barriers to entry, and the capital requirements for entry, with the exception of advertising costs, were small. The Court must at least explain why the threat of such entry and the presence of small competitors in existing regional markets cannot be considered the predominant, and unaffected, form of competition. To establish its point, the Court must either minimize the importance of such competition or show why it would be substantially lessened by the merger.

[25] Bain's pioneering study of barriers to entry, Barriers to New Competition, recognized that such barriers could be surmounted at different price levels by different potential entrants. Thus even without change in the nature of the barriers themselves, the market could become more insulated through loss of the most likely entrant simply because the prevailing market price would have to rise to a higher level than before to induce entry.

I do not find convincing as presented. The second possible effect is that a reasonably probable entrant has been excluded from the market and a measure of horizontal competition has been lost. Certainly the exclusion of what would promise to be an important independent competitor from the market may be sufficient, in itself, to support a finding of illegality under § 7, when the market has few competitors. The Commission, however, expressly refused to find a reasonable probability that Procter would have entered this market on its own, and the Sixth Circuit was in emphatic agreement. The Court certainly cannot mean to set its judgment on the facts against the concurrent findings below, and thus it seems clear to me that no consequence can be attached to the possibility of loss of Procter as an actual competitor.

Thus I believe, with all respect, that the Court has failed to make a convincing analysis of the difficult problem presented, and were no more to be said in favor of the Commission's order I would vote to set it aside.

The Court, following the Commission, points out that this merger is not a pure "conglomerate" merger but may more aptly be labelled a "product-extension" merger. No explanation, however, is offered as to why this distinction has any significance and the Court in fact declares that all mergers, whatever their nature, "must be tested by the same standard." But no matter what label is attached to this transaction, it certainly must be recognized that the problem we face is vastly different from those which concerned the Court in *Brown Shoe,* and *United States v. Philadelphia National Bank.* And though it is entirely proper to assert that the words of § 7 are the only standard we have with which to work, it is equally important to recognize that different sets of circumstances may call for fundamentally different tests of substantial anticompetitive effect.

At the outset, it seems to me that there is a serious question whether the state of our economic knowledge is sufficiently advanced to enable a sure-footed administrative or judicial determination to be made *a priori* of substantial anticompetitive effect in mergers of this kind. It is clear enough that Congress desired that conglomerate and product-extension mergers be brought under § 7 scrutiny, but well versed economists have argued that such scrutiny can never lead to a valid finding of illegality.

Lending strength to this position is the fact that such mergers do provide significant economic benefits which argue against excessive controls being imposed on them. The ability to merge brings large firms into the market for capital assets and encourages economic development by holding out the incentive of easy and profitable liquidation to others. Here, for example, the owners of Clorox, who had built the business, were able to liquefy their capital on profitable terms without dismantling the enterprise they had created. Also merger allows an active management to move rapidly into new markets bringing with its intervention competitive stimulation and innovation. It permits a large corporation to protect its shareholders from business fluctuation through diversification, and may facilitate the introduction of capital resources, allowing significant economies of scale, into a stagnating market.

At the other end of the spectrum, it has been argued that the entry of a large conglomerate enterprise may have a destructive effect on competition in any market. The big company is said to be able to "outbid, outspend or outlose the small one. . . ." Thus it is contended that a large conglomerate may underprice in one market, adversely affecting competition, and subsidize the operation by benefits accruing elsewhere.[26] It is also argued that the large company generates psychological pressure which may force smaller ones to follow its pricing policies, and that its very presence in the market may discourage entrants or make lending institutions unwilling to finance them.[27] While "business behavior is too complex and varied to permit of a single generalized explanation," these observations do indicate that significant dangers to competition *may* be presented by some conglomerate and product-extension mergers. Further, congressional concern in enacting § 7 extended not only to anticompetitive behavior in particular markets, but also to the possible economic dominance of large companies which had grown through merger. Thus, while fully agreeing that mergers of this kind are not to be regarded as something entirely set apart from scrutiny under § 7, I am of the view that when this Court does undertake to establish the standards for judging their legality, it should proceed with utmost circumspection. Meanwhile, with this case before us, I cannot escape the necessity of venturing my own views as to some of the governing standards.

In adjudicating horizontal and vertical combinations under § 7 where the effects on competition are reasonably obvious and substantiality is the key issue, the responsible agencies have moved away from an initial emphasis on comprehensive scrutiny and opted for more precise rules of thumb which provide advantages of administrative convenience and predictability for the business world.[28] A conglomerate case, however, is not only too new to our experience to allow the formulation of simple rules but also involves "concepts of economic power and competitive effect that are still largely unformulated." This makes clear the need for "full investigation and analysis, whatever the cost in delay or immediate ineffectiveness." Certainly full scale investigation is supported by the considerations adverted to earlier in this opinion and the basic fact that "the statute does not leave us free to strike down mergers on the basis of sheer speculation or a general fear of bigness."

Procter, contending that the broadest possible investigation is required here, and noting "the relative poverty of [economic] information about industrial institutions and the relations among different company complexes, as well as the sketchiness of our understanding of methods of competition in specific industries and

[26] But see Turner, Conglomerate Mergers and Section 7 of the Clayton Act, 78 Harv. L. Rev. 1313, 1340. "[T]he belief that predatory pricing is a likely consequence of conglomerate size, and hence of conglomerate merger, is wholly unverified by any careful studies. . . ."

[27] But see Cook, Merger Law and Big Business: A Look Ahead, 40 N.Y.U.L. Rev. 710, 713. "Of course, the conglomerate cases are the best examples of the exotic restraints. Here mere speculation on what either common sense or judiciously selected economists might lead one to infer is apparently enough to prevent a merger. One reads these opinions with growing incredulity. They imply that big businesses have so much strength and such deep pockets that they simply could not lose out in competition with smaller companies. . . . One does not need a statistical survey to know that this is simply not the way the world is."

[28] In so doing the Court has moved away from the original recommendations in the Report of the Attorney General's National Committee to Study the Antitrust Laws, which concluded that "it will always be necessary to analyze the effect of the merger on relevant markets in sufficient detail, given the circumstances of each case, to permit a reasonable conclusion as to its probable economic effect." Report, at 123. But the development of specific criteria was aided by a degree of experience which does not exist in conglomerate cases, where the caution to analyze in detail seems particularly sound.

markets," has insisted throughout this proceeding that anticompetitive efforts must be proved *in fact* from post-merger evidence in order for § 7 to be applied. The Court gives little attention to this contention, but I think it must be considered seriously both because it is arguable and because it was, in a sense, the main source of difference between the Commission and the Sixth Circuit.

In its initial decision, the Commission remanded the proceeding to the Examiner for the express purpose of taking additional evidence on the post-merger situation in the liquid bleach industry. The Commission first held that the record before it, which contained all the information upon which the second Commission decision and the Court rely, was insufficient to support the finding of a § 7 violation. The Commission's subsequent opinion, handed down by an almost entirely changed Commission, held post-merger evidence generally irrelevant and "proper only in the unusual case in which the structure of the market has changed radically since the merger. . . ." Market structure changes, rather than evidence of market behavior, were held to be the key to a § 7 analysis.

In support of this position, the Commission noted that dependence on post-merger evidence would allow controls to be evaded by the dissimulation of market power during the period of observation. For example, Procter had been aware of the § 7 challenge almost from the date of the merger, and it would be unrealistic, so reasoned the Commission, to assume that market power would be used adversely to competition during the pendency of the proceeding.

The Commission also emphasized the difficulty of unscrambling a completed merger, and the need for businessmen to be able to make at least some predictions as to the legality of their actions when formulating future market plans. Finally, the Commission pointed to the strain which would be placed upon its limited enforcement resources by a requirement to assemble large amounts of post-merger data.

The Sixth Circuit was in disagreement with the second Commission's view. It held that "[a]ny relevant evidence must be considered in a Section 7 case. . . . The extent to which inquiry may be made into post-merger conditions may well depend on the facts of the case, and where the evidence is obtained it should not be ignored." The court characterized as "pure conjecture" the finding that Procter's behavior might have been influenced by the pendency of the proceeding.

[Focus on Premerger Market Structure]

If § 7 is to serve the purposes Congress intended for it, we must, I think, stand with the Commission on this issue. Only by focusing on market structure can we begin to formulate standards which will allow the responsible agencies to give proper consideration to such mergers and allow businessmen to plan their actions with a fair degree of certainty. In the recent amendments to the Bank Merger Act, Congress has indicated its approval of rapid adjudication based on premerger conditions, and all agency decisions hinging on competitive effects must be made without benefit of post-combination results. The value of post-merger evidence seems more than offset by the difficulties encountered in obtaining it. And the post-merger evidence before us in this proceeding is at best inconclusive.

Deciding that § 7 inquiry in conglomerate or product-extension merger cases should be directed toward reasonably probable changes in market structure does not, however, determine how that inquiry should be narrowed and focused. The Commission and the Court isolate two separate structural elements, the degree of concentration in the existing market and the "condition of entry." The interplay of these two factors is said to determine the existence and extent of market power, since the "condition of entry" determines the limits potential competition places on the existing market. It must be noted, however, that economic theory teaches that potential competition will have no effect on the market behavior of existing firms unless present market power is sufficient to drive the market price to the point where entry would become a real possibility.[29] So long as existing competition is sufficient to keep the market price below that point, potential competition is of marginal significance as a market regulator. Thus in a conglomerate or product-extension case, where the effects on market structure which are easiest to discover are generally effects on the "condition of entry," an understanding of the workings of the premerger market cannot be ignored, and, indeed, is critical to a determination of whether the visible effects on "condition of entry" have any competitive significance.

The Commission pinned its analysis of the premerger market exclusively on its concentration, the large market share enjoyed by the leading firms. In so doing the Commission was following the path taken by this Court in judging more conventional merger cases, *e.g., United States v. Philadelphia Nat'l Bank,* and taking the position favored by the great weight of economic authority. The Sixth Circuit discounted the Commission's analysis because of the presence of some 200 small competitors in the market. The Court bases its agreement with the Commission and its rejection of the Court of Appeals' position on Clorox's alleged domination of the market. But domination is an elusive term, for dominance in terms of percentage of sales is not the equivalent of dominance in terms of control over price or other aspects of market behavior. Just as the total number of sellers in the market is not determinative of its operation, the percentage of sales made by any group of sellers is similarly not conclusive. The determinative issue is, instead, how the sellers interact and establish the pattern of market behavior. The significance of concentration analysis is that it allows measurement of one easily determined variable to serve as an opening key to the pattern of market behavior.

I think that the Commission, on *this* record, was entitled to regard the market as "oligopolistic" and that it could properly ignore the impact of the smaller firms. I hasten to add, however, that there are significant "economic dissents" from oligopoly analysis in general and stronger arguments that if its principles "are justified in some cases, they are not justified in all cases. In adjudicating § 7 questions in a conglomerate or product-extension merger context where the pattern of behavior in the existing market is apt to be crucial, I would, therefore, allow the introduction by a defendant of evidence designed to show that the actual operation of the market did not accord with oligopoly theory, or whatever other theory the Commission desires to apply. In other words, I believe that defendants in § 7 proceedings are entitled, in the case of conglomerate or product-extension mergers, to build their

---

[29] Thus Bain points out that in a competitive market where market price is presumed to be cost-based the threat of entry should not affect market price because each firm is presumed to make its pricing decisions without considering their impact on the market as a whole. Even in an oligopolistic market in which each seller must assume that its price actions will have marketwide effect, the threat of entry serves to limit market price only when the optimum return would be obtained at a price sufficient to induce entry. So long as the optimum price is below the entry-triggering price, the threat of entry has no real impact on the market.

own economic cases for the proposition that the mergers will not substantially impair competition.

For example, had Procter desired to go beyond demonstrating the mere presence of small competitors and attempted to show that the prices of unadvertised bleaches which were cost-determined set an effective ceiling on market price through the mechanism of an acceptable differential,[30] I think that the Commission would have been obliged to receive and evaluate the proof. But to challenge effectively the presumption which the Commission is entitled to draw from general economic theory, a defendant must present, in my opinion, not only contradictory facts but a more cogent explanation of the pattern of market behavior.

If the proof as a whole establishes that pricing power may be exercised by a firm or firms in the market—that prices may be raised in the long run over competitive prices—then the Commission may legitimately focus on the role of potential competition and the "condition of entry." In so doing, however, a new difficulty is encountered. The threat of potential competition merely affects the range over which price power extends. Potential competition does not compel more vigorous striving in the market, nor advance any other social goal which Congress might be said to have favored in passing § 7.[31] Thus it may legitimately be questioned whether even a substantial increase in entry barriers creates a substantial lessening of competition or tendency to monopoly as required by § 7.

Two justifications for the use of entry barriers as a determinant under § 7 can be given. The first is that an increased range over which pricing power may be exercised is contrary to the mandate of § 7 because Congress' use of the word "competition" was a shorthand for the invocation of the benefits of a competitive market, one of which is a price close to average cost. Such an approach leads to the conclusion that economic efficiencies produced by the merger must be weighed against anticompetitive consequences in the final determination whether the net effect on competition is substantially adverse. The second justification is found in the tendency to monopoly clause of § 7. Certainly the clearest evil of monopoly is the excessive power the monopolist has over price. Since "antitrust operates to forestall concentrations of economic power which, if allowed to develop unhindered, would call for much more intrusive government supervision of the economy," increased power over price should be attackable under § 7. For these reasons I conclude that

[30] There was evidence in the record that the liquid bleach market had three separate price levels, one for nationally advertised brands (Clorox and Purex) another for regional brands, and a third for local brands. There was also some testimony by officials of the companies producing the unadvertised regional and local brands, which sold at a lower price than Clorox and Purex, that their prices were determined by their costs. Some witnesses also testified that sales of unadvertised brands were extremely price elastic, and Bain's study of the related soap industry would lend support to that observation. Bain, Barriers to New Competition, Appendix D, at 283. Thus, an argument might have been made that because of this price consciousness the prices of advertised brands could not greatly exceed those of regional and local brands, and therefore costs served as the ultimate determinant of market price. On the other hand, there is testimony in the record that the pricing policy of some unadvertised producers was to follow the price of Clorox and maintain a differential sufficient to provide adequate sales.

[31] Potential entry does not keep "a large number of small competitors in business," even if that goal could be considered desirable. In fact, by placing a ceiling on market price it may serve to drive out small competitors who may be relatively inefficient producers. Potential entry does not control the market share of dominant firms or prevent them from expanding their power to force others to accede to their practices.

the Commission may properly find a conglomerate or product-extension merger illegal under § 7 because it substantially increases pricing power in the relevant market.

Given the development of a case against the merger in this area, however, the problem of efficiencies raised above must still be faced. The Court attempts to brush the question aside by asserting that Congress preferred competition to economies, but neglects to determine whether certain economies are inherent in the idea of competition. If it is conceded, as it must be, that Congress had reasons for favoring competition, then more efficient operation must have been among them. It is of course true that a firm's ability to achieve economies enhances its competitive position, but adverse effects on competitors must be distinguished from adverse effects on competition. Economies achieved by one firm may stimulate matching innovation by others, the very essence of competition. They always allow the total output to be delivered to the consumer with an expenditure of fewer resources. Thus when the case against a conglomerate or product-extension merger rests on a market-structure demonstration that the likelihood of anticompetitive consequences has been substantially increased, the responsible agency should then move on to examine and weigh possible efficiencies arising from the merger in order to determine whether, on balance, competition has been substantially lessened. Where detriments to competition are apt to be "highly speculative" it seems wisest to conclude that "possibilities of adverse effects on competitive behavior are worth worrying about only when the merger does not involve substantial economies. . . ." The Court must proceed with caution in this area lest its decision "over the long run deter new market entry and tend to stifle the very competition it seeks to foster." Four important guides to the adjudication of conglomerate or product-extension mergers under § 7 seem to come forward. First, the decision can rest on analysis of market structure without resort to evidence of post-merger anticompetitive behavior. Second, the operation of the premerger market must be understood as the foundation of successful analysis. The responsible agency may presume that the market operates in accord with generally accepted principles of economic theory, but the presumption must be open to the challenge of alternative operational formulations. Third, if it is reasonably probable that there will be a change in market structure which will allow the exercise of substantially greater market power, then a prima facie case has been made out under § 7. Fourth, where the case against the merger rests on the probability of increased market power, the merging companies may attempt to prove that there are countervailing economies reasonably probable which should be weighed against the adverse effects.

The Commission's decision did, I think, conform to this analysis. A review of the points the Commission relied upon is next required.

The Commission first attempted a catalogue of all the possible effects of the merger on competition, many of which were "to an important degree psychological." Most of these "effects" were speculations on the impact of Procter's ability to obtain advertising discounts and use its financial resources for increased sales promotion. Others were predictions as to the possible responses of retailers and competitors to Procter's entry and expected promotional activities. These were, as the Court of Appeals said, speculative at best but the Commission did not place great reliance on them in reaching its ultimate conclusion.

To hold the merger unlawful, the Commission relied on five factors which taken together convinced it that "substantial" anticompetitive consequences could be expected. A "substantial" impact was said to be "significant and real, and discernible not merely to theorists or scholars but to practical, hard-headed businessmen."

The relevant factors were (1) the excessive concentration in the industry at the time of the merger and the commanding market position of Clorox, (2) the relative disparity in size and strength between Procter and the firms in the liquid bleach industry, (3) the position of Procter in other markets, (4) the elimination of Procter as a potential competitor, and (5) the nature of the "economies" expected from the merger. The net of these factors was to establish a substantial effect on the market structure variable involved, condition of entry.

Because Clorox had 48.8% of the premerger market and six firms made 80% of the sales, the Commission's conclusion that the market was oligopolistic and Clorox was the price leader must be sustained on this record where no alternative formulation of market operation was attempted. The Commission's position is aided by actual evidence in the record supporting its hypothesis. Officials of other bleach companies appearing in the proceedings testified that their prices were established with regard to Clorox's price and uniformly regarded Clorox as the leading competitor in the market. The foundation was thus adequate for a consideration of probable changes in the "condition of entry."

Procter was indisputably many times the size of any firm in the liquid bleach industry and had great financial resources. Its advertising budget was more than 20 times that of Clorox and the scale of its expenditures qualified it for quantity discounts from media as well as enabling it to purchase expensive but advantageous advertising outlets. The record clearly showed that "pre-selling" through advertising was a requisite for large scale liquid bleach operations, and thus the difference between Procter's advertising power and that of Clorox was important to a potential entrant. The expenditure on advertising which would have to be undertaken by a potential entrant in order to capture an acceptable market would vary with the tenacity of response to be expected from existing competitors. The greater the expenditure required, the higher the price to be commanded would have to be before entry would be undertaken.[32] In this regard the substitution of Procter for Clorox was a substantial change.

Procter's strong position in other product markets is equally relevant to the probability of change in the "condition of entry." It would be unrealistic, however, to attach substantial importance to Procter's extensive financial resources unless Procter were able to bring them to bear in the liquid bleach industry. If Procter were hard pressed along all fronts of its operation, competitors could safely assume that increased pressure in the liquid bleach industry would not provoke a strong response, simply because financial resources could not be diverted to that purpose. Procter, however, was conducting highly profitable operations in other markets and had demonstrated its ability to bring large resources to bear in intensive competitive campaigns by its successful introduction of Comet cleanser and various toothpastes on a nationwide scale. Proof of demonstrated ability to mobilize and

---

[32] This is the "lesson" of the incident in Erie, Pennsylvania, where Clorox was able to repel Purex's assault on its market position. Purex's initial success showed that part of the market could be captured, but Procter's response made clear that the beachhead could not be maintained without continued heavy advertising expenses. Unless the price commanded was expected to be quite high, these advertising expenditures could not be sustained.

utilize large financial resources seems to me required if the introduction of such resources into the market is alleged to have a substantial effect. Such proof exists in this record.

Procter's role as a potential entrant was also related, by the Commission, to the "condition of entry." The Commission had "no occasion to speculate on such questions as whether or not Procter . . . would in fact have entered the bleach industry on its own. . . ." It merely noted that Procter's growth pattern, financial resources, experience in the field and management policies made it the most favorably situated potential entrant. Thus the Commission reasoned that Procter might have been induced to enter the liquid bleach market when that market had a prevailing price level lower than that necessary to attract entry by more remote competitors. The limitation potential competition places on pricing policies depends on the barriers to entry facing particular competitors, and increased insulation can stem not only from changes which make it more costly for any firm to enter the market, but also from limitation of the class of entrants to those whose entry costs are high. At first blush, a serious inconsistency seems to arise between the Commission's analysis of this potential competition, and its expressed fear that the merger might turn the field into one of big business competition by inducing other large firms to seek entry into the market. If Procter's entry could be shown to have increased rather than decreased the likelihood of additional entry then it could hardly be attacked because of adverse effect on the "condition of entry." And I think it irrelevant whether further entry might be by small or large firms. Although there are those who attach a talismanic significance to small firm competition, I do not believe that competition between dynamic well-managed large companies is less desirable than any other form. However, there is nothing in the record to show that the Commission's discussion of this point was more than mere speculation, and I cannot attach any real significance to it.

The Commission's analysis of the economies involved in this case is critical and I regret that the Court refrains from commenting upon it. The Commission— in my opinion quite correctly—seemed to accept the idea that economies could be used to defend a merger, noting that "[a] merger that results in increased efficiency of production, distribution or marketing may, in certain cases, increase the vigor of competition in the relevant market." But advertising economies were placed in a different classification since they were said "only to increase the barriers to new entry" and to be "offensive to at least the spirit, if not the letter, of the antitrust laws." Advertising was thought to benefit only the seller by entrenching his market position, and to be of no use to the consumer.

I think the Commission's view overstated and oversimplified. Proper advertising serves a legitimate and important purpose in the market by educating the consumer as to available alternatives. This process contributes to consumer demand being developed to the point at which economies of scale can be realized in production. The advertiser's brand name may also be an assurance of quality, and the value of this benefit is demonstrated by the general willingness of consumers to pay a premium for the advertised brands. Undeniably advertising may sometimes be used to create irrational brand preferences and mislead consumers as to the actual differences between products,[33] but it is very difficult to discover at what point advertising ceases to be an aspect of healthy competition.

[33] The Commission found, for example, that Clorox was identical to other liquid bleaches. Procter contended, and the Court of Appeals concluded, that Clorox employed

It is not the Commission's function to decide which lawful elements of the "product" offered the consumer should be considered useful and which should be considered the symptoms of industrial "sickness." It is the consumer who must make that election through the exercise of his purchasing power. In my view, true efficiencies in the use of advertising must be considered in assessing economies in the marketing process, which, as has been noted, are factors in the sort of § 7 proceeding involved here.

I do not think, however, that on the record presented Procter has shown any true efficiencies in advertising. Procter has merely shown that it is able to command equivalent resources at a lower dollar cost than other bleach producers. No peculiarly efficient marketing techniques have been demonstrated, nor does the record show that a smaller net advertising expenditure could be expected. Economies cannot be premised solely on dollar figures, lest accounting controversies dominate § 7 proceedings. Economies employed in defense of a merger must be shown in what economists label "real" terms, that is in terms of resources applied to the accomplishment of the objective. For this reason, the Commission, I think, was justified in discounting Procter's efficiency defense.

For the reasons set forth in this opinion, I conclude that the Commission was justified in finding that the Procter-Clorox merger entails the reasonable probability of a substantial increase in barriers to entry and of enhancement in pricing power in the liquid bleach industry and that its order must be upheld.

ANHEUSER-BUSCH

The question presented is whether certain pricing activities of respondent, Anheuser-Busch, Inc., constituted price discrimination within the meaning of Section 2(a) of the Clayton Act, 38 Stat. 730, as amended by the Robinson-Patman Act.

Section 2(a) provides in pertinent part:

> That it shall be unlawful for any person engaged in commerce, in the course of such commerce, either directly or indirectly, to discriminate in price between different purchasers of commodities of like grade and quality, where either or any of the purchases involved in such discrimination are in commerce, where such commodities are sold for use, consumption, or resale within the United States or any Territory thereof or the District of Columbia or any insular possession or other place under the jurisdiction of the United States, and where the effect of such discrimination may be substantially to lessen competition or tend to create a monopoly in any line of commerce, or to injure, destroy, or prevent competition with any person who either grants or knowingly receives the benefit of such discrimination, or with customers of either of them. . . .

This controversy had its genesis in a complaint issued by the Federal Trade Commission in 1955, which charged respondent, a beer producer, with a violation of § 2(a). The complaint alleged that respondent had "discriminated in price between different purchasers of its beer of like grade and quality by selling it to some of its customers at higher prices than to other[s]"; that, more specifically, respondent had lowered prices in the St. Louis, Missouri, market, without making similar price reductions in other markets; that this discrimination had already diverted sub-

---

superior quality controls. The evidence seemed to indicate that the regional and national brands were very similar, but that some local brands varied in strength.

stantial business from repondent's St. Louis competitors; that it was "sufficient" to have the same impact in the future; that there was a "reasonable probability" it would substantially lessen competition in respondent's line of commerce; and that it might also tend to create a monopoly or to injure, destroy, or prevent competition with respondent. Thus the complaint described a pricing pattern which had adverse effects only upon sellers' competition, commonly termed primary-line competition, and not upon buyers' competition, commonly termed secondary-line competition.

Both the hearing examiner and, on appeal, the Commission held that the evidence introduced at the hearing established a violation of § 2(a). The Commission found the facts to be as follows:

Respondent, a leading national brewer,[34] sells a so-called premium beer, which is priced higher than the beers of regional and local breweries in the great majority of markets, although both the price of respondent's beer and the premium differential vary from market to market and from time to time. During the period relevant to this case, respondent had three principal competitors in the St. Louis area, all regional breweries: Falstaff Brewing Corporation, Griesedieck Western Brewing Company, and Griesedieck Brothers Brewery Company. In accord with the generally prevailing price structure, these breweries normally sold their products at a price substantially lower than respondent's.

In 1953, most of the national breweries, including respondent, granted their employees a wage increase, and on October 1, 1953, they put into effect a general price increase. Although many regional and local breweries throughout the country followed suit by raising their prices, Falstaff, Griesedieck Western, and Griesedieck Brothers maintained their pre-October price of $2.35 per standard case. Although respondent's sales in the St. Louis area did not decline, its national sales fell, along with industry sales in general.

On January 4, 1954, respondent lowered its price in the St. Louis market from $2.93 to $2.68 per case, thereby reducing the previous 58¢ differential to 33¢. A second price cut occurred on June 21, 1954, this time to $2.35, the same price charged by respondent's three competitors. On January 3, 1954, the day before the first price cut, respondent's price in the St. Louis market had been lower than its price in other markets,[35] and during the period of the price reductions in the St.

---

[34] Anheuser-Busch ranked second nationally in gross sales in 1952 and 1955, and first in 1953 and 1954.

[35] The following table discloses the degree of this price spread:

St. Louis, Mo.	$2.93
Chicago, Ill.	3.44
Cincinnati, Ohio	3.75
Houston, Tex.	3.70
Bronx, N.Y.	3.68
Kearney, Nebr.	3.68
St. Joseph, Mo.	3.17
Buffalo, N.Y.	3.60
Baltimore, Md.	3.62
Washington, D.C.	3.65
Detroit, Mich.	3.55
Boston, Mass.	3.69
Kansas City, Mo.	3.15

continued

Louis area, respondent made no similar price reductions in any other market. In March, 1955, respondent increased its St. Louis price 45¢ per case, and Falstaff, Griesedieck Western, and Griesedieck Brothers almost immediately raised their prices 15¢, which re-established a substantial differential. This ended the period of alleged price discrimination.

The Commission concluded:

> As a result of maintaining higher prices to all purchasers outside of the St. Louis area and charging the lower prices, as reduced in 1954, to only those customers in the St. Louis area, respondent discriminated in price as between purchasers differently located.

Since, as will appear, it is this aspect of the decision which concerns us, it is necessary only to sketch summarily the remaining elements in the Commission's decision. The Commission's finding of competitive injury was predicated to a substantial degree upon what it regarded as a demonstrated diversion of business to respondent from its St. Louis competitors during the period of price discrimination. For example, by comparing that period with a similar period during the previous year, the Commission determined that respondent's sales had risen 201.5%, Falstaff's sales had dropped slightly, Griesedieck Western's sales had fallen about 33%, and Griesedieck Brothers' sales had plummeted about 41%. In tabular form, the relative market positions of the St. Louis sellers were as follows:

	Dec. 31 1953	June 30 1954	Mar. 1 1955	July 31 1955
Respondent	12.5	16.55	39.3	21.03
Griesedieck Brothers	14.4	12.58	4.8	7.36
Falstaff	29.4	32.05	29.1	36.62
Griesedieck Western	38.9	33.	23.1	27.78
All others	4.8	5.82	3.94	7.21

The Commission rejected respondent's contention that its price reductions had been made in good faith to meet the equally low price of a competitor within the meaning of the proviso to § 2(b) of the Robinson-Patman Act, and also found respondent's attack upon the examiner's cease-and-desist order to be meritless. The Commission thereupon adopted and issued that order, with only slight modification.[36]

St. Paul, Minn.	3.53
Sioux Falls, S. Dak.	3.50
Denver, Colo.	. . .
San Francisco, Calif.	3.79
Los Angeles, Calif.	3.80

[36] "It Is Ordered, that the respondent, Anheuser-Busch, Inc., a corporation, and its officers, representatives, agents and employees, directly or through any corporate or other device, in the sale of beer of like grade and quality, do forthwith cease and desist from discriminating, directly or indirectly, in price, between different purchasers engaged in

On review, the Court of Appeals set aside the order. We granted certiorari, 361 U.S. 880, because a conflict had developed among the Courts of Appeals on a question of importance in the administration of the statute.

The limited nature of our inquiry can be fully appreciated only in the light of the correspondingly narrow decision of the Court of Appeals, which rested entirely upon the holding that the threshold statutory element of price discrimination had not been established. Thus the Court of Appeals did not consider whether the record supported a finding of the requisite competitive injury, whether respondent's good faith defense was valid, or whether the Commission's order was unduly broad. We have concluded that the Court of Appeals erred in its construction of § 2(a) and that the evidence fully warranted the Commission's finding of price discrimination. Respondent would have us affirm nonetheless on any of the alternative grounds it strongly urged below. While this is, to be sure, an appropriate course of action under proper circumstances, we believe that it would be unwise for us to grapple with these intricate problems, the solution to which requires a careful examination of a voluminous record, before they have been dealt with by the Court of Appeals. Therefore, the case will be remanded, and of course nothing in this opinion should be interpreted as intimating a view upon the remaining aspects of the controversy.

A discussion of the import of the § 2(a) phrase "discriminate in price," in the context of this case, must begin with a consideration of the purpose of the statute with respect to primary-line competition. The Court of Appeals expressed some doubt that § 2(a) was designed to protect this competition at all, but respondent has not undertaken to defend that position here. This is entirely understandable. While "precision of expression is not an outstanding characteristic of the Robinson-Patman Act," it is certain at least that § 2(a) is violated where there is a price discrimination which deals the requisite injury to primary-line competition, even though secondary-line and tertiary-line competition are unaffected. The statute could hardly be read any other way, for it forbids price discriminations "where the effect . . . may be substantially to lessen competition or tend to create a monopoly *in any line of commerce,* or to injure, destroy, or prevent competition with any person *who either grants* or knowingly receives the benefit of such discrimination, or with customers of either of them." (Emphasis added.)

The legislative history of § 2(a) is equally plain. The section, when originally enacted as part of the Clayton Act in 1914, was born of a desire by Congress to curb the use by financially powerful corporations of localized price-cutting tactics which had gravely impaired the competitive position of other sellers.[37] It is, of

---

the same line of commerce, where either, or any, of the purchases involved in such discrimination are in commerce, as 'commerce' is defined in the Clayton Act, by a price reduction in any market where respondent is in competition with any other seller, unless it proportionately reduces its prices everywhere for the same quantity of beer."

[37] "Section 2 of the bill . . . is expressly designed with the view of correcting and forbidding a common and widespread unfair trade practice whereby certain great corporations and also certain smaller concerns which seek to secure a monopoly in trade and commerce by aping the methods of the great corporations, have heretofore endeavored to destroy competition and render unprofitable the business of competitors by selling their goods, wares, and merchandise at a less price in the particular communities where their rivals are engaged in business than at other places throughout the country. . . . In the past it has been a most common practice of great and powerful combinations engaged in commerce—notably the Standard Oil Co., and the American Tobacco Co.,

course, quite true—and too well known to require extensive exposition—that the 1936 Robinson-Patman amendments to the Clayton Act were motivated principally by congressional concern over the impact upon secondary-line competition of the burgeoning of mammoth purchasers, notably chain stores. However, the legislative history of these amendments leaves no doubt that Congress was intent upon strengthening the Clayton Act provisions, not weakening them, and that it was no part of Congress' purpose to curtail the pre-existing applicability of § 2(a) to price discriminations affecting primary-line competition.

The federal courts, both before and after the amendment of § 2(a), have taken this view of the scope of the statute in cases involving impairment of primary-line competition. In fact, the original focus of § 2(a) on sellers' competition was so evident that this Court was compelled to hold explicitly, contrary to lower court decisions, that the statute was not *restricted* to price discriminations impeding primary-line competition, but protected secondary-line competition as well. The Court sustained a treble damage judgment in favor of a competing seller which was based partly upon a violation of § 2(a).

Thus neither the language of § 2(a), its legislative history, nor its judicial application countenance a construction of the statute which draws strength from even a lingering doubt as to its purpose of protecting primary-line competition. But the rationale of the Court of Appeals appears to have been shaped by precisely this type of doubt. The view of the Court of Appeals was that, before there can be a price discrimination within the meaning of § 2(a), "[t]here must be some relationship between the different purchasers which entitles them to comparable treatment." Such a relationship would exist, the Court reasoned, if different prices were being charged to *competing* purchasers. But the Court observed that in this case all *competing* purchasers paid respondent the same price, so far as the record disclosed. Consequently, the court concluded that, even assuming the price cuts "were directed at [Anheuser-Busch's] local competitors, they were not *discriminatory*." [38]

This qualification upon the applicability of § 2(a) to primary-line competition cases is in no way adumbrated by the prevailing line of relevant decisions. In *Mead's Fine Bread Co.*, in *Maryland Baking Co.*, and in *Porto Rican American Tobacco Co.*, violations of § 2(a) were predicated upon injury to primary-line competition without reliance upon the presence or absence of competition among purchasers as a relevant factor. And in *Muller & Co.*, while there was evidence that the purchasers in question were competing, the court explicitly rejected the notion that this was a necessary element of a violation in a primary-line case.

More important, however, is the incompatability of the Circuit Court's rule with the purpose of § 2(a). The existence of competition among buyers who are

---

and others of less notoriety, but of great influence—to lower prices of their commodities, oftentimes below the cost of production in certain communities and sections where they had competition, with the intent to destroy and make unprofitable the business of their competitors, and with the ultimate purpose in view of thereby acquiring a monopoly in the particular locality or section in which the discriminating price is made...." H.R. Rep. No. 627, 63d Cong., 2d Sess. 8. See also S. Rep. No. 698, 63d Cong., 2d Sess. 2–4.

[38] There is a dispute as to whether the Commission adopted a finding by the examiner which related to the purpose of the price reductions. Since we conclude that the issue of predatory intent is irrelevant to the question before us, it is unnecessary for us to resolve this dispute.

charged different prices by a seller is obviously important in terms of adverse effect upon secondary-line competition, but it would be merely a fortuitous circumstance so far as injury to primary-line competition is concerned. Since, as we have indicated, an independent and important goal of § 2(a) is to extend protection to competitors of the discriminating seller, the limitation of that protection by the alien factor of competition among purchasers would constitute a debilitating graft upon the statute.

Although respondent's starting point is the same as that of the Court of Appeals—that a price discrimination is not synonymous with a price difference—its test of price discrimination is somewhat broader. Respondent concedes that a competitive relationship among purchasers is not a prerequisite of price discrimination, but maintains that at least there must be "proof that the lower price is below cost or unreasonably low for the purpose or design to eliminate competition and thereby obtain a monopoly." Since such a finding is lacking here, respondent argues that it cannot be said that there was price discrimination.

Respondent asserts that its view is supported by legislative history, court decisions, and reason. Respondent relies heavily, as did the Court of Appeals, upon a statement made during Congress' consideration of the Robinson-Patman legislation by Representative Utterback, a manager of the conference bill which became § 2(a). In this rather widely quoted exegesis of the section, Representative Utterback declared that "a discrimination is more than a mere difference," and exists only when there is "some relationship . . . between the parties to the discrimination which entitles them to equal treatment." Such a relationship would prevail among competing purchasers, according to the Congressman, and also "where . . . the price to one is so low as to involve a sacrifice of some part of the seller's necessary costs and profit," so that "it leaves that deficit inevitably to be made up in higher prices to his other customers." [39] Respondent also cites expressions in the legislative history of the Clayton Act which reflect Congress' concern over classic examples of predatory business practices. Moreover, respondent maintains that the principle it advances has found expression in the decisions of the federal courts in primary-line competition cases, which consistently emphasize the unreasonably low prices and the predatory intent of the defendants. Respondent also urges that its view is grounded upon the statutory scheme of § 2(a), which penalizes sellers only if an anticompetitive effect stems from a *discriminatory* pricing pattern, not if it results merely from a low price. Thus, the argument goes, unless there is proof that high prices in one area have subsidized low prices in another, the price differential does not fall within the compass of the section. In such a case, it is contended, § 3 of

---

[39] The statement in full is as follows:

"In its meaning as simple English a discrimination is more than a mere difference. Underlying the meaning of the word is the idea that some relationship exists between the parties to the discrimination which entitles them to equal treatment, whereby the difference granted to one casts some burden or disadvantage upon the other. If the two are competing in the resale of the goods concerned, that relationship exists. Where, also, the price to one is so low as to involve a sacrifice of some part of the seller's necessary costs and profit as applied to that business, it leaves that deficit inevitably to be made up in higher prices to his other customers; and there, too, a relationship may exist upon which to base the charge of discrimination. But where no such relationship exists, where the goods are sold in different markets and the conditions affecting those markets set different price levels for them, the sale to different customers at those different prices would not constitute a discrimination within the meaning of this bill."

the Robinson-Patman Act may be applicable, but not § 2(a).[40] Finally, respondent argues that, unless its position is accepted, the law will impose rigid price uniformity upon the business world, contrary to sound economics and the policy of the antitrust laws.

The trouble with respondent's arguments is not that they are necessarily irrelevant in a § 2(a) proceeding, but that they are misdirected when the issue under consideration is solely whether there has been a price discrimination. We are convinced that, whatever may be said with respect to the rest of §§ 2(a) and 2(b)—and we say nothing here—there are no overtones of business buccaneering in the § 2(a) phrase "discriminate in price." Rather, a price discrimination within the meaning of that provision is merely a price difference.

When this Court has spoken of price discrimination in § 2(a) cases, it has generally assumed that the term was synonymous with price differentiation. In *Federal Trade Comm'n v. Cement Institute* the Court referred to "discrimination in price" as "selling the same kind of goods cheaper to one purchaser than to another." And in *Federal Trade Comm'n v. Morton Salt Co.* the Court said, "Congress meant by using the words 'discrimination in price' in § 2 that in a case involving competitive injury between a seller's customers the Commission need only prove that a seller had charged one purchaser a higher price for like goods than he had charged one or more of the purchaser's competitors." The commentators have generally shared this view.

These assumptions, we now conclude, were firmly rooted in the structure of the statute, for it is only by equating price discrimination with price differentiation that § 2(a) can be administered as Congress intended. As we read that provision, it proscribes price differences, subject to certain defined defenses,[41] where the effect of the differences "may be substantially to lessen competition or tend to create a monopoly in any line of commerce, or to injure, destroy, or prevent com-

---

[40] Section 3 provides:
"It shall be unlawful for any person engaged in commerce, in the course of such commerce, to be a party to, or assist in, any transaction of sale, or contract to sell, which discriminates to his knowledge against competitors of the purchaser, in that, any discount, rebate, allowance, or advertising service charge is granted to the purchaser over and above any discount, rebate, allowance, or advertising service charge available at the time of such transaction to said competitors in respect of a sale of goods of like grade, quality, and quantity; to sell, or contract to sell, goods in any part of the United States at prices lower than those exacted by said person elsewhere in the United States for the purpose of destroying competition, or eliminating a competitor in such part of the United States; or, to sell, or contract to sell, goods at unreasonably low prices for the purpose of destroying competition or eliminating a competitor."

[41] In addition to the statutory provisions regarding injury to competition there are other relevant portions of the statute, such as the seller's § 2(b) defense of "showing that his lower price . . . was made in good faith to meet an equally low price of a competitor. . . ." And a proviso to § 2(a) states:
"That nothing herein contained shall prevent differentials which make only due allowance for differences in the cost of manufacture, sale, or delivery resulting from the differing methods or quantities in which such commodities are to such purchasers sold or delivered. . . ." And still another proviso to § 2(a) states:
"That nothing herein contained shall prevent price changes from time to time where in response to changing conditions affecting the market for or the marketability of the goods concerned, such as but not limited to actual or imminent deterioration of perishable goods, obsolescence of seasonal goods, distress sales under court process, or sales in good faith in discontinuance of business in the goods concerned."

petition with any person who either grants or knowingly receives the benefit" of the price differential, "or with customers of either of them."

In other words, the statute itself spells out the conditions which make a price difference illegal or legal, and we would derange this integrated statutory scheme were we to read other conditions into the law by means of the nondirective phrase, "discriminate in price." Not only would such action be contrary to what we conceive to be the meaning of the statute, but, perhaps because of this, it would be thoroughly undesirable. As one commentator has succinctly put it, "Inevitably every legal controversy over any price difference would shift from the detailed governing provisions—'injury,' 'cost justification,' 'meeting competition,' etc.—over into the 'discrimination' concept for *ad hoc* resolution divorced from specifically pertinent statutory text."

In the face of these considerations, we do not find respondent's arguments persuasive. The fact that activity which falls within the civil proscription of § 2(a) may also be criminal under § 3 is entirely irrelevant. The partial overlap between these sections, which was to a significant extent the by-product of the tortuous path of the Robinson-Patman bills through Congress, has been widely recognized.

The other materials adduced by respondent do no more than indicate that the factors in question—predatory intent and unreasonably low local price cuts—may possibly be relevant to other matters which may be put in issue in a § 2(a) proceeding. For example, it might be argued that the existence of predatory intent bears upon the likelihood of injury to competition, and that a price reduction below cost tends to establish such an intent. Practically all of the legislative materials and court decisions relied upon by respondent are explicable on this basis, since hardly any of them are concerned specifically with the meaning of price discrimination. Moreover, many of the legislative expressions cited by respondent may merely be descriptive of the prototype of the evil with which Congress dealt in § 2(a), rather than delineative of the outer reach of that section. A possible exception is the statement of Representative Utterback. But the primary function of statutory construction is to effectuate the intent of Congress, and that function cannot properly be discharged by reliance upon a statement of a single Congressman, in the face of the weighty countervailing considerations which are present in this case.

Nothing that we have said, of course, should be construed to be the expression of any view concerning the relevance of the factors stressed by respondent to statutory standards other than price discrimination. We wish merely to point out, on the one hand, why respondent's arguments in our view are not pertinent to the issue at bar, and, on the other, that we are not foreclosing respondent from urging in the Court of Appeals that such arguments are material to issues not now before us.

What we have said makes it quite evident, we believe, that our decision does not raise the specter of a flat prohibition of price differentials, inasmuch as price differences constitute but one element of a § 2(a) violation. In fact, as we have indicated, respondent has vigorously contested this very case on the entirely separate grounds of insufficient injury to competition and good faith lowering of price to meet competition. Nor is it relevant that the Commission did not proceed upon the basis of the respondent's price differentials which existed prior to the period in question in this case. This choice is committed to the discretion of the Commission; and it may well be that the Commission did not believe the remaining statutory elements could be established with respect to other differentials. Our interest is solely with this case, and at this stage of the litigation that interest is confined exclusively to identifying and keeping distinct the various statutory standards which are part of the § 2 (a) complex.

The judgment of the Court of Appeals is reversed and the case is remanded to that court for further proceedings not inconsistent with this opinion.

CHAPTER 13

Long-Term Investment Decisions: Capital Budgeting

Management faces two separate but related tasks in working toward its goal of maximizing the value of the firm: (1) It must use existing resources in an optimal manner; (2) it must decide when to increase or reduce the firm's stock of resources. We have not yet explicitly separated these tasks, although our emphasis has been on the first one. Now we explicitly consider the decision to add to the stock of resources, or the decision process known as *capital budgeting*.

Capital budgeting consists of the entire process of planning expenditures whose returns are expected to extend beyond one year. The choice of one year is arbitrary, of course, but it is a convenient cutoff for distinguishing between classes of expenditures. Obvious examples of capital outlays are expenditures for land, buildings, and equipment and for permanent additions to working capital (especially inventories) associated with plant expansion. An advertising or promotion campaign or a program of research and development is likely also to have an impact beyond one year, and hence to come within the classification of capital budgeting expenditures.

In a very real sense capital budgeting integrates and fuses the various elements of the firm. Although the financial manager generally has administrative control of the capital budgeting process, the effectiveness of the process itself is fundamentally dependent on inputs from all major departments. Because a sales forecast is always required, the marketing department has a key role in the process. Because operating costs must be estimated, the production, engineering, and purchasing departments are involved. The initial outlay, or investment cost, must be estimated; again engineering and purchasing must supply inputs. Funds must be procured to finance the project, and obtaining these funds and estimating their cost are major tasks of the financial manager. Finally, these various estimates must be drawn together in the form of a project evaluation. Although the finance department generally writes up the evaluation report, top management sets the standards of acceptability and ultimately makes the decision to accept or reject the project.

Our first task in this chapter is to describe the mechanics of the capital budgeting process. Then we discuss in some detail the key roles of the marketing, production, and finance departments in the process. The entire process is illustrated by examining a complex, comprehensive capital budgeting problem in Chapter 14.

A SIMPLIFIED VIEW OF CAPITAL BUDGETING

Capital budgeting is, in essence, an application of a classic proposition from the economic theory of the firm; namely, a firm should operate at the point where its marginal revenue is just equal to its marginal cost. When this rule is applied to the capital budgeting decision, marginal revenue is taken to be the rate of return on investments, and marginal cost is the firm's cost of capital.

A simplified version of the concept is depicted in Figure 13-1(a). The horizontal axis measures the dollars of investment during a year; the vertical axis shows both the percentage cost of capital and the rate of return on projects. The projects are denoted by the boxes—Project A, for example, calls for an outlay of $3 million and promises a 17 percent rate of return; Project B requires $1 million and yields about 16 percent; and so on. The last investment, Project G, simply involves buying 4 percent government bonds, which may be purchased in unlimited quantities. In Figure 13-1(b) the concept is generalized to show a smoothed investment opportunity schedule, the curve labeled IRR.[1]

The curve MCC designates the marginal cost of capital, or the cost of each additional dollar acquired for purposes of making capital expenditures. As it is drawn in 13-1(a), the marginal cost of capital is constant at 10 percent until the firm has raised $13 million, after which the cost of capital be-

---

[1] The investment opportunity schedule measures the yield or rate of return on each project. The rate of return on a project is generally called the *internal rate of return* (*IRR*). This is why we label the investment opportunity schedules *IRR*. The process of calculating the *IRR* is explained in Appendix A.

Figure 13-1   Illustrative Capital-budgeting Decision Process: (a) Discrete Investment Projects; (b) A Smoothed Investment Opportunity Schedule

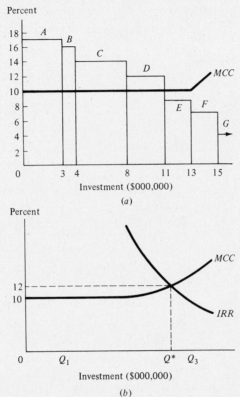

(a)

(b)

gins to rise. To maximize profits, the firm should accept Projects A through D, obtaining and investing $11 million, and reject E, F, and G. The smoothed, generalized curves in Part b indicate that the firm should invest Q^* dollars during the year. Here, the marginal cost of capital, the cost of the last dollar raised, is 12 percent, the same as the rate on the last project accepted.

APPLICATION OF THE CONCEPT

At the applied level, the capital budgeting process is much more complex than the preceding example would suggest. Projects do not just appear. A continuing stream of good investment opportunities results from hard thinking, careful planning, and, often, large outlays for research and development. In addition, some very difficult measurement problems are involved—the revenues and costs associated with particular projects must be estimated, frequently for many years into the future, in the face of great uncertainty.

Finally, some difficult conceptual and empirical problems arise over the methods of calculating rates of return and the cost of capital. Businessmen are required to take action, however, even in the face of problems such as these, and the capital budgeting procedure described in this chapter is designed to aid in this decision process.

Investment Proposals

Aside from the actual generation of ideas (no small task itself) the first step in the capital budgeting process is to assemble a list of the proposed new investments, together with the data necessary to appraise them. Although practices vary from firm to firm, proposals dealing with asset acquisitions are frequently grouped according to the following categories:

1. Replacements
2. Expansion: additional capacity in existing product lines
3. Expansion: new product lines
4. Other

These groupings are somewhat arbitrary, and it is frequently difficult to decide the appropriate category for a particular investment. In spite of such problems, the scheme is widely used, and with good reason.

Ordinarily, replacement decisions are the simplest to make. Assets wear out and become obsolete, and they must be replaced if production is to continue. The firm has a very good idea of the savings in cost obtained by replacing an old asset, and it knows the consequences of nonreplacement. All in all, the outcomes of most replacement decisions can be predicted with a high degree of confidence.

Examples of the second investment classification are proposals for the addition of more machines of the kind already in use, or the opening of another branch in a city-wide chain of food stores. Expansion investments are frequently incorporated in replacement decisions. To illustrate—an old, inefficient machine may be replaced by a larger and more efficient one.

A degree of uncertainty, sometimes extremely high, is clearly involved in expansion, but the firm at least has the advantage of examining past production and sales experience with similar machines or stores. When it considers an investment of the third kind, expansion into new product lines, little if any experience data are available on which to base decisions. To illustrate—when Union Carbide decided to develop the laser for commercial application, it had very little information on either the development costs or the specific applications to which lasers could be put. Under such circumstances, any estimates must at best be treated as very inexact approximations.

The "other" category is a catchall and includes intangibles; an example is a proposal to boost employee morale and productivity by installing a recorded-music system. Pollution-control devices are another example of the "other" category. Major strategic decisions, such as plans for overseas expansion or mergers, might also be included here, but more frequently they are treated separately from the regular capital budget. The same concepts, however, are involved in merger analysis, overseas expansion, and the like, as in "regular" investment analysis.

Administrative Details

The remaining aspects of capital budgeting concern administrative matters. As we move away from replacement decisions, and as the sums involved increase, approval at higher levels within the organization are typically required. One of the most important functions of the board of directors is to approve the major outlays in a capital budgeting program, because such decisions are crucial for the future well-being of the firm.

The planning horizon for capital budgeting programs varies with the nature of the industry. When the economic lifespan of major pieces of equipment is projected to be twenty or more years, the planning period is likely to be correspondingly long; electric utilities are an example of such an industry. When technology in the industry requires from eight to ten years to develop a new major product, as in certain segments of the aerospace industry, a correspondingly long planning period is also necessary.

After a capital budget has been adopted, payments must be scheduled. Characteristically, the finance department is responsible for scheduling payments and for acquiring funds to meet payment schedule requirements. In addition, the finance department is primarily responsible for cooperating with the members of operating divisions to compile systematic records on the uses of funds and the uses of equipment purchased in capital budgeting programs. Effective capital budgeting programs require such information as the basis for periodic review and evaluation of capital expenditure decisions—this is the feedback and control phase of capital budgeting.

MECHANICS OF CAPITAL BUDGETING[2]

Capital budgeting is, in essence, an application of the basic valuation model first introduced in Chapter 1.[3]

$$\text{Value} = \sum_{t=1}^{n} \frac{\text{Total Revenue}_t - \text{Total Cost}_t}{(1+k)^t} = \sum_{t=1}^{n} \frac{\text{Profit}_t}{(1+k)^t}. \quad (13\text{-}1)$$

[2] A knowledge of compound interest is necessary for an understanding of this section. Students who have not covered compound interest in other courses or who have forgotten it should read through the relevant sections of Appendix A.

[3] Other evaluation methods, generally shortcut or rule-of-thumb techniques designed to simplify the capital budgeting process, are also employed by many firms. Among these methods are: (1) payback; (2) average, or accounting, rate of return; (3) internal rate of return; and (4) profitability index. Under certain conditions these other techniques result in reasonably good evaluations in the sense that they make the same accept-reject decisions as the *NPV* method. However, the *NPV* technique described here is the only method that is theoretically correct and which will always lead to correct project selection recommendations. For a further discussion of alternative capital budgeting techniques, *see* J. F. Weston and E. F. Brigham, Appendix A to Chapter 10, "Differences between the Major Discounted Cash Flow Capital Budgeting Techniques," in *Managerial Finance*, 5th ed., Dryden Press, 1975.

Equation 13-1 applies to the entire firm; in this equation profit represents the firm's total after-tax income, and k, which is based on an appraisal of the firm's overall riskiness, represents the average cost of capital to the firm.[4]

When the present value model is used in capital budgeting, it is applied to a single project rather than to the firm as a whole.[5] In brief, the procedure is as described below:

1. Estimate the expected net cash flows from the project. Depending on the nature of the project, these estimates will have a greater or lesser degree of riskiness. For example, the benefits from replacing a piece of equipment used to produce a stable, established product can be estimated more accurately than those from an investment in equipment to produce a new and untried product.

2. Estimate the expected cost, or investment outlay, of the project. This cost estimate will be quite accurate for purchased equipment— cost is equal to the invoice price plus delivery and installation charges—but cost estimates for other kinds of projects may be highly uncertain or speculative. To illustrate, in 1968 Rolls-Royce estimated that it could develop a jet engine for a new aircraft at a cost of about $156 million and signed a contract to develop the engine. By 1970 the company had spent in excess of the original estimate and made a new cost projection of $324 million. In 1971 the estimated cost of development was increased once again to $600 million before the company went bankrupt, with the engine still far from completion.

3. Determine an appropriate discount rate, or cost of capital, for the project. The cost of capital is considered in detail later in the chapter, but for now it may be thought of as being determined by the riskiness of the project; that is, by the uncertainty of the expected profits and the investment outlay.

4. Find the present value of the expected profits, and subtract from this figure the estimated cost of the project.[6] The resulting figure is defined as the net present value (NPV) of the project. If the NPV

---

[4] In order to abstract from unnecessary complications that might hinder an understanding of the fundamental elements of capital budgeting, we shall generally assume in this chapter (1) that all sales are for cash, (2) that all costs except depreciation are cash expenses, and (3) that the depreciation charges reported as costs are calculated by what accountants call the "annuity method" of figuring depreciation and are actually set aside in a cash "reserve for depreciation." This permits us to abstract from a myriad of accounting details and to concentrate on the basic elements of capital budgeting theory.

[5] Note that a "project" can consist of a single asset such as a truck, a group of similar assets such as a new fleet of trucks, or a group of dissimilar assets which are used in concert and are evaluated as a single project. An example of the last group is a proposal to invest in a fleet of trucks, a warehouse, and a maintenance shop—all for the purpose of establishing an in-house delivery system as a replacement for a contract delivery service presently being used.

[6] If costs are spread over several years this fact must be taken into account. Suppose, for example, that a firm bought land in 1970, erected a building in 1971, installed equipment in 1972, and started production in 1973. One could treat 1970 as

is greater than zero, the project should be accepted; if it is less than zero, the project should be rejected. In equation form:

$$NPV_i = \sum_{t=1}^{n} \frac{R_{it}}{(1 + k_i)^t} - C_i, \qquad (13\text{-}2)$$

where NPV_i is the NPV of the ith project, R_{it} represents the expected net cash flows of the ith project in the tth year, k_i is the risk-adjusted discount rate applicable to the ith project, and C_i is the project's investment outlay, or cost.[7]

To see that this procedure of accepting only investment projects for which the net present value is positive is in fact an application of the marginal analysis illustrated in Figure 13-1, consider briefly the determination of the yield or internal rate of return on an investment. *The internal rate of return is defined as that interest or discount rate which equates the discounted present value of the future receipts of a project to the initial cost or outlay.* The equation for calculating the internal rate of return is simply the NPV formula set equal to zero. That is:

$$NPV_i = \sum_{t=1}^{n} \frac{R_{it}}{(1 + k_i^{*})^t} - C_i = 0.$$

Here the equation is solved for the discount rate, k_i^{*}, which produces a zero net present value or, alternatively, which causes the sum of the discounted future receipts to equal the initial cost. That discount rate is the internal rate of return or yield earned by the project.

Because the net present value equation is a complex polynomial, it is extremely difficult and in many cases impossible to solve for the internal rate of return on an investment. For this reason a trial-and-error method is typically employed. One begins by arbitrarily selecting a discount rate with which to calculate the net present value of the project. If the NPV is positive, then the internal rate of return must be greater than the interest or discount rate used, and another *higher* rate would be tried. Similarly, if the NPV is negative, this implies that the internal rate of return on the project is lower than the discount rate, and the NPV calculation must be repeated using a lower discount rate. This process of changing the discount rate and recalculating the net present value is continued until the discounted present value of the future cash flows is approximately equal to the initial cost. The interest rate that brings about this equality is the yield or internal rate of return on the project.

Now consider again the decision rule which states that a firm should accept only projects whose net present values are positive when the firm's

---

the base year, comparing the present value of the costs as of 1970 to the present value of the benefit stream as of that same date. For ease in exposition we shall assume in this chapter that all costs are incurred immediately and that profits occur annually at the end of each future year.

[7] If the cost of capital is expected to vary over time, this fact could be taken into account by designating k_{it} as the cost of capital for the ith project in the tth year.

risk-adjusted cost of capital, k_i, is used as the discount rate. In this model, k_i, the risk-adjusted discount factor, is the firm's marginal cost of capital and is, therefore, the rate of "interest" that must be paid on the funds invested in a project. As we have seen from the discussion of the calculation of internal rates of return or yields on an investment, if the net present value of a project, calculated using the firm's cost of capital as the discount rate, is positive, this implies that the yield on the project is greater than the cost of capital. Likewise, if the *NPV* is negative, the implication is that the internal rate of return is less than the cost of capital. Thus, it is clear that the *NPV* decision technique which limits acceptable projects to those whose net present values, using k_i as the discount rate, are positive, is one based essentially on a comparison of the marginal cost of capital and the marginal yield, or return, on the investment.

Illustration of the *NPV* Technique

To illustrate the *NPV* evaluation technique, assume that a firm has two investment opportunities, each costing $1,000 and each having the expected profits shown in Table 13-1.

Let us further assume that the cost of each project is known with certainty, but the expected profits of Project *B* are riskier than are those of Project *A*.[8] After giving due consideration to the risks inherent in each proj-

Table 13-1   Expected Profits from Projects *A* and *B*

Year	A	B
1	$500	$200
2	400	400
3	300	500
4	100	600

[8] Specifically, the coefficient of variation, which was seen in Chapter 3 to equal the standard deviation of any expected profit figure divided by the expected profit itself, is higher for each figure in Project *B* than for the corresponding figure in Project *A*. For example, σ_{A1}, the standard deviation of profits for Project *A* in Year 1, might be $200, meaning that there is a 68 percent probability that the actual profits during that year will lie between $300 and $700 ($= 500 \pm \$200$); σ_{B1}, on the other hand, might be $100. The coefficients of variation (ν_A and ν_B) for the two projects would be calculated as:

$$\nu_{A1} = \frac{\sigma_{A1}}{\$500} = \frac{\$200}{\$500} = 0.40,$$

$$\nu_{B1} = \frac{\sigma_{B1}}{\$200} = \frac{\$100}{\$200} = 0.50.$$

Since Project *B* has a higher coefficient of variation, its profit in Year 1 is more risky than that of Project *A*. We assume that the coefficients of variation are similar in other years, so *B* is riskier than *A*.

ect, management has determined that A should be evaluated with a 10 per-cent cost of capital, with a 15 percent cost of capital for the riskier Project B.

Equation 13-2 can be restated as Equation 13-3, using Project A as an example, for ease of calculations:

$$NPV_A = \sum_{t=1}^{n} \frac{P_{At}}{(1+k_A)^t} - C_A$$

$$= \left[\frac{P_{A1}}{(1+k_A)^1} + \frac{P_{A2}}{(1+k_A)^2} + \frac{P_{A3}}{(1+k_A)^3} + \frac{P_{A4}}{(1+k_A)^4} \right] - C_A$$

$$= \left[(P_{A1}) \left(\frac{1}{1+k_A} \right)^1 + (P_{A2}) \left(\frac{1}{1+k_A} \right)^2 + (P_{A3}) \left(\frac{1}{1+k_A} \right)^3 \right.$$

$$\left. + (P_{A4}) \left(\frac{1}{1+k_A} \right)^4 \right] - C_A$$

$$= [(P_{A1} \cdot IF_{A1}) + (P_{A2} \cdot IF_{A2}) + (P_{A3} \cdot IF_{A3}) + (P_{A4} \cdot IF_{A4})] - C_A.$$

$$(13\text{-}3)$$

Values for the interest factors, the IF terms, are found in Appendix A. For example, IF_{A2}, the interest factor for the present value of $1 due in two years discounted at a 10 percent rate, is .83.

Equation 13-3 for both projects is given in tabular form in Table 13-2. Project A's NPV is $80 and Project B's is $150. Since both projects have positive NPVs, both earn a rate of return in excess of their costs of capital—the marginal rate of return is greater than the marginal cost of capital, in the sense of Figure 13-1. If the two projects are independent, they should both be accepted, because each adds more to the value of the firm than its cost: Project A increases the value of the firm by $80 over what it would be if the project is not accepted; Project B increases the firm's value by $150. If the projects are mutually exclusive, B should be selected, because it adds more to the firm's value than does A.

Table 13-2   Calculating the Net Present Value (NPV) of Projects with $1,000 Cost

	Project A				Project B		
Year	Profit	IF (10%)	PV of Profit	Year	Profit	IF (15%)	PV of Profit
1	$500	0.91	$ 455	1	$200	0.87	$ 174
2	400	0.83	332	2	400	0.76	304
3	300	0.75	225	3	500	0.66	330
4	100	0.68	68	4	600	0.57	342
	PV		$1,080		PV		$1,150
	Less Cost		−1,000		Less Cost		−1,000
	NPA_A		$ 80		NPV_B		$ 150

MATHEMATICAL PROGRAMMING APPROACHES TO CAPITAL BUDGETING

Ordinarily, firms operate as illustrated in Figure 13-1; that is, they take on investments to the point where the marginal returns from investment are just equal to their marginal cost of capital. For firms operating in this way the decision process is as described in the above example—they make investments having positive net present values, reject those whose net present values are negative, and choose between mutually exclusive investments on the basis of the higher net present value. For many capital budgeting problems, however, the use of the *NPV* concept for analyzing capital budgeting decisions is far more complex than the illustration suggests. For example, the capital budgeting problem may require analysis of mutually exclusive projects with different expected lives or with substantially different initial costs. When these conditions exist, the net present value criterion as discussed above may not result in the selection of projects that maximize the value of the firm.

A similar complication arises when the firm sets an absolute limit on the size of its capital budget in any one year and this limit is less than the level of investment that would be undertaken on the basis of the criteria described above. The rationale behind such "capital rationing," as it is called, stems from a number of factors. First, it is sometimes a fallacy to consider that what is true of the individual parts will be true of the whole. Although individual projects appear to promise a relatively attractive yield, when they are taken together difficulties might arise in achieving all the favorable results simultaneously. One problem is that other firms in the same industry may be engaging in similar capital expenditure programs in an attempt to increase their capacity or, by cost and price reductions, to obtain a larger share of the product market. For a given growth rate in the industry, it is obviously impossible for every firm to obtain increases in sales that would fully utilize all the capital expenditure projects being undertaken.[9]

A second problem is that, although individual projects promise favorable yields, to undertake a large number of projects simultaneously might involve a very high rate of expansion by the individual firm. Such substantial additional personnel requirements and organizational problems may be involved that overall rates of return will be diminished. Top management, at some point in the capital budgeting process, must therefore make a decision regarding the total volume of favorable projects that may be successfully undertaken without causing a significant reduction in the prospective returns from individual projects.

A third reason for limiting the capital budget, and one that perhaps better meets the strict definition of "capital rationing," is the reluctance of

---

[9] A case in point is the Portland cement industry since 1950. For a convenient summary *see* Bruce T. Allen. "Vertical Integration and Market Foreclosure: The Case of Cement and Concrete," *Journal of Law and Economics,* April 1971.

some managements to engage in external financing (borrowing, or selling stock). One management, recalling the plight of firms with substantial amounts of debt in the 1930s, may simply refuse to use debt. Another management, which has no objection to selling debt, may not wish to sell equity capital for fear of losing some measure of voting control. Still others may refuse to use any form of outside financing, considering safety and control to be more important than additional profits. These are all cases of capital rationing, and they result in limiting the rate of expansion to a slower pace than would be dictated by "purely rational profit-maximizing behavior."

Under conditions of capital rationing, the net present value criterion may again give a ranking of projects that does not maximize the value of the firm. Further, when the possibility that investment opportunities in the future may provide substantially better (or worse) returns than those available today is coupled with capital rationing, the capital budgeting process is complicated even further. Complication arises because the reinvestment of cash flows from current projects is dependent on investment opportunities that become available over their lives.[10]

Correct capital budgeting decisions under the more complex conditions cited above require that the net present value concept be expanded through a mathematical programming approach. As a first step in examining such a programming method, consider a procedure that can at least conceptually improve on our decision in the capital rationing case. Figure 13-2 gives a matrix of investments in alternative projects, as well as cash flows from the projects. The values in the cells of the matrix are the net cash flows attributable to Projects $A, B, \ldots, Z$ over Years $1, 2, \ldots, n$. The rows of the matrix thus represent the investment opportunities available during the relevant time horizon, and the columns represent the net cash flows from all projects during a given year. The cash flows in a particular cell can be either positive or negative. A negative cash flow represents an investment; a positive cash flow represents the benefits resulting from the investment.

Figure 13-2 simply describes the investment opportunities open to the firm—the capital projects it can take on. If no capital rationing is imposed, the firm will be able to take on all economically desirable projects. If it is further assumed that the cost of capital is constant, the straightforward *NPV* method can be used to determine which of the available projects should be accepted in each year. The whole concept of Figure 13-2 is totally unnecessary in this case.

Suppose, however, that the firm is subject to capital rationing. Specifically, assume that it has an initial amount of money available for investment at the beginning of Year 1. It can invest this amount but no more. Further, assume that the funds available for investment in future years must come

---

[10] The *NPV* criterion assumes implicitly that these cash flows are reinvested at the cost of capital, an assumption that is clearly inappropriate when capital rationing prevents the firm from investing up to the point at which the internal rate of return, or yield on investment, is just equal to the marginal cost of capital.

Figure 13-2 Matrix of Future Investment Opportunities

Years

Projects	1	2	3	4	5	6	7	8	9	10	11	12	13	14	15
A	R_{a1}	R_{a2}	R_{a3}												
B	R_{b1}	R_{b2}	R_{b3}	R_{b4}											
C	R_{c1}	R_{c2}	R_{c3}	R_{c4}	R_{c5}	R_{c6}	R_{c7}								
D		R_{d2}	R_{d3}	R_{d4}	R_{d5}	R_{d6}	→								
E		R_{e2}	R_{e3}	⋯											
F		R_{f2}	R_{f3}	⋯											
G		R_{g2}	R_{g3}	⋯											
H			R_{h3}	⋯											
I			R_{i3}	⋯											
J			R_{j3}	⋯											
K				R_{k4}	⋯										
L				R_{l4}	⋯										
M				R_{m4}	⋯										
N					R_{n5}	⋯									
O					R_{o5}	⋯									
P					R_{p5}	⋯									

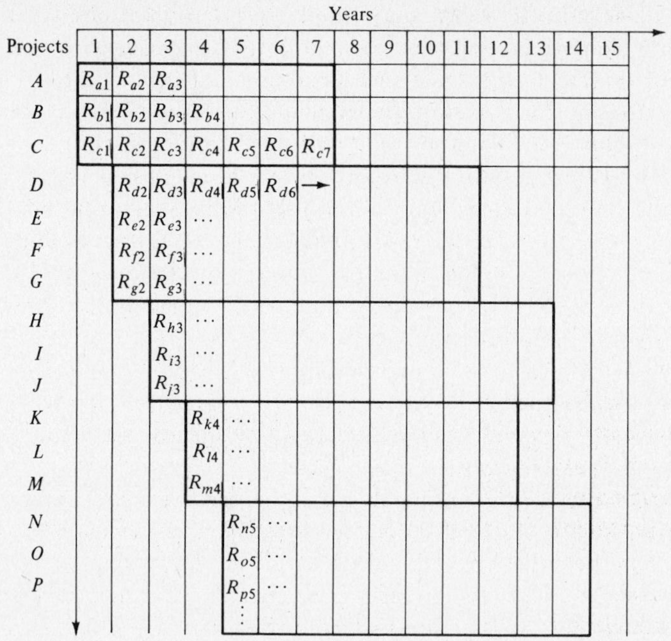

from cash generated from investments in the past. The funds available for investment in Year 2 will therefore depend on the set of investments chosen in Year 1; investment funds available in Year 3 will depend on cash throw-off from investments in Years 1 and 2; and so on.

If the projects available for investment in Year 2 are more profitable than those available in Year 1—that is, if they have higher internal rates of return—the firm should perhaps select investments in Year 1 that will have fast paybacks, making funds available for the profitable investment opportunities in Year 2. This is, however, only an approximation. Conceptually, the firm should select its investments in each year (subject to the capital rationing constraint) so as to maximize the net present value of all future cash flows. These cash flows should be discounted at the firm's cost of capital.[11]

If the investment opportunities are infinitely divisible—for example, if the investment opportunities are securities such as stocks or bonds that could be purchased in larger or smaller quantities—the firm could use linear programming to determine the optimal set of investment opportunities. If

---

[11] Actually, each project should be discounted at an appropriate risk-adjusted discount rate if they vary in riskiness.

such opportunities are not infinitely divisible—and in capital budgeting they typically are not—a more complex procedure known as *integer programming* must be used to find the optimum investment strategy.[12] Regardless of the computational process used to solve the problem, the firm should seek to find the set of investment opportunities that maximizes the *NPV* of the firm as a whole without exceeding the capital rationing constraint.

The mathematical programming approach can also handle the difficulties that arise because of interdependence between capital budgeting projects. For example, the program can be structured to insure that only one of a set of mutually exclusive projects is included in the final capital budget selection. This is done by adding a constraint equation to the problem that limits the total selection from those mutually exclusive projects to no more than one.[13]

Likewise, the selection of projects whose inclusion in the capital budget is dependent on selection of a second project can also be handled within a mathematical programming approach. An investment in jet engine maintenance equipment by an airline that is considering investing in its first jet aircraft is an example of such a project. The firm can invest in the maintenance equipment and perform its own engine maintenance, or it can contract with an outside concern for engine upkeep. The choice between these two alternatives is dependent on, among other things, their relative costs and the availability of alternative uses for investment funds. It is also totally dependent on a decision to purchase the jet aircraft, because without them the maintenance equipment would be of little value to the airline. A constraint equation in the programming model can insure that the maintenance equipment investment is accepted only if the jet aircraft are also included in the capital budget.[14]

In summary, the mathematical programming extension of the *NPV* provides a conceptual capital budgeting model which allows a firm to explicitly take into account the many complexities that arise in actual investment decision problems. Its implementation in real-world capital budgeting processes has been limited in the past because of limitations on input information and computational difficulties. These problems are being rapidly overcome as management information systems are developed to improve the informational flow for managerial decision making and as computer tech-

[12] H. Martin Weingartner—in *Mathematical Programming and the Analysis of Capital Budgeting Problems,* Prentice-Hall, Englewood Cliffs, N.J., 1963—has shown how integer programming can be used in capital budgeting decisions. To this point, however, information and computer processing requirements have limited the use of the approach on real-world capital budgeting problems.

[13] It is possible that none of those projects would be included in the optimal package of investments.

[14] This does not mean that the engine maintenance equipment will be automatically included if the jets are selected; it merely means that without the jets the maintenance equipment investment will be ruled out.

nology advances, thus making the complex analysis practicable. The programming approach to capital budgeting is likely to become an important management decision tool in the near future.

STEPS IN THE CAPITAL BUDGETING PROCESS

The information requirements referred to above indicate that the complexity of the capital budgeting decision extends far beyond the mechanical process required to evaluate investment alternatives. In fact, almost all the topics covered in this book must be brought to bear on important capital budgeting decisions. Demand functions, production functions, and cost functions must all be estimated and analyzed. Market structures may have to be appraised, both for use in determining how competitors are likely to react to major decisions and for the antitrust implications of particular courses of action; antitrust analysis is especially important if the action involves an investment in another firm or a joint venture with another company. Regulated firms are subject to special problems in their long-term investment programs, and almost all manufacturing companies are undergoing appraisals of the costs of and benefits accruing from investments in pollution-control equipment.

Demand Forecasts

The first step in most capital budgeting decisions is to make an estimate of future demand. The need for this step is obvious in expansion decisions, but it is also a vital part of replacement, modernization, and pollution-control investments. A worn-out machine should not be replaced unless demand for its output will continue for some time into the future; a plant should be closed rather than equipped with pollution-control equipment if demand for the plant's output is weak.

Cost Forecasts

Once the demand function has been estimated, the next step is to determine the operating cost function. This procedure frequently involves a knowledge of production theory, input factor markets, and statistical cost estimation. And, although we abstract from these considerations in this chapter, accurate cost analysis is also heavily dependent on such accounting-based topics as depreciation, inventory valuation procedures, and tax considerations.

Profit Forecasts

The third step in the process is to integrate the demand and cost functions in order to locate the optimal output level and the expected annual profits at this output. Although firms are often unable to obtain sufficiently accurate demand and cost data to actually employ the optimization calculus, they do, nevertheless, implicitly go through the process subjectively. Further, firms are increasingly setting up systems to generate the data necessary for optimization, and more and more of them are constructing simulation models, with demand and cost functions as key components, to appraise major investment proposals.

Cost of Capital

Determining the firm's cost of capital for use as the appropriate discount rate is an essential part of the capital budgeting process. The cost of capital is a complex subject, which is discussed in detail in finance courses, and a thorough treatment of the topic is far beyond the scope of this book. Accordingly, we shall merely summarize some of the important elements of the cost of capital theory as it is developed in finance.

Firms raise funds in the form of long-term and short-term debt, the sale of preferred stock, the sale of common stock, and by retaining earnings.[15] Each source of funds has a cost, and these costs are the basic inputs in the cost of capital determination.

Cost of Debt   If a firm borrows $100,000 for one year at 6 percent interest, its before-tax dollar cost is $6,000 and its before-tax percentage cost is 6 percent. *The cost of debt is defined as the rate of return that must be earned on debt-financed investments in order to keep unchanged the earnings available to common shareholders.* The before-tax cost of debt turns out to be the interest rate on debt; if the firm borrows, and invests the borrowed funds to earn a before-tax return just equal to the interest rate, the earnings available to common shareholders remain unchanged.

Interest payments on debt are deductible for income tax purposes, but dividends paid on preferred stock and common stock are not. It is necessary to account for this tax deductibility by adjusting the cost of debt to an after-tax basis. The deductibility of interest payments means, in effect, that the federal government pays part of a firm's interest charges. This reduces the cost of debt capital as follows:

$$\text{After-tax Cost of Debt} = (\text{Interest Rate}) \times (1.0 - \text{Tax Rate}).$$

Assuming that the firm's marginal tax rate is 50 percent, the after-tax cost of debt will be one-half the interest rate.

Note that the cost of debt is applicable to *new* debt, not to the interest on old, previously outstanding debt. In other words, we are interested in the cost of new debt, or the *marginal* cost of debt. The primary concern with the cost of capital is to use it in a decision-making process—the decision whether to obtain capital to make new investments. The fact that the firm borrowed at high or low rates in the past is irrelevant.[16]

---

[15] Funds are also obtained by sales of convertibles and warrants, by leasing, from government agencies, and so on, but we shall abstract from these details.

[16] The fact that the firm borrowed at high or low rates in the past is important

Cost of Preferred Stock Preferred stock is a hybrid between debt and common stock. Like debt, preferred stock carries a fixed commitment by the corporation to make periodic payments; in liquidation, the claims of the preferred stockholders take precedence over those of the common stockholders. Unlike debt, however, failure to make the preferred dividend payments does not result in bankruptcy. Preferred stock is thus somewhat more risky *to the firm* than common stock, but it is less risky than bonds. Just the reverse holds for investors. To the investor, preferred is less risky than common, but more risky than debt.

The definition of the cost of preferred stock is similar to that of the cost of debt: It is that rate of return that must be earned on preferred stock-financed investments in order to keep unchanged the earnings available to common shareholders. This required rate of return turns out to be the preferred dividend per share (D_P) divided by the net price that the firm could realize from the sale of one share of a new issue of preferred stock(P_n):

$$\text{Cost of Preferred Stock} = \frac{D_P}{P_n}.$$

Since the dividends paid on preferred stock are not deductible for income tax calculation, the before-tax and after-tax costs of preferred stock are identical.

Cost of Equity[17] *The cost of equity capital is defined as the minimum rate of return that must be earned on equity-financed investments to keep unchanged the value of the existing common equity.* In other words, if 10 percent is a corporation's cost of equity capital, the value of the equity used to finance an investment will exceed its cost if—and only if—the internal rate of return on the investment exceeds 10 percent. This is an opportunity cost concept. If investors can find investments of similar risk outside the firm that yield at least 10 percent—that is, if their opportunity cost of funds tied up in the business is 10 percent—they do not want the firm to invest equity capital to yield less than 10 percent.

Although one can use involved, highly complicated procedures to empirically estimate the cost of equity capital, satisfactory estimates may in general be obtained in either of two relatively simple ways:

1. Recognize that the cost of capital of a risky security such as a common stock consists of a riskless rate of return (R_F) plus a risk premium (P):

$$k = R_F + P.$$

in terms of the effect of the interest charges on current profits, but this past decision is not relevant for current decisions. For current financial decisions, only current interest rates are relevant.

[17] "Equity" is defined to *exclude* preferred stock. Equity, or net worth, is the sum of capital stock, capital surplus, and earned surplus (the accumulated retained earnings).

The risk free return is typically taken to be the interest rate on U.S. government securities. Various procedures are available for estimating P for different securities, but a discussion of them goes beyond the scope of this book.[18]

2. An alternative procedure, the use of which is recommended in conjunction with the one described above, is to estimate the basic required rate of return as[19]:

$$\text{Rate of Return} = \frac{\text{Dividends}}{\text{Price}} + \text{Expected Growth Rate}$$
$$k = \frac{D}{P} + g.$$

The rationale for this equation is that stockholder returns are derived from dividends and capital gains. The total of the dividend yield plus the expected growth rate over the next five to ten years gives an estimate of the total returns that stockholders probably expect in the future from a particular share of stock. Growth rate expectations can be obtained from security analysts.

The two procedures generally give similar results.

Weighted Cost of Capital   Suppose a particular firm's after-tax cost of debt is estimated to be 4 percent (the interest rate on new debt issues is 8 percent and the firm's marginal income tax rate is 50 percent); its cost of equity is estimated to be 12 percent; and the decision has been made to finance next year's projects by selling debt. The argument is sometimes advanced that the cost of these projects is 4 percent, because debt will be used to finance them.

This position contains a basic fallacy. To finance a particular set of projects with debt implies that the firm is also using up some of its potential for obtaining new low-cost debt. As expansion takes place in subsequent years, at some point the firm will find it necessary to use additional equity financing or else the debt ratio will become too large. In other words, the interest rate on debt is not the firm's true opportunity cost of this kind of capital.

To illustrate this point, suppose the firm has a 4 percent cost of debt and a 12 percent cost of equity. In the first year it borrows heavily, using up its debt capacity in the process, to finance projects yielding 5 percent. In the second year it has projects available that yield 9 percent, almost twice the return on first-year projects, but it cannot accept them because they would

---

[18] *See* Weston and Brigham, *op. cit.*, Chapter 19, for a discussion of risk premium estimates.

[19] The "growth rate" here is the growth in the price of the firm's stock, but if the dividend payout rate is constant, and if the dividend capitalization rate (k) remains unchanged, earnings, dividends, and the stock price all grow at the same rate.

have to be financed with 12 percent equity money. To avoid this problem the firm should be viewed as an on-going concern, and its cost of capital should be calculated as a weighted average of the various sources of funds it uses: debt, preferred stock, and equity. The proper set of weights to be employed in computing the weighted average cost of capital is determined by the optimal financial structure of the firm.

In general, the risk to investors is lowest on debt, next lowest on preferred stock, and highest on common stock; because of risk aversion, therefore, debt is the lowest cost source of funds and equity the highest cost source. Risk increases as the percentage of total capital obtained in the form of debt increases, since the higher the debt level, the greater the probability that adverse conditions will lower earnings to the point where the firm is unable to pay its interest charges and to pay off debt issues as they mature. The fact that interest rates on debt are lower than the expected rate of return (dividends plus capital gains) on common stock causes the overall, or average, cost of capital to the firm to decline as the percentage of capital raised as debt increases. However, the fact that more debt means higher risk offsets this effect to some extent. As a result, it is generally felt that the average cost of capital (1) declines at first as a firm moves from zero debt to some positive amount of debt; (2) hits a minimum, perhaps over a range rather than at some specific amount of debt; and then (3) rises as an increase in the level of debt drives the firm's risk position beyond acceptable levels. Thus, there is an optimal amount of debt for each firm, an amount of debt which minimizes its cost of capital and maximizes its value.[20]

Figure 13-3 shows, for a hypothetical industry, how the cost of capital changes as the debt ratio increases.[21] (The average cost of capital figures in the graph are calculated in Table 13-3.) In the figure each dot represents one of the firms in the industry. For example, the dots labeled 1 represent Firm 1, a company with no debt. Since it is financed entirely with 12 percent equity money, Firm 1's average cost of capital is 12 percent. Firm 2 uses 10 percent debt in its capital structure and has a 3 percent after-tax cost of debt and a 12.2 percent cost of equity; a risk premium of 0.2 percent has been added to the required return on equity to account for the additional risk of financial leverage. Firm 3 uses 20 percent debt, and also has a 3 percent cost of debt and a 12.5 percent cost of equity. Firm 4 has a 13 percent cost of equity and a 3.5 percent cost of debt. It uses 30 percent debt, and providers of debt capital feel that because of the added risk of financial leverage at this high debt level, they should obtain higher yields on the firm's securities. In this particular industry the threshold debt ratio that begins to worry creditors is about 20 percent. Below 20 percent debt, creditors

---

[20] This is a controversial subject, but virtually all authorities agree that, because of the deductibility of interest for income tax purposes, if for no other reason, there is an optimal capital structure for any given firm. Determining this optimal structure is, however, a most difficult matter.

[21] For ease in exposition, it is assumed that firms have no preferred stock.

Figure 13-3   Hypothetical Cost of Capital Schedules for an Industry

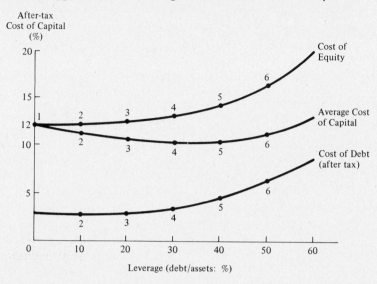

are totally unconcerned about any risk induced by debt; above 20 percent they are aware of the higher risk and require compensation in the form of higher rates of return.

In Table 13-3 the debt and equity costs of the various firms are averaged on the basis of their respective proportions of the firm's total capital. Firm 1 has a weighted average cost equal to 12 percent; Firm 2 has a weighted average cost of 11.3 percent; Firm 3 has a weighted cost of 10.6 percent; and Firm 4 has a weighted cost of 10.15 percent. These weighted costs, together with those of the other firms in the industry, are also plotted in Figure 3-3. We can see that firms with approximately 30 percent debt in their capital structure have the lowest weighted cost of capital. Accordingly, proper calculation of the weighted cost of capital requires that the cost of equity for a firm in the industry be given a weight of 0.70, and that debt be given a weight of 0.30.

SUMMARY

Capital budgeting is the process of planning expenditures where the returns or benefits are expected to extend beyond one year. Capital budgeting decisions are among the most important faced by a firm's management because of both the size of the expenditures and the long-term nature of the commitments involved. It is a difficult process because one is dealing with estimates of events which are going to occur some distance in the future.

Capital budgeting decision making requires an integration of all the elements of the firm. Demand projections must be developed for the firm's products. Produc-

Table 13-3 Calculation of Average Cost of Capital for Hypothetical Firms with Different Debt Ratios

		Percent of Total (1)	Component Cost (2)	Weighted Cost (1) × (2) −100 (3)
Firm 1	Debt	0	3.0	0.00
	Equity	100	12.0	12.00
		100%	Average Cost	12.00%
Firm 2	Debt	10	3.0	0.30
	Equity	90	12.2	11.00
		100%	Average Cost	11.30%
Firm 3	Debt	20	3.0	0.60
	Equity	80	12.5	10.00
		100%	Average Cost	10.60%
Firm 4	Debt	30	3.5	1.05
	Equity	70	13.0	9.10
		100%	Average Cost	10.15%
Firm 5	Debt	40	4.5	1.80
	Equity	60	14.0	8.40
		100%	Average Cost	10.20%
Firm 6	Debt	50	6.0	3.00
	Equity	50	16.0	8.00
		100%	Average Cost	11.00%
Firm 7	Debt	60	8.5	5.10
	Equity	40	19.5	7.80
		100%	Average Cost	12.90%

tion and cost relationships have to be analyzed. Personnel requirements must be estimated. The funds necessary to support the investment project have to be procured.

Capital budgeting decisions should be made by comparing the marginal return on investment with the marginal cost of capital. The net present value (*NPV*) technique was shown to be a theoretically correct method for analyzing investment proposals.

For certain complex capital budgeting situations—those involving capital rationing, mutually exclusive, and closely interrelated projects—the *NVP* approach may be inappropriate for project selection. Mathematical programming techniques are being developed which improve decision making in these complex circumstances.

Calculation of the cost of capital for use in the net present value model is a difficult problem. Proper decision making requires that a weighted average of the costs of the various types of capital employed by the firm should be used for all capital budgeting decisions.

QUESTIONS

13-1   The economics of input combination tells us that factors should be used in proportions such that the marginal product/price ratios for all inputs are equal. For capital management policy this implies that the marginal net cost of debt should be equal to the marginal net cost of equity at the optimal capital structure. Yet, we typically see firms issuing debt at interest rates significantly below the yields investors are estimated to require on the firm's equity shares. Does this mean that these firms are not operating with optimal capital structures? Explain.

13-2   New York City licenses taxicabs in two classes: (1) for operation by companies with fleets, and (2) for operation by independent driver-owners having only one cab. It also fixes the rates that taxis charge. For many years now no new licenses have been issued in either class. There is an unofficial market in the "medallions" that signify the possession of a license. A medallion for an independent cab now sells for about $17,000 in this market.

a)   Discuss the factors determining the price of a medallion. For concreteness, conjecture at the numerical values of the various components that together can be summarized in a price of $17,000.

b)   What factors would determine whether a change in the fare fixed by the city would raise or lower the price of a medallion?

c)   Cab drivers, whether hired by companies or as owners of their own cabs, seem unanimous in opposing any increase in the number of cabs licensed. They argue that an increase in the number of cabs, by increasing competition for customers, would drive down what they regard as an already unduly low return to drivers. Is their economic analysis correct? Who would benefit and who would lose from an expansion in the number of licenses issued at a nominal fee?

PROBLEMS

13-1   Terri-Built, Inc., plans to introduce a new line of paint brushes. Three alternative designs, each requiring a different production setup, having a different variable cost, selling at a different price, and having a different expected annual sales volume are available. Relevant data on each model are given below:

	Model A	Model B	Model C
Price	$ 5.00	$ 6.00	$ 7.00
Direct cost per unit	$ 2.00	$ 2.30	$ 2.50
Annual unit sales volume	800,000	650,000	450,000
Annual marketing costs	$ 90,000	$ 75,000	$ 55,000
Investment required to produce annual sales volume	$2,000,000	$1,500,000	$1,000,000

Assume the following facts: (1) The company's marginal tax rate is 50 percent; (2) each project is expected to have a six-year life; (3) the firm uses straight line depreciation; (4) the average cost of capital is 10 percent; (5) the projects are of about the same riskiness as the firm's other business; and (6) the company has already spent $60,000 on research for the new venture —this amount has been capitalized and will be written off over the life of the project.

a) What is the expected net cash flow each year? (*Hint:* Cash flow equals net profits after taxes plus depreciation and amortization charges.)

b) What is the net present value of each project? Which project, if any, should be selected?

c) Suppose that Terri-Built's primary business is quite cyclical, moving up and down with the economy; while paint brush sales are expected to be countercyclical, moving up when large numbers of men are laid off work and use their time to fix up their homes. Further, suppose that the $5 brushes are expected to be most countercyclical. Might this have any bearing on your decision?

13-2 Venture Corporation is considering investing $50,000 in facilities to produce a new product. The product is sold in an essentially competitive market structure at a price of $390 per unit. Assume that the facility will have a total cost function with fixed costs of $5,000 annually (in addition to depreciation on the facility which is computed in a straight-line manner) and variable costs given by the equation:

$$\text{Variable Costs} = -\$10X + \$2X^2.$$

If the facility is expected to have an economic life of ten years (and a salvage value of $0), should the firm make the investment if its after-tax cost of capital is 12 percent? (Assume a 50 percent income tax rate for Venture Corporation.)

13-3 The Maskor Company must choose between two mutually exclusive investment projects. Each project costs $6,000 and has an expected life of four years. Annual net cash flows from each project begin one year after the initial investment is made and have the following characteristics:

	Probability	Annual Net Cash Flow
Project *A*	0.05	$2,200
	0.40	3,300
	0.25	3,800
	0.30	3,600
	1.00	
Project *B*	0.15	$ 300
	0.35	3,700
	0.22	6,900
	0.28	6,200
	1.00	

Maskor has decided to evaluate the riskier project at a 14 percent cost of capital and the less risky project at 12 percent.

a) What is the expected value of the annual net cash flows from each project?

b) What is the risk-adjusted *NPV* of each project?

SELECTED REFERENCES

Brigham, Eugene F. *Readings in Managerial Finance.* New York: Holt, Rinehart and Winston, 1971. Selections in Part II, Capital Budgeting, and Part III, Cost of Capital.

Johnson, Robert W. *Financial Management,* 4th ed. Boston: Allyn and Bacon, 1971, Chapters 8 and 11.

Van Horne, James C. *Financial Management and Policy,* 3d ed. Englewood Cliffs, N.J.: Prentice-Hall, 1974, Chapters 3, 4, 5, and 6.

Weingartner, H. Martin. *Mathematical Programming and the Analysis of Capital Budgeting Problems.* Englewood Cliffs, N.J.: Prentice-Hall, 1963.

Weston, J. Fred, and Eugene F. Brigham. *Essentials of Managerial Finance,* 3d ed. New York: Holt, Rinehart and Winston, 1971, Chapters 11, 12, and 20.

———. *Managerial Finance,* 5th ed. New York: Dryden Press, 1975, Chapters 7, 8, and 11.

CHAPTER 14

The Westfall Company:
An Integrated Case
in Managerial
Decision Making

In this chapter we illustrate most of the principles and techniques developed throughout the text with an integrated case. Demand and cost forecasting, production functions, market structures, and capital budgeting are all discussed, and the case shows how these topics are applied in an integrated manner in actual business decisions.

BACKGROUND

The Westfall Company is a manufacturing and retailing concern with headquarters in the Chicago area. Originally a furniture manufacturer, by 1974 Westfall had become a highly diversified corporation, partly through merger and partly through internal expansion of product lines.

Because the firm is highly diversified, Westfall's management feels strongly that decisions should be decentralized. Accordingly, each major division—furniture, appliances, mobile homes, prefabricated houses, camping equipment, and a retailing operation that handles furniture and appliances—is headed by a vice-president, who reports directly to the president of the corporation, Martin Glass. In addition to the operating divisions,

Westfall also has a corporate staff which oversees the divisions and insures that the operation of each division is consistent with overall corporate policy.

The most important single function of the corporate staff, which is headed by Allen Bruce, executive vice-president, deals with capital budgeting. Glass and Bruce both feel that, while the divisional vice-presidents should be given a relatively free hand in running their divisions, the central staff must decide how the corporation's funds are to be allocated among its divisions.

Until 1969 the furniture division had generated the largest cash flows and had been allowed to keep most of this money (aside from paying its share of the corporate dividends), in spite of the fact that certain other divisions had earned a higher rate of return on invested capital. When Glass and Bruce assumed their current positions in that year, they instituted a new capital budgeting process requiring divisions to justify their requests for long-term investment funds on the basis of the net present value technique. This action reduced the share of the capital budget allocated to the furniture division.

Auditors from the corporate staff follow up on the accepted projects to see that the actual cost and revenue figures are reasonably close to the projected figures. It is expected that even though individual projects may deviate from the estimates, divisional figures, on the average, should approximate the projections. If any division consistently overestimates revenues or underestimates costs, this is considered an indication of optimistic bias which will cause too much of Westfall's available funds to be invested in that division. Conversely, if revenues are consistently underestimated or costs overestimated, this indicates a conservative bias and an underallocation of funds to the division.

Westfall employs a salary-plus-bonus system for compensating its three hundred top executives, with the bonus consisting partly of cash and partly of stock. The total bonus is determined in two steps. First, a "basic profit" equal to 10 percent of assets is computed. Second, 25 percent of all profit in excess of the "basic profit" goes into the "bonus pool." To illustrate, in 1973 Westfall's total assets were $1 billion and its net profits after taxes were $130 million. Accordingly, $7.5 million, representing 25 percent of $30 million, the amount by which profits exceeded 10 percent of assets, went into the bonus pool. The total bonus was then allocated among the corporate officers and staff, as well as the divisional executives, in accordance with the evaluation by the bonus committee composed of three outside members of the board of directors. Each division's profits, rate of return on invested capital, growth rate in profits, and correlation between budget and performance were the key factors used in evaluating divisional personnel, while headquarters personnel were evaluated on total corporate performance. On the average, over the past few years the three hundred officers covered by the bonus plan have received about one-half of their total compensation as regular salary and one-half under the bonus program.

CAPITAL BUDGETING PROCESS

Divisional managers usually have their own staffs prepare capital budgeting requests for the coming year, and these requests must be completed by October 1st of the current year. The managers review these proposals, then forward them to corporate headquarters by November 1st. The corporate staff automatically approves all projects amounting to less than $25,000 and all replacement projects amounting to less than $100,000. Projects exceeding these limits, but under $200,000, can be approved by the financial vice-president, Elliot Neff. Projects costing between $200,000 and $1 million are approved by the executive committee consisting of the president, the executive vice-president, the financial vice-president, and the six divisional vice-presidents. Projects involving over $1 million are first cleared by the executive committee, then referred for final approval to the board of directors.

Capital budgeting requests generally have been completed without assistance from the corporate staff—the divisional budget officers follow a standard format prescribed by the financial vice-president and supply him with any supplemental data requested in his review process. Recently, however, Neff issued a memo indicating that a new budget analyst, a recent MBA graduate with training in managerial economics, was available to assist divisional budget officers with large project analyses, and Tom Watson, budget officer for the mobile home division, decided to accept Neff's offer.

In recent years the mobile home division (MHD), Westfall's star performer, has earned a return on investment averaging 23 percent, as against 13 percent for the entire corporation, and has experienced a growth rate of about 20 percent, in contrast to 8 percent for the whole firm. This superior performance reflects, in part, the fact that the mobile home industry is growing faster than any other industry in which Westfall operates. Because of MHD's good growth opportunities and high rate of return, the corporate staff welcomes budget requests from the division. However, the staff officers, and also the MHD executives, are concerned about the possibility that high returns earned in the industry are causing so much expansion by existing firms, and attracting so many new firms, that profit margins may be seriously eroded in the future.

This question of whether increased competition in the mobile home industry will erode profit margins also plagues investors, so mobile home producers currently find it necessary to pay relatively high rates of interest on long-term borrowed funds, and they think that their costs of equity capital are correspondingly high. The Westfall executives are not at all sure that this pessimistic forecast is justified for their own company; in fact, a substantial majority of the board of directors feels that Westfall's established position and expertise in related industries, such as furniture and modular prefabricated houses, assures its continued success in the mobile home field. Management agrees, however, that, right or wrong, investors take a dim view of the mobile home industry. Accordingly, MHD is required to evaluate projects using a 12 percent cost of capital versus an average of 10 percent for other divisions.[1]

Tom Watson, the MHD budget officer, writes up the formal funds requests, reviews them with the divisional vice-president, and sends them to corporate headquarters. The MHD operating personnel, especially the production people, initiate expenditure requests by providing Watson with selected cost and revenue data on standard forms supplied by corporate headquarters. If the request is for the replacement of inoperative equipment, it is approved immediately on the assumption that revenues would certainly exceed costs.[2] Requests for funds to replace obsolete equipment with newer, more efficient machines require estimates of cost savings and equipment costs, which Watson uses to calculate the project's net present value.

Expansion requests require both sales and cost data, and these figures are developed jointly by marketing and production people. Typically, expansion takes place after the salesmen have turned in orders for more mobile homes than can be delivered, order backlogs have developed, customers have begun to ask about delivery delays, salesmen have complained to the sales manager, and he has expressed concern to the divisional vice-president. After this sequence of events, the divisional vice-president meets with the

---

[1] Westfall determines its cost of capital in the following manner: It believes that its optimal capital structure calls for 70 percent equity and 30 percent debt. The company currently pays 8 percent for debt (4 percent after taxes), and the estimated equity capitalization rate is 12.5 percent. Using these figures, the weighted cost of capital is determined:

$$30\% \times 4.0 = 1.20$$
$$70\% \times 12.5 = 8.75$$
$$\text{Average} \quad \overline{\underline{9.95\%}}$$

The 9.95 percent estimated cost of capital is rounded to 10 percent.

Top management judges that the retailing operation involves the lowest degree of risk—profits in this division have been quite stable over the years—and that the mobile home division involves the most risk because of uncertainty over the future state of competition in the industry. The other divisions are thought to be equally risky with one another. Accordingly, the retail division is assigned an 8 percent cost of capital for capital budgeting purposes; the mobile home division is given a 12 percent cost; and each of the other divisions has a 10 percent cost. Since MHD and retailing use about the same amount of capital, the corporate average is 10 percent.

[2] The standard argument against formal evaluation of such requests is to ask what the incremental costs and revenues would be if a broken drive motor is replaced on the main MHD assembly line. The motor would cost about $1,500, while the incremental profits resulting from its purchase would be the *entire* profit from the plant, because the plant could not operate without the drive motor. Obviously, the present value of these incremental profits far exceeds the $1,500 cost of the motor.

sales manager and the plant engineer, and all three jointly determine what can be done to increase output. In the past increasing output has generally meant addition of new assembly stations, adding to capacity to produce some key component, or the like. The incremental sales revenue, operating costs, capital outlays, and useful life of the new equipment have been estimated and given to Watson for use in preparing his formal project request. Watson, whose background is in cost accounting, has spent many hours asking probing questions about cost and revenue data, because his own career evaluation depends in part on the ex post accuracy of MHD's capital project requests.

Until recently the procedure used for estimating costs and revenues had never concerned Watson—he had felt that the expert judgments of the production and sales personnel on whom he relied constituted a reasonable means of forecasting the key variables. Further, he had not questioned the *NPV* project evaluation technique or the cost of capital assigned to the MHD by the corporate staff. Two recent events, however, caused Watson to have second thoughts about these established practices. First, he attended a meeting called by Neff, the financial vice-president, in which Neff introduced all the divisional budget officers to his new assistant, Roger Blum. Neff made it clear that Blum was available to assist the divisions both in refining their budgeting procedures and in evaluating specific large projects. After the meeting Watson talked informally with Blum. He came away convinced that Blum was a very capable person and that some of the procedures Blum advocated might well help Watson improve his division's cost and revenue estimates.

The other event which prompted Watson's second thoughts about his procedures was the major project currently under active consideration in the MHD—a new manufacturing facility to be located in Atlanta, which would add substantially to the division's capacity. Presently, MHD's production is concentrated in a single plant located in Chicago, where expansion has been undertaken on the piecemeal basis described above. MHD personnel believe, however, that long-term demand warrants more capacity and that the new capacity should be added in the southeast, where mobile home demand is growing especially rapidly.

Both Watson and his boss, Ed Phillips, the MHD vice-president, have qualms about the expansion plans. Although they feel that the expansion is probably justified, they acknowledge the possibility that other firms in the industry are contemplating similar expansion moves and that serious excess capacity may develop. Further, they wonder if the proposed Atlanta plant represents the optimum means of expanding. Some engineers on the production staff have voiced the opinion that it would be preferable to build several smaller plants located throughout the southeast, in Richmond, Memphis, Orlando, and New Orleans, in addition to Atlanta.

This latter method of expansion appeals to Watson and Phillips for several reasons. First, they could build new plants as actual demand occurs

—the single Atlanta plant, to realize its full cost-saving potential, would have to be built with its full capacity installed at the time of its completion.[3] Second, total transportation costs would certainly be reduced by locating plants close to all the major markets. Third, constructing a series of small plants, with construction phased over several years, would place a lighter burden on the corporation's available funds. (Allen Bruce, Westfall's executive vice-president, has made it plain to all divisions that funds will be both scarce and expensive during the following year or two.)

The marketing personnel have also expressed doubts about the proposed expansion. The company has always followed the practice of offering a full line of mobile homes, expensive models as well as inexpensive ones. The general sales manager, while agreeing that this plan has worked well previously, has questioned its wisdom for the future. He has stated, with the support of his regional sales managers, that the trend is toward higher quality and more expensive mobile homes, and has suggested that the proposed expansion should be used as an opportunity to upgrade the firm's product line.

This upgrading represents a major decision, because the configuration of the new plant would be significantly different for high-quality products. Specifically, if the decision is made to go for the deluxe mobile home market, more precision tools would be required, copper rather than plastic plumbing would be used, and so on. Further, labor would require more training, and more inspectors would be needed, and for both of these reasons it would be difficult and expensive to lay off employees during periods when demand might be slow. Accordingly, production of the more expensive homes would probably be continued during sales slowdowns, so extra storage capacity would be required. All things considered, Watson and Phillips have concluded that if the decision is made to concentrate on production of deluxe mobile homes, the required capital outlay would be considerably larger and the fixed cost component of total cost would also be higher.[4]

With these thoughts in mind, Watson arranged for Neff and Blum to visit the MHD office to discuss the proposed expansion. At the ensuing meeting among Watson, Neff, Blum, and Phillips, it was decided that because of the significance of the proposal to the corporation, as well as the complexities of the proposal, Blum should be assigned to the MHD for an extended period. He and Watson should decide on the data needed to eval-

---

[3] This statement somewhat oversimplifies the case, but the reader should *assume* that the Atlanta plant must be built with full capacity and that it is not feasible to install additional capacity to meet increases in demand in this plant.

[4] The Chicago plant can produce either deluxe or standard mobile homes, and currently about 8,000 expensive models and 10,000 inexpensive models are turned out there. This flexibility is costly, however, because the assembly lines must be modified extensively to alter the output mix. Because of the difficulties in making these production changes and also because of sales and advertising considerations, it seems imperative to have the southeastern plant or plants concentrate on either high-priced or low-priced products, but not on both.

uate the expansion alternatives, the best way of obtaining these data, and how it should be analyzed. Blum would then return to corporate headquarters, but he would remain on call to assist Watson as the need arose. Phillips assured the group that the marketing and engineering staffs of the MHD would cooperate fully. This cooperation would be especially important, because requests for capital expenditures would be due in corporate headquarters in four months. Neff stated that while such large projects are generally considered on an ad hoc basis, in view of the general shortage of funds and the fact that other divisions are also expected to be seeking extraordinarily large amounts of money, every effort should be made to submit the request on schedule.

DEMAND ESTIMATES

Blum and Watson agreed that the imprecise, judgmental estimating procedures previously used are inappropriate for the present decision—because the construction of the new plant, or plants, together with the related working capital, would require an outlay of approximately $25 million, a decision of this magnitude requires very careful and serious consideration. And because the board of directors would certainly review the proposal carefully, both Blum and Watson know that its reception—as well as the subsequent conformity of events to projections—will have a major bearing on their careers.

They decided to attack first the question of demand, setting up demand functions for both the entire industry and for Westfall's MHD, and separate functions for total, high-priced and low-priced mobile homes. Blum and Watson recognized that their estimates were subject to error, so they wanted several different projections, which could be compared with one another and could be used to check the consistency of their estimates.

A great many factors affect the demand for mobile homes, but Watson and Blum believed the key variables to be the following:

1. *Price:* P_{HX} = Industry average wholesale price of high-priced mobile homes

   P_{LX} = Industry average wholesale price of low-priced mobile homes

   P_{HW} = Westfall's average price of high-priced homes

   P_{LW} = Westfall's average price of low-priced homes

2. *Advertising:* A_W = Westfall's MHD advertising expenditures

   A_X = Total industry advertising expenditures

   A_{HX} = Industry advertising expenditures on high-priced mobile homes

   A_{LX} = Industry advertising expenditures on low-priced mobile homes

3. *Income:* I = Per capita income (national average)

4. *Credit terms:* $C =$ Index of credit terms for mobile homes. The higher the index, the more liberal the credit terms. (*Base:* $100 = 1957$–1959 average)

5. *Time:* $T =$ A trend factor which incorporates trends in population and other demographic factors, tastes, and the like. $T_1 = 1950, T_2 = 1951, \ldots, T_{25} = 1974.$

Using data from 1950 through 1974 available from the industry trade association, corporate reports, the U.S. Department of Commerce, and various other sources, Blum and Watson fitted the following equations for total industry demand (Q_T) in units[5]:

$$Q_T = a_1 + b_1 P_{HX} + c_1 P_{LX} + d_1 A_X + e_1 I + f_1 C + g_1 T, \qquad (14\text{-}1)$$

$$Q_T = a_2 P_{HX}^{b_2} P_{LX}^{c_2} A_X^{d_2} I^{e_2} C^{f_2} T^{g_2}. \qquad (14\text{-}2)$$

Table 14-1 Demand Functions—Mobile Homes

Industry
  Total demand

$$Q_T = 101{,}837 - 1.2P_{HX} - 1.5P_{LX} + 0.025A_X + 0.3I + 0.36C + 0.02T. \qquad (14\text{-}3)$$

  Deluxe

$$Q_{HX} = 15{,}063 - 1.3P_{HX} + 0.04P_{LX} + 0.028A_{HX} + 0.32I + 0.60C + 0.03T. \qquad (14\text{-}4)$$

  Standard

$$Q_{LX} = 81{,}694 - 1.8P_{LX} + 0.07P_{HX} + 0.024A_{LX} + 0.2I + 0.28C + 0.01T. \qquad (14\text{-}5)$$

Westfall
  Deluxe

$$Q_{HW} = 1{,}410 - 1.35P_{HW} + 0.05P_{LW} + 0.001P_{HX} + 0.002P_{LX} + 0.01A_W \\ + 0.00356A_X + 0.25I + 0.32C + 0.035T. \qquad (14\text{-}6)$$

  Standard

$$Q_{LW} = 1{,}796 - 1.75P_{LW} + 0.06P_{HW} + 0.003P_{LX} + 0.004P_{HX} + 0.02A_W \\ + 0.0019A_X + 0.23I + 0.27C + 0.02T. \qquad (14\text{-}7)$$

---

[5] Certain data were considered to be relatively accurate; other data were known to be crudely estimated. For example, total unit sales (Q) were relatively accurate, as were the per capita income and credit term figures. Advertising expenditures, on the other hand, were estimated for the whole industry by applying to the entire industry the average advertising/sales ratio of a few companies which report this figure. The breakdown between high- and low-priced homes followed a standard industry procedure, but obviously the decomposed figures were less accurate than the total ones.

Blum and Watson used as an independent variable the ratio cost of conventional housing/cost of mobile homes, but found it to be so highly correlated with the time variable that it was deleted from the regression equations. Some multicollinearity among other independent variables was also encountered, and tests for autocorrelation of the residuals were inconclusive. Blum and Watson were aware of these problems and of the difficulties they could cause in interpreting the regression results. They therefore placed great stress on the "reasonableness" of the final results as viewed by old-timers, and

The linear model, Equation 14-1, was found to provide the better fit—its R^2 and t ratios (standard error divided into the regression coefficient) were higher. The estimated demand functions for both the industry and Westfall are given in Table 14-1.

The demand functions in the table were used to obtain sales projections, which were generated in the following manner: First, estimates of all the independent variables were made for each of the projected years. United States government projections were used for income; credit terms were assumed to continue at the 1975 level; advertising expenditures for both Westfall and the industry were assumed to continue growing at the same rate as during the period 1965-1975; and prices were assumed to continue increasing at the 1965-1975 rate. The values used for each of the independent variables, in both 1975 and 1980, are given in Table 14-2.

Table 14-2 Independent Variable Values

	1975	1980
Industry		
P_{HX}	\$ 11,200	\$ 13,650
P_{LX}	\$ 6,100	\$ 7,400
A_X	\$4,800,000	\$8,400,000
A_{HX}	\$2,800,000	\$4,600,000
A_{LX}	\$2,000,000	\$3,800,000
I	\$ 2,200	\$ 2,780
C	150	150
T	1975	1980
Westfall		
P_{HW}	\$ 11,500	\$ 14,670
P_{LW}	\$ 6,500	\$ 8,300
P_{HX}	\$ 11,200	\$ 13,650
P_{LX}	\$ 6,100	\$ 7,400
A_W	\$ 500,000	\$ 900,000
A_X	\$4,800,000	\$8,400,000
I	\$ 2,200	\$ 2,780
C	150	150
T	1975	1980

Next, the equations given in Table 14-1 were combined with the data given in Table 14-2 to generate the demand projections for 1975 and 1980 that are in Table 14-3. Projections for the other years (1976-1979) in the forecast period were generated in the same way, and projected demand for the mobile home division for the period 1975-1980 is shown in Table 14-4.

---

also took the statistical problems into account when applying their risk adjustments in the final capital budgeting process.

Table 14-3 Standard and Deluxe Demand Projections

	Regression Coefficient (1)	1975 Independent Variable (2)	1975 Product (1) × (2) (3)	1980 Independent Variable (4)	1980 Product (1) × (4) (5)
Industry: Deluxe					
Intercept			15,063		15,063
P_{HX}	−1.3	$ 11,200	(14,560)	$ 13,650	(17,745)
P_{LX}	0.04	$ 6,100	244	$ 7,400	296
A_{HX}	0.028	$2,800,000	78,400	$4,600,000	128,800
I	0.32	$ 2,200	704	$ 2,780	890
C	0.6	150	90	150	90
T	0.03	1975	59	1980	59
Projected Demand			80,000		127,453
					≈127,000
Industry: Standard					
Intercept			81,694		81,694
P_{HX}	0.07	$ 11,200	784	$ 13,650	956
P_{LX}	−1.8	$ 6,100	(10,980)	$ 7,400	(13,320)
A_{LX}	0.024	$2,000,000	48,000	$3,800,000	91,200
I	0.2	$ 2,200	440	$ 2,780	556
C	0.28	150	42	150	42
T	0.01	1975	20	1980	20
Projected Demand			120,000		161,148
					≈161,000
Westfall: Deluxe					
Intercept			1,410		1,410
P_{HW}	−1.35	$ 11,500	(15,525)	$ 14,670	(19,805)
P_{LW}	0.05	$ 6,500	325	$ 8,300	415
P_{HX}	0.001	$ 11,200	11	$ 13,650	14
P_{LX}	0.002	$ 6,100	12	$ 7,400	15
A_W	0.01	$ 500,000	5,000	$ 900,000	9,000
A_X	0.00356	$4,800,000	17,088	$8,400,000	29,000
I	0.25	$ 2,200	550	$ 2,780	695
C	0.32	150	48	150	48
T	0.035	1975	69	1980	69
Projected Demand			8,988		21,765
				≈9,000	≈22,000

Table 14-3 Standard and Deluxe Demand Projections (*continued*)

		1975		1980	
	Regression Coefficient (1)	Independent Variable (2)	Product (1) $\times$ (2) (3)	Independent Variable (4)	Product (1) $\times$ (4) (5)
Westfall: Standard					
Intercept			1,796		1,796
P_{LW}	−1.75	$ 6,500	(11,375)	$ 8,300	(14,525)
P_{HW}	0.06	$ 11,500	690	$ 14,670	880
P_{LX}	0.003	$ 6,100	18	$ 7,400	22
P_{HX}	0.004	$ 11,200	45	$ 13,650	55
A_W	0.02	$ 500,000	10,000	$ 900,000	18,000
A_X	0.0019	$4,800,000	9,120	$8,400,000	15,960
I	0.23	$ 2,200	506	$ 2,780	639
C	0.27	150	41	150	41
T	0.02	1975	39	1980	39
Projected Demand			10,880 ≈11,000		22,907 ≈23,000

Table 14-4 Demand Projections, 1975-1980 ("Normal" Economic Conditions)

	1975	1976	1977	1978	1979	1980
Industry						
Total	200,000	216,000	232,000	251,000	271,000	288,000
Deluxe	80,000	89,000	96,000	109,000	117,000	127,000
Standard	120,000	127,000	136,000	142,000	154,000	161,000
Westfall, Total MHD*						
Deluxe	9,000	11,000	13,000	15,000	19,000	22,000
Standard	11,000	13,000	15,000	16,000	19,000	23,000
Westfall, Southern Operations Only						
Deluxe	1,000	3,000	5,000	7,000	11,000	14,000
Standard	1,000	3,000	5,000	6,000	9,000	13,000

* The figures give projected *demand*, assuming that the Table 14-2 values of the independent variables are accurate. However, Westfall's *sales* of either high-priced or low-priced homes will be *less than* the demand. The company plans to build capacity to produce *either* high-priced *or* low-priced units, but not both. Accordingly, sales will be less than projected demand for the product type whose capacity is not expanded.

Blum and Watson also used the data to generate a set of demand curves for high-priced and low-priced mobile homes. The procedure used is shown in the following calculation for the 1975 deluxe model demand curve:

$$Q_{HW} = 1,410 - 1.35P_{HW} + 0.05P_{LW} + 0.001P_{HX} + 0.002P_{LX} + 0.01A_X$$
$$+ 0.00356A_X + 0.25I + 0.32C + 0.035T.$$

$$Q_{HW} = 1,410 - 1.35P_{HW} + [0.05(6,500) + 0.001(11,200)$$
$$+ 0.002(6,100) + 0.01(500,000)$$
$$+ 0.00356(4,800,000) + 0.25(2,200)$$
$$+ 0.32(150) + 0.035(1,975)].$$

$$Q_{HW} = 24,525 - 1.35P_{HW}, \text{ or } P_{HW} = 18,167 - 0.74Q_{HW}.$$

The complete set of demand curves is shown in Table 14-5. The demand curves given in the table can be used to generate a set of marginal revenue curves in the manner illustrated here for high-priced mobile homes in 1975:

Demand Curve: $P_{HW} = 18,167 - 0.74Q_{HW}$.
Total Revenue Curve: $TR_{HW} = 18,167Q_{HW} - 0.74Q^2_{HW}$.
Marginal Revenue Curve: $MR_{HW} = \dfrac{dTR_{HW}}{dQ_{HW}} = 18,167 - 1.48Q_{HW}$.

Table 14-5 Westfall Demand Curves

1975	Deluxe Model	$P_{HW} = 18,167 - 0.74Q_{WH}$
	Standard Model	$P_{LW} = 12,786 - 0.57Q_{LW}$
1980	Deluxe Model	$P_{HW} = 30,967 - 0.74Q_{HW}$
	Standard Model	$P_{LW} = 21,443 - 0.57Q_{LW}$

The marginal revenue curves associated with the other demand curves were calculated in the same way and are presented in Table 14-6.

Table 14-6 Westfall Marginal Revenue Curves

1975	Deluxe Model	$MR_{HW} = 18,167 - 1.48Q_{HW}$
	Standard Model	$MR_{LW} = 12,786 - 1.14Q_{LW}$
1980	Deluxe Model	$MR_{HW} = 30,967 - 1.48Q_{HW}$
	Standard Model	$MR_{LW} = 21,443 - 1.14Q_{LW}$

DEMAND FOR THE SOUTHERN PLANT'S OUTPUT

The demand projections shown in Table 14-4 are for Westfall's entire MHD —the Chicago plant as well as the new Southern plant. Blum and Watson recognized that, for capital budgeting purposes, they needed to determine the *incremental* sales attributable to the new plant. Accordingly, for planning purposes they assumed that the Chicago plant would continue to produce at the 1975 projected rate—10,000 standard and 8,000 deluxe mobile homes—and would sell this output at the prices given in Table 14-2. The difference between total projected demand and Chicago output is the estimated demand for Southern output. These figures are given in the lower section of Table 14-4.[6]

If the MHD should decide to establish a two-price system, with the Table 14-2 prices charged by the Chicago plant for sales in the Midwest region and another price in the Southern region, how would this affect demand? Certainly a lower price would stimulate demand and a higher price would depress it, but by how much? Blum and Watson decided, after discussions with the sales manager, to handle the problem of the Southern plant's demand function as follows: First, they assumed that if the Southern district should charge the same price as the Chicago division, Southern demand, Q_S, would be equal to Table 14-3 and Table 14-4 values minus Chicago output. If, however, Southern prices should differ from Chicago prices, demand would be higher if a lower price were charged, and lower if a higher price were set. The relationship they used is graphed in Figure 14-1. Here Q_W designates Westfall's total demand for either high-priced or low-priced homes, Q_C denotes the Chicago plant's output, P_S is the Southern division's price, and P_W is the Chicago price. The slope of the demand curve for the Southern plant's output is assumed to be the same as that for the Chicago plant— -0.74 for high-priced mobile homes and -0.57 for low-priced mobile homes.

The procedure is illustrated with 1975 data for high-priced homes.

First, note that Q_{HW} is estimated at 9,000 units. If the Southern facility charges \$11,500, the estimated value of P_{HW} for 1975, then Q_{HS} will be total estimated demand, 9,000, minus Chicago output, 8,000, or 1,000. Sales will increase by 1.35 units for every \$1 price reduction or fall by 1.35 units for every \$1 price increase. If the Southern price is lowered to zero, demand will (according to the linear approximation equation) increase by 15,525 units ($= 1.35 \times 11,500$), so the Q_{HW} intercept is 16,525 ($= 15,525 + 1,000$). The deluxe model demand curve for 1975 is, therefore:

$$Q_{HS} = 16{,}525 - 1.35P_{HS}, \text{ or } P_{HS} = \$12{,}241 - \$0.74Q_{HS}.$$

[6] The Southern plant demand figures are modified at a later stage in the analysis. At present, prices are simply the 1975 projected figures, increased by a trend percentage. Later in the analysis, when cost functions have been developed, a profit-maximizing price/output combination is calculated; and there is no reason to believe that this price/output combination will agree perfectly with the Tables 14-2, 14-3, and 14-4 values.

Figure 14-1   Demand for Southern Production

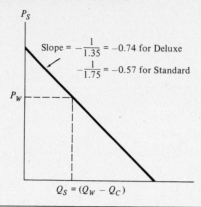

Table 14-7   Southern District Demand and Marginal Revenue Curves

1975: Deluxe
$$P_{HS} = 12{,}241 - 0.74Q_{HS}$$
$$MR_{HS} = 12{,}241 - 1.48Q_{HS}$$

  Standard
$$P_{LS} = 7{,}071 - 0.57Q_{LS}$$
$$MR_{LS} = 7{,}071 - 1.14Q_{LS}$$

1980: Deluxe
$$P_{HS} = 25{,}041 - 0.74Q_{HS}$$
$$MR_{HS} = 25{,}041 - 1.48Q_{HS}$$

  Standard
$$P_{LS} = 15{,}729 - 0.57Q_{LS}$$
$$MR_{LS} = 15{,}729 - 1.14Q_{LS}$$

The Southern district demand curves can be used to develop marginal revenue curves. The procedure is illustrated below for high-priced mobile homes, 1975:

$$TR_{HS} = 12{,}241Q_{HS} - 0.74^2_{HS}.$$
$$MR_{HS} = \frac{dTR_{HS}}{dQ_{HS}} = 12{,}241 - 1.48Q_{HS}.$$

The Southern district demand and marginal revenue curves for 1975 and 1980, calculated as described above, are given in Table 14-7.

COST ESTIMATES

Cost estimates were needed for high-priced and low-priced mobile homes for the proposed large Atlanta plant and for a series of smaller plants located in various southeastern cities. After extended discussions Blum and Watson decided to approach the question of cost estimation in two ways: (1) they would themselves conduct a statistical cost analysis for the industry; (2)

they would have the MHD engineering department develop an engineering cost study to generate functions showing the total and average costs for different plant sizes and at different operating levels. They planned to compare the two sets of estimates and to use any major differences as indications that further study was necessary.

STATISTICAL COST ANALYSIS

The combined backgrounds of both men—Watson's in cost accounting and Blum's in economics and statistics—provided useful insights into the question of statistical cost estimation. They agreed that the best approach, from a theoretical standpoint, would be to follow these steps: (1) They would examine the production function for mobile home manufacturing; (2) they would examine the nature of input prices; (3) they would combine the results of these two examinations to derive a theoretical cost function; and (4) they would statistically estimate the parameters of the cost function, using least squares regression analysis.

Production Function
In the production of mobile homes, as in most other manufacturing operations, it seems reasonable to assume that the production function of a single plant will be of the form shown in Figure 14-2. Here the production function exhibits first increasing, then decreasing, returns to scale. The firm would build additional plants rather than expand the single plant into the region of decreasing returns.

Figure 14-2   Assumed Form of the Production Function for a Single Plant

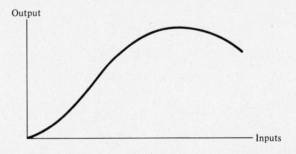

Cost Functions
A preliminary investigation suggested that the prices of inputs other than the fixed plant and equipment would be approximately equal in all geographic areas contemplated as plant sites. Further, since Westfall would not be an especially large employer in any of the areas, Blum and Watson decided

that it would be appropriate to assume that input prices would be invariant with respect to output. Labor and materials costs were, however, expected to rise over time because of inflationary pressures.

Fixed costs would be higher for the large Atlanta plant than for any single small plant, but it was not completely clear at this stage of the analysis whether total fixed costs would be greater for the single large plant or for the series of smaller plants. Also, Blum and Watson noted that certain elements of "fixed" costs would be constant over time, but other elements would rise. Depreciation charges were placed in the first category; property taxes, supervisory personnel salaries, utilities, and the like were placed in the second.

On the basis of these assumptions about the production functions and input prices, Blum and Watson concluded that the total cost function for the large Atlanta plant would probably have the general shape of the hypothetical TC curve shown in Figure 14-3. FC_L represents the fixed costs. The

Figure 14-3 Hypothetical Total Cost Functions for a large Plant and a Series of Small Plants

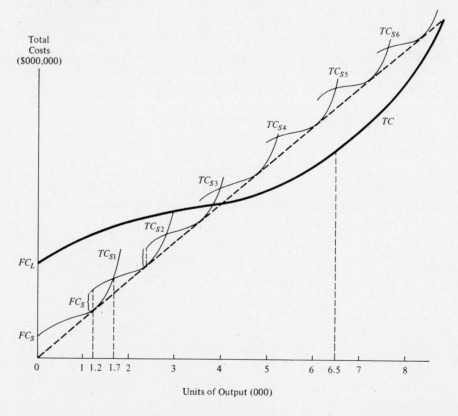

slope of TC first declines, then rises, indicating that marginal costs first decline, then rise. The average cost per unit—measured by the slope of a line from the origin to TC—declines until output reaches about 6,500, is equal to marginal costs (the slope of the TC curve) at this output, and then begins to rise.

The situation is somewhat different for the series of small plants. The curve TC_{S1} in Figure 14-3 designates the total cost function for one small plant. TC_{S1} has the same general shape as TC, but the fixed costs for the small plant (FC_S) are much lower and the curve turns up sharply at a lower output. The optimal, or minimum average cost, output, is about 1,200 units; average cost per unit rises rather sharply beyond this production level.

Suppose Westfall builds one small plant, then adds another, similar plant when the first one is operating at its minimum average cost output. Total cost will jump by the amount of fixed costs (FC_S) incurred by the second plant, plus any variable costs incurred by the second plant. Accordingly, the total costs of the firm will be represented by TC_{S2} for outputs beyond 1,700 (and before a third plant is built). Assuming additional plants can be added continuously and without economies or diseconomies of overhead (that is, overhead cost savings offset costs of coordination), the firm's total cost function, assuming it elects to build a series of small plants, is represented by the scalloped curve.

The average and the marginal curves associated with these hypothetical total cost curves are shown in Figure 14-4.[7] The following points should be noted:

1. The marginal and the average cost curves for the series of small plants are constant and equal to one another beyond an output of about 1,200 units.
2. The cost per unit is higher for the large plant up to an output of about 3,800 units, and lower beyond this production level.
3. The average cost curve for the large plant declines to an output of about 6,500 units, at which point $MC = AC$, and rises beyond that level.
4. At some high output, probably about 12,000 units, the average cost per unit at the large plant will exceed that of the series of small plants.

Figures 14-3 and 14-4 are strictly hypothetical—Blum and Watson constructed them purely to illustrate intuitively the general nature of the cost functions they expected to find in their later empirical studies.

Changes in Cost Functions over Time

Although input prices are assumed to be invariant with respect to output in any given production period, inflationary pressures may be expected to

---

[7] The scallops in the small plant total cost curve are ignored in Figure 14-4.

Figure 14-4 Average and Marginal Cost Functions for a Large Plant and a Series of Small Plants

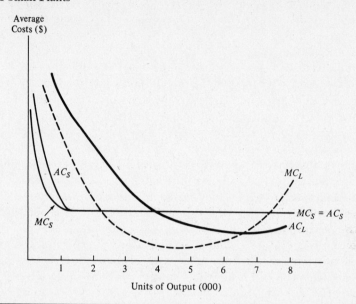

cause input prices to rise over time. These rising prices will have the effect of shifting all the cost functions upward. If fixed input prices (plant managers' salaries, property taxes, and so on) rise by the same percentage as variable factor prices, the shifts will be parallel. If "fixed" input prices rise less than proportionately to increases in variable factor prices, the shifts will not be parallel.

Fitting Long-run Statistical Cost Functions

When Blum and Watson first began their joint project, Blum was convinced that they would be able to fit a statistical cost curve that would provide a great deal of insight into the decision problem at hand. He had written his master's thesis on cost estimation in the electric utility industry, and he planned to use the same procedures for mobile home production. Watson at first played the role of the cautious accountant, but Blum's enthusiasm eventually prevailed. Accordingly, Blum and Watson initially planned to give considerable weight to the statistical cost estimates.

This initial decision was reinforced by a related experience with statistical cost functions. The MHD's cost accounting department, with the assistance of the management services department of a large accounting firm, had recently completed a short-run statistical cost study for use in setting standard costs at various output levels. The results of this analysis, which employed multiple regression techniques to study the relationship between monthly variable costs and monthly output, holding constant other factors —such as wage rates, material costs, machine down-time, and the like—had proved quite useful for short-run planning purposes. The regression statistics had been "good"—the R^2 was high; the standard errors of the coefficients were low; and the model had proved to be an accurate forecaster of short-run costs.

The results of the long-run statistical cost study were quite different. Blum and Watson initially decided, on the basis of theoretical considerations along the lines of Figures 14-3 and 14-4, to fit a cubic cost function of the following kind:

$$TC = a + bQ - cQ^2 + dQ^3 + eX_1 + fX_2 + \cdots. \tag{14-8}$$

Here TC is total costs, Q is output in units, and the X variables represent other independent variables included in the cost function to hold constant such factors as wage rates for firms operating in different areas, age of plant facilities, differences in output (for example, standard versus deluxe mobile homes), and the like.

Blum pointed out to Watson that they would need these data on at least fifteen firms but preferably twenty-five to thirty firms, and that they would use the standard regression program available in Westfall's central computer facilities to estimate the parameters a, b, c, and so on. Further, Blum felt that they should estimate the parameters for a number of different years—say, each year from 1965 through 1974—to determine whether the parameters were stable. If they were, then more confidence could be placed in the use of the cost function as a predictor of the cost/output relationship in the years ahead.

When Blum finished explaining his plan of attack, Watson laughed. Where, he asked, could they possibly get the required data on five firms, much less fifteen? Although the trade association listed thirty-seven manufacturers as members, in addition to Westfall, *cost data in the required form were not available on even one of them.* Twenty-six members, all small, privately owned firms that produced only mobile homes, would not disclose their cost data.[8] The remaining eleven members were all publicly owned corporations, so they did report certain financial data to stockholders, *but these firms were all multiproduct companies, and they did not provide a breakdown of costs by type of product.*

Watson was about to point out the difficulties they would encounter "holding constant factors other than output" even if they had complete access to their competitors' books, but Blum gave up, muttering something

---

[8] Selected information was made available to a national certified public accounting firm hired by the trade association to develop data useful to all members, but this information was treated as highly confidential by the CPA firm. A report based on the data was published by the trade association, but information in it was too highly aggregated to be of any use in a regression study. For the regression study data were needed on *individual* firms, and none were available.

about information in the mobile home industry not being nearly so good as that in the electric utility industry. With that, they abandoned the idea of a statistical cost study and turned their attention to the engineering cost estimates.

ENGINEERING COST ESTIMATES

The MHD engineering staff, under orders from Phillips to expedite the study, worked with equipment manufacturers to determine the optimum kinds of machinery, assembly line setups, and so forth for various levels of operation. Labor requirements, raw materials usage, power costs, transportation charges, and the like were then calculated for the optimum plant associated with each production level. The total of these variable costs, divided by the various output figures, resulted in an engineering estimate of the average variable cost curve.

Some amount of fixed cost is associated with each plant size—the larger the plant, the higher the fixed costs.[9] The total fixed costs plus total variable costs *at the output for which the plant was designed* divided by the optimal output gives the average total cost for that output, and the set of minimum *ATCs* for various outputs defines the long-run average cost curve (*see* Figure 8-6).

Relatively early in the game the MHD chief engineer pointed out to Watson and Blum that he would need some approximate target output figure before he could develop a cost function. In view of the time limitations, not to mention the costs of making the estimates, it was simply not feasible to develop very many short-run cost functions for use in constructing a long-run cost function that covered a wide range of output. The *LRAC* curve would have to be estimated over a more limited range.

After much discussion it was decided that the engineers would design the plants for 1980 production levels and would develop short-run cost functions based on target outputs of 6,000, 8,000, and 10,000 units for the large plant; and 1,000, 1,500, and 2,000 for each of the small plants. Based on preliminary estimates of 1980 demand, these seemed to be reasonable ranges of outputs for that year.

Preliminary analyses of these cost functions revealed that the 8,000-unit design would clearly be the most efficient plant for Atlanta and that the 1,500-unit plant would be optimal for the other locations. The physical size of the acreage under option in Atlanta was insufficient for a plant designed to produce more than 8,000 units annually, but the cost and output

---

[9] For example, a plant designed to produce 2,000 units would require X welders, Y paint spray stations, and so forth. A plant designed for 4,000 units would require a larger amount of capital equipment. Similarly, the smaller plant would have fewer supervisory personnel on the payroll, lower property taxes, and so on. As a result, the total fixed costs would be smaller for the smaller plant.

capacity of a high-speed injection moulding unit on which the larger plant's efficiency was largely based made it unreasonable to warrant building a 6,000-unit plant. In the case of the outlying plants, it was quickly decided that a plant designed for under 1,000 units a year would be grossly inefficient, while one designed for 2,000 units would require the plant to ship to distant markets at a high cost, thus offsetting a principal advantage of the multiple-plant plan—its low transportation cost. Accordingly, the engineering department developed in final form only four cost functions for each year: (1) large plant, deluxe; (2) large plant, standard; (3) small plant,

Table 14-8   Engineering Cost Functions

Large Plant
1975	High Price	$TC_{HS} = \$31,350,000 + \$6,270Q_{HS} + \$0.27Q_{HS}^2$
	Low Price	$TC_{LS} = \$15,700,000 + \$4,700Q_{LS} + \$0.078Q_{LS}^2$
1980	High Price	$TC_{HS} = \$40,000,000 + \$7,000Q_{HS} + \$0.35Q_{HS}^2$
	Low Price	$TC_{LS} = \$20,000,000 + \$5,000Q_{LS} + \$0.10Q_{LS}^2$

Small Plants
1975 *	High Price	$TC_{HS} = \$\ 4,000,000 + \$1,350Q_{HS} + \$8.82Q_{HS}^2$
	Low Price	$TC_{LS} = \$\ 2,000,000 + \$\ \ 600Q_{LS} + \$4.80Q_{LS}^2$
1980 †	High Price	$TC_{HS} = \$37,000,000 + \$6,500Q_{HS} + \$0.85Q_{HS}^2$
	Low Price	$TC_{LS} = \$17,000,000 + \$4,000Q_{LS} + \$0.628Q_{LS}^2$

* Assumes that only one small plant will be built in 1975 and four other plants will be added in 1976-1980.

† Assumes that all five small plants are completed. Further assumes that production is divided equally among the plants.

Figure 14-5   General Shape of the Engineering Cost Functions (Total Costs)

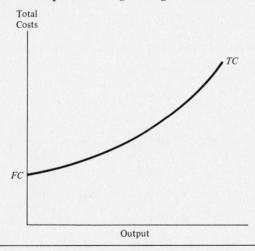

deluxe; and (4) small plant, standard. Table 14-8 presents these functions for 1975 and 1980, and Figures 14-5 and 14-6 show the general shapes of the total cost functions and their associated average and marginal costs.

The marginal cost curve associated with each total cost curve in Table 14-8 is simply the first derivative of the TC curve. Thus, for the large plant, deluxe homes, 1975, the marginal cost curve is calculated as:

$$TC_{HS} = \$31,350,000 + \$6,270Q_{HS} + \$0.27Q_{HS}^2.$$
$$MC = \frac{dTC_{HS}}{dQ_{HS}} = \$6,270 + \$0.54Q_{HS}.$$

Other marginal cost curves were calculated similarly and are shown in Table 14-9.

Figure 14-6   General Shape of the Engineering Cost Functions (Average and Marginal Costs)

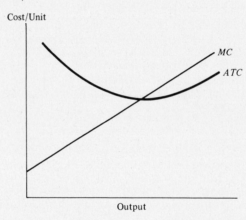

Table 14-9   Marginal Cost Curves

Large Plant

1975	Deluxe	$6,270 + 0.540Q_{HS}$
	Standard	$4,700 + 0.156Q_{LS}$
1980	Deluxe	$7,000 + 0.70Q_{HS}$
	Standard	$5,000 + 0.20Q_{LS}$

Small Plants

1975	Deluxe	$1,350 + 17.64Q_{HS}$
	Standard	$600 + 9.60Q_{LS}$
1980	Deluxe	$6,500 + 1.70Q_{HS}$
	Standard	$4,000 + 1.25Q_{LS}$

ESTIMATING NET PRESENT VALUES FOR ALTERNATIVE PLANTS AND PRODUCTS[10]

Profits

Given the demand and cost functions, Blum and Watson next calculated the expected profits for each of the four alternatives: Atlanta plant, deluxe mobile homes; Atlanta plant, standard mobile homes; multiple plants, deluxe models; multiple plants, standard models. They made this calculation by setting $MR = MC$ to estimate the optimal output for the Southern plant, then used this output to determine revenues, costs, and profits.

To illustrate, the demand curve for deluxe mobile homes for 1975 was found earlier to be $P_{HS} = 12,241 - 0.74Q_{HS}$. Using this equation, Blum and Watson found MR as follows:

$$TR_{HS} = P_{HS} \cdot Q_{HS} = (12,241 - 0.74Q_{HS})Q_{HS} = 12,241Q_{HS} - 0.74Q_{HS}^2.$$

$$MR_{HS} = \frac{\partial TR_{HS}}{\partial Q_{HS}} = 12,241 - 1.48Q_{HS}.$$

The 1975 total cost function for the deluxe model Atlanta plant was seen in Table 14-8 to be:

$$TC_{HS} = \$31,350,000 + \$6,270Q_{HS} + \$0.27Q_{HS}^2,$$

with the associated marginal cost curve:

$$MC_{HS} = \$6,270 + \$0.54Q_{HS}.$$

To estimate the optimal output, Blum and Watson set $MR_{HS} = MC_{HS}$:

$$MR_{HS} = 12,241 - 1.48Q_{HS} = 6,270 + 0.54Q_{HS} = MC_{HS}$$
$$2.02Q_{HS} = 5,971$$
$$Q_{HS} = 2,956.$$

An output of 2,956 units could be sold at a price of $10,054, which they calculated from the demand function as follows:

$$P_{HS} = 12,241 - 0.74(2,956)$$
$$= \$10,054.$$

The costs, revenues, and profits at the optimal price/output points

---

[10] As noted earlier, this case is simplified by abstracting from the difficulties presented by depreciation and other noncash charges. We assume, most unrealistically, that all costs other than depreciation are paid as they occur and that a depreciation reserve fund is set up and increased each year by a "depreciation payment" calculated to permit replacement of assets as they wear out. Making these assumptions permits us to concentrate on *economic* issues rather than on issues covered in accounting and finance courses.

Also, as will be noted later, revenues and costs are determined for three different economic conditions: good, normal, and bad. The equations presented in this section are all based on normal conditions, but it should be realized that Blum and Watson conducted a similar, though less complete analysis for good and bad conditions.

were estimated next. The calculations for deluxe model production, 1975, Atlanta plant, are given below as an illustration[11]:

Step 1. Revenue $= P \cdot Q = (\$10,054)(2,956)$
$$= \$29,719,624.$$

Step 2. Costs $= \$31,350,000 + \$6,270(2,956) + \$0.27(2,956)^2$
$$= \$31,350,000 + \$18,534,120 + \$0.27(8,737,936)$$
$$= \$31,350,000 + \$18,534,120 + \$2,359,243$$
$$= \$52,243,363.$$

Step 3. Before-tax Profit (loss) $= \$29,719,624 - \$52,243,363$
$$= (\$22,523,739).$$

Step 4. After-tax Profits (loss) $= (\$22,523,739) \times 0.5$
$$= (\$11,261,870)$$
$$\approx (\$11,262,000).$$

Thus, an after-tax loss of $11,262,000 was projected for the first year of operations, assuming (1) normal economic conditions, and (2) that a large plant is built in Atlanta to produce deluxe mobile homes. Similar calculations were performed to determine the projected after-tax profits for the other processes and in other years and under other economic conditions; these projections are given in Table 14-10.

Project Life

Although the engineering department estimated that the effective service life of the equipment would be approximately fifteen years, because of uncertainties about the rate of obsolescence they admitted that this was only a rough guess. Also, the engineers suggested that the plant structures, regardless of the production process adopted, would probably require extensive modifications to render them suitable for continual operations after about fifteen years. These considerations, combined with questions about the long-run nature of the demand for mobile homes, suggested to Blum and Watson that they should use a 1989 estimated terminal date for the project. Accordingly, they decided to project the 1980 profits for an additional nine years.

Terminal Value

The land, buildings, and equipment would undoubtedly have some value at the end of 1989, the projected terminal date of the project, but how much value? If Westfall should modernize the plant and continue the operation, the value would be quite high; in view of the probable level of inflation, the

---

[11] The tax calculation assumes (1) a 50 percent tax rate, and (2) that losses are offset by profitable operations in other divisions.

Table 14-10 Southern Operation After-tax Profit Projections for "Normal," "Good," and "Bad" Economic Conditions (dollars in thousands)*

	1975	1976	1977	1978	1979	1980	1981-1989
"Normal" Conditions							
Atlanta Plant							
High Price	($11,262)	($2,710)	($ 637)	$3,369	$13,495	$17,325	$17,325
Low Price	($ 6,766)	($4,408)	$1,257	$ 627	$ 4,417	$11,476	$11,476
Small Plants							
High Price	($ 449)	($ 418)	$1,348	$3,933	$ 6,118	$ 8,526	$ 8,526
Low Price	($ 25)	($ 20)	$ 564	$2,961	$ 4,556	$ 5,854	$ 5,854
"Good" Conditions							
Atlanta Plant							
High Price	($ 6,757)	($1,126)	$1,282	$5,054	$18,243	$22,854	$22,854
Low Price	($ 4,060)	($1,807)	$ 529	$1,934	$ 7,846	$16,788	$16,788
Small Plants							
High Price	($ 260)	$ 12	$2,921	$5,600	$ 9,273	$13,385	$13,385
Low Price	($ 10)	$ 39	$1,346	$4,210	$ 6,911	$ 8,952	$ 8,952
"Bad" Conditions							
Atlanta Plant							
High Price	($16,019)	($4,821)	($1,528)	($ 23)	$ 8,342	$13,048	$13,048
Low Price	($ 7,003)	($5,054)	($1,547)	($ 29)	$ 4,168	$10,951	$10,951
Small Plants							
High Price	($ 1,821)	($ 938)	($ 72)	$1,927	$ 4,723	$ 5,938	$ 5,938
Low Price	($ 332)	($ 65)	($ 11)	$2,382	$ 4,141	$ 5,563	$ 5,563

* For purposes of analysis, assume that all profits are earned at the *end* of the year in question.

Table 14-11 Terminal Value Estimates

"State of Nature"	Terminal Value (1)	Probability (2)	(1) × (2) (3)	Expected Terminal Value = Sum of (3) (4)
Atlanta Plant				
Good: Continued Use, Low Repair Cost	$21,000,000	.2	$4,200,000	
Normal: Continued Use, Higher Repair Cost	$15,000,000	.6	$9,000,000	
Bad: Operation Discontinued, Plant Abandoned	($ 1,000,000)	.2	$(200,000)	$13,000,000
Multiple Plants (five plants)				
Good: Continued Use, Low Repair Cost	$20,000,000	.2	$4,000,000	
Normal: Continued Use, Higher Repair Cost	$10,000,000	.6	$5,400,000	
Bad: Operation Discontinued, Plants Abandoned	$ 3,100,000	.2	$ 600,000	$10,000,000

land value could easily be three times the 1974 purchase price and the buildings could likewise be worth close to their cost of construction, even considering necessary renovation. On the other hand, if technology should change to the extent that the buildings were no longer usable, and if the neighborhood in which the plant is located should deteriorate badly, the cost of closing the plant could even exceed its worth, giving rise to a *negative* terminal value. On the basis of the experience of Westfall's other operations, Watson and Blum decided to base the projected 1989 terminal value on the probability estimates given in Table 14-11.

Project Costs

Estimates of the required outlays for plant and equipment shown in Table 14-12 were obtained from the engineering department. The cost of the raw land for the Atlanta plant was known with certainty, but there was a degree of uncertainty about this cost in the other cities. Site preparation costs, as well as the cost of completing the buildings, could vary considerably depending on soil conditions, the weather, strikes during construction, and the like. Some equipment would be purchased at known catalogue prices, but other equipment would be built on contract; and, depending on technical problems that might be encountered, these costs could vary greatly. Finally, break-in costs would be incurred as bugs were worked out of the processing and assembly facilities, and again, depending on technical factors, these costs could range from modest to quite high.

For the multiple-plant project, the cost of one plant was estimated. Since only one plant will be built in 1975, with the others scheduled for construction in later years, the costs of the four later plants must be discounted back to the present to determine a present value cost-of-investment figure comparable to the cost given for the Atlanta plant. For reasons explained in the following section, a 14 percent discount rate was used to determine the present value of these costs.

Blum and Watson attempted to pin the engineers down to a somewhat narrower range of possible costs, but the engineers stated flatly that this was the best they could do in view of the time constraints, and that even if the time constraints were relaxed, they would not be able to estimate costs much more precisely.

Cost of Capital

The MHD had been assigned a 12 percent cost of capital for use as a discount rate in capital budgeting. As was noted earlier, this rate was questioned; Blum and Watson felt for several reasons that the discount rate should be re-examined. In the first place, the 12 percent rate had been applied to Chicago plant investments, which were probably less risky than the completely untried Southern division operation. Second, there would be less risk in the multiplant approach than in the large Atlanta plant approach for

Table 14-12 Estimated Costs of Building and Equipping Plants (thousands of dollars)

Atlanta Plant	Plant Cost (1)	Probability (2)	(1) × (2) (3)	Expected Cost = Sum of (3) (4)
High Price				
High Estimate	$40,000	0.10	$ 4,000	
Median Estimate	29,000	0.80	23,200	$29,500
Low Estimate	23,000	0.10	2,300	
Low Price				
High Estimate	$30,000	0.10	$ 3,000	
Median Estimate	26,000	0.80	20,800	$25,600
Low Estimate	18,000	0.10	1,800	

Multiple Plants	Plant Cost	Probability	Possible Cost	Expected Cost for One Plant	Present Value of Expected Cost for Five Plants
High Price					
High Estimate	$12,000	0.10	$1,200		$ 7,300 + $7,300 (*IF*)
Median Estimate	7,000	0.80	5,000	$7,300	= $ 7,300 + $7,300 (2.91)
Low Estimate	5,000	0.10	500		= $28,543
Low Price					
High Estimate	$10,000	0.10	$1,000		$ 6,200 + $6,200 (*IF*)
Median Estimate	6,000	0.80	4,800	$6,200	= $ 6,200 + $6,200 (2.91)
Low Estimate	4,000	0.10	400		= $24,242

Notes: (1) All costs for the Atlanta plant will be incurred in 1975. For analysis purposes, assume all costs incurred at the *beginning* of the year.

(2) The same costs are estimated for each of the small plants. One plant will be built each year from 1975 through 1979. Assume that all costs are incurred at the *beginning* of the year in which a plant is built. Further, inflationary increases in construction and equipment costs are assumed to be offset by lower start-up costs as information increases, so plant costs remain constant for the five years. A discount rate of 14 percent is used; the reason for using this rate is explained in the following section, "Cost of Capital."

the simple reason that, if cost and demand projections were not borne out for the first small plant, the remainder of the project could be abandoned or otherwise modified.

In addition, the Atlanta plant would require a large sum of money almost immediately, whereas construction for the smaller plants would be phased over five years. To raise the amount of money required for the Atlanta plant, Westfall would probably have to float a stock issue and incur substantial underwriting costs; the smaller amount of funds required for the small plants could probably be raised at a lower cost through retained earnings and debt issues. In this connection, Neff, the financial vice-president, has already indicated that, although other divisions are expected to be seeking an especially large amount of funds during the next year or two, long-range projections suggest that these extraordinary demands will tapor off after 1976. From this it might be assumed that Westfall's cost of capital will be higher in 1975 and 1976 than it has been in the past or is likely to be in the future.

For these reasons Blum and Watson reached the following tentative decision. Since the large Atlanta plant project is riskier than most MHD projects, riskier than the multiple-plant project, and will require an especially large amount of funds at a time when funds are both scarce and expensive, this project should be evaluated with a 16 percent cost of capital. Because the multiple small plant is riskier than most MHD projects, but less so than the large plant, and because funds are probably more expensive now than they have been in the past, this project should be evaluated with a 14 percent cost of capital. When informed of this decision, Neff agreed that it appeared reasonable, and authorized the use of the new cost-of-capital figures for the specific proposals.

Present Value of Inflows

The next step in the decision process was to calculate the present values of the expected net cash inflows—the "profits" plus the residual value—of the several alternatives. This calculation, for the deluxe model, Atlanta plant, is found as follows:

$$
\begin{aligned}
PV &= \sum_{t=1}^{n} \frac{P_t}{(1+k)^t} = \sum_{t=1}^{n} P_t IF_t \\
&= \frac{(\$11{,}262)}{1.16} + \frac{(\$2{,}710)}{(1.16)^2} + \frac{(\$637)}{(1.16)^3} + \frac{\$3{,}369}{(1.16)^4} \\
&\qquad\qquad + \frac{\$13{,}495}{(1.16)^5} + \sum_{t=6}^{15} + \frac{\$17{,}325}{(1.16)^t} + \frac{\$13{,}000}{(1.16)^{15}} \\
&= -\$11{,}262(0.86) - \$2{,}710(0.74) - \$637(0.64) + \$3{,}369(0.55) \\
&\qquad\qquad + \$13{,}495(0.48) + \$17{,}325(2.30) + \$13{,}000(0.11) \\
&= \$37{,}510{,}000.
\end{aligned}
$$

Other present values were developed in like manner and are presented in Column 1 of the decision trees described below.

Decision Trees

The information developed thus far was used to construct the decision trees shown as Figures 14-7 and 14-8. From the starting box, two branches emerge —the Atlanta plant and the multiple plants. Regardless of which branch is

Figure 14-7 Decision Tree for Deluxe Model

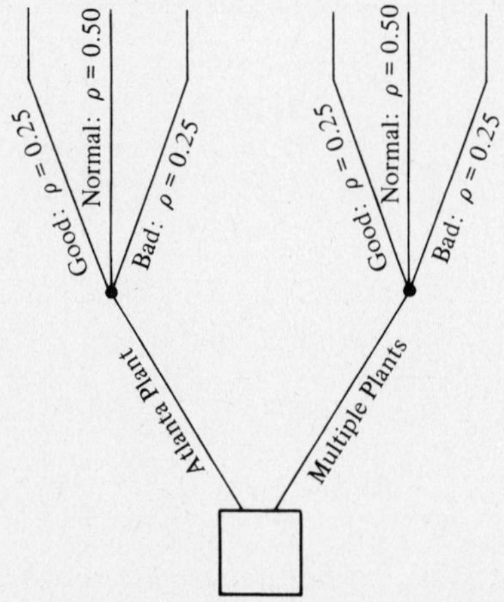

Possible Present Value ($000) (1)	Expected Plant Cost ($000) (2)	Possible Net Present Value ($000) (3) = (1) − (2)	Conditional Probability (4)	(5) = (3) × (4)	Expected Net Present Value ($000) (6) = Σ (5)
$60,807	$29,500	$31,307	0.25	$7,827	
$37,510	$29,500	$8,010	0.50	$4,005	$8,374
$15,669	$29,500	$(13,831)	0.25	$(3,458)	
$48,966	$28,543	$20,423	0.25	$5,106	
$30,207	$28,543	$1,664	0.50	$832	$3,126
$17,297	$28,543	$(11,246)	0.25	$(2,812)	

Atlanta Plant
Good: $\rho = 0.25$
Normal: $\rho = 0.50$
Bad: $\rho = 0.25$

Multiple Plants
Good: $\rho = 0.25$
Normal: $\rho = 0.50$
Bad: $\rho = 0.25$

Figure 14-8   Decision Tree for Standard Model

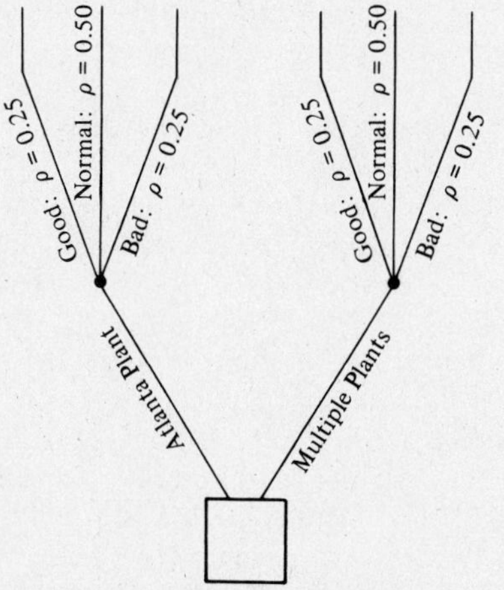

Possible Present Value ($000) (1)		Expected Plant Cost ($000) (2)	Possible Net Present Value ($000) (3) = (1) − (2)	Conditional Probability (4)	(5) = (3) × (4)	Expected Net Present Value ($000) (6) = Σ (5)
Atlanta Plant						
Good: ρ = 0.25	$41,482	$25,600	$15,882	0.25	$3,971	
Normal: ρ = 0.50	$20,405	$25,600	$(5,195)	0.50	$(2,598)	$(925)
Bad: ρ = 0.25	$16,408	$25,600	$(9,192)	0.25	$(2,298)	
Multiple Plants						
Good: ρ = 0.25	$34,074	$24,242	$9,832	0.25	$2,458	
Normal: ρ = 0.50	$21,727	$24,242	$(2,515)	0.50	$(1,258)	$(293)
Bad: ρ = 0.25	$18,270	$24,242	$(5,972)	0.25	$(1,493)	

taken, the probability is 0.25 that economic conditions in the mobile home industry will be good, 0.50 that conditions will be normal, and 0.25 that conditions will be bad. Depending on the state of the economy, the "profits" will vary, as will the *PV* of the profit streams: These figures are given in Column 1 of the tree diagrams. The expected plant costs, taken from Table 14-12, are given in Column 2, and the *NPV* for each branch is given in Column 3. The conditional probabilities, representing in this case the various economic climates, are multiplied by the possible *NPV*s to develop Column 5; and the sum of the Column 5 figures for each branch represents the expected value of the branch. For the deluxe model, Atlanta plant, the *NPV* is $8.374 million.

FINAL DECISION

The last remaining tasks faced by Blum and Watson were (1) to decide on the best course of action, and (2) present (and defend) their choice to Westfall's officers and directors.

QUESTIONS

14-1 Westfall uses the average rate of return on investment as one of its criteria for rewarding division managers. What problems can you think of that would be associated with this usage? Would the same problems arise if the average rate of return was used as a basis for allocating funds among divisions?

14-2 Do you feel that the profit-sharing plan, as described in the case, is well designed to cause Westfall's officers to behave in a manner consistent with the stockholders' best interests? Consider the effects of the plan on each of the following:

a) Efficient operations in production and sales departments.

b) Financial efficiency in the sense of seeking an optimal capital structure.

c) Capital budgeting efficiency in the sense of taking on new projects if, and only if, by doing so the value for the firm's *existing* stockholders is increased.

d) Would the plan's effectiveness be altered if

(i) bonuses were given only in the form of stock,

(ii) bonuses were given only in the form of cash,

(iii) the bonus policy was broadened to include more employees,

(iv) the policy was made more restrictive to cover fewer employees, and

(v) the bonuses of divisional executives were made solely a function of their division's profitability?

e) Accounting policy within the firm, especially with regard to transfer pricing, depreciation, and inventory evaluation.

f) Personnel transfers among divisions and the time span of major projects (long-run, slow payout versus short-run, fast payout projects).

14-3 Do you agree with the general procedure used for determining the cost of capital assigned to the different divisions? Specifically:
  a) Is the weighted average approach reasonable?
  b) Suppose Westfall's management strongly believes that "the stock market" is wrong and that less risk should be assigned to mobile home production than to most other manufacturing operations. Would this affect the way the firm should calculate its divisional cost of capital?
  c) Suppose the reverse is true—investors assign a low degree of risk to mobile home production, but management considers the MHD to be a very risky operation. What effect should this have on the assigned cost of capital to divisions?

14-4 How would each of the following affect the cost of capital that should be used by a division?
  a) Interest rates rise because the Federal Reserve System tightens the money supply.
  b) The stock market suffers a sharp decline, and Westfall stock falls from $75 to $30 a share without, in management's judgment, any decline in the company's future earnings expectations.
  c) The firm decides that it can move from 30 percent to 50 percent debt without affecting the interest rate on debt or the cost of equity capital.
  d) The firm's rate of expansion increases to the point where it must raise substantial sums of new equity capital by selling common stock. Previously, only retained earnings and debt had been used to finance expansion. (The cost of floating new stock issues is estimated to be 20 percent of the funds raised, giving consideration to necessary underpricing that will be required to sell new stock issues.)

14-5 MHD executives, as well as investors, are concerned about possible overcapacity in the mobile home manufacturing industry. Do you think that the industry trade association could perform a service for the firms in the industry by collecting statistics on existing capacity and planned expansions and making this information available to member firms? How would firms use such information, and might there be any antitrust implications?

14-6 Consider the advertising expenditures variables, and answer the following questions:
  a) What are the pros and cons to breaking down advertising into that devoted to deluxe demand and to standard demand, as was done in the demand estimates for the industry, instead of using a single figure?
  b) Suppose Westfall's advertising expenditures in 1978 are actually twice the projected amount. What effect will this have on Westfall's demand for deluxe mobile homes?
  c) Notice that the regression coefficients for all advertising variables are positive. How would you interpret this finding?
  d) Suppose the regression coefficients in Equations 14-6 and 14-7 were larger for A_X than for A_W. How would you interpret this finding? Would it seem reasonable?
  e) Does Westfall's advertising program appear to be more effective for deluxe homes than for standard homes? What about industry advertising? How does Part a of this question bear on your answers here?

14-7 Consider the credit variable and answer the following questions:

a) If the Federal Reserve Board tightened credit, how would this action affect the demand for mobile homes?

b) Is Westfall's deluxe demand or standard demand more sensitive to credit terms? What about the industry as a whole?

c) Some state-controlled savings and loan associations have the power to make loans for the purchase of mobile homes. Should Westfall and other companies lobby in Congress to have this power extended to Federal S & Ls? How would this action affect the demand functions?

14-8 Would the total industry demand (Q_T) be 101,837 units if all the independent variables in Equation 14-3 took on the value 0?

14-9 The regression coefficient for T in Equation 14-6 is larger than that in Equation 14-7. Does this *necessarily* mean that the demand for deluxe mobile homes is growing faster than that for standard homes?

14-10 Firms frequently employ price competition and nonprice competition simultaneously by advertising price reductions. Does this practice have any implications for the choice between Equations 14-1 and 14-2? What do the empirical findings with regard to the fit of the two equations have to say for the practice; that is, should Westfall coordinate advertising and price reductions, or treat them as independent actions?

14-11 The hypothetical average cost functions shown in Figure 14-3 indicate that the average cost of production will be higher if the large plant is built and production exceeds about 12,000 units. Can you think of a reason why this result would probably *not* occur?

14-12 Construct two hypothetical graphs to illustrate the total, average, and marginal cost curves as they are likely to shift over time for the large plant. Assume that "fixed" costs rise less than proportionately to variable costs.

14-13 Short-run statistical cost studies have been reported for a wide variety of industries, ranging from autos to Xerox machines. Long-run cost studies, on the other hand, have been restricted to a handful of industries such as banks, savings and loans, insurance companies, utilities, and steel. Why do you suppose so many more short-run than long-run studies have been conducted?

14-14 Do you think that the engineers were justified in developing just the eight cost functions shown in Table 14-8, or should they have developed a more complete set of functions? Explain the advantages and disadvantages of developing these additional functions.

14-15 Compare the cost curves presented in Figures 14-3 and 14-4 with those in Figures 14-5 and 14-6.

a) Which set is "more reasonable"?

b) Are the curves shown in Figures 14-5 and 14-6 short-run or long-run curves?

c) How could the MC curve in Figure 14-6 possibly represent the marginal costs for a set of small plants when Figure 14-4 shows that the MC curve for a series of small plants should be represented by a horizontal line?

14-16 The price called for under the $MR = MC$ conditions for the deluxe, Atlanta plant in 1973 is substantially below the Chicago price. What assumption about the market for mobile homes is implicit in this decision? What problems might this create? Would you recommended the lower price?

14-17   Would you recommend the use of a probability distribution for the life of the project?

14-18   Does it seem reasonable to use the same probability of occurrence distributions for terminal values for the Atlanta plant as for the five smaller plants?

14-19   How might you improve the decision tree branch for the multiplant option? (*Hint:* Consider what you as an MHD manager might do if, after constructing the initial small plant, demand turned out to be very low.)

14-20   What recommendations should Blum and Watson make to the board of directors?

APPENDIX A

Compound Interest[1]

The time value of money—the fact that a dollar due in the future is worth less than a dollar in hand today—plays an important role in economics. Originally worked out by mathematical economists, the concepts of compounding and discounting are widely used today in all aspects of business and economics. Accordingly, it is useful to have a good grasp of the techniques presented in this appendix.[2]

COMPOUND INTEREST

Assume that you deposit $1,000 in a bank that pays 4 percent interest compounded annually. How much will you have at the end of one year? To treat the matter systematically, let us define the following terms:

---

[1] This appendix is adapted from Weston and Brigham, *Managerial Finance,* 5th ed., The Dryden Press, New York, 1975.
[2] Only two sections of this appendix—"Present Value" and "Present Value of an Annuity"—are absolutely necessary to an understanding of the text material and to the working of the problems in this book.

P = principal, or beginning amount.
i = interest rate.
I = dollar amount of interest earned during a period.
V = ending amount, or the sum of $P + I$.

V may now be calculated as:

$$
\begin{aligned}
V &= P + I \\
&= P + Pi \\
&= P(1 + i).
\end{aligned} \tag{A-1}
$$

The last form of the equation shows that the ending amount is equal to the beginning amount times the factor $(1 + i)$. In the example, where $P = \$1,000$ and $i = 4\%$, V is determined as:

$$V = \$1,000(1.0 + 0.04) = \$1,000(1.04) = 1,040.$$

If the $\$1,000$ is left on deposit for five years, to what amount will it have grown at the end of the period? Equation A-1 can be used to construct Table A-1, which provides the answer. Note that V_2, the balance at the end of the second year, is found as:

$$
\begin{aligned}
V_2 &= P_2(1 + i) \\
&= P_1(1 + i)(1 + i) \\
&= P_1(1 + i)^2.
\end{aligned}
$$

Similarly, V_3, the balance after three years, is found as:

$$
\begin{aligned}
V_3 &= P_3(1 + i) \\
&= P_1(1 + i)^3.
\end{aligned}
$$

In general, V_n, the compound amount at the end of any Year n, is found as:

$$V_n = P(1 + i)^n. \tag{A-2}$$

This is the fundamental equation of compound interest, and it can readily be seen that Equation A-1 is simply a special case of Equation A-2 where $n = 1$.

Table A-1 Compound Interest Calculations

Year	Beginning Amount (P)	$\times$	$(1 + i)$	$=$	Ending Amount (V)
1	$1,000		1.04		$1,040
2	1,040		1.04		1,082
3	1,082		1.04		1,125
4	1,125		1.04		1,170
5	1,170		1.04		1,217

Table A-2 Compound Value of $1

Year	1%	2%	3%	4%	5%	6%	7%	8%	9%	10%
1	1.010	1.020	1.030	1.040	1.050	1.060	1.070	1.080	1.090	1.100
2	1.020	1.040	1.061	1.082	1.102	1.124	1.145	1.166	1.188	1.210
3	1.030	1.061	1.093	1.125	1.158	1.191	1.225	1.260	1.295	1.331
4	1.041	1.082	1.126	1.170	1.216	1.262	1.311	1.360	1.412	1.464
5	1.051	1.104	1.159	1.217	1.276	1.338	1.403	1.469	1.539	1.611
6	1.062	1.126	1.194	1.265	1.340	1.419	1.501	1.587	1.677	1.772
7	1.072	1.149	1.230	1.316	1.407	1.504	1.606	1.714	1.828	1.949
8	1.083	1.172	1.267	1.369	1.477	1.594	1.718	1.851	1.993	2.144
9	1.094	1.195	1.305	1.423	1.551	1.689	1.838	1.999	2.172	2.358
10	1.105	1.219	1.344	1.480	1.629	1.791	1.967	2.159	2.367	2.594
11	1.116	1.243	1.384	1.539	1.710	1.898	2.105	2.332	2.580	2.853
12	1.127	1.268	1.426	1.601	1.796	2.012	2.252	2.518	2.813	3.138
13	1.138	1.294	1.469	1.665	1.886	2.133	2.410	2.720	3.066	3.452
14	1.149	1.319	1.513	1.732	1.980	2.261	2.579	2.937	3.342	3.797
15	1.161	1.346	1.558	1.801	2.079	2.397	2.759	3.172	3.642	4.177

While it is necessary to understand the derivation of Equation A-2 in order to understand much of the material in the remainder of this appendix, the concept can be applied quite readily in a mechanical sense. Tables have been constructed for values of $(1+i)^n$ for wide ranges of i and n. Table A-2 is illustrative; Table A-9, at the end of the appendix, is a more complete one.

Letting *IF* (Interest Factor) $= (1+i)^n$, Equation A-2 may be written as $V = P(IF)$. It is necessary only to refer to an appropriate interest table to find the proper interest factor. The correct interest factor for the above illustration is found in Table A-2. Look down the year column to 5, then across this row to the appropriate number in the 4 percent column to find the interest factor—1.217. Then, using this interest factor, we find the compound value of the $1,000 after five years as:

$$V = P(IF) = \$1,000(1.217) = \$1,217.$$

Notice that this is precisely the same figure that was obtained by the long method in Table A-1.

Present Value

Suppose you are offered the alternative of either $1,217 at the end of five years or X dollars today. There is no question but that the $1,217 will be paid in full (perhaps the payer is the United States government) and, having no current need for money, you would deposit the X dollars in a bank paying a 4 percent dividend. (Four percent is defined as your "opportunity cost.") How small must X be to induce you to accept the promise of $1,217 five years hence?

Referring to Table A-2, we find that the initial amount of $1,000 growing at 4 percent a year yields $1,217 at the end of five years. Hence, you should be indifferent in your choice between $1,000 today and $1,217 at the end of five years. The $1,000 is defined as the *present value* of $1,217 due in five years when the applicable interest rate is 4 percent.

Finding present values (or discounting, as it is commonly called) is simply the reverse of compounding, and Equation A-2 can quite readily be transformed into a present value formula. Dividing both sides by $(1+i)^n$ and dropping the subscript n from V_n, we have:

$$\text{Present Value} = P = \frac{V}{(1+i)^n} = V \left[\frac{1}{(1+i)^n} \right]. \qquad \text{(A-3)}$$

Tables have been constructed for the term in brackets for various values of i and n. Table A-3 is an example; a more complete table, Table A-10, is found at the end of the appendix. For the illustrative case being considered, look down the 4 percent column to the row for Year 5. The figure shown there, .822, is the interest factor used to determine the present value of $1,217 payable in five years, discounted at 4 percent.

$$
\begin{aligned}
P &= V(IF) \\
&= \$1,217(0.822) \\
&= \$1,000.
\end{aligned}
$$

COMPOUND VALUE OF AN ANNUITY

An annuity is defined as a series of payments of a fixed amount for a specified number of years. Each payment occurs at the end of the year.[3] For

---

Table A-3   Present Value of $1

Year	1%	2%	3%	4%	5%	6%	7%	8%	9%	10%	12%	14%	15%
1	.990	.980	.971	.962	.952	.943	.935	.926	.917	.909	.893	.877	.870
2	.980	.961	.943	.925	.907	.890	.873	.857	.842	.826	.797	.769	.756
3	.971	.942	.915	.889	.864	.840	.816	.794	.772	.751	.712	.675	.658
4	.961	.924	.889	.855	.823	.792	.763	.735	.708	.683	.636	.592	.572
5	.951	.906	.863	.822	.784	.747	.713	.681	.650	.621	.567	.519	.497
6	.942	.888	.838	.790	.746	.705	.666	.630	.596	.564	.507	.456	.432
7	.933	.871	.813	.760	.711	.665	.623	.583	.547	.513	.452	.400	.376
8	.923	.853	.789	.731	.677	.627	.582	.540	.502	.467	.404	.351	.327
9	.914	.837	.766	.703	.645	.592	.544	.500	.460	.424	.361	.308	.284
10	.905	.820	.744	.676	.614	.558	.508	.463	.422	.386	.322	.270	.247

---

[3] If the payment is made at the beginning of the period, each receipt simply shifts back one year. The annuity is then called an *annuity due;* the one in the present dis-

Figure A-1   Graphic Illustration of an Annuity: Compound Sum

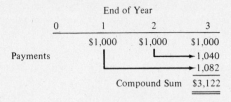

example, a promise to pay $1,000 a year for three years is a three-year annuity. If a person receives such an annuity and deposits each annual payment in a savings account paying 4 percent interest, how much will he have at the end of three years? The answer is shown graphically in Figure A-1. The first payment is made at the end of Year 1; the second at the end of Year 2; and so on. The last payment is not compounded at all; the next to last one is compounded for one year; the second from the last for two years; and so on back to the first, which is compounded for $n-1$ years. When the compound values of each of the payments are added, their total is the sum of the annuity. For the example, this total is $3,122.

Expressed algebraically, with S_n defined as the compound sum, R as the periodic receipt, and n as the length of the annuity, the formula for S_n is:

$$\begin{aligned} S_n &= R(1+i)^{n-1} + R(1+i)^{n-2} + \ldots + R(1+i)^1 + R(1+i)^0 \\ &= R[(1+i)^{n-1} + (1+i)^{n-2} + \ldots + (1+i)^1 + 1] \\ &= R[IF]. \end{aligned}$$

The expression in brackets has been given values for various combinations of n and i. An illustrative set of these annuity interest factors is shown in Table A-4; a more complete set may be found in Table A-11 at the end of the appendix.

To find the answer to the three-year $1,000 annuity problem, refer to Table A-4, look down the 4 percent column to the row for the third year, and multiply the factor 3.122 by $1,000. The answer is the same as the one derived by the long method illustrated in Figure A-1.

$$\begin{aligned} S_n &= R \times IF \\ &= \$1,000 \times 3.122 = \$3,122. \end{aligned} \qquad \text{(A-4)}$$

Notice that the *IF* for the *sum of an annuity* is always larger than the number of years the annuity runs.

---

cussion, where payments are made at the end of each period, is called a *regular annuity* or, sometimes, a *deferred annuity*.

Table A-4   Sum of an Annuity of $1 for N Years

Year	1%	2%	3%	4%	5%	6%	7%	8%
1	1.000	1.000	1.000	1.000	1.000	1.000	1.000	1.000
2	2.010	2.020	2.030	2.040	2.050	2.060	2.070	2.080
3	3.030	3.060	3.091	3.122	3.152	3.184	3.215	3.246
4	4.060	4.122	4.184	4.246	4.310	4.375	4.440	4.506
5	5.101	5.204	5.309	5.416	5.526	5.637	5.751	5.867
6	6.152	6.308	6.468	6.633	6.802	6.975	7.153	7.336
7	7.214	7.434	7.662	7.898	8.142	8.394	8.654	8.923
8	8.286	8.583	8.892	9.214	9.549	9.897	10.260	10.637
9	9.369	9.755	10.159	10.583	11.027	11.491	11.978	12.488
10	10.462	10.950	11.464	12.006	12.578	13.181	13.816	14.487

PRESENT VALUE OF AN ANNUITY

Suppose you are offered the following alternatives: a three-year annuity of $1,000 a year or a lump-sum payment today. You have no need for the money during the next three years, so if you accept the annuity you would simply deposit the receipts in a savings account paying 4 percent interest. How large must the lump-sum payment be to make it equivalent to the annuity? The graphic illustration shown in Figure A-2 will help to explain the problem.

The present value of the first receipt is $R[1/(1+i)]$; the second is $R[1/(1+i)^2]$; and so on. Defining the present value of an annuity of n years A_n, we may write the following equation:

$$
\begin{aligned}
A_n &= R\ \frac{1}{(1+i)^1} + R\ \frac{1}{(1+i)^2} + \ldots + R\ \frac{1}{(1+i)^n} \\
&= R\left[\frac{1}{(1+i)} + \frac{1}{(1+i)^2} + \ldots + \frac{1}{(1+i)^n}\right] \qquad \text{(A-5)} \\
&= R[IF].
\end{aligned}
$$

Figure A-2   Graphic Illustration of an Annuity: Present Value

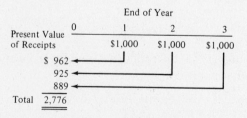

Table A-5   Present Values of an Annuity of $1

Year	1%	2%	3%	4%	5%	6%	7%	8%	9%	10%
1	0.990	0.980	0.971	0.962	0.952	0.943	0.935	0.926	0.917	0.909
2	1.970	1.942	1.913	1.886	1.859	1.833	1.808	1.783	1.759	1.736
3	2.941	2.884	2.829	2.775	2.723	2.673	2.624	2.577	2.531	2.487
4	3.902	3.808	3.717	3.630	3.546	3.465	3.387	3.312	3.240	3.170
5	4.853	4.713	4.580	4.452	4.329	4.212	4.100	3.993	3.890	3.791
6	5.795	5.601	5.417	5.242	5.076	4.917	4.766	4.623	4.486	4.355
7	6.728	6.472	6.230	6.002	5.786	5.582	5.389	5.206	5.033	4.868
8	7.652	7.325	7.020	6.733	6.463	6.210	5.971	5.747	5.535	5.335
9	8.566	8.162	7.786	7.435	7.108	6.802	6.515	6.247	5.985	5.759
10	9.471	8.983	8.530	8.111	7.722	7.360	7.024	6.710	6.418	6.145

Again, tables have been worked out for the interest factor, the term in brackets. Table A-5 is illustrative of the more complete set of interest factors found in Table A-12 at the end of the appendix. From this table, the *IF* for a three-year 4 percent annuity is found to be 2.775. Multiplying this factor by the $1,000 annual receipt gives $2,775, the present value of the annuity. This figure departs from the long method answer shown in Figure A-2 only by a rounding difference.

$$A_n = R \times IF$$
$$= \$1,000 \times 2.775 \qquad (A\text{-}6)$$
$$= \$2,775.$$

Note that the *IF* for the present value of an annuity is always *less than* the number of years the annuity runs, whereas the *IF* for the sum of an annuity is *greater than* the number of years.

ANNUAL PAYMENTS FOR ACCUMULATION OF A FUTURE SUM

Suppose we want to know the amount of money that must be deposited at 5 percent for each of the next five years in order to have $10,000 available to pay off a debt at the end of the fifth year. Dividing both sides of Equation A-4 by *IF*, we obtain:

$$R = \frac{S_n}{IF}.$$

Looking up the interest factor for five years at 5 percent in Table A-4 and dividing this figure into $10,000, we find:

$$R = \frac{\$10,000}{5.526} = \$1,810.$$

Thus, if $1,810 is deposited each year in an account paying 5 percent interest, at the end of five years the account will have accumulated $10,000.

ANNUAL RECEIPTS FROM AN ANNUITY

Suppose that on September 1, 1975, you receive an inheritance of $7,000. The money is to be used for your education and is to be spent during the academic years beginning September 1976, 1977, and 1978. If you place the money in a bank account paying 4 percent annual interest and make three equal withdrawals at each of the specified dates, how large can each withdrawal be so as to leave you with exactly a zero balance after the last one has been made?

The solution requires application of the present value of an annuity formula, Equation A-6. Here, however, we know that the present value of the annuity is $7,000, and the problem is to find the three equal annual payments when the interest rate is 4 percent. This calls for dividing both sides of Equation A-6 by IF to derive Equation A-7:

$$A_n = R(IF). \tag{A-6}$$

$$R = \frac{A_n}{IF}. \tag{A-7}$$

The interest factor (IF) is found in Table A-5 to be 2.775, and substituting this value into Equation A-7 we find the three equal annual withdrawals to be $2,523 a year:

$$R = \frac{\$7,000}{2.775} = \$2,523.$$

This particular kind of calculation is used frequently in setting up insurance and pension plan benefit schedules and in finding the periodic payments necessary to retire a loan within a specified period. For example, if you want to retire in three equal annual payments a $7,000 bank loan drawing interest at 4 percent on the unpaid balance, each payment would be $2,523. In this case, you are the borrower and the bank is "buying" an annuity with a present value of $7,000.

DETERMINING INTEREST RATES

In many instances the present values and the cash flows associated with payment streams are known but the interest rate is not. For example, suppose a bank offers to lend you $1,000 today if you will sign a note agreeing to pay the bank $1,217 at the end of five years. What rate of interest will you be paying on the loan? The answer to this question requires the use of Equation A-2:

$$V_n = P(1+i)^n = P(IF). \tag{A-2}$$

Simply solve for *IF*, then look up this value of *IF* in Table A-2 (or A-9) under the row for the fifth year:

$$IF = \frac{V_n}{P} = \frac{\$1,217}{\$1,000} = 1.217.$$

Looking across the row for the fifth year, we find the value 1.217 in the 4 percent column; therefore, the interest rate on the loan is 4 percent.

Exactly the same approach is taken to determine the interest rate implicit in an annuity. For example, suppose a bank will lend you $2,775 provided you sign a note in which you agree to pay the bank $1,000 at the end of each of the next three years. What interest rate is the bank charging you? To answer the question, solve Equation A-6 for *IF*, then look up the *IF* in Table A-5 (or A-12):

$$A_n = R \times IF$$
$$IF = \frac{A_n}{R} = \frac{\$2,775}{\$1,000} = 2.775. \qquad \text{(A-6)}$$

Looking across the third-year row, we find the factor 2.775 under the 4 percent column; therefore, the bank is lending you money at 4 percent.

PRESENT VALUE OF AN UNEVEN SERIES OF RECEIPTS

Recall that the definition of an annuity includes the words *fixed amount*—in other words, annuities deal with constant, or level, payments or receipts. Although many economic decisions do involve constant payments, many important decisions are concerned with uneven flows of cash. Consequently, it is necessary to expand the present analysis to deal with varying payment streams. Because most of the applications call for present value, not compound sums or other figures, this section is restricted to the present value (*PV*).

To illutrate the calculating procedure, suppose someone offers to sell you a series of payments consisting of $300 after one year, $100 after two years, and $200 after three years. How much would you be willing to pay for the series, assuming the appropriate discount rate (interest rate) is 4 percent? To determine the purchase price, simply compute the present value of the series. The calculations are worked out in Table A-6.

The receipts for each year are shown in the second column; the discount factors (from Table A-3) are given in the third column; and the product of these two columns, the present value of each individual receipt, is given in the last column. When the individual present values in the last column are added, the sum is the present value of the investment, $558.90. Under the assumptions of the example, you should be willing to pay this amount for the investment.

If the series of payments had been somewhat different—say $300 at the

Table A-6 Calculating the Present Value of an Uneven Series of Payments

Year	Receipt	×	Interest Factor	=	Present Value
1	$300		.962		$288.60
2	100		.925		92.50
3	200		.889		177.80
			Present Value of Investment		$558.90

end of the first year, then nine annual payments of $100 each—we would probably want to use a different procedure for finding the present value of the investment. We could set up a calculating table, such as Table A-6, but because most of the payments are part of an annuity, we may use a short cut. The calculating procedure is shown in Table A-7, and the logic of the table is diagramed in Figure A-3.

Section 1 of the table deals with the $300 received at the end of the first year; its present value is found to be $288.60. Section 2 deals with the nine $100 payments. In 2(a) of the table the value of a $100, nine-year, 4 percent annuity is found to be $743.50. However, the annuity does not start until *next* year—that is, the first receipt under the annuity comes in two years—so it is worth less than $743.50 today. Specifically, it is worth the

Table A-7 Calculating Procedure for an Uneven Series of Payments that Includes an Annuity

1. *PV* of $300 due in 1 year $300(0.962) $288.60
2. *PV* of nine-year annuity with $100 receipts
   a) *PV* at beginning of next year
     $100(7.435) = $743.50
   b) *PV* of $743.50 = $743.50(0.962)   715.25
3. *PV* of total series $1,003.85

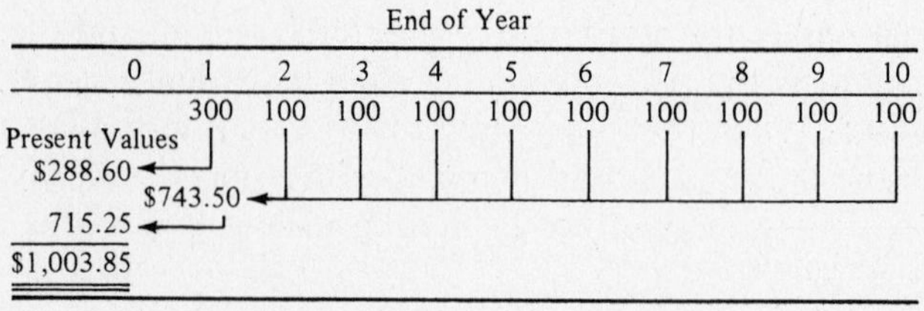

Figure A-3 Graphic Illustration of Present Value Calculations

present value of $743.50, discounted back one year at 4 percent, or $715.25; this calculation is shown in 2(b) of the table. When the present value of the initial payment is added to the present value of the annuity component, the sum is the present value of the entire investment, or $1,003.85.

SEMIANNUAL AND OTHER COMPOUNDING PERIODS

In all the examples used thus far it has been assumed that returns were received once a year, or annually. For example, in the first section of this appendix, dealing with compound values, it was assumed that funds were placed on deposit in a bank and grew by 4 percent a year. However, suppose the advertised rate had been 4 percent compounded *semiannually*. What would this have meant? Consider the following example.

A person deposits $1,000 in a bank savings account and receives a return of 4 percent compounded semiannually. How much will he have at the end of one year? Semiannual compounding means that interest is actually paid each six months, a fact taken into account in the tabular calculations in Table A-8. Here the annual interest rate is divided by 2, but twice as many compounding periods are used because interest is paid twice a year. Comparing the amount on hand at the end of the second six-month period, $1,040.40, with what would have been on hand under annual compounding, $1,040, shows that semiannual compounding is better from the standpoint of the saver. This result occurs because he earns interest on interest more frequently.

General formulas can be developed for use when compounding periods are more frequent than once a year. To demonstrate this, Equation A-2 is modified as follows:

$$V_n = P(1+i)^n \qquad \text{(A-2)}$$

$$V_n = P\left(1+\frac{i}{m}\right)^{mn} \qquad \text{(A-8)}$$

Here m is the number of times a year compounding occurs. When banks compute daily interest, the value of m is set at 365 and Equation A-8 is applied.

Interest tables can be used when compounding occurs more than once a year. Simply divide the nominal, or stated, interest rate by the number of

---

Table A-8 Compound Interest Calculations with Semiannual Compounding

Period	Beginning Amount (P)	×	(1 + i)	=	Ending Amount
1	$1,000.00		(1.02)		$1,020.00
2	1,020.00		(1.02)		1,040.40

times compounding occurs in a year, and multiply the years by the number of compounding periods a year. For example, to find the amount to which $1,000 will grow after five years if semiannual compounding is applied to a stated 4 percent interest rate, divide 4 percent by 2 and multiply the five years by 2. Then refer to Table A-2 (or Table A-9) under the 2 percent column and in the row for the tenth year. You find an interest factor of 1.219. Multiplying this by the initial $1,000 gives a value of $1,219, the amount to which $1,000 will grow in five years at 4 percent compounded semiannually. This compares with $1,217 for annual compounding.

The same procedure is applied in all the cases covered—compounding, discounting, single payments, and annuities. To illustrate semiannual compounding in finding the present value of an annuity, for example, consider the case described in the above section on the present value of an annuity— $1,000 a year for three years, discounted at 4 percent. With annual compounding (or discounting) the interest factor is 2.775, and the present value of the annuity is $2,775. For semiannual compounding look under the 2 percent column and in the Year 6 row of Table A-5 to find an interest factor of 5.601. This amount is now multiplied by one-half of $1,000, or the $500 deposited each six months, to get the present value of the annuity—$2,800. The payments come a little more rapidly—the first $500 is paid after only six months (similarly with other payments), so the annuity is a little more valuable if payments are received semiannually rather than annually.

By letting m approach infinity, Equation A-8 can be modified to the special case of *continuous compounding*. Continuous compounding, while useful in developing theoretical models, has not been used frequently in practical applications. Moreover, its development is highly technical and requires the use of integral calculus. We have therefore elected not to treat it in this book.[4]

---

[4] For a discussion of continuous compounding, *see Managerial Finance*, 5th ed., The Dryden Press, Hinsdale, Illinois, 1975, Appendix to Chapter 9.

COMPOUND INTEREST TABLES

Table A-9 Compound Sum of $1

Period	1%	2%	3%	4%	5%	6%	7%
1	1.010	1.020	1.030	1.040	1.050	1.060	1.070
2	1.020	1.040	1.061	1.082	1.102	1.124	1.145
3	1.030	1.061	1.093	1.125	1.158	1.191	1.225
4	1.041	1.082	1.126	1.170	1.216	1.262	1.311
5	1.051	1.104	1.159	1.217	1.276	1.338	1.403
6	1.062	1.126	1.194	1.265	1.340	1.419	1.501
7	1.072	1.149	1.230	1.316	1.407	1.504	1.606
8	1.083	1.172	1.267	1.369	1.477	1.594	1.718
9	1.094	1.195	1.305	1.423	1.551	1.689	1.838
10	1.105	1.219	1.344	1.480	1.629	1.791	1.967
11	1.116	1.243	1.384	1.539	1.710	1.898	2.105
12	1.127	1.268	1.426	1.601	1.796	2.012	2.252
13	1.138	1.294	1.469	1.665	1.886	2.133	2.410
14	1.149	1.319	1.513	1.732	1.980	2.261	2.579
15	1.161	1.346	1.558	1.801	2.079	2.397	2.759
16	1.173	1.373	1.605	1.873	2.183	2.540	2.952
17	1.184	1.400	1.653	1.948	2.292	2.693	3.159
18	1.196	1.428	1.702	2.026	2.407	2.854	3.380
19	1.208	1.457	1.754	2.107	2.527	3.026	3.617
20	1.220	1.486	1.806	2.191	2.653	3.207	3.870
25	1.282	1.641	2.094	2.666	3.386	4.292	5.427
30	1.348	1.811	2.427	3.243	4.322	5.743	7.612

Period	8%	9%	10%	12%	14%	15%	16%
1	1.080	1.090	1.100	1.120	1.140	1.150	1.160
2	1.166	1.186	1.210	1.254	1.300	1.322	1.346
3	1.260	1.295	1.331	1.405	1.482	1.521	1.561
4	1.360	1.412	1.464	1.574	1.689	1.749	1.811
5	1.469	1.539	1.611	1.762	1.925	2.011	2.100
6	1.587	1.677	1.772	1.974	2.195	2.313	2.436
7	1.714	1.828	1.949	2.211	2.502	2.660	2.826
8	1.851	1.993	2.144	2.476	2.853	3.059	3.278
9	1.999	2.172	2.358	2.773	3.252	3.518	3.803
10	2.159	2.367	2.594	3.106	3.707	4.046	4.411
11	2.332	2.580	2.853	3.479	4.226	4.652	5.117
12	2.518	2.813	3.138	3.896	4.818	5.350	5.926
13	2.720	3.066	3.452	4.363	5.492	6.153	6.886
14	2.937	3.342	3.797	4.887	6.261	7.076	7.988
15	3.172	3.642	4.177	5.474	7.138	8.137	9.266
16	3.426	3.970	4.595	6.130	8.137	9.358	10.748
17	3.700	4.328	5.054	6.866	9.276	10.761	12.468
18	3.996	4.717	5.560	7.690	10.575	12.375	14.463
19	4.316	5.142	6.116	8.613	12.056	14.232	16.777
20	4.661	5.604	6.728	9.646	13.743	16.367	19.461
25	6.848	8.623	10.835	17.000	26.462	32.919	40.874
30	10.063	13.268	17.449	29.960	50.950	66.212	85.850

Table A-9 (concluded)

Period	18%	20%	24%	28%	32%	36%
1	1.180	1.200	1.240	1.280	1.320	1.360
2	1.392	1.440	1.538	1.638	1.742	1.850
3	1.643	1.728	1.907	2.067	2.300	2.515
4	1.939	2.074	2.364	2.684	3.036	3.421
5	2.288	2.488	2.932	3.436	4.007	4.653
6	2.700	2.986	3.635	4.398	5.290	6.328
7	3.185	3.583	4.508	5.629	6.983	8.605
8	3.759	4.300	5.590	7.206	9.217	11.703
9	4.435	5.160	6.931	9.223	12.166	15.917
10	5.234	6.192	8.594	11.806	16.060	21.647
11	6.176	7.430	10.657	15.112	21.199	29.439
12	7.288	8.916	13.215	19.343	27.983	40.037
13	8.599	10.699	16.386	24.759	36.937	54.451
14	10.147	12.839	20.319	31.961	48.757	74.053
15	11.974	15.407	25.196	40.565	64.359	100.712
16	14.129	18.488	31.243	51.923	84.954	136.97
17	16.672	22.186	38.741	66.461	112.14	186.28
18	19.673	26.623	48.039	85.071	148.02	253.34
19	23.214	31.948	59.568	108.89	195.39	344.54
20	27.393	38.338	73.864	139.38	257.92	468.57
25	62.669	95.396	216.542	478.90	1033.6	2180.1
30	143.371	237.376	634.820	1645.5	4142.1	10143.

Period	40%	50%	60%	70%	80%	90%
1	1.400	1.500	1.600	1.700	1.800	1.900
2	1.960	2.250	2.560	2.890	3.240	3.610
3	2.744	3.375	4.096	4.913	5.832	6.859
4	3.842	5.062	6.544	8.352	10.498	13.032
5	5.378	7.594	10.486	14.199	18.896	24.761
6	7.530	11.391	16.777	24.138	34.012	47.046
7	10.541	17.086	26.844	41.034	61.222	89.387
8	14.758	25.629	42.950	69.758	110.200	169.836
9	20.661	38.443	68.720	118.588	198.359	322.688
10	28.925	57.665	109.951	201.599	357.047	613.107
11	40.496	86.498	175.922	342.719	642.684	1164.902
12	56.694	129.746	281.475	582.622	1156.831	2213.314
13	79.372	194.619	450.360	990.457	2082.295	4205.297
14	111.120	291.929	720.576	1683.777	3748.131	7990.065
15	155.568	437.894	1152.921	2862.421	6746.636	15181.122
16	217.795	656.84	1844.7	4866.1	12144.	28844.0
17	304.914	985.26	2951.5	8272.4	21859.	54804.0
18	426.879	1477.9	4722.4	14063.0	39346.	104130.0
19	597.630	2216.8	7555.8	23907.0	70824.	197840.0
20	836.683	3325.3	12089.0	40642.0	127480.	375900.0
25	4499.880	25251.	126760.0	577060.0	2408900.	9307600.0
30	24201.432	191750.	1329200.0	8193500.0	45517000.	230470000.0

Table A-10 Present Value of $1

Period	1%	2%	3%	4%	5%	6%	7%	8%	9%	10%	12%	14%	15%
1	.990	.980	.971	.962	.952	.943	.935	.926	.917	.909	.893	.877	.870
2	.980	.961	.943	.925	.907	.890	.873	.857	.842	.826	.797	.769	.756
3	.971	.942	.915	.889	.864	.840	.816	.794	.772	.751	.712	.675	.658
4	.961	.924	.889	.855	.823	.792	.763	.735	.708	.683	.636	.592	.572
5	.951	.906	.863	.822	.784	.747	.713	.681	.650	.621	.567	.519	.497
6	.942	.888	.838	.790	.746	.705	.666	.630	.596	.564	.507	.456	.432
7	.933	.871	.813	.760	.711	.665	.623	.583	.547	.513	.452	.400	.376
8	.923	.853	.789	.731	.677	.627	.582	.540	.502	.467	.404	.351	.327
9	.914	.837	.766	.703	.645	.592	.544	.500	.460	.424	.361	.308	.284
10	.905	.820	.744	.676	.614	.558	.508	.463	.422	.386	.322	.270	.247
11	.896	.804	.722	.650	.585	.527	.475	.429	.388	.350	.287	.237	.215
12	.887	.788	.701	.625	.557	.497	.444	.397	.356	.319	.257	.208	.187
13	.879	.773	.681	.601	.530	.469	.415	.368	.326	.290	.229	.182	.163
14	.870	.758	.661	.577	.505	.442	.388	.340	.299	.263	.205	.160	.141
15	.861	.743	.642	.555	.481	.417	.362	.315	.275	.239	.183	.140	.123
16	.853	.728	.623	.534	.458	.394	.339	.292	.252	.218	.163	.123	.107
17	.844	.714	.605	.513	.436	.371	.317	.270	.231	.198	.146	.108	.093
18	.836	.700	.587	.494	.416	.350	.296	.250	.212	.180	.130	.095	.081
19	.828	.686	.570	.475	.396	.331	.276	.232	.194	.164	.116	.083	.070
20	.820	.673	.554	.456	.377	.312	.258	.215	.178	.149	.104	.073	.061
25	.780	.610	.478	.375	.295	.233	.184	.146	.116	.092	.059	.038	.030
30	.742	.552	.412	.308	.231	.174	.131	.099	.075	.057	.033	.020	.015

Period	16%	18%	20%	24%	28%	32%	36%	40%	50%	60%	70%	80%	90%
1	.862	.847	.833	.806	.781	.758	.735	.714	.667	.625	.588	.556	.526
2	.743	.718	.694	.650	.610	.574	.541	.510	.444	.391	.346	.309	.277
3	.641	.609	.579	.524	.477	.435	.398	.364	.296	.244	.204	.171	.146
4	.552	.516	.482	.423	.373	.329	.292	.260	.198	.153	.120	.095	.077
5	.476	.437	.402	.341	.291	.250	.215	.186	.132	.095	.070	.053	.040
6	.410	.370	.335	.275	.227	.189	.158	.133	.088	.060	.041	.029	.021
7	.354	.314	.279	.222	.178	.143	.116	.095	.059	.037	.024	.016	.011
8	.305	.266	.233	.179	.139	.108	.085	.068	.039	.023	.014	.009	.006
9	.263	.226	.194	.144	.108	.082	.063	.048	.026	.015	.008	.005	.003
10	.227	.191	.162	.116	.085	.062	.046	.035	.017	.009	.005	.003	.002
11	.195	.162	.135	.094	.066	.047	.034	.025	.012	.006	.003	.002	.001
12	.168	.137	.112	.076	.052	.036	.025	.018	.008	.004	.002	.001	.001
13	.145	.116	.093	.061	.040	.027	.018	.013	.005	.002	.001	.001	.000
14	.125	.099	.078	.049	.032	.021	.014	.009	.003	.001	.001	.000	.000
15	.108	.084	.065	.040	.025	.016	.010	.006	.002	.001	.000	.000	.000
16	.093	.071	.054	.032	.019	.012	.007	.005	.002	.001	.000	.000	
17	.080	.060	.045	.026	.015	.009	.005	.003	.001	.000	.000		
18	.089	.051	.038	.021	.012	.007	.004	.002	.001	.000	.000		
19	.060	.043	.031	.017	.009	.005	.003	.002	.000	.000			
20	.051	.037	.026	.014	.007	.004	.002	.001	.000	.000			
25	.024	.016	.010	.005	.002	.001	.000	.000					
30	.012	.007	.004	.002	.001	.000	.000						

Table A-11 Sum of an Annuity of $1 for N Periods

Period	1%	2%	3%	4%	5%	6%
1	1.000	1.000	1.000	1.000	1.000	1.000
2	2.010	2.020	2.030	2.040	2.050	2.060
3	3.030	3.060	3.091	3.122	3.152	3.184
4	4.060	4.122	4.184	4.246	4.310	4.375
5	5.101	5.204	5.309	5.416	5.526	5.637
6	6.152	6.308	6.468	6.633	6.802	6.975
7	7.214	7.434	7.662	7.898	8.142	8.394
8	8.286	8.583	8.892	9.214	9.549	9.897
9	9.369	9.755	10.159	10.583	11.027	11.491
10	10.462	10.950	11.464	12.006	12.578	13.181
11	11.567	12.169	12.808	13.486	14.207	14.972
12	12.683	13.412	14.192	15.026	15.917	16.870
13	13.809	14.680	15.618	16.627	17.713	18.882
14	14.947	15.974	17.086	18.292	19.599	21.051
15	16.097	17.293	18.599	20.024	21.579	23.276
16	17.258	18.639	20.157	21.825	23.657	25.673
17	18.430	20.012	21.762	23.698	25.840	28.213
18	19.615	21.412	23.414	25.645	28.132	30.906
19	20.811	22.841	25.117	27.671	30.539	33.760
20	22.019	24.297	26.870	29.778	33.066	36.786
25	28.243	32.030	36.459	41.646	47.727	54.865
30	34.785	40.568	47.575	56.805	66.439	79.058

Period	7%	8%	9%	10%	12%	14%
1	1.000	1.000	1.000	1.000	1.000	1.000
2	2.070	2.080	2.090	2.100	2.120	2.140
3	3.215	3.246	3.278	3.310	3.374	3.440
4	4.440	4.506	4.573	4.641	4.770	4.921
5	5.751	5.867	5.985	6.105	6.353	6.610
6	7.153	7.336	7.523	7.716	8.115	8.536
7	8.654	8.923	9.200	9.487	10.089	10.730
8	10.260	10.637	11.028	11.436	12.300	13.233
9	11.978	12.488	13.021	13.579	14.776	16.085
10	13.816	14.487	15.193	15.937	17.549	19.337
11	15.784	16.645	17.560	18.531	20.655	23.044
12	17.888	18.977	20.141	21.384	24.133	27.271
13	20.141	21.495	22.953	24.523	28.029	32.089
14	22.550	24.215	26.019	27.975	32.393	37.581
15	25.129	27.152	29.361	31.772	37.280	43.842
16	27.888	30.324	33.003	35.950	42.753	50.980
17	30.840	33.750	36.974	40.545	48.884	59.118
18	33.999	37.450	41.301	45.599	55.750	68.394
19	37.379	41.446	46.018	51.159	63.440	78.969
20	40.995	45.762	51.160	57.275	72.052	91.025
25	63.249	73.106	84.701	98.347	133.334	181.871
30	94.461	113.283	136.308	164.494	241.333	356.787

Table A-11   (concluded)

Period	16%	18%	20%	24%	28%	32%
1	1.000	1.000	1.000	1.000	1.000	1.000
2	2.160	2.180	2.200	2.240	2.280	2.320
3	3.506	3.572	3.640	3.778	3.918	4.062
4	5.066	5.215	5.368	5.684	6.016	6.362
5	6.877	7.154	7.442	8.048	8.700	9.398
6	8.977	9.442	9.930	10.980	12.136	13.406
7	11.414	12.142	12.916	14.615	16.534	18.696
8	14.240	15.327	16.499	19.123	22.163	25.678
9	17.518	19.086	20.799	24.712	29.369	34.895
10	21.321	23.521	25.959	31.643	38.592	47.062
11	25.733	28.755	32.150	40.238	50.399	63.122
12	30.850	34.931	39.580	50.985	65.510	84.320
13	36.786	42.219	48.497	64.110	84.853	112.303
14	43.672	50.818	59.196	80.496	109.612	149.240
15	51.660	60.965	72.035	100.815	141.303	197.997
16	60.925	72.939	87.442	126.011	181.87	262.36
17	71.673	87.068	105.931	157.253	233.79	347.31
18	84.141	103.740	128.117	195.994	300.25	459.45
19	98.603	123.414	154.740	244.033	385.32	607.47
20	115.380	146.628	186.688	303.601	494.21	802.86
25	249.214	342.603	471.981	898.092	1706.8	3226.8
30	530.312	790.948	1181.882	2640.916	5873.2	12941.0

Period	36%	40%	50%	60%	70%	80%
1	1.000	1.000	1.000	1.000	1.000	1.000
2	2.360	2.400	2.500	2.600	2.700	2.800
3	4.210	4.360	4.750	5.160	5.590	6.040
4	6.725	7.104	8.125	9.256	10.503	11.872
5	10.146	10.846	13.188	15.810	18.855	22.370
6	14.799	16.324	20.781	26.295	33.054	41.265
7	21.126	23.853	32.172	43.073	57.191	75.278
8	29.732	34.395	49.258	69.916	98.225	136.500
9	41.435	49.153	74.887	112.866	167.983	246.699
10	57.352	69.814	113.330	181.585	286.570	445.058
11	78.998	98.739	170.995	291.536	488.170	802.105
12	108.437	139.235	257.493	467.458	830.888	1444.788
13	148.475	195.929	387.239	748.933	1413.510	2601.619
14	202.926	275.300	581.859	1199.293	2403.968	4683.914
15	276.979	386.420	873.788	1919.869	4087.745	8432.045
16	377.69	541.99	1311.7	3072.8	6950.2	15179.0
17	514.66	759.78	1968.5	4917.5	11816.0	27323.0
18	700.94	1064.7	2953.8	7868.9	20089.0	49182.0
19	954.28	1491.6	4431.7	12591.0	34152.0	88528.0
20	1298.8	2089.2	6648.5	20147.0	58059.0	159350.0
25	6053.0	11247.0	50500.0	211270.0	824370.0	3011100.0
30	28172.0	60501.0	383500.0	2215400.0	11705000.0	56896000.0

Table A-12 Present Value of an Annuity of $1

Period	1%	2%	3%	4%	5%	6%	7%	8%	9%	10%
1	0.990	0.980	0.971	0.962	0.952	0.943	0.935	0.926	0.917	0.909
2	1.970	1.942	1.913	1.886	1.859	1.833	1.808	1.783	1.759	1.736
3	2.941	2.884	2.829	2.775	2.723	2.673	2.624	2.577	2.531	2.487
4	3.902	3.808	3.717	3.630	3.546	3.465	3.387	3.312	3.240	3.170
5	4.853	4.713	4.580	4.452	4.329	4.212	4.100	3.993	3.890	3.791
6	5.795	5.601	5.417	5.242	5.076	4.917	4.766	4.623	4.486	4.355
7	6.728	6.472	6.230	6.002	5.786	5.582	5.389	5.206	5.033	4.868
8	7.652	7.325	7.020	6.733	6.463	6.210	5.971	5.747	5.535	5.335
9	8.566	8.162	7.786	7.435	7.108	6.802	6.515	6.247	5.995	5.759
10	9.471	8.983	8.530	8.111	7.722	7.360	7.024	6.710	6.418	6.145
11	10.368	9.787	9.253	8.760	8.306	7.887	7.499	7.139	6.805	6.495
12	11.255	10.575	9.954	9.385	8.863	8.384	7.943	7.536	7.161	6.814
13	12.134	11.348	10.635	9.986	9.394	8.853	8.358	7.904	7.487	7.103
14	13.004	12.106	11.296	10.563	9.899	9.295	8.745	8.244	7.786	7.367
15	13.865	12.849	11.938	11.118	10.380	9.712	9.108	8.559	8.060	7.606
16	14.718	13.578	12.561	11.652	10.838	10.106	9.447	8.851	8.312	7.824
17	15.562	14.292	13.166	12.166	11.274	10.477	9.763	9.122	8.544	8.022
18	16.398	14.992	13.754	12.659	11.690	10.828	10.059	9.372	8.756	8.201
19	17.226	15.678	14.324	13.134	12.085	11.158	10.336	9.604	8.950	8.365
20	18.046	16.351	14.877	13.590	12.462	11.470	10.594	9.818	9.128	8.514
25	22.023	19.523	17.413	15.622	14.094	12.783	11.654	10.675	9.823	9.077
30	25.808	22.397	19.600	17.292	15.373	13.765	12.409	11.258	10.274	9.427

Period	12%	14%	16%	18%	20%	24%	28%	32%	36%
1	0.893	0.877	0.862	0.847	0.833	0.806	0.781	0.758	0.735
2	1.690	1.647	1.605	1.566	1.528	1.457	1.392	1.332	1.276
3	2.402	2.322	2.246	2.174	2.106	1.981	1.868	1.766	1.674
4	3.037	2.914	2.798	2.690	2.589	2.404	2.241	2.096	1.966
5	3.605	3.433	3.274	3.127	2.991	2.745	2.532	2.345	2.181
6	4.111	3.889	3.685	3.498	3.326	3.020	2.759	2.534	2.339
7	4.564	4.288	4.039	3.812	3.605	3.242	2.937	2.678	2.455
8	4.968	4.639	4.344	4.078	3.837	3.421	3.076	2.786	2.540
9	5.328	4.946	4.607	4.303	4.031	3.566	3.184	2.868	2.603
10	5.650	5.216	4.833	4.494	4.193	3.682	3.269	2.930	2.650
11	5.938	5.453	5.029	4.656	4.327	3.776	3.335	2.978	2.683
12	6.194	5.660	5.197	4.793	4.439	3.851	3.387	3.013	2.708
13	6.424	5.842	5.342	4.910	4.533	3.912	3.427	3.040	2.727
14	6.628	6.002	5.468	5.008	4.611	3.962	3.459	3.061	2.740
15	6.811	6.142	5.575	5.092	4.675	4.001	3.483	3.076	2.750
16	6.974	6.265	5.669	5.162	4.730	4.033	3.503	3.088	2.758
17	7.120	5.373	5.749	4.222	4.775	4.059	3.518	3.097	2.763
18	7.250	6.467	5.818	5.273	4.812	4.080	3.529	3.104	2.767
19	7.366	6.550	5.877	5.316	4.844	4.097	3.539	3.109	2.770
20	7.469	6.623	5.929	5.353	4.870	4.110	3.546	3.113	2.772
25	7.843	6.873	6.097	5.467	4.948	4.147	3.564	3.122	2.776
30	8.055	7.003	6.177	5.517	4.979	4.160	3.569	3.124	2.778

PROBLEMS

A-1   Show how the factor .864, which is the factor used to determine the present value of a sum due in three years when the interest rate is 5 percent, is derived.

A-2   What is the discount factor for each of the following?
  a)   A sum due in 1 year discounted at 5 percent.
  b)   A sum due in 2 years discounted at 5 percent.
  c)   A sum due in 3 years discounted at 5 percent.
  d)   A sum due in 1 year discounted at 10 percent.
  e)   A sum due in 2 years discounted at 10 percent.
  f)   A sum due in 3 years discounted at 10 percent.

A-3   Find the present value of each of the following:
  a) $100 due in 3 years at 5 percent.
  b) $1 due in 3 years at 5 percent.
  c) $1,000 due in 3 years at 10 percent.

A-4   Find the value of a bond that promises to pay $100 at the end of each of the next three years when the appropriate discount rate is: a) 5 percent. b) 10 percent.

APPENDIX B

Forecasting

Two key functions of management for any organization are *planning* and *control*. The firm must plan for the future. Planning for the future involves the following steps:

1. Determine the product and geographic markets where the firm can earn the highest returns.[1]
2. Forecast the level of demand in these markets under different conditions of price, promotional activities, competition, and general economic activity levels.
3. Forecast the cost of producing different levels of output under conditions of changing technology, wage rates, and raw materials prices.
4. Decide on the optimum operating plan; that is, the value-maximizing plan.
5. Engage in capital acquisition programs, labor training programs, and so forth in order to implement the general corporate plan.

[1] If the economic system is functioning properly this also means finding the markets where the firm can make the largest contribution to society. Properly employed, tax and other incentive programs can help to increase the correlation between achievement of social and private goals.

Once the plan has been determined, it must be carried out in the *control*, or *operating*, phase of the activity of the enterprise. Quite obviously, planning and control are closely related; in practice, they are often inseparable. Operating procedures, or the process of control, must be geared to the firm's plans. If the forecasts about demand or about the cost of the input factors of production, technology, and the like that go into the plan are seriously in error, then the plan will be no good and the control phase will also break down.

In view of the key role of forecasting in managerial decisions, it is not surprising that forecasting per se is emphasized in managerial economics. In this appendix we describe and illustrate several of the more useful techniques employed in forecasting.

FORECASTING METHODOLOGIES

Many techniques are available for use in forecasting economic variables. They range from simple, often somewhat naïve, and relatively inexpensive procedures to methods that are quite complex, difficult to use, and very expensive. Some forecasting techniques are basically quantitative; others are qualitative. The various forecasting techniques can be divided into the following five broad categories:

1. Trend projection or curve fitting
2. Barometric, or leading indicator, methods
3. Econometric models
4. Input-output analysis
5. Survey techniques

It is impossible to state unequivocally that one or another of these procedures is superior to the others. The best one for a particular task depends in large part on a number of factors in each specific forecasting problem. Some of the important factors that must be considered include:

1. The distance into the future that one must forecast.
2. The lead time needed for making decisions.
3. The level of accuracy required.
4. The nature of the relationships involved in the forecasting problem.

Some techniques—for example, barometric and survey methodologies—are well suited for short-term projections. Others require more lead time and are therefore more useful for long-run forecasting. Within each class of forecasting techniques, the level of sophistication is also quite variable. Typically, the greater the sophistication, the higher the cost. If the level of accuracy needed in the projection is low, less sophisticated methods may provide adequate results at minimal cost. The remainder of this appendix is devoted to an examination of each of the five basic forecasting methods.

TREND PROJECTION, OR EXTRAPOLATION

Probably the most frequently employed forecasting methodology is one variously known as *extrapolation, trend projection, curve fitting,* or—as it is more affectionately called in the profession—the *lost-horse method.* The technique basically involves assuming that future events will follow along an established path or, alternatively, that past patterns of economic behavior prevail sufficiently to justify using historical patterns to predict the future. This forecasting technique acquired the "lost-horse" nomenclature because it is analogous to the way in which a farmer seeks a lost horse. He proceeds to the spot where the horse was last seen and then searches in the direction it was heading. An economic forecaster using this technique looks at the historical pattern of travel of the variable he is interested in and then projects, or forecasts, that it will continue moving along the path described by its past movement.

The many variations of forecasting by trend projection are all predicated on an assumption of a continuing relationship between the variable being projected and the passage of time, so all of them employ time-series data. An economic time series is a sequential array of the values of an economic variable. Time series of sales and cost data, income statistics, population, and the gross national product (*GNP*) are all examples of economic time series.

All time series, regardless of the nature of the economic variable involved, can be described by the following four characteristics:

1. *Secular trend,* or the long-run increase or decrease in the series.
2. *Cyclical fluctuations,* or rhythmic variations in the economic series.
3. *Seasonal variation,* or variations caused by weather patterns and/ or social habits that produce an *annual* pattern in the time series.
4. *Irregular or random influences,* or unpredictable shocks to the system—such as wars, strikes, natural catastrophes, and so on.

These four patterns are illustrated in Figure B-1, where (a) shows secular and cyclical trends in sales of women's clothing, and (b) shows (1) the seasonal pattern superimposed over the long-run trend (which, in this case, is a composite of the secular and cyclical trends); and (2) random fluctuations around the seasonal curve.

Time Series Analysis

Time series analysis can be as simple as projecting or extrapolating the unadjusted trend. Applying either graphic analysis ("by eye" fitting) or least squares regression techniques,[2] one can use historical data to determine the

---

[2] The least squares regression technique of estimation is examined in detail in Chapter 5.

Figure B-1 Time Series Characteristics: (a) Secular Trend and Cyclical Variation in Women's Clothing Sales; (b) Seasonal Pattern and Random Fluctuations

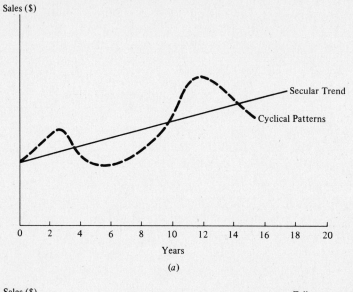

(a)

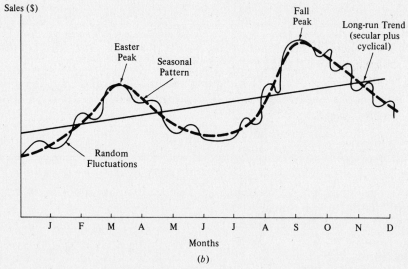

(b)

average increase or decrease in the series during each time period, and then
project this rate of change into the future.

Since extrapolation techniques assume that a variable will follow its
established path, the problem is to determine accurately the appropriate
trend curve. In theory one could fit any complex mathematical function to

the historical data and extrapolate to estimate future values. In practice, however, one typically finds linear, simple power, or exponential curves used for economic forecasting.

Selection of the appropriate curve is guided by both empirical and theoretical considerations. Empirically, it is a question of finding the curve that best fits the historical movement of the data. Theoretical considerations intervene when logic dictates that a particular pattern of future events must prevail. For example, output in a particular industry may have been expanding at a constant rate historically but, due to known resource limitations, one might use a declining growth rate model to reflect the slowing down of growth that must ultimately prevail.

The trending procedure is illustrated in Figure B-2, where the gross national product (*GNP*) time-series data given in Table B-1 are graphed. Fitting a linear trend to the data and extending it allows one to project *GNP* at various dates in the future. The projected *GNP* for 1975, for example, is $1.3 trillion, and for 1980 it is $1.6 trillion. Note, however, that this projection of future *GNP* is based on a *linear* trend line which implies that *GNP* is increasing by a constant dollar amount each year. While an assumption of a constant absolute annual change is quite appropriate for some economic variables, there are several alternative assumptions that may more accurately describe the way many economic series change over time.

One widely used alternative model is the constant growth rate, or constant *rate* of change, model. Sales revenues for many products—as well as *GNP*, per capita income, and population—are all examples of economic variables whose change over time appears to be proportional rather than constant in absolute amount.

Table B-1   United States Gross National Product, 1960-1973 (current dollars)

Year	GNP (billions)
1960	503.7
1961	520.1
1962	560.3
1963	590.5
1964	632.4
1965	683.9
1966	743.3
1967	793.5
1968	865.7
1969	930.2
1970	977.1
1971	1055.5
1972	1155.2
1973	1289.1

Figure B-2 United States Gross National Product, 1960-1973 (current dollars)

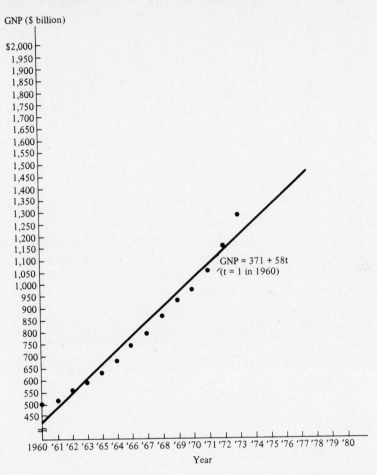

The constant *rate* of change, or proportional change, model involves determining the average historical rate of change in the variable and projecting that rate into the future. This is essentially identical to the compounding of value model discussed in Appendix A. For example, if a firm is projecting its sales for five years into the future and if it has determined that sales are increasing at an annual rate of 10 percent, the projection would simply involve multiplying the 10 percent interest factor for five years times current sales. Assuming current sales are $1 million, the forecast of sales five years from now would be:

$$\text{Sales in Year 5} = \text{Current sales} \times (1 + \text{growth rate})^5$$
$$= \$1,000,000 \times (1.10)^5$$
$$= \$1,000,000 \times 1.61$$
$$= \$1,610,000.$$

More generally, the constant rate of change projection model can be stated as follows:

Value t Years in the Future = Current Value $\times$ $(1 +$ Rate of Change$)^t$.

Just as one can estimate the constant annual change in an economic time series by fitting historical data to a linear regression model of the form $Y = a + bt$, so, too, one can estimate the annual growth rate in a constant rate of change projection model using the same technique. In this case the growth rate is estimated using linear regression by fitting historical data to the logarithmic transformation of the model. For example, if one were to formulate a constant growth rate model for *GNP* it would take the form:

$$GNP_t = GNP_0 \cdot (1 + g)^t. \qquad \textbf{(B-1)}$$

Here *GNP* t years in the future is assumed to be equal to *GNP* today, GNP_0, compounded at a growth rate g for a period of t years. Taking logarithms of both sides of Equation B-1 results in the expression:

$$\text{Log } GNP_t = \text{Log } GNP_0 + \text{Log } (1 + g) \cdot t. \qquad \textbf{(B-2)}$$

Note that Equation B-2 is an expression of the form:

$$Y_t = a + bt,$$

where $Y_t = \text{Log } GNP_t$, $a = \text{Log } GNP_0$, and $b = \text{Log } (1 + g)$; hence, its parameters ($\text{Log } GNP_0$ and $\text{Log } (1 + g)$) can be estimated using the least squares regression technique.

Applying this technique to the *GNP* data in Table B-1 results in the regression model:

$$\text{Log } GNP_t = 6.1079 + .0724\, t, \qquad \textbf{(B-3)}$$

or, equivalently:

$$GNP_t = \text{Antilog } 6.1079\ (1.075)^t = 449\ (1.075)^t. \qquad \textbf{(B-4)}$$

In this model, 449 billion dollars is the adjusted *GNP* for $t = 0$ (which would be 1959, since the first year of data used in the regression estimation ($t = 1$) was 1960); and 1.075 is the quantity one plus the average annual rate of growth, or increase in *GNP*, indicating that GNP has been increasing by 7.5 percent annually.[3]

---

[3] Another frequently used form of the constant growth rate model is based on a *continuous* (as opposed to annual) compounding assumption. This model is expressed by the exponential equation:

$$Y_t = Y_o e^{gt},$$

and its logarithmic equivalent is:

$$\text{Log } Y_t = \text{Log } Y_0 + gt.$$

Thus, with the exponential growth assumption, the regression model's estimate of the slope coefficient, g, is a direct estimate of the continuous rate of growth. For example, in the *GNP* regression model, Equation B-3, the parameter .0724 ($= 7.24\%$) is a direct estimate of a continuous compounding growth rate for *GNP*.

To forecast *GNP* in any future year using this model, one would subtract 1959 from the year being forecast to determine t, the number of years to compound the growth rate in Equation B-4. For example, a forecast of *GNP* in 1975 would be made as follows:

$$t = 1975 - 1959 = 16$$
$$GNP_{1975} = 449 \ (1.075)^{16}$$
$$= 449 \times 3.1796$$
$$= 1.4 \text{ trillion dollars.}$$

Similarly, a *GNP* forecast for 1980 would be:

$$t = 1980 - 1959 = 21$$
$$GNP_{1980} = 449 \ (1.075)^{21}$$
$$= 2.0 \text{ trillion dollars.}$$

The extreme importance of selecting the correct structural form for a trending model can be demonstrated by comparing the *GNP* projections that result from the two models we have examined. Recall that with the constant absolute annual change model *GNP* was projected to be \$1.3 trillion and \$1.6 trillion in 1975 and 1980, respectively. These projections compare with the \$1.4 trillion *GNP* projection for 1975 and the \$2.0 trillion forecast for 1980 obtained with the constant growth rate model. Notice that difference in the near-term forecasts (1975) is quite small relative to the difference in the 1980 projections. This points up the fact that if an economic time series is growing at a constant *rate* rather than increasing by a constant absolute amount—and *GNP* does appear to exhibit this characteristic[4]—then forecasts based on a linear trend model will tend to become less and less accurate the further out into the future one projects.

Although trend projections can provide very adequate estimates for some forecasting purposes, a number of serious shortcomings in the technique limit its usefulness for many purposes. First, trend projections are typically more useful for intermediate to long-term forecasting than for short-run estimation. The reason lies in the inability of the technique to predict cyclical turning points or fluctuations. Second, trend projections implicitly assume that the historical relationships involved in the time series will continue into the future. This is not always the case. There are many examples of the disastrous effects of using this forecasting method just prior to 1929, 1937, and 1968. Finally, trend analysis entails no analysis of causal relationships and, hence, offers no help in analyzing either why a particular series moves as it does, or what the impact of a particular policy decision would be on the future movement of the series.

[4] We state that the constant growth rate assumption for modeling *GNP* appears more consistent with reality because the fit of the logarithmic regression model, as measured by the coefficient of determination ($R^2 = .996$), was better for that model structure than for the linear model ($R^2 = .966$).

Introducing Seasonal Factors

For many economic projections an analysis of seasonal and cyclical fluctuations can vastly improve short-term forecasting results. There are several techniques for estimating seasonal variations. For example, if monthly sales data for a particular product indicate that, on the average, December sales are 20 percent above the trend line, a seasonal adjustment factor of 1.20 can be applied to the trend projection to forecast sales in that month. Likewise, if it is found that February sales had on average been 20 percent below the trend, an adjustment factor of 0.80 would be applied in projecting February sales. To illustrate, annual sales might be forecast at $1.2 million, or $100,000 a month. When the seasonal factor is introduced, however, December sales would be projected at $120,000 ($= \$100,000 \times 1.20$) and February sales at $80,000 ($= \$100,000 \times 0.8$). Inventory production requirements could be scheduled accordingly.

Cyclical Variations

Determination of cyclical patterns is very similar to that for seasonal patterns. Here the interest is on rhythmic patterns that occur over a period of years. While a few industries appear to have rhythmic oscillations that repeat with enough regularity to be considered cycles—home construction is frequently cited—these are probably the exception rather than the rule. Further, statistical problems make any breakdown of a time series into trend and cycle components tenuous at best. Most analysts today recognize that both secular trend and cycle are typically generated by a common causal mechanism, and therefore separation of the two does not lead to unambiguous forecasts. Moreover, the timing and amplitude of cycles are inconsistent over time, making cyclical adjustments difficult if not impossible.

BAROMETRIC METHODS

Although cyclical patterns in most economic time series are so erratic as to make simple projection a hazardous short-term forecasting technique, there is evidence that a relatively consistent relationship exists between the movement of *different* economic variables over time. In other words, even though no single economic series exhibits a consistent pattern of movement over time, it is often possible to find a second series (or group of series) whose movement is closely correlated to that of the first. Should the forecaster have the good fortune to discover an economic series that *leads* the one he is attempting to forecast, he can use the leading series as a barometer for forecasting short-term change, just as a meteorologist uses changes in a mercury barometer to forecast changes in the weather.

There is evidence that this barometric, or leading, indicator approach to business forecasting is nearly as old as business itself. More than two thousand years ago merchants used the arrival of trading ships as indicators of business activity. Over one hundred years ago Andrew Carnegie is re-

Table B-2 Leading, Coincident, and Lagging Economic Time Series

Leading Indicators

Average work week—Production workers, manufacturing
Average weekly initial claims—State unemployment insurance
Index of net business formation
New orders—Durable goods industries
Contracts and orders—Plant and equipment
New building permits—Private housing
Change in manufacturing and trade inventories
Industrial materials prices
Stock prices—500 common stocks
Corporate profits, after taxes
Ratio of price to unit labor cost—Manufacturing
Changes in consumer installment debt

Roughly Coincident Indicators

Employees on nonagricultural payrolls
Unemployment rate—Total
GNP in current dollars
Industrial production
Personal income
Manufacturing and trade sales
Sales of retail stores

Lagging Indicators

Unemployment rate—15 weeks and over
Business expenditures—New plant and equipment
Book value—Manufacturing and trade inventories
Labor cost per unit of output—Manufacturing
Commercial and industrial loans outstanding
Bank rates on short-term business loans

ported to have used the number of smoking industrial chimneys to forecast business activity and hence the demand for steel. Today, the barometric approach to forecasting has been refined considerably, primarily through the work of the National Bureau of Economic Research and the U.S. Department of Commerce. *Business Conditions Digest*, a monthly publication of the Department of Commerce, provides extensive data on a large number of business indicators. Table B-2 lists twenty-five leading, coincident, and lagging economic time series which are contained in that data.

Barometric Forecasting

As indicated above, barometric, or indicator, forecasting is based on the observation that there are lagged relationships between many economic time series. That is, changes in some series appear to consistently follow changes in one or more other series. The theoretical basis for some of these leads and lags is obvious. For example, building permits issued precede housing starts, and orders for plant and equipment lead production in durable goods industries. The reason is that each of these indicators refers to plans or commitments for the activity that follows. Other barometers are not so directly related to the economic variable they forecast. An index of common stock prices, for example, is a good leading indicator of general business activity. Although the causal relationship here is not readily apparent, stock prices reflect an aggregation of profit expectations by businessmen and others, and hence a composite expectation of the level of business activity.

Theoretically, barometric forecasting requires the isolation of an economic time series that consistently leads the series being forecast. Once this relationship is established, forecasting directional changes in the lagged series is simply a matter of keeping track of movement in the leading indicator. Actually, several problems prevent such an easy solution to the forecasting problem. First, few series *always* correctly indicate changes in another economic variable. Even the best leading indicators of general business conditions forecast with only 80 to 90 percent accuracy. Second, even the indicators that have good records of forecasting directional changes generally fail to lead by a consistent period. If a series is to be an adequate barometer, it not only must indicate directional changes but, additionally, must provide a constant lead time. Few series meet the test of lead time consistency. Finally, barometric forecasting suffers in that, even when leading indicators prove to be satisfactory from the standpoint of consistently indicating directional change with a stable lead time, they provide very little information about the magnitude of change in the forecast variable.

Composite and Diffusion Indexes

Two techniques that have been used with some success to overcome at least partially the difficulties in barometric forecasting are composite indexes and diffusion indexes. *Composite indexes* are weighted averages of several leading indicators. The combining of individual series into a composite index results in a series with less random fluctuation, or "noise." The smoother composite series has a lower tendency to produce false signals of change in the predicted variable.

Diffusion indexes are similar to composite indexes. Here, instead of combining a number of leading indicators into a single standardized index, the methodology consists of noting the percentage of the total number of leading indicators that are rising at a given point in time. For example, if twelve individual indicators have all proved to be relatively reliable leading indicators of steel sales, a diffusion or "pressure" index would show the percentage of those indicators which are increasing at the present time. If seven are rising, the diffusion index would be seven-twelfths, or 58 percent; with only three rising, the index would register 25 percent. Forecasting with diffusion indexes typically involves projecting an increase in the economic variable if the index is above 50—that is, when over one-half of the individual leading indicators are rising—and a decline when it is below 50.

Even with the use of composite and diffusion indexes, the barometric forecasting technique is a relatively poor tool for estimating the magnitude of change in an economic variable. Thus, although it represents a significant improvement over the extrapolation technique for short-term forecasting, where calling the turning points is necessary, the barometric methodology is not really suitable for all forecasting problems.

ECONOMETRIC MODELS

Econometric methods of forecasting combine the extrapolation and the barometric techniques. Econometric modeling consists of a combination of economic theory and mathematical and statistical tools to analyze economic relationships. The use of econometric forecasting techniques has several distinct advantages over the alternative methods. For one, it forces the forecaster to make explicit his assumptions about the interrelationships between the variables in the economic system being examined. In other words, the forecaster must deal with *causal* relationships. This process reduces the probability of logical inconsistencies in the model and thus increases the reliability and acceptability of the results.

A second advantage of econometric methods lies in the consistency of the technique from period to period. The forecaster can compare his forecasts with actual results and use the insights gained from this comparison to improve his model. That is, by feeding past forecasting errors back into the model, the forecaster can obtain new parameters which should improve future forecasting results.

The output form of econometric forecasts is another major advantage of this technique. Since econometric models provide estimates of the actual values for the forecasted variables, the models indicate not only the direction of change but also the magnitude of change. This is a significant improvement over the trend extrapolation technique, which fails to predict turning points, and the barometric approach, which provides little information about the magnitude of changes.

Perhaps the most important advantage of econometric models relates to their basic characteristic of *explaining* economic phenomena. In the vast majority of business forecasting problems, management has some degree of control over many of the variables present in the relationship being examined. For example, in forecasting sales of a product, the firm must take into account both the price it will charge and the amount it has spent and will spend on advertising, as well as many other variables over which it may or may not have any influence. Only by thoroughly understanding the interrelationships involved can management hope to forecast accurately and to make optimal decisions as it selects values for the controllable variables.

Single Equation Estimation

Many of the firm's forecasting problems can be solved adequately with single equation econometric models. The first step in developing an econometric model is to express the hypothesized economic relationship in the form of an equation. For example, in constructing a model for forecasting sales of new automobiles, one might hypothesize that automobile demand (Q) is determined by price (P), disposable income (Y_d), population (Pop), personal liquidity (L), availability of credit (C), and advertising expenditures (A). A linear model expressing this relationship could be written as follows:

$$Q = a_0 + a_1P + a_2Y_d + a_3\,Pop + a_4L + a_5C + a_6A. \qquad (\textbf{B-5})$$

Once the economic relationship has been expressed in equation form, the next step in econometric modeling is to estimate the parameters of the system, or values of the a's in Equation B-5. The most frequently used technique for parameter estimation is the application of the method of least squares regression analysis with either historical or cross-sectional data.[5]

Once the parameters, or coefficients, of the model have been obtained, forecasting with a single equation model consists of obtaining the values for the independent variables in the equation and then evaluating the equation for those values. This means that an econometric model that is to be used for forecasting purposes must contain independent or explanatory variables whose values for the forecast period can be readily obtained.

Multiple Equation Systems

Although in numerous instances business problems can be analyzed adequately with a single equation model, in many other cases the interrelationships involved are so complex that they require the use of multiple equation systems. In these systems we refer to the variables whose values are determined by the model through the simultaneous solution of the equations as *endogenous,* meaning originating from within, and to those determined outside, or external to, the system as *exogenous.* The values of endogenous variables are determined within the model; the values of exogenous variables are "given" externally. Endogenous variables are equivalent to the dependent variable in a single equation system; the exogenous variables are equivalent to the independent variables.

Multiple equation econometric models are composed of two basic kinds of equations, identities and behavioral equations. Identities or definitional equations express relationships that are true by definition. The statement that profits (π) are equal to total revenue (TR) minus cost (TC) is an example of an identity:

$$\pi = TR - TC. \qquad (\textbf{B-6})$$

Profits are *defined* by the relationship expressed in Equation B-6; the equation is true by definition.

[5] The least squares technique is examined in detail in Chapter 5, where its use in empirical demand estimation is studied, and again in Chapter 9, where it is applied to statistical cost analysis. "Historical data" refers to time-series data, as in Table B-1; "cross-sectional data" refers to data at a single point in time for a sample of firms, individuals, or other units of observation.

The second group of equations encountered in econometric models, behavioral equations, reflect hypotheses about how the variables in the system interact with one another. Behavioral equations may indicate how individuals and institutions are expected to react to various stimuli, or they may be technical as, for example, a production function that indicates the technical relationships in the production system.

Perhaps the easiest way to illustrate the use of a multiple equation system is to examine a simple three-equation model of a national economy. Actual econometric models used for forecasting general business conditions have many more equations than this, but the three-equation system does provide insight into the technique without being so complex as to become confusing. The three equations are:

$$C_t = a_1 + b_1 \, GNP_t + u_1, \qquad \text{(B-7)}$$
$$I_t = a_2 + b_2 P_{t-1} + u_2, \qquad \text{(B-8)}$$
$$GNP_t = C_t + I_t + G_t, \qquad \text{(B-9)}$$

where:

$$C = \text{Personal Consumption Expenditures}$$
$$I = \text{Net Capital Investment}$$
$$P = \text{Profits}$$
$$G = \text{Government Expenditures for Goods and Services}$$
$$GNP = \text{Gross National Product}$$
$$a, b = \text{Parameters of the Equations}$$
$$u = \text{Stochastic Disturbance Terms}$$
$$t = \text{Current Time Period}$$
$$t-1 = \text{Previous Time Period}$$

Equations B-7 and B-8 are behavioral hypotheses. The first hypothesizes that current period consumption is a function of the current level of gross national product; the second, that current net capital investment depends on profits in the previous period. The last equation in the system is an identity. It defines gross national product as being equal to the sum of personal consumption expenditures, net capital investment, and government expenditures.

The stochastic terms in the behavioral equations—the u's—are included in recognition of the fact that the hypothesized relationships are not exact. In other words, other factors, including random disturbances, are not accounted for in the system, and these factors affect the size of personal consumption expenditures and of net capital investment. So long as these stochastic elements are randomly distributed and their net effects are canceled —that is, the expected value of each stochastic term is zero—they do not present a barrier to empirical estimation of the parameters. However, if the error terms are not randomly distributed, the parameter estimates will be biased and the reliability of forecasts made with the model will be questionable. Furthermore, even though the error terms are random, if the error terms are large the model will not forecast very accurately.

Empirical estimation of the parameters—that is, the a's and b's in Equations B-7 and B-8—of multiple equation systems requires the use of statistical techniques that go beyond the scope of the text.[6] We can, however, illustrate the use of such a system for forecasting purposes after the parameters have been estimated.

To forecast next year's gross national product for the economic system represented by our illustrative model, we must be able to express GNP in terms of only those variables whose values are known at the moment the forecast is generated. Consider the manipulations of equations in the system necessary to accomplish this.

Substituting Equation B-7 into B-9—that is, replacing C_t with Equation B-7—results in[7]:

$$GNP_t = a_1 + b_1 GNP_t + I_t + G_t. \qquad \text{(B-10)}$$

A similar substitution of Equation B-8 for the variable I_t produces:

$$GNP_t = a_1 + b_1 GNP_t + a_2 + b_2 P_{t-1} + G_t. \qquad \text{(B-11)}$$

Collecting terms and isolating GNP in Equation B-11 gives:

$$(1 - b_1)GNP_t = a_1 + a_2 + b_2 P_{t-1} + G_t,$$

or, alternatively:

$$\begin{aligned} GNP_t &= \frac{a_1 + a_2 + b_2 P_{t-1} + G_t}{1 - b_1} \\ &= \frac{a_1 + a_2}{1 - b_1} + \frac{b_2}{1 - b_1} P_{t-1} + \frac{1}{1 - b_1} G_t. \end{aligned} \qquad \text{(B-12)}$$

Equation B-12 now relates current GNP to the previous period's profits and to current government expenditure. Assuming that government spending on goods and services, which is exogenous to the system, can be adequately projected for the forthcoming period from budget and appropriations data currently available in government publications, Equation B-12 provides us with a forecasting model that takes into account the simultaneous relationships expressed in the multiple equation system.

INPUT-OUTPUT ANALYSIS[8]

A highly versatile forecasting method known as *input-output analysis* provides perhaps the most complete examination of all the complex interrelationships within an economic system. Input-output analysis shows how an

---

[6] *See* Chapter 10 of W. J. Baumol's text, *Economic Theory and Operations Analysis*, 3d ed. (Prentice-Hall Inc., Englewood Cliffs, N.J., 1972) for an introduction to several of these techniques.

[7] The stochastic terms (u's) have been dropped from the illustration, since their expected values are zero. The final equation for GNP, however, is stochastic in nature.

[8] This section draws heavily from "Input-Output Structure of the U.S. Economy: 1967," *Survey of Current Business*, February 1974.

increase or a decrease in the demand for one industry's output will affect other industries. For example, an increase in the demand for trucks will lead to increased production of steel, plastics, tires, glass, and other materials. The increase in the demand for these materials will have secondary effects. The increase in the demand for glass, for example, will lead to a further increase in the demand for steel, as well as for trucks used in the manufacture of glass, steel, and so on. Input-output analysis traces through all these interindustry relationships to provide information about the total impact on all industries of the original increase in the demand for trucks.

Input-output forecasting is based on a set of tables that describe the interrelations between all the component parts of the United States economy. The construction of input-output tables is a most formidable task; fortunately, however, such tables are available from the Office of Business Economics, U.S. Department of Commerce. To use the tables effectively, one must understand their construction. Accordingly, the construction of these tables, as well as the use of input-output tables, is examined in this section.

Nature of Input-Output Tables

The starting point for constructing input-output tables is the set of accounts on which the nation's *GNP* is based; the basic accounts are listed in Table B-3. The table shows that *GNP* is equal to the sum of the national income accounts, Items 1-9, or, alternatively, to the sum of final product flows to consuming sectors, Items 10-13.

Input-output tables break down the income and the product account

Table B-3 List of National Income and Product Accounts Used to Construct *GNP*

National Income Accounts	
1. Compensation of Employees	
2. Proprietor's Income	
3. Rental Income of Persons	
4. Corporate Profits and Inventory Valuation Adjustment	
5. Net Interest	Gross National Product
6. Business Transfer Payments	
7. Indirect Business Tax and Nontax Liability	
8. Less: Subsidies Less Current Surplus of Government Enterprises	
9. Capital Consumption Allowances	
Final Product Accounts	
10. Personal Consumption Expenditures	
11. Gross Private Domestic Investment	
12. Net Export of Goods and Services	Gross National Product
13. Government Purchases of Goods and Services	

data and provide information about interindustry transactions. Table B-4 is an example of a simplified input-output table. It is a matrix of the same gross national product data contained in Table B-3, but with the addition of a (shaded) section showing all the interindustry transactions as well.[9] The industry-to-industry flows in the shaded area depict the input-output structure of the economy. For example, the manufacturing row, Row 4, shows the sales by manufacturing firms to other manufacturing firms, to each of the other industries, and also to final users. Thus, Cell 4, 2 shows sales from manufacturers to mining companies; Cell 4, 4 from manufacturers to other manufacturers; and Cell 4, 7 from manufacturers to service firms such as banks, entertainment companies, and the like. The manufacturing column, Column 4, shows the sources of goods and services purchased by manufacturers for production, as well as the value added in their production of output. For example, Cell 2, 4 shows manufacturing firms' purchases from mining companies; and Cell 6, 4 shows the manufacturing firms' purchases from the transportation industry.

Since interindustry sales are included in the value of the products sold to various final consumers, they must be omitted from the measurement of total gross national product. That is, to avoid double counting, producer-to-producer sales must be excluded from the determination of GNP. The same is true when calculating GNP by use of the national income accounts; interindustry transactions must be eliminated to avoid redundancy. Accordingly, the entire shaded area of Table B-4 is ignored when GNP is determined: GNP is calculated either as the total of all the cells shown in the Final Markets columns or as the total of cells in the Value Added rows.

Uses of Input-Output Analysis

Input-output analysis has a variety of applications, ranging from forecasting the sales of an individual firm to probing the implications of national economic programs and policies. The major contribution of input-output analysis is that it facilitates measurement of the effects on all industrial sectors of changes in demand in any one sector.

The usefulness of input-output analysis can be illustrated by the following example, which shows the effect of an increase in consumer demand for passenger cars. The first effect of the change in demand is an increase in the output of the automobile industry; there are further impacts, however. The increase in auto output necessitates more steel production, which in turn requires more chemicals, more iron ore, more limestone, and more coal. Auto production also requires other products, and demand will increase for upholstery fabrics, synthetic fibers, plastics, and glass. There will be still further reactions; for example, the production of synthetic fibers and other

---

[9] Although the illustrated input-output table has only eight industry classifications, actual 1967 Office of Business Economics input-output tables are far more complex, containing nearly 370 separate industry classifications.

Table *B-4* Input-Output Flow Table

| | Interindustry Transactions | | | | | | | | Final Markets (National Product Accounts) | | | |
	Agriculture (1)	Mining (2)	Construction (3)	Manufacturing (4)	Trade (5)	Transportation (6)	Services (7)	Other (8)	Persons (9)	Investors (10)	Foreigners (11)	Government (12)
Interindustry Transactions												
Agriculture (1)									Personal Consumption Expenditures (Account 10)	Gross Private Domestic Investment (Account 11)	Net Exports of Goods and Services (Account 12)	Government Purchases of Goods and Services (Account 13)
Mining (2)				2, 4								
Construction (3)												
Manufacturing (4)		4, 2		4, 4			4, 7					
Trade (5)												
Transportation (6)				6, 4								
Services (7)												
Other (8)												
Value Added (National Income Accounts)												
Employees (9)	Compensation of Employees (Account 1)											
Owners of Business and Capital (10)	Profit-type Income and Capital Consumption Allowances (Accounts 2, 3, 4, 5, 6, 9)*											
Government (11)	Indirect Business Taxes and Current Surplus of Government Enterprises, and So Forth (Accounts 7, 8)											

Gross National Product

* Account numbers refer to the national income and product accounts of Table B-3.

chemicals will lead to increased demand for electricity, containers, and transportation services. Input-output analysis traces this intricate chain reaction throughout all industrial sectors and measures the effects, both direct and indirect, on the output of each of the industries.

The industry outputs derived in this way can be used for estimating related industry requirements. For example, with supplementary data the estimated output of each industry can be translated into requirements for employment or for additional plant and equipment. Or, bolstered by information on the geographic distribution of industries, input-output analysis can also shed light on the regional implications of changes in national *GNP*.

Recognizing the unique ability of input-output analysis to account completely for the complex interaction among industries, many businesses have been guided in their decision making by this analysis. For example, input-output has been used to evaluate market prospects for established products, to identify potential markets for new products, to spot prospective shortages in supplies, to add new dimensions and greater depth to the analysis of the economic environment in which the firms can expect to operate, and to evaluate investment prospects in various industries.

Input-output analysis has also been employed in the decision-making processes of government agencies at every level. A notable federal application has been in the study of the long-term growth of the economy and its implications for manpower requirements. Input-output has also been used to calculate the impact of United States exports and imports on employment in various industries and regions. A number of state and local governments have sponsored the construction of input-output tables for use in evaluating the effects of different paths of economic development. Others have used input-output to study the industrial impact of alternative tax programs. In one state input-output is the central element in a large-scale system for forecasting demographic and economic variables, and also serves as an aid in planning land use, expenditure and revenue programs, industrial development, and so on.

Moreover, many regions throughout the country have been increasingly concerned about the adequacy of water resources. Input-output is being used as part of a total system to measure the industrial requirements for water. The analysis is particularly helpful in identifying the activities that generate important demands for water, not only as direct users but also because their suppliers of materials, power, and other inputs also require water.

Forecasting with Input-Output Tables

It should be obvious that the data required to construct an input-output system are most numerous, and the analysis necessary to trace the intricate interrelationships is almost overwhelming. Because of the enormous costs of setting up and maintaining input-output tables, individual firms, even the largest ones, typically rely on U.S. Department of Commerce tables rather than construct their own. But firms can and do extend the published tables and apply them to their own unique situations. For example, a company such as Du Pont, which operates in a number of the 367 industries covered in the Department of Commerce tables, could estimate its share of each of the relevant markets and use this information to estimate the impact of a specific change on Du Pont per se. Similarly, long-run trends could be projected through input-output analysis, and, depending on the forecasts for specific markets, Du Pont could decide which areas appear most promising and then concentrate its long-range plans in these areas.

For any of these uses, however, it is necessary to understand thoroughly the nature of an input-output system. To facilitate such an understanding we trace through a very simple hypothetical economy containing only three producing sectors. Table B-5 provides the basic national accounting data for the hypothetical system. The upper section contains the detailed interindustry relationships necessary for construction of input-output tables; the lower section gives the national income and product accounts that make up *GNP*.

Table B-6 shows all this information reformulated in an input-output matrix for the system. The Producers rows contain information about the distribution of output. For example, Industry A produces and sells a total of $130 billion, with $10 billion going to other firms in Industry A, $2 billion to Industry B, $50 billion to Industry C, $40 billion to individuals for personal consumption, and $28 billion to the government. As is shown in the Producers columns, firms in Industry A buy $10 billion of goods and services from other A firms and $3 billion from B firms, pay $100 billion in wages, and have $17 billion left for depreciation and profits. Gross national product can be obtained from the input-output table by summing either the Total Value Added section or the Final Markets sector. Cells in the producer-to-producer section of the matrix are eliminated to avoid double counting.

For forecasting purposes, two additional types of matrices are constructed from the Producers' section of Table B-6. One is the percentage distribution of gross output matrix, which indicates where each industry sells its products and, thus, how dependent it is on various sectors of the system. Table B-7 shows the percentage distribution matrix for this hypothetical economy. Each element in that table is found by dividing the corresponding element in Table B-6 by its row total. For example, the 8 percent in element A, A was found by dividing the $10 billion of sales Industry A makes to itself by the $130 billion total sales of that industry. The 4 percent in Cell B, A indicates that Industry B sells 4 percent of its output to Industry A.

A second type of input-output matrix derived from the producer-to-producer sector of Table B-6, the *direct* and *total requirement* tables, are especially useful when individual firms are making demand forecasts. Table B-8 is the direct requirements table for the hypothetical economy. The entries in each column show the dollar inputs required directly from each industry given in the rows to produce $1 of output. Industry C, for example, requires direct inputs costing 56¢ from Industry A and 17¢ from Industry B to produce an additional $1 of output. These direct requirement figures are

Table B-5 National Accounting Data for a Hypothetical Economy (dollars in billions)

Industry Production Accounts

Industry A	Receipts		Expenses + Profits	
	Sales to Industry A	$ 10	Purchases from	
	Sales to Industry B	2	Industry A	$ 10
	Sales to Industry C	50	Purchases from	
	Sales to Persons	40	Industry B	3
	Sales to Government	28	Wages (employee	
			compensation)	100
			Depreciation	10
			Profits	7
		$130		$130

Industry B				
	Sales to Iudustry A	$ 3	Purchases from	
	Sales to Industry C	15	Industry A	$ 2
	Sales to Persons	30	Purchases from	
	Sales to Government	20	Industry C	25
	Sales to Exports	2	Wages (employee	
			compensation)	25
			Depreciation	8
			Profits	10
		$ 70		$70

Industry C				
	Sales to Industry B	$ 25	Purchases from	
	Sales to Persons	65	Industry A	$50
			Purchases from	
			Industry B	15
			Wages (employee	
			compensation)	20
			Profits	5
		$ 90		$90

National Income and Product Accounts

Wages	$145	Personal Consump-		
Profits	22	tion Expenditures	$135	
Depreciation	18	Government	48	
		Exports	2	
	$185		$185	

found by dividing each element in the industry columns in Table B-6 by the column total. Thus, the 0.08 figure for the first-row, first-column element in Table B-8 is found by dividing the $10 billion of purchases among Industry A firms by the $130 billion total found in the first column of Table B-6.

Table B-6 Input-Output Matrix for a Hypothetical Economy (billions of dollars)

		Producers			Final Markets			Row Totals
		A	B	C	Personal Consumption	Government	Exports	
Producers	A	10	2	50	40	28		130
	B	3		15	30	20	2	70
	C		25		65			90
Value Added	Wages	100	25	20				145
	Profit plus Depreciation	17	18	5				40
	Column Total	130	70	90	135	48	2	

$GNP = \$185$

$GNP = \$185$

Table B-7 Percentage Distribution of Gross Output

Percentage Sales to Each Consuming Sector

Producing Industry	Industry A	Industry B	Industry C	Persons	Government	Export	Total
A	8	1	38	31	22	0	100
B	4	0	21	43	29	3	100
C	0	28	0	72	0	0	100

The direct requirements matrix in Table B-8 permits systematic examination of all the interrelationships among the various industries and final demand sectors. For example, assume that Industry A is expected to produce $1 million of output for sale to final consumers. Using the first column of Table B-8, we can see that Industry A will use $80,000 ($1,000,000 × 0.08) of its own production in the process of manufacturing the $1 million of output for final consumption. Thus, the industry must actually produce a minimum of $1.080 million of output. Production of $1.080 million of output by A also requires $21,600 ($1,080,000 × 0.02) from Industry B. As shown by the 0.00 element in the last row of the first column, Industry A requires no direct inputs from Industry C. Calculating the total effect of the original $1 million final demand for A's output requires further analysis. Note that Industry A requires $21,600 in inputs from Industry B. To meet this requirement, B needs inputs of $648 ($21,600 × 0.03) from Industry A and $7,776 ($21,600 × 0.36) from Industry C. These requirements, in turn, must be fed back into the system to determine the second-round effects, which in turn produce further reactions as the cycle continues. Each successive reaction is smaller than the preceding one, and the reactions converge on the final effects of the original demand.

Table **B-8**   Direct Requirements per Dollar of Gross Output

Supplying Industry	Producing Industry		
	A	B	C
A	0.08	0.03	0.56
B	0.02	0.00	0.17
C	0.00	0.36	0.00

Table B-9 presents the *total requirements*—direct plus indirect—for the hypothetical economy.[10] Each column in the table shows the inputs required, both direct and indirect, by the producing industry; each row shows the demand that supplying industries can expect per dollar of final consumption demand. To continue our illustration of a $1 million final consumer demand for the output of Industry A, we see that, in order to produce the $1 million to meet final demand, Industry A production must total $1.09 million; Industry B, $.03 million; and Industry C, $.01 million. In total, production must amount to $1.13 million to supply $1 million of final output of Product A, with the $.13 million being the product required to produce the $1 million final output.

This illustration of the construction and use of input-output tables indicates the versatility and power of the technique in a variety of forecasting situations. It should be apparent at this point that a large part of that versatility depends on the detail contained in the basic input-output

[10] The total requirements tables provide the solution values, or the values on which the chain reaction converges. The mathematics of the solution is described in W. H. Miernyk, *The Elements of Input-Output Analysis* (New York: Random House, 1965).

Table B-9 Total Requirements (Direct plus Indirect) per Dollar of Output for Final Consumption

Supplying Industry	Producing Industry		
	A	B	C
A	1.09	0.27	0.66
B	0.03	1.07	0.19
C	0.01	0.39	1.07

matrix. That is, the finer the industry distinctions in the input-output tables, the more valuable they are for forecasting purposes.

The 1967 input-output table for the United States economy, recently completed by the Office of Business Economics, segments the industrial sector of the system into nearly 370 industry categories, as did the 1963 table. This compares with a classification into only 86 separate industries for earlier input-output tables. The much greater detail provided by these latest tables vastly increases their value to managerial decision makers and should lead to much greater use of the techniques of input-output analysis for industry and firm forecasting purposes.

SURVEY TECHNIQUES

Survey techniques constitute another useful forecasting tool, especially for short-term projections. Surveys generally involve use of interviews or mailed questionnaires asking business firms, government agencies, and individuals about their future plans. Business firms plan and budget virtually all their expenditures in advance of actual purchases or production. Surveys asking about capital budgets, sales budgets, and operating budgets can thus provide much information that is useful for forecasting. Government units also prepare formal budgets well before the actual spending is done, and surveys of budget material, Congressional appropriations hearings, and the like can provide a wealth of information to the forecaster. Finally, even individual consumers usually plan expenditures for such major items as automobiles, furniture, housing, vacations, and education well ahead of the purchase date, so consumer intention surveys can provide valuable indications of future spending on consumer goods.

While surveys do provide an alternative to the quantitative forecasting techniques, they are generally used to supplement rather than replace quantitative analysis. Survey information may be all that is obtainable in certain forecasting situations—for example, when a firm is attempting to project the demand for a new product. The absence of historical sales data prevents econometric modeling of the system, and frequently not enough is known about the product's sales characteristics to allow use of the barometric approach. More often, surveys are used in conjunction with the quantitative methods. The value of survey techniques as a supplement to econometric modeling methods stems from two factors. First, a nonquantifiable psychological element is inherent in most economic behavior, and surveys are especially well suited to pick up this phenomenon. Second, econometric models generally assume stable consumer tastes and the like, and if these factors are actually changing, survey data may reveal the changes.

Surveys for Forecasting Various Classes of Expenditures

Many useful surveys for forecasting business activity in various sectors of the United States economy are published periodically by private and government units. Some of these are discussed in this section.

Plant and Equipment Expenditures Surveys of businessmen's intentions to expand plant and equipment are conducted by the U.S. Department of Commerce, the Securities and Exchange Commission, the National Industrial Conference Board, McGraw-Hill, Inc., *Fortune* magazine, and various trade associations such as the Edison Electric Institute and the American Gas Association.

Inventory Changes and Sales Expectations The U.S. Commerce Department, *Fortune* magazine, McGraw-Hill, Inc., Dun and Bradstreet, and the National Association of Purchasing Agents all survey businesspeople's expectations about future sales levels and their plans for inventory changes. These surveys, while not nearly so accurate as those for long-term investment, provide a useful check on other forecasting methods.

Consumer Expenditures The consumer intentions surveys of the Census Bureau, the University of Michigan Research Center, and the Sindlinger-National Industrial Conference Board all provide information on planned purchases of specific products—such as automobiles, housing, and appliances. In addition, these surveys often indicate consumer confidence in the economy and, thereby, spending expectations in general. Attempts are being made to quantify all aspects of survey data and to incorporate this information directly into econometric models. Although some success is being achieved with these attempts, a great deal of judgment is still required. Forecasting is becoming a "science," but it still contains elements of "art."

PROBLEMS

B-1 You are presented with the following time-series data for the gross national product (*GNP*):

Year	GNP (in billions)
1955	$398.0
1960	503.7
1965	683.9
1969	932.1

Determine the *GNP* growth rate between the years 1955-1960, 1955-1965, and 1955-1969.

B-2 The following figures constitute annual sales for Jackson's Department Store:

Year	Sales
1962	239,000
1963	266,000
1964	287,000
1965	315,000
1966	353,000
1967	384,000
1968	427,000
1969	462,000
1970	520,000
1971	575,000
1972	628,000

a) Forecast sales for 1973 and 1977, using the constant rate of change model.

b) Forecast sales for 1973 and 1977 by graphic analysis.

c) Compare the two forecasts. Which one do you think is more accurate?

B-3 The Acme Book Company's economist believes that sales in any given month are related to consumers' incomes during the preceding month.

a) Write an equation for next month's sales, using the symbols S = sales, Y = income, t = time, a_0 = constant term, a_1 = regression slope coefficient, and u = random disturbance.

b) Now assume that sales in this month increase by the same percentage as income increased during the preceding month. Write an equation for predicting sales.

c) If last month's income was $2 billion and this month's sales are $400,000, what should sales amount to next month if income this month is $2.1 billion? Use the equation developed in Part b.

B-4 The quantity demanded of Product A in any given week is inversely proportional to the sales of Product B in the previous week; that is, if sales of B rose by X percent last week, sales of A can be expected to fall by X percent this week.

    a)   Write the equation for next week's sales of A, using the symbols $A =$ sales of Product A, $B =$ sales of Product B, $t =$ time. Assume there will be no shortages of either product.

    b)   Two weeks ago 200 units of Product A and 150 units of Product B were sold. Last week 160 units of A and 180 units of B were sold. What would you predict the sales of A and B to be this week?

    c)   What is the significance of the error term? What property must the error term have to allow use of regression results in forecasting?

B-5 In July 1969 the management of the Sund Corporation was evaluating the merits of building a new plant in order to fulfill a new contract with the federal government. The alternative to expansion is to use additional overtime or to reduce other production or to do both. The company manufactures a wide range of parts for aircraft, automotive, and agricultural equipment industries and will want to add new capacity only if the economy appears to be expanding. Forecasting the general economic activity of the United States, therefore, is of obvious interest to the company as an input in the decision process.

    The firm has collected the data and has estimated the relationships for the United States economy shown below:

Last Year's Total Profits (all corporations) $P_{t-1} = \$80$ billion
This Year's Government Expenditures $G = \$120$ billion
Annual Consumption Expenditures $C = \$60$ billion $+ 0.70(Y) + u$
Annual Investment Expenditures $I = \$4$ billion $+ 0.85(P_{t-1}) + u$
Annual Tax Receipts $T = 0.25$ (GNP)
National Income $Y = GNP - T$
Gross National Product $GNP = C + I + G$

Assume that all random disturbances average out to zero, and forecast each of the above variables through the simultaneous relationships expressed in the multiple equation system.

APPENDIX C

Check Figures for Selected
End-of-Chapter Problems

In this appendix we provide some check figures, typically the final numerical answer to most of the end-of-chapter problems. These "solutions" will prove useful in showing whether your approach to the problem is correct. They will not help you solve the problems, as no intermediate steps are provided.

CHAPTER 2

2-1 a) $TR_9 = 1962$, $MR_3 = 262$, $MR_6 = 238$, $MR_{11} = -42$, $AR_4 = 248$, $AR_9 = 218$, $AR_{12} = 152$

2-2 a) $MR_{53} = 48$, $MR_{57} = 44$, $MC_{54} = 43$, $MC_{57} = 47$, $\pi_{53} = 1021$, $\pi_{57} = 1021$, $M\pi_{54} = 3$, $M\pi_{57} = -3$, $M\pi_{58} = -5$

2-4 a) $\dfrac{dY}{dX} = 4, \dfrac{d^2Y}{dX^2} = 0$

   b) $\dfrac{dY}{dX} = 50 - .6X, \dfrac{d^2Y}{dX^2} = -.6$

   c) $\dfrac{dY}{dX} = 50 - 10X + 3X^2, \dfrac{d^2Y}{dX^2} = -10 + 6X$

d) $\dfrac{dY}{dX} = 4X - 4, \dfrac{d^2Y}{dX^2} = 4$

e) $\dfrac{dY}{dX} = \dfrac{-X^2 + 6}{X^4}, \dfrac{d^2Y}{dX^2} = \dfrac{2X^2 - 24}{X^5}$

f) $\dfrac{dY}{dX} = 54 + 72X + 24X^2, \dfrac{d^2Y}{dX^2} = 72 + 48X$

2-5 a) Y_{max} at $X = 200$;

    b) Y_{max} at $X = -10$, Y_{min} at $X = 20$

2-6 a) TR_{max} at $Q = 10$;

    b) MR_{max} at $Q = 3.33$

    c) $AR = MR$ at $Q = 5$

2-7 a) π_{max} at $Q = 55$

2-8 a) $\dfrac{\partial Y}{\partial X} = -2 + Z, \dfrac{\partial Y}{\partial Z} = -3 + X + 2Z$

    b) $\dfrac{\partial Y}{\partial X} = 3 + 2Z - 2X, \dfrac{\partial Y}{\partial Z} = 1 + 2X - 2Z$

    c) $\dfrac{\partial Y}{\partial X} = 2X + WZ, \dfrac{\partial Y}{\partial Z} = WX - 4WZ + 1, \dfrac{\partial Y}{\partial W} = XZ - 2Z^2$

    d) $\dfrac{\partial Y}{\partial X} = 3.2X^{-0.6}Z^{0.6}, \dfrac{\partial Y}{\partial Z} = 4.8X^{0.4}Z^{-0.4}$

2-9 $EOQ = \sqrt{\dfrac{2\phi X}{C}}$

2-10 a) $A = 8, B = 6$

    b) $A = 11, B = 9$

    c) 3

2-11 a) $A = 14, B = 41, TR = \$3,920$

2-12 a) $A = 10, B = 10$

    b) $\lambda = 100$

Kantell Engineering Case
1) $F \approx 3$
2) $Q = 72,864$
3) $\pi = \$2,604,000$

CHAPTER 3

3-1 a) $E(\pi_1) = \$500,000$; $E(\pi_2) = \$350,000$

    c) $\nu_1 = .51$; $\nu_2 = .28$

    d) strategy #1 = 24.1 utils; strategy #2 = 22.8 utils

3-2 a) Expected annual cash flow: Alternative #1 = \$3,440

                                      Alternative #2 = \$3,600

    b) $NPV_1 = \$6,905$; $NPV_2 = \$6,933$

    c) $\alpha_1 = .957$; $\alpha_2 = .917$

    d) $NPV_1 = \$6,903$; $NPV_2 = \$6,934$

3-3 c) $E(\pi_A) = \$1,640; E(\pi_B) = \$1,460$
     d) $\nu_A = .77; \nu_B = 1.27$

3-4 b) $E(\text{Value}_A) = \$186,803$
         $E(\text{Value}_B) = \$\ 62,150$
         $E(\text{Value}_C) = \$124,793$

3A-1 b) $E(\pi_A) = \$3,750; E(\pi_B) = \$5,625$
      c) $E(\text{Loss}_A) = \$2,000; E(\text{Loss}_B) = \$125$
      d) $\$125$

3A-2 d) .5
      e) $NPV(\text{savings}) = \$1,195.50$

CHAPTER 4

4-1 a) \$200 per ton;
     b) 250 tons per day;
     c) \$333.33
     d) 1000 tons;
     f) -1.5

4-2 a)

Income	Quantity demanded (units)
\$2,000	500
3,000	700
4,000	900
5,000	1,100
6,000	1,300

     b) $\epsilon_{I=4,000} = 0.889; \epsilon_{I=6,000} = 0.923$
     c) $E_I = 0.833$ for 2,000 to 3,000 range
         $E_I = 0.917$ for 5,000 to 6,000 range

4-3 a) (1) b, (2) c, (3) f

4-4 a) $Q_{1975} = 1,190; Q_{1976} = 1,161$
     b) $Q_{1975} = 1,129$ with competitors price change

4-5 a) substitutes
     b)

P_X	Y (units)
\$100	1,060
80	1,048
60	1,036
40	1,024

     c) $\epsilon_{P_X} = .0458$ at $P_X = \$80$
         $\epsilon_{P_X} = .0234$ at $P_X = \$40$
     d) $E_{P_X} = .0512$ for \$100 to \$80 range
         $E_{P_X} = .0291$ for \$60 to \$40 range

4-6 a) 1.084
     b) at \$16.76, 10,000 pairs will be sold
     c) $TR_{7,000} = \$140,000$; $TR_{10,000} = \$167,000$

4-7 a) $\epsilon_{P(\text{Airtight})} = -1.0$; $\epsilon_{P(\text{Longlife})} = -.60$
     b) $E_{P_X} = .71$

CHAPTER 5

5-1 c) $Q \approx 28,000 - 2,800P$

5-2 c) $\epsilon_P = -3.67$
     d) $\epsilon_{P_X} = .67$
     e) 12 to 18

5-3 a) $\epsilon_P = -1.01$
     b) $\epsilon_A = +.12$
     c) $\epsilon_I = +.885$
     d) $\epsilon_{P_X} = +.51$

5-4 a) $E_{P(\text{average})} = -.276$
     b) $E_{A(\text{average})} = .277$
     c) $E_{P_X(\text{average})} = .153$
     d) $\epsilon_{P(\text{average})} = -.1569$
         $\epsilon_{A(\text{average})} = .145$
         $\epsilon_{P_X(\text{average})} = .090$
     e) $\epsilon_P = -.144$, $\epsilon_A = .134$, $\epsilon_{P_X} = .097$

CHAPTER 6

6-2 a) decreasing
     c) 3
     e) constant

6-4 a) constant
     b) constant
     c) decreasing
     d) increasing
     e) constant
     f) decreasing
     g) constant

6-5 a) $n = .9$, decreasing
     b) $n = p + q$
     c) $n = 1.8$, increasing
     d) $n = 2.0$, increasing
     e) $n = 1.0$, constant

6-6 a) $C = 2/3L$
     b) $L = 2C$
     c) yes

6-7   a) $n = 2$, increasing
      b)   85,900 units per week
      c) $MP_C = 620$, $MP_L = 980$

6A-1   a) $X = 1.5Y$
      b) $X = 125$, $Y = 83.33$, $Q = 62,975$, $\lambda = 128$
      c)   128 units
      d) $X \approx 111.25$, $Y \approx 74.2$, Cost = 890.2, $\lambda = .0089$

CHAPTER 7

7-1   a) $K = 2L$
      c) $MP_L = 1/9$ up to $L = 9/4\ K$, 0 beyond;
           $MP_K = 1/4$ up to $K = 4/9\ L$, 0 beyond, Constant returns to scale
      d) $4Q_X$ requires $36L$ and $16K$: $16\ Q_X$ requires $144L$ and $64K$
      e)   4 units
      f) $MP_K = \frac{1}{4}$, $MP_L = 0$

7-2   b) $C = 8$, $D = 12.67$; $Q_X = 20.67$
      d) $V_O = .33$, $V_L = .2$, $L_A = .899$, $L_B = .165$
      f)   (1) C
          (2) 63 1/3 units increase

7-3   a) $Y = 6$, $X = 4$, $\pi = \$32,400$ (maximum monthly profit)
      b) $V_A = \$1.50$ per unit, $V_B = \$6.00$ per unit, $V_C = 0$
      c)   decrease

7-4   b) $V_{NG} = 10$, $V_{FO} = 5$; $L_{P_B} = 7.5$, $L_{P_A} = 0$, $F = 16.67$, $P_A = 8.33$,
           $P_B = 0$, $\pi = 1,750$

7-5   b) $S = 1$ ton, $C = 4$ tons, $S_{CA} = 400$, $S_R = 4,000$, Cost $= \$420$
      c) $V_P = .04$, $V_T = 60$

CHAPTER 8

8-2   a)   The relevant costs for the decision are materials cost, direct labor,
           variable overhead and opportunity cost of foregone profits.
      b)   If accepted, Zipsaw would decrease profits by $150,000.

8-3   Edgewood should make B-0012 and save $500,000.

8-4   Dropping Ling would reduce profits by $80,000.

8-5   a)   The price cut should be made.

8-6   a) $TFC = \$375,000$
      b)   an increase of 57,143 gross would be needed

8-7   a) $TC = \$85,000 + \$.75\ Q$
      b) $TC = \$85,000 + \$.80\ Q$
      c)   an increase of 8,333 units would be needed
      d) $Q = 137,500$, $P = \$1.90$

8-8   b) $X = 120$ units of output; $Q = 4{,}344$ units of output; and maximized $\pi = \$22{,}840$

8-9   b)   25,000 units
      c) $\pi = \$5{,}000$
      d)   D.O.L. $= 6$
      e) -60%

8-10   a)   20,000 units
      b)   D.O.L. $= 2$
      c) 40%
      d)   increase D.O.L.
      e)   decrease D.O.L.
      f)   increase D.O.L. to 2.67

CHAPTER 10

10-1   b) $P = \$1.875$, $Q_D = Q_S = 37{,}500$

10-2   a)   (1) $Q = 20$ units (2) $AC = \$240$ (3) $\pi = \$8{,}000$
      c)   (1) $Q = 10$ units (2) $AC = MC = \$140$ (3) $P = AC = \$140$

10-3   a) $Q = 2{,}050$ units
      b) $\pi = \$4{,}052{,}500$
      c) $P = \$2{,}450$
      d) $P = \$2{,}250$; $Q = 2{,}250$; $\pi = \$4{,}012{,}500$
      e)   The industry is not currently in equilibrium.
           In equilibrium: $P = \$787.50$, $Q \approx 387$ units, $\pi = \$0$

10-4   a) $Q_1 = 2.5$, $Q_2 = 1$, $Q_T = 3.5$; $\pi_1 = \$21.50$, $\pi_2 = \$4.50$, $\pi_T = \$26$
      b) $Q_1 = 1.25$, $Q_2 = .75$, $Q_T = 2$; $\pi_1 = \$18.82$, $\pi_2 = \$13.70$, $\pi_T = \$32.52$

10-5   b)   oligopolistic
      c) $Q = 20$, $P = \$20$, $\pi = \$50$
      d) $Q = 20$, $P = \$20$
      e) $Q = 17$, $P = \$20.75$
      f)   yes

10-6   b) $Q_L = 12{,}771$; $P_L \approx \$85{,}000$
      c) $S_F = 10{,}250$

10-7   a)   (1) $Q = 500$, $P = \$100$; (2) $Q = 100$, $P = \$90$
      c) $P = \$90$
      d) $P = \$100$
      e) $P = \$90$
      f) $100 is the cost of uncertainty
      h)   differentiated oligopoly

CHAPTER 11

11-1   Tucson Electronic should accept the order because incremental profit contribution is $16,000.

11-2 Poulton should accept the offer because the incremental profit contribution is $190,000.

11-3 a) $.52

b) $.81 per eight pack

11-4 Incremental profit: Offer #1 $56,000; Offer #2 $52,000

11-5 b) $MR_{(aggregate)} = MC$, $P_1 = \$260$, $P_2 = \$210$,
$MR_1 = MR_2 = \$20 = MC$, $Q_1 = 30$, $Q_2 = 38$, $\pi = \$4,420$

c) $P_1 = P_2 = \$229.20$, $Q_1 = 33.84$, $Q_2 = 34.16$, $\pi = \$4,225$

11-6 b) (1) only in Market A (2) $Q_A = 6\ 2/3$, $P = \$18.33$ (3) $\pi = \$26.70$

c) (1) in both Markets A and B; (2) $Q_A = 10.8$, $Q_B = 13.2$, $P_A = \$14.20$,
$P_B = \$6.70$, $\pi_T = \$89.00$

d) (1) in both Markets A and B, (2) $\pi_T = \$44.00$

11A-1 a) (1) $Q = 50$, (2) $P = \$42.50$, (3) $\pi = \$150$

b) (1) $Q = 27.78$, $P_T = \$35.78$; (2) $\pi_{Mfg} = (\$305.50)$, $\pi_{Dist} = \$208.50$;
(3) $\pi_{Firm} = (\$97.00)$, $247 less than in Part (a); (5) $P_T = \$18$,
(6) $\pi_{Dist} = \$900$, $\pi_{Mfg} = (\$750)$

11A-2 a) $Q = 29.5$, $P_T = \$69$

b) $P_T = \$190$; HPD will purchase 22.78 units and ESD will sell 67.22 externally

c) $P_T = \$99.60$, $P_{Ext} = \$255.30$; HPD will purchase 27.8 units and ESD will sell 17 units externally

CHAPTER 12

12-1 a) $Q = 15$ million tons, $P_A = \$500$ per ton

b) $\pi_A = \$1,575$ million

c) above-normal profits, a 31.5% rate of return

d) $Q = 22.5$ million tons, $P_A = \$425$

e) $\pi_A = \$731.25$ million, above-normal profits

f) losses of $269 million per year would be incurred

12-2 a) $Q_A = 59$, $Q_B = 50$, $P_A = \$541$, $P_B = \$50$; 59 units of output will be produced and 9 units of B will be dumped.

b) $Q_A = 57$, $Q_B = 55$, $P_A = \$543$, $P_B = \$45$; 57 units of output will be produced and 2 units of B will be dumped.

c) $13.34

12-3 a) $A = 34.3$ hours, $B = 54.3$ hours

b) $A = 53.3$ hours, $B = 40$ hours

c) cost of restriction $= \$38.00$

12-4 a) $L = 2,375,000 - 250,000P_L$

b) labor demand would be reduced by 250,000 manhours each year.

12-5 a) $ROI = 13.8\%$

b) $P = \$26$

CHAPTER 13

13-1   a)   Net annual cash inflows:
             Model A $1,326,666
             Model B   1,295,000
             Model C   1,073,333
       b) $NPV_A = \$3,777,630; NPV_B = \$4,139,725; NPV_C = \$3,674,365$

13-2 $NPV = \$6,500$, so Venture should undertake the investment.

13-3   a)   Expected annual cash flow:
             Project A $3,460
             Project B   4,594
       b) $NPV_A = \$4,508$ $NPV_B = \$7,387$

APPENDIX A

A-2   a)   .952
      b)   .907
      c)   .864
      d)   .909
      e)   .826
      f)   .751

A-3   a) $PV = \$86.40$
      b) $PV = \$.864$
      c) $PV = \$751.00$

A-4   a)   Value $= \$315.20$
      b)   Value $= \$331.00$

APPENDIX B

B-1   1955-1960 $\approx 5\%$ growth rate
      1955-1965 $\approx 5.5\%$ growth rate
      1955-1969 $\approx 6.25\%$ growth rate

B-2   Forecasted sales: 1973 $= \$691,000$, 1977 $= \$1,012,000$

B-3   a) $S_{t+1} = a_o + a_1 Y_t + u$

      b) $S_{t+1} = \dfrac{Y_t}{Y_{t-1}} (S_t) + u$

      c) $S_{t+1} = \$420,000 + u$

B-4   a) $A_{t+1} = \dfrac{B_{t-1}}{B_t} (A_t) + u$

      b) $A_{t+1} = 133.33$

B-5 $I = \$72$ billion, GNP $= \$531$ billion, $C = \$339$ billion, $T = \$133$ billion, $Y = \$398$ billion

INDEX